# International Security

*Also by Michael E. Smith*

EUROPE'S FOREIGN AND SECURITY POLICY: The Institutionalization of Cooperation

GOVERNING EUROPE'S NEIGHBOURHOOD: Partners or Periphery? (co-author/co-editor)

EUROPEAN SECURITY (editor)

EUROPE'S COMMON SECURITY AND DEFENCE POLICY: Capacity-Building, Experiential Learning, and Institutional Change

# International Security

## Politics, Policy, Prospects

2nd Edition

**Michael E. Smith**

 macmillan education    palgrave

First edition 2010

Second edition 2017
Published by PALGRAVE

Palgrave in the UK is an imprint of Macmillan Publishers Limited, registered in England, company number 785998, of 4 Crinan Street, London, N1 9XW.

Palgrave is a global imprint of the above companies and is represented throughout the world.

Palgrave® and Macmillan® are registered trademarks in the United States, the United Kingdom, Europe and other countries.

ISBN 978-1-137-58293-5 hardback
ISBN 978-1-137-58292-8 paperback

This book is printed on paper suitable for recycling and made from fully managed and sustained forest sources. Logging, pulping and manufacturing processes are expected to conform to the environmental regulations of the country of origin.

A catalogue record for this book is available from the British Library.

A catalog record for this book is available from the Library of Congress.

Printed and bound by CPI Group (UK) Ltd, Croydon, CR0 4YY

*For Olivia Rose*
*with hopes for a happy and secure future*

# Contents

# List of Tables, Figures and Boxes

## Tables

## Figures

## Boxes

# List of Abbreviations

| | |
|---|---|
| ABM | Anti-Ballistic Missile Treaty |
| ACMD | UK Advisory Council on the Misuse of Drugs |
| AFSJ | EU Area of Freedom, Security, and Justice |
| AIDS | Acquired Immune Deficiency Syndrome |
| ANZUS | Australia–New Zealand–US Treaty |
| ASEAN | Association of Southeast Asian Nations |
| ATF | US Bureau of Alcohol, Tobacco, Firearms, and Explosives |
| AU | African Union |
| BIS | Bank for International Settlements |
| BLWP | Blinding Laser Weapons Protocol |
| BRIC | Brazil, Russia, India, China |
| BWC | Biological Weapons Convention |
| C4I | Command, Control, Communications, Computers, and Intelligence |
| CCW | UN Conference/Convention on Certain Conventional Weapons |
| CDC | US Centers for Disease Control |
| CDO | Collateralized Debt Obligation |
| CEMAC | Economic and Monetary Union of Central African States |
| CFC | Chlorofluorocarbon |
| CFE | Treaty on Conventional Forces in Europe |
| CFSP | EU Common Foreign and Security Policy |
| CIA | US Central Intelligence Agency |
| CIS | Commonwealth of Independent States |
| CSCE | Conference on Security and Cooperation in Europe |
| CSDP | EU Common Security and Defence Policy |
| CSTO | Collective Security Treaty Organization |
| CTBT | Comprehensive Test Ban Treaty |
| CW | Conventional Weapon |
| CWC | Chemical Weapons Convention |
| DDoS | Distributed Denial-of-Service |
| DEA | US Drug Enforcement Administration |
| DoD | US Department of Defence |
| DoJ | US Department of Justice |
| DoS | Denial-of-Service |
| DoT | US Department of the Treasury |
| DHKP/C | Revolutionary People's Liberation Party/Front (Turkey) |
| DHS | US Department of Homeland Security |

| | |
|---|---|
| DRC | Democratic Republic of the Congo |
| EBA | European Banking Authority |
| ECOWAS | Economic Community of West African States |
| EFSA | European Food Safety Authority |
| ELN | National Liberation Army (Colombia) |
| EMA | European Medicines Agency |
| ENP | European Neighbourhood Policy |
| ESDP | European Security and Defence Policy |
| ESSENCE | Electronic Surveillance System for the Early Notification of Community-Based Epidemics |
| ETA | Euskadi Ta Askatasuna (Spain) |
| EU | European Union |
| Euratom | European Atomic Energy Community |
| FARC | Revolutionary Armed Forces of Colombia |
| FATF | Financial Action Task Force |
| FAO | UN Food and Agriculture Organization |
| FBI | US Federal Bureau of Investigation |
| FCC | US Federal Communications Commission |
| FDI | Foreign direct investment |
| FSB | Financial Stability Board |
| FTO | Foreign Terrorist Organization |
| G2 | Group of Two |
| G3 | Group of Three |
| G7 | Group of Seven |
| G8 | Group of Eight |
| G20 | Group of 20 |
| G77 | Group of 77 |
| GAR | Global Alert and Response |
| GATT | General Agreement on Tariffs and Trade |
| GCHQ | UK Government Communications Headquarters |
| GHG | Greenhouse Gas |
| HIPC | Heavily Indebted Poor Country |
| HIV | Human Immunodeficiency Virus |
| HMO | Health Maintenance Organization |
| HTML | Hypertext Markup Language |
| HTTP | Hypertext Transfer Protocol |
| HUJI-B | Harakat ul-Jihad-i-Islami/Bangladesh |
| IAEA | International Atomic Energy Agency |
| ICANN | Internet Corporation for Assigned Names and Numbers |
| ICAO | International Civil Aviation Organization |
| ICBL | International Campaign to Ban Landmines |
| ICBM | Intercontinental Ballistic Missile |
| ICC | International Criminal Court |
| ICE | US Immigrations and Customs Enforcement Agency |

| | |
|---|---|
| ICRC | International Committee of the Red Cross |
| IDP | Internally Displaced Person |
| IEA | International Energy Agency |
| IFI | International Financial Institution |
| IMF | International Monetary Fund |
| IMO | International Maritime Organization |
| INDC | Intended Nationally Determined Contributions |
| INF | Intermediate Range Nuclear Forces Treaty |
| Interpol | International Criminal Police Organization |
| IO | International Organization |
| IOM | International Organization for Migration |
| IoT | Internet of Things |
| IPCC | UN Intergovernmental Panel on Climate Change |
| IRA | Irish Republican Army |
| ISP | Internet Service Provider |
| IT | Information Technology |
| JEM | Jaish-e-Mohammed |
| JTF | Joint Task Force |
| LDC | Less Developed Country |
| LOAC | Law of Armed Conflict |
| LTTE | Liberation Tigers of Tamil Eelam |
| M&A | Mergers and Acquisitions |
| MAD | Mutual Assured Destruction |
| MBD | Million Barrels a Day |
| MEA | Multilateral Environmental Agreement |
| MIRV | Multiple Independently Targetable Re-entry Vehicle |
| MLAT | Mutual Legal Assistance Treaty |
| MNC | Multinational Corporation |
| MOCG | Mobile Organized Crime Group |
| NAFTA | North American Free Trade Agreement |
| NASA | US National Aeronautics and Space Administration |
| NATO | North Atlantic Treaty Organization |
| NCA | UK National Crime Agency |
| NGO | Non-Governmental Organization |
| NHS | UK National Health Service |
| NORML | National Organization for the Reform of Marijuana Laws (US) |
| NSA | US National Security Agency |
| NWS | Nuclear Weapon State |
| NNWS | Non-Nuclear Weapon State |
| NPT | (Nuclear) Non-Proliferation Treaty |
| OAS | Organization of American States |

| | |
|---|---|
| OECD | Organisation for Economic Co-operation and Development |
| ONDCP | US Office of National Counterdrug Policy |
| OPEC | Organization of the Petroleum Exporting Countries |
| PIJ | Palestinian Islamic Jihad |
| PKK | Kurdistan Workers' Party |
| PLF | Palestine Liberation Front |
| PLO | Palestine Liberation Organization |
| PMC | Private Military Contractor |
| POW | Prisoner of War |
| R2P | Responsibility to Protect |
| SALT | Strategic Arms Limitation Treaty |
| SARS | Severe Acute Respiratory Syndrome |
| SEATO | Southeast Asia Treaty Organization |
| SOCA | UK Serious Organised Crime Agency |
| START | Strategic Arms Reduction Treaty |
| TNT | Trinitrotoluene |
| UK | United Kingdom |
| UN | United Nations |
| UN FCCC | UN Framework Convention on Climate Change |
| UN-Habitat | United Nations Human Settlements Programme |
| UNHCR | UN High Commissioner for Refugees |
| UNSC | UN Security Council |
| US | United States |
| USAMRIID | US Army Medical Research Institute of Infectious Diseases |
| USSR | Union of Soviet Socialist Republics |
| UV-B | Ultraviolet-B rays |
| WHO | World Health Organization |
| WMD | Weapons of Mass Destruction |
| WTO | World Trade Organization |
| WWI | World War I |
| WWII | World War II |
| XDR-TB | Extreme Drug Resistant Tuberculosis |

# Preface

When the first edition of this book was being drafted, the world was suffering the effects of the 2008 global economic crisis, one of the new or human security topics covered in detail in this volume. In the realm of more traditional security affairs, the US was well into its 'War on Terror' targeted primarily against al-Qaeda. At the same time, a new Democratic presidential administration under Barack Obama was inaugurated in January 2009; among other things, Obama pledged to end some of the more controversial security policies of his predecessor, George W. Bush. He also hoped to 'reboot' US relations with Russia and the Arab world after years of mistrust. Now that the Obama administration has left office, it does not require the expertise of a political scientist to see that not only did America fail to achieve these goals, it (along with its major strategic partners) also failed to assert effective leadership on a number of other security issues, so that the world seems to have been in an almost-constant state of turmoil since 2009: the 'Arab Spring' revolutions, the use of chemical weapons in Syria, the eurozone crisis, the rise of Islamic State, Russia's annexation of Crimea, tensions in the South China Sea, a major outbreak of Ebola, terrorist attacks around the world, a massive refugee crisis in the Middle East and Europe, an attempted *coup d'état* in Turkey, successful coups elsewhere, and the UK's vote to leave the EU after more than four decades of membership, despite the appeals of other EU member states and America.

These events clearly challenge the high hopes of some scholars and policy-makers about the prospects for a more peaceful and democratic international system after the Cold War. Moreover, given the ongoing disputes about how to prioritize among the many serious problems currently facing the international community, security specialists – whether academics or policy-makers – must work even harder to make international security a *discipline* rather than just a 'topic' or 'subject', so that its insights can help us to not just analyse individual security problems and solutions, but also understand how the politics of one problem relates to other problems, and how difficult it is for real-world policy-makers to cope with these varying pressures *simultaneously*. These political calculations often involve international and domestic factors for all major stakeholders, and intensive interactions between public and private (or non-state) interests, two major themes of this volume. Public–private linkages in particular have become even more salient after the Obama administration, not to mention the rest of the world, was stunned by two revelations made by low-level employees in the US security apparatus. The first involved the publication of thousands of secret US diplomatic documents in 2010 (the WikiLeaks or 'Cablegate' scandal), and the second in 2013 involved America's extensive spying and surveillance activities targeted at American citizens and US allies, among others. These events almost certainly undermined America's reputation in world politics; for some critics, Obama's campaign slogan of 'Yes, we can' became the practice of 'Yes, we scan' once he assumed the world's most powerful office. Even worse, as this volume goes to press the US has elected Donald Trump, a reality TV celebrity with no political experience, as its president, and he has questioned many long-standing US security policies, such as America's security commitment to its European and Asian allies. If Trump follows through on such ideas, the state of international security affairs could become even more unstable, or at least more unpredictable, than it already is.

As with the first edition, then, a central concern with politics and policy still provides the basic organizing framework of this volume. Above all, it focuses on combining insights from rigorous empirical research on international security with sharp analytical concepts and lessons drawn from what might seem to be unrelated or distinct problems and policies. Accomplishing this task generally involves giving the practice of international security affairs more attention than one tends to find in more theoretically focused texts, some of which are barely distinguishable from texts on international relations theory that already fill the bookshelves. I also assume that many, if not most, students of international relations expect to work as practitioners in the public or private sectors, rather than as academics, so this volume views theory as a means to an end rather than an end in itself. This also involves noting when theories seem to be based on outdated, incomplete, or simply unproven beliefs about how people tend to act regarding international security.

In addition, this book offers three distinctive features to help introduce international security studies to upper-level undergraduate and postgraduate students who have a basic knowledge of international relations:

First, it offers a single, novel, analytical framework applied across all of the topical chapters. This framework does not involve or advance a single theory, but rather interprets all major international security problems in terms of several more general political factors and dynamics that tend to recur in the contemporary practice of international security affairs and world politics more generally.

Second, it offers more comprehensive issue coverage than found in some other texts on international or global security, and includes equal attention to traditional topics related to military force, as well as a range of less traditional topics, many of which are associated with non-state actors (such as terrorists and organized criminal groups), or new referent objects (such as environmental problems). Many of these non-traditional topics are also associated with broader concepts such as human security or the new security agenda; however, rather than examine them in a single chapter I have chosen to handle them as the international community generally does: as a series of loosely related problems rather than as a core and unified part of the international security agenda. Equally importantly, the political attention given to these various topics, as *security* problems, varies widely as well (Hameiri and Jones, 2013), which is why I disaggregate the human/new security agenda into several chapters in the last part of this volume.

Third, as the focus here is on *international* security affairs, rather than global security, security studies, strategic studies or defence policy, the text also provides for a more coherent treatment of the relationship between national/domestic, regional and international political factors that combine, in various ways, to produce some kind of 'international community consensus' regarding a specific security problem. This variation among levels of analysis, though with the concept of 'international security' always at the core, is especially relevant for examining the rise of non-traditional international security issues and the expanded range of ways to deal with all types of international security problems, which often involve striking a balance between unilateral and multilateral approaches, between 'international' and 'regional' efforts, and between public authority and private involvement in the field.

Finally, in this edition, I have made some important changes to help keep the text current as a teaching and research tool for courses on international security and related subjects. The most visible change is the addition of a new chapter on cybersecurity/cyberwar, which has emerged as a key policy concern of many stakeholders and as a new research topic for security analysts. The second main change is the addition of 'mini-case studies' in each empirical chapter; these cases provide additional insights into how the politics of certain security problems function in the real world facing high-level decision-makers. Each of these case studies has also generated its own research literature, so they can be used as examples in lectures, tutorials and discussion groups. Third, I have provided lists of core texts at the end of each main topical chapter to provide guidance on further reading. Finally, I have also expanded and updated the theoretical discussion in Chapter 2, as well as the empirical/research material in all other chapters and the Conclusion, so that the central points made in each chapter should remain relevant for some time to come. Overall, the volume is still structured to map easily onto a standard, 12–16 week, one-term course on international security or security studies, for those who have had some introductory training in international relations (history and theory). In my own teaching, each week generally involves a lecture on a central security problem (such as interstate war) and a lecture on a related case study (such as the Persian Gulf War), supplemented by tutorials focused on readings from the research literature, particularly current journal articles.

That said, and given this range of topics and a finite amount of space in which to examine them, my main goal here is to provide a broad overview or 'grand tour', using a common set of questions and processes for each topic. Each chapter, however, cites more than enough examples and sources from other works to give students enough intellectual ammunition to continue the conversation outside the classroom and back in the real world, where things are infinitely more complicated and interesting.

MICHAEL E. SMITH
*Aberdeen*

# Acknowledgements

I would like to acknowledge the extensive assistance provided by Steven Kennedy and Stephen Wenham at Palgrave Macmillan throughout the preparation of this book and its first edition; they were very helpful in supporting the overall approach and the treatment of specific topics covered in this volume, and I am grateful for their thoughtful input. Chloe Osborne provided expert editorial assistance to help me finalise the final draft, and I also appreciate the comments provided by anonymous reviewers on earlier drafts. Although they did not always agree with each other, nor I with them in some cases, their advice informed numerous aspects of the book, from the general approach to specific conceptual and factual details. I hope the final product respects their concerns, which I am sure will be shared by many others who teach this topic.

Speaking of teaching, I would also like to thank my own students from years past. The lectures I composed and then inflicted upon them provided extremely rough first drafts for many of the chapters in this volume, and their responses in the classroom served as a very helpful sounding board regarding my approach to this topic.

Finally, a word of thanks to my family, particularly the person to whom this book is dedicated: my daughter Olivia. As this book is about the protection of valued things, Olivia, along with my wife Penny, reminds me every day of what really should take priority in our increasingly hectic lives, even though that may not seem to be the case when I am at my desk stubbornly working on a project like this.

The author and publishers wish to thank the following for giving permission to use copyright material in this book: C. S. Lewis Pte Ltd for the extract on p. xxi, Cambridge University Press for Tables 5.2 and 5.3, MIT Press Journals for Tables 5.5 and 7.1 and Taylor & Francis for Table 8.1, Jeff Koterba for the cartoon in Chapter 3, Steve Greenberg for the cartoons in Boxes 4.1, 5.1 and 10.1, Ingrid Rice for the cartoon in Box 6.1, Tom Toles for the cartoon in Box 7.4, Bob Englehart for the cartoon in Box 8.1, Tim Kelly for the cartoon in Box 9.1, Linda Causey for the cartoon in Box 11.1, Patrick Chappatte for the cartoon is Box 12.2, Arcadio Esquival for the cartoon in Box 13.1.

Of all tyrannies, a tyranny sincerely exercised
for the good of its victims may be the most oppressive. ...
[T]hose who torment us for our own good will torment us without end,
for they do so with the approval of their own conscience.

C. S. Lewis, *God in the Dock,* © C. S. Lewis Pte Ltd 1970

# Part I

## Questions and Concepts

# Chapter 1

# International Relations and International Security

Wars, arms races and weapons of mass destruction. Terrorism, insurgencies and suicide bombings. Genocides, infectious diseases and refugee crises. Oil depletion, global climate change and economic collapse. Drug trafficking, cyberwar and piracy. These and other international security problems make disturbing headlines on a regular, even relentless, basis. In fact, the list of such problems seems so extensive that if economics is the original 'dismal science' then the study of international security must be a very close second (Kapstein, 2002–3). Yet this field can also be as exciting as it is depressing, for it forces us to examine two critical questions about the human condition: *what do we really value*, and *how far will we go* to protect those valued things? One might even say we cannot comprehend other philosophical questions about our existence, purpose and destiny until these fundamental questions have been addressed – that is, until we feel more *secure*.

International security also occupies a central position in the broader academic discipline of international relations, yet there have been dramatic changes in the scope and content of these subjects since they emerged a century ago. During the early part of the twentieth century, the study of international relations focused on security affairs, particularly the problem of war. Today, however, the discipline includes a wider range of research fields: international security, international political economy, international organizations and institutions, international law, foreign policy analysis and area or regional studies. Each of these fields in turn has produced its own sub-fields, many of which pay varying degrees of attention to security issues. However, while the subject matter of international relations grew in the decades after World War II (WWII), the topic of international security within that discipline remained fairly narrowly construed – mainly in terms of international war and strategy – for most of the twentieth century. Three twentieth-century conflicts in particular – the two world wars and the Cold War – helped to maintain this more narrow focus even as other problems emerged.

However, even during the Cold War, some scholars began questioning the strategic, war-focused approach to international security and to related fields within international relations (Ullman, 1983). America's inability to prevail in Vietnam despite its preponderance of military power; the rise of new centres of power in Asia, Europe and elsewhere; the increasing prominence of non-state actors and international institutions; and the transformation of environmental, economic, health and other 'low politics' issues into 'high politics' security problems were key factors that challenged the traditional military-focused view of international security. Calls to expand the subject even more grew dramatically starting in the late 1980s with the end of the Cold War and the collapse of the Soviet Union, and since that time the field of international security has endured a great deal of fragmentation and contestation, more so perhaps in the past two decades than at any other time in its history.

This situation creates multiple challenges for those who research and teach international security studies (Walt, 1991; Baldwin, 1997; Betts, 1997; Buzan, 2007). However, if we approach international security as a distinct academic discipline with its own unique research agenda, then two simple premises follow: first, that in undertaking any field of academic enquiry one must start by fundamentally problematizing the core concerns of that field while excluding other issues or holding them constant as working assumptions. Once these core concerns have been addressed through a combination of theoretical innovation and empirical research, we can then relax the initial working assumptions and extend the boundaries of the field into new or related areas of enquiry. The second premise is that despite the plethora of theories, concepts and topics that increasingly complicate, if not confuse, the study of international security, there is in fact a single common thread running through most scholarly works on the topic, no matter how narrowly or broadly defined. That thread involves the idea that 'security' is not just a social concept worthy of intense academic study; it is also a problem to be regularly managed or controlled by human communities if they hope to survive. The term 'control', in turn, implies some degree of power or authority, or in other words: politics.

## International security: politics, policy and prospects

Defining international security as an academic subject first involves considering three related debates about the appropriate boundaries of the field. The first debate involves how to balance the analysis of tangible trends, decisions and policies against speculation about what the world should be doing about certain security problems, whether actual or potential. More simply, this is the question of balancing description/explanation (or empirical theory) against prescription/advocacy (or normative theory), although both approaches are related. The second debate involves the appropriate frame of reference in terms of who or what, exactly, should be secured, and how. Specifically, 'international security' can be conceived more narrowly as states (meaning their governments, territories, citizens and sovereign rights) and the state system itself, or far more broadly in terms of just about any valued thing on the planet. The third debate involves the role of force or violence in identifying major threats and in determining the most effective response to dealing with those threats. Again, this question can be framed more narrowly in terms of military threats met with a military response, or more broadly in terms of a range of threats, both military and non-military, met with a much wider range of policies.

As this volume is concerned with examining the state of international security studies based on contemporary thinking and practice, I must justify how my treatment of the topic addresses these three debates. First, this volume focuses on empirical research regarding the determination of whether certain problems 'qualify' as international security concerns. No community can devote its full attention to all policy problems all of the time, so we need to understand the general processes of selection by which security priorities are set by such communities. Second, I am concerned with the collective management of security problems once they have been identified as such. As problem management involves politics and policy, it is appropriate to structure the discussion around the role of states as key referent objects to be protected, whether in terms of their territories, their citizens, their governments or their sovereignty as political communities – or all of the above. States are not only charged with providing security for their citizens, they also have the authority to set public priorities, make security policy, apply force and extract private resources, in terms of physical and human capital, from the societies they ostensibly protect (Evans, Rueschemeyer and Skocpol, 1985; Ikenberry, Lake and Mastanduno, 1988).

Of course, in speaking of 'states' acting or deciding, I actually mean 'governments', which in turn means the officials charged with providing a range of services in exchange for our allegiance. To the extent that international security problems, whether in part or in total, are explicitly delegated to states for resolution, we must pay attention to processes of national policy formation and international cooperation when analysing those problems. Thus, although many *potential* security problems and referent objects may appear on the scene or attract the attention of security specialists, my primary concern here is with how these problems are 'politicized' (that is, made an explicit object of political action) into important international security issues. Finally, once states have become involved, it then follows that their policies can be backed up by the threat of force as they continue to claim a monopoly on the legitimate use of violence (Weber, 1918). Although some security scholars define 'force' or 'violence' in military terms, this volume takes a broader view to encompass policing, border control, travel restrictions and other types of official force to determine just how seriously the international community defines a specific threat (Jentleson, 2002).

Based on these considerations, this volume advances a *political analysis* approach, as compared to a *public policy* or *strategic analysis* approach, to international security, although these approaches are related. As I shall discuss in Chapter 3, a political analysis approach starts with the interests, power resources and activities or behaviours of the major political actors involved in the management of international security affairs. It assumes that such actors have conflicting interests, security and otherwise, and multiple demands on their attention and resources. Interest definition and threat perception, which factor into all international security problems, are inherently political processes; they can change in light of domestic and international circumstances. Actors involved in these issues must also pay attention not only to international politics but also to national or domestic politics, often simultaneously, in a kind of 'two-level' political process (Putnam, 1988). Conversely, a policy or strategic approach starts with the nature of the security problem or strategic game itself – as 'objectively' defined by the analyst – and then determines the mix of resources that should be mobilized to manage that problem, or to play that strategic 'game', most effectively (Schelling, 1966; Kennedy, 1991). Obviously politics, or competition about power or status or influence, is involved in both approaches, yet the key question is how we prioritize these political contests: as a fundamental dynamic governing all major aspects of international security affairs, or as an *ad hoc* peripheral concern used, along with a range of other variables, to explain why actors effectively managed (or failed to manage) a security problem.

This volume incorporates politics as an essential dynamic behind a full range of contemporary international security problems. Yet the ways by which political debates influence outcomes will vary depending on the key referent objects or values to be secured, on the role of force as a means to secure those values and on the range of actors, problems or issues to be defined as threats. In light of these considerations, we shall need to adopt a variable rather than rigid approach to these definitional questions, starting with the more orthodox, narrow and traditional views about international security (state-centric, focusing on military force and defining issues in relation to threats to state survival) and moving on to more contested, broader and somewhat less orthodox or less traditional views (non-state-centric, using other policy tools in addition to or instead of military force and defining issues relative to other values beyond state survival). This approach – treating international security as an academic discipline bound by a range of variously contested views about core conceptual and empirical elements – generally informs the selection and presentation of the problems covered in the volume. Therefore I begin with the traditional treatment of international war as a core security concern in Chapter 4 and then broaden the debate with each successive chapter to encompass other issues often grouped under the more general label of the new international security agenda, which encompasses 'human' or 'societal' or 'non-traditional' security.

A political approach to international security is also justified by several other considerations. One is that the term 'security' itself is often applied deliberately as a political tactic to stifle debate, assume more power or gain control over resources; therefore we must be sensitive to this possibility throughout the discussion. State actors in particular assume a special capacity to define issues as 'security' problems, which may then undermine the ability of other actors to question how those problems should be governed (Ikenberry, Lake and Mastanduno, 1988). They may also claim that such problems, once defined, should then be considered as 'above politics', or depoliticized, a claim which itself is inherently political in nature. In this volume, no international security issues are inherently 'above politics'. States also claim a monopoly over security-related information, or intelligence, not normally privy to many other actors (although this claim itself is under threat, as we shall see in Chapter 8). This monopoly, combined with other factors outlined in Chapter 3, means we must be *more* rather than less sensitive to fundamental political questions operating 'behind the scenes': who benefits from the protection of certain values, who governs and who pays? In other words, who wins and who loses in the high-stakes global politics of international security?

A second consideration is that the analysis of security often involves 'worst case' scenarios and assumptions. Once an issue has been framed as a security concern, policy-makers often think about the most terrible outcomes in order to avoid the maximum potential damage surrounding that threat. Typically this means thinking about the risks or damage caused by the most extreme situations, no matter how improbable those scenarios might be. In addition, this type of mentality might involve thinking the worst of an enemy or other adversary (Jervis, 1976). Sometimes this kind of thinking is just prudent planning by well-meaning policy specialists; at other times, however, it may be a political tactic to prioritize one security problem, or one branch of government, over another. Again, the political analysis of international security means we must assume that all actors involved, no matter how well-meaning they may seem, typically possess a range of motives in adopting certain policies about security problems, not all of which are directly related to merely 'solving' that problem. Politics means that larger questions of status or influence or control are always involved in security affairs, and in ways that go well beyond the need to manage a given problem to the satisfaction of those who hope to be made secure by their political authorities.

Finally, security policies can be further prone to politicization in light of many other considerations, not least of which is the political status such policies confer on certain actors, or the various resources those policies allow one to control. If security policies are meant to protect or maintain a current state of affairs (that is, a 'status quo posture') then actors who do not benefit from the status quo, such as the current distribution of global wealth, may find it difficult to protect their interests or promote change in such a system. Conversely, if security policies attempt to change the current state of affairs (that is, a 'revisionary posture'), as in the case of 'regime change', then this too will benefit some actors at the expense of others. Neither policy will necessarily improve *international* security, although the distribution of costs and benefits may change dramatically and can then be interpreted by some actors as a positive outcome for the international community.

In addition to the politics/policy-oriented approach to the topic, this volume is structured in light of three other major themes. These themes will be developed more fully in Chapter 2, yet it is worth flagging them here to help set the stage. The first theme involves the relationship between international and national (including domestic or homeland) security. As the title indicates, this volume is explicitly concerned with *international security* affairs rather than *security studies* or *national/homeland security*. Obviously there are no clear distinctions between these levels of analysis, and security problems that begin at the national level can easily migrate to the transnational and international levels (and vice versa). I shall return to this point in more detail in the following chapters, yet it should be clear at the outset that the most important criterion for including certain topics in this volume is that they have been *explicitly defined as international security problems by a critical mass of both scholars and policy-makers*. This also means that these problems have inspired specific bodies of theoretical and empirical research we can draw upon in the chapters to follow. The term 'international' need not mean or imply 'global' either (that is, in the sense of affecting the entire planet or all of humanity); only that a problem has been identified by authoritative international actors as important enough to require the sustained and focused attention of many states and other international actors.

A second theme running throughout this volume involves the specific relationship between state and non-state actors in managing various international security problems covered in later chapters. As I have noted, although this volume assumes a core role for states, it also pays close attention to state-based international organizations (IOs), including more traditional military alliances (such as the North Atlantic Treaty Organization, or NATO) and regional IOs that address certain security problems (such as the European Union, or EU). It also attempts to incorporate the role of non-state actors as threats, referent objects or even security providers. As I shall discuss further in Chapter 3, these non-state actors might take the form of non-governmental organizations (NGOs), private firms (especially multinational corporations, or MNCs), terrorist groups, organized criminal gangs and others depending on the security issue at hand.

A third and final theme involves the relationship between public and private authority, or states and markets. Here things get somewhat more complicated, but also more representative of contemporary politics and economics, as the borderline between 'public' and 'private' activity is becoming increasingly blurred, even in the realm of international security affairs. Public officials must be responsive to private demands for more security as well as to threats arising from the private sector; these processes become more complicated as new issues are added to an ever-expanding agenda. Equally interesting is the growing role of private actors in *providing* security services, either directly or indirectly. The *direct* private supply of security services typically takes the form of private military contractors (PMCs), who may supply material and services, including armed personnel, to governments. In other words, 'non-state' actors can be contracted to take on 'state-like' functions, even to the extent of using force. The 2003 war in Iraq in particular involved a very large number of PMCs amounting to thousands of individuals (Spearin, 2003; Singer, 2007), all of whom provide services similar to those of traditional national armies, yet this trend has been evident for years. In 1991, for example, there was roughly one PMC employee for every 100 US soldiers; ten years later – before the 2003 Iraq war – the figure had already risen to about ten PMCs per 100 soldiers. This trend is even more difficult to measure, but just as important, in terms of analysing the public–private balance regarding many new security issues, such as organized crime and pandemic disease.

The *indirect* private supply of security services might involve the role of medical firms, banks, internet service providers (ISPs) and other companies who assist governments with their expertise. Individual citizens and firms may also hire their own security services to protect their interests, conduct investigations or recover lost assets, which can involve the use of armed personnel with quasi-policing capabilities. Security has always been big business, and the use of mercenaries and privateers by states and firms has a long and complicated history (Thomson, 1990). Yet the modern expansion of private involvement ranging from arms manufacturers to armed security providers has greatly increased the profits to be earned from international security. To the extent that these profits involve the legal extraction of resources from individual citizens in the form of tax revenues, public oversight becomes an issue. These trends, all of which have been growing over the past few decades, make it increasingly difficult to determine the appropriate, effective and legal lines of authority and accountability we typically associate with government activities. Moreover, they mean we need to take a critical look at how states actually exercise their (supposed) monopoly over their (supposedly) legitimate use of violence; in other words, violence can be, and has been, subcontracted or outsourced to other actors, not all of whom can easily be made accountable. The same holds true of other security activities covered in this volume, in both traditional and non-traditional problem areas.

## Theory and research design in international security

As we shall see in Chapter 2, the expansion of international security as a field of study has been accompanied by a similar expansion of theories and concepts. These theories can be based on widely diverging views about not just the fundamentals of international security but about knowledge creation, or epistemology, itself. What we study is strongly influenced by what we want, what we value and what we think is right; ignoring these facts can greatly complicate the pursuit of knowledge, particularly in the social sciences. Realism in particular has been dominant in part because it helped to legitimize the conduct of certain states during the Cold War, when international security developed into a distinct field of study. More generally, scholars often study war because they want to end wars, or make them less likely or destructive, or make their own state's victory in war more likely, not merely because war is a fascinating example of human behaviour.

This tendency to offer incomplete or quick prescriptions in addition to, or even instead of, furthering our basic understanding of international security affairs is directly related to the fact that security is often driven by current events, and can involve high-stakes issues of life and death. These facts can profoundly influence the kinds of research that specialists conduct; the dramatic rise of terrorism studies and the debate over cyber-security in the past decade are major examples, as with the dramatic rise of strategic (nuclear) studies in the 1950s. Yet these problems and events do not automatically lead to a specific theory; instead, one's choice of (or predilection for) a theory strongly preconditions how one frames or *problematizes* a research question. Thus the choice of one's theory must not be taken lightly, nor taken for granted; it should be made as explicitly as possible in any respectable research effort, and then defended.

As international security is very value-laden as a discipline, it can be difficult to study objectively or scientifically. One must constantly be aware of the value claims of the researcher, particularly when they are not stated at the outset (and often they are not). In addition, the modern study of international security can be extremely complex, and involve history, politics, economics, culture, law, ethics, military studies, geography, strategy, technology and many other factors. Although I defend a political approach to the topic in more detail in Chapter 3, it should be clear at the outset that answering specific research questions about international security might involve concepts or factors from all of these areas. Yet how do we organize all of these disciplines and, more importantly, compare our findings with those of other researchers? In other words, how do we defend our own truth claims against competing views? With the systematic and rigorous use of theory and data, or empirical research.

To begin, empirical research or knowledge production generally starts with a specific question (or a set of related questions). Although this initial question can be specific or general (that is, explaining one war or all wars), most research is typically oriented towards the creation of cumulative knowledge, which means the researcher must think about how to *generalize* the facts or findings specific to one case in terms of drawing broader lessons from it, then test and gradually build upon those lessons by looking at other related cases or evidence. This is where theory comes in, and the problem of generalizability raises the more specific question of inductive versus deductive research designs. An *inductive* approach would attempt to examine evidence or data first and then try to draw general conclusions based on certain patterns within the evidence. *Deductive* research designs reverse this process: they start with a theory (or set of theoretical causal propositions, usually known as *hypotheses*), then attempt to find evidence to support or reject that theory. In doing so they attempt to relate individual phenomena (such as a specific war) to larger classes of phenomena (such as all wars or political violence) in order to prove theoretical linkages between them.

One might assume that an inductive approach is best as it (supposedly) reduces the chance of bias on the part of the researcher, yet a critical problem here is that the study of social phenomena is fundamentally different from the study of natural phenomena. As there are no social laws equivalent to physical laws in the universe, there really is no such thing as 'purely inductive' (that is, totally objective or atheoretical) social science research. The study of international security therefore is not like that of the physical or natural sciences, where experiments and other inductive observations, even unintentional ones, can often yield insightful theoretical findings. One must also be aware of the so-called 'inductivist illusion', as cultural anthropologist Claude Lévi-Strauss (1963) once put it. This illusion is that social facts will 'speak for themselves' if one merely collects enough data; the reality, however, is that empirical observations and experience rarely, if ever, lead directly to non-trivial, robust and convincing causal explanations. They may yield puzzles, questions and even educated guesses (hypotheses) to help generate 'quasi-theories' or 'pre-theories' but not much more. In fact, in the social sciences one could easily be overwhelmed by a mass of useless detail depending on where one looks: public opinion polls, archives, statistics, voting records, newspaper articles, elite interviews, and so on. Especially when studying highly complex social phenomena like wars and disease and poverty, one must be prepared to generalize first, and then attempt to find supporting evidence later through the use of specific methodologies to reduce the possibility of bias: this is the process of rigorous deductive empirical research. In other words, it is better to be explicit 'up front' about one's views of the world and attempt to control them through a clear research design than assert that one is going to look at a topic with completely fresh eyes and (supposedly) defend no values whatsoever. In this volume, then, 'theory' simply means a *proposed* explanation whose status is still conjectural in contrast to well-established propositions that are regarded as reporting matters of actual fact. More persuasive theories will inspire a specific research programme, which then attempts to prove, disprove or revise the theory at hand to help accumulate knowledge and move academic enquiry forward (Rosenau and Rosenau, 2000).

Theories and the research programmes they inspire can also vary in terms of their scope, which introduces another consideration into the effort. At one end of the spectrum, theories as defined above, can apply to large classes of events or long periods of historical time or to basic features of the human condition, such as the role of violence in politics, whose specific form can vary widely depending on the circumstances. This approach is often termed 'grand theory' or 'macro-theory' and some scholars believe that such an approach is both possible and desirable within the realm of international relations (Waltz, 1979). At the other end of the scale one can construct explanations that are far narrower, or 'micro-theories', that apply to a much smaller class of events or even to single events, such as a unique decision. Obviously there is a trade-off here: grand theories may be very ambitious yet they may be nearly impossible to prove or test empirically, or so abstract that they cannot explain most of the 'day-to-day' behaviours that concern international security specialists. Conversely, micro-level theories might be so unique to one case that it becomes difficult to generalize across time and space in hopes of making better use of the findings.

To deal with these problems, this volume attempts to find some common ground between these contending positions regarding grand versus micro-level theories. This generally involves paying attention to 'middle-range' theories to explain more specific, though still quite generalizable, questions, such as: is one geographic region or type of governing regime more prone to war than others? What factors increase the likelihood of foreign military intervention in a civil war? What accounts for the defeat or disappearance of some terrorist groups but not others? And so on. Then, as one builds up knowledge within these middle-range areas, it might be possible – and more persuasive – to build grand theory from the bottom up, as it were, with solid concepts and empirical evidence about causal relationships among various factors, rather than from the top down. This approach avoids the pretensions of grand theory by adopting a more modest scope of analysis, such as a shorter historical period, as with the dynamics of the Cold War, or a smaller class of phenomena, such as security relations among democratic states, but one still wide enough to draw meaningful generalizations across a range of events as compared to more micro-level theories. Much of the research cited throughout this volume involves precisely this compromise between grand international relations theories and more micro-level theories of single foreign policy decisions or policies.

## Evolution of the international security research agenda

The need for a general analytical framework to understand, and teach, contemporary international security affairs can be seen in the evolution of the research agenda over the past two decades. Although this volume takes for granted the ideas that international security is not a 'self-evident' end in itself, and that it can be contested like any other social goal or political problem, this was not always the case. We should remember that the field, particularly in the US (Smith, 2002), largely developed in response to the Cold War, which included the assimilation of the 'lessons' of the interwar period. During the Cold War era, scholars and policy-makers focused on a unique and highly competitive bilateral relationship where the possession of strategic nuclear weapons, and the possibility of total global destruction, created a permanent shadow of fear unlike anything experienced in any other adversarial relationship in history. However, the fact that the superpowers ended their conflict without ever resorting to a 'hot' war, particularly one involving nuclear weapons, meant that analysts had a very limited amount of information on which to base their predictions and recommendations. In addition, the novelty of a bilateral *nuclear* strategic competition would almost certainly raise questions about whether lessons from the management of that relationship really could apply to other contemporary problems of international security.

This highly unique Cold War combination – an unprecedented type of deadly strategic rivalry coupled with limited empirical data about how to conduct such a relationship – resulted in an overwhelming reliance on the assumption of unitary and rational state (that is, government) action, where both superpowers attempted to avoid the same two least desired outcomes: global thermonuclear war (that is, mutual assured destruction, or MAD), and defeat or submission at the hands of the other party. In hopes of avoiding these extremes, analysts devised a range of hypothetical strategic scenarios or 'games' to help guide national policies on weapons development and deployment, alliance creation and maintenance (Walt, 1991), military intervention and even economic policy, such as the use of trade or financial embargoes (Mastanduno, 1993), in the absence of actual knowledge, historical or otherwise, about how a bilateral strategic nuclear competition might end (Oye, 1986).

As we shall see in Chapter 2, the legacy of the Cold War analytical agenda still influences international security studies and provides much of the background scholarly material for the more traditional problems covered in this volume. This legacy, however, raises two critical problems. First, many of the theoretical arguments about the Cold War rivalry, particularly the question of how states might conduct a nuclear war (Kahn, 1960), simply could not be supported by empirical evidence as no two countries have ever attacked *each other* with nuclear weapons (so far!). Second, any supposed lessons about power and credibility generated by the Cold War in general or the US–Soviet relationship in particular may not be applicable to the kinds of security threats, and the range of possible responses, now confronting decision-makers, such as the crisis in Syria (Mitton, 2015). These problems are compounded by our limited knowledge about how actors – state officials and otherwise – are likely to manage non-traditional security threats. The result is that some researchers might be tempted to conclude that each contemporary international security problem must be treated on its own merits, as a self-contained analytical puzzle, and that the search for underlying processes or principles that transcend individual security problems is futile. Such an attitude, of course, may also contribute to the overall fragmentation and disorganization of the discipline, yet if the security agenda itself is increasingly fragmented and disorganized, so that virtually any topic is 'fair game' as a security concern, then we can hardly expect academic researchers to do much better.

The problem of finding a consensus about fundamental principles in researching international security is even more complicated in light of the overwhelming focus in the discipline on *Western* values, security problems and analytical tools. To the extent that the roots of contemporary international security studies, if not international relations in general, are found in Cold War policy debates, US scholars in particular helped to set the agenda for international relations as 'an American social science' (Hoffman, 1977; also see Wæver, 1998), although various European schools of thought increasingly challenged that dominance. As we shall see in the next chapter, the dominance of the realist school of thinking about international security is difficult to disentangle from the politics of the Cold War, although most realist scholars insist that its insights are based on deeper historical 'patterns' or 'processes' in world politics extending back centuries.

Thus it is no surprise that studies of nuclear policies, crisis decision-making and alliance politics tended to dominate the international security research agenda for much of the Cold War period. Why concern yourself with the emergence of a new infectious disease in sub-Saharan Africa that fatally depresses the immune system when the superpowers had tens of thousands of nuclear warheads on constant alert? Why devote attention to organized crime when America and its allies apparently faced communist-supported insurgencies in a range of hotspots around the globe? And why study global climate change as a potential threat when actual US/Soviet intervention in less developed countries (LDCs) threatened to disrupt important sources of raw materials and change the global balance of power? This tendency is still reflected in some scholarly works and academic journals, which treat the subjects of 'US national security policy' and 'international security' as virtually synonymous. If we are indeed still living in a 'unipolar moment' (Krauthammer, 1990–1; Mastanduno, 1997; Beckley, 2011–12; Brands, 2016) where America's wealth and military power put it in a class of its own as a great power, if not a superpower, then the US is better positioned than other actors in setting the international security agenda, even though its influence may have declined in recent years. On some topics, then, it is tempting to conclude that 'international security' is largely what the US and its allies say it is. However, although this volume stresses the political analysis of international security affairs, and pays special attention to the role of leading states such as the US, it does not fall into the trap of prioritizing American views on all security issues for several reasons.

First, as noted above, even during the Cold War some scholars were attempting to broaden the agenda of policy issues and theoretical concepts in international security well beyond the realist focus on strategic superpower military confrontation. Second, it became clear to many scholars that US influence could vary widely across topics, and that the chief measure of US political power – military force, or 'hard power' – can either be stretched too thin or be completely ineffective for certain types of security problems. The possibility that America is becoming overstretched as the dominant power, or may even be in terminal decline, while other powers, such as China, assert themselves, also calls into question the idea that international security is largely synonymous with America's interests (Kupchan, 1998). Third, even with America's dominant military might, other actors are catching up to the US in terms of various forms of 'soft power' (Nye, 2005) – finance, trade, reputation, values and so on – that may be very useful for addressing many contemporary security problems. Fourth, to the extent that America desires some degree of international support for its policies, it must attempt to find allies and build stable coalitions; these activities allow other actors to play key roles in turning US rhetoric into global reality. Fifth and perhaps most interestingly, the US is most certainly not a monolithic actor. No respectable study of US policy and policy-making would deny that multiple actors attempt to speak for the US, even in the realm of foreign/security policy, and not always with a single voice; or that US policies are often contradictory and may even work at cross purposes; or that the US policy process in security affairs can be just as politicized as in other policy domains, so that numerous actors within the US must compete to set the agenda and control key resources. As we shall see in Chapter 3, these political processes, which are at work in varying ways in all states, can seriously undermine national leadership, and the broader assumption of unitary rational state action, over international security affairs (Hill, 2003).

To summarize, the overall tone of this volume is sceptical, and the overall analytical approach is political. It is sceptical because I take very little for granted in analysing contemporary international security problems, and I attempt to treat them with a common analytical framework that interprets all international security threats according to the same standards. It is political because the process of determining what is protected from what types of harm by what means is inherently power-oriented. No political actor has the capacity to manage all security problems equally effectively all of the time, so we must understand the political process of choice in the face of competing values and priorities. Power is always required to collectively define valued things and then to marshal the resources needed to protect those valued things (Easton, 1965), even when the need to do so seems abundantly self-evident to a political community – which is rarely the case. As we shall see in the next chapter, most alternative approaches to international security are in fact power-oriented; they merely adopt a different view of power and assume different referent objects or values as compared to more traditional theories.

Similar attempts to frame international security problems through normative theories based on human rights or justice or equity also tend to reinforce Western, and even transatlantic or European, values rather than 'universal' values about what all people should value across space and time. This conceit among some scholars and policy-makers about 'fundamental' values and the actual international community to be protected from harm will become increasingly apparent as we traverse the range of contemporary security problems covered in this volume, and will be examined in more detail in the conclusion. Moreover, actors in many cultures will sacrifice freedom, justice, equity and other Western/liberal values for all kinds of other values, and not just security of life and property; these include religion, social unity or stability, fairness, status and others. In fact, international security can be defined as much by a clash of values as by a harmony of them, so we need to consider how international power is marshalled to put one set of values ahead of another, which requires some form of political analysis. Before attempting such an analysis, however, we need to understand the more general evolution and current context of the field of international security as an academic discipline and as a set of policy objectives. This task is taken up in the next chapter.

# Chapter 2

# Theory, Research and International Security: Continuity and Change

The dramatically altered academic preoccupations of contemporary international security studies deserve more attention as all of the security problems covered throughout this volume must take into consideration certain intellectual legacies and other factors, though these may operate quite differently depending on the issue at hand. Since these factors are so pervasive, we should consider them at length here to avoid a repetitive discussion of them in the chapters devoted to specific security problems. However, we must also keep in mind what has *not* changed in recent years regarding international security studies. New theories based on realism and liberalism are being developed in this realm, even as alternative approaches claim to challenge the intellectual hegemony of these two enduring paradigms. Similarly, certain aspects of the Cold War still condition debates about international security and must be kept in mind even as new issues are added to the agenda.

The next three sections of this chapter examine these dynamics in terms of international security studies prior to the Cold War, during the Cold War and after the Cold War. In addition, each section examines both intellectual trends and the major empirical problems of international security that influenced those trends. The intellectual trends involve two major dimensions: a general expansion in major approaches to international relations/security beyond the realist–liberal dichotomy, and a shift in focus among various levels of analysis when attempting to delineate the field. The empirical problems also reflect a general expansion throughout these periods, beginning with the problem of international war in the early part of the twentieth century and expanding to include a number of non-traditional threats. The fourth and final section of the chapter is a more focused treatment of two key contemporary concepts whose implications are still being debated: globalization and human security. A critical debate regarding both of these concepts involves whether the role of the state has been undermined or enhanced as the major reference point for the study of international security, and whether it should be replaced by other referent objects, such as the individual or society.

## International security studies in the interwar period

Although it can be difficult to disentangle the subject matter of international relations and international security in the decades prior to the Cold War, as both disciplines were generally preoccupied with the question of international war, it is worth keeping in mind some of the nuances in scholarly thinking about that subject before the advent of WWII. Although a great deal of such thinking during this period (and beyond) can be framed in terms of a debate between realism and liberalism and their associated dichotomies (that is, war/peace, determinism/free will, practice/theory, pessimist/optimist, real world/ideal world, bureaucrat/intellectual, right/ left, conservative/radical and politics/ethics) (Carr, 1964; Baldwin, 1993), it is also worth keeping in mind the existence, even during these years, of alternative approaches to the topic – such as Marxism – that continue to inspire scholarly work in the discipline.

As international relations emerged as an academic discipline after World War I (WWI), a conflict unprecedented in human history, it is no surprise that the core concern was to prevent another such conflict from ever taking place. However, scholars quickly became divided regarding how to diagnose the major causes of WWI and, in turn, consider what types of policy prescriptions would be most effective to avoid another such conflagration. Initially, many placed their hopes in the liberal ideal of collective security, in the form of a security guarantee offered by the new League of Nations. The creation of the League, which was championed in particular by US President Woodrow Wilson, himself a constitutional scholar, was inspired by one major form of liberalism – institutional or regulatory or legal liberalism – that still influences contemporary international relations theory. This view tends to focus on customs, rules, laws and institutions as key components of international security and cooperation; some scholars in fact still use the term 'Grotian' liberalism after Hugo Grotius, a Dutch thinker who developed some fundamental concepts of the law of nations.

This idea of *collective security* as governed by international agreement had its roots in the emergence of what is now known as the modern Law of Armed Conflict (LOAC) regime (or *international humanitarian law*). The LOAC began to consolidate following the American Civil War and the wars of German unification, when new actors in the form of transnational peace societies, such as the International Committee of the Red Cross (ICRC), the International Peace Bureau and the Interparliamentary Union began to lobby for controls on the conduct of war and for the peaceful resolution of disputes. In the face of these concerns, the 1899 and 1907 Hague Conventions attempted to set down rules to govern warfare and, hopefully, make it more 'humane', in line with Western liberal values. These instruments served to both define an emerging norm of humanitarian warfare and justify possible constraints on warfighting that might

violate that norm. Following WWI, when many of these norms were violated, the international community attempted to take a stronger stance by
devising an instrument, the 1928 Kellogg–Briand Pact (also known as the
Pact of Paris), that required signatories to 'renounce' warfare as an instrument of national policy. Negotiated by the US Secretary of State (Kellogg)
and the French Foreign Minister (Briand), the pact, ultimately signed by
61 states, entered into force in 1929 and remains part of international law
to this day.

In general, the idea was that states could entrust their security to the
League of Nations and other such legal instruments, and therefore would
not have to resort to unilateral war-making to defend themselves. Further,
any state acting in an 'aggressive' manner would risk the collective punishment of the League, which would also involve itself in many other problems
discussed in this book, such as refugees and health. One immediate problem, however, was the failure of the US Senate to ratify the League treaty
owing to its collective security provisions; this refusal deprived the League
of support from one of the most important major powers. Moreover, the
League's approach to collective security came under increasing stress in
the face of the threat of fascism during the 1930s, as the League failed
to deter aggression on the part of Germany, Italy and Japan (Housden,
2012; Pedersen, 2015). Related efforts by other states, such as the UK
and France, to negotiate with rather than punish or oppose such regimes,
became known as *appeasement* (Press, 2004); this strategy of offering unilateral concessions to deter threats made by another has taken on very
negative connotations that persist to this day.

For some scholars, these events demonstrated the primary defect of
a liberal approach to international security: the problem of enforcing
collective norms or laws (Carr, 1964). This view intensified in the face
of a major international economic crisis in the 1930s; rather than work
together to effectively manage the problem, the major powers ultimately
resorted to unilateral self-help in the form of tariff barriers and competitive currency devaluations in an attempt to force the costs of adjustment
onto their trading partners; this is known as a *beggar-thy-neighbour* strategy. If everyone adopts this strategy, however, the result is a kind of trade
or tariff war (Conybeare, 1987), whereby the economic crisis can become
far worse, and last much longer, than it might have. Officials from this
period cannot plead ignorance on this point either; when the US fired the
first shots of the trade war in the form of the Smoot-Hawley Tariff Act
of 1930, a petition against the Act signed by 1,028 economists failed to
persuade President Hoover to veto it. Other states retaliated in kind, and
the international economy descended into the Great Depression.

The gulf that emerged in the 1930s between liberal theory and the
practice of international security allowed realist scholars to assert themselves in a manner that persists to this day, and helped to inspire the

initial evolution of what came to be known as security studies (Ekbladh, 2011–12). In fact, realism remains the most important general theory of international security and many other theories considered throughout this volume have been framed, implicitly or explicitly, either to fill in the gaps neglected by realists or to undermine the entire realist edifice. In the years prior to WWII, realism expanded from *classical realism*, which focused on negative aspects of human nature as an explanation for war (Waltz, 1959), towards what came to be known as *defensive realism*, which generally stressed the importance of national self-help as IOs such as the League could not be trusted to provide security in an anarchic international system (Morgenthau, 1948). National self-help, in turn, requires a certain degree of material power to convert into military force; this is generally known as a *balance-of-power* strategy. Such a strategy could involve *internal balancing* (that is, building up resources domestically), *external balancing* (that is, searching for allies with similar security problems), or both, in the form of *omni-balancing* (David, 1991). However, realists at this time were unclear on just how much power would be enough to balance against a rival. This question, among others, would receive much greater attention during the Cold War, especially after the start of a superpower nuclear arms race.

Finally, a third strand of thinking endured throughout this period: Marxism. In fact, Marxism deserves credit as the first truly modern theory of international relations, and as a precursor to more recent critical theories (see 'International Security Studies After the Cold War' below), many of which owe a debt to Marxist thought. As with all approaches discussed in this chapter, Marxism has its own permutations and areas of contention, yet it does possess a relatively coherent core of assumptions and principles. Most of these can be traced back to several key works, particularly Karl Marx's *Communist Manifesto* (1838) and Vladimir Lenin's *Imperialism: The Highest Stage of Capitalism* (1916), plus the ideas found in anti-imperialist works such as John Hobson's *Imperialism* (1902). As Marx himself was more concerned with domestic politics than international politics, Hobson and Lenin looked to the experience of the Boer War and WWI, as well as other 'imperialist' wars among competing colonial powers, as their inspiration for a Marxist theory of international relations. In their interpretation, Marxism came to reflect a mix of both realist and liberal traditions: with realism, it shares a key focus on the material basis of power where the most powerful actors are the owners of capital, yet it also shares with liberalism a somewhat utopian view of a more peaceful and egalitarian future for humanity, whereby nation-states, and the wars they regularly instigate in the face of scarce resources, will ultimately wither away.

For Marxists, the only effective way to break this cycle of exploitation and dominance is to replace the global capitalist system with a socialist one, so that the poor (or *periphery*) states will be able catch up to the rich (or *core*) states (Wallerstein, 1984). Of course, changing the global economic order is much easier said than done, and there are really only three major Marxist options here: 1) a world socialist revolution as more states become socialist through domestic processes; 2) the adoption of *autarky* by periphery states (that is, they attempt to break their dependency on core states by raising trade barriers, pursuing import-substituting industrialization or forming producer cartels for certain raw materials, such as oil); or 3) a gradual reform of the system into a more egalitarian one, using collective bargaining tactics among the poorer states. These approaches are not mutually exclusive, of course, and leaders sympathetic to Marxism have often followed the second and third options while waiting for the global socialist revolution to occur.

To summarize, although all three theories above focused mainly on the problem of international war, they did so by using different levels of analysis and by recommending different policy prescriptions. Liberalism mostly took the form of institutional/regulatory/legal liberalism, involving a new formal security organization created at the international system level (the League of Nations). Realism maintained its traditional focus on material power but began to shift from an emphasis on human nature towards national power and self-help (or from the individual level to the national/domestic level). Marxism, finally, stressed the global context, rather than the state level, as the most important level of analysis, and can be seen as the first truly systemic or structural theory of international relations/security. The Marxist focus on class divisions within capitalist states manifested itself at the international level in the uneven development of rich states (primarily in the North) and poor states (primarily in the South). Two consequences then follow: the division in the global ownership of capital breeds a potential for colonial conflicts between the North and the South, while competition among northern states breeds imperialist wars among them. These themes appear in different forms in the major variants of Marxist theory throughout the twentieth century, such as world systems theory, neo-Gramscian theory and dependency theory.

A final point to keep in mind about this period is that the focus on war and armaments – a clear legacy of WWI – overshadowed other issues that today would almost certainly be considered major international security problems. One obvious example is the Great Depression; it was severe, but the world had suffered previous economic downturns in 1873–8 and 1893–7, so policy-makers expected to be able to cope with the 1930s crisis without defining it as a security threat. A second example involves conflicts and human rights abuses in less developed parts of the world, most of which were colonial possessions and therefore did not 'qualify' as important locales for international security considerations. A third example is the threat of pandemic disease, mainly in the form of the 1917–18

influenza that killed as many as 50 million people. Not only was this problem not identified as an 'international security' problem; policy-makers in
several countries even suppressed news of it for fear of creating a panic and
thus undermining the war effort. Spanish authorities, however, reported
honestly about the problem, which is why the pandemic is known to this
day as 'Spanish flu'. A final example involves the problem of civil war, and
again Spain provides the best example. The Spanish Civil War of 1936–9
is known today as a kind of 'dress rehearsal' for WWII, as it took the
form of a clash between democratic (or republican) and authoritarian (or
nationalist) forces, with German/Italian support for the nationalists and
Soviet support for the republicans. However, despite the heavy death toll –
over 500,000 killed – in one of the largest states in Europe, and despite
the involvement of many outside volunteers on both sides, the League of
Nations again failed to halt the violence and the war was not treated as
a major threat to international security. The democratically elected Spanish republican government eventually succumbed to nationalist forces on
1 April 1939, ushering in a period of authoritarian rule under General
Francisco Franco that lasted until 1978 – one of the longest dictatorships
in modern history.

## International security studies and the Cold War

Problems associated with a liberal institutional approach to international
security in the form of the League of Nations, as well as various non-
aggression and arms control agreements, were clearly on the minds of
scholars and policy-makers as WWII wound down and the Cold War
warmed up in the late 1940s. The Cold War was a global conflict, and
it consumed vast resources – material and intellectual – on the part of all
players. And, for the first time in the history of military conflict, the main
rivals in the Cold War *each* had the capability, many times over, to wreak
catastrophic destruction. The fact that each side of the Cold War was also
associated with a distinct political ideology – liberalism in the West and
communism in the East – also turned the rivalry into not just a military
competition but also a political contest for hearts and minds across the
globe, which involved the use of reputation, legitimacy, symbols and even
culture (Saunders, 2001) as political tools and as major referent objects to
be protected. This process also involved a somewhat awkward transition
from former Western allies into enemies (China and the USSR) and former
Western enemies into allies (Germany, Italy and Japan).

   More specifically, the rise of a global superpower rivalry between the
post-WWII East and West helped to inspire new realist works on an old
question: how much power would enable the US and its allies to deter or

defeat an attack by the Soviet Union and/or China? As power must be maintained to ensure survival in a competitive and anarchic international system, power-balancing requires states to constantly measure their status and power *vis-à-vis* their main rivals; this tendency became known as the *relative gains problem* (Grieco, 1990; Powell, 1991; Snidal, 1991). However, such 'tit-for-tat' balancing behaviour can produce a second problem: the *security dilemma,* or the tendency for efforts to increase one's own security to cause others to behave likewise, which then reduces security for everyone (Herz, 1950; Jervis, 1978). This is a core principle behind the realist view of arms races or trade/tariff wars, and such an emphasis on international system-level factors, instead of domestic or individual-level factors (Waltz, 1959; see also Brodie, 1973), took the form of increasingly complex debates about how to strike a balance between general environmental or contextual variables (such as anarchy or the balance of power) and more specific national/domestic variables (such as regime type, bureaucratic politics, organizational cultures, interest groups, public opinion and so on).

As Figure 2.1 shows, the possible combinations of theory and level(s) of analysis are virtually endless once one starts to 'open up' any one of the nearly 200 states in the current international system (for example, see Allison, 1971; Small and Singer, 1976; Andreski, 1980; Doyle, 1983; Chan, 1984; J. Snyder, 1984 and 1991; Weede, 1984; Doyle, 1986; and Russett, 1990).

Although most theories discussed in this volume focus on the systemic/ structural to the national/domestic levels, it is also possible to examine individual-level factors to add more detail to the analysis; these factors might include human nature; biological factors; gender; and (especially) psychological factors, such as personality or character traits, cognition

---

1. Systemic/Global (all states)

2. Structural (balance-of-power dynamics, economic/financial markets, networks)

3. Regional

4. Sub-regional

5. National/Domestic (comparative politics; comparative foreign policy)

6. State institutions (governments, bureaucracies, officials)

7. Societal institutions (interest groups, parties, firms, civil society)

8. Individuals: psychology/personality, gender, biology

---

Figure 2.1   *Levels of analysis in international relations*

and perception/misperception, decision-making under conditions of crisis or stress, the role of images or biases held by key leaders and so on (Janis, 1972; Jervis, 1976; George, 1980; Barber, 1992). The advent of gene-mapping in recent years has even led some scholars to explore the controversial notion of 'genopolitics', or how specific genes might influence certain types of political behaviour, such as voting (Fowler and Dawes, 2013). However, as these levels are merely a way of structuring the major variables of interest to a particular analyst, there is no 'correct' number of levels to adopt. The use of these levels can be likened to changing the lens on a microscope to view a living cell: the cell doesn't change, but new structures and processes will come into view as you change the magnification. The same principle applies here, and one might miss something important at one level by focusing too long somewhere else; hence more sophisticated analyses of international security often combine various levels of analysis into a single explanation.

Despite the potential utility of these various levels in understanding international security in general and the Cold War in particular, the first half of the Cold War era was characterized by a balance-of-power strategy on both sides. Although America had planned to demobilize most of its military forces after WWII, Soviet actions in Czechoslovakia, Poland, Hungary, Greece, Iran and Turkey soon convinced the US that a total withdrawal of its forces from Europe might embolden the Soviets in a manner similar to Nazi expansion in the 1930s. In response, the US developed a strategic nuclear deterrent and what became a global system of alliances to defend itself (Macdonald, 1995–6). Thus, starting in 1949, the US created NATO, the Southeast Asia Treaty Organization (SEATO), the Australia–New Zealand–US Treaty (ANZUS) and other bilateral arrangements such as the US security commitments to Israel and Taiwan. The Soviet bloc adopted a similar approach, resulting in two main superpower alliance systems – NATO and the Soviet-led Warsaw Treaty Organization (Warsaw Pact) – each with its own mix of conventional and nuclear forces.

However, once this overall balance-of-power strategy was in place – framed as containment (of Soviet expansion) and deterrence (of a Soviet attack against the West) – it became necessary to defend and refine it in light of subsequent political, economic, technological and even cultural changes. These measures generally involved reliance on deterrence with both conventional weapons and, increasingly, weapons of mass destruction (WMD) to protect each superpower bloc. To maintain this overall balance of power, an intense nuclear rivalry developed between both sides as each attempted to achieve nuclear superiority over the other (that is, the ability to *win* a nuclear war). Such superiority, if achieved, was also expected to provide bargaining leverage over the rival side. To complicate the situation even further, *no one on earth really knew how a nuclear war would be conducted*, as no such war had ever taken place. Here, then, is where a new generation of post-war international security scholars and strategic studies scholars possibly could play a role. Many such scholars first attempted to measure and document, systematically, how states conducted war with each other as a way to gain insights into strategic rivalries like the Cold War. This effort became part of the larger 'behavioural revolution' in American social science in the 1950s, which focused on the use of empirical evidence, or experience, experiment and observation, to understand the human condition. In security studies, huge efforts were expended to construct large databases on war and various related topics, such as the Correlates of War project, the Conflict and Peace Databank and others.

Although we shall revisit some of these studies in later chapters in this volume, it is worth noting at this point the crucial role of arms racing in international security studies during the Cold War. Here special attention was paid to so-called 'strategic' nuclear weapons: those whose range and power could enable the defeat of an enemy's military forces so completely that the enemy government surrenders. The pursuit of this objective resulted in the possession of over 10,000 strategic warheads by each of the two main rival states during the Cold War. The other declared nuclear powers at the time – China, France and the UK – never had more than a few hundred warheads each, so the rivalry clearly was a US–Soviet contest. The rivalry over strategic warheads was compounded by other contests regarding tactical nuclear weapons, nuclear delivery systems, missile defences, conventional forces, economic performance and even civil defence plans, as each side tried to find that unique edge over the other. Accordingly, the literature during this period is overwhelmingly dominated by analyses of these various rivalries regarding technological advances or strategic doctrines made by either side. Relatively less attention was paid to what type of world we would have, if any, following a strategic nuclear exchange (i.e. a *nuclear winter*; see Baum, 2015), or to the actual political objectives that would be served by gaining true nuclear superiority over one's rival, if such a thing were actually possible. In other words, the Cold War was effectively becoming *an end in itself*, rather than a means to some other end, or to some other type of world order, as occurs with most other conventional military rivalries or conflicts.

As a reflection of this tendency, we can see various studies of whether global 'structures' of power – such as those based on a 'preponderance' of power (that is, a *unipolar* system in which one state dominates) or a 'balance' or 'parity' of power (that is, a *bipolar* or *multipolar* system) – are inherently more or less stable or peaceful (Niou, Ordeshook and Rose, 1989; Wagner, 1994). However, the arguments and findings of this research are still inconclusive in terms of determining which type of system is more stable, meaning the absence of war among major powers, and whether states might actually reject balancing in favour of 'bandwagoning' (that is, allying with a stronger state to share in the spoils of war or avoid conquest). Some argued that unipolar systems dominated by a single major power, or hegemon, are more stable (Keohane, 1984; Jervis, 2009), especially when such a major power can fend off all major competitors (at a minimum) and effectively control the international agenda (at a maximum). Others, however (Layne, 1993 and 2006), argued that such orders ultimately invite the rise of competing powers, and thus conflict, as other states attempt to displace the 'king of the hill'. Measuring polarity primarily in terms of material power also ignores the high social costs of maintaining legitimacy and avoiding hypocrisy on the part of the hegemon (Finnemore, 2009). If these arguments have merit, then multipolar systems may be the most stable in the long term as they provide many coalition-building opportunities for states to balance against any state attempting to dominate the system (Deutsch and Singer, 1964). This view, however, is contradicted by arguments pointing out that multipolar Europe has been the site of the most destructive wars in history. In addition, the lack of a superpower war during the Cold War led some analysts to argue that bipolar systems are the most stable. To support this position, Kenneth Waltz developed a new realist, or 'neo-realist', approach to the international system, which supplements anarchy with two other structural factors: the number of great powers (that is, unipolar, bipolar or multipolar), and the distribution of power among them (Waltz, 1979; also see Keohane, 1986).

However, Waltz's view about the pacifistic effects of a bipolar system is highly problematic for several reasons. Specifically, the fact that the two superpowers of the Cold War did not fight a 'hot war' *in this case* does not mean such a war is unlikely in all such situations. For example, would a bipolar Nazi–Soviet nuclear rivalry have been as stable as the US–Soviet contest? Also, even if we interpret the Cold War as a state of 'long peace' (that is, stability) between the superpowers and their major allies (Gaddis, 1986), the Cold War still involved a high degree of political violence among and within other states in the form of proxy wars, as in the two Koreas, Vietnam, Angola, Afghanistan, El Salvador and others. Moreover, the relative rarity of bipolar (and unipolar) systems in general, and the near impossibility of deliberately transforming one type of system into another, mean that these types of analyses can tell us relatively little about specific policy recommendations concerning many contemporary security problems. In addition, more recent work on the question of balancing of any type has argued that a balance of power – assuming it does not involve the threat of nuclear weapons – may actually *increase* the propensity of adversaries to go to war (Moul, 2003).

Beyond this preoccupation with material power structures, the Cold War study of international security was complicated further by various attempts to deal with a problem noted earlier: the lack of data regarding an actual nuclear war. In response, a number of security scholars turned to game theory, computer simulations and statistical analyses, many of which were produced by the US-based RAND Corporation starting in the 1950s. The use of game theory as a guide to strategic Cold War interactions was particularly problematic: it can be manipulated to produce a variety of decision or strategic outcomes depending on the initial assumptions adopted by the game's creator. Assuming a worst case scenario based on realist assumptions – meaning no communication with the other side, no outside actor to enforce agreements and no possibility of repeated plays – would yield so-called *prisoner's dilemma*-type strategic games, where the dominant strategy for both sides is to defect (that is, cheat the other side) rather than cooperate and risk defeat at the hands of an adversary. These assumptions about actors and preferences could be manipulated in countless ways to produce optimal game strategies for various strategic situations, such as *stag hunt* or *chicken* (Oye, 1986), yet these exercises could not escape the basic fact that a simulated game is not like the real world of decision-making, especially under the shadow of nuclear war.

Compounding these analytical difficulties regarding superpower nuclear rivalry, scholars also had to adapt to the changing strategic situation *between* the superpowers, as well as *within* each superpower bloc, starting in the 1960s. Between the superpowers, the advent of *thermonuclear* weapons (or hydrogen bombs) and various delivery methods for those weapons required scholars to reassess their predictions of how the Cold War competition might proceed. In particular, the 1962 Cuban missile crisis suggested that some of the stricter assumptions about game theory-type situations might not operate in an actual nuclear confrontation. Specifically, during this crisis both sides were more than willing to negotiate – that is, communicate while trusting each other not to launch a pre-emptive strike – before risking even a *conventional* confrontation (a naval battle near Cuba). The crisis was resolved peacefully, and put both sides on a path to greater cooperation involving arms control, management of regional conflicts and other initiatives, such as scientific cooperation and joint space exploration. Scholars therefore had to contend with a Cold War that consisted of an active strategic nuclear rivalry coupled with apparently productive cooperation, including what Gaddis (1986) has termed 'superpower rules of engagement' about their various spheres of influence; this situation was difficult to explain with any single narrow theoretical view, whether realism or otherwise (also see Gowa and Wessell, 1982; and George, 1983).

Additional puzzles arose within each superpower bloc. First, *both* superpowers had difficulties in leading their allies to adopt similar policy positions regarding various strategic goals. The US found it difficult to convince its European allies to spend more on defence, or to pursue certain weapons systems (such as the 'neutron bomb') or strategies, or to expand NATO 'out of area' (such as into the Middle East), or to deny certain technologies or other resources to the Soviet bloc, or to avoid the pursuit of more peaceful relations with the Eastern European countries within that bloc (Deporte, 1986; Mastanduno, 1988). West Germany's more cooperative policy of *Ostpolitik* towards the Soviet bloc, and Western Europe's support for the more general Conference on Security and Cooperation in Europe (CSCE) process, were two key examples of this difference in views. Similarly, the Soviets had their own problems within the communist bloc, such as China's pursuit of a different form of communism coupled with various border disputes (the 'Sino-Soviet split'); the anti-Soviet movements in Hungary, Czechoslovakia and Poland through the late 1950s to early 1980s; and finally, the USSR's difficulties in supporting other (supposedly indigenous) communist movements in Africa, Central/South America, Afghanistan and elsewhere. Second, a number of states simply refused to play the Cold War 'game' according to superpower rules. Some states created the 'non-aligned movement' to avoid having to support one side or the other, while other states, such as Egypt, India and Turkey, became adept at playing one side against the other in order to receive political support and/or economic/military aid.

Ultimately, these various empirical trends regarding relations between, within and outside the two superpower blocs converged in the 1980s and resulted in a relatively peaceful end to the Cold War, the democratic transitions among central and Eastern European states, and finally, the disintegration of the Soviet Union itself. A related puzzle is that after a brief debate about what policy to adopt *vis-à-vis* the former Soviet Union and its allies (which included the option of attempting to *prevent* a total Soviet collapse, which amounted to a status quo posture), the West decided to mount a massive aid operation to support these countries after decades of policies designed to defeat them. The EU was charged with coordinating this aid, which gave it a special role in facilitating political and economic transitions in most former communist countries in Europe. These events and policies suggested to many scholars that the materialist view of superpower rivalry adopted by many Cold War era scholars was far less important perhaps than an economic, societal or ideational view of security. In response, they began to articulate a range of competing, even critical, viewpoints to help explain what seemed to be missing in the Cold War view of security studies, as well as to pave the way towards a broader and far more eclectic way to think about this topic during the immediate post-Cold War era and beyond.

## International security studies after the Cold War

As noted in Chapter 1, the transition from the Cold War to the post-Cold War era has been accompanied by a wide-ranging reconsideration of the entire field of international security (Chipman, 1992; Gray, 1992; Buzan,

Table 2.1   *Major approaches to international security studies*

|  | Referent object | View of power | View of truth | Main security research focus |
|---|---|---|---|---|
| 1. Realism | States | Material | Objective | Power-balancing |
| 2. Liberalism | Social groups | Varies | Objective | Learning/ institutions |
| 3. Marxism | Economic classes | Material | Objective | Capitalist problems, socialist alternatives |
| 4. Social constructivism | Social structure, human agents | Socially constructed | Subjective | Reproduction of social order |
| 5. Critical theory | Humans and the earth | Varies | Subjective | Emancipation of all humans from harm or fear |
| 6. Feminist theory | Gender | Masculinist vs. feminist | Subjective | Gender neutrality/ equity, specificity or dominance |

1997). On the theoretical side, one important trend involves the reinvigoration of liberalism; a second trend involves the rise of at least three general schools of thought – social constructivism, critical security studies and feminist theory – that must be added to the traditional triumvirate of realism, liberalism and Marxism. On the empirical research side, we can see a reframing of the international security research and policy agenda to go well beyond the traditional concerns of war and armaments; this also involves expanding the topic to include all major levels of analysis as noted above. These major schools of thought are summarized in Table 2.1.

## Theoretical trends

As we shall see in the sub-section on 'empirical trends' below, the end of the Cold War inspired a range of liberal interpretations of that event; these views can also be applied to other contemporary international security issues. Today in fact there are multiple versions of liberalism beyond the institutional/regulatory/legal liberalism discussed above; these are summarized in Table 2.2 later in the chapter. Democratic/republican liberalism is especially important and will be examined further in Chapter 4; it focuses on the idea that democratic states tend not to go to war, or even to credibly threaten war, against each other to resolve their disputes (Howard, 1978; Doyle, 1983). It also influences the subfield of peace and conflict studies, which focuses on the conditions for a stable peace among former or potential adversaries (Galtung, 1996; Barash and Webel, 2002; Dunn, 2005). An important version of social liberalism involves the idea of *security communities*, whereby shared values, trust and a common understanding of problems can bind a set of actors together, as in Karl Deutsch's classic view of the North Atlantic security community (Deutsch et al., 1957). A more recent version involves *epistemic communities*, or knowledge-based networks of specialists with shared beliefs about scientific/technical policy problems. Such communities may be especially important in the management of security problems involving a high degree of scientific knowledge, such as infectious disease (Haas, 1992a). Modern regulatory liberalism (sometimes known as 'neo-liberalism') looks to the construction of international public law and the creation of multilateral institutions (or 'international regimes') such as the UN system (particularly the UN Security Council, or UNSC), the EU or the International Criminal Court (ICC) to help govern common problems (Keohane and Nye, 1977; Krasner, 1983; Barnett and Finnemore, 2004); some have argued that this rule-centred approach to collective security still persists even after the War on Terror of 2001 and onwards (Frederking, 2003).

Debates over various forms of realism noted above have also persisted since the end of the Cold War (Parent and Rosato, 2015), while other realists have attempted to update and adapt their theories. For example, *offensive realism* assumes that states, particularly the major powers, seek dominance or hegemony rather than 'mere' security in order to protect themselves against any potential rising power, so they will pursue power maximization strategies in dealing with their closest competitors (Mearsheimer, 2001). Such a transition from defensive to offensive realism among the major powers could create new conflicts where none had existed before, resulting in what Mearsheimer calls the 'tragedy' of great power politics. However, other theorists have attempted to combine key insights of liberal and realist theory, and in doing so offer a more optimistic view about the prospects of international cooperation in economic and security affairs. The so-called 'English School' of international relations theory accepts that a lack of world government can make it difficult for states to cooperate, but also argues that effective cooperation is still possible thanks to other social values or practices shared by a community, such as common roots in Roman law or Western/Christian civilization, or a more general sense of cosmopolitanism (Buzan, 1993; Linklater and Suganami, 2006). All sustained social interaction requires basic customs and norms to function effectively; this is no less true of the international system – or the 'anarchical society' – in the view of English School theorists (Bull, 2001), a position that attempts to link the core insights of realism (i.e. no world government) and liberalism (i.e. a need for rules). In this light, some have argued that rather than a multipolar world, we are headed towards a 'multi-order world' organized largely by nested or overlapping institutions, which again reflects the liberal side of English School theorizing (Flockhart, 2016).

Although realism, liberalism and, to a lesser degree, Marxism continue to inspire various types of research in international security studies, alternative approaches have appeared in recent years. Some of these new approaches might also fall under the general heading of 'normative' international relations theory (Cochran, 2000), but this term is somewhat misleading. All social theories are normative to some degree; the question really is about how we balance or problematize the relationship between the measurement and analysis of 'what is' against the question of 'what should be' in our interpretation of a particular issue. The three major alternatives considered in the rest of this section – social constructivism, critical theory (or critical security studies) and feminist theory – adopt different views on this question and may blur the line between analysis and advocacy. There are also major divisions within these general approaches, which may undermine their persuasiveness in terms of challenging existing approaches and/or offering major new insights into international security.

For example, social constructivism can be considered to some degree as a form of social liberalism. However, unlike social liberalism, which generally focuses on the progressive or cooperative aspects of increased social contacts, social constructivism claims to be more neutral on this point and focuses on static structures rather than progressive change (Hopf, 1998; Wendt, 1999). It simply argues that social structures can either reinforce or undermine peaceful relations depending on how interactions between 'agents' (or actors) and 'structures' (or social systems) create a common social reality (Wendt, 1992; Katzenstein, 1996). However, this circular or tautological approach to causality – structure conditions agents whose speech acts create the structure they inhabit – can make it difficult to generate convincing explanations of specific events. Thus, and like all structural theories, social constructivism can be indeterminate in terms of how a single social structure produces multiple outcomes, political or otherwise. It also shares with neorealism the problem of explaining how one structure can change into another, or how agents can assert leadership or otherwise innovate in such structured social configurations.

Even more problematic is a broader school of thought known as 'critical theory' or 'critical security studies' (Cox, 1981; Leonard, 1990; Booth, 2005), which is the most incoherent of the six major approaches noted above as it shares a high degree of commonality with several other approaches (particularly liberalism, social constructivism and Marxism) but also exhibits a number of contradictory aims and claims. It developed in the mid-1990s as an attempt to broaden the research and policy agenda for post-Cold War security studies (Krause and Williams, 1997), although it is not exactly clear why an entirely new school of thought was required to achieve this aim. Advocates of critical security studies were especially concerned about the focus on the state and the role of military force; these concerns were often (though not exclusively) framed as an attack on realism. More importantly, the approach developed initially in hope of changing our views and practices regarding 'security' in various ways; in this sense it is far more normative in purpose than liberalism, social constructivism and even Marxism. In fact, some critical security theorists (Wyn Jones, 1999) even link themselves to the Frankfurt School of neo-Marxism, which focuses on Marxism as a tool for change (or as a political ideology) rather than as a 'scientific' theory of historical processes. Finally, critical security theory claims to offer a more philosophical or holistic interpretation of international security by examining fundamental values, terms or ideas that supposedly influence both the positivist research agenda of security scholars and any policies derived from that agenda. It attempts to do so by focusing on human beings as the key unit of analysis, and by attempting to 'emancipate' them from not just 'threats' but from all physical and human constraints (such as the core concepts of realism) that prevent people from realizing their full potential. In this sense it has clear sympathies with the human security agenda discussed in the last section of this chapter, given its central concern with justice, equality, identity and freedom (Williams, 1998).

As with elements of the more orthodox theories noted above, this volume attempts to draw upon some of the major insights of critical theory in keeping with my goal of questioning all aspects of individual security problems. However, some central claims of this school can be subject to criticism as well, particularly since the discipline was already expanding, even during the Cold War, to include other topics beyond war, while a focus on the state can include the various components of the state (particularly institutions and people/citizens). In addition, critical security studies confuses the distinction between empirical/positivist theory and normative/ethical theory; Booth (2005: 30) also asserts that the approach attempts to 'stand outside' prevailing structures/ideologies in order to understand them (i.e. a claim of objectivity), but then states that 'critical theorizing does not make a claim to objectivity'. In addition to this confusion about how to assert and evaluate truth claims using critical theory, while also balancing objectivity against subjectivity, the approach says little about how certain values or constraints arise in the first place, or how to change one value system into another. Many critical theorists also present their arguments in the spirit of universalism (that is, *all humans* need to be 'emancipated'), yet these views are in fact closely associated with well-established liberal ideas about the social contracts that bind certain human communities, especially in the Western world. Finally, the stress on language and discourse in critical security studies (as in social constructivism) implies that we can change 'reality' simply by changing the way we talk about it; the so-called 'Welsh School' and 'Copenhagen School' of security studies share this tendency. These two schools in particular are more similar than their names imply (see Browning and McDonald, 2011), although the Welsh School tends to stress 'emancipation' more generally while the Copenhagen School focuses more narrowly on how certain referent objects or issues become transformed into security problems, often by elites (see the special issue of *Security Dialogue*, 42/4–5, 2011). Other scholars similarly stress 'ontological security' among various actors (that is, a durable identity or sense of order/continuity), which has been framed in security studies in terms of stable relations among states, state practices that may produce anxiety, or the absence of fear among individuals, among other things (Steele, 2005; Mitzen, 2006; Croft, 2012).

The heavy focus on discourse across most critical approaches, however, could seem very naive (if not outright harmful) when facing the harsh reality of a military attack or deadly pandemic. In fact, the reason many international security theorists still focus on the state as a key – but not only – unit of analysis is precisely because states are explicitly charged with managing various problems associated with global order; they also claim the so-called monopoly on the legitimate use of force/violence to address those problems (Weber, 1918). This is not just a theoretical or philosophical claim either; individuals often first look to states (as reflected in public opinion polls and election dynamics) to protect them from the various problems covered in later chapters, although state involvement does not preclude a role for other actors, such as IOs or private firms, depending on the problem at hand. In addition, when states fail to manage these problems effectively, their leaders may be punished by their own citizens, whether in terms of losing office in democratic states or losing their lives in authoritarian states. These factors limit critical theory's prospects for advancing a coherent research agenda and influencing public policy. Instead, this approach risks regressing into a self-referential intellectual cul-de-sac – at least in the realm of security affairs, where most humans tend to fear death and destruction – in which its adherents make bold truth claims about social relations without bothering to verify those claims (and any policies that might result from them) through the use of rigorous empirical research designs. As we shall see in the discussion of human security below and in Chapter 5, the so-called 'Responsibility to Protect' norm was inspired by this kind of thinking – i.e. making *individuals* the key referent objects of security – yet in practice this norm has been almost completely ignored by the international community because it faces competition in the form of other 'real-world' interests at stake. Thus, although critical security studies certainly offers useful insights on the evolution of the field, its focus on 'thick description' and narratives can undermine its impact in terms of devising theoretical concepts that can be generalized across time and space. In this sense the approach has more in common with the fields of history and philosophy than with other social science disciplines, although some critical theorists, such as those of the Paris School (representing a 'political sociology' of security studies), attempt to incorporate a focus on practice and shared knowledge into their analyses (Bigo, 2013). As we shall see in the next chapter, this link between discourse/ideas/knowledge, actual practice and power/politics will play a key role in how the specific security problems covered in the rest of this volume are presented.

One final alternative approach, feminist theory, is based on the role of identity in general, and gender in particular, and here there are sympathetic links to other theories, particularly Marxism, constructivism and critical security studies (Tickner, 1992; Jones, 1996; Murphy, 1996; Tickner, 1997; Keohane, 1998; Steans, 1998). Many of these scholars are motivated by a general recognition that the role of women has been marginalized in international security studies, which appears to them as a very 'masculine' discipline given its focus on violence and threats. To address this imbalance, feminist scholars have devised a range of arguments about how gender might influence the theory and practice of security studies, as women could bring new points of view and new skills to the domain. Yet, as with all schools of thought discussed in this volume, there are problems and disputes regarding the feminist/gender agenda. For example, one strain of feminist theory, which might be called liberal feminism, involves the idea that more attention should be paid to women as objects and subjects of action in international relations (Enloe, 1990); this view is relatively uncontroversial. Other feminist theorists are associated more with critical theory, arguing that women may be more concerned than men about the future of the human race because of their social roles as mothers and caregivers. They would be more cooperative and resolve their disputes peacefully, so we might see less violent conflict if women were permitted more of a role in decision-making (Zalewski and Papart, 1998). A third major variant might be termed radical feminism; this view argues that men have made the world a far less safe and happy place, so we all might be better off if women took more control (Fukuyama, 1998). After all, men are responsible for most of the violence in society in terms of both crime and war. In addition, public opinion polls and voting statistics generally indicate that women do have different attitudes towards war and peace as compared to men (Goldstein, 2001). In the view of all of these thinkers, the discourse on international relations (war, security, violence and power) is inherently masculine, and contributes to a great deal of suffering. A truly matriarchal world would be better and more stable for everyone, resulting not in a democratic peace, but a *feminine* peace.

However, as feminist theorists disagree among themselves about the precise relationship between gender and security, there is no clear policy consensus here. One major problem is the question of whether we are aiming for gender neutrality/equality, gender specificity or gender dominance. Gender neutrality/equality tries to take gender out of the equation by asserting that we should simply make sure that women's voices are heard as clearly as those of men throughout the international security policy-making arena (Melander, 2005). Gender specificity, however, asserts that men and women have different, though equally important, priorities and abilities, and society would be better off if this full range of human potential was utilized. Finally, gender dominance sees women as inherently more virtuous than men; therefore our policies should explicitly reject the current 'masculine' approach to international security and adopt a more 'feminine' one. It is unclear how such a state of affairs should be realized, although the first two approaches might be more feasible in terms of legal measures (that is, electoral rules, employment laws and so on). The fact that some states explicitly legislate for the inclusion of more women in public life shows that these ideas are taken seriously in some polities, as in Scandinavia.

Also, it must be kept in mind that gender, like class or ethnicity or nationality, comprises only part of one's identity or self-interest, and is certainly not the only or even primary basis upon which key decisions are made. Individuals play multiple roles in life, often at the same time, and not all of these roles are linked to gender. Therefore gender must be considered alongside many other motivations for, or justifications of, political behaviour, such as survival, economic welfare, nationalism, ethnic identity, religion, history, national myths and so on, not all of which are 'masculine' in nature. Finally, it is not clear that the goal of examining weak or under-represented populations (such as women, children, ethnic minorities and so on) requires an entirely new theory of international relations, as opposed to adapting current theories. However, the idea that men and women may make different calculations about using violence or aggression to achieve their goals is certainly worth exploring, whether in the realm of interpersonal/social relations or international security (McDermott, 2015); the same holds true for gender differences regarding economic/trade affairs (Mansfield, Mutz and Silver, 2015). Even so, framing 'violence' beyond physical violence to include mental/emotional harm makes it difficult to make far-reaching claims about the 'inherent' qualities of men and women when it comes to interpersonal relations, pacifism and cooperation. Moreover, the facts that women are playing greater roles in combat today (in both 'regular' armies and irregular/insurgent forces; see Duncanson and Woodward, 2016), and have even perpetrated sexual violence in conflict zones (Cohen, 2013), mean that gender-based approaches to security, like all conceptual approaches, must pay constant attention to empirical trends and adjust their arguments accordingly.

Table 2.2 summarizes some of the major competing theories, as relevant to international security, within the six general schools of thought noted above. Although some scholars insist that some of these theories represent completely unique approaches to the discipline, a closer examination of their core assumptions along two key dimensions (the role of

**Table 2.2**   *Competing theories relevant to international security studies*

| | Violence is central (hard/material power, mainly WAR-MAKING) | Violence is not central (soft/ideational/social power, mainly RULE-MAKING) |
|---|---|---|
| Positivist (explanation first, usually based on empirical evidence) | * Classical realism (anarchy, states, self-help)<br>* Defensive realism (balance of power)<br>* Offensive realism (preponderance of power)<br>* Neorealism (anarchy, structure of state power)<br>* Marxism/historical materialism | * Classical/Ethical liberalism (human rights)<br>* Legal/Institutional liberalism (laws/rules/norms)<br>* Social liberalism (personal/group relationships, knowledge communities)<br>* Economic/Commercial liberalism (markets/transactions)<br>* Democratic/Republican liberalism (absence of war among democracies/credible commitments among democracies)<br>* Neoliberalism (anarchy, international institutions/regimes to enforce promises)<br>* English School (socio-cultural factors that promote international order)<br>* Social constructivism |
| Post-positivist or interpretivist (ethics/advocacy first) | * Frankfurt School/Neo-Marxism<br><br>* Feminism (anti-patriarchy; women as excluded/peaceful)<br><br>* Copenhagen School/Securitization theory | * Feminism (pro-inclusion; women as equals)<br><br>* Critical theory/Post-modernism/Welsh School<br><br>* Paris School/political sociology |

physical violence versus the role of norms/rules, and the goal of explanation versus advocacy) clearly reveals that there are more similarities than differences at work here. In other words, they can be viewed as branches of more general theories rather than as entirely new approaches to the subject. Throughout this volume, we shall see how some of these ideas inspire specific explanations and policies regarding certain international security problems. Although some approaches noted above pay less attention to causality in favour of more interpretivist narratives, the chapters that follow will attempt to draw causal links between problems and policies. In other words, to bring about change through policy, one must be concerned with whether a decision (such as military intervention) actually produces a desired outcome (such as ending a civil war). This focus on causality, in turn, means we must also pay close attention to some kind of evidence when evaluating international security (for example, how do we know whether, or why, a civil war has ended?), which brings us to the evolution of empirical trends in the discipline since the end of the Cold War.

## Empirical trends

These new theories have also provoked a new series of debates in areas that received little or no attention during the Cold War. One debate involves a reassessment of the Cold War itself in light of the extraordinary changes that led to the collapse of the Soviet Union and of new information that came to light as a result of that collapse (Baldwin, 1995). Here one of the most important arguments involved the limits of systemic/structural theories in explaining the changes in Soviet foreign policy following the ascent of Mikhail Gorbachev as General Secretary of the Communist Party of the Soviet Union in 1985 (Koslowski and Kratochwil, 1994; Lebow and Risse-Kappen, 1995). Depending on one's personal views, these systemic theories were either merely indeterminate or completely wrong about how the Cold War might end. Among all systemic theories, realism attracted the most criticism during the immediate aftermath of the Cold War owing to its dominance among leading security and strategic studies scholars.

One argument along these lines was that international anarchy is not as pernicious as realists assume; in fact, some international regions today (such as the EU) possess far more hierarchical authority and stability than some states (such as Somalia), which tend towards chronic *domestic* anarchy (Milner, 1992). In other words, the (supposedly) threatening effects of international anarchy can be mitigated through a variety of mechanisms, as we shall see later in this section. The Cold War also ended without a great power war, which led analysts to take a closer look at domestic factors as key causes of international change. In a similar vein, others criticized realism for being too deterministic, fatalistic and pessimistic. It seemed to leave no room for humans to improve their situation by any means other than power-balancing and major power war, which goes against a basic justification for modern social science: that greater understanding will help us find policies to aid and improve the human condition, or the idea of *progress* (Adler and Crawford, 1991). Finally, these limitations of realism should make it clear that 'mono-causal' explanations of any international phenomena, or those based on a single factor or variable, such as anarchy or class or gender, are always indeterminate and must be supplemented with other concepts or factors; this is especially true of realism, Marxism and feminism.

A number of analysts also pointed to the difficulty of using systemic/ structural level explanations of the key changes in Soviet foreign policy that led to the end of the Cold War, particularly Gorbachev's 'new thinking' on foreign policy after 1985: the withdrawal of Soviet forces from

Afghanistan, the relaxation of Soviet controls on its Eastern European client states and the rejection of a military rivalry with the US. Soviet military capabilities had not declined in a dramatic fashion; although the Soviet economy was having difficulties that suggested a need for some policy reform, this did not require a revolutionary change in foreign policy. In fact, the Soviets could have muddled through for years; many much weaker states manage to do just that (Brown, 2009). In addition, another major communist state – China – was undergoing even worse economic problems yet did not attempt such a dramatic change in its ideology. Nor did the Soviet Union experience a crisis of the type that might lead to a fundamental rejection of long-held foreign policy positions; some modest economic reform would have been more pragmatic in terms of maintaining a realist strategy. In short, although the US kept up the pressure on the Soviets in the area of military spending, there simply was not enough relative Soviet economic or military decline to explain the changes that led to a fundamental rethinking of Soviet foreign policy.

In terms of applying more specific liberal ideas to the question of the end of the Cold War, one such explanation focused on the role of transnational and transgovernmental linkages – or social liberalism – between the Soviet leadership and the outside world, where new ideas about how to manage the US–Soviet rivalry spread between a 'liberal internationalist community' and sympathetic political actors within the Soviet Union. This community included arms control specialists, peace activists, policy analysts and public interest groups, all of whom attempted to influence Gorbachev (Breslauer, 1987; Risse-Kappen, 1994). Similarly, others focused on Gorbachev himself as the key catalyst in ending the Cold War, which further undermines the idea that systemic factors and balance-of-power dynamics govern international security. In this view, Gorbachev was part of a new, much younger generation of Soviet leaders after the 'old guard' WWII generation – Brezhnev, Andropov and Chernenko – passed from the scene (and from the earth) between 1982 and 1985. Gorbachev's apparent openness to new views, his personal commitment to change the Soviet Union in fundamental ways and his overt rejection of the superpower rivalry ultimately led to the end of the Cold War (Meyer, 1988; Checkel, 1993; Stein, 1994; Snyder, 2005).

This reassessment of the Cold War was followed by a high degree of speculation about the future of world politics, and the role of security studies within it. A brief moment of liberal 'end of history' optimism about a peaceful 'new world order' (Fukuyama, 1992) quickly gave way to far more sober assessments about the persistence of violence in international relations, as reflected by the 1991 Persian Gulf War; the collapse of Yugoslavia; a horrific genocide in Rwanda that claimed 800,000 lives; a series of other state failures and civil wars throughout the developing world; a number of small-scale terrorist attacks against a variety of targets; the stubborn persistence of the Israeli–Palestinian conflict and the emergence of an overt nuclear rivalry between India and Pakistan. These events were then overshadowed by higher-profile terrorist attacks on the US, Spain and the UK between 2001 and 2005, all of which led directly to a US-led war against the Taliban-controlled government of Afghanistan in late 2001, as well as a US-led war against Iraq in the spring of 2003. These more traditional security problems, among others, have helped to maintain realism as a major school of international security studies even while inspiring some of the alternative views discussed above. These views have since been applied to all levels of analysis in the field.

For example, at the systemic level, scholars have attempted to consider the distribution of power among the leading states of the system as a guide to future patterns of conflict and cooperation. One major concern involves the question of whether America's dominant position will persist for long or, instead, decline so that the US is a sole 'non-hegemonic' superpower, or merely one among several great powers, or even overshadowed, partially or completely, by a new hegemonic power, such as China (Shambaugh, 1996; Goldstein, 1997–8; Shambaugh, 1999; Christensen, 2001 and 2006; Brooks and Wohlforth, 2015–16). Along with China, states such as Brazil, India and Russia are provoking much speculation about their roles as regional hegemons (at a minimum) and global leaders (at a maximum). These four states are often grouped as the 'BRIC bloc' by some scholars, and cooperation among China, India and Russia in particular is likely to have major implications for future security affairs on the Euro-Asian continent.

A related post-Cold War systemic trend to keep in mind throughout this volume is the growing role of more specialized international regimes, whether based on specific functional tasks or geographic regions, in managing certain security problems. In functional terms, the creation in 1996 of an organization to implement the Comprehensive Test Ban Treaty shows that it is possible to delegate important security functions to a highly specialized international agency (see Chapter 6). In geographical terms, the expanding role of the EU as a global economic, political and now security actor is the most prominent example, as the EU now includes 28 member states (see Box 2.1), representing about 25 per cent of global GDP, or around $17 trillion (slightly ahead of US GDP), although the UK is expected to leave the EU soon. The EU also controls its own regional currency (the euro), foreign/security policies and military capabilities (Smith, 2003; Howorth, 2007).

These changes have created various complications regarding the maintenance of NATO in general and the US–European relationship in particular, in areas that extend well beyond NATO's traditional role of defence through deterrence for its 28 member states. The EU is attempting to develop new relationships with all non-EU states on its borders, some of which, such as Libya and Syria, have experienced very difficult relations with the US (Weber, Smith and Baun, 2007). Although the US and the

**Box 2.1   EU member states, 2016**

| | | |
|---|---|---|
| Austria | Germany | Poland |
| Belgium | Greece | Portugal |
| Bulgaria | Hungary | Romania |
| Croatia | Ireland | Slovakia |
| Cyprus | Italy | Slovenia |
| Czech Republic | Latvia | Spain |
| Denmark | Lithuania | Sweden |
| Estonia | Luxembourg | UK (voted to leave in 2016) |
| Finland | Malta | |
| France | Netherlands | |

EU often claim to have similar positions on the security issues discussed in this volume, a closer look often reveals some major conflicts of both strategy and tactics. This is most obvious where America's global War on Terror is concerned, yet it extends to many other contemporary security problems and further highlights the possibility of regional approaches to international security using methods different from traditional alliances or collective security arrangements.

Similar experiments in regional integration and security cooperation have been taking place among former members of the Soviet Union (involving the Soviet-led Commonwealth of Independent States, or CIS), among various East Asian states and elsewhere, all of which call into question the idea of a *single* systemic world order as the key organizing principle in the construction of theories of international relations/security. The expansion of functionally oriented institutions (that is, those devoted to a specific set of policy tasks), such as NATO (see Box 2.2) or the Organisation for Economic Co-operation and Development (OECD) (Box 2.3), which

**Box 2.2   NATO member states, 2016**

| | | |
|---|---|---|
| Albania | Greece | Poland |
| Belgium | Hungary | Portugal |
| Bulgaria | Iceland | Romania |
| Canada | Italy | Slovakia |
| Croatia | Latvia | Slovenia |
| Czech Republic | Lithuania | Spain |
| Denmark | Luxembourg | Turkey |
| Estonia | Netherlands | UK |
| France | Norway | US |
| Germany | | |

---

## Box 2.3   OECD member states, 2016

| | | |
|---|---|---|
| Australia | Hungary | Poland |
| Austria | Iceland | Portugal |
| Belgium | Ireland | Slovakia |
| Canada | Israel | Slovenia |
| Chile | Italy | South Korea |
| Czech Republic | Japan | Spain |
| Denmark | Luxembourg | Sweden |
| Estonia | Mexico | Switzerland |
| Finland | Netherlands | Turkey |
| France | New Zealand | UK |
| Germany | Norway | US |
| Greece | | |

---

consists of 34 of the richest states in the world, also calls into question the relationship between traditional state-centric approaches and more liberal or constructivist methods of cooperation in security affairs, as well as the increasingly complicated relationship between economics and security.

The contemporary study of international security is made even more complicated by various changes at the national or domestic level of analysis, some of which result directly from the systemic/regional trends noted above. One critical issue involves the consolidation of political and economic reforms in many former communist states, a process which has obvious implications for their security policies. Although a number of these states, particularly those who have joined the EU, have functioned fairly successfully since their transitions, others have not fared so well and may revert to more authoritarian systems. Russia in particular has provoked a great deal of speculation along these lines since the Boris Yeltsin era (1991–9), thanks to the control of the Russian economy by a set of extremely powerful oligarchs, strict controls on the media and public protest, Russia's response to the Chechen rebellion, a high degree of corruption and organized crime and various foreign policy actions such as the war with Georgia during the summer of 2008 and the annexation of Crimea in 2014. China too has been engaging in a long-term reform process, mostly associated with its transition to a 'socialist market' economy, and these reforms may intensify pressures for more political freedoms in ways similar to what happened during Gorbachev's reform era during the late 1980s. Finally, after 2011 domestic politics in the Middle East provoked public unrest in many states across the region (the 'Arab Spring') in ways that spilled over into international security affairs; these events triggered a range of problems that will be covered in the chapters to follow.

A related trend at the domestic level involves the blurring of the distinctions between international and domestic politics, and between public and private affairs, as more actors become involved in international security issues, whether as threats or victims or security providers – or all three (Bobbitt, 2008). Here we see the increasing 'internationalization' of what used to be mainly domestic problems and agencies (criminal justice, public health, money laundering and so on) for the purposes of achieving international security, and the blurring of the distinction between public authority and private activity, as with the role of PMCs, private charities, MNCs or NGOs in international security affairs, all of which undermine the state-centric view of international security as found in the traditional literature.

Finally, the individual level of analysis has seen several important trends that will impact the future of international security studies, whether directly or indirectly. One broad change at this level involves simple demographics, along several dimensions. Here we see the intensification of cleavages between urban and rural populations, between younger and older populations and between richer and poorer populations. Simply put, many poorer states have much younger and more urban populations than richer states, and much higher rates of population growth, which will put greater pressures on a range of public services (such as employment, sanitation, transportation, nutrition and family planning) for the states least able to afford them. To the extent that these states fail to manage these demographic changes, political conflict and security dilemmas will proliferate in the developing world. When these changes occur in poorer Islamic states, which has been the case in recent years, the prospect of some type of conflict with broader problems of international security is even more likely. This last trend in turn highlights the lingering importance of cultural and ideational factors, rather than mere material factors, in analysing various security problems. Although some more strident observers have framed these factors in terms of a 'clash of civilizations' (Huntington, 1997) or a rise of 'Islamo-fascism' (Podhoretz, 2007), we still need to take seriously the idea that different cultures will make different calculations about the costs and benefits of various courses of action, a prospect which further undermines the use of narrow, or at least Western, assumptions about international security largely based on Euro-American values (such as liberalism) or analytical tools (such as game theory).

## Globalization and human security

Many of the above trends, which affect most of the issues discussed later in this volume, can be framed in terms of two more general, and related, processes: globalization and the idea of 'human security'. However, there is still a great deal of confusion regarding both of these concepts; moreover, the research literature on these topics is still far too limited and indeterminate to reach firm conclusions.

## The globalization debate

The term 'globalization' is often confused with other concepts, such as Westernization, secularization, democratization, consumerism, materialism, modernity and market capitalism, which can pose a problem for rigorous empirical analysis. Although these factors are linked, globalization can be more effectively considered in a much broader sense than international interdependence, whereby changes in one state – whether positive or negative – can affect another state, and vice versa (Keohane and Nye, 1977). Interdependence, however, is usually framed in bilateral or regional terms, and is generally state-centric, while globalization implies a much higher degree of 'interpenetration' among a much wider range of actors – public and private – across a wider range of issue areas: social, political, economic, ideational and so on (Rosenau, 1996; Cha, 2000; Mittelman, 2000 and 2002). More specifically, globalization is often measured in terms of several core empirical trends, including:

1.  trade flows in goods, services and intellectual property
2.  global financial mobility
3.  increasing foreign direct investment (FDI)
4.  innovations in technology, particularly involving communications and transportation
5.  flows of new ideas and norms
6.  a greater convergence of prices, and even tastes, in the form of a single global market; and
7.  cross-border travel and migration (both legal and illegal).

These trends, however, do not manifest themselves to the same degree across each other or across states; for example, financial globalization is very extensive and fast-paced (see Chapter 10), while migration flows are relatively more limited in size and scope (see Chapter 13). The other measures of globalization listed above fall somewhere between these extremes. Nor are states equally equipped to cope with the pressures of globalization (that is, maximizing its benefits while reducing its risks). More powerful states, such as OECD members, are much less vulnerable to some of the risks of globalization relative to LDCs. However, for the purpose of analysing contemporary security affairs, the key point is that globalization *reduces* the ability of states to unilaterally protect themselves in terms of identifying and responding to specific security threats, and therefore *increases* the need for states to cooperate to manage the threats that result from greater openness. In addition, globalization means that apparently small or isolated problems (such as a virus), or apparently weak actors (such as private citizens), can have a disproportionate impact on international security. Of course, states can always consider raising barriers to trade, travel and other aspects of globalization, yet this can be a fairly radical solution as other states could retaliate in kind and thus erode over-all global economic efficiency. It is always a possibility, however, so we must be aware that states could attempt to stop globalization in its tracks, at least temporarily, in the face of a major security crisis such as an infectious disease pandemic.

The fact that states vary widely in their vulnerability to such problems also means their propensity to cooperate with each other will vary widely. The US in particular, for example, often acts as if it can afford to 'go it alone' to cope with many of the security challenges caused or exacerbated by globalization. Other states, however, may act in a completely opposite fashion and believe that only multilateral solutions will be effective, which in fact is a major rationale behind the gradual expansion of the EU over the past five decades. Yet effective multilateral solutions can take much time to implement, which is why unilateral action on the part of the major powers can be so tempting. The challenge, of course, is to find a middle ground between these positions to maximize the effective international cooperation required to cope with security problems; this point will be examined further in Chapter 3.

In addition, globalization also radically alters the traditional view of international security affairs across several dimensions. As we have seen, these dimensions include an expanded role in security affairs for 'low politics' problems (such as economics), non-state or private actors and domestic factors. The rise of private actors in security affairs is a very important trend related to globalization, and will be examined in more detail in Chapter 3. Here we need only note that globalization makes it increasingly difficult to police all of their activities, even just their legal ones. Criminal non-state actors are in fact one of the most difficult new security threats for states to cope with, as we shall see later in this volume. As always, these changes as related to the overall globalization of security affairs will vary widely across states and across security issue areas, so it is not possible to point to any stable solution, whether in terms of empirical analysis or policy recommendations. Instead, they must be incorporated into specific security problems on a case-by-case basis and then analysed accordingly.

For example, analysts of less traditional international security problems, such as public health, economic or environmental issues, have always been aware of the trends noted above, so they take for granted the idea that private behaviours within domestic polities can have a dramatic impact on certain international problems. For them, globalization merely intensifies trends that have always been with us; it represents a change of degree rather than of kind. For those who analyse more traditional international security issues involving war and the use of military force, however, globalization challenges their orthodox, state-centric, internationally oriented assumptions about how security is defined and pursued.

The globalization of the arms industry is a key case in point. Rather than state ownership of this industry, globalization has created an increasingly transnational and largely private defence technology and industrial base, including technology transfers, international subcontracting, international joint venture companies, cross-border mergers and acquisitions (M&As), licensed production and multinational co-development of weapons systems. In the past, arms industries tended to be wholly national in their activities, with ownership, design, research and development, manufacture and procurement all kept within a single country, sometimes even owned or controlled by the government. The end of the Cold War, however, has put downward pressures on defence budgets and led many firms to seek markets and economic relationships elsewhere – or to *globalize*. For example, around 1970 there were no joint ventures, no strategic alliances and only one M&A involving defence firms. By the early 1990s, however, there were 31 joint ventures, 23 strategic alliances and no less than 80 M&As involving defence firms (Bitzinger, 1994). Globalization here also means increasing competition against the major powers by new suppliers: Brazil, Israel, Singapore, South Africa, South Korea and Taiwan. The pace of these changes has accelerated in recent years; major arms-producing states must 'go global or go out of business' (Adams, 1992).

Traditional state-centric views of military security are similarly challenged by how globalization facilitates threats by non-state actors, such as terrorists and criminals. These actors existed before globalization, of course, yet various aspects of globalization have greatly expanded their scope of operations. Some aspects can involve a more general form, such as a backlash against US/Western values related to globalization (such as secularization or consumerism) that aid terrorist recruitment, or a more specific form, such as the use of communications/transportation networks to clandestinely acquire funds or arms (Gulke, 1995). As with the arms industry, we can see a shift from state support of terrorists to a more 'self-generating' style of international terrorism, with diverse economic and ideational means of support allowing organizations to recruit members, plan attacks and carry them out well away from their base of operations or even without any discernible base of operations (Cronin, 2002–3). Any response that exacerbates negative feelings about globalization in general or the West in particular will only make things worse, which is why revelations regarding US military abuses during the 2003 Iraq war, plus America's use of rendition and torture tactics, have been so explosive. It is also important to keep in mind that these trends are not confined to the developing world or to Islamic states: recent years have seen an increasingly high degree of alienation about globalization even in advanced industrialized states. Thus, if citizens even in rich states are increasingly uneasy about the unintended consequences or downside of globalization, the situation in LDCs must seem even more frustrating.

## The human security debate

A second important trend in contemporary international security is even more controversial: whether globalization will undermine the very state system on which the current international order is based (Falk, 1997), which may involve the ascendance of the idea of human security. This idea generally represents a return to the individual level of analysis as the main referent object in security studies, and a rejection of the traditional focus in the discipline on the national/domestic or international levels (that is, states and the state system). However, as with globalization, 'human security' means different things to different analysts (MacLean et al., 2006; Tadjbakhsh and Chenoy, 2007).

One of the most widely cited views of human security is the 2003 *Final Report of the UN Commission on Human Security*, which notes ten ways to improve human security on a global basis. These goals are:

Protecting people in violent conflict
Protecting people from the proliferation of arms
Supporting the security of people on the move
Establishing human security transition funds for post-conflict situations
Encouraging fair trade and markets to benefit the extreme poor
Working to provide minimum living standards everywhere
According higher priority to ensuring universal access to basic health care
Developing an efficient and equitable global system for patent rights
Empowering all people with universal basic education
Clarifying the need for a global human identity while respecting the freedom of individuals to have diverse identities and affiliations.

Based on these goals, which are often summarized more simply as 'freedom from fear and want', it is easy to see that human security is a policy agenda that packages or even 'rebrands' certain UN goals concerning economic development and human rights as *security* problems. Several of these measures are linked in some way to conflict situations and criminal activities, which will be examined at length in this volume, particularly in Part III. The emergence of what may be a new international norm – the 'Responsibility to Protect' (or R2P) any threatened individuals in conflict zones and similar insecure situations – can also be linked to the human security agenda, as we shall see in Chapter 5. Other human security goals are directly associated with non-traditional security threats, especially involving health and migration, and will be examined in Chapters 9 to 13. Finally, the last three goals – on patent rights, universal education and the need for a 'global human identity' – are simply not important priorities on the current international security agenda and will not be examined at length in this volume.

As a policy agenda, then, human security is not especially controversial. However, when framed as a critique of the orthodox view of international security, or – worse – as a kind of theory of security politics, the situation becomes far more complicated. The single most important problem here is the claim by some human security enthusiasts that a focus on individuals or humans in general should displace the more traditional focus on the state and the state system. This view misses the point for two reasons. First, the traditional 'state-centric' view of international relations/security can already encompass the needs of humans; after all, the term 'state' itself is a social construct that generally includes at least four critical components: territory, government, citizens/residents and legal sovereignty. So if human security really refers to the needs of humans defined as specific social groups or populations (for example, those lacking in basic health care or education), then the traditional focus on the state, which by definition includes their populations, can also easily incorporate such goals. Second, and more importantly, the entire concept of human security is really a question of priorities, and the fact is that human security is quite meaningless without some effective authority to provide protection from fear and want. Since we have no world government, the task of providing human security falls to states and state-based IOs, but this point in turn implies that the state system itself must be secure from other threats. If the state system faces other more important threats, however, then human security as such will remain a low priority on the international security agenda, which is precisely the current state of affairs. This can easily be seen in the more limited resources and attention devoted to the human security agenda (Part III of this volume) as compared to the more traditional international security agenda (Part II of this volume), which involves the much greater use of military/police forces.

Similarly, empirical research that focuses on the direct link between human security, globalization trends and the state can take many forms, but is far too imprecise at present to summarize easily. This is due mainly to the wide variety of referent objects and processes that one could examine, which is always the problem with research at the individual level of analysis. For example, some analysts have focused on the increasing difficulties faced by states in collecting tax revenues in a world of increasing global financial movements (Paris, 2003), while others have focused more broadly on the rise of 'sovereign-free' actors and forces that challenge the ability of states to perform their usual functions (Rosenau, 1990), such as societal/national security and the maintenance of economic stability. These processes may result in what Strange (1996) has called a 'retreat of the state' in world politics. While this volume, and much of the literature cited within it, generally assumes the maintenance of the state system for the foreseeable future, it also accepts that states are not the only important actors in the realm of international security affairs, that states can manifest weakness or incompetence and that the globalization of various security problems – some of which are now framed as part of the human security agenda – increasingly challenges the ability of all states – even the US – to act unilaterally to cope with them.

## Summary

This chapter has attempted to consolidate a number of arguments regarding the contemporary study of international security as a prelude to the various issues covered later in the volume. It noted the continuing relevance of the levels of analysis approach as a way to frame different causal variables used to explain international security affairs, as well as the lingering Cold War mindset still seen in modern scholarship, particularly for issues involving war and military affairs. Against these more traditional views about international security, however, the chapter also noted the rise of several other theoretical and empirical trends that increasingly challenge the state-centric, 'high politics' view of international security affairs as conducted within an anarchical international system. These trends may be seen at all major levels of analysis – systemic/international, domestic/national and individual/human – and may be framed more generally in terms of an ongoing process of globalization, which essentially blurs the distinctions among these levels and thus greatly complicates our pursuit of *international* security. The rise of institutionalized multilateral approaches to international security, as well as the role of non-state or private actors within this realm, are especially important trends in many of the topics covered in this volume and will be treated in more detail in chapters to come.

It is worth bearing in mind, however, that some more traditional theorists – and not just realists – still prefer to define this topic as a domain controlled largely by states using their monopoly on the legitimate use of violence, rather than in terms suggested by the trends covered in this chapter. In their view, switching the focus from states (especially the major powers) to institutions, non-state actors or (worse) more general forces or trends related to globalization and smaller-scale human populations only helps to fragment the discipline and reduce the possibility of any conceptual advances within it. As a result, there is even less hope of building a useful knowledge base for international security affairs as scholars increasingly talk past each other using concepts, terms and evidence – or no evidence at all – exclusive to their own theoretical views. This understandable attitude about the apparent lack of discipline within the discipline of international security, coupled with the empirical trends and the plethora of contending theories covered in this chapter, make it increasingly difficult to summarize and teach the field to others – and to write a volume such as this. Fundamentally, however, understanding 'security' is about *setting priorities*, a process involving all of the actors, values and other factors discussed throughout this chapter. To address this problem of prioritization, we must get back to basics in a sense, and rediscover the *fundamental role of politics* in international security affairs in a more general sense than in the terms suggested by the theories and arguments discussed above. This critical task is undertaken in the next chapter.

## Chapter 3

# The Politics of International Security

Imagine the following scenario: a huge explosion occurs at a major population centre in the US, resulting in thousands of deaths and injuries. Within minutes – hopefully – an army of officials from various agencies descends upon the scene. These officials represent the local police and fire departments, the medical community, the Federal Bureau of Investigation (FBI), the Bureau of Alcohol, Tobacco, Firearms and Explosives (ATF), and possibly counter-terrorism experts from the local and federal authorities. The initial response of these officials was inspired by the same event – the explosion – yet their professional interest in the disaster varies quite widely. Medical personnel are interested in caring for the wounded; police and fire officials are interested in securing the area and rescuing survivors; FBI and ATF personnel are interested in finding and protecting the evidence of a crime scene, such as witness statements and physical evidence, that could be used in a court of law; and counter-terrorism experts are interested in quickly assigning responsibility for the attack, if appropriate, to some domestic or international terrorist group. Local, state and national politicians are likely to appear at some point, and they may wish to blame other politicians (mainly in the opposition party, of course) for failing to prevent the attack in the first place. These people are all making a 'correct' response based on their interests, training and areas of responsibility, yet it is also clear that their goals might not just conflict with, but even undermine each other.

Now imagine the same scenario at the international level, with an attack or similar destructive event involving multiple states that attracts a variety of international actors in addition to the domestic ones noted above: these include officials from IOs such as the UN and NGOs such as the ICRC, as well as private citizens, activists and firms that might be victims of violence or providers of security services (or both), and so on. In addition to these actors with a direct interest in the event, we might also factor in other actors, such as politicians, the media and even the criminal or terrorist organizations themselves who may have caused the mayhem, either directly or indirectly, in the first place. What we have, then, is not just a range of complementary and competing interests, but also a range of professional skills and even 'world views' possessed by these actors that help to define, in their view, the nature of the problem and the appropriate response to it. In other words, we have a colossal international coordination problem involving multiple actors with varying degrees of interest, and varying types of power resources, that must be managed effectively to preserve international security.

As these dynamics apply to every security issue covered in this volume, it makes sense to approach them with a single analytical framework to help isolate their commonalities and differences. This chapter offers such a framework for understanding modern international security issues as part of a distinct research programme within the context of international relations and political science. Such a research programme is generally oriented towards answering this basic question: how and why are specific choices made (or likely to be made) regarding a potential international security problem? While some security issues, such as global thermonuclear war or a deadly influenza pandemic, might involve an obvious physical threat to human existence, how humans interpret that threat and, more importantly, devise ways to manage it, are contested processes. In addition, security problems vary widely in terms of their negative impacts, and that variation may undermine the formation of an international consensus about how to handle them. Although numerous factors – historical, cultural, technological, social and economic – may help us answer the 'how and why' question posed above, this chapter offers a 'first cut' set of *political* concepts and processes to help structure the presentation of each of the international security problems covered later in the volume.

This approach also involves incorporating insights from a range of general theories, and shifting among various levels of analysis. These changes in focus, however, are justified by the limits of adopting any single conceptual perspective or level of analysis as the most important reference points, as noted in Chapter 2. Structural theories, such as neorealism or social constructivism, aim to isolate and explore various contextual dimensions in international security; however, they vary in terms of how they define structure, which then conditions their arguments about causal relationships. Ultimately, then, if the concept of 'structure' has any use at all, it means that states with *different* domestic characteristics will nonetheless *tend to act similarly* in a given international structure. Also, these similar behaviours should change if a structure changes from one type into another. Conversely, if these behaviours do not occur, then we must look elsewhere – or revise our notion of a 'structure' – to explain such discrepancies.

Another reason for shifting among theories and levels of analysis depending on the problem at hand involves the notion of *constraints* versus *opportunities*, and *permissive/situational* versus *active/dispositional* causes. For example, the systemic/structural level might be viewed most effectively as a general incentive structure for behaviour: it rewards some behaviours (or provides opportunities for action) and punishes others (or provides constraints on action). In other words, the system or structure can act as a permissive cause: it *permits* certain outcomes to happen (or makes them more likely; a situational cause), but it does not *determine* whether they will happen in a specific case. To explain the latter, we need to look at active causality – or the dispositions of actors – which requires, in turn, far more detailed levels of political analysis. This focus on dispositions, opportunities and decision-making also means putting 'normal' human beings back at the centre of analysis, as opposed to focusing on impersonal factors (such as armaments or geography) or viewing humans as caricatures based on single variables (such as economic class or gender) that receive much attention in the literature, as we saw in Chapter 2.

## The politics of international security: basic assumptions

Before turning to the specifics of this approach, we need to keep in mind five basic working assumptions regarding the politics of international security.

### The role of consensual knowledge

To begin, this volume attempts to determine the scope of generally accepted empirical reality surrounding a number of specific international security problems. While the meanings and values attached to that reality can vary widely, a political analysis of security must still begin by attempting to determine what aspects of the problem are thought to be broadly understood as facts – or as *consensual knowledge* – by a critical mass of security scholars, policy-makers and other informed observers, and what aspects are politically contested. This relationship between consensual and contested knowledge is often in flux depending on the problem at hand and the actors involved, as we shall see with the topics covered in the rest of this volume. However, this variation in terms of consensual knowledge across different security issues can provide us with an initial impression of the scope and degree of political conflict likely to be involved in the management of that problem by the key actors involved.

As noted in Chapter 2, some scholars associated with the Copenhagen School of security studies, as well as more critical theories, refer to the creation of such consensual knowledge largely as a subjective and discursive process of 'securitization' (Buzan, Wæver and De Wilde, 1998). I am sympathetic to this view of the 'malleability' of various security problems as they are being defined, or 'framed', by certain actors; however, the approach used throughout this volume attempts to strike a balance between more objective (or material/historical) and more subjective (or discursive/ideational) sources of international consensual knowledge regarding individual security problems. In other words, to be successful and convincing at the *international* level of analysis, where there is no single central authority or source of leadership, the process of securitization may require the more intensive or creative use of various types of empirical data, new information and other persuasive resources by a wider range of actors (Wood and Vedlitz, 2007) than that suggested by the more 'self-referential' process of securitization theory (that is, a 'security problem' is simply what powerful government officials say it is). Moreover, the process of 'securitization' does not end the political debate about how to manage a certain 'securitized' problem; it merely takes it in new directions and changes the stakes involved, as we shall see.

## The assumption of rationality

Additionally, this volume assumes *rationality* at the level of *individual* human beings. The rational actor assumption is one of the most misunderstood concepts in all social science, especially international relations (Kahler, 1998; Walt, 1999; Brown, 2000; MacDonald, 2003), where scholars often make the mistake of distinguishing between 'rationalist' and 'non-rationalist' theories (and 'non-rationalism' is often equated with social constructivism). This is a false and highly misleading dichotomy; most contemporary theories of international relations, including social constructivist theories, make some use of the rational actor assumption. As used in this volume, and in most empirical social science research, this assumption merely means that individuals attempt to choose the most feasible alternative course of action, given various constraints (economic, cognitive and otherwise), to realize their goals in any social setting (Elster, 1986). If we abandon this assumption, a theoretically informed explanation of social behaviour becomes virtually impossible; this is precisely why some analyses derived from critical theory and other post-positivist or anti-positivist approaches can seem so inconclusive or indeterminate. However, our reliance on the rational actor assumption requires two additional caveats.

First, the assumption of rationality as used in much contemporary social science research tends to stress *bounded rationality*. This simply means that actors may not have perfect information about the situation at hand, or they may have too much information to process effectively, or they may have conflicting information from various sources (i.e. cognitive limits). Under such conditions, individuals often look to elite opinion, arguments and expertise to help interpret, or 'frame', an issue (Druckman, 2004) as a political problem or a security threat. These dynamics clearly are at work when examining most, if not all, international security problems. Moreover, assuming that people *as individuals* are rational does not mean that people *in the aggregate* (states, political parties, firms, bureaucracies and so on) are similarly rational; in fact, it is the capacity of organizations and institutions to undermine or conflict with the information processing of individuals that provides much of the empirical material for political science. Under these circumstances, actors often engage in *satisficing* behaviours, meaning they willingly settle for what appears (in the view of a detached observer) to be a sub-optimal outcome owing to the complexity of the situation at hand. It is also worth noting that actors do not possess unlimited resources when making policy choices; trade-offs are typically involved and these can similarly result in sub-optimal (but still *rational*) decisions.

Second, the use of bounded rationality means that actors can, and frequently do, make 'bad' decisions. Making mistakes or bad decisions, even in the face of new information, does not necessarily mean an actor is behaving irrationally. On the contrary, the fact that actors often pursue a range of (sometimes conflicting) goals means that a bad decision viewed in one context can still be a good decision in another context. In international security affairs, where the need to demonstrate resolve or to satisfy important domestic constituents can be very intense, and where it can be very difficult to calculate the costs and benefits of various courses of action (especially in a crisis situation), the pursuit of what may seem to be a self-defeating policy according to one standard may in fact serve an equally important, and rational, goal according to another standard. This approach to how 'normal' human beings make decisions, even in the context of a crisis situation, is sometimes referred to as 'soft' rationality (or *reasonable choice*), which is distinct from the 'hard' rationality typically assumed by traditional economic or game theory approaches to social choice (Grofman, 2001). 'Hard' rationality also tends to make more use of easily measurable quantitative data (such as surveys or military spending) rather than qualitative factors (such as history or ideas). A reasonable choice approach simply asks: is the outcome explainable afterwards based on the information – both quantitative and qualitative – that the actors had at the time they made their decision? To answer this question, however, we also need to understand what they want when they decide: the problem of interests and preferences.

## Interests and preferences

The problem of conflicting goals noted above leads to the third fundamental assumption of this volume: that actor *interests and preferences are not fixed but can vary widely*. The term *interests* refers to the value at stake regarding a problem (such as stable energy supplies), while the term *preferences* refers to the specific policies used to protect the value at stake (such as favouring diplomacy over military action). We also should note that the rational actor assumption *by itself* says nothing about these interests and preferences, or how actors may order them in relation to each other. In fact, major theories of international relations do not vary in their assumption of rationality; instead they vary in the assumptions they make about the sources and ordering of actor interests or preferences. Realists might assume actors place territorial security above all other values, while social constructivists might assume actors place the need for social inclusion above all other values, yet both theories share the assumption that actors will attempt to realize those preferences in a rational fashion. In addition, most actors actually share many common interests in international security affairs, yet they cannot agree on how to meet those threats – a question of divergent preferences or policy positions. This volume assumes, therefore, that there is rarely an inherent reason to privilege one interest or preference over another; moreover, even if we did assume one interest (such as territorial defence) over all others, there are costs and trade-offs involved in various choices, and actors calculate those trade-offs differently. Our key analytical problem, then, involves mapping the interests and preferences of certain actors, and determining the power resources they can bring to bear upon those interests and preferences.

## International security and collective action

As our fourth operating assumption, this volume generally approaches international security as various sets of 'collective action problems'. This is a generic term for public policy problems that cannot be solved effectively by a single actor. By definition, international security as a subject matter involves problems that threaten multiple actors and collective values in the international system, and that generally do not respect borders (that is, they are difficult to contain in one state). Such common problems, then, are likely to require some degree of collective action to be handled with any degree of effectiveness. This assumption is justified in light of the inherent dynamics of the security dilemma and the more general trends related to globalization discussed earlier in this volume, plus the specific features of modern international security problems to be discussed in the chapters that follow. Modern security threats are often transnational in nature and therefore require increasing levels of international cooperation – collective action – to manage them effectively. To some degree, in fact, international security can be viewed as an international public good, although it is questionable whether individual security problems do in fact meet the standards of public goods theory.

In economics, for example, some argue that the international regimes for money, trade and intellectual property rights (among others) provide benefits to all states and should therefore be protected and respected by all. Is this also the case with international security? The short answer for many of the topics covered in this volume is: no. Specifically, a 'true' public good, whether national or international, must be both *indivisible* (that is, one actor's consumption of the good does not reduce the amount available to others) and *non-excludable* (that is, individual actors within a system cannot be prevented from enjoying the good, otherwise it would be a private or club good). A commons good is divisible (that is, it can be used up) but non-excludable; fishing on the high seas is one example of a global commons good (Ostrom, 1990). Figure 3.1 shows these types of goods.

One classic example of a true public good is a lighthouse: its light cannot be overconsumed by ships approaching it, nor can its light be subdivided to favour some ships over others. It can be turned off, of course, but this would put all ships at risk at night and thus defeat its purpose. Clean air in open spaces also qualifies as a public good. In international security affairs, we actually find that most benefits of international security cooperation are in fact either indivisible and/or excludable (as in the case of alliance systems) and therefore do not protect all states. There are some possible exceptions in this volume: the avoidance of global thermonuclear war; the benefits of combating certain environmental problems, such as ozone depletion and climate change; and responding to a major infectious disease outbreak. The benefits of managing these types of problems are generally both indivisible and non-excludable, although in some cases the vulnerability to harm still varies widely, as with for example small island states in the face of global climate change (see Chapter 11). Similarly, a world completely free of WMD might qualify as an international public good, yet we shall see in Chapter 6 why this is unlikely to be achieved.

In any event, collective action does not happen automatically; it requires political leadership and power at the national and international levels. This of course is the key insight regarding international anarchy: not that the global system is completely chaotic and ungovernable, but that institutions for interest mediation, preference aggregation, collective action

|  |  | Indivisible? | |
|---|---|---|---|
|  |  | Yes | No |
| Non-excludable? | Yes | Public good | Commons good |
|  | No | Private good | Club good |

Figure 3.1   *Types of collective goods*

and decision implementation *at the international level* typically have less authority than, and are not hierarchically organized like, institutions within states. Under such conditions, actors are either tempted to 'free-ride' on the efforts of others and contribute as little as possible, or they attempt to 'pass the buck' and wait for someone else to take the initiative (Christensen and Snyder, 1990). In both cases, collective action regarding a specific problem can easily be undermined. To avoid these pathologies, some actor(s) must take responsibility for defining and managing international security problems; they do not solve themselves. This cold 'logic of collective action' (Olson, 1974) requires us to pay some degree of attention to the problems of leadership, including the resources by which, and the principles or rules under which, such leadership is exercised.

## Leadership and power

This leads to our fifth and final assumption: that an effective understanding of leadership in the face of modern international security problems requires us to adopt a fairly broad definition of *political power*. Power can be defined most basically as the authority or ability to exert influence over other actors in a given social setting, yet as used in this volume it takes on several additional features. First, our approach to power must vary according to the problem context and the actors involved, as discussed in more detail later. What might be an effective use of one type of power in one setting might be ineffective, or even counterproductive, in another. The problem of *collectively* determining what types of power are most effective and appropriate for what types of policy problems is indeed one of the key analytical puzzles in international security studies. Second, power must also be defined in relational terms to determine its full potential causal impact as related to international security problems. For example, some analysts distinguish between (general) 'structural' power and (specific) 'instrumental' power. Structural power is the ability to set the basic rules of the game for everyone in a social system, while instrumental power involves the exercise of influence over specific actors for a specific purpose (Barnett and Duvall, 2005). The effectiveness of both types of power can vary widely depending on whether the targets of influence are thought to be allies, competitors or enemies. Third, this volume adopts the distinction between hard and soft power as discussed in Chapter 1. Thus, a mere accounting of guns and bombs possessed by an actor does not get one very far with many of the problems discussed in this volume. Our approach to power and leadership, therefore, must vary depending on the specific security problem under consideration.

To summarize, careful readers may see that this volume applies a mix of realist, liberal and even social constructivist and critical views. Like realism, the approach in this volume respects the problems of collective action under anarchy and the role of material or physical reality in conditioning the ways actors engage with each other. Unlike realism, however, it does not privilege the security of one value and the principle of self-help over all other values and concepts, or assume that material power – weapons – is the most effective, appropriate or cost-efficient way of handling most security challenges. We cannot even assume that human life is the basic value at stake, since this then raises the question: whose lives should be protected if all humans cannot be protected equally all of the time, which is clearly the case in world politics? As with liberalism, this volume accepts the need for international cooperation in managing most security problems and pays much attention to the role of multilateral institutions in facilitating such cooperation. Unlike liberalism, however, it does not assume that institutions or laws reflect universal values, or that actors are not easily tempted to use (or reject) institutions for more self-interested purposes (which may or may not then facilitate international cooperation). In fact, actors often completely ignore institutional norms or international law, especially where security is at stake, which is why a 'pure' liberal approach to international security is as unrealistic as a 'pure' realist approach is too simplistic. Finally, as with social constructivist and critical theories, this volume problematizes the wide range of values, interests/preferences and power resources possessed by major actors in the modern international system. Unlike such theories, however, this volume does not ignore or downplay the existence of certain material or historical facts at work in the modern world, and attempts therefore to strike a pragmatic balance between the physical reality and the social or discursive reality facing the actors within that world.

Keeping the five assumptions above well in mind as we proceed through the chapters to follow, a 'first cut' political analysis of the how and why of contemporary international security problems involves answering four basic questions, or performing four analytical tasks. These tasks involve:

1.  determining the degree of consensual knowledge, if any, regarding the nature of the value–threat relationship involved with a particular (or potential) security problem
2.  assessing various features of the actors involved in that problem
3.  framing the global management of that problem as a series of international collective action problems
4.  analysing the political aspects of any policy evaluation that results from such collective action.

The rest of this chapter discusses these tasks in turn.

## The value–threat relationship and international security

As this volume is largely concerned with the politics of international security, we must first attempt to determine the extent to which a specific security problem involves material interests or physical threats to certain values or interests that are treated as empirical givens by various actors. In other words, to what extent does the security issue at hand involve some degree of consensual knowledge about threats to certain values across the international community? As I suggested above, to a large degree such knowledge is socially constructed; however, it is also true that physical measurement or direct experience with a phenomenon can make the social construction of consensual knowledge far more likely. A high degree of such knowledge, in turn, may reduce the scope for politicization when addressing a specific security issue, and possibly even turn it into a more technical or administrative problem. Security problems related to infectious diseases, for example, may involve so much specialized knowledge that political actors may delegate a great deal of authority to technical experts (that is, those with a very high degree of consensual knowledge) such as epidemiologists and public health officials. Where such consensus is lacking, however, we are likely to see far more political contestation about the empirical reality of the problem to be addressed.

More specifically, we can attempt to assess the degree of such consensual knowledge along at least four parameters.

### Destructive scale

To what extent does a phenomenon involve human deaths or injuries, or physical damage to or destruction of property or other valued things? The protection of human lives and resources critical to human life is a central topic in many analyses of security affairs (as 'existential' interests), yet consensual knowledge about the specific scale of destruction if certain threats are not managed can vary widely depending on the issue at hand. As noted earlier, the field of international security is generally oriented towards worst case scenarios; however, consensus views about the degree of damage associated with a threat – even a worst case one – are not always easy to achieve, and obviously can vary depending on the perspective of the actors in question. For some issues, such as an ongoing interstate military conflict, there may be a general sense of agreement about the destructive consequences involved as deaths mount, refugees scatter and property is destroyed. For other issues, however, such as an infectious disease outbreak, the scale of destruction may be far more hypothetical or conceptual in nature, and consensual knowledge about the appropriate response may be harder to generate.

In a related vein, some 'valued things' can be more physical in nature (such as territory and people) and more easily conceptualized in terms of what is to be protected, while other values are more abstract in nature (such as 'civilization' or 'states') and might therefore involve far more contention over how damage to them should be defined and measured by the international community. Finally, values of a physical nature can further be conceptualized as either zero-sum or more positive-sum resources. Territorial disputes in particular often have a zero-sum character – a gain for one actor must be at the expense of another actor – which is why they are often so violent and protracted; the Israel–Palestine conflict is one obvious example of this dynamic. Perceptions of joint gains (or positive-sum outcomes), however, as in the case of increasing global markets or the reduction of global warming, may improve the prospects for cooperation.

## Geographic and temporal scope

To what extent is the threat to a certain value cross-border or international in nature, and how long might the damage last if the threat is not effectively curtailed? International security problems typically involve multiple states, yet there is no practical consensus on the number of states that must be threatened for an issue to qualify as an *international* security problem, rather than a bilateral or multilateral one. A threat facing a small number of powerful states can often be more easily framed as an international security problem than a threat facing a large number of weak states, which is why I favour a political approach throughout this volume, and prefer the term 'international' rather than 'global' security.

Determining the long-term effects of damage can be equally problematic, as it may involve forecasting with data sources that are lacking, unreliable or merely disputed by various actors. For issues where there is limited direct experience, or where the time horizon extends far into the future, such as global climate change, achieving a consensus on the temporal scope of the threat might be even more difficult. Further, any security problem that involves human behaviour to some degree – known as *anthropogenic* threats – will require knowledge about trends in that behaviour before a collective forecast can be used to generate threat assessments and policy prescriptions. All of the problems discussed in this volume are largely anthropogenic threats, which is why we do not consider natural disasters (for example) by themselves as 'international security' problems. Even with a 'naturally occurring' problem such as a deadly infectious disease, the key problem is not just the features of the virus, but the behaviour of the humans infected by it – in other words, an anthropogenic threat. A final consideration here is that most actors tend to focus on short- or medium-term problems rather than long-term ones. Politicians in fact are often criticized precisely because they are reluctant to see beyond the next election; an even less charitable view is that political actors will actually prefer to impose costs on future generations rather than on today's voters. This problem is particularly acute in the case of international economic affairs (see Chapter 10), yet it applies to other issues as well. Immediate crises therefore often take precedence over long-term planning, especially when an election looms, which is a perfectly rational *political* calculation even though it might be a sub-optimal *policy* one.

## Likelihood

How likely is it that the threat will materialize if measures are not taken to prevent or counteract it? This aspect of the threat–value relationship is just as important as the others, yet it gets much less attention than debates regarding the scale and scope of potential destruction. And when comparing across threats, say for the purposes of committing scarce resources, one must balance the destructive scale/scope of threats against the propensity that they will actually occur. Again, this often involves forecasting, which requires some type of reliable data. Trends in military spending, weapons proliferation, infectious disease mortality, resource depletion and so on must be collated and analysed in hopes of producing some consensual knowledge about whether a threat will manifest itself. However, where the threat results from decisions made by other humans, such as government officials or criminals, it is not enough to know facts about material capabilities; we must know something about *intent* as well. This problem – analysing intent in addition to capabilities to determine the likelihood of a threat materializing – is one of the most difficult aspects of a political approach to international security, but also is precisely why such an approach is justified. The key point is that, to the extent there is *some* consensual knowledge regarding the likelihood of a threat materializing, the scope for political contestation may be greatly reduced. Unfortunately, however, this is rarely the case for most of the problems in this volume, although some do involve a fairly high degree of consensual knowledge regarding the question of likelihood.

## Recovery

Finally, if a security threat actually materializes in the form of damage or destruction, to what extent is such destruction permanent or even catastrophic? And to what extent can any recovery be made if the problem is not handled effectively? This factor is obviously related to the issues of scale/scope noted above, yet the prospects for recovery – and their associated costs – can vary widely across international security issues. A recovery from global nuclear war or catastrophic climate change might indeed be impossible, while recovery from a breakdown in computer networks might be costly but still manageable. The ability to create back-up systems or procedures (or 'redundancies') is one obvious way to manage this problem. The ability to develop substitutes for certain valued things, such as fossil fuels, is another possible solution for certain security problems. In addition, individual states and other actors can vary widely in their ability to handle any recovery efforts, which should have an impact on how they interpret the destructive potential of threat to their security. Still, to the extent that actors can agree that the global damage resulting from the materialization of some threat is both catastrophic and irreversible, common action to manage that threat may be more likely.

In short, if there is fairly widespread agreement on these questions, then the potential for politicization is somewhat lessened and the possibility of collective action is somewhat greater. What they may add up to, in fact, is an overall international sense of *urgency* about the problem; a condition that may be difficult to measure but that still generally involves agreement on the four factors noted above. If there is little or no agreement here – no sense of urgency – then the scope for politicization increases and the need for leadership to build consensus and take action, if any, is that much greater. This is precisely why efforts to reframe international security in terms of societal security, human security, soft security and so on can be so difficult, as we shall see in later chapters. In addition, such a lack of consensual knowledge regarding these factors may also mean that a leading political actor may be subjected to higher standards of effectiveness and legitimacy – or even rejected completely as a leader – if he or she miscalculates one or more of these factors, or attempts to mislead others. This is why activities involving intelligence gathering and analysis, public watchdogs (such as NGOs), journalistic reporting, academic research and other forms of (potentially) global consensual knowledge can play such a strong supporting role in the problems covered in this volume.

To be sure, such consensual knowledge can be manufactured, manipulated and even politicized in a variety of ways; policy-makers can ignore or inflate intelligence estimates for their own interests just as they can any other pieces of information they encounter ('threat inflation'). US Secretary of State Colin Powell's 2003 presentation to the UN about Iraq's supposed WMD capability, which justified the American-led war on that country, will go down in history as an infamous example of such behaviour. Although Powell himself may have been acting in good faith, the 'intelligence' he presented to the international community had been politically manipulated to an unprecedented degree by the White House and its political supporters at home and abroad. In fact, US congressman Henry Waxman later cited at least 237 exaggerated or dubious claims made by the Bush administration about Iraq's alleged possession of WMD, a staggering figure by any standard. As the sources of such intelligence findings are also typically secret, it can be difficult for other political actors to challenge them (Holt, 1995; Lowenthal, 2003; Johnson and Wirtz, 2004).

This misuse of evidence can occur not just in traditional areas like war, but also with non-traditional security issues like economic instability and drug trafficking. There is also a potential trap here: if authorities start to use certain types of evidence to justify their policies, then it becomes harder for them to disavow the evidence if it contradicts them later. It also means that *future* problems of a similar nature may be discounted as threats by the international community owing to a lack of trust about the intelligence claims made by certain actors. To complicate this problem, in most countries there are a number of intelligence agencies and other sources of security-related information, often competing with each other for resources and power. Political, economic and military intelligence estimates are usually produced by different bureaucracies with varying agendas. Political actors must make sense of it all, and they may not always agree on the final analysis; the various warnings prior to 9/11 regarding a possible foreign terrorist attack within the US are a prime case in point (see Chapter 7). Political actors can also specifically direct, or 'task', intelligence agencies to stress some types of security threats or sources of evidence over others, which can easily create a bias regarding the information that results. Still, attempting to determine whether there is *some* degree of empirical (that is, relatively uncontested) support regarding the fundamentals of an international security issue is the first – but only the first – analytical step in understanding how it might be handled by the international community.

## Stakeholders and international security

In the section above I referred to 'actors' in various places without specifying their precise natures. This task is undertaken in this section, which generally adopts what might be called a 'stakeholder' approach to the analysis of international security. To a some degree, all people on the planet might be viewed as stakeholders in this domain; however, the fundamental point of a political analysis involves recognizing the obvious, though possibly unpleasant, truth that some stakeholders have far more influence than others, no matter how unfair or illegitimate this may seem. Yet, as I also noted above, a stakeholder approach does not mean we privilege military power, and those who hold it, as the only or even primary source of influence on these problems. What I mean by stakeholder in this context simply refers to a range of political actors who generally: 1) act on behalf of or in the name of larger entities (such as governments, citizens, firms, international organizations, terrorist groups); and 2) commit far more of their attention, time and other resources to security matters as compared to average citizens, firms and other actors. As in the business world, the label of 'stakeholder' can be claimed by any number of interested parties; in a political analysis, however, this claim must be backed up with some degree of power/authority and sustained politically motivated action *vis-à-vis* competing stakeholders. One might also frame this distinction as a difference between active and passive stakeholders. The former play a key role in the political processes discussed in the section below and thus receive more attention in this volume; the latter play an indirect role as voters or objects of action and will receive somewhat less attention. More specifically, the active stakeholders analysed at length in this volume will be defined according to several key parameters.

## Principal stakeholders

Active or principal stakeholders are routinely and directly involved in the 'everyday business' of international security affairs, largely by virtue of their roles and power resources, and they can take the form of interpreters of, providers of, threats to, targets of or victims of international security. As these forms involve states to some degree, every chapter in this volume will take for granted their key role as political stakeholders. The five permanent members (or P5) of the UNSC – China, France, Russia, the UK and the US – are especially important for many of the problems considered in this volume. A similar major power grouping is the Group of 7, or G7, bloc, which involves the finance ministers of Canada, France, Germany, Italy, Japan, the UK and the US; the G7 began meeting formally in 1976. Between 1998 and 2014, the G8 bloc added Russia to the G7 states and involved heads of government rather than finance ministers; an EU representative usually attends G7 and G8 meetings as well. However, Russia's involvement in the G8 was suspended after its annexation of Crimea (see Chapter 4), although the G8 itself was not officially dissolved. Some now also speak of a G2 world (China and the US) or a G3 world (the G2 plus the EU), while many other groupings (such as the G20 or the G77) are involved in specific security matters, as we shall see later. Relative to other stakeholders, then, states and state-based coalitions or IOs tend to possess a very wide range of power resources, both hard and soft, by which to influence the international security agenda, and must choose how to apply these resources to various security problems as defined in this volume.

However, it is somewhat simplistic to speak merely of 'states' acting in the abstract, so this volume also considers, where necessary, two major state components: *national governments* (and their supporting agencies, including military and intelligence services) which generally enjoy executive authority, and *legislative or representative bodies*, which may have budgetary, treaty ratification or veto powers (among other domestic powers) over decisions made by national governments. The US Senate's critical examination – and occasional rejection – of various security-related treaties discussed in this volume is a case in point (Auerswald, 2006).

The stakeholder approach to 'actorness' in this volume also includes a *societal component*, largely in the form of organized groups with a shared interest (political parties, firms, think tanks and so on) or other non-state actors who may assert some influence in international security. This societal component also includes non-state actors at the international level, such as transnational advocacy NGOs (for example, Amnesty International or Greenpeace) or activist networks (such as the International Campaign to Ban Landmines) that may involve themselves in certain policy issues (Keck and Sikkink, 1998). Some of these groups, which number in the thousands, function as major MNCs, with operating budgets in the hundreds of millions of dollars and offices or missions in dozens of states around the globe. However, they do not exert similar degrees of influence, and therefore must be analysed on a case-by-case basis depending on the security problem at hand. Nor should it be assumed that such NGOs are more legitimate than any other stakeholders; the term 'non-governmental' implies some distance from, or impartiality towards, states, yet many NGOs are partly funded by states, must often deal with states where they operate, and can perform state-like functions, not all of which will positively impact a security problem. Like the expanded use of PMCs in recent years, NGOs are simply part of a larger trend towards the privatization of many state functions, and they can be as corrupt, inefficient and unaccountable as any other stakeholders working in the realm of international security.

## Interests and preferences

Stakeholders cannot exert decisive influence in international security without power, yet one cannot analyse power effectively without knowing something about its source, purpose and context. This is where disputes regarding interests and preferences can come into play. Stakeholders can disagree about interests or preferences, or both, in which case a high degree of political manoeuvring will be necessary to bring about a consensus on a certain problem. As noted earlier, a political analysis of international security does not in fact require that we assume a similar ranking of interests and preferences across various stakeholders; on the contrary, we should assume conflicts among them. This approach is also contrary to most realist analyses, which assume that concerns about security will always dominate other interests.

Although security concerns might not be prioritized equally among key stakeholders, and although such conflicts over interests might seem potentially limitless (which is why realism assumes security interests will dominate), these problems can be simplified to some degree depending on the international security problem at stake. For many modern international security problems, such conflicts of interest at the global level can be framed as East–West cleavages (where 'East' can refer to the communist world, Asia or the Islamic world), North–South cleavages, West–West (or transatlantic) cleavages and a cleavage between the US/West and the rest of the world (or 'the West versus the rest'). As we shall see throughout this volume, one of the main factors behind these cleavages – or different perceptions of security interests and threats – involves a more fundamental difference in vulnerability. International security problems do not impact all states in the same way, and these differences in vulnerability must always be factored into the analysis. In addition, interest/preference cleavages based on different values, variation in vulnerability and other factors may also vary over time, in different arenas or during different types of political debates as discussed later in this chapter. This means we may need to pay close attention to factors such as (for example) electoral cycles, interest group pressures, global market dynamics, technological change or bureaucratic politics, depending on the problem at hand.

## The use of force

Stakeholder views about this question are somewhat unique to the political analysis of security problems, which are more likely to involve the use of force as compared to other international problems. In fact, some would identify international security problems precisely by whether violence is involved in defining or managing them (Walt, 1991); therefore it makes sense to consider whether stakeholder views about the use of force vary within the context of individual security problems. In other words, even if a set of stakeholders fully agrees on the nature of the value–threat relationship, some of them may feel strongly that the problem can be resolved peacefully, or with less punitive measures such as economic sanctions, rather than with a resort to military force. This debate therefore involves calculations about the utility, ethics and costs of military force; such calculations often vary, as always, according to the stakeholders and security problems at hand. Even so, a very high degree of consensus on this topic might reflect a clear 'dilemma of common aversion' (Stein, 1982): an outcome that virtually all stakeholders in a social setting might wish to avoid at virtually any cost (for example, global thermonuclear war or pandemic disease).

As we shall see throughout this volume, however, this degree of consensus is actually quite rare; moreover, even where we find it many other factors – political and otherwise – must be examined to determine the likely response of the international community. Once we determine stakeholder views on this dimension, along with their power resources, we can then determine the scope for political bargaining, and therefore the potential for agreement, regarding various security problems. In addition, we need to define 'force' as broadly as possible when examining how actors may respond to contemporary security problems, which means not just overt military force (such as land, air and naval forces), but also covert action, special forces, police forces and highly controversial measures such as assassination, torture, kidnapping or hostage-taking. Finally, these capabilities, as always, can vary widely not just among states but also among non-state actors, and can therefore greatly intensify political disputes regarding their effectiveness and appropriateness, whether among security providers or security threats.

## Public–private domains and levels of jurisdiction

Finally, the nature of contemporary international security problems requires that we pay some attention to stakeholder views about the appropriate or effective relationship between public and private approaches to international security, and to the related problem of the appropriate or effective level of jurisdiction. Traditional or orthodox approaches to security affairs tend to focus primarily or exclusively on public or official activities (war-making by states) at the international level of jurisdiction or legality. However, contemporary security problems often involve complicated overlaps, and even contradictions, between these realms of activity. PMCs governed under the domestic jurisdictions of their home countries can be involved in foreign interstate or intrastate wars, and public IOs/NGOs can assert influence over private activities within states (even states that are not members of such organizations; a complex phenomenon known as 'extraterritoriality'). Further, political stakeholders can and do strongly disagree about the appropriate and effective balance between these public–private and international–domestic domains, which can then complicate the search for a solution to common international security problems. Thus, even where we might find a fairly high degree of consensus regarding the three stakeholder factors noted above, common ground might still be lacking regarding this element of an international security problem, which would then complicate international cooperation efforts. Indeed, debates over the appropriate response to a specific security problem often involve the question of jurisdiction: should the problem be handled by an international organization with legal authority, or by individual states, or by some combination?

## Political debates about international security

An obvious problem in determining stakeholder views about the factors above is that such views can change over time, sometimes drastically (as with a change in government, for example). A related problem is that such

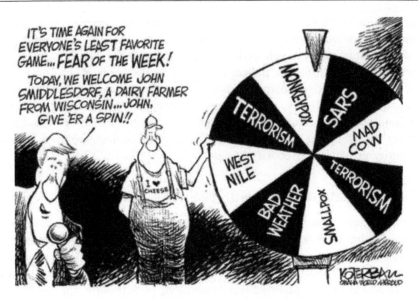

*How does the international community choose among so many competing problems?*

views can be misrepresented deliberately by stakeholders for the purposes of strategic bargaining or outright deception. One way to manage these problems is to focus on a shorter time span in hope of reducing excessive variation regarding the power resources, interests/preferences and other stakeholder attributes noted above. Thus in the chapters that follow I focus most of my attention on contemporary problems of international security (that is, the post-Cold War period). A second way to manage stakeholder variation is to disaggregate international security problems into a series of linked political debates. While these debates are presented as phases in the political management of a security problem, it should be obvious that these phases lack discrete boundaries; instead they quite often 'shade' into each other. In addition, the process suggested here is not entirely linear and unidirectional; setbacks and divergences often occur depending on a wide range of political and other factors. However, our analysis must start somewhere, and this section attempts to isolate some of the key political debates involved in bringing a security problem to life at the global level. These phases of debate involve agenda-setting, framing alternative policies, and the politics of policy choice.

## International agenda-setting

Agenda-setting is not quite the same as merely generating publicity or raising awareness about a security concern, although these activities can be important. Instead, it refers to the political act of making an international security problem a regular topic of focused attention among the key stake-holders as defined above. One obvious problem here is that many security problems may be defined initially as national (or possibly bilateral or regional) security problems, whether in terms of the value to be protected or the threat to be managed. In these cases, the state in question may make an effort to 'export' its problem to the international level in hopes of managing it better, or of simply sharing the costs with other stakeholders. However, this type of 'problem transference' involves risks as well, since the international community may not adopt the same response desired by the state or other stakeholder(s) responsible for the agenda-setting.

A second consideration is that stakeholders vary in terms of their ability and authority to set the agenda, although this phase of the process is arguably the most open and transparent as compared to later phases. Normally government stakeholders are responsible for determining the international security agenda; however, the increasing range and complexity of modern security problems as covered in this volume allow for a wider range of potential agenda-setters (such as technical experts or NGOs). This is where *credibility* can be a key source of power for stakeholders attempting to set the international security agenda. In other words, do they have access to relevant and trustworthy knowledge about the value–threat relationship at issue, and do they have a track record of effectively analysing that issue? Obviously states (particularly their intelligence and related agencies) claim a high degree of credibility regarding the international security agenda; however, this credibility is not absolute for reasons noted above, and other stakeholders might have an opportunity to help set the agenda depending on the topic at hand.

In addition, the process of initial agenda-setting for any security problem involves making some critical assumptions or arguments about the nature of the value–threat relationship, which often includes an effort to generate or consolidate some consensual knowledge. This initial agenda-setting can be an extremely vague process as well; if a high degree of uncertainty remains regarding either the value or threat at stake here, then each later phase of the process – assuming it does proceed – becomes that much more complicated and contentious. This is an especially important point to keep in mind throughout this volume as security stakeholders are often responding to the fears of their constituents when setting the agenda, and the politics of fear can generate many unintended consequences, such as overreaction or a misdirection of resources. Fear can also create threats or enemies where they did not exist before and/or can be manipulated deliberately by stakeholders for various reasons (Ramadan and Shantz, 2016). Finally, even if a security problem becomes part of the international security agenda, we still need to understand why some problems stall at this stage while others receive far more attention and resources on the part of the international community.

## Framing a range of policy alternatives

The first indication that a security problem might result in some significant attention by the international community (beyond mere 'cheap talk' or do-nothing summitry) is when key political stakeholders begin debating definite policy options rather than merely discussing whether the problem exists in the first place. The debate over policy options can involve a number of parameters. One critical aspect involves the question of unilateral versus multilateral solutions (or local versus global solutions); even if considerable consensus exists about the nature of an international security problem, stakeholders may still prefer to handle it at the national level for a variety of reasons. If the stakes are especially high, and/or if the threat varies widely across different stakeholders, then the stakeholders facing the greatest threat might not trust others to be as diligent or effective in managing the problem. These political considerations regarding the virtues of unilateral versus multilateral responses are often compounded by institutional, legal, technical or other policy-related debates, such as the appropriate level of jurisdiction as discussed above. For some traditional security concerns, such as those involving interstate war, national governments typically play the central role as policy managers. For other problems, such as those involving cybersecurity or organized crime, subnational stakeholders and processes (including private firms) may become as important as central governments. In both cases, however, some degree of delegation to, or involvement of, an IO may help to take the problem from the 'deliberation' to the 'action' phase.

A second general parameter regarding policy options involves the equally difficult debate regarding what type of policy tool to apply to the problem at hand, and the appropriate 'target' of the policy. Policy tools, which require appropriate material resources on the part of relevant stakeholders, might involve diplomatic, economic (financial aid and trade) and military measures. In addition, all of these options can be framed as both positive and negative measures (or as 'carrots and sticks'), and in terms of more passive/defensive versus more active/offensive measures. Positive measures would include diplomatic support for issues valued by the target stakeholder in question, financial aid, trade access, technical support or military aid (such as providing arms or a security guarantee, including membership of an alliance). Negative measures would involve the denial of these valued resources, criminal charges and punishments, and possibly the most controversial policy tool of all: various types of military action against the target stakeholder in question. In general, passive/defensive measures are easier and cheaper to implement than more active/offensive measures, which typically require more multilateral cooperation. This volume, therefore, is primarily concerned with more active and multilateral approaches to specific international security problems, such as the formation of alliances (an active multilateral measure) as opposed to fixed fortifications or national airline passenger screening (passive unilateral measures) in response to an international security problem.

Most international security problems also involve debates about some type of policy mix, which would include whether to apply different types of tools to different aspects of the problem (such as a balance between carrots and sticks), or whether to escalate the level of punishment if certain results – assuming those results can be agreed – are not achieved. Offering a series of increasing incentives is also possible, such as an increase in trade or a relaxation of sanctions. Finally, the target of the policy is linked to the question of direct versus indirect threats. Direct threats to security usually involve deliberate stakeholder behaviours (such as terrorist attacks) that can be clearly identified and targeted by the international community as the main source of the problem. Indirect threats are far more complicated: they might involve the behaviours of various stakeholders (particularly non-state actors) that produce *negative externalities* (i.e. spillover or knock-on effects) that are not intended to threaten others but still do so, and may therefore be framed (and targeted) as international security problems. Indirect threats also include many anthropogenic phenomena, such as economic or environmental trends, that cannot be traced easily to a single source or cause, which makes the process of targeting the problem that much more difficult and politically contentious.

## Policy choice

This is typically the most difficult aspect of a policy debate, and failure here often explains why some potential international security problems stall without resolution (that is, result in deadlock or stalemate). Debating problems and options is one thing, but finding or even forcing agreement on a single policy (or set of policies) is quite another, especially if a set of stakeholders attempts to use consensus or unanimity as a normal decision rule. The general options suggested above can involve a wide range of costs and benefits for certain stakeholders even though the problem at hand involves 'international' security affairs; these costs and benefits become much clearer once the international community begins to focus on options at one level of jurisdiction (if any) with one set of stakeholders (assuming multilateral rather than unilateral action). If the stakeholders are indeed agreed on the virtues of collective action over, or in addition to, unilateral action, then a specific policy choice may result from several political processes. These may include some form of hegemonic leadership, where a single powerful stakeholder (typically a state) agrees or offers to take on much of the burden of the policy choice, or a 'coalition of the willing', where a set of stakeholders agrees to manage the problem collectively. In addition, policy choice can be facilitated by outright bargaining over a range of options, which might include *log-rolling* deals (i.e. trading favours across policy issues, even ones not directly related to the security issue at hand) and/or the provision of *side payments* (i.e. offering specific incentives to stakeholders who might otherwise oppose a policy option).

It is possible, of course, that the degree of consensual knowledge about the nature of a security problem, as based on (for example) technical data, could lead directly to a single policy choice, but this rarely happens for most security problems. It is also possible that some stakeholder(s) might unilaterally decide on a course of action, even while debating the problem with others, and then attempt to defend that action as one taken for the benefit of the international community at large. Policy choice also involves not just the question of tools and targets; it also often involves questions regarding the balance between policy tools, who will pay what costs for certain policies, whether to impose a timetable of implementation and what types of outcomes are expected by the policy. Finally, use of the term 'choice' here implies full agreement among a set of political stakeholders, but the situation is rarely so neat and tidy for many questions of international security. Instead, as suggested by the discussion of bounded rationality noted above, what we usually find is a sub-optimal, even conflicting, *set of choices* based as much, or more, on parochial political concerns than on an ideal, objective analysis of how to apply what resources to what aspects of what type of international security problem. This I why I favour a broad political analysis over a narrow strategic or public policy analysis in this volume.

## The politics of policy effectiveness

The final aspect of a political analysis of an international security problem involves evaluating the effectiveness or performance of any policy that has been agreed, whether by states, IOs or any other stakeholders. This question, however, is so important and potentially contentious that it requires a separate set of political considerations. The objective here is to determine the extent to which a policy (or set of policies) is responsible for the effective management or eradication of a specific threat to international security. Specifically, if the policy seems to be working as desired by its creators, then why exactly is that the case (that is, to what extent is the policy responsible for success, as opposed to, or in addition to, other factors that might be responsible)? Or, if the policy does not seem to be working, then why is that the case? How stakeholders, particularly government officials who wish to stay in power, answer these questions can, as always, be a politically contentious process. Therefore we need to have a general understanding of the different ways policy performance or success can be framed in the realm of international security.

The first consideration is the extent to which the policy (or set of policies) has actually been implemented as agreed by the stakeholders in question. With many issues involving international cooperation, implementation is largely left to individual states and their governments; IOs in this case may simply monitor their behaviour and attempt to impose some type of limited sanctions (typically 'naming and shaming') for states or other stakeholders that defect from their commitments. Failure to implement an agreed policy may take the form of voluntary defections (if the stakeholder deliberately refused to comply) or involuntary defections (if the stakeholder intended to comply in good faith but could not because of a variety of reasons, such as a lack of financial or administrative capacities) (Cole, 2015). More effective collective policies will have clear provisions for not only monitoring stakeholder compliance but also for distinguishing between voluntary and involuntary defections, and then applying some type of appropriate punishment.

In addition, for some security problems, states may be more willing to delegate their authority to global or regional IOs or other public 'watchdogs', which may then enjoy a fair degree of autonomy in terms of managing the problem at hand. In either case, policy implementation still involves the devotion of resources to a problem as long as it persists. However, most security problems discussed in this volume are open-ended in nature, with no clear endpoint. These problems are especially difficult as the political coalitions that first agreed on a solution can change dramatically over time and thus upset whatever policy consensus had been achieved. National elections or other changes in senior leadership are the most obvious source of such interruptions of a long-term policy consensus; in addition, crises, changes in technology, economic trends and other factors can easily interfere with the formulation and implementation of collective solutions. For some issues, however, such as eradicating a certain disease, it is possible that some type of timetable and division of labour can be agreed until the problem has been solved to the satisfaction of those attempting to manage it, which may reduce the possibility of a disruption in implementation owing to either voluntary or involuntary defections.

Assuming, however, that the stakeholders have implemented the policy in good faith as agreed (which is often a heroic assumption in international relations), then how do we know the policy is working as intended? Again, this is often a political calculation as much as a technical one. Here stakeholders have several options for defending the apparent effectiveness of a policy once it has been implemented.

The simplest option might be termed the 'total victory' standard: this involves completely eliminating the threat or problem as defined by the international community. This option is most obviously associated with military conflicts, as in 'winning' a war or removing an aggressive government from office. But it also might be applied in terms of capturing a specific terrorist, destroying a specific terrorist group or a specific criminal organization, compelling a certain stakeholder to reverse its behaviour or eliminating a specific disease through extensive global vaccination programmes. However, as always there are complications; for example, to what extent can the absence of a Soviet invasion of Western Europe be attributed to NATO? In other words, proving the effectiveness of a policy in terms of something that did *not* happen, or something that supposedly would have happened (such as a terrorist attack) if the policy had not been pursued (or *counterfactual reasoning*) can be especially politically contentious; scholars will be arguing for decades about whether NATO, rather than other factors, actually prevented a Soviet invasion of Western Europe (assuming the Soviets always intended such an attack, which is also debatable), just as scholars still debate whether World Wars I and II were preventable if the right action had been taken in time.

For many international security problems, then, a 'total victory' standard of policy evaluation is inappropriate. Instead, one might adopt a 'historical trends' standard, which involves choosing a historical reference point and measuring policy performance against that point. The goal, of course, is to demonstrate that one's policy was directly responsible (or at least partly responsible) for the desired change in outcomes. Obviously this option involves political debates in terms of choosing the appropriate starting (or similar reference) point, and the choice of appropriate metrics to evaluate it. For many security problems covered in this volume such a 'trends' approach is often the most likely option and may in fact be written into the policy itself. For example, statistics on general terrorist or criminal activity, environmental factors, disease patterns, migration, economic growth and so on can be applied in the service of evaluating a particular policy. Even if the statistics seem to demonstrate success – a reduction in crime, car bombings or whatever – we still must attempt to take the next step and determine whether the policy itself was responsible, as opposed to other factors. This is also why *causality* must be an important part of any theoretical approaches to the systematic study of international security, a fact that is often neglected (or rejected completely) by some scholars, as in the case of normative or critical approaches. Finally, and in keeping with the notion of bounded rationality, the problems of contradictory data, missing data or even manufactured data also exist, all of which must be evaluated and interpreted, opening the door, once again, to political manipulation.

A third option is perhaps the most difficult of all: this might be termed the 'comparative metrics' standard of policy performance. It involves evaluating the performance of a policy relative to some other standard or reference point besides (or in addition to) a previous point in time. For some issues, as with the historical trends approach, this method is not so far-fetched. For example, nutrition experts might argue that an average human being requires a minimum of 1,200–1,800 calories of food per day to survive; countries whose populations fail to meet that standard are said to be at risk even if general historical trends show a gradual increase in caloric intake. Other technical standards involving sanitation, access to clean water, carbon emissions or even per capita income might be employed in the service of a policy evaluation of a certain security problem. Where such technical standards are lacking, however, we will expect to find a great deal of political contention regarding an appropriate comparative standard against which to measure an international security policy. This is the situation, in fact, with many normative or critical approaches to international security, which (in addition to their neglect of causality) often attempt to apply standards based on justice, fairness, human dignity, emancipation or similar concepts that cannot be so easily measured and defined, and thus agreed, by the international community.

With all these approaches, a truly comprehensive policy evaluation would also include the negative consequences of one's policy, and in doing so produce a 'net assessment' of whether the policy is producing the desired benefits, and whether those benefits outweigh the costs. This assessment might be framed in terms of 'efficiency,' in the sense that the chosen course of action is cost-effective relative to other possible solutions. However, this standard is rarely achieved in international security owing to the high stakes and complex issues involved, and to the pressures of decision-making in stressful or crisis situations. Instead, a more pragmatic approach to the net assessment of international security policies would simply attempt to balance their benefits with their costs, not evaluate all possible solutions in every single choice situation. Ideally, this evaluation would also include the cost of doing nothing (which should have been addressed during the formative stage of the policy as well), even if it is not very clear whether any action would make the situation better regarding the security problem at issue. We also would do well to remember an old phrase from medical ethics – 'First, do no harm' – when attempting to 'solve' a particular international security problem. Thus, even if a policy seems to be achieving its goals as agreed by the international community, we still might see some political contention over whether the results are actually worth the effort, or whether we have reached a point of diminishing marginal returns on the policy, or whether it is harming some stakeholders more than helping others. For example, one might argue about the effectiveness of a policy based on military costs, economic costs, social/ political costs (that is, cohesion, reputation and so on), and even the costs of negative externalities related to a policy (cost paid by third parties, such as collateral damage to civilians or environmental damage resulting from fossil fuels).

Finally, we must also keep in mind that such evaluations of effectiveness and acceptable costs can change, especially for longer-term policies. In invading Afghanistan in pursuit of Osama bin Laden following the 9/11 attacks in 2001, President Bush said the US would 'smoke him out' of his hiding place and practically stop at nothing to capture the man. Two years later, having failed to capture bin Laden, Bush seemed to have given up and said he 'didn't think about him very much' any more. Was this an admission of policy failure or an attempt to change the policy goals (or both)? In addition, such changes can occur not only within individual stakeholders but also among sets of stakeholders, whether states, IOs, NGOs and so on. This fact can introduce an even greater level of uncertainty, and therefore potential politicization, into the process of policy-making. The rational desire of political stakeholders to claim credit for successful policies, and to deny their roles in unsuccessful ones, means it may be easier to redefine 'success', and/or to shift the blame for failure to other stakeholders, than to prove actual measures of (supposed) effectiveness as noted above. Since success has many parents who claim credit while failure is an orphan, we would also do well to keep in mind how different stakeholders use competing benchmarks for their own political ends rather than for the benefit of the international community.

## Summary

Given the indeterminate nature of general theories of international relations in explaining the full range of security issues covered in this volume, this chapter has outlined a range of basic political considerations – about the nature of the problem, the stakeholders involved, the policy options discussed and agreed and the evaluation of any agreed policy – to structure the discussion of each of the major security problems covered in the rest of this volume. For each issue, we shall primarily be concerned about this set of questions: who decides what valued things should be protected, with what means and with what measures of success? It should be made clear at the outset, however, that not all aspects of these questions as discussed in this chapter will be applied equally across security issues. Their emphasis will vary widely depending on the issue or policy at hand. Moreover, as this is a research-oriented volume,

I shall frame these political considerations, as far as possible, in light of current, and largely (but not exclusively) empirical research depending on the topic. Most theorists of international security probably share a desire to improve the human condition in some way, yet we still need to have a comprehensive diagnosis of the full range of problems associated with this field before offering any solutions to them, whether based on positivist/empirical or normative/ethical theories. The rest of this volume is written in this spirit. We begin with two chapters devoted to the most prominent and long-standing problem in the study of international security: war.

## Part II

# The Traditional International Security Agenda

## Chapter 4

# Interstate War

The problem of war has attracted more scholarly attention than any other topic in the history of international security studies, so it is appropriate to begin our discussion here. However, there is an astonishingly wide range of ways to conceptualize this question. One can examine the propensity for organized violence at all major levels of analysis, from individual human beings to the international system level, and reach different conclusions about the causal dynamics involved without ever considering the relationships between these levels. On another dimension, one can examine the normal 'steady state' or 'default position' of the international system: is it peace or war? In other words, is war the normal state of affairs, so that we have to explain when peace 'breaks out'? Or is war the exception, not the rule, in everyday political life, as most states and humans seem to be at peace with each other most of the time? And yet a third, but no means final, general aspect of war in international security is that it can be conceived as both a problem and a solution. As long as national defence (that is, unilateral war-making) is allowed by the rules of international law under certain conditions, the problem of war in international security affairs may be better framed as an analysis of the conditions under which armed conflicts become a security concern at the international level of analysis, and the conditions under which the use of military force is deemed acceptable by the international community.

Accordingly, this chapter will concern itself less with the historical evolution of war or the conduct of wars and focus instead on the politics of the relationship between war – as a problem and a solution – and international security. In keeping with the analytical framework discussed in the previous chapter, this approach first involves the treatment of war as a *deliberate*, though not necessarily *effective*, product of human decisions. Although some observers might speak of unnecessary, inadvertent or even accidental wars, most wars are in fact deliberate (Reiter, 1995) and can be, or have been, justified rationally, both before and/or after the fact, according to a range of goals. War may be very costly in human terms, and almost always involves random or unforeseeable problems (the 'fog of war'), yet states are still willing to take a gamble on it for a variety of reasons beyond merely fighting for the sake of fighting. And although most wars, particularly among modern democratic polities, involve some degree of controversy about their ends and/or means, they continue to occur on a regular basis and governments can often manage to overcome a great deal of domestic opposition to their military policies, at least in the short to medium term. This dual contrary recognition – of the highly destructive nature of modern wars yet also of the need for states to arm themselves ostensibly to avoid such wars – informs a great deal of theorizing about war, especially among realists.

## Interstate war and international security

In the context of international security, war can be defined most generally as highly organized political violence – involving discipline and leadership – conducted with armed force, and typically involves well-defined social groups, usually states or sub-units within states. Although the concept of war can easily shade into other forms of political violence, in this chapter the term is used in the more traditional sense of a military conflict between two or more social groups that results in widespread destruction in the form of killing and property damage. In this chapter we shall focus primarily on the problem of international (or interstate) war; in the next chapter we shall turn our attention to civil (or intrastate) war and imperial/colonial (or extrastate) war. Obviously they can be linked: interstate conflicts can cause, or be caused by, intrastate wars and vice versa. In addition, it may be difficult to determine whether an armed conflict is primarily an international or domestic problem, which then affects the range of possible responses or solutions. The dissolution of Yugoslavia is one such example, yet armed conflicts in many unstable regions of the world, such as sub-Saharan Africa, share this problem. However, to examine this topic in a systematic fashion, I shall concentrate on the interstate dimensions of armed conflict in the discussion below, keeping in mind the obvious linkage to intrastate wars to be covered in the next chapter.

We begin with an examination of whether any significant consensual knowledge exists regarding the nature of this problem. Fortunately, we possess a huge amount of data about the characteristics of wars in databases such as the Correlates of War project, the Conflict and Peace Databank, the Armed Conflict Dataset and similar efforts (Richardson, 1960; Blainey, 1973; Russett, 1972; Singer and Small, 1972; Snyder and Diesing, 1977; Singer, 1980; Levy, 1983; Holsti, 1996). Unfortunately, however, these data have been manipulated in an endless variety of ways to assert certain, and often conflicting, points of view; this is partly due to the wide range of ways to apply statistical techniques to quantitative data (Beck, King and Zeng, 2000). At a minimum, the question of whether any specific war is, or might become, an *international* security problem is contingent to some degree on three types of consensual knowledge: first, the actual and/or potential destructiveness of the war; second, beliefs about the cause(s) of the war, particularly in terms of determining why it is being fought and what outcome might result if one or another party prevails; and third, the costs involved in taking action to end the war and/or limit its destructiveness, as determined by various stakeholders in the international community. In the rest of this section I focus on the first area of consensual knowledge; in the rest of the chapter I address the second and third aspects of it.

## Destructive scale

Consensual knowledge about the destructive scale of interstate wars begins with the recognition that modern wars can be not only extremely violent and damaging; they tend now to be more violent than those of previous centuries. The advent of total war in particular during WWI greatly expanded the destructive scale and scope of conflict well beyond what had been experienced throughout prior human history. A second and related fact of modern war involves the recognition that the use of WMD, particularly nuclear weapons, could *catastrophically* expand the destruction if used in any type of conflict. More specific details about such damage are provided in Chapter 6 on weapons proliferation; here we need only point out that most security analysts would agree that any conflict threatening to escalate from conventional weapons to WMD poses a major risk to the international community. The vicious Iran–Iraq War during the 1980s, and the more recent civil war in Syria, where chemical weapons were used in both instances, indicate that this possibility is unfortunately not just a theoretical one. Now that over a dozen states possess some WMD capability, we must always keep in mind the potential use of such weapons in the event of an armed conflict.

Beyond these points, the analysis becomes far more problematic when turning from general trends to more specific cases. All wars are inherently destructive, but not all wars are interpreted as major international security threats. Surveying the vast amount of data on wars it is clear that individual armed conflicts can vary dramatically in terms of their destructive scale, which is often measured in terms of 'severity' (overall number of battle deaths) and 'intensity' (battle deaths per one million population). While these figures can vary from a severity of a few hundred battle deaths to over tens of millions, academic analyses often define an interstate war as an international armed conflict involving an intensity of at least 1,000 battle deaths (Levy, 1983). This, however, is quite an arbitrary threshold and can be measured against many other indicators. Also, suffering during a war can involve combatants and non-combatants, a distinction which is not always appreciated by the parties to a conflict – or even by many security scholars, who focus primarily on battle deaths. Indeed, the recent US-led wars against Afghanistan and Iraq resulted in the creation of a category of 'enemy non-combatants', which can be targeted by the US for capture and imprisonment in a manner similar to normal enemy combatants (prisoners of war, or POWs), but (apparently) without the usual legal protections enjoyed by POWs. This policy has prompted a number of legal battles inside and outside the US that are yet to be resolved (Slim, 2008). In addition to this wide range in destructive potential across wars, during the course of a specific conflict it can be difficult to determine the actual degree of damage involved. If truth is the first casualty of war, then reliable data about the conduct of ongoing wars are always suspect, and can be manipulated for a variety of purposes.

## Geographic and temporal scope

Beyond the question of sheer numbers of deaths or injuries or other physical damage, wars vary widely in terms of their geographical and temporal scope. They can be either bilateral (or *dyadic*) or multilateral, or start bilaterally and then grow into a multilateral, even global, conflict. Interstate wars are, by definition, cross-border in nature, and therefore always potentially threaten international security. If we assume the destructive scope expands with the number of states involved, then any war that starts as, or threatens to expand into, a multilateral one could be considered a greater threat than a bilateral war, all else being equal. Similarly, if we assume the destructive scope across space and time greatly expands when the parties involved possess considerable resources to convert into military power, then this fact too may suggest the presence of a major security threat, as does the possession of WMD by one or all parties to a conflict. Thus, a war between India and Pakistan – two states with large populations and WMD capabilities that have gone to the brink of war with each other – is far more likely to be seen as a major threat to international security than a war between, say, two small sub-Saharan African states. Such a war, if it includes WMD, is also likely to involve long-term damage to humans and the environment, which heightens its status as a threat to international security.

These assumptions actually inform a great deal of theoretical work on interstate war, much of which focuses on so-called great power, hegemonic, major or systemic wars. In the history of modern war since the sixteenth century, the most damaging wars have tended to involve several of the most powerful states at a given time (Wright, 1965; Levy, 1983; Diehl, 1985; Mearsheimer, 2001). Beyond their destructive scale and geographic/temporal scope, these wars also tend to reshape the basic international order following a long period of destruction. In fact, one early such major power war, the Thirty Years' War (1618–48), led to the creation of the modern state system (or the *Westphalian order*) according to several general principles that persist to this day: national sovereignty, non-intervention in domestic affairs, diplomatic immunity and extraterritoriality. Table 4.1 lists the major power wars that tend to attract the most attention of theorists of international war.

Table 4.1 *Select major power wars*

| War | Dates | Ratio of major powers involved | Intensity | Severity |
|---|---|---|---|---|
| War of Dutch Independence/Spanish Armada | 1585–1609 | 3/5 | 1,060 | 190,000 |
| Thirty Years' War | 1618–48 | 6/7 | 20,000 | 2,000,000 |
| Dutch War of Louis XIV | 1672–8 | 6/7 | 3,600 | 300,000 |
| War of the League of Augsburg | 1688–97 | 5/7 | 6,900 | 700,000 |
| War of the Spanish Succession | 1701–13 | 5/6 | 12,500 | 1,300,000 |
| War of Jenkins' Ear/Austrian Succession | 1738–48 | 6/6 | 3,400 | 400,000 |
| Seven Years' War | 1755–63 | 6/6 | 9,100 | 1,000,000 |
| French Revolutionary and Napoleonic Wars | 1792–1815 | 6/6 | 21,000 | 2,500,000 |
| World War I | 1914–18 | 8/8 | 58,000 | 7,700,000 |
| World War II | 1939–45 | 7/7 | 94,000 | 13,000,000 |

*Source*: Adapted from data in Levy (1983).

Although this table clearly indicates that the leading states in the system have indeed fought a series of wars (averaging two or three per century since the 1500s) with an increasing level of destructive intensity and severity since the 1800s, beyond these facts our consensual knowledge about such major power wars begins to wither. In fact, most analysts of such wars cannot agree on several basic measures: how many powers must be involved to define such a war; whether such wars should be defined in terms of their causes or effects (or both); whether to combine separate wars into single conflict; how to incorporate alliances into such measurements and many other factors (Levy, 1983). Moreover, if one analyses *all interstate wars* above a certain destructive threshold fought since the 1500s, the potential for disagreement becomes even more acute. Similarly, the acquisition of nuclear weapons by several major powers today also seriously calls into question the utility of using past major power wars as a guide to modern theory or policy. Even realists strongly disagree about whether nuclear weapons will reduce the propensity for war among major powers (see Waltz, 1981 versus Gilpin, 1989). Some scholars have even suggested that major power war is now virtually unthinkable, if not completely obsolete, owing to the assured destructive potential of nuclear weapons and other factors (Mueller, 1989; Jervis, 1990; Kaysen, 1990).

## Likelihood

This debate about the propensity for modern war is not confined to the question of WMD, and predicting the likelihood and dynamics of a specific war is in fact one of the most difficult analytical problems in the study of international security. Although some studies of war focus on the condition of international anarchy as a key cause of interstate war – in the sense that wars occur because the international system cannot prevent them (Waltz, 1989) – this view should be considered more of a background or permissive contributor to the general problem of interstate war rather than as an active cause of a specific conflict. A second common starting point involves the question of power relationships between a set of potential adversaries. War obviously requires resources, so analysing the power resources of leading states might shed some light on their propensity to fight each other. Much of the literature associated with defence/strategic studies, in fact, attempts to assess war–power relationships in terms of various types of weapons systems, as well as doctrines for their use. This type of research, as found in the *Journal of Strategic Studies* and *Arms Control* (now *Contemporary Security Policy*), can involve assessments of weapons (including various forms of WMD) based on their ability to launch a surprise attack ('offensive' weapons), defend geographic space ('defensive' weapons), deny the movements of opposing forces (as with 'no-fly zones'), defeat opposing weapons systems, defeat insurgencies and other factors. More recent work along these lines focuses on cyberwarfare, as we shall see in Chapter 8.

More generally, measures of military spending also receive a high degree of attention, and it is possible to generate rankings of states based on this factor alone (see Table 4.2). It also seems fairly clear that a rising threat of foreign armed conflict plays a major factor in causing states to increase their spending on armaments (Nordhaus, Oneal and Russett, 2012). Clearly the US leads the world on this measure in terms of absolute spending, as well as on overall GDP for any single state: around $17.91 trillion in 2015, representing around one-fifth of the global economy. In fact, US military spending alone ($600 billion) accounts for more than one-third of global military spending ($1.776 trillion), a fact that clearly places America in a category by itself under this standard: the sole military superpower. Yet these figures, of course, do not tell us much about whether and how these resources will be used, which is partly why some analysts also debate the role of supposed power structures – unipolar, bipolar and multipolar – to explain a system's general propensity for war, as discussed in Chapter 2. A related approach to major power war suggests that power-balancing dynamics could even be analysed as 'cycles' of peace and conflict; 'long cycle' theory for example assumes that the victor in a major power war will enjoy a period of hegemonic leadership and peace, until several other powers rise up to challenge its position. Then a new major war cycle, with a new hegemon in power, begins (Modelski, 1978; Thompson, 1983; also see Farrar Jr., 1977; Doran and Parsons, 1980). 'Power transition' theories (Organski, 1968; Gilpin, 1981; Howard, 1983; Väyrynen, 1983; Houweling and Siccama, 1988; Kim, 1989) and Marxist-inspired 'world systems' theory (Chase-Dunn, 1981; Wallerstein, 1984) make similar arguments about the effects of uneven economic growth and technological change among major powers on their propensity for war-making, but do not assume the regularity of cycles as suggested by long cycle theory. In both views, uneven economic growth among major powers typically results in a conflict between status quo (or satisfied) states, that benefit from, and thus want to preserve, the existing order, and revisionist (or dissatisfied) states, that might risk war to change it. The conduct of Germany and Japan in particular, two major rising (that is, revisionist) powers in the early 1900s, has been framed in these terms; a similar analysis might be made of contemporary China, although there are conflicting views on whether such a rise will lead to conflict with other powers, particularly the US (Christensen, 2001; Goldstein, 2013; Johnston, 2013; Khong, 2013–14; Brooks and Wohlforth, 2015–16). Similarly, America's commitment to aid Taiwan's defence may become very problematic if China asserts its claims over the island with military force (Kastner, 2015–16), while others have argued that some form of

Table 4.2   *States ranked by military expenditures, 2014*

|  | Military expenditures in billions of US dollars | Military expenditures as a per cent of GDP |
|---|---|---|
| 1. United States | 610 | 3.5 |
| 2. China | 216 | 2.1 |
| 3. Russia | 84.5 | 4.5 |
| 4. Saudi Arabia | 80.8 | 10.4 |
| 5. France | 62.3 | 2.2 |
| 6. United Kingdom | 60.5 | 2.2 |
| 7. India | 50 | 2.4 |
| 8. Germany | 46.5 | 1.2 |
| 9. Japan | 45.8 | 1.0 |
| 10. South Korea | 36.7 | 2.6 |

*Source*: Stockholm International Peace Research Institute, 2015 Fact Sheet.

US–China accommodation on this and other issues might be possible to avoid a larger conflict (Liff and Ikenberry, 2014; Glaser, 2015).

Problems with using simple measures of power alone to predict the propensity of war have inspired related work on threat perception as an indicator of war-proneness. This involves linking a capability analysis (that is, power measures) to an analysis of *intent*. Walt's (1987 and 1988) 'balance of threat' theory, for example, argues that a power analysis must be integrated with several other factors, such as geographic proximity, expressions of aggressive intentions and measures of the offence–defence balance (that is, if an adversary possesses or develops weapons that seem to give an advantage to the offence, or attacking first (see Quester, 1977; Levy, 1984; Van Evera, 1998; Glaser and Kaufman, 1998; Van Evera, 1999). Some scholars have focused on public opinion, such as a desire for revenge, as a way to explain why some democracies are more war-prone than others (Stein 2015), while territorial disputes are also thought to be an important determinant in predicting the likelihood of war among all types of states (Senese and Vasquez, 2003), in part owing to their 'zero-sum' nature: a gain for one side is a loss for the other. However, even when we find some degree of consensus that certain states are dramatically increasing their military spending, or are developing new types of weapons systems, or are supporting more belligerent governing regimes, it does not automatically follow that war is more likely, or that such a war will be interpreted as a major threat to *international* security. As

always, these are also political, rather than simply quantitative, determinations. For example, China is currently exhibiting an upward trend
in its military spending, yet politicians and scholars still debate whether
the Chinese intend to use these resources to attack, deter or otherwise
threaten other states. Recent events in the South China Sea, however, suggest that the Chinese are intent on using their military power to establish
more control over the region, largely because of the oil reserves there;
this type of 'resource conflict', which may lead to war, is covered in more
detail in Chapter 11.

## Recovery

Finally, as one of the most destructive security problems covered in this
volume, most scholars generally agree that war involves very high-cost
and long-term recovery efforts. These tasks can take years if not a generation or more, particularly when the war in question is a major power
conflict. As always, the greater the scale and scope of destruction as noted
above, the more difficult and costly the recovery efforts. If WMD are used,
then recovery efforts might in fact be impossible, or too costly, to manage
once (for example) radiation damage has occurred. Since we have never
experienced an actual exchange of nuclear weapons in war, but only a
unilateral nuclear attack by the US on Japan, the determination of recovery costs is somewhat speculative. However, decades of nuclear weapons
tests have decisively confirmed that a nuclear war would cause irreversible
damage in, if not the total destruction of, the states involved, as well as of
other states, depending on the quantity and types of weapons used. These
factors explain the general interest of the international community in preventing a nuclear war, above all other types of war, from breaking out. As
we shall see in Chapter 6, one form of this international interest involves
the multilateral control of arms proliferation; other policies devoted to the
management of war are covered below in the section on interstate war as
a policy problem.

## Stakeholder factors

Given the limitations above regarding the degree of consensual knowledge
about the general propensity towards interstate war, we must also consider in more detail various key stakeholders and their preferences regarding this problem. This task in turn is made considerably easier if we start
by treating war as a deliberate political decision rather than as an accident
or mistake. As already noted, most theories of war assume rational calculations about the costs and benefits of using violence to achieve one's
goals, although those calculations may turn out to be incorrect.

## Principal stakeholders

Accordingly, some analyses of war focus more specifically on the stakeholders directly involved in war-related decisions rather than, or in addition to, the passive background conditions, such as anarchy or power differentials, that might make war more likely. Regarding interstate war, these stakeholders can be framed in a more abstract sense as states, or more specifically as the high officials who make decisions on behalf of states (or similar social groupings). Regarding intrastate war, however, the stakeholder situation becomes far more complex, as we shall see in Chapter 5. For those who focus on the role of states in general, much attention has been devoted to the question of what types of states are likely to initiate wars. In this vein, scholars have examined factors such as ideology, political culture, religion, economic system and so on as a guide to whether a particular state might be more war-prone than another, yet empirical studies have shown no consistent relationship between these attributes and war-making (Wright, 1965; Singer and Small, 1972).

A related approach examines the question of government (or 'regime') type, in the belief that leaders of democracies are more peaceful than those of non-democracies (Doyle, 1983, 1986 and 1997; Russett, 1993; Dixon, 1994). Although this 'democratic peace' literature has suggested that twentieth-century democracies tend not to fight other states if they believe them to be democracies (that is, perceptions may matter more than democratic reality (see Owen, 1994 and Oren, 1995), they will however initiate wars against non-democracies. Moreover, prior to 1914, there seems to be no statistically significant relationship between democracy and war (Morgan, 1993; Farber and Gowa, 1995; Gowa, 1995), while others have criticized the causal logic of this theory in terms of the focus on peaceful conflict resolution and accountable leaders (Rosato, 2003). In proportional terms, democratic states have also been involved in as many wars as non-democratic states, and, once involved in a war, democracies can be as violent as any other types of states (Chan, 1984; Levy, 1989; Layne, 1994; Spiro, 1994). Democracies are also just as likely as non-democracies to target civilians during war (Valentino, Huth and Croco, 2006). States undergoing a *transition* to democracy might also be more war-prone than other states according to some scholars (Mansfield and Snyder, 1995). Similarly, the idea that democracies are more effective than non-democracies in terms of war-making and making 'credible commitments' to act has provoked some debate, but as always the findings strongly depend on how the evidence is chosen and manipulated (Lake, 1992; Desch, 2008; Downes and Sechser, 2012). Other studies have similarly challenged the idea that democracies are better able than non-democracies to signal their foreign policy intentions, which may undermine the idea that autocratic elites cannot be held accountable for their actions (and thus must be confronted or punished by outside actors) (Weeks, 2008).

Another line of thinking examines the supposedly militaristic, expansionistic, revisionist or aggressive (now 'rogue') tendencies of certain states, an approach which can be combined with the question of regime type. However, there is no common definition in the literature of these terms, and they can easily be manipulated to produce contrary findings. If 'revisionist' states are supposedly more war-prone than 'status quo' states, then one can switch those labels for a certain state depending on the historical period or state interests one examines. And if one relaxes the term 'expansionistic' to include economic or even cultural expansionism in addition to, or instead of, territorial expansionism, then even peace-loving democracies can be accused of expansionistic or even militaristic tendencies, as Marxist and critical studies of war remind us. Some analysts have also examined the question of weak or failed states to determine whether such states are more or less likely to initiate wars, and again the findings are contradictory: wars can result from all types of states, whether weak or strong, successful or failing, and so forth (although weak or failed states are often linked to domestic political conflict; see Chapter 5). It does appear, however, that 'buffer states', or those caught between two major rivals (such as Belgium, the Koreas and Poland), are more likely to suffer from conquest or occupation than others, although this phenomenon (or 'state death') has virtually ceased since 1945 (Fazal, 2004). Similarly, a supposed mismatch between the state (that is, its government) and nation (that is, its citizens) can possibly explain the war propensity for specific states or regions, such as the Middle East (Miller, 2006). Finally, not all failing states have initiated wars, a fact which again creates analytical problems for this school of thought. Even in the case of multi-ethnic states, which are supposedly less stable than states with a single dominant ethnic group according to some analysts, the argument breaks down in the face of stable multi-ethnic states such as Switzerland, a point we shall examine in more detail along with other attributes of weak or failed states in the next chapter.

## Interests and preferences

Given the high costs of modern wars in particular, it might be assumed that governments prefer to avoid war unless they face a major existential threat to their survival. This can be framed in terms of the physical demise of the state(s) involved – state death through occupation or conquest – if the threat is not repelled. The history of war provides numerous examples of such dynamics; since the dawn of human civilization, thousands of political units united by geography, history and culture have been destroyed or broken up in a modern international system with over seven billion people, representing over 6,000 languages, that still numbers only around 200 sovereign states. A more focused analysis also found that 50 of 202 states, or about 25 per cent, have 'died' at some point in the past two centuries as a result of military conquest (Fazal, 2004). And in countless other cases smaller political groupings, such as city-states, principalities and localized ethnic groups, have been 'absorbed' into stronger states, so that they virtually disappear as political entities at the international level. Some groups may still actively, and even successfully, resist this treatment, which may result in civil wars or insurgencies, as we shall see in later chapters.

A related concern, particularly for the major powers, involves whether a threat could produce a fundamental change in the international order, as in the discussion of great power or hegemonic wars noted above (Keohane, 1969; Jervis, 1979). Hegemonic orders are not equal; the character of the victorious state(s) can have a profound effect on the nature of the international order it dominates. For example, a post-WWII Nazi or Soviet hegemony would have functioned very differently from the more liberal post-war order that formed as a result of US leadership (Ruggie, 1982). Thus, if the capacity to make war is in fact the single most important factor in determining the survival, and prosperity, of any large political entity in world politics, as well as the maintenance of a given international order, then those entities (states) will share a fundamental interest in improving their capacity to make, and to credibly threaten, war against each other, which includes securing reliable supplies of war-related natural resources such as oil (Krasner, 1978). This general recognition, however, still does not solve the problem of effectively determining whether a state will cause, or become involved in, a specific war. To answer this question we must turn our attention to decision-making dynamics among actors responsible for planning and conducting wars.

The most direct approach here involves 'expected utility' theory (Bueno de Mesquita, 1981 and 1989; Brito and Intriligator, 1985; Morrow, 1985; Hussein, 1987), which generally frames a specific decision for war as a cost–benefit analysis. If the expected benefit of going to war (that is, the 'utility function' of a war) seems to outweigh the expected costs of surrendering or otherwise avoiding war, then a rational actor should choose war. This calculation can include expectations about costs and benefits well into the future, which allows the theory to incorporate notions of 'preemptive war' (to stop an expected *imminent* attack) and – more controversially – even 'preventative war' (to defeat an expected *rising* challenger or threat) (Bell and Johnson, 2015), although some scholars have argued that such wars are in fact extremely rare (Reiter, 1995). It also allows us to consider that an expectation of victory is not necessary to begin or join a war, only that a state might believe it would be better off having fought a war under its own terms than having a war forced upon it under less favourable conditions. Japan did not necessarily expect to defeat the US in

WWII when it attacked American forces at Pearl Harbor, but it did hope to gain more in the course of fighting a war than it would have suffered in the face of an extended American oil embargo (Sagan, 1989).

Beyond this simple proposition, however, lies a range of difficult analytical problems involving how officials actually calculate these costs and benefits based on the information at their disposal *before* the war, which in turn requires more detailed knowledge about specific preferences (beyond a simple interest in 'security') than is typically provided by expected utility theory. In addition, modern states, even non-democratic ones, are composed of multiple decision-makers who often hold conflicting preferences when facing such a difficult choice as war, so we might also need to examine how these stakeholders aggregate their preferences into a single decision about war. The fact that it is possible for some states to 'calibrate' their use of military force at a level lower than total war (i.e. 'limited war') plays a role here as well, as some stakeholders might believe it would be more cost-effective to achieve a limited aim, with limited means, as compared to a total war seeking the complete defeat of an opponent (see the Persian Gulf War case study below). In addition to the temptations of limited war, which could involve new technologies such as drones (see Chapter 7) or computer viruses (see Chapter 8), the possibility of misperception or miscalculation owing to a range of factors, including psychological limitations under stressful conditions, can also seriously complicate the predictions of expected utility theory (Jervis, 1976). Finally, if stakeholders attempt to negotiate to avoid war, which is often the case (Morrow, 1992), then they may have a rational incentive to misrepresent their preferences and overstate their capabilities to achieve a better bargain, which can make war more likely (Fearon, 1995). To the extent that parties to a dispute have an interest in inflating their capabilities or disagreements *vis-à-vis* other actors (for example, to deter an attack or to gain bargaining leverage), it may become very difficult to determine a difference between bluffing and an impending attack. And a bluff or threat, of course, can always escalate into an actual conflict.

To address some of these problems, analysts have attempted to incorporate domestic politics into their models, in ways considerably more sophisticated than democratic peace theory or expected utility theory. One major approach examines the role of elite 'mindsets' and bureaucratic or strategic cultures that govern official thinking about war-making. For example, the rapid escalation of WWI from a minor crisis in the Balkans into a major global war is often explained in part as a consequence of the 'cult' or 'ideology' of the offensive, or a belief that a strategic advantage lies with the side that strikes first, assuming that it possesses offensive capabilities such as transport systems, weapons and doctrines (Posen, 1984; Snyder, 1984; Van Evera, 1984, 1986 and 1999); similar beliefs have been cited as a factor behind the US–Soviet strategic rivalry (Johnston, 1995).

In addition, these calculations increasingly consider the domestic costs and benefits of war in addition to their external aspects. At a minimum, domestic political factors might tempt elites into overstating the nature of the threat (threat inflation) or manipulating other types of information in order to build support for a war (Fearon, 1994). This dynamic clearly was at work, particularly in the US and the UK, in the months prior to the 2003 attack on Iraq (Kaufmann, 2004; Mueller, 2006). At a maximum, some wars have been explained as an effort to distract domestic audiences from other problems within the state, under the belief that an external enemy or threat will help bind a people together and increase support for the government. Although the empirical evidence for this view is quite limited, and the causal arguments are unclear (Wilkenfeld, 1973; Skolnick Jr., 1974; Stein, 1976; Tarar, 2006), it still persists in the literature as the 'scapegoat', or 'diversionary', theory of war and has been applied to cases as varied as the Russo-Japanese War, WWI and the Falkland Islands War (Dassel, 1998), as well as to both democratic and authoritarian regimes (Pickering and Kisangani, 2005). Finally, once a state enters into a war, for whatever reasons, domestic political support may increase in line with the so-called 'rally around the flag' effect, which has been especially well-documented in the US (Mueller, 1973; Ostrom and Job, 1986; Stoll, 1987) but may also apply to the UK (Lai and Reiter, 2005). Some analysts have also examined electoral cycles to determine whether involvement in war is more likely during an impending election; although there is some evidence for this proposition in democratic states, it cannot be conclusively demonstrated that a desire for electoral gain is a critical factor in leading politicians to go to war. Moreover, in democratic polities anti-war stakeholders can attempt to increase the costs of going to war, and therefore may induce caution on the part of pro-war politicians (Gaubatz, 1991 and 1999).

## The use of force

As the discussion thus far has implied, political calculations about war generally take for granted the idea that, when facing an existential threat in the form of a military attack, a state is not only permitted but expected to resist its attacker with deadly force. In fact, if any security problem covered in this volume is likely to lead to a military response, the threat of interstate war is it. Thus, if it is true that no global government or international armed force can be relied upon to protect states from each other, then realists are correct in assuming some degree of self-help in dealing with such problems. The liberal-inspired international legal system supports this view, as the UN Charter (1945) specifically affirms the right of individual or collective self-defence under its Article 51 provisions. Moreover, the question of whether a threatened state will receive assistance from its allies or other supporters is partly a function of whether those allies think it deserves their support by continuing to resist an invading or attacking force. For example, the US became far more willing to provide military aid to the British as they continued to successfully resist a Nazi air attack during the Battle of Britain in 1940.

Using force in the face of armed attacks also involves the question of deterrence. Many strategists point out that the best way to avoid war is to develop military forces strong enough to deter a foreign military attack (Mearsheimer, 1983; Morgan, 2003), rather than adopt a strategy of appeasement, although it has also been argued that selective appeasement can be a perfectly rational strategy in the face of multiple adversaries (Treisman, 2004). Here it is also possible to speak of various types of deterrence, such as *direct* versus *indirect deterrence* and *passive/defensive deterrence* versus *active/offensive deterrence*. Direct deterrence is intended to protect oneself from attack, while indirect (or extended) deterrence applies to third parties or even entire regions. Passive deterrence measures might involve fixed fortifications, mine fields, tank traps and other efforts to control one's territory and discourage an attack. Active deterrence measures can involve the threat of nuclear weapons or conventional weapons to discourage an adversary from attacking, whether by targeting the adversary's military forces (or *counterforce targeting*), its civilian infrastructure (or *countervalue targeting*) or both (*mixed* or *dual-use targeting*).

A related approach involves a strategy of *denial* (or *containment*), which attempts to contain or block the efforts of an adversary to gain influence beyond its own territory. With this strategy a state must try to counteract the diplomatic, economic and military policies of its adversaries in critical areas of the world (such as the oil-rich Middle East), a policy that may also produce crises or even wars. This type of policy can be especially problematic, if not entirely counterproductive, when the state in question also hopes to maintain an economic relationship with its potential adversary, which is precisely why the Bush administration's policy of 'congagement' with China (that is, containment plus engagement) was so difficult to implement, and seemed so contradictory to many observers – including the Chinese.

## Public–private domains and levels of jurisdiction

In the realm of international war, we have noted the dominance of national self-help as a fundamental principle given the lack of a firm universal security guarantee provided by some international actor. Self-help also involves the dominance of public authority over private interests when a legitimate decision for war is taken. However, two considerations increasingly complicate this traditional view of public (or state) dominance in the realm of war-making. The first involves the role of private firms in developing weapons systems and selling arms around the world, as mentioned in Chapter 2. This trend has been in evidence at least since the late nineteenth century, and has only intensified with each passing decade (Brandes, 1997). The problem was raised after WWI and again during the early years of the Cold War – in President Eisenhower's recognition of an 'iron triangle' of influence, or a 'military-industrial complex', among armaments firms, defence policy-makers and members of Congress – yet there was little empirical evidence that such arrangements create or intensify nationalistic or militaristic policies. They most certainly can contribute to waste and overspending, however, which may have an indirect effect on military readiness and the responses of other actors, as in the form of an arms race.

A second and more intriguing aspect of the public–private relationship in war-making involves the recruitment of private actors. The use of mercenaries and privateers seemed to be on the decline by the late nineteenth century with the rise of mass citizen armies and professional soldiers, followed by investment in strategic nuclear forces during the Cold War (Percy, 2007). However, since the end of the Cold War we have seen a dramatic increase in the use of so-called 'neo-mercenaries', or modern transnational security providers and other PMCs, in both international and domestic wars. These firms include Blackwater (now Xe Services), DynCorp, Executive Outcomes, Military Professional Resources Incorporated, STTEP and many others (Scahill, 2008). Proponents of PMCs (including the PMCs themselves) argue that modern warfare requires unorthodox and flexible methods, while critics note that the privatization of armed force raises a number of difficult questions regarding the legal status and oversight of PMCs. In this regard international law tends to focus on pirates, colonists and state trading companies, not the explicit delegation of government military functions to PMCs (Chesterman and Lehnardt, 2007).

One issue involves how to determine the nature of combatants if PMCs are armed and in harm's way (though they might not be playing a combat role): should they be treated as civilians by both sides or are they legitimate military targets (Doswald-Beck, 2007)? A second question involves the question of accountability: if PMCs abuse their authority, should they fall under the military or civilian rules of justice (Lehnardt, 2007)? Moreover, as private actors, PMCs are permitted to lobby government officials regarding the nature of their role and deployments, which reverses the normal patterns of civilian control over the military in democratic polities (Isenberg, 2007; Leander, 2007). Although several scholars have examined these questions (Avant, 2005; Chesterman and Lehnardt, 2007; Cockayne, 2007; Pelton, 2007; Singer, 2007; Van Meegdenburg, 2015), there is no consensus on how to answer them. In the meantime, we have in fact seen empirical evidence of the problems noted above, such as the role of certain PMC employees in running criminal enterprises during peacekeeping missions (as in the Balkans in the 1990s), or in committing human rights abuses against local civilians (as in Iraq after 2003). And the fact that the murder of four Blackwater employees in Fallujah in March 2004 prompted a US attack on that city suggests that states are in fact willing to resort to extraordinary measures to protect their PMCs, as compared to 'normal' civilians.

## Interstate war as a policy problem

Although the general destructiveness of interstate war suggests its importance as a focal point in security studies, the fact is that not all interstate wars are treated equally. Thus, in addition to the general areas of consensual knowledge noted above about the dangers of international war, here we need to consider how specific interstate wars are treated as multilateral security problems by the international community.

### Agenda-setting

How does an interstate war become an international security problem? As noted above, questions about the scale and scope of destruction are one way to predict whether an international conflict will attract the attention of other states. As it is virtually impossible in the modern world to keep a large-scale war or other major international problem from remaining a secret owing to the globalization of communications, we might expect that rising awareness by the international community about body counts and other measures of conflict might increase the propensity for taking action. In this sense agenda-setting for interstate wars is almost 'automatic' owing to the high degree of consensual knowledge already in place about the destructiveness of modern wars. If the parties to an interstate war are embedded in their own alliance networks, their allies must also choose whether to join the fight, a dynamic which may also increase the propensity of the international community to pay more attention to a certain war (assuming, of course, that these commitments are public rather than private). Yet outside of these larger-scale conflicts, which are in fact quite rare relative to limited wars and intrastate wars, the situation becomes far more complicated.

Specifically, if the major powers – particularly the P5 of the UNSC – do not feel directly threatened by a localized interstate war, then they may attempt to take a more hands-off approach and, possibly, delegate the problem to other stakeholders, whether states or IOs (particularly regional ones). This may end their focused attention to the war unless the conflict shows clear signs of expanding its destructiveness in certain ways, such as geographic scope (involving more states) and/or destructive scale (involving civilians or perhaps questions of human rights abuses). We saw precisely this dynamic in the case of the collapse of Yugoslavia, where various secessionist movements very quickly grew into a civil war, then into a localized interstate war among the former major regions (now states) of Yugoslavia. While the Europeans devoted considerable resources to resolving this conflict, other powers, such as the US, exhibited much less interest until the conflict dragged on and started to generate large refugee flows into the rest of Europe, as well as human rights abuses. Conversely, interstate wars in other places such as sub-Saharan Africa occur on a regular basis but do not threaten the interests of the major powers as compared to wars on the Eurasian continent. This same dynamic generally holds true for international attention to civil conflicts around the world, as we shall see in Chapter 5. Similarly, any war that threatens to involve the use of WMD, particularly nuclear weapons, will undoubtedly loom large on the international security agenda, which is why the international community (particularly the US) tends to pay close attention to resolving conflicts between India and Pakistan (Yusuf and Kirk, 2016).

## Framing policy alternatives

As we have seen, among all types of international security problems the problem of interstate war in particular lends itself to assumptions about self-help and autonomy (that is, unilateralism), as states may be reluctant to trust their territorial security and basic existence to any other actor. However, even in this realm few states can afford to 'go it alone' completely when drawn into an interstate war, and multilateral options soon become more attractive. It is often possible, of course, to negotiate some alternative to war, usually through an exchange of some type ('logrolling'), such as territory or support for certain policies. This may also involve arbitration by a neutral third party; this option is especially likely if international law is very clear on the nature of the dispute, as in the case of certain territorial claims (Huth, Croco and Appel, 2011). It is also possible to complement a negotiation with economic incentives, either in the form of inducements (such as foreign aid or other side payments) or punishments (sanctions). Finally, the parties can also attempt to invoke various diplomatic or legal options inspired by regulatory liberalism. One such approach involves arms control and disarmament, a topic we shall examine more closely in Chapter 6. As discussed in Chapter 2, a second set of legal options involves measures to ban or outlaw war as a national policy tool, and the related use of non-aggression pacts among certain sets of states (involving a promise not to attack each other) or pledges of 'no first use' regarding certain weapons (particularly WMD). Finally, a third set of legal measures involves the question of controlling the conduct of war itself, as in the form of the modern LOAC regime.

Specifically, although states are legally permitted to use military force to deal with external attacks on their territory, this right is not unlimited. Most such actions are supposed to be governed under the modern LOAC according to the *jus ad bellum* criteria regarding the decision to use force, and the *jus in bello* criteria regarding warfighting itself (Lang Jr., Pierce and Rosenthal, 2004). The *jus ad bellum* criteria, for example, involve a just cause (such as protecting one's citizens from an armed attack), the use of legitimate state authority to decide a war and the use of force as a last resort once peaceful measures have been exhausted. The *jus in bello* criteria, which are intended to apply to any armed conflict no matter how it began, involve the principle of discrimination between combatants and non-combatants, the principle of proportionality in that military force must not be excessive in relation to the threat being repelled and the principle of military necessity when choosing targets, so that damage to civilians is minimized. These rules also govern certain aspects of weapons development and deployment, a topic we shall examine more extensively in Chapter 6. However, devising and enforcing such rules are two separate things, as we shall see below in the discussion of policy effectiveness.

Although diplomacy and legal/economic measures, such as economic sanctions or arms embargoes, are often deployed in the early stages of a potential military conflict, if these fail – which is often the case owing to the inherent difficulties of sustaining a multilateral sanctions regime (Pape, 1997 and 1998; Baldwin, 1999–2000; Elliott, Hufbauer and Schott, 2008; Early, 2009) – then states must resort to stronger military measures. These generally involve dynamics of either power-balancing or bandwagoning *vis-à-vis* adversaries (Walt, 1985), as described in Chapter 2. In cases where states are unsure about the intentions and capabilities of the potential allies and adversaries surrounding them, a related multilateral alternative involves collective security, where the nature of the threat and the nature of the commitment to oppose that threat are more vague than in an alliance system, and collective security is activated (in principle) in a less automatic fashion than in an alliance system (Kupchan and Kupchan, 1995).

Finally, if deterrence fails and a resort to force is necessary in a situation of interstate war, another set of options presents itself. Here one can envision military tools ranging in cost and intensity along a scale from the use of special operations forces, to aerial bombing or drone/missile attacks, to a more limited or low-intensity war (limited in terms of the types of armed forces used, the geographic scope of the war or the war objectives of the combatants) that might not involve the complete defeat of an opponent, to a full-scale air/naval/land war including invasion, regime change and possibly long-term occupation and reconstruction (i.e. total war), as in the cases of Japan and Germany after WWII, or the recent American-led wars in Iraq and Afghanistan. Similarly, in situations where direct intervention is not desirable for whatever reason (such as domestic political opposition), states might resort to the use of private actors, such as NGOs or PMCs, to deliver assistance or provide security.

## Policy choice

It can be somewhat inappropriate to speak about free choice here, as if various stakeholders, states and otherwise have the luxury to decide whether to join a specific war. However, states in particular do normally plan for the possibility of war, which involves the preventative measures discussed in this section.

Although the rest of this chapter stresses contemporary responses to interstate war as an international security problem, it is first worth recalling the overall arc of thinking about this topic over the past century. The most important point involves a general lack of confidence, as discussed in Chapter 2, in the more liberal approaches to the threat of armed force, starting with the emergence of the LOAC regime and related efforts to ban war. These measures obviously failed to prevent, or even to reduce the destructiveness of, either WWI or WWII, yet the idea of attempting to govern war through regulatory liberalism persists among both scholars and international legal experts.

However, although the LOAC remains in force and has been periodically revised (as through the Geneva Conventions consolidated in 1949 and the creation of the ICC in 2002), and although the UNSC, like the League of Nations before it, is charged with providing collective security for all UN members that respect the UN Charter, the legacy of modern industrialized warfare still discourages states who possess enough power from abandoning more realist-inspired approaches to the threat of war. As we saw in Chapter 2, during the Cold War the two most powerful states on both sides of the superpower conflict adopted formal alliance systems – NATO and the Warsaw Pact – to deter an attack against each other. Thus, a major tendency for threatened states is to form alliances – that is, to balance against other powerful states rather than to bandwagon with them – provided they perceive a great enough threat according to the criteria noted earlier and are not so weak that they must join the winning side at all costs (Rothstein, 1968). As several analysts have noted (Zimmerman, 1969; Morgan, 1985; Walt, 1988), this behaviour contradicts the claims of some Western and Soviet Cold Warriors that states would be easily tempted to join the perceived rising threat (that is, bandwagon with the Soviet Union) rather than join other states under the US security umbrella.

Although the end of the Cold War and the collapse of the Soviet Union brought an end to the Warsaw Pact, and SEATO was dissolved in 1977, several other alliances are still in place. NATO in particular remains a centrepiece of transatlantic security, and has gradually expanded its membership and functions since the end of the Cold War. In addition to its traditional focus on the territorial defence of its member states, NATO also plans to play a greater role in managing other, less traditional, security threats, such as terrorism and human trafficking. In a related manner, the EU has been developing its own Common Foreign and Security Policy (CFSP) and Common Security and Defence Policy (CSDP), and has undertaken a range of limited policing and military operations, as well as civilian security operations, most of which deal with the problem of intrastate, rather than interstate, war (Howorth, 2003; Smith, 2003; Anderson and Seitz, 2006; Howorth, 2007; Bailes, 2008). It has also developed a European Neighbourhood Policy (ENP) to help facilitate cooperation in a range of policy areas, including security, among 15 states (plus the Palestinian Authority) surrounding the EU (Weber, Smith and Baun, 2007). However, the CSDP (and the ENP) still lacks a formal security guarantee in the form of NATO's Article V, which pledges all NATO members to treat an armed attack on one of them as an attack on all of them, which then invokes an obligation of collective defence. The EU also does not provide for any type of collective nuclear deterrence policy even though two of its member states (France and the UK) possess nuclear weapons. Since the end of the Cold War, recent EU treaties do provide for a weak mutual assistance or 'solidarity' clause in the event of an armed attack involving an EU member state (including terrorist attacks), yet this is far from the assurance provided by NATO's own Article V. However, one such provision (Article 42.7 of the 2007 Lisbon Treaty) was invoked for the first time when France suffered a terrorist attack in Paris in November 2015 (see Chapter 7).

The former Soviet Union has also developed its own regional collective security system, in the form of the Commonwealth of Independent States (CIS) Collective Security Treaty Organization (CSTO). There are, however, some strains in this arrangement, owing to Russia's dominance of both the CIS in general and the CSTO in particular, although NATO is also not immune to the inherent problems associated with maintaining alliances of the type elaborated in Table 4.3.

Before turning to the effectiveness of multilateral policies regarding the threat of interstate war, it is worth recalling the dominance of unilateral approaches on the part of the superpowers during and after the Cold War. The Soviets took unilateral military action on a number of occasions to protect their interests; in some cases these actions were directed against their own Warsaw Pact allies (Hungary, 1956; Czechoslovakia, 1969); in others they involved actions against states outside the Pact (Afghanistan, 1979). The US has been equally if not more active in deploying military force around the globe, chiefly in the form of limited wars as defined above.

Table 4.3   *Current major regional security arrangements*

| | |
|---|---|
| ANZUS | US and Australia; Australia and New Zealand |
| NATO | 28 member states (see Chapter 2 for the full list) |
| CSTO | Armenia, Belarus, Kazakhstan, Kyrgyzstan, Russia, Tajikistan and Uzbekistan |
| Council for Peace and Security in Central Africa | Angola, Burundi, Cameroon, Central African Republic, Chad, Democratic Republic of the Congo, Equatorial Guinea, Gabon, Republic of the Congo, Rwanda, São Tomé and Principe |
| Shanghai Cooperation Organization | China, Kazakhstan, Kyrgyzstan, Russia, Tajikistan and Uzbekistan |

Since WWII these conflicts include: Korea (1950s); Vietnam (1960s–70s); Cyprus (1975); Lebanon (1976, 1983); Korea (1976); Zaire (1978); Iran (1980); Central America (1980s); Libya (1981, 1986); Sinai (1982); Egypt (1983, 1985); Chad (1983); Bolivia (1986); Kuwait (1987); Philippines (1989); Persian Gulf/Iraq (1991); Somalia (1992–3); Haiti (1994); Bosnia (1990s) and Kosovo (1999). The 1991 Persian Gulf War was the first post-Cold War limited war, and played a role in influencing later conflicts of various types (see the case study in Box 4.1).

However, these wars may be illegal in US domestic law and international law, as they are often undeclared wars, while a supposedly 'limited' war can easily blend or expand into another (through processes such as 'task expansion', 'target drift' or 'mission creep'). An equally troubling policy, from the perspective of multilateral security affairs, is the advent of the so-called 'Bush doctrine' following the 9/11 terror attacks; this doctrine asserts America's right to engage in preventative war to secure itself, particularly where a threat of WMD and/or international terrorism may be involved. Obviously if all the major powers engage in such a policy – as some (such as China and Russia) have considered – then the entire international system could be at risk (Kegley and Raymond, 2003).

## The politics of policy effectiveness

How well has the international community coped with the problem of interstate war since the end of the Cold War? The first consideration involves the question of implementation. A chronic problem of international cooperation is the gap between the creation and implementation of collective policies, and this is especially true regarding efforts to govern international warfare. As we have seen, liberal approaches to international war have been especially prone to criticism. The shocking nature of total war during WWI quickly exposed a wide gap between principles and practice regarding new technologies and the rules of war. Despite the Hague ban on chemical weapons, which involved various loopholes, an estimated 200,000 tons of such weapons were used in WWI (Prentiss, 1937), resulting in thousands of casualties. Following this war, the creation of the League of Nations and the Kellogg–Briand Pact could not prevent the Japanese attack on Manchuria in 1931, the Italian invasion of Abyssinia (now Ethiopia) in 1935 and the German actions against Austria, Czechoslovakia and Poland in the late 1930s which precipitated WWII – even though the Italians, the Germans and the Japanese had signed these instruments.

The role of the UNSC in preventing interstate war following WWII must be seen in an equally critical light, as it has always been highly prone to deadlock and thus inaction owing to repeated clashes during the Cold War between the two communist P5 states – the Soviet Union and China – and the three democratic P5 states (France, the UK and the US). Although there have been exceptions (see the Persian Gulf War case study), this problem persists and efforts to make the UNSC more representative of the international community – for example, by allowing states such as Germany and Japan to become permanent members – have failed so far. However, other liberal measures such as the LOAC regime and its associated Geneva Conventions continue to endure and even expand in an attempt to make warfare more 'civilized,' as with the 1977 Protocols I and II to the Geneva Conventions of 1949 codifying the principle that the methods or means of warfare are not unlimited. Yet it too has come under pressure owing to problems related to conflicts among LDCs and America's pursuit of the War on Terror.

Ultimately, the history of warfare and weapons proliferation in the twentieth century demonstrates that the LOAC still has serious limits as a mechanism to govern modern warfare and therefore it has been supplemented on a regular basis with weapons-specific agreements (see Chapter 6). Similarly, the ICC, created in 2002 to prosecute war-related crimes such as genocide, crimes against humanity and war crimes (and potentially crimes of aggression as well) (Sands, 2016), has focused almost exclusively on domestic abuses of power in its investigations rather than the problem of interstate war (see Chapter 5). More problematically, major powers such as China, India, Russia and the US refuse to participate in the work of the ICC, so any deterrent or compellent effects of the ICC on interstate or intrastate war are likely to remain weak (although 123 other states have acceded to the Rome Statute, which created the ICC).

## Box 4.1    The 1991 Persian Gulf War

*Several factors were behind the Persian Gulf War, but the threat to global oil supplies was critical.*

If large-scale or great power interstate war has become very rare compared to the time before the Cold War, the same cannot be said for limited interstate wars. These wars attempt to limit the destruction in terms of the number of states involved, the types of weapons (i.e. air power alone), the objectives of the war or some combination of these. One key example that still influences contemporary security affairs is the 1991 Persian Gulf War. It was launched by a coalition led by the US to force Iraq to retreat from its August 1990 invasion of Kuwait, under the pretence of an oil reserve dispute.

Several aspects of this war are particularly relevant to international security studies. One is that most limited wars launched by the US are in fact 'undeclared wars' as they have not involved a formal declaration of war by the US Congress. This was true of the Persian Gulf War, although President Bush did receive 'authorization' from both houses of Congress after a controversial public relations campaign funded in part by the government of

→

Realist approaches based on power-balancing, alliance networks and collective security involve their own problems regarding implementation, particularly in multipolar systems (Liska, 1962; Wolfers, 1962; Modelski,

$\rightarrow$

Kuwait. Although human rights abuses were the among the reasons stated for launching the war, there is little doubt that Iraq's potential control of Persian Gulf oil reserves was the critical factor. This is evident in a second important aspect of the case: how the war was legally authorized by the UN as well, with widespread support among the permanent and rotating members of the UNSC. Importantly, the USSR and China, as P5 members, could have blocked the UN resolution, yet in this case the USSR supported the resolution while China merely abstained from voting. Such support enabled the US to build a large coalition of nearly one million troops to compel Iraq leader Saddam Hussein to retreat from Kuwait.

Obviously this attempt at compellence (Operation Desert Shield) failed, which raises another aspect of the case: the question of why did Iraq choose to fight the US? As Janice Gross Stein (1992) argues, although the US had moved military forces into the Gulf, Hussein still did not believe that an invasion was credible in light of recent US interventions in the Middle East (particularly Lebanon). Even before his own invasion of Kuwait, he had received mixed signals from US officials about whether America would become involved in his dispute with the tiny country. After President Bush received his authorization, Hussein still did not back down – even with the help of mediators like France and the USSR – because he then felt that the US was going to overthrow his regime no matter what. In other words, 'limited war' involves different perceptions by the belligerents involved; these can easily change as a crisis escalates, and misperception can then increase the probability of conflict, as some have argued about this case (Duelfer and Dyson, 2011). This same pattern of mistrust and misperception influenced the 2003 Iraq War, with much larger stakes for both sides (Lake, 2010–11).

A final aspect is the legacy of the war (Operation Desert Storm). Thanks to overwhelming air power, it was over in just six weeks with limited coalition casualties; this result influenced a debate over air power in another conflict at the end of the decade: NATO's war in Kosovo (see Chapter 5). America's refusal to overthrow Hussein raised another set of questions in the aftermath of 9/11: should the US have made this a total war from the start, so that disputes over WMD would not have surfaced as they had? However, this would have undermined coalition support for the war at the time, which raises a final aspect: the fact that despite widespread moral support, the US still had to commit the largest number of military forces and use pressure and even side payments (such as debt relief for Egypt) to encourage other states to support the effort (Bennett, Lepgold and Unger, 1994). Without this leadership, the war almost certainly would not have happened, even though all coalition members shared a common interest in protecting Persian Gulf oil reserves.

1963; Holsti et al., 1973; Snyder, 1984 and 1997). One involves the 'free-riding' problem, in the sense that not all partners in an alliance may be willing and able to contribute the resources for maintaining it. For example, the US has consistently asked for more burden-sharing on the part of its NATO allies, chiefly in the form of more spending on defence (Beer, 1972; Kennedy, 1979; Sandler and Forbes, 1980; Sloan, 1985; Calleo, 1987; Domke, Eichenberg and Kelleher, 1987); more recently, this question has been reframed in terms of whether NATO is still necessary in the post-Cold War era (Oneal, 1990; Glaser, 1993; Art, 1996). Similarly, America's efforts to expand NATO's remit to include out-of-area problems such as South West Asia (particularly the Persian Gulf and, since 9/11, Afghanistan) met with considerable opposition on the part of European allies; even though the Europeans generally supported greater NATO attention to the Gulf region in the 1980s and beyond, they have been reluctant to commit greater resources to that effort and other tasks, such as 'humanitarian' missions (Kupchan, 1988; Lepgold, 1998). The US was also forced to suspend its treaty obligations to New Zealand after 1985 when that state refused to permit nuclear-powered or nuclear-armed ships from entering its waters, while the first major contemporary attempt to reverse an interstate invasion, the 1991 Persian Gulf War, had similar problems regarding burden-sharing (see the case study).

More recently, although a new German governing coalition argued in 2009 for the removal of about 200 US nuclear weapons still remaining on European soil in an effort to reduce NATO's emphasis on nuclear deterrence, the annexation in 2014 by Russia of Crimea (part of Ukraine) reminded all NATO allies of the continued importance of the Atlantic Alliance, as balance-of-threat theory would predict. In response to this violation of a 1994 agreement between the UK, US and Russia (the Budapest Memorandum), NATO pursued a policy of reassurance to its Eastern allies (such as more troops, equipment and training exercises), while Montenegro is currently pursuing membership and Finland and Sweden (among others) are debating membership. However, it is still unlikely that NATO would threaten a major war in Europe to defend a non-member state (such as Ukraine or Georgia), so the situation has become a stalemate for the time being. At the same time, however, Russia is attempting to work with the US and other Western countries to resolve a major intrastate war in Syria (Lundgren, 2016), which (among other problems) is partly responsible for the rise of Islamic State, a violent political movement seeking to establish its own sovereign state in the region (see Chapter 5).

The free-riding problem is compounded by other problems when a war changes from a possibility to an actuality. One is that alliances can be prone to 'chain-ganging' or entrapment dynamics, which involves the alliance partners being dragged into a war they might not otherwise want to fight owing to the actions of their alliance partners. WWI is often cited as an example of chain-ganging, as two opposing alliance systems facilitated the expansion of a small local conflict – a dispute between Austria–Hungary and Serbia – into a much larger war between Austria–Hungary/Germany and France/Russia/the UK (among other parties). An opposite problem, 'buck-passing', occurs when each alliance partner might look to the others to take the lead in opposing a common threat (Christensen and Snyder, 1990). WWII is cited as a prime example of buck-passing, as an anti-German alliance led by France and the UK refused to act – it passed the buck – through the 1930s until it was too late to prevent Hitler's war machine from attacking Poland.

More recently, concerns about buck-passing may be partly responsible for the EU's development of its own CSDP capability, which is intended to be independent of NATO (and thus the US). In the first two NATO military actions in its history, Kosovo in 1999 and Afghanistan in 2003 onwards, the US clearly played a dominant role and supplied the largest proportion of military forces. The US, of course, claims the 2003 Afghan war was supported by a multinational force, yet most of its supporters were in fact smaller states rather than major powers, and/or they contributed only a small number of troops; among the major powers only the UK was willing to commit around 45,000 troops (at first). Fears about chain-ganging in Afghanistan were especially prominent in Germany, particularly after German military commanders launched an airstrike in September 2009 that killed dozens of civilians. This was the deadliest attack by Germany since WWII and it immediately sparked major protests in that country about the wisdom of participating in the NATO operation. In addition, and as with the 1991 Persian Gulf War, the US still had to resort to providing billions of dollars in financial incentives to encourage contributions to the effort. The case of Iraq also raises the issue of preventative war as a policy option for states powerful enough to instigate one. As noted above, such a war does not involve the question of an imminent attack on the state believing itself to be at risk, and falls outside the realm of just war theory (or the LOAC).

Thus, most of the multilateral arrangements for managing interstate war, such as realist approaches (power-balancing and alliances) as well as liberal approaches (the UN Security Council and the LOAC regime), involve various limitations and have not always been implemented as intended by their creators. States are still too easily tempted into defecting from these arrangements, whether voluntarily or involuntarily, when a war turns from a possibility to an actuality. Responses to interstate war based on hegemonic leadership are similarly flawed: neither the UK nor the US during their (supposed) hegemonic eras was able to prevent various wars among their competitors; neither state was able to offer credible security guarantees to other major powers; and neither state was able to prevent the rise of other peer competitors, such as Germany, Japan and the US during Britain's hegemony and the Soviet Union, and now China, during America's rise to unipolarity/hegemony. And while the US certainly has more military power than other major powers today, it cannot convert that power into hegemonic dominance over other actors, while its economic power is now rivalled by the EU and (soon) that of China (see Chapter 10).

In terms of our three general standards for overall effectiveness noted in Chapter 3 – total victory, historical trends and comparative metrics – the evidence varies. The total victory standard is the most problematic. Obviously the general problem of interstate war has not been eliminated and is unlikely to disappear any time soon. States will continue to resort to war as long as they believe the benefits of making war will outweigh the costs, even if that determination is prone to miscalculation or if they expect to lose the war. Similarly, efforts by the international community to handle specific interstate wars have produced a mixed record since the end of WWII. If the Cold War was the major international security concern of the post-war era, then it appears as if the Western capitalist states prevailed over their communist adversaries without resorting to a hot war, which is often cited as a victory for deterrence in general and the US/NATO in particular. However, analysts will continue to debate this question for years to come, particularly since communism is still with us and China is emerging as a major power in its own right, which may precipitate another Cold War if the US views China as more of a threat than it actually may be (Christensen, 2006), or vice versa. We shall return to this point in the chapters on cybersecurity (Chapter 8), economic security (Chapter 10) and environmental/resource security (Chapter 11), three areas where US–China disputes are intensifying.

The total victory standard has been especially problematic in light of the two most recent interstate wars involving multiple actors: Afghanistan and Iraq. Although the governments of these states were overthrown fairly quickly, the subsequent processes of occupation, state-building and counter-insurgency call into question whether anything like a total victory can be achieved in such cases (Ricks, 2006). In a comprehensive analysis of military occupations Edelstein (2008) shows that only about 27 per cent of such occupations (7 out of 26) since 1815 could be seen as successful. Successful occupations require the pacification of fierce resistance to the effort in both the occupied country and the occupying country, which is often far away. If a common external threat (namely another state) is involved, an occupation is more likely to succeed as it would be viewed by the occupied state as the lesser of two evils. So the simple provision of more resources or resolve may not be enough to succeed, as Afghanistan and Iraq clearly demonstrate, while other successful cases have not required huge resources. Also, unilateral occupations are less legitimate, and thus enjoy less support in occupied and occupying states, than multilateral ones. So the best chance may be a true *multilateral* occupation in the face of a clear external threat, but this of course depends on the complex politics of threat assessment as outlined in Chapter 3.

The more general historical trends standard regarding modern war, however, is fairly clear and somewhat more optimistic: major power wars have declined considerably since WWII and may be unlikely in the near to medium future. In addition, it also appears that the prospect of state death has declined greatly in the years since WWII, so that most states do not face the tough choice between appeasement and defeat, except in rare cases. These trends, however, are probably due less to any specific multilateral security policies – whether realist or liberal – than to other systemic factors at work during the twentieth century: the horrible experience of two world wars; the prospect of MAD during the Cold War; the fact that most major powers today are status quo rather than revisionist states; a high degree of economic interdependence among major powers (even between the US and China, unlike between the US and USSR during the Cold War); the continued possession of WMD by most of the major powers; a much greater ability to monitor international behaviour owing to reconnaissance technology; and other factors.

In other words, major power stability is quite overdetermined according to some scholars (Gaddis, 1986; Mueller, 1988), so that specific security policies pursued by these actors may actually be quite superfluous and wasteful – or even counterproductive. The apparently pacifistic effects of nuclear weapons in particular sit somewhat uneasily with the international efforts devoted to nuclear non-proliferation (see Chapter 6). A related question is whether America's attempts to maintain its own military dominance *vis-à-vis* its 'peer competitors' like China will provoke those states into taking riskier actions, whether unilateral or multilateral, than they might otherwise prefer. Similarly, India and Pakistan continue to clash on a low-intensity level, particularly in response to terrorist activities in either state such as the 2008 Mumbai attacks, yet they too seem to realize the danger that a full-scale war could escalate into a nuclear one and constrain themselves accordingly (Hagerty, 1995–6). However, smaller-scale interstate wars are still with us, and the international community still generally adopts a case-by-case response to such wars, particularly when they are more a result of 'spillover' from domestic conflicts rather than a form of international 'aggression' (see Chapter 5).

Finally, by adopting a comparative metrics standard it is also clear that the overall violence resulting from major wars seems to have peaked with WWII – a major peak to be sure – after several hundred years of gradual escalation. Today most organized political violence is in fact a result of civil wars and related domestic conflicts, not major interstate wars. However, it is also worth noting that the decline of major power wars, as well as the peaceful end of the Cold War, depended to a large degree on the role of MAD, which essentially is a mutual suicide pact that still places the entire world at risk. It is also an extremely dangerous form of mutual deterrence given the inherent problems of command

and control over nuclear weapons (Sagan, 1993), not to mention the possibility of nuclear terrorism. And while MAD may have helped to prevent a US–Soviet 'hot war' against each other, both sides had factored nuclear weapons into their war planning so that any small crisis still threatened to escalate into a major conflict (George, 1983; Garthoff, 1985). The Soviets secretly possessed tactical nuclear weapons in the 1960s and might have used them in a confrontation over Cuba (Dobbs, 2009), while European states deliberately kept their conventional weapons at a level lower than that of the USSR to convince the Soviets that any war in Europe would quickly 'go nuclear', an outcome that (hopefully) would continue to deter the USSR. In addition, the existence of MAD did not prevent the Americans and the Soviets from intervening militarily in their own spheres of influence, as neither side was willing to risk a nuclear war to stop such acts.

## Summary

As noted in Chapter 2, the study of interstate war still occurs to a large extent under the intellectual shadow of the Cold War. Yet even in this case – where scholars and others still argue over the outcome of this conflict – it is now abundantly clear that the two superpowers, and to a lesser extent their allies, spent far too much to deter a threat with a low probability of materializing (Lebow and Stein, 1995). Credible mutual deterrence – in the form of an assured second strike capability – was achieved by the early 1970s (if not sooner) by both superpowers, so much of the spending on weapons development and procurement, not to mention other conventional military resources devoted to the Cold War, was largely superfluous. The Cold War thus perfectly illustrates how easily an international security threat can be politicized and manipulated as an electoral issue to score points, mainly (but not exclusively) at the domestic level. It thus serves as a major warning any time another supposed existential threat to national or international security manifests itself, whether in the form of terrorism, cybersecurity, infectious disease, global warming or other issues.

In the two decades since the end of the Cold War, we are indeed fortunate that major power wars seem to be a thing of the past – for now. However, if a war of any type is essentially 'policy by other means' (Clausewitz, 1968) then an enduring solution to the problem of interstate war would be as difficult to develop as a general solution to the problem of policy or politics. Even if such a solution were theoretically possible, as in the form of a more representative global government with a strong police or military force, it likely would be unacceptable to the major powers in the system. Instead, most pragmatic approaches to the problem of war are based on two very simple but important points: first, war is most fundamentally a contest of arms, and second, the nature of that contest depends to a large degree on the resources of the contestants, which includes their supporters and opponents outside the war. As there is little chance of a major power war in the modern world owing to the possession of nuclear weapons by several major powers (among other factors), the only alternative derived from power-based approaches is to form counterbalancing coalitions on a case-by-case basis to prevent or stop an interstate war, or to act unilaterally in situations where the other major powers are unable or unwilling to get involved. While these efforts may contribute to international security in an indirect fashion, the fact remains that such efforts are largely a response by the major powers to protect their own interests rather than the interests of the international community, no matter how strenuously they may argue otherwise. And while most of the major powers continue to extol the virtues of international law and the peaceful resolution of disputes, they are also perfectly willing to resort to violence in case an interstate dispute threatens the international order, which now may include making a preventative war against a possible threat in addition to making a pre-emptive war against an actual one.

This fact in turn highlights another unpleasant fact regarding organized political violence in the contemporary world: the presence of a fairly clear divide between a rich and secure zone of peace among the stronger powers, particularly in the North, and a zone of poverty, violence and insecurity among the weaker powers in the South. As noted above, most of the stronger and richer states are generally status quo powers, and prefer to maintain the global capitalist order they created after WWII. However, over four-fifths of the world's population is located in the poorer parts of the world, including China and India, and these people may resort to violence in order to improve their living standards and political prospects, which often involves upsetting the status quo and even challenging the legitimacy of the modern state system and global economic order (they may also resort to fleeing to the richer states, as we shall see in Chapter 13). If the concerns of these individuals are not met, and if their national governments cannot contain or otherwise address their demands, the potential that certain states will descend into chaos and violence becomes that much greater. This dynamic is in fact one of the most prevalent problems in contemporary international security, as it involves the question of intrastate or civil violence and the possibility of deliberate international intervention – armed and otherwise – into the domestic affairs of sovereign states. This topic is the subject of Chapter 5, and should be considered as the second half of our discussion regarding the problem of war in international security.

## Further reading

Geoffrey Blainey (1973). *The Causes of War*. New York: Free Press.
Bruce Bueno de Mesquita (1981). *The War Trap*. New Haven: Yale University Press.
Robert Gilpin (1981). *War and Change in World Politics*. New York: Cambridge University Press.
Chris Hables Gray (1997). *Post-Modern War: The New Politics of Conflict*. London: Routledge.
K. J. Holsti (1996). *The State, War, and the State of War*. Cambridge: Cambridge University Press.
Michael Howard (1983). *The Causes of Wars*. Cambridge: Harvard University Press.
Jack S. Levy (1983). *War in the Modern Great Power System*. Lexington: University Press of Kentucky.
John Mueller (1989). *Retreat from Doomsday: The Obsolescence of Major War*. New York: Basic Books.
Robert I. Rotberg and Theodore K. Rabb (eds.) (1989). *The Origin and Prevention of Major Wars*. Cambridge: Cambridge University Press.
J. David Singer and Melvin Small (1972). *The Wages of War, 1816–1965*. New York: Wiley.
Stephen Van Evera (1999). *Causes of War: Power and the Roots of Conflict*. Ithaca: Cornell University Press.
John Vasquez (2012). *What Do We Know About War?* Lanham, MD: Rowman & Littlefield.
Kenneth N. Waltz (1959). *Man, the State, and War: A Theoretical Analysis*. New York: Columbia University Press.
Quincy Wright (1965). *A Study of War*. Chicago: University of Chicago Press.

# Chapter 5

# Intrastate War

The problem of intrastate instability has emerged as one of the most significant security issues in the post-war era, and can be linked, directly or indirectly, to many other problems. Moreover, the vast majority of these conflicts take place in LDCs, which raises difficult questions about how to close the security gap between rich and poor states, and whether rich states should become involved in such conflicts. The 1994 Rwandan genocide alone resulted in the vicious slaughter of over 800,000 people, and many other intrastate conflicts since 1945 have involved similar patterns of destruction. The problem of intrastate war in turn can be linked to a more general problem of weak or failed states, which can take a variety of forms depending on one's definition. Problems in such states can spill over to, or be exacerbated by, external actors or external phenomena such as disease or famine; these complex processes can have major implications for international security. Similarly, whether the international community – in the form of aid workers, PMCs, military peacekeepers or civilian state-builders – becomes involved in a domestic conflict is also a contested process and involves many more complications than the largely state-centric focus of our discussion about interstate war.

As with the previous chapter, our primary concern here is the conditions under which intrastate conflicts become international security problems. There are of course multiple forms of organized violence that occur at the intrastate level, such as mob violence, organized crime, low-level insurgencies and terrorism, resistance and separatist movements, *coups d'état* and the like. Most of these lower-scale problems will be covered in more detail in later chapters, particularly those involving terrorism (Chapter 7) and organized crime (Chapter 9). Accordingly, the rest of this chapter will examine the question of intrastate war in particular, which involves paying close attention to the nature and functioning of modern states. This focus continues the discussion begun in the previous chapter about various state attributes, such as regime type, which might contribute to intrastate conflict and cause it to escalate into an international concern. Similarly, as we are still dealing with the question of war in international security affairs, the discussion must pay especially close attention to the role of armed force as a possible solution. This can involve not only the balance of domestic forces in determining the outcome of an intrastate conflict but also the thorny question of outside armed intervention, and for reasons that might go well beyond traditional interpretations of threats to international security.

## Intrastate war and international security

The question of whether an intrastate war (also known as civil, internal or domestic war) might be interpreted as a threat to international security first depends on whether any consensual knowledge exists regarding the general nature of such conflicts. Here we immediately run into difficulties, as political scientists themselves find it challenging to distinguish an intrastate war from other types of domestic organized violence, and even to distinguish among types of intrastate wars. Therefore a single, concise definition that covers all apparent cases of modern intrastate wars still eludes us. One common reference (Small and Singer, 1976) defines such a war as any armed conflict that involves: a) 'military action internal to the metropole' (that is, the state's boundaries); b) the 'active participation of the national government'; and c) 'effective resistance by both sides'. This raises the question of what type of national government involvement is necessary to distinguish a 'true' intrastate war from either one-sided state-sponsored violence (as with militias rather than national forces, for example in Kenya from 1991 to 1993), or complete state failure/collapse (such as Somalia after 1991) (Sambanis, 2004). Assuming the national government is stable enough to deploy military forces, an intrastate war can in principle be distinguished from interstate wars, as discussed in the previous chapter. 'Extrastate' wars, however, are more complicated, as they can occur not only during empire-building but also during decolonization as the imperial power retreats; the 2008–9 war in Gaza between Israel and Hamas could be interpreted as either an intrastate or extrastate war, as can the Russian intrastate war in Chechnya in the 1990s, while the Russia–Georgia war in 2008 could be viewed as either an interstate or extrastate war. In addition, in the contemporary era many intrastate and extrastate conflicts also involve terrorism, insurgency or other forms of low-intensity war; this topic will be addressed in more detail in Chapter 7.

### Destructive scale

As with interstate war, many analysts adopt an annual death threshold of 1,000 battle deaths to define an intrastate war. This is the approach used by the widely cited Correlates of War database, which informs many empirical studies. However, many domestic conflicts, particularly in smaller states, do not meet this threshold on an annual basis yet would still be considered intrastate wars based on the definition above. If one adopts a more nuanced approach and uses a range of deaths over time rather than an absolute annual threshold, this results in a list of around 140–5 intrastate wars since WWII, with an average number of 144,000 deaths for each war (Regan, 2002; Sambanis, 2004). This means, in turn, that well over 20 million people – mostly civilians – have died in these wars since the end of WWII, which represents one of the most destructive trends, in terms of human lives lost, of all the issues covered in this volume. Thus the average intrastate war can be extremely destructive in human costs, even if it has little or no chance of involving other states.

In addition to the high death toll, recent analyses also pay increasing attention to the other costs associated with domestic conflict, particularly in terms of harm to civilians through injury or displacement, and the more general difficulty of distinguishing between combatants and non-combatants. As an intrastate war by definition typically involves state and non-state military forces, whose loyalties can change or even overlap depending on the circumstances, any intrastate war potentially puts all citizens of the state in question at risk – even those who hope to remain uninvolved. This tendency in turn leads to a consideration of the human rights aspects of such wars, which stem from the use of torture, rape, child soldiers, mutilation, ethnic cleansing and even genocide as a state descends into violent political suicide. In fact, these types of behaviours in particular, rather than the absolute death count, may be more responsible for provoking international involvement in a given intrastate war if recent experience is any guide. A growing body of research on ethnic intrastate wars in particular argues that conflicts motivated by disputes between ethnic groups (that is, groups bound by various cultural ties, such as language, history or religion) are especially violent and difficult to resolve, as compared to ideological intrastate wars, where loyalties are supposedly less rigid and passionate (Kaufmann, 1996; Brown et al., 2001; King, 2001; Snyder, 2001; Gurr and Harff, 2002). These disputes may also be more likely in states exhibiting a high degree of economic inequality and/or political exclusion among major ethnic groups (Cederman, Wimmer and Min, 2010; Cederman, Weidmann and Gleditsch, 2011).

Conversely, intrastate wars in states with a very high degree of ethnic homogeneity, such as Vietnam, tend to result in stronger state institutions once the war is finished (Taylor and Botea, 2008). Intrastate wars involving religion as an area of dispute have become especially prevalent and violent since WWII, and a very high proportion of such wars – around 80 per cent according to one analysis (Toft, 2007) – involve Islam; this was the case even before the eruption of intrastate violence across the Islamic world during the Arab Spring revolutions after 2010, in Tunisia, Egypt, Libya, Syria, Jordan, Yemen, Bahrain and (to a lesser extent) Saudi Arabia. Empirical analysis also suggests that states suffering from ethno-political violence are more likely to use force – and use it first – in an international dispute against a state without such problems (Trumbore, 2003). These are important claims to keep in mind as we examine the various rationales offered for intervening in such conflicts. There is, unfortunately, no short-age of opportunities for making such determinations; for example, only a few years after the end of the Cold War no less than 50 ethnic conflicts were being fought around the world, of which 13 had each caused more than 100,000 deaths by the mid-1990s (Gurr, 1994).

## Geographic and temporal scope

A second consideration involves the scope of an intrastate war, which can easily extend to other states, whether directly in the form of military engage-ments on border regions or indirectly in the form of refugee flows, trade in contraband (such as arms), environmental destruction or other sources of damage and instability. An intrastate war can also tempt a neighbour-ing state to intervene in support of either the national government or its opponents; in a worst case scenario a neighbouring state can even attempt to assert full control over another state stricken by domestic conflict, a fact always at the forefront of government calculations regarding armed chal-lenges to its authority. Moreover, some entire regions are prone to intra-state wars and other types of domestic conflict, so that an intrastate war in one state can easily invite or provoke the involvement of multiple neigh-bouring states (Levy, 1989); sub-Saharan Africa, the Middle East and Asia are especially prone to this dynamic given their complex webs of unde-fended borders and ethnic identities. This possibility can quickly turn a sin-gle domestic or intrastate conflict into a multilateral international conflict, which in turn makes it more likely to be viewed as a threat to international security. Table 5.1 summarizes some of these types of conflicts in terms of their relationship to other states or nationalist/ethnic groups:

**Table 5.1   *Types of war involving intrastate conflict***

| Type | Characteristics |
| --- | --- |
| Intrastate/civil war | Armed conflict among two or more groups within a state vying for control of that state (English Civil War). |
| Irredentist war | A state attempts to take territory from another state, on the pretence of protecting its own nationals within, or recovering its former territory from, the state under attack (Germany in Sudetenland/Czechoslovakia). |
| Secessionist war | An armed group within a state seeks to break free of that state and achieve independence or join with another state (US Civil War; Yugoslavia). |
| War of unification | Several armed groups in different territories seek to join together into a single state or join with another state (Wars of German unification). |

It is also important to bear in mind the temporal scope of intrastate wars. While interstate wars in the modern era rarely last for more than a few years and typically involve some type of legal instrument to symbolize their official cessation, intrastate wars can last for decades and might not involve a clear beginning and end point. In fact, many such conflicts start with very low levels of violence and escalate (or the reverse), or they might involve long periods of low violence where it may seem that no war is taking place (known as a 'frozen conflict'); these tendencies are related to the problems noted above regarding how to define an intrastate war. The recently ended intrastate conflict in Sri Lanka, for example, lasted for over 25 years and varied in intensity over that period, yet still resulted in more than 80,000 official deaths. Many such wars, therefore, are very ambiguous in terms of measuring their level of violence over time, or precisely when they start or finish, or how they might shade into acts of terrorism, insurgency, genocide, organized crime, mob violence or even interstate war – factors which necessarily complicate the determination of whether such a conflict should be treated as a threat to international security. Even when an intrastate conflict ends, the resulting peace can be defined in negative terms (the mere absence of war) or more positive terms (the absence of war plus a stable negotiated settlement of the issues at stake) (Fortna, 2004). Lack of clarity on these points can greatly obscure the findings of any particular study of intrastate war, and the policy recommendations that might result.

In all cases, however, this longer period of conflict relative to interstate wars tends to add to the overall destructiveness of intrastate conflicts, particularly since groups fighting in intrastate wars tend to fight to the bitter end unless some outside party attempts to broker an agreement (Walter, 1997). One might also note the opportunity costs of an ongoing intrastate war: the lost productivity and investment suffered by a state as a result of long-term violence and instability. Finally, a very long-term period of domestic conflict, particularly where the national government does not effectively control certain regions of its national territory (as in Colombia, Ethiopia and Sudan), might turn that territory into a safe haven for organized criminal activities, domestic or international terrorists, and other threatening non-state actors. Therefore even if a given intrastate war shows no signs of either spilling over to another state or of causing extensive human rights abuses, the international community may still consider it a threat to security owing to these other intrastate war opportunists.

## Likelihood

There is no doubt that intrastate war is still a widespread phenomenon in contemporary world politics. As noted above, the international system has experienced around 145 intrastate wars since the end of WWII, plus

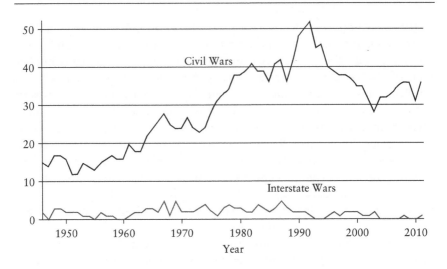

**Figure 5.1    *Types of wars, 1946–2011***
*Source:* Uppsala Conflict Data Program Armed Conflict Dataset v. 4-2012.

dozens of other assorted cases of domestic political conflict; Figure 5.1 shows the huge disparity between the incidence of interstate wars versus intrastate wars since WWII. This prevalence of intrastate/civil conflict means that in any given year over the past six decades we might find anywhere from ten to 50 ongoing intrastate wars at various levels of intensity. However, if predicting the likelihood of an interstate war breaking out among a given set of states is difficult, predicting the propensity for any single state to descend into intrastate war or violent domestic conflict is even more challenging. This question is in fact one of the major growth areas in the study of political violence and there is no shortage of theories (Tilly, 1978; Rule, 1988; Gurr, 1994; Lichbach, 1995; David, 1997). In keeping with the empirical trends involving ethnic war as noted above, a number of scholars have examined the role of ethnic nationalism as a likely cause of intrastate war, particularly when such groups desire their own state (Van Evera, 1994).

A more general set of hypotheses about intrastate war involves the question of weak, failed or failing states, where one finds a partial or complete collapse of state authority often accompanied by widespread political violence. In 1994 a US government State Failure Task Force attempted to forecast such problems in a kind of early warning system; members of the project defined 'state failure' as consisting of revolutionary war ('sustained military conflicts between insurgents and central governments'), genocides/politicides ('sustained policies by states and their agents and, in intrastate wars, by contending authorities that result in the deaths of a substantial portion of members of communal or political groups') and adverse or disruptive regime transitions (including 'state collapse, periods of severe regime instability and shifts toward authoritarian rule') (Esty et al., 1998). The project identified 127 state failures between 1955 and 1998 (which corresponds roughly with the 100+ number of intrastate wars in the post-war era) and used extensive statistical techniques to test 31 possible variables, in various combinations, that might predict state failure. Subsequent work in this area (King and Zeng, 2001) has resulted in a basic model of state failure, which involves six clusters of variables: overall level of democracy, legislative effectiveness, trade openness, infant mortality, military population and population density. To summarize the model, it predicts that state failure is more likely when the level of democracy is low, the legislature is non-existent or ineffective, trade is low or non-existent, infant mortality is high, the military population (and thus the number of weapons) as a proportion of overall population is high and the population density is high. The model quantifies these variables so that it is possible to make probability estimates of state failure for specific cases (as summarized in Table 5.2).

Conversely, the model can also be used to predict state 'non-failure' (state 'success' or internal stability) as summarized by the predictions in Table 5.3.

This type of work also shows that some earlier explanations about state failure, such as the role of economic growth as a source of conflict (Huntington, 1968) or past experience as a failed state, are generally not

Table 5.2  *Highest probability of state failure, and failure observed*

| State | Failure probability | Failure observed (year) |
|-------|--------------------|-----------------------|
| Senegal | 0.5307 | 1991 |
| Kyrgystan | 0.4563 | 1995 |
| Kazakhstan | 0.4147 | 1997 |
| Cambodia | 0.4122 | 1997 |
| Georgia | 0.3913 | 1998 |
| Armenia | 0.3470 | 1994 |
| Guinea-Bissau | 0.3214 | 1998 |
| Thailand | 0.2787 | 1991 |
| Zambia | 0.2348 | 1996 |
| Georgia | 0.2285 | 1991 |

*Source:* King and Zeng (2001).

**Table 5.3**  *Lowest probability of state failure, and failure did not occur*

| State | Failure probability | Non-failure observed (year) |
|---|---|---|
| Finland | 0.0014 | 1992 |
| Sweden | 0.0015 | 1994 |
| Estonia | 0.0015 | 1997 |
| Finland | 0.0016 | 1993 |
| Switzerland | 0.0016 | 1993 |
| Switzerland | 0.0016 | 1994 |
| Norway | 0.0017 | 1993 |
| United Kingdom | 0.0017 | 1991 |
| United Kingdom | 0.0017 | 1994 |
| United Kingdom | 0.0017 | 1996 |

*Source:* King and Zeng (2001).

supported by the data. However, as always, no model is perfect, and a change on a single variable can greatly affect a forecast. The model, for example, incorrectly predicted a low probability of state failure in Algeria, Haiti and Sierra Leone in 1991, and in Bosnia–Herzegovina and the Democratic Republic of the Congo in 1992. Still, given the lively debate in the literature over the past two decades about the relationship between various aspects of state strength and security (Migdal, 1988; Desch, 1996), this work helps to reorient the discussion more towards prediction than mere description or explanation.

## Recovery

Finally, as we might expect, the recovery time following an intrastate war can be extremely lengthy, even when such a war has been concluded with a formal peace agreement respected by all parties. Obviously the recovery time will depend on the scale of destructiveness, particularly in terms of the length of the war and whether the war was confined to a certain geographic region or, conversely, involved the entire country. If outside aid or investment are lacking following an intrastate war, recovery can take years if not decades. Even more problematic are cases where an intrastate war has not been concluded with either a decisive victory or a workable peace agreement; in such wars no recovery is possible until the conflict has been brought to a clear end. In states suffering from such a situation, such as Colombia and (until recently) Sri Lanka, the affected areas are essentially closed off from the rest of the state and function as lawless areas subject to the control of rebel groups. Thus, and as with interstate wars, the terms under which an intrastate war has been concluded are extremely important in determining the future stability and recovery of the affected state in question (Boyle, 2014). In most cases, intrastate wars end with a decisive victory by either the national government forces or the rebels, and the terms of peace are generally imposed by the victorious party. In a minority of cases, however, a negotiated peace between the forces may result and will require some provisions regarding enforcement and compliance if neither side has achieved a decisive victory over the other. These in fact are the most difficult cases to resolve and typically require intensive outside intervention if peace and recovery are to be achieved, as we shall see.

## Stakeholder factors

One major problem regarding intrastate conflict, as suggested above, is the sheer number of various types of stakeholders who can involve themselves in the war and whose preferences need to be taken into consideration when a settlement, if any, is negotiated. This problem is difficult enough in a conflict involving a single rebel group; in cases involving multiple rebel groups the chances for a stable settlement are even more remote, as with the collapse of Yugoslavia into multiple states throughout the 1990s.

### Principal stakeholders

As intrastate wars are a type of organized violence, our discussion of key stakeholders begins with the types of organized groups that might initiate or participate in such violence. These groups generally involve, on the one hand, the national governments who are typically attempting to defend the state and, on the other hand, various types of rebel or resistance movements who seek a range of goals. As with the study of interstate war, national government actors can be disaggregated into executive authorities and military bureaucracies, meaning political elites or regime officials. One critical issue in a failed state or intrastate war is whether the military supports or opposes the government regime in a given state. Military rebellions or *coups d'état*, where the regime is overthrown and replaced by a new leader (often one with military links or support), are still a major threat in some LDCs; Thailand (2006), Honduras (2009) and Egypt (2013) are recent examples, along with an attempted coup in Turkey (2016). If, however, the military supports the governing regime, which is typically the case, then our attention turns to the organized non-state stakeholders who might threaten the state in question. These groups can involve rebel or resistance movements, warlords, criminal organizations, local militias, ethnic groups and many other forms of armed opposition to a governing regime. However, as we shall see in the next section, the preferences of these groups can vary widely, which influences the extent to which they represent a threat to a given state or the international community.

It is also worth keeping in mind the role of external stakeholders in either supporting or opposing a specific intrastate war or failing state. Other states, particularly those in close proximity to the state in question, may attempt to influence the situation by supporting or opposing the governing regime. In some extreme cases another state will attempt to overthrow the government of a weak or failed state, as with the US in Grenada and Panama, Ethiopia in Somalia or with various European colonial powers in many less developed parts of the world (particularly Africa). Outside states can also deliberately create or exacerbate instability in weak states for various reasons, as with Russia in Ukraine, which involved Russia's annexation of Crimea in 2014. Various IOs and NGOs, such as humanitarian aid groups, may also develop an interest in a certain intrastate war and become involved, which often raises the question of taking sides between the various factions involved. For example, in Rwanda the influential NGO *Médecins Sans Frontières*, which provides medical care in LDCs, found its leadership split over how to maintain impartiality between pro-Hutu and pro-Tutsi factions (Orbinski, 2008). Finally, as with modern interstate wars, recent years have seen a dramatic rise in the involvement of various private stakeholders on behalf of either the governing regime or the opposition movement(s). This phenomenon can dramatically complicate the prospects for resolving an intrastate conflict and will require further attention later in this chapter.

## Interests and preferences

Fighting in a major intrastate war is somewhat similar to fighting in an interstate war under anarchy: domestic institutions have broken down and the chief prize is to capture control of the national government and restore unitary authority. In a sense, such states are facing an 'insecurity dilemma' (Job, 1992) owing to various domestic problems, rather than a security dilemma produced by the actions of other states. Even under these circumstances, however, rationalist theories of intrastate war would still claim the parties are driven by the same cost–benefit calculations that occur during an interstate war (Holl, 1993; Wagner, 1993; Zartman, 1993; Mason and Fett, 1996). An alternative view based on ideas or identity argues that intrastate wars involve more intense values and emotions than interstate conflicts, particularly when related to the ethnic composition of the state involved, and cannot be ended so easily through negotiation and compromise (Randle, 1973; Horowitz, 1985; Burton, 1987). This view, however, is somewhat in decline as an exploratory tool for theorizing across intrastate wars, although ethnic concerns might play a supplementary role in the analysis of a specific war.

Some analysts have explored the question of whether we are now witnessing a distinction between old and new intrastate war styles since the end of the Cold War: 'new' civil or intrastate wars (also known as 'post-modern' conflicts; see Gray, 1997 and Duffield, 1998) are supposedly more criminal, economic and predatory in nature, as opposed to the public, political and ideological nature of 'old' intrastate wars. Or in other words, old intrastate wars tend to involve collective grievances while new intrastate wars involve private looting and vast 'networks of profit' (King, 2001). New intrastate wars are also supposedly more violent and lack the broad popular support of major societal groups as compared to previous intrastate wars (Snow, 1996; Kaldor, 1999; Collier, 2000). Both the UN and the World Bank have also asserted this view about the nature of new intrastate wars (Annan, 1999). Table 5.4 summarizes some of the major distinctions between 'old' and 'new' intrastate wars, as argued by some of these scholars.

As with identity and ethnicity, however, these views about 'new' intrastate wars should not be overstated: previous intrastate wars often involved a criminal element in the sense of attempting to secure control of valuable resources or property, while new intrastate wars usually involve a political or ideological element that might be easily overlooked by outsiders. This possibly false distinction is also problematic if it leads to demands for military intervention on the basis of incorrect assumptions about the true nature of modern intrastate wars (Mueller, 2000; Kalyvas, 2001).

A closer look at the specific preferences of the various stakeholders reveals they can be analysed in terms of basic political calculations. For example, if the government is facing a true intrastate war as defined above,

Table 5.4   *'Old' and 'new' intrastate wars*

| 'Old' intrastate wars | 'New' intrastate wars |
| --- | --- |
| Ideological | Criminal |
| Political | De-politicized |
| Collective/public | Private |
| 'Noble' | Predatory |
| Justice-seeking | 'Loot-seeking' or 'rent-seeking'; banditry; warlordism |

it will generally stop at nothing to put down the rebellion. However, two other possibilities exist depending on the conflict at hand. First, the national government may be willing to accept some or all of the demands of the rebel movement if the government feels it cannot achieve victory. This calculation can be strongly affected by outside intervention, as we shall see in the discussion of policy options below. Second, the national government itself might be split in terms of its preferences, so that a consistent position cannot be determined. One common source of such a split involves disagreement among the civilian and military elites; civilians might be more willing than the military to negotiate a compromise (or vice versa), which might tempt military elites into overthrowing the government in order to save the state. This pattern of 'spoiler problems' among competing groups in conflict states (Stedman, 1997) is fairly common in less democratic societies, such as Central and South America, where the military is expected to play a dominant role in defending the state from domestic rebellion. For example, the *coup d'état* in Honduras was justified by its military as a move to prevent the sitting president, Manuel Zelaya, from attempting to change the Honduran constitution to allow him to serve beyond the legal limit of a single four-year term.

The goals of the rebels are equally variable, and might be ranged along a continuum from greater recognition as a sub-national group or region, to more political freedoms or autonomy within the state, to full separation from the state in question (that is, separatist or independence movements), to complete capture and control of the state in question. This array of preferences can be complicated further by two factors: the involvement of multiple rebel groups who might share conflicting goals, and/or the fact that these goals might change over time depending on the conduct of the war and any concessions made by the national government (Cunningham, 2011). For example, rebel groups may increase their ambitions if they sense an easy victory over the national forces, so that a bid for more autonomy expands into a full-scale separatist movement, or a separatist movement becomes an attempt to overthrow the national government. In all cases of intrastate war, the main power resources for these groups centre on their military resources, particularly weapons and human capital, which usually gives an edge (at least initially) to the national government unless the rebel movement enjoys unusually wide support throughout the state and/or some degree of physical security as a result of geography. Local knowledge is also important, particularly in situations where the rebel groups can exploit private information about the terrain, climate, demographics and other factors in areas where they operate. In cases where the rebels are not strong enough to fight directly with the national forces, the war may become a smaller-scale insurgency or terror campaign, an alternative we shall explore in more detail in Chapter 7.

Finally, the various outside parties noted above may possess unique interests or preferences regarding the outcome of an intrastate war. Other states, IOs, NGOs and private stakeholders may become involved not necessarily to support or oppose the governing regime but to enhance their own security, earn profits from the sale of scarce goods, build new economic or political ties (or maintain existing ones), meet their alliance commitments, promote international norms, prevent other stakeholders from playing a dominant role and even enhance their own international or domestic position (Mullenbach, 2005; Fordham, 2008). British and French involvement in sub-Saharan Africa, for example, can be attributed to some of these motives (Regan and Aydin, 2006), while America's surprise decision in 1992 to intervene in Somalia has been attributed to domestic political calculations by the Bush administration just prior to Clinton's assumption of the presidency in 1993, rather than to the nature of the crisis of Somalia in particular (Western, 2002). Russia's recent policies towards some former Soviet republics involve these narrow national interests as well, mainly in terms of keeping them within Russia's sphere of influence rather than allowing them to draw closer to NATO and/or the EU. Even NGOs are not immune to this dynamic; their views about the nature of new intrastate wars may have inspired their opposition to the 1999 Sierra Leone peace agreement, as they believed the rebels were violent criminals rather than political activists and thought it was immoral to grant them an amnesty and invite their participation in a new government. Conversely, the peace agreement in Northern Ireland was criticized by the same groups on precisely the opposite grounds: that the peace deal did *not* allow the participation of IRA members in the new government (Kalyvas, 2001). The critical point is that these stakeholders are likely to have multiple and even conflicting preferences regarding a specific intrastate war; and the greater the number of external stakeholders involved, the greater the likelihood that their preferences will clash with each other in terms of finding a solution. These factors, which currently are very prominent in the tragic case of Syria, are especially critical when considering external intervention in a given intrastate war. As many such interventions today are multilateral in nature, the possibility that the outside parties will conflict with each other over the priorities of the intervention, or over more parochial matters such as differences in their military cultures (Soeters and Manigart, 2008) becomes that much greater.

## The use of force

Governments, whether democratic or authoritarian, facing open revolt by armed citizens are typically more than willing to resort to deadly force to maintain control. They will often vigorously assert their right to handle such problems as they see fit, and expect others to respect their sovereign right of non-interference when intrastate war threatens. A response that does not involve deadly force is possible of course; this generally means some form of negotiation or settlement between the parties to either avoid or end an intrastate war. However, the dominant tendency with contemporary intrastate wars is for the parties to fight to the bitter end rather than to negotiate a peaceful settlement. Of 40 intrastate wars ending between 1940 and 1990, 16 (40 per cent) resulted in decisive government victory; 16 (40 per cent) resulted in decisive rebel victory; and eight (20 per cent) resulted in a successful settlement (Walter, 1997).

This general tendency for the international community to let most intrastate wars resolve themselves – or to 'self-stabilize' – through a decisive victory does not preclude the possibility of intervention by outsiders in some cases, which can create endless complications. The level of complexity is partly a function of whether a foreign stakeholder is invited to help by some or all parties to the conflict; in cases where a foreign stakeholder is actively opposed by some major party – whether a rebel group or the national government – the situation can become extremely unstable and violent. This, however, is precisely the danger we often face when the international community attempts to insert itself into an intrastate conflict in the name of regional or international security, or of other universal goals, such as human rights.

## Public–private domains and levels of jurisdiction

A final consideration about the general nature of intrastate war involves the increasingly complex balance between public and private domains of action as well as levels of jurisdiction, whether international, national or sub-national, in dealing with this problem. Obviously the central government will assert its public authority at the national and sub-national levels when facing such a threat, yet the nature of intrastate war easily blurs the distinction between the public and private domains for several reasons. One is that the government may rely upon private militia groups, whether officially or unofficially, as a way to deal with the rebels. This tactic may expand the scope of the conflict and complicate the pursuit of a settlement if such groups cannot be controlled effectively by the state. A second problem is that rebel movements themselves are typically composed of private citizens rather than public military officials, although there can be some overlap between these spheres. This means the movement must develop its own quasi-public status in attempting to recruit and train its own soldiers from among ordinary citizens, as well as extract resources from society to fund itself. As noted above, some analysts view this as 'criminal' rather than 'political' activity as they believe it represents material gain for its own sake, yet all armies – public and private – require funds and must find ways to 'tax' their resource base effectively, even if this requires the vicious punishment of innocent civilians. This activity is especially prevalent in areas rich in natural resources such as diamonds or oil, or where illegal drugs are grown; the terms 'narco-guerrillas' or 'narco-terrorism' are sometimes used to refer to the latter phenomenon.

The public–private balance becomes even more complicated if *foreign* private stakeholders involve themselves, which brings the international level of jurisdiction into the mix. The most common form of such private intervention involves the delivery of humanitarian aid by various types of NGOs, such as CARE or the ICRC. However, as with interstate war, the role of PMCs in intrastate wars has also increased markedly in recent years; some even argue that PMCs could have acted more quickly and effectively than the UN to save lives in places like Rwanda and Liberia if they had been allowed to operate (O'Brien, 2007). Even foreign businesses have been asked to contribute to peace processes in weak states where they operate, as with a UN request made to foreign oil firms operating in Angola in 2001 (Haufler, 2004). However, there is no such thing as purely 'neutral' humanitarian aid; this designation always depends on the perceptions of the recipients (or their enemies), not just the good intentions of the aid providers (Lischer, 2003). Even PMCs could be viewed as the enemy if political allegiances shift within the state, which is often the case (McIntyre and Weiss, 2007). This finding also applies to efforts by the UN, the US and other powerful stakeholders to 'rebuild' failed states. A related point is that although an intrastate war seems to primarily involve the domestic–national level of jurisdiction, this level can be threatened from below and above depending on the nature of the intrastate war: some rebel or even terrorist movements may become so powerful that they emerge as viable global actors in their own right, and make claims regarding their diplomatic or legal status that can further undermine the national governments they oppose, as happened with the Palestine Liberation Organization (PLO) after the 1993 Oslo Accords signed by the PLO and Israel. Islamic State in Syria/Iraq/Libya is attempting to achieve this status as well in terms of creating an independent Islamic caliphate (Fromson and Simon, 2015; Byman, 2016; Gerges, 2016; Saideman, 2016) by controlling territory, recruiting fighters, using extreme violence (including sexual violence), producing various forms of foreign media (through its 'al-Hayat' arm) and even minting a unique form of currency (a new gold dinar). These efforts make Islamic State seem more like a well-organized rebel/secessionist movement in its willingness to attack military forces, as opposed to a loosely organized or decentralized 'traditional' terrorist organization focusing primarily on attacks on civilians (see Chapter 7); the Islamist group Boko Haram is attempting the same thing in Nigeria, though on a much smaller scale.

## Intrastate war as a policy problem

The question of how the international community should respond to a given intrastate war often amounts to the question of whether the state should be kept whole, which generally means supporting the national government, or should instead be broken into smaller parts or be encouraged to allow other less drastic forms of regional independence, which generally means supporting resistance or rebel movements. As this determination is often made by the major powers of the system, there is an inherent bias towards the status quo regarding any incidence of intrastate war, which translates as support for the national government rather than the rebel groups. Major powers generally do not want to risk the complications involved in allowing states to break into smaller units, particularly when they have their own rebel or separatist movements to contend with (as in China, India, Pakistan and Russia). There are exceptions, of course, as with the peaceful 'velvet divorce' of Czechoslovakia in 1993, which created the new Czech and Slovak Republics. However, the dominant tendency is to favour national unity for fear of a painful break-up, as reflected during the early stages of one of the most violent and complicated state failures since the end of the Cold War: the collapse of Yugoslavia. Most major powers attempted to keep the state intact, which involved a belief that a national Yugoslavian identity could still ultimately triumph over various ethnic ones. This approach, however, quickly became impossible once the level of violence had escalated to atrocities and ethnic cleansing. Even so, disagreements about the Balkans linger in world politics, as with the ongoing disputes among many states over recognizing the independence of Kosovo (see the case study in Box 5.1).

This question about unity versus dissolution reflects a more fundamental problem: that there is nothing inherently sacrosanct about the administrative divisions within and among states. Instead, they developed as a result of multiple political conflicts and a range of other very idiosyncratic historical factors (Krasner, 1995–6), few of which were legitimate in the eyes of many people within those states. In fact, in the past century there has been considerable variation in the support of the major powers for the 'national self-determination' of minority groups within states (or empires) versus a desire to keep multi-ethnic states as they are; it is only since the advent of the UN Charter after WWII that the international community has become biased towards an emphasis on state unity and stability rather than on the right of ethnic groups or other national minorities to form their own states (Barkin and Cronin, 1994). The Cold War also had a kind of 'chilling effect' on the aspirations of some nationalist groups to pursue independence, as these efforts could be opposed by one superpower or the other. At the same time, however, the settlements imposed by the victors of major wars, as well as the related processes of colonization and decolonization, have left a bitter legacy of weak, fragmented or otherwise unstable states in many parts of the world, particularly in the South. This fact is important to keep in mind whenever calls are made for outside stakeholders (particularly the Western liberal states) to intervene for the purpose of rebuilding or otherwise pacifying the state in question.

## Agenda-setting

Although the *general* problem of intrastate war is widely recognized as a matter of international security, the question of how a *specific* intrastate conflict attracts the attention of the international community is very complex. Like the problem of interstate wars, this is frequently a determination made by the major powers who take an interest in certain intrastate wars for various reasons – not always related to security – noted above, although these states may be encouraged along this path by IOs, NGOs and the media. An intrastate conflict might also attract the attention of a major power which desires to maintain political and/or economic control over its immediate sphere of influence, as with the US in the Western hemisphere and Russia in the territory of the former Soviet Union (Fordham, 2008). Global or regional IOs may become involved in an intrastate war in order to preserve their autonomy or merely to gain experience in handling such problems; the EU in particular demonstrated this tendency with its EU-led peacekeeping/conflict resolution missions since 2003 (Ginsberg and Smith, 2007; Smith, forthcoming). Studies of NGOs have shown that even they are motivated not just by the human rights or security problems in the state in question, but also desire to raise their own profiles, set international standards and maximize their advocacy and funding opportunities when choosing to pay attention to a particular intrastate conflict (Ron, Ramos and Rodgers, 2005).

It is also important to recognize the efforts of the weak state in question to set the agenda and thus either encourage or discourage involvement by the international community. As the normal tendency for most governments is to reject outside intervention in favour of retaining national autonomy and control, the question becomes: under what conditions might the government of a weak state voluntarily agree to involvement by a foreign stakeholder? The literature on this topic suggests several factors, such as the costs and duration of the conflict, the presence of historical ties between the foreign stakeholder and the conflict state in question, the expectation on the part of the conflict state government that the involvement will be successful and the amount of resources the foreign stakeholder offers to devote to the problem. Intensive statistical analysis of intrastate war mediation, for example, suggests that the willingness to accept mediation rises as a function of the duration of the war in question (except when the war drags on for around 20 years or more) and the reputation of the actor offering mediation, as measured for example by previous success at mediation (Greig and Regan, 2008). These studies suggest that agenda-setting regarding international involvement in intrastate wars involves a complicated set of interactions – based on calculations related to historical, political and economic factors – between the prospective intervening parties and the warring parties of the conflict state in question.

In rare cases where foreign intervention occurs without an invitation on the part of the warring parties, as with (for example) a situation where mass homicide is being committed or sponsored by the government (Pape, 2012), the situation on the ground can become extremely dangerous. This outcome may become more likely in light of recent thinking regarding the nature of weak states and the obligations of the international community to become more involved. Ever since the Rwandan genocide and the ethnic cleansing of the Balkans, the R2P norm has emerged as a justification for intervention in certain conflicts. The primary consideration here is the presence of serious human rights abuses among the parties to an intrastate war; a second consideration is the inability or unwillingness of the national government in question to stop the violence. In these cases, various international stakeholders may decide to intervene even against the wishes of the national government, and even where an international security threat, as traditionally defined, seems to be lacking (Posen, 1996; Moore, 1998; Chesterman, 2001; Chatterjee and Scheid, 2002; Finnemore, 2003; Holzgrefe and Keohane, 2003; Lang Jr., 2003; Welsh, 2004; Carpenter, 2005; Krain, 2005). This norm also involves the question of human security and role of individual human beings, rather than governments or national unity, as the key referent objects to be secured. However, *calling* for such action and *taking* such action are two very separate things, as we shall see.

## Framing policy alternatives

All wars are easier to start than to terminate, and intrastate wars can be the most difficult of all to bring to a peaceful conclusion. As noted above, the normal tendency in such wars is a fight to the death of one side or the other if no outside help is offered. The problem of a weak state facing a multi-ethnic intrastate war is especially toxic, as the governing regime is not strong enough to maintain any order and the ethnic groups are often unwilling to consider any power-sharing arrangement even if order could be restored. For international stakeholders who pay close attention to a specific intrastate war or failed state, the post-war history of intrastate war suggests only a few options.

One option is to do nothing and stay out. This option tends to favour the stronger group of adversaries in the state, which is usually the national government or its proxies (such as state-supported militias), assuming the national military supports the governing regime. In these cases, the choice of non-intervention tends to favour the status quo, which is often very tempting for outside stakeholders (particularly the major powers). Often this option also involves an arms embargo imposed by some foreign stake-holders, as in the case of Yugoslavia. This policy also tends to favour the national government as it usually possesses more weapons and organizational strength than the rebel groups (although this is not always the case; see Park, 2015). Taken together, such measures typically facilitate the use of more violence by the governing regime, especially if it tends not to enjoy other sources of legitimacy or political influence to encourage national unity. This also tends to encourage the suppression of minority ethnic communities, unless they can be 'assimilated' into a broader national identity, a very difficult task for weak multi-ethnic states. It is so difficult, in fact, that the national government may be strongly tempted to remove or even kill certain populations rather than attempt to integrate them into the state. Such a policy can also create massive refugee flows and force foreign stakeholders to reconsider their 'hands-off' approach (i.e. hoping for self-stabilization), as we shall see in Chapter 13.

A second option for outsiders is to help negotiate to keep the state intact. However, this is also difficult for reasons noted above. Intrastate wars are in fact much less likely than interstate wars to end in a negotiated settlement; 55 per cent of interstate wars that ended between 1940 and 1990 were resolved by bargaining, while only 20 per cent of intrastate wars ended in the same manner (Walter, 1997). Most intrastate wars in fact end by the surrender or destruction of one side or the other, often because it is difficult if not impossible for the parties themselves to make credible guarantees to each other regarding a settlement. In theory, parties to an intrastate war may find some common bargaining space to end their conflict; in practice, however, any agreement to disarm, demobilize and reintegrate former rebels usually puts the weaker party at risk, especially when the government is unwilling or unable to enforce the peace agreement impartially and/or prevent retribution by various groups. Even when reintegration of rebels (rather than punishment) is pursued in good faith, it requires sustained efforts on the part of all stakeholders, as well as favourable socio-economic conditions in the long term (Phayal, Khadka and Thyne, 2015); in some cases, such reintegration into a new national army may even create more problems than it is worth (Krebs and Lick-lider, 2015–16). This potential security deficit for rebel groups when negotiating with the central government is the main difference between typical interstate and typical intrastate wars: the parties in an interstate war can usually retain independent military forces (although they may be reduced in size) so that they are not completely defenceless, while rebel groups in an intrastate war typically must lay down their arms and put themselves at the mercy of not just the government, but of any other groups that may have supported the state.

In situations where the central government is not trusted to respect a peace agreement, the rational option for the rebel side is to fight as hard as possible to overthrow the government and take over its military forces, unless some third party (a foreign force) can guarantee its security (Lake and Rothchild, 1996; Walter, 1997). This latter option can take various forms under Chapter VI of the UN Charter: observer missions (often unarmed); peacekeeping missions (usually lightly armed for self-defence only) and multidimensional peacekeeping or state-building missions (which involve armed troops plus other support elements devoted to institution-building, elections-monitoring, humanitarian aid delivery and other tasks). Some missions might not involve the consent of the warring parties, in which case they are known as peace enforcement missions. These are also authorized under Chapter VII of the UN Charter. It is similarly possible to conceive of some form of 'international trusteeship' over a weak state, which involves the taking over of a state's administrative functions by an outside authority such as the UN (Herbst, 1996–7; Fearon and Laitin, 2004; Fortna, 2004). The origins of this option extend back to the League of Nations era, which involved League protectorates (or 'mandates') over certain territories, such as Palestine and South West Africa (now Namibia), which were remnants of the defeated Ottoman and German empires after 1918.

A third option is to negotiate some form of separation between the parties, or even total dissolution of the state. Some observers have argued that where intrastate wars involve a strong element of ethnic conflict, it may be desirable to separate the communities into defensible ethnic enclaves, a view sometimes referred to as 'partition theory'. This may be an attractive option particularly when tales of atrocities surface and harden the loyalties of various factions (Kaufmann, 1996 and 1998). Partition theorists also argue that ethnic intrastate wars typically discourage individuals from joining a competing ethnic group based on appeals to ideology or other more inclusive values; instead, they are essentially prisoners of their own ethnic group and must assert their interests against competing ethnic groups. Rather than attempt to restore or rebuild weak or failed states, then, which might allow massacres, ethnic cleansing or genocide to continue, partition theorists argue that a better option may be the creation of independent national homelands based largely on ethnicity. This option was followed in Kosovo, as we shall see in the case study below. In addition, others have argued that where a settlement is not possible, rebel victories may result in a more stable post-war peace as compared to victory by the national government or a settlement imposed from the outside (Toft, 2010).

## Policy choice

How does the contemporary international community tend to respond to the problem of intrastate war? Scholars have examined this question by analysing both sides of the intervention equation: the characteristics of intrastate wars that might inspire intervention, and the characteristics of the foreign stakeholders who might intervene.

Regarding the nature of the intrastate wars, we should reiterate the point above that most such wars tend to end as a result of a decisive victory by one side or the other. Based on the 100 or more intrastate wars that have ended since WWII, the chance for victory is split about equally between the government and the rebel forces. In most cases, therefore, the international community has tended to adopt a 'hands-off' attitude to these conflicts, although token offers of diplomatic or economic support might be made. This was partly a result of a preoccupation by the major powers with the Cold War, which placed a low priority on intrastate wars unless they involved a major element of ideological rivalry (for example, pro-communist versus anti-communist forces). Even in these cases, as in Central/South America, Asia and sub-Saharan Africa, outside stakeholders typically preferred to involve themselves in an indirect fashion, by sending aid and military/technical assistance for example, rather than intervene directly for the purpose of ending the war. In a sense, the superpowers respected each other's regional sphere of influence and tried to prevent any proxy wars between capitalism and communism from escalating into a superpower confrontation, especially after the Cuban missile crisis (Gaddis, 1986).

In addition, the Cold War rivalry complicated any efforts by the UN system to get more involved in certain intrastate conflicts, as the UNSC could easily be deadlocked over such a decision if the US and the USSR (and/or China) failed to agree. As a result, the number of UN peace operations in intrastate wars during the Cold War – such as those in Cyprus, the Golan Heights and Lebanon – was very small relative to the total number of ongoing intrastate wars. In addition, statistical analyses of the relationship between the characteristics of intrastate wars and the provision of peacekeeping forces have generally discounted several war-related factors (such as the presence of an identity conflict, a formal peace agreement or a high degree of violence) that have been suggested as reasons why the international community might be tempted to intervene (Fortna, 2004). However, the same work does suggest that missions are more likely if a conflict tends to drag on in the form of a stalemate. Others have argued that government-biased and rebel-biased interventions should be examined as distinct phenomena rather than as a single type of policy, as 66 out of 140 conflicts studied (based on the dataset in Regan, 2002) resulted in a government-biased intervention, while 59 were rebel-biased.

Government-biased intervention was also more likely in ideological rather than identity-based conflicts, while rebel-biased intervention is equally likely in both types of conflicts. Shared borders (or a 'neighbourhood effect') also seem to increase the prospects of a rebel-biased intervention (Gent, 2008).

Regarding the nature of the intervening actors, it is clear that the international community has started to pay far more attention to weak states, failed states and intrastate conflicts since the end of the Cold War, following on from decades of UN peacekeeping experience (Guéhenno, 2015). Security analysts are increasingly realizing that many contemporary threats can be related in one form or another to the problem of intrastate conflict; such threats include not just interstate war and terrorism, but also less traditional problems such as organized crime, environmental degradation, infectious disease, arms trafficking and many others. As a result, the international community seems more willing than ever before to devote resources to the question of weak states, which includes various forms of outside intervention or aid by a range of both state and non-state actors.

In fact, the problem of intrastate conflict is so important today that it is possible to see the emergence of two general international norms in this area. As noted above, one involves the R2P norm (International Commission on Intervention and State Sovereignty, 2002), which partly justified NATO's so-called humanitarian military intervention in Kosovo (see the case study in Box 5.1). A second and related norm involves the idea of preventative measures to head off such problems before they erupt into intrastate war. Both the UN (Annan, 1999) and the EU (Council of the EU, 2003), for example, have identified this concern as an important aspect of their policies regarding weak or failing states. These more anticipatory policies, such as the state failure project noted above, are also closely related to the more general human security agenda. In other words, it may be far more effective, and cheaper, to get involved in a weak state as early as possible rather than wait for it to collapse into violence and chaos.

As always, however, the key problem is deciding on which states to 'save'. Even with a general recognition regarding the potential regional or global implications of intrastate conflict, the international community can still find it difficult to determine when and how to intervene, and for what purposes. In most cases, the preference is to attempt to preserve the state, which means the outsiders must help the warring factions to reach a stable settlement and thus share the national territory of their state. However, to provide a credible security guarantee in such states, the foreign peacekeepers must have a strategic interest in upholding their promise to protect the parties, whether for security reasons, colonial ties, economic ties or alliance commitments. They must also have a credible military force willing and able to protect the disarming groups and punish those who violate the peace treaty; this degree of force usually means a state, or coalition of states (such as organized by the UN), powerful enough to commit resources to the fight, keep all the warring parties at bay and sustain the effort until the parties can secure themselves (Walter, 1997; Doyle and Sambanis, 2000). These are extremely high barriers to a successful peacekeeping operation, even for states as powerful as the US, and easily explain why many such operations, even multinational ones, experience difficulties (Howe, 1996–7) – assuming they can be organized at all. All of these factors may come into play when assessing the outcomes of individual peacekeeping operations, as we shall see in more detail in the discussion of policy effectiveness below.

Still, one of the most remarkable trends in international security since the end of the Cold War is the increasing willingness of various actors to take on these challenges, which may or may not involve UN resources or even UN endorsement. In fact, most intrastate war peace operations since the end of the Cold War have not involved the UN but rather other organizations or coalitions of states, as Table 5.5 indicates.

As we can see, although the UN is still the dominant player (Price and Zacher, 2004), other IOs are now more willing to take the lead, as with the Economic and Monetary Union of Central African States (CEMAC) in the Central African Republic, the Economic Community of West African States (ECOWAS) in Liberia and Côte d'Ivoire, the African Union (AU) in Burundi and Darfur (Sudan) and the EU in Macedonia, the Democratic Republic of the Congo (DRC), Bosnia, Chad and the Central African Republic (Smith, forthcoming). The UN also attempted to intervene in Syria's civil war in 2012 but the mission was quickly suspended in the face of rapidly escalating violence. The EU's efforts are especially interesting, as the missions in the DRC and Chad are obviously well removed from the European continent and thus did not involve a direct threat to EU interests (unlike the missions authorized by the AU, CEMAC and ECOWAS, which did involve a threat to Africa). The EU also worked closely with the UN in these cases, as well as in the most recent intervention in the Central African Republic. The US has similarly decided to increase its profile in one major trouble spot – Africa – by creating in 2007 a formal 'African Command' military unit, headquartered in Germany, with a local base in Djibouti (Camp Lemonnier). It has not yet been tasked with a major peacekeeping or humanitarian operation; however, this command has resorted to the use of drone surveillance/strikes in certain parts of Africa (such as the Central African Republic, Mali, Somalia and Uganda), while 300 US troops have been deployed to Cameroon to fight the Boko Haram militia (see the special issue of *Contemporary Security Policy* on the African Command, 30/1, 2009). Finally, some missions have required a certain degree of political coordination between various IOs to materialize, as with Bosnia and Kosovo (UN and NATO), the DRC and Chad (UN and EU) and Côte d'Ivoire (UN and ECOWAS). Afghanistan is a special

Table 5.5    *Peace operations in intrastate wars, 1991–2014*

| Date created | Location | Authorizing body | Operational command |
|---|---|---|---|
| 1991 | Western Sahara | UN | UN |
| 1992 | Georgia/South Ossetia | Russia–Georgia–South Ossetia | Russia |
| 1994 | Georgia | UN | UN |
| 1994 | Georgia/Abkhazia | CIS | Russia |
| 1996 | Bosnia | UN | NATO |
| 1999 | Kosovo | UN (civilian) | UN |
| 1999 | Kosovo | UN (military) | NATO |
| 1999 | Democratic Rep. of the Congo | UN | UN |
| 1999 | Sierra Leone | UN | UN |
| 2000 | Sierra Leone | UK–Sierra Leone | UK |
| 2001 | Burundi | South Africa–Burundi | South Africa |
| 2002 | Macedonia | NATO | NATO |
| 2002 | East Timor | UN | UN |
| 2002 | Central Africa Republic | CEMAC | CEMAC |
| 2002 | Côte d'Ivoire | France | France |
| 2003 | Liberia | UN | UN |
| 2003 | Macedonia | EU | EU |

→

case and not treated as an intrastate war; it collapsed following a US-led invasion in 2001, which was followed by UN/NATO involvement after 2002–3 but with primary control exercised by the US.

One final option, which tends not to receive much consideration, is the outright separation of the warring groups as recommended by partition theorists. The general rejection of this option is due primarily to the concerns about stability noted above. In addition, empirical studies of the partition thesis have found that partition, on the rare occasions it has occurred (as with the partition of India and Pakistan in 1947, or the independence of Kosovo in 2008), has not always resulted in more peace and stability between the warring groups (Sambanis, 2000; Kuperman, 2004; Sambanis and Schulhofer-Wuhl, 2009). Some argue further that ethnic identities are not permanent but can be deliberately changed or combined by religious conversion and/or intermarriage between ethnic groups. In this light the partition solution may be inappropriate and even excessive; at any rate, it is not usually a viable option for the international

| → | | | |
|---|---|---|---|
| 2003 | Democratic Rep. of Congo | UN | EU/France |
| 2003 | Burundi | AU | AU |
| 2003 | Liberia | ECOWAS | ECOWAS |
| 2003 | Côte d'Ivoire | UN–ECOWAS | ECOWAS |
| 2003 | Solomon Islands | Australia–Solomon Islands | Australia |
| 2004 | Côte d'Ivoire | UN | UN |
| 2004 | Darfur, Sudan | AU | AU |
| 2004 | Haiti | UN | UN |
| 2004 | Bosnia | UN | EU |
| 2004 | Burundi | UN | UN |
| 2008 | Chad | UN | EU |
| 2010 | Democratic Rep. of Congo | UN | UN |
| 2011 | Darfur, Sudan | UN | UN |
| 2011 | Libya | UN | Coalition (led by France, UK, US, and NATO forces) |
| 2012 | Syria | UN | UN (suspended) |
| 2013 | Mali | UN | UN |
| 2014 | Central African Republic | UN | UN/EU |

*Source:* Bellamy and Williams (2005), updated by the author.

community in most cases of intrastate war, and the ongoing difficulties involved in creating a Palestinian state provide additional evidence of the wide gap between the theory and practice of permanent partition. It is also important to keep in mind the issues of post-conflict justice and reconciliation, which can rekindle an intrastate war if not handled correctly. Although this issue is generally under the direct jurisdiction of the state(s) involved, the ICC was created in 1998 specifically to deal with such problems if those states are unwilling or unable to prosecute those accused of crimes against humanity, genocide or war crimes. The ICC entered into effect in 2002 and currently has 124 state parties to it despite the refusal of certain states (such as China, India, Israel and the US) to join it. However, although the ICC is a major symbolic effort regarding international justice, it has managed to investigate only eight weak states (Central African Republic, Côte d'Ivoire, Darfur/Sudan, the DRC, Kenya, Libya, Mali and Northern Uganda) and indict only 39 people despite complaints about crimes in 139 states.

> ## Box 5.1    Humanitarian military intervention in Kosovo

*Humanitarian crises often invite calls for firm action, yet the use of military force may do more harm than good.*

One ongoing legacy of post-Cold War politics in the Balkans involves the unusual status of Kosovo, a disputed province of the former Yugloslav republic (now state) of Serbia. Populated primarily by ethnic Albanians, Kosovo launched a bid for independence from Serbia in the mid-1990s, which involved the use of attacks against Serb police forces by militants, such as the Kosovo Liberation Army (KLA). Serbia fought back, and the violence escalated with claims of atrocities, including ethnic cleansing and terrorism, on both sides. By 1999 Kosovo was the largest humanitarian crisis in Europe since WWII, with 250,000 people displaced from their homes. As a US-led NATO military campaign had managed to halt earlier ethnic violence over Bosnia–Herzegovina, many observers called for similar action in Kosovo. However, Serbs opposed such outside intervention as they feared it might embolden Kosovo's bid for independence even more – which is

→

## The politics of policy effectiveness

As the empirical record clearly demonstrates, in any given year since WWII there are numerous ongoing intrastate wars that afford opportunities for the international community to help stem the violence. Yet the record also

$\rightarrow$
exactly what happened. In this way, outside support created a kind of moral hazard situation, by increasing a risk (KLA rebellion) that might not have escalated otherwise (Kuperman, 2008).

Serbian President Slobodan Milošević refused to accede to NATO's initial demands for a settlement to the conflict, which included the deployment of NATO forces in Serbia itself. In response, the US and NATO launched a 78-day bombing campaign against Serb targets in Kosovo and Serbia. This action, however, was extremely controversial because the bombing – which applied mixed or dual-use targeting – effectively killed many Serbian civilians to protect ethnic Albanian civilians. NATO forces even mistakenly attacked an Albanian refugee convoy (believing it to be a Serbian military one), killing around 50 people, and mistakenly bombed several other targets, including the Chinese embassy in Belgrade. The war also exposed major rifts among NATO allies (Martin and Brawley, 2001). Although some analysts believe the air campaign alone forced Milošević to back down, others argue that NATO was preparing a credible ground campaign if bombing failed (Byman and Waxman, 2000; Posen, 2000; Stigler, 2002–3; Gentry, 2006); Milošević may also have been losing support within Serbia (Lake, 2009). A settlement was reached by mid-1999, yet although Milošević 'won' in the sense that NATO troops were not based in Serbia, the intervention ultimately led to a temporary UN trusteeship over Kosovo (1999–2008). As Serbia had feared, this precipitated Kosovo's 'official' bid for independence in February 2008, a move that divided the UNSC and is still unrecognized by 85 UN member states.

Thanks to this legacy, today Kosovo is still a fragile quasi-state subject to the authority of outside parties. The EU for example runs its largest 'rule of law' mission (EULEX Kosovo) in the region to help reform state institutions, while NATO maintains a residual force (KFOR) of nearly 5,000 troops to preserve the peace between Kosovo and Serbia – which still views Kosovo as a breakaway province. With just 1.8 million citizens and a weak economy, the area is also known as a major hub of organized crime thanks to its instability. Thus, Kosovo has been a kind of international protectorate for nearly two decades, and the case led to lingering debates over the wisdom, and legality, of both the bombing campaign and its effects on the way the province pursued independence (Roberts, 1999; Daalder and O'Hanlon, 2000; Kay, 2004). In other words, what is the ultimate goal of 'humanitarian' military intervention (i.e. to save lives or punish aggressors) and what happens if such an intervention ultimately rewards a violent separatist movement, such as the KLA, with its own independent state?

demonstrates that, until fairly recently, the international community was generally content to take a relatively passive role unless a specific conflict invited the interference by some outside stakeholder, and often for reasons only marginally related to *international* security. Fortunately this situation seems to be changing for the better, as virtually all major players that compose the international community now agree that the passive 'wait and see' approach regarding weak states and internal war is no longer tenable in light of many of the contemporary security problems covered in this volume. Thus, compared to the situation just a decade ago we now see a greater willingness for various actors to become more involved in these conflicts, even to the extent of organizing their own military and state-building operations.

However, once involvement is decided, what factors then determine compliance by outside and inside parties? Fortunately, in cases where outside actors do commit themselves to a multilateral peace operation or a similar intervention, they usually tend to follow through to complete the mission. It is worth keeping in mind, too, that compliance with implementation also involves the attitude of the warring parties on the ground; the evidence is quite clear that if all of the warring parties invite or agree to some outside help, as with accepting a formal peacekeeping mission, the odds of implementation are that much greater. In some cases this initial commitment can require foreign actors to send resources for years or even decades, as in the UN peacekeeping mission in Cyprus – in place since 1964. The effectiveness of foreign peacekeeping operations in reducing the violence is also enhanced when military forces are emphasized over police or civilian observers, according to one major study (Hultman, Kathman and Shannon, 2014).

In addition, as most interventions are devoted to keeping the state intact rather allowing it to fragment, the dominant tendency for modern interventions is to introduce some type of pluralist political system into the state, whereby various organized political actors within the state have a reasonable chance of pursuing their interests against each other. Although this can be seen as a form of mission creep or task expansion in the sense that a simple or short-term peacekeeping mission can expand into a complicated and long-term state-building operation, many analysts now generally recognize that peacebuilding and state-building are essentially the same process, particularly where weak or failed states are involved (which is often the case). Thus, in attempting to reform the state to avoid future intrastate wars, outside parties must often make a difficult choice between a more democratic system, which invites participation but might also be less stable, and a more authoritarian system, which discourages participation but might be able to keep the state at peace. This trade-off is in fact one of the most difficult problems in maintaining the cohesion of an intervening coalition, and is especially problematic in unstable Muslim states (such as Iraq and Afghanistan), where elections can easily bring to power more Islamist regimes who tap into the anti-Western sentiments among their populations.

Taking a closer look at the three general ways to assess the success of various policy options, it is possible to apply the total victory standard to some cases, which means that a particular intrastate war has been stopped with a peace agreement or similar pact among the warring parties (Lick-lider, 1993). As noted, in most cases where an intrastate war ends (about 80 per cent of the cases between 1940 and 1990), it is through a total victory for one side or the other. Half of the time the government won, and half of the time the rebels prevailed, although a rebel victory seems to be less likely in identity-based intrastate wars fought along ethnic lines than ideological ones (Gent, 2008). In these cases, therefore, a hands-off policy on the part of the international community resulted in a war ending on its own (although it might have been extremely destructive during its course). However, over 100 other intrastate wars were still ongoing during roughly the same period, so for these stalemate cases the outlook looks very grim indeed unless an outside party intervenes.

This point then begs the question: do such interventions, which tend to take place in the more difficult cases (that is, stalemates; see Gent, 2008), actually create peace? Before answering this question, it is worth bearing in mind that the odds of success are often working against the peace-keepers, which is partly why such missions are so difficult to organize in the first place. In one of the more sophisticated analyses of this question, which attempts to take into consideration the degree of difficulty involved in 115 specific peacekeeping missions analysed, Fortna (2004) concluded that international intervention does help make peace more likely to last, and to last longer, and therefore is worth the effort as a means of preventing a future intrastate war. However, the degree of success (that is, how long the peace lasts and whether a stable state is created) is always highly contingent on the factors noted above regarding the resources and will of the peacekeepers, as well as the relationship between democratic participation and a credible solution to the domestic insecurity dilemma – which may be at odds with each other, especially when either the national government and/or the separatists are divided rather than united when they attempt to negotiate (Cunningham, 2011).

Taking a historical trends view of this problem, the bad news is that weak states in general and intrastate conflicts in particular show no dramatic signs of becoming less prevalent. It seems that weak states will be with us for quite some time and will pose a constant challenge to international security as defined by the major problems in this volume. It also seems that stopping some intrastate wars may be beyond the capacity of the international community, as seems to be the case in Syria. However, the good news is that since most major actors now agree on the general problem of failed or weak states, they are much more willing to intervene in such states than just a few years ago. They are also more willing to take proactive or preventative measures to deal with such problems, although it may be quite some time for evidence regarding the performance of this strategy to become apparent. The increased prominence of regional approaches to this problem, as through regional IOs or 'coalitions of the willing', often operating under UN auspices, is especially encouraging, although there certainly have been cases (such as Liberia from 1990 to 1996) where a regional effort simply was not forceful enough to create a long-term peace (Howe, 1996–7). These efforts are successful mainly when the state in question recognizes that it has a problem and invites outside help; lacking such an invitation, an outside intervention risks becoming a major disaster, even when launched for 'humanitarian' rather than 'peace-keeping' objectives, as with the 1993 US/UN intervention in Somalia.

More generally, other scholars have noted that America's success at state-building in post-war Germany and Japan must be balanced against its failures since the late nineteenth century (Brownlee, 2007); one comprehensive study calculated a 26 per cent success rate for US-led reconstruction efforts since the late nineteenth century (Pei, 2003). In addition, outsiders who become involved in an intrastate conflict, whether invited or not, must also recognize that there is no such thing as a completely neutral intervention; any assistance usually helps one party against another, either to keep the state whole or to break it up. Also, efforts by outsiders, whether they support or oppose the national government, can actually backfire and strengthen the support of hardliners within various groups as they attempt to create their own domestic order (Snyder and Ballentine, 1996; Coyne, 2006). For example, as Yugoslavia started to break up in the early 1990s, its prime minister (Milan Panić) was facing a presidential election against hardliner Slobodan Milošević. Panić ran on a platform of democratization, economic reform, and ending the war in Bosnia – all of which would help lift UN sanctions. Milošević accused him of pandering to foreign interests and Panic´ lost with only 34 per cent of the vote (Gagnon Jr., 1994–5; Kaufmann, 1996).

Finally, a comparative standards approach to the problems of intrastate conflict would vary widely depending on the region in question. One major example on the positive side of the ledger is the failure of most Central/East European states to descend into interstate/intrastate war and ethnic conflict after 1990. In that case it seems the prospect of NATO and EU membership – which were conditioned on democratic stability and a resolution of border/ethnic problems – had a far more pacifying effect on Europe in general and on potential EU member states (as well as on a reunified Germany after 1990) in particular than expected by some realists (Mearsheimer, 1990; Glaser, 1993; Larrabee, 1993; Waltz, 1993; Art, 1996), although others had suggested such a possibility (Snyder, 1990; Van Evera, 1990–1). This positive impact of institutional membership on the resolution of conflicts has been especially important in the cases of Hungary and Romania, who managed to solve their ethnic/border problems peacefully since the end of the Cold War (Linden, 2000), while the prospect of European integration has not completely solved the problem of lingering tensions across the Balkans.

In other regions, particularly Africa and Asia, the problem of intrastate war stubbornly persists as long as states reserve the right to solve their own domestic problems as they see fit. Until (or if) the preventative measures noted above start to take effect, in the more short term we must hope that national governments will recognize as quickly as possible when they face a serious rebellion and invite outside assistance earlier rather than wait for a clear stalemate to develop between the warring parties, by which time thousands of innocent lives are likely to have been lost. This willingness, in turn, depends in large part upon the credibility and power – or overall reputation – of potential foreign assistance providers, which is why the UN, the EU, the US and other major players must think very carefully about how their decisions regarding involvement (or not) are interpreted in the target states. This will be an especially difficult task for the US in light of its previous reputation as a state-builder and its recent attacks in Afghanistan and Iraq (not to mention its controversial use of drone strikes), and may provide an opening for other stakeholders to play a greater role, which already seems to be happening on the part of the AU, ECOWAS and the EU.

## Summary

After decades of focusing on the Cold War superpower rivalry, the international community seems to be waking up to the security threats posed by weak states and intrastate conflicts. Although the Cold War had the *potential* to destroy the lives of millions (if not billions) of people if it ever turned into a 'hot war', intrastate wars have in fact produced such a terrible outcome, with over 20 million dead and countless millions wounded since the end of WWII. As tragic as that is, it is by no means clear that interventions by various types of outside actors would have ceased or reduced the violence in specific cases. It is clear, however, that intrastate wars and weak/failed states are directly and indirectly related to many of the security problems covered in this volume, as well as many other problems involving global governance. And although there is now widespread recognition of this fact among most security scholars and policy-makers, the international community as a whole still finds it difficult to determine whether to act in specific cases. The choice to act, as well as the success of that action, depends on a complex mix of attributes involving the nature of the intrastate conflict, the nature of the actor or coalition that hopes to stop it and whether the intervention is biased towards the government or rebel forces.

In another sense the problem is essentially one of free-riding: major powers may collectively recognize the dangers of a Somalia or Bosnia or Rwanda, yet will refrain from taking decisive action in the hopes that some other actor will take the risks of attempting to stem the violence. For example, the ongoing civil conflict in Darfur (western Sudan) has resulted in over 300,000 deaths since 2003, yet the international community has failed to mount a successful operation to stop the violence, some of which amounts to genocide according to the US – but not the UN or the AU. Civil war in Syria has also resulted in an estimated 400,000 dead since 2011, yet no sustained peacekeeping effort has been launched. And when foreign stakeholders do decide to take action, the reasons are frequently based on factors or interests that may have little to do with the actual international security threat posed by a weak or failing state. Western powers typically invoke the goals of democratization and human rights in justifying interventions, yet they will also support despots and authoritarian regimes to serve their interests (Gardner, 2009).

This policy in turn has major implications not just for intrastate conflicts but also for terrorism, crime and other international security problems. However, this fact alone does not mean that such interventions will fail, only that the stakeholders who undertake a more self-interested intervention must then work very hard to bolster the legitimacy and credibility of their efforts in three basic ways: by increasing the multilateral contributions to their efforts, by securing the endorsement of the UN and/or other legitimate IOs and by negotiating an invitation on the part of the warring parties to help solve their problem. On the positive side, more actors than ever before are willing to take a chance on helping weak or failing states early in the hopes of heading off problems later. This increased willingness to intervene to stop violence at the source in some cases also overlaps with another appealing option concerning how to manage the threat of war: controlling weapons proliferation, the topic of Chapter 6.

## Further reading

Michael J. Boyle (2014). *Violence After War: Explaining Instability in Post-Conflict States*. Baltimore: Johns Hopkins University Press.
Michael Brown, Owen R. Coté Jr., Sean M. Lynn-Jones and Steven E. Miller (eds.) (2001). *Nationalism and Ethnic Conflict*. Cambridge: MIT Press.
Jean-Marie Guéhenno (2015). *The Fog of Peace: A Memoir of International Peacekeeping in the 21st Century*. Washington, DC: Brookings Institution Press.
Ted Robert Gurr and B. Harff (2002). *Ethnic Conflict in World Politics*. Boulder: Westview.
Donald L. Horowitz (1985). *Ethnic Groups in Conflict*. Berkeley: University of California Press.

Roy Licklider (ed.) (1993). *Stopping the Killing: How Civil Wars End*. New York: New York University Press.

James B. Rule (1988). *Theories of Civil Violence*. Berkeley: University of California Press.

Donald M. Snow (1996). *Uncivil Wars: International Security and the New Internal Conflicts*. Boulder: Lynne Rienner.

Jack Snyder (2001). *From Voting to Violence: Democratization and Nationalist Conflict*. New York: W.W. Norton.

# Chapter 6

# Weapons Proliferation

The analysis of weapons proliferation as a distinct international security problem can be viewed as an adjunct to our discussion of military conflict. The focus here, however, is somewhat narrower, as we are concerned primarily with the properties and diffusion patterns of weapons themselves rather than with their use during a conflict. Although the central concern of this chapter is with Cold War and post-Cold War developments, we should keep in mind that arms control is very much a late nineteenth/early twentieth-century phenomenon that predates the advent of nuclear weapons. Measures introduced in the pre-WWI era – which involved both conventional weapons (CW) and WMD – still influence modern debates over weapons proliferation, and concepts from this period have been revived, reinterpreted or expanded in light of recent technological developments.

For both CW and WMD, the question of controlling proliferation can be divided further into debates about 'vertical' versus 'horizontal' proliferation. *Vertical proliferation* describes the growth in numbers of certain weapons and related advancements in weapons technologies that might pose a problem for international security. *Horizontal proliferation* refers to an expansion in the number of actors who possess such weapons. Finally, a third dimension to the debate involves the question of state versus non-state actors. While states are typically the 'official' stakeholders authorized to develop and deploy certain weapons, non-state actors such as firms and terrorists may also play leading roles as both sources of new weapons technologies and as international threats if they acquire certain weapons. A related general point is that while weapons proliferation is typically defined as a military-strategic issue, the global arms trade is also a major source of financial revenue, for both industrialized states and LDCs, which introduces some important economic considerations into the analysis.

## Weapons proliferation and international security

After the experience of two world wars and the Cold War, there is today a fairly high degree of consensual knowledge regarding certain aspects of weapons proliferation; such knowledge keeps this problem very high on the international security agenda. In the most general sense, there is a wide appreciation of the rapid pace of technological change, and of the negative consequences of certain technologies as defining features of the twentieth century. When applied to weapons development, such advances – especially when they occur during a major war – often outpace the construction of global norms or rules intended to govern their use or diffusion.

Leaving aside for the moment the question of intentional use, there is more consensual knowledge regarding the effects of weapons systems based on test data, battlefield experience and computer simulations. A sad but undeniable lesson of twentieth-century warfare is that human beings from both democratic and authoritarian states have not just the ability but also the sheer will to engage in mass destruction, using both WMD and CW. Weapons that facilitate such mass destruction do exist in a variety of forms, are possessed by a variety of states, are desired by other states and non-state actors and cannot be 'uninvented'; these material and historical facts help explain why various disarmament campaigns or efforts to out-law war can be very difficult to implement at the international level. Even if just one actor, no matter how well-intentioned, possesses a new type of 'ultimate weapon', then other actors will feel themselves at risk – the security dilemma at work once again. However, decades of more specific arms control measures also show that deliberate, though modest, efforts can be taken to reduce our reliance on WMD in particular, which could have a corresponding impact on patterns of proliferation. Obviously not all stakeholders will agree to such measures; hence we also need some way of creating a normative consensus among actors who would prefer to deploy or even use such weapons in the service of their own interests.

## Destructive scale

Concerns about weapons development since the Industrial Revolution have inspired numerous studies regarding the destructive potential of mecha-nized, widescale, total war. The Hague conventions of 1899 and 1907 were inspired in part by fears about excessively destructive new weapons, and norms devised under these pacts still inform current debates on this issue. As a result of continued testing and refinement, with WMD in par-ticular we find wide variation in terms of their destructive potential, their costs, their availability, their lethality, their susceptibility to countermeas-ures, and other factors, all of which influence their utility and desirability as weapons of war. They can also involve both 'high-tech' devices (high-yield nuclear weapons delivered by missiles) and 'low-tech' devices (chem-ical weapons made from chlorine or other widely available substances, or 'dirty bombs' using basic explosives laced with radioactive substances). Nuclear weapons naturally receive the most attention as a modern inter-national security problem. One type involves *fission* weapons, which use a chemical explosive to split a fissile material (usually U-235 or plutonium) and create a nuclear explosion. Weapons of this type – the original 'atomic bombs' – were dropped by the US on Hiroshima and Nagasaki in Japan in 1945. Today bombs of this size are considered low-yield (or 'tactical' or 'battlefield') weapons, with the explosiveness equivalent to 20–50 kilotons (kt) of the high explosive trinitrotoluene (TNT). The US expected to enjoy a monopoly with this weapon for at least ten years, yet the Soviet Union managed to explode its first atomic bomb in 1949 thanks to a combination of espionage and experimentation. Two further developments raised the stakes even higher: the advent of *fusion* weapons (that is, thermonuclear or hydrogen bombs) and the advent of intercontinental ballistic missiles (ICBMs) in 1959; this combination of a higher-yield bomb combined with a delivery system that can range as far as several thousand miles is often referred to as a 'strategic' nuclear weapon. The yield of thermonuclear weapons can range from 1–100 *million* tons (megatons, or mt) equivalent of TNT; the resulting explosion can easily destroy an entire city. On 31 October 1952 the US detonated its first hydrogen bomb, which naturally led the Soviets to develop their own. Less than a decade later, on 30 October 1961, the Soviet Union managed to detonate the largest man-made explosion in history: about 53mt. By the early 1960s, then, both super-powers possessed such weapons in enough quantities to ensure they could retaliate after a first strike – resulting in the prospect of MAD – and the so-called 'nuclear revolution' was complete (Jervis, 1990). There have also been more than 2,000 nuclear tests since 1945, more than half of which were conducted by the US. The introduction in the 1970s of multiple independently targetable re-entry vehicles (MIRVs), which allow for up to a dozen or more nuclear bombs to be placed on a single missile, raised the stakes even higher. Each nuclear bomb, or 'warhead', could then be sent to a different target to maximize the missile's destructive power, and also to foil any anti-missile defences in the target state.

    The direct effects resulting from an attack by weapons of this type would be deaths in the range of thousands or millions depending on the target (population density, building solidity and so on), the size/type of the weapon and the conditions of its delivery (weather, altitude at detonation, terrain and so on). A 'dirty bomb' obviously would not be as severe but could serve as an effective mass terror weapon once victims realized they had been exposed to radiation. Explosions resulting from fission/fusion weapons also create extreme effects in terms of blast pressure, thermal radiation and residual radiation that can last for decades. Most initial deaths are caused by blast pressure and heat exceeding the temperature on the sun's surface (greater than 6,000°C or 11,000°F); a 1mt bomb would kill or seriously wound about 50 per cent of the people located within five miles of the blast. Nuclear explosions also create electromagnetic pulses (also known as the 'Compton effect') capable of knocking out electrical devices many hundreds of miles away from the actual detonation site. Finally, nuclear bombs can be designed to intensify their radiation effects rather than their blast/heat effects (so-called 'enhanced radiation weapons' or 'neutron bombs'), which damage 'soft' targets like humans and animals but could leave 'hard' targets like buildings and bridges intact.

Chemical and biological weapons are obviously less destructive than nuclear weapons to buildings and other structures but can be nearly as deadly. An estimated 200,000 tons of chemical weapons were used in WWI, causing extraordinary suffering and death on the part of thousands of combatants (Prentiss, 1937). In the interwar period, poison gas was used by several powers despite the Hague prohibitions: the Spanish in Morocco, the Italians in Ethiopia, the Soviet Union against its own people and the Japanese in China (and considered by the British in Mesopotamia). While the major powers avoided the use of biological/chemical weapons against each other during WWII, owing mainly to fears of retaliation, the Germans used poison gas against millions of their Holocaust victims during that conflict, while the use of 'strategic bombing', 'fire-bombing' and short-range ballistic missiles (such as Germany's V-2) showed that high-explosive CW could be even more effective at mass destruction than chemicals or germs, as seen with the attacks against Coventry, London, Hamburg, Nuremburg, Dresden, Tokyo and elsewhere.

As Table 6.1 summarizes, modern chemical agents take a wide variety of forms, such as nerve agents, blistering agents, asphyxiating/choking agents and toxic agents (ricin) which can either kill or incapacitate. The sarin nerve agent attacks made by the Aum Shinrikyo ('Supreme Truth') religious cult in a Tokyo subway in 1995 killed 12 people and injured about 6,000 others, causing widespread panic. Biological weapons are equally varied and might include anthrax, brucellosis, cholera, bubonic plague, the Marburg virus, smallpox, tularaemia, typhus, yellow fever and many other agents, either uniquely or in combination. Not all of these biological agents have been deployed as weapons, however. Even so, a smallpox pandemic might result in up to 30 per cent fatalities of any (unvaccinated) population that is directly attacked. The Japanese deployed plague-infected fleas in China in 1940, while the 2001 anthrax attacks in the US, which used the postal service as a delivery system, killed five people, infected several others and practically shut down the US Congress and much of Washington for several days (Miller et al., 2002; Guillemin, 2005). The leading suspect in these attacks, an American biodefence researcher, killed himself in 2008, so this case might never be solved conclusively, although it did have an impact on America's general public health/pandemic preparedness (see Chapter 12). Most recently, two chemical weapon attacks using sarin took place in Syria in August 2013; although most evidence pointed to the Syrian military as the perpetrators after a UN investigation, the incident is still

**Table 6.1  Major chemical/biological weapons**

| Type | Exposure | Symptoms | Protection |
|---|---|---|---|
| Nerve agents (sarin, tabun, soman, VX) | Inhalation, skin/eye contact | Nasal discharge, wheezing, chest convulsions, respiratory failure, twitching, coma | Injection of atropine antidote |
| Blistering agents (mustard, lewisite, phosgene) | Inhalation, skin contact | Skin burns, throat pain, coughing, internal organ damage, conjunctivitis | Protective mask/clothing, decontamination |
| Asphyxiating/choking agents (chlorine, hydrogen cyanide) | Inhalation | Throat pain, coughing, asphyxiation | Protective mask/clothing, decontamination |
| Ricin (chemical/biological agent) | Inhalation, ingestion | Inhaled: fever, chest tightening, cough, nausea / Ingestion: vomiting, abdominal cramps, severe diarrhoea | No vaccine or antitoxin available |
| Anthrax (biological agent) | Inhalation, ingestion, skin contact | Inhalation: flu-like symptoms / Ingestion: symptoms like food poisoning / Skin contact: lesions | Vaccine, antibiotics |
| Botulinum (biological agent) | Skin wounds, ingestion | Blurred/double vision, nausea, paralysis, respiratory failure, vomiting | Antitoxin injection |
| Bubonic plague (biological agent) | Aerosol inhalation, flea bites | Chills, fever, cramps, seizures, swollen glands | Antibiotics |

disputed. This attack killed at least several hundred people, and Syria's government agreed to turn over its remaining chemical weapons under a deal brokered by the US and Russia.

## Geographic and temporal scope

Modern delivery systems for WMD make them truly global threats. They can be delivered across the planet via strategic bombers and missiles launched from air, land or sea. Smaller 'suitcase' nuclear bombs have been developed for clandestine transport to their targets. The nature of biological weapons greatly adds to the geographic scope of destruction; viruses and bacteria do not respect borders and can be carried via humans and animals, even without their awareness in some cases. The temporal scope of damage resulting from nuclear explosions is especially long; debris or other materials can be irradiated by the nuclear blast and distributed as nuclear fallout throughout the atmosphere long after the explosion, which can damage crops, water supplies and animals. Some biological weapons, such as anthrax spores, can similarly lie dormant and even undetected for years until they infect a victim. Beyond these technical factors, the scope of potential destruction is expanded further by the number of states possessing such capabilities, and this is where the major efforts regarding weapons proliferation tend to be focused.

Possession of weapons is only part of the problem, however. Another concern involves patterns of arms sales, and here the situation is equally troubling. As noted in Chapter 2, increasing economic globalization also means increasing competition among arms suppliers, which now include the major powers and various new suppliers: Brazil, Israel, North Korea, Singapore, South Africa, South Korea and Taiwan. All P5 states of the UNSC, as well as several OECD member states, are major arms exporters, which creates a clear conflict of interest on their part as both suppliers and regulators of the global arms trade. Further, transfer patterns have shifted from a transatlantic orientation towards a more North–South axis, where developing countries enter into partnerships with major arms producers. Even more troubling from an international security perspective is that LDCs are establishing their own indigenous arms industries, particularly for small arms and light weapons, and then exporting their weapons to other LDCs (Parker, 1999). This activity will have obvious implications for attempts to control conflicts among and within these states, and could also add to lower-intensity problems such as terrorism and crime. It is also increasingly difficult to police arms transfers from new state suppliers to the developing world (Bitzinger, 1992; also see the special issue of *Contemporary Security Policy*, 29/1, 2008).

## Likelihood

At this point consensual knowledge about the likelihood of damage resulting from weapons proliferation becomes far more problematic. We know
what might happen as a result of a nuclear explosion, for example, but
what states can be trusted with such destructive power? And what factors
determine whether states (or other actors) will not only deploy but actually use WMD? Nuclear weapons in particular have been used in wartime
by only one state: the US against Japan. Since then what we think we
know about these weapons largely results from unilateral weapons testing, computer simulations and theoretical models. And, thankfully, the
international community has never experienced an actual nuclear war;
such a war might also be the last thing we experience. These facts have led
to a great deal of speculation, often political and hypothetical rather than
empirical in nature, regarding the likelihood of the threat, as opposed to
the scale of destruction if the threat materializes. In other words, we need
to know something about intent in addition to mere capabilities, and consensual knowledge about the intentions of a specific actor is often lacking
at the international level.

One obvious way to avoid this problem is simply to focus on the number or types of weapons thought to exist (vertical proliferation) and the
states (or other actors) that possess them (horizontal proliferation) as
proxies for measuring the likelihood of the threat. Since so many WMD
were (and still are) in the possession of just two states, measures taken
by those states alone to control their vertical proliferation could have a
dramatic impact on the overall levels of destructive power threatening the
planet. Since the end of the Cold War, however, increasing attention has
been paid to the problem of horizontal proliferation among both states
and non-state actors. For WMD, the current 'scorecard' regarding various
state proliferators is summarized in Table 6.2.

For example, North Korea exploded a Hiroshima-sized (10–20kt)
nuclear weapon in May 2009, much greater than its 1kt test in 2006. It
also test-fired six short-range missiles at that time, and may have an effective long-range (4,100 miles) missile capability soon, which could reach
Alaska. Pyongyang also claimed it had placed a peaceful communications
satellite in orbit. Similarly, Iran is now thought to be capable of producing
a nuclear weapon within six months of taking a decision to do so, according to a UN report of June 2009, and has tested missile technology that
could be used to deliver such weapons (although its nuclear programme
is on hold). As noted in Chapter 4, if such states are viewed as especially
aggressive – or 'rogue' – then the international community may develop a
special interest in them, as has been the case with North Korea and Iran.

In the past two decades we also have seen the emergence of 'proliferation rings' and related activities involving the illegal diffusion of WMD

**Table 6.2**  ***States with known or suspected* WMD *capabilities (post-Cold War)***

| | Nuclear weapons (warheads) | Chemical weapons | Biological weapons |
|---|---|---|---|
| Albania | | 16 tons; destroyed in 2007 under the rules of the CWC | |
| China | 260 | Probable | Probable |
| Egypt | | Probable | |
| France | 300 | Probable | Probable; possesses smallpox virus |
| India | 110–20 | Possesses unknown quantities of various agents | |
| Iran | Near capable | Probable; has acceded to CWC but made no declarations of stockpiles | Possible |
| Israel | 100–200 | Probable | Probable |
| Libya | | Possesses unknown quantities of various agents; declared 23 tons of mustard gas in 2004 after acceding to the CWC | |
| Myanmar | | Probable | Possible |
| North Korea | Less than 10 | Possesses unknown quantities of various agents | Probable |
| Pakistan | 120–30 | Probable | Possible |
| Russia | 4,700 | Declared stockpiles of 40,000 tons of various agents; very small portion destroyed since acceding to CWC | Possesses unknown quantities of various agents (including smallpox) |
| Serbia | | Probable | |
| South Africa | | Claims to have destroyed stockpiles in early 1990s | Claims to have destroyed stockpiles in early 1990s |
| Sudan | | Possible | Possible |
| Syria | | Possesses unknown quantities of various agents | Possible |
| Taiwan | | Possible | Possible |
| United Kingdom | 215 | Possesses unknown quantities of various agents | Possesses unknown quantities of various agents |
| United States | 4,500 | Declared 31,500 tons of various agents in 1997; claims to have destroyed 45 per cent of this stockpile under CWC | Possesses unknown quantities of various agents (including smallpox) |
| Vietnam | | Probable | |

*Note:* Warhead numbers include both tactical and strategic nuclear weapons, and both 'operational' and 'reserve' weapons.

*Source:* Federation of American Scientists, Status of World Nuclear Forces (2014).

technologies, sometimes with the collusion of organized criminal gangs (Chestnut, 2007; Langewiesche, 2007). In 1997 former Russian national security advisor Aleksander Lebed claimed his military had lost 100 'suitcase' bombs, each with a yield of 10kt. In 1998 an al-Qaeda agent, Mamdough Mamud, was arrested for attempting to buy enriched uranium in Europe. In 2004 analysts began investigating proliferation rings following the revelation that Pakistani scientist A. Q. Khan might have provided nuclear technology and bomb designs to North Korea, Iraq, Iran, Libya and Syria. These activities, plus the related problem of securing former Soviet (now Russian) nuclear facilities, materials and even scientists (Bukharin, 1997), created major problems for those involved in arms control and further intensified the post-Cold War focus on horizontal, rather than vertical, proliferation (Braun and Chyba, 2004; Clary, 2004; Albright and Hinderstein, 2005; Allison, 2006). However, even where analysts agree on patterns of either vertical or horizontal proliferation, global consensus often breaks down regarding the intentions of certain new proliferators. While most people might agree on the need to prevent terrorists from acquiring WMD, what about other states that claim a legitimate right to secure themselves with such technologies, as the P5 of the UNSC do? This problem – analysing intentions and rights in addition to capabilities in terms of threat definition – is one of the most difficult aspects of a political analysis of proliferation (Sagan and Waltz, 2003).

## Recovery

Finally, WMD in particular involve long-term, irreversible and potentially catastrophic effects that could threaten the entire planet even if used in a limited capacity. Nuclear weapons create gamma rays and other forms of residual radiation that can cause cancer in victims and their offspring; similar long-term and possibly irreversible damage would be made to plants, animals, food and water supplies, the atmosphere and so on. The term 'nuclear winter' has been suggested to describe the devastating effects of a nuclear exchange, involving severe cold and reduced sunlight for months or years. The capacity of radiation-type weapons to cause sterility or injure future generations of children is an especially egregious characteristic. Major accidents at nuclear power plants provide additional evidence of the kinds of long-term damage that can result from contamination. For example, the worst such accident in history, at the Chernobyl nuclear power plant in Ukraine in 1986 (part of the USSR at the time), resulted in 31 deaths, extensive pollution in Lake Baikal and in various Siberian rivers, the evacuation of 130,000 people, hundreds of hospitalizations, clean-up costs of $20 billion and counting and radioactive contamination spread around the globe.

Even if a nuclear explosion does not cause cancer in a victim, exposure to radiation can cause painful burns and other radiation illnesses, as well as damage the body's overall capacity to heal itself. Chemical weapons can produce burns or blindness (among other long-term injuries) in victims that do not die immediately, while disfigurement or other disabilities related to all types of weapons can cause suffering long after the event, for both combatants and non-combatants, depending on the conditions under which the weapon was delivered. And both chemical and (especially) biological weapons can spread far beyond the primary targets where they are used depending on weather conditions and population movements. This degree of long-term and indirect or 'collateral' damage – beyond the immediate effects of WMD noted above – generates additional pressures for the maintenance of norms or so-called 'taboos' against the use of such weapons (Price, 1995; Tannenwald, 2005). Others, however, have questioned the actual strength of such taboos in some cases, such as chemical weapons (Dolan, 2013) and nuclear weapons (Press, Sagan and Valentino, 2013).

## Stakeholder factors

Before turning to specific efforts to manage such problems, we must first examine various attributes of the specific stakeholders involved in weapons proliferation.

### Principal stakeholders

As suggested above, states play the leading role in terms of developing, deploying and diffusing weapons around the globe. This is especially true regarding WMD, and nuclear weapons in particular, and America more than any other country has played a leading role in not just developing nuclear weapons but also working to inhibit their spread to other stakeholders (Gavin, 2015). However, even in the case of nuclear weapons we often find several competing stakeholders at work within the major states involved: heads of government, legislatures, cabinet ministries or bureaucracies and the military services. In addition to disputes within governments that may produce incoherent or contradictory policies, weapons proliferation involves important societal stakeholders as well, particularly defence firms that develop and sell such weapons to a range of buyers. Many weapons technologies also involve a complex 'dual-use' problem, meaning they have both civilian and military applications, and thus both civilian and military stakeholders. Allowing some applications while controlling or prohibiting others can be extremely difficult, even when the government of a particular state agrees on the proper balance between the civilian and military uses of a weapons-related technology.

A third key stakeholder, or set of stakeholders, involves what might be termed the 'global arms control community', consisting of scientists (such as the Pugwash Group and the Union of Concerned Scientists), IOs, NGOs, and even more specialized interest groups, such as the Campaign for Nuclear Disarmament and the International Campaign to Ban Anti-Personnel Landmines, that call for restrictions on, or total disarmament of, certain weapons (see the case study, Box 6.1). *The Bulletin of the Atomic Scientists*, for example, has published an ongoing 'doomsday clock' since 1947 to visualize how close the world is to nuclear disaster; at the time of writing (2016), the clock stands at three minutes to midnight (nuclear war) – the most dangerous setting since 1983 during the Cold War. A final set of stakeholders might be termed the 'new proliferators', which are primarily states and certain non-state actors (such as terrorist groups) that specifically attempt to develop or acquire certain weapons even in the face of controls established by other international stakeholders (Lavoy et al., 2000). These efforts, of course, largely inspire the current policy focus on horizontal, rather than vertical, proliferation.

## Interests and preferences

Although we might assume that most of the state-related stakeholders above share an interest in preventing a global catastrophe, and are more or less willing to place some restrictions or prohibitions on certain weapons, the political reality is far more complex. Regarding interests, one obvious problem is that some terrorist groups do seem willing to use, or threaten to use, WMD if they could acquire such technology. Suicide terrorism in particular takes on an entirely new dimension if one considers a suicide bomber equipped with a WMD rather than a mere conventional explosive, although there are other conceptual problems surrounding the designation of suicide terrorists (see Chapter 7). For other stakeholders, we might first consider their security interests as served by certain weapons, whether for deterrence and/or defence/warfighting. As already discussed in Chapters 4 and 5, these can vary quite widely and can be defined differently, or prioritized differently, by stakeholders between and within states. To the extent that the security interests of these stakeholders can be satisfied without resorting to vertical or horizontal weapons proliferation, through alliances or other security guarantees for example, then international security might be enhanced. More problematic, however, is the role of weapons in enhancing broader *political* objectives of certain stakeholders, such as the status or independence of individual bureaucracies, military services or even entire governments (Sagan, 1996–7). Security guarantees or similar incentives might not serve the political interests of new proliferators if status or reputation, at the international and/or domestic level, is a key consideration.

We must also consider the economic or technological interests at stake here, which primarily affect defence firms but also many other stakeholders in the military-industrial complex or iron triangle of defence/technology firms, military services and political officials, especially legislators with high defence spending in their districts. This type of public/private and political/economic collusion is especially pronounced in the arms industry; for example, American and British officials made major efforts as early as WWI to acquire weapons-related technologies from the defeated Germans and apply them in the service of both public and private interests, as in the chemical and aerospace industries (Kennedy, 2004); this process was repeated on an even larger scale by the major allied powers after WWII. In some cases, even democratic governments will go to the extent of temporarily nationalizing private firms to support national security goals. Scientists are no less immune to the temptations of government research grants for new technologies or large-scale weapons programmes, such as national missile defences, and can be persuaded to develop weapons that they may later regret. Economic interests may also be reflected in light of the high costs of starting and maintaining a credible WMD programme, particularly a nuclear one, which can be considerable when weapons delivery systems are also taken into consideration. Thankfully, most states seem to believe the economic and political costs outweigh the benefits, so they engage in self-restraint.

Finally, the question of preferences – assuming a fairly high degree of common interest in preventing a certain type of weapons proliferation – often hinges on the question of whether to use military force to discourage proliferation by a certain stakeholder. This issue is examined in more detail in the next section.

## The use of force

Following on from the discussion of stakeholder interests, views about the role of force in managing this problem can also vary widely. While many stakeholders might seriously consider the use of violence to deter or counteract the *actual or imminent use* of WMD, using force to prevent *proliferation alone* is quite another matter. Ever since the earliest attempts at arms control, some stakeholders have viewed arms control with great suspicion and think a resort to force is the only effective approach. Israel, the US and the UK in particular still argue the necessity of using force to stop the proliferation of WMD, while others – states, IOs, NGOs and other stakeholders – either reject the use of violence or view it only as a last resort after other measures, diplomatic and economic, have been exhausted. Stakeholders willing to resort to violence will therefore view arms control measures as a way to identify possible targets: states that either refuse to sign such agreements or that sign agreements then defect from them might then be singled out for some form of retaliation. Thus, even where we might find a great deal of consensus regarding the nature of the value–threat relationship, the appropriate response to the problem is where collective action breaks down, as with the case of the 2003 Iraq war. All multilateral arms control measures therefore must address the role of force and other sanctions in punishing defectors (or in forcing countries to sign agreements in the first place), as we shall see in the discussion of policy issues below.

## Public–private domains and appropriate levels of jurisdiction

The dual-use nature of many weapons technologies greatly complicates modern arms control efforts. For all types of modern WMD – nuclear, chemical and biological – there are often legitimate civilian applications and most advanced states have some degree of industrial infrastructure to turn a civilian industry into a military one. This transformation is most difficult for nuclear weapons, but even here some degree of technology transfer is possible and most recent nuclear proliferators acquired some aspects of their nuclear technology from existing suppliers. For chemical and biological WMD, the dual-use problem is even more acute owing to the wide availability of certain materials, a large technical knowledge base, a large number of private firms and a large consumer market for certain chemical and biological products or services. Arms control measures must take these factors into consideration if they are to be effective and legitimate. The role of private firms and consumers also varies across certain CW, not all of which, of course, are framed as proliferation problems. Some CW, such as firearms, have a very large civilian market base and therefore might be extremely difficult to police across borders, while others, such as tanks or artillery pieces, might be easier to control through a bilateral or multilateral arms agreement, such as the Conventional Forces in Europe Treaty.

The question of jurisdiction also complicates the debate between unilateral versus bilateral versus multilateral controls on proliferation; in other words, who should be responsible for implementing arms control measures? As arms agreements are negotiated between states and involve a core aspect of their sovereignty, they are often reluctant to delegate extensive powers, particularly relating to monitoring and sanctions, to IOs or other potentially 'supranational' bodies. Delegating such powers to NGOs or private firms is also usually out of the question, although such stakeholders may be involved in specific phases of agenda-setting or allowed very specific implementation tasks, such as mine-clearing. Even at the regional level, where the EU in particular created an agency to help govern nuclear technologies – the European Atomic Energy Community (or Euratom) – EU member states were reluctant to delegate significant powers to it

(Dawe, 2004). As a result of these concerns, particularly among the major powers, today only one type of weapon – nuclear weapons – involves a fairly extensive regime involving inspections and policing, making them the exception to the rule about the reluctance to delegate certain powers to the international community. Even here, there are major political disagreements involving the actual implementation of such rules, as we shall see in the discussion of policy effectiveness below.

## Proliferation as a policy problem

As with most of the topics covered in this volume, weapons proliferation is a basic, even fundamental, human activity. As we have seen, key stakeholders can vary widely in their views about the relationship between the possession of certain weapons and the likelihood they will be used to threaten international security. To a large degree, distinguishing between 'acceptable' proliferators or weapons, and 'unacceptable' proliferators or weapons, has more to do with the nature of the stakeholders making that distinction than with the specific features or diffusion patterns of the weapons in question. The following three stages of political debates may help to illuminate why this is so.

### Agenda-setting

International experience with various weapons during the twentieth century helps keep proliferation very high on the international security agenda. Multiple security problems are thought to result from unchecked horizontal and vertical proliferation, particularly of WMD: arms races, conflict spirals, various types of wars, industrial accidents, environmental damage, nuclear blackmail and terrorist attacks (Perry, 2015). Another view, however, holds that *greater* proliferation of WMD, mainly nuclear weapons, might actually *enhance* international security (Waltz, 1981 and 1990) because fear of mutual destruction should inspire cautionary behaviours, and even cooperation, as occurred between the superpowers towards the end of the Cold War. This view, however, is politically controversial, especially in light of the chance that terrorists could take advantage of greater proliferation, and therefore is not a feasible policy option. A closer look at actual agenda-setting here reveals that it is largely the innovators, which tend to be the advanced industrialized states, who attempt to control the ownership and diffusion patterns of new weapons systems, in an effort to protect themselves rather than, or in addition to, the international community at large. For many weaker and poorer states, the issue of weapons proliferation is a concern but is far less important to them than other problems, such as domestic instability or economic underdevelopment. Even where weapons proliferation is a concern for such states, they might prefer to focus on CW rather than WMD, as small arms and related CW, such as cluster bombs, anti-personnel mines and fragmentation weapons, regularly cause many deaths in the developing world.

Agenda-setting in this realm, therefore, tends to stress the as yet unrealized threat of a single blast that could kill thousands or even millions rather than on the actual thousands of deaths and injuries among poor countries that occur on a regular basis. And for some weaker states, not to mention terrorist groups, the only problem of weapons proliferation is that they lack the technologies possessed by the stronger states, and will attempt to acquire them through legal or illegal measures. The mere characteristics of certain weapons, therefore, can tell us very little about how such weapons will be managed as specific international security problems by the international community. Instead, we need to know more about the relationship between those who prefer to control such weapons and those who seek to acquire them, a relationship that reveals itself in the policy options suggested by the international community.

One key trend to highlight regarding agenda-setting and weapons proliferation is the increasingly prominent role played by NGOs or similar transnational social movements, which attempt to erode the monopoly on this topic usually held by states and their officials, especially military or technical experts (Wittner, 2009). Although such groups have attempted to assert their voices over weapons proliferation since even before the 1899 Hague Conference, global agenda-setting regarding some recent arms control pacts, such as those for blinding laser weapons and anti-personnel landmines (see the case study below), seems to have involved an extraordinarily high degree of attention and involvement by NGOs (Cameron, 1999; Anderson, 2000; Rutherford, 2000; Long, 2002). However, getting a topic on the international security agenda and achieving a firm global agreement are two separate things, as can be seen with the resistance by some major powers to the imposition of controls or bans on cluster bombs, small arms and the overall global arms trade.

## Framing policy alternatives

As international security problems related to weapons proliferation have been on the global agenda for over 100 years, the international community has produced a range of options to manage such problems. As we saw in Chapter 4, one way to control or limit such weapons is through the general LOAC regime, particularly the *jus in bello* criteria regarding principles governing warfighting and its associated weapons and tactics. Weapons that violate such criteria, such as WMD, should not be developed by parties to the regime in the first place, which should help mitigate proliferation. The issue of strategic bombing is also directly relevant to the evolution of this debate; it is especially revealing how such bombing, which is a major military option for the US and its allies, is generally excluded from discussions regarding weapons proliferation and the 'official' designation of a WMD (Legro, 1995; Pape, 1996; Biddle, 2002). Strategic bombing campaigns nearly always result in considerable collateral damage to civilians, yet apparently do not violate the norm to discriminate between civilian and combatant targets as required by the *jus in bello* criteria. The same problem is currently occurring with America's combat use of unmanned aerial vehicles or drones, such as the MQ-1 Predator or MQ-6 Reaper, in Afghanistan, Iraq, Yemen and Pakistan, which have produced numerous civilian casualties but are not subject to any specific legal prohibition. As over two dozen states now possess, or are developing, such systems, the legal consequences of 'drone warfare' will undoubtedly become more prominent (Benjamin, 2012).

Beyond the role of the LOAC and the controversial question of strategic bombing, the indirect approach to proliferation has been bolstered by several other options. The first of these simply involves unilateral self-policing or self-restraint, whereby states simply decide on their own not to develop or deploy certain weapons. This option in fact largely explains why we see much less proliferation, especially of WMD, than we might otherwise expect in an anarchic, self-help system. Considering that the vast majority of the 193 UN member states seem to have little or no desire to acquire WMD, especially nuclear weapons, the factors behind self-restraint probably deserve more analytical attention than we see at present (although see Solingen, 1994; Sagan, 1996–7). These factors could be framed in terms of expected utility theory, where the costs of possessing WMD today outweigh the benefits, and/or in terms of liberal or social constructivist arguments, where the possession of certain WMD is widely viewed by the international community as illegitimate (Price, 1995; Tannenwald, 2005).

A related unilateral option involves efforts by certain stakeholders, principally states, to impose their own norms and sanctions against certain proliferators. This can extend to maintaining one's own WMD deterrent or relying on 'extended deterrence' provided by an ally, and/or developing unilateral countermeasures such as hardened facilities, missile defences, vaccinations/cures and so on. Especially powerful countries, such as the US, can and do take unilateral measures to control proliferation, as America did with the MacMahon Act of 1946, which prohibited the export of nuclear materials, equipment or technology to any nation. This approach can also extend to unilateral military action, as with Israel's bombing of a suspected nuclear facility at Osirik in Iraq in 1981, or coalitions organized by one or a few states, as with the Iraq

War in 2003 and the Joint Comprehensive Plan of Action agreed with Iran in 2015. These measures are actually quite rare, and are typically framed as a 'last resort' policy option and as an adjunct to, rather than a replacement for, multilateral policies.

Thus, although arms control can be achieved through unilateral measures, the nature of the security dilemma, among other factors, typically requires explicit bilateral or multilateral agreements to help manage specific weapons. In general, such measures can take the form of mere controls, which allow some stakeholders to hold and transfer some weapons to certain stakeholders, and outright bans, which explicitly prohibit weapons or tactics for all signatories. The fact that no single state can typically enjoy a long monopoly over most weapons systems is a key driver of collective efforts to stem proliferation; this tendency for new technologies to diffuse beyond the wishes of their innovators is yet another major consequence of globalization. During the Cold War, for example, when vertical proliferation between the two superpowers dominated the agenda, bilateral US–Soviet pacts attempted to rein in their arms race and had a corresponding positive impact on international security. However, unilateral US efforts to prevent the Soviets from acquiring other technologies often encountered opposition from European and other states (Mastanduno, 1993). This type of transatlantic proliferation dispute is now being repeated with China, which has not been privy to the US–Soviet efforts and feels unconstrained by them (Garrett and Glaser, 1995–6). A similar dynamic is occurring in the context of cybersecurity, as we shall see in Chapter 8.

## Policy choice

If we focus mainly on collective efforts, while keeping unilateral measures in mind, one immediate political problem here is the tendency for buck-passing and free-riding. If the international effort, taken as a whole, to control weapons proliferation is viewed as a public collective good, then stakeholders may be tempted to pass the buck in the hope that some other stakeholder will assume the costs of organizing cooperation, or to free-ride in the hope of enjoying the benefits without directly contributing to their costs. Both behaviours often result in the under-provision of security, making the problem of leadership in the area of arms control especially acute. This leadership problem is similar to that involving the creation of alliances, as we saw in Chapter 4. While mere self-interest might lead states to sign up to a provision to control weapons proliferation, they are far less willing to assume the costs of monitoring and, especially, sanctioning potential defectors. Nor do they wish to be monitored or sanctioned themselves if they find it necessary to deploy or use a certain banned weapon.

This disjuncture between negotiating and enforcing an arms agreement has existed since the first major effort, the *Hague Declaration of 1899 Concerning Asphyxiating Gases*, which was summarily violated by some of the belligerents in WWI. Following WWI, all major powers – France, Germany, Italy, Japan, the Soviet Union, the UK and the US – continued their pursuit of WMD programmes of various types. A 1922 Washington Arms Conference Treaty would have banned chemical weapons outright but was rejected by France and never went into effect; three years later the major powers did agree on a Chemical and Bacteriological Weapons Convention, also known as the 1925 Geneva Protocol, to ban the use of such weapons in warfare, though it was not ratified by the US Senate until 1975. The problem of enforcing arms control agreements persisted throughout the interwar period, and again with the advent of bilateral efforts during the Cold War. One virtue of bilateral efforts, of course, is that the focus on only two countries may at least help reduce the problem of monitoring compliance, although sanctions are another matter.

Thus, we see a strong tendency towards bilateral efforts regarding nuclear weapons in particular, beginning in 1943 at the Anglo-American Quebec Conference where the US and the UK, along with Canada, agreed to prevent nuclear information and materials from passing to third parties; this idea then grew into a policy of comprehensive denial. During the Cold War, we also see a fairly extensive range of primarily bilateral US–Soviet agreements regarding nuclear weapons after both sides essentially realized the existence of a 'nuclear stalemate' at their 1955 Geneva Summit, the first superpower bilateral summit to take place since the end of WWII. These agreements initially attempted to limit the areas where such weapons could be deployed ('non-armament' treaties), then placed a cap on the absolute numbers of such weapons to be held by the superpowers ('arms control' treaties), then allowed for an actual reduction of certain types of weapons as the Cold War came to an end ('limited disarmament' treaties). These pacts, most of which were largely negotiated by the superpowers but allowed for accession by other states, are summarized in Table 6.3.

In addition, a SALT II agreement of 1979 would have reduced (rather than merely capping) nuclear arsenals at about 2,250 delivery vehicles on both sides. However, the US Senate refused to ratify the agreement after the Soviet invasion of Afghanistan later that year. Both sides did begin to implement its provisions and SALT II was later supplanted by the START talks. A START III treaty would have reduced the cap even further, to about 2,000–2,500 strategic warheads for each side; it was abandoned in favour of the 2002 Moscow Treaty. This treaty, in turn, was replaced by the New START agreement in 2010, which limited Russian and American nuclear arsenals to no more than 1,550 warheads each.

Table 6.3  *Major nuclear-related arms control agreements*

| Agreement | Key provisions | Status |
|---|---|---|
| 1959 Antarctic Treaty | Prohibits military activity, weapons testing or deployment in Antarctica. | 53 parties; entered into force in 1961. |
| 1963 Partial Test Ban Treaty (or Limited Test Ban Treaty) | Prohibits nuclear testing in the atmosphere and under water. | 125 parties; entered into force in 1963. |
| 1967 Outer Space Treaty | Prohibits the deployment of nuclear weapons in space. | 104 parties; entered into force in 1967. |
| 1968 Nuclear Non-Proliferation Treaty (NPT) | Prohibits acquisition of nuclear weapons by non-nuclear weapons states. | 190 parties; entered into force in 1970. |
| 1972 Strategic Arms Limitation Treaty (SALT I) | Froze the number of ICBMs at 1972 levels for each superpower. | Entered into force in 1972. |
| 1972 Anti-Ballistic Missile Treaty | Limited both superpowers to the deployment of two anti-ballistic missile sites within their countries (reduced to only one each in 1974). | Entered into force in 1972; the US withdrew unilaterally in 2002. |
| 1987 Intermediate Range Nuclear Forces (INF) Treaty | Eliminated an entire class of nuclear weapons and their delivery systems from US and Soviet nuclear arsenals in Europe: those with a range of 300–3,400 miles. | Entered into force in 1988. |
| 1991–3 Strategic Arms Reduction Treaties (START I and II). | START I barred the signatories from deploying more than 6,000 warheads each; START II reduced the cap to 3,500 warheads on each side and also banned the use of MIRVs on ICBMs. | Entered into force in 1992. Parties: Belarus, Kazakhstan, the US, Russia, Ukraine. |
| 1996 Comprehensive Test Ban Treaty | Establishes a total ban on all nuclear explosions for the signatories. | 183 signatories; 164 ratifications. However, 44 named states must sign and ratify the treaty for it to enter into force, which has not happened. |
| 2002 Treaty on Strategic Offensive Reductions (SORT, or the Moscow Treaty) (replaced by New START) | Aimed to reduce the aggregate number of warheads possessed by Russia and the US to 1,700–2,200 each by 31 December 2012. | Signed and ratified by both parties; entered into force in 2003. |
| 2002 Hague Code of Conduct Against Ballistic Missile Proliferation | Aims to restrain or regulate the spread of ballistic missile technology (used to deliver warheads). | 134 signatories; entered into force in 2002. |
| 2010 New START | Aims to limit the number of deployed strategic nuclear warheads by Russia and the US to 1,550 each by 2018. | Signed and ratified by both parties; entered into force in 2011. |

The long legacy of US–Soviet agreements, which were negotiated primarily, if not exclusively, in the interests of the superpowers, also helped to pave the way for multilateral agreements on various WMD, starting with the Nuclear Non-Proliferation Treaty (NPT). This instrument basically comprises a bargain between nuclear 'haves' and 'have-nots'. States with a declared nuclear weapons capability (nuclear weapons states, or NWS) agree that all states have a right to the peaceful uses of nuclear technology and may provide such technology to non-nuclear weapons states (NNWS) that sign the NPT. The NWS also agree to pursue disarmament of their own nuclear weapons while NNWS agree not to pursue their own nuclear weapons capability or to assist other NNWS in such pursuits. Nearly all states in the international system have acceded to the NPT regime, which currently includes 190 signatories (including the Holy See and Palestine). The NPT is supported further by the International Atomic Energy Agency (IAEA), which administers a so-called 'safeguards regime' to monitor and inspect the nuclear programmes and fissile materials of NPT signatories. More recently, the Comprehensive (Nuclear) Test Ban Treaty (CTBT) attempts to ban all nuclear testing by its signatories; these states have also proceeded with the creation of a CTBT Organization, which involves 337 monitoring sites around the world able to detect nuclear explosions. This organization, based in Vienna, has begun its work even though the CTBT has not yet officially entered into force (see the section on policy effectiveness below).

For other WMD, two multilateral instruments attempt to control chemical and biological weapons: the 1972 Biological Weapons Convention (BWC) and the 1993 Chemical Weapons Convention (CWC). Both were follow-up efforts to the 1925 Geneva Protocol and took years of negotiation to realize. At present 173 states have ratified or acceded to the BWC, which prohibits the development, production, transfer and stockpiling of bacteriological and toxic weapons; it thus governs both horizontal and vertical proliferation. Unusually for a multilateral arms agreement, the BWC applies to private parties as well as to states, yet this attempt at more comprehensive policing has in fact helped to undermine efforts to add a verification or compliance regime to the protocol, as we shall see in the section on policy effectiveness below. The CWC, which includes 192 parties, prohibits similar activities in the realm of chemical weapons. However, it does include a verification mechanism in the form of an Organization for the Prohibition of Chemical Weapons, an IO established in 1997 that is linked to, but independent of, the UN system. The BWC and CWC regimes both attempt to classify various substances depending on their suitability as weapons, or as components of weapons, and have loopholes to allow the holding of small amounts for defensive research purposes. They also link to efforts regarding international public health security, as we shall see in Chapter 12.

Finally, conventional weapons are largely governed under the terms of the 1980 UN Conference on Certain Conventional Weapons (the CCW Convention). In addition, a 1992 US–Soviet agreement, the Treaty on Conventional Forces in Europe (CFE), was instituted to help limit or reduce CW stockpiles in Europe towards the end of the Cold War. While the CFE Treaty included an elaborate system for inspections and verification between the parties, the more general CCW Convention, like the BWC, is largely a self-policing system under international humanitarian law and parties are expected to follow its rules in good faith without submitting to external verification procedures. In recent years, the CCW Convention has been invoked to help create arms control measures for specific CW, such as the 1995 Blinding Laser Weapons Protocol (BLWP) and the 1997 Convention on the Prohibition of the Use, Stockpiling, Production or Transfer of Anti-Personnel Mines and Their Destruction (or the Ottawa Convention). There are currently 105 parties to the BLWP, which entered into force in 1998, and 162 parties to the Ottawa Convention, which entered into force in 1999. Of the P5 members of the UNSC, France and the UK are parties to both measures, while China, Russia and the US are parties to the BLWP but not to the Ottawa Treaty. In fact, ratification of the BLWP was one of the very first acts of the Obama administration when it assumed office in January 2009, after the Bush and Clinton administrations neglected to steer it through the Senate for over ten years. Obama was unable to take action on another emerging CW problem, the question of banning cluster munitions, which disperse hundreds of 'bomblets' over a wide area and can easily kill or injure non-combatants. The effort to ban such weapons, known as the 'Oslo process', resulted in an international treaty in 2008: the Convention on Cluster Munitions. This Convention, which entered in force in 2010, has the support of 98 parties (including most EU member states); however, as with the Ottawa Treaty, China, Russia and the US have not acceded to the ban on cluster munitions.

Before examining multilateral efforts to enforce arms agreements, we should first reiterate that unilateral self-restraint is the foundation of international cooperation regarding weapons proliferation. The vast majority of states do not possess WMD and therefore are not directly involved in the proliferation of such weapons. Major powers have occasionally attempted to lead by example in this area as well, as with the UK's unilateral renunciation of chemical and biological warfare in 1956, followed by America's unilateral renunciation of chemical weapons and biological warfare under President Nixon's administration. In addition, most WMD agreements negotiated between the US and the Soviet Union were implemented in good faith through self-policing by the parties, supported by inspections of facilities in some cases.

The INF Treaty is a key example; by the treaty's deadline of 1 June 1991, a total of 2,692 such weapons had been destroyed; 846 by the US and 1846 by the Soviet Union. The CFE was also implemented in good faith through the first half of the 1990s, while the US–Russian Cooperative Threat Reduction Program of 1992 works to dismantle WMD and their infrastructure within former Soviet states; it has resulted in the destruction of over 6,000 warheads and several thousand WMD delivery vehicles. However, although START I and START II were ratified by both parties, only START I was implemented in good faith; implementation of START II and a proposed START III, as well as the more recent Moscow Treaty, ran into difficulties due to America's continued pursuit of its own national missile defence system and the related decision by President Bush to unilaterally withdraw from the Anti-Ballistic Missile (ABM) Treaty in 2002. This was the first time the US had withdrawn from such an important and long-standing arms control treaty, a move that clearly undermined US–Russian arms control cooperation and which will almost certainly intensify global competition (and thus proliferation) regarding national missile defences and related technologies, on ground or in space (Sauer, 2003). Under the Obama administration, however, the US and Russia managed to agree to the New START pact noted above.

Regarding other WMD, the US has been reluctant to provide the BWC with an inspection and verification regime similar to those for the CWC, the NPT and the CTBT, although the vast majority of other BWC signatories would like to establish such a regime. As the BWC applies to private stakeholders as well as to public facilities, the US fears that an inspection regime would undermine its lead in certain biological and pharmaceutical technologies. These fears are also shared by major interest groups, such as the Pharmaceutical Research and Manufacturers of America. In the realm of conventional arms control there are no inspection regimes whatsoever for recent pacts on blinding laser weapons or anti-personnel mines, and adherents to these agreements must rely on good faith, mutual trust and self-policing to implement them. This aspect of certain arms agreements can be extremely problematic; even after the US renounced chemical and biological warfare in the early 1970s, the public later learned that the CIA kept stockpiles of these agents, supposedly unknown to the president. The US Army Medical Research Institute of Infectious Diseases (USAMRIID) also keeps some agents, including smallpox, on hand, for what it claims are defensive research purposes only. During the 1980s, scientists in Iraq purchased four strains of anthrax from a US firm with the approval of the US Department of Commerce, while the 2001 anthrax attacks in the US are believed to have used a strain of the virus developed at USAMRIID. Thus, if the world's most powerful democracy has such difficulties with implementing arms control agreements in good faith, then we may have little hope for other, supposedly less responsible and accountable, states.

A final point to note here is that even with inspections and verification regimes in place, the international community has no uniform system for

## Box 6.1   The international campaign to ban landmines

*Despite powerful opposition, the ICBL was a major global achievement.*

International advocacy groups in favour of arms control have existed for over 100 years. Their influence, however, varies widely and can be difficult to measure against other factors, such as the power and expertise of the many stakeholders involved in weapons development. For example, dozens of well-organized groups, such as Global Zero and European Nuclear Disarmament, have attempted to eliminate nuclear weapons for decades without much success. Yet under some conditions these groups can play a critical role in persuading states to rethink their attitudes and policies regarding certain weapons, even ones that have played a (supposedly) useful role in international security. One major example of this phenomenon that has attracted the attention of a number of scholars involves anti-personnel landmines (Price, 1998; Cameron, 1999; Anderson, 2000; Long, 2002). The global effort to restrict these weapons also resulted in a Nobel Peace Prize (1997) for

→

punishing defectors to these regimes, or for forcing states to join them in the first place. Such a decision to punish certain states is always political and therefore almost always controversial. Even the most important arms control regime of all, the NPT/IAEA regime, has to rely on UNSC

→
the International Campaign to Ban Landmines (ICBL) and its leader, Jody Williams.

This effort began in the 1980s when Williams encountered the devastating harm caused by landmines while working on development projects in Central America. Landmines are a cheap and effective way to control territory, yet their destructive effects persist long after a conflict has ended. Framing landmines as a global 'epidemic' because of their deployment in dozens of countries (mostly in the developing world), Williams worked with the UN to coordinate the efforts of major IOs as well as 1,300 NGOs in 90 countries to persuade the international community to ban the use of these weapons (Rutherford, 2000; Carpenter, 2011). This was an uphill battle, as landmines were cheap, legitimate and produced by dozens of countries for decades before the ICBL. More importantly, leading powers such as the P5 of the UNSC actively opposed, or did not support, such a ban on a weapon that had been considered effective and legitimate for decades. However, with the use of a global public campaign, the ICBL managed to convince the vast majority of states that anti-personnel landmines violated two central norms of humanitarian warfare (*jus in bello*): they did not distinguish effectively between civilians and combatants (the principle of 'discrimination'), and their destructive effects outweighed their military benefits (the principle of 'proportionality'). To highlight these problems, the ICBL focused on the harm done to children and farmers in the developing world. The campaign also enlisted the support of celebrities, such as Diana, Princess of Wales (the UK), to help raise awareness of their cause.

The efforts led in 1997 to the Ottawa Convention (see main text), and the number of mine-related casualties has dropped by thousands since the Convention entered into effect in 1999. Some leading P5 states, such as France and the UK, also reversed their positions and eventually supported the Ottawa Convention. However, around 4,000 victims still suffer each year from mines and other explosive remnants of war, so the ICBL has not been a complete success. China, Russia and the US (along with over 30 other states) also refuse to sign up to the ban, and the landmine problem persists in many parts of the world (especially Africa and South Asia). Yet the ICBL did 'beat the odds' in terms of changing the minds of many policy-makers and military experts on this issue; it also influenced other campaigns against certain conventional weapons, such as cluster munitions, small arms and blinding laser weapons. A similar effort is now underway regarding the use of unmanned aerial vehicles (drones) as weapons of war.

resolutions to punish defectors. This is often extremely difficult to achieve based on the unilateral veto power of each of its P5 members, all of which are declared NWS, plus the requirement that at least nine of the total members of the UNSC (the P5 plus at least four of its ten non-permanent members) support the resolution. If such a resolution does not pass, states may resort to their own extra-legal efforts, unilateral or multilateral, to punish certain states or other stakeholders for their alleged weapons activities, as in the case of the 2003 Iraq War.

## The politics of policy effectiveness

How well has all of this worked, and how do we know it? One key point to keep in mind is that the status of arms agreements is partially a function of larger patterns of stability and security. In other words, the fact that most states keep their arms control obligations during periods of peace should not lead us to believe that such willingness will survive during wartime. Once one side believes the other has broken, or is about to break, the agreement then arms agreements may be quickly abandoned. On the far more positive side, however, it is also worth emphasizing the point that the vast majority of states seem to want nothing to do with WMD; for them arms control measures are largely superfluous and have no direct causal influence. This profound opposition to certain WMD for some states has even manifested itself in the form of 'nuclear weapons-free zones'. Several such zones exist today, among 33 states in Latin America (the 1967 Treaty of Tlatelolco), 13 states in the South Pacific (the 1985 Treaty of Rarotonga) and ten states in South East Asia (the 1995 Treaty of Bangkok). In Africa, 40 states have ratified the 1996 Treaty of Pelindaba to prohibit nuclear weapons on their continent; this pact finally entered into force in 2009. Similarly, five countries of the former Soviet Union (Kazakhstan, Kyrgysztan, Tajikistan, Turkmenistan and Uzbekistan) finished negotiations in September 2002 to establish a Central Asian nuclear weapons-free zone; this pact (the Treaty of Semipalatinsk) also entered into force in 2009. Thus, if the decision to deploy certain weapons can be the result of a variety of factors (or 'overdetermined'), then the decision *not* to deploy can be overdetermined as well, meaning any single effort (such as multilateral arms control) is not as important as the full range of cost–benefit calculations involved for each stakeholder: political/economic and domestic/international.

A second general point is that non-proliferation measures *by themselves* seem to have little impact on states intent on acquiring certain weapons, such as Israel, India, Pakistan and North Korea, in the absence of an explicit punishment threatened by major powers (Ahmed, 1999; Ganguly, 1999). All four of these countries are not part of the NPT regime and of the basic bargain behind it; therefore they may claim a 'right' to develop weapons technologies as they see fit. Only North Korea, however, has been singled out for special criticism by the major powers regarding its nuclear ambitions, owing of course to the political relationship between its government and other states rather than to the special characteristics of WMD themselves. After a North Korean nuclear test in May 2009, all P5 members of the UNSC agreed to strengthen the sanctions regime against that state. Even China 'resolutely opposed' the test and agreed to the new sanctions, which include controversial stop-and-search powers to allow states to inspect North Korean vessels suspected of violating the ban on North Korean weapons exports created by the new sanctions regime. Even so, North Korea conducted two more tests (2013 and 2016), threatened to launch pre-emptive strikes against its enemies and has launched a rocket into space.

Israel and Pakistan, however, have not been punished for their programmes, while India has actually enjoyed even greater access to American dual-use nuclear technology since it exploded its first weapon. Similarly, Iran, which is a party to the NPT regime, including the IAEA safeguards, continues to assert its right to develop civilian nuclear technology under NPT rules (Hadian, 2008; Inbar, 2008). In another rare move, the UNSC, acting on advice from the IAEA, decided in 2005 that Iran's programme violated the terms of its adherence to the NPT. Sanctions were imposed on the country and the idea of a military strike was debated among some policy experts. However, as noted above, Iran agreed in 2013 to limit its nuclear programme and allow access to IAEA inspectors in exchange for a lifting of the sanctions. This pact is in the process of implementation. Even so, and despite this one (potential) case of success, where horizontal non-proliferation among states is concerned it could easily be argued that modern multilateral arms control efforts actually have very little direct impact. They are intended primarily for the 'fence-sitters': states that have (or had) a capability or interest in deploying, but have yet to do so for a variety of reasons relating to arms control or otherwise. Such states might include Argentina, Brazil, Libya, South Africa and a number of former Soviet republics.

An equally incongruous assessment might be made of US–Soviet/Russian arms control pacts. Although they have resulted in an overall decrease in WMD held by those countries, the destructive power represented by the thousands of nuclear weapons still held by the US and Russia (plus other NWS), which they continue to refuse to give up, means it cannot be said that a 50 per cent or 75 per cent reduction in warheads has increased international security by similar proportions. And as the US continues to support India, Russia did the same for Iran's suspected programme until the agreement noted above. Both the INF and CFE treaties may also be under threat, after Russian President Vladimir Putin stated that they no longer serve Russian interests, which can be interpreted as a threat to withdraw from these treaties in response to America's effort to pursue a missile defence programme in Europe. In September 2009, Obama stated that he would cancel this programme, but insisted that Russian opposition was not a factor in his decision; the US also planned to continue modern-izing its nuclear arsenal, as did China, France, Russia and the UK. In 2007, Putin explicitly suspended Russia's observance of the CFE Treaty, citing NATO's enlargement as a precipitating reason (Fatton, 2016); as noted in Chapter 4, Russia's annexation of Crimea in 2014 has increased pres-sures for greater defence spending in NATO, which may negatively impact arms reduction efforts with Russia. Similarly, while agreements prohibit-ing weapons in Antarctica and outer space have been implemented suc-cessfully, mainly due to self-restraint on the part of the signatories, these agreements may be under threat on several fronts: from US missile defence efforts, increasing competition by stakeholders with growing space pro-grammes (such as Brazil, China, India, Japan, Russia and the EU) and intensifying disputes over the (supposedly) common resources found in the Antarctic region and elsewhere (see Chapter 11).

Thus, in terms of our three standards for effectiveness noted in Chapter 3 – total victory, historical trends and comparative metrics – the evidence varies widely. While total international disarmament of all WMD might be somewhat unrealistic to implement and monitor owing to the ease with which industrial facilities can be adapted for chemical or biological weapons production, there has been a revival of the idea of global *nuclear* disarmament (Cirincione, 2007), as in the form of the so-called 'global zero' option suggested by Obama in an April 2009 speech in Prague. Although Moscow was receptive to this idea in principle, and while it may be more technically feasible to implement as compared to bans on other types of WMD, it is still politically impractical on an inter-national scale as it would require the abandonment of nuclear weapons by not just all of the P5 states, but also recent proliferators, such as India, North Korea and Pakistan, as well as 'undeclared' or clandestine nuclear powers, such as Israel. This in turn would require two international capa-bilities that are currently lacking: credible security guarantees for a num-ber of states and a much stronger inspection/punishment regime than the NPT/IAEA. Until these problems are solved, which would require more sustained and coherent leadership by the UNSC than it has ever provided in the past, the 'global zero' option will be little more than a pleasant notion, like that of outlawing war itself or pledging a 'no first use' policy on WMD on the part the US or other NWS (Gerson, 2010). However, we have seen some success with more modest 'total victory' approaches to proliferation, such as non-armament zones, nuclear weapons-free zones in various regions, bans on chemical/biological warfare and certain CW, and, above all, with overall self-restraint on the part of most states in the inter-national system regarding the acquisition of WMD. A more pragmatic cap on nuclear weapons, of perhaps 200–300 strategic nuclear weapons for each declared nuclear power, might also be achievable if the P5 states can agree to it.

With a historical trends standard, the overall numbers of various WMD, and their delivery systems, have declined considerably since the 1970s, as have CW stockpiles in Europe in particular, owing mainly to efforts by the two superpowers and their allies. This contraction in vertical proliferation of WMD has not been equalled in terms of horizontal proliferation; while some states (Argentina, Brazil, Libya, South Africa, Ukraine, Kazakhstan and Belarus) have abandoned their programmes or weapons, others have pursued or continued to pursue them: Israel, India, Pakistan, North Korea and Iran, plus of course the ongoing programmes of the P5 states. Nuclear testing, however, has declined considerably since the first two decades of the Cold War, yet again this is due more to unilateral self-restraint than to the provisions of the CTBT. All NWS were already phasing out nuclear tests by the 1990s, and as noted above, the vast majority of states never intended to make a nuclear explosion in the first place. Now the chief battle over the CTBT is between its supporters and the major 'hold-outs,' who refuse to restrain themselves from testing largely owing to their fundamental disagreement over which states should be allowed to join the 'nuclear club'.

Specifically, North Korea, India and Pakistan have not signed or ratified the treaty; while China, Colombia, Egypt, Indonesia, Iran, Israel and the US still must ratify it. And despite the attention currently seen towards Iran and North Korea, Pakistan may be even more problematic as a new NWS owing to its inherent instability, militarism and susceptibility to Islamist influence, especially since the US invasion of Afghanistan (Jones, 2003; Weaver, 2003); it may soon even be the first weak or failing state to possess nuclear weapons, a threat arguably more dangerous than that posed by a nuclear Iran or North Korea. Another potential problem, which is only indirectly addressed by the LOAC regime and the Geneva Conventions, concerns 'innovation proliferation', or the ongoing efforts by major powers (especially the P5) to develop and/or improve more effective weapons of various types, such as 'pain' weapons, drones, non-lethal weapons, autonomous weapons and so on. As the tendency is to develop weapons first then to determine their legal/ethical consequences, the possibility always exists that a fearsome new weapon will be unleashed upon the world before the international community can determine how to control it. This is precisely what happened most recently with blinding laser weapons, so that the Ottawa Treaty to control such weapons still has far too many loopholes to serve as an effective restraint.

Finally, in terms of comparative standards, we might be thankful that we have witnessed neither a large-scale war involving WMD, nor a nuclear strike or exchange between states, nor a major terrorist attack involving WMD. However, the analysis conducted above suggests that these positive 'non-events' probably owe far more to national political calculations, such as fears of arms racing or retaliation, or even to mere good fortune, than to the specific multilateral arms control measures discussed in this chapter. The one 'wild card' in this assessment, of course, involves the prospects of a terrorist acquisition of WMD (Allison, 2006). Obviously terrorists are not parties to arms agreements, but it is hoped that the efforts above might indirectly reduce their ability to acquire nuclear weapons or fissile materials. We should not have the same hope about controls on biological or chemical weapons owing to factors about such weapons and their controls already noted above. A more direct effort here involves efforts to monitor and punish terrorist activities in general, a topic addressed in the next chapter of this volume.

## Summary

A comprehensive net assessment of international policy on weapons proliferation is largely a story of wishful thinking, double standards and mixed messages, resulting in overall inconsistency regarding the range and effectiveness of various arms control and disarmament measures. It involves wishful thinking in three ways: that some 'ultimate weapon' will give a state a clear long-term advantage over its rivals; that major powers will eventually agree to completely abandon their WMD to serve the greater good and that arms agreements can be effective without robust monitoring and verification measures. All three of these wishful thoughts are demonstrably false. The problem of weapons proliferation also involves clear double standards: arms control has as much to do with the diffusion of technology from advanced industrialized states to their own allies as it does with the indigenous development of technology within LDCs. If the advanced states are not willing to rigorously police their own weapons development and diffusion activities, or do not agree on which stakeholders to isolate as unacceptable proliferators, the arms control regime quickly breaks down.

Based on the actual behaviours of a handful of advanced industrial states, which develop, stockpile, upgrade and deploy various WMD, as well as use or sell CW that may violate the LOAC, while refusing to allow other states to do so, it is difficult to escape the conclusion that arms control, even during the Cold War, is largely a means to maintain a clear power disparity between the 'haves' and the 'have-nots.' In other words, arms control regimes are little more than an institutionalized form of technological discrimination between the major and minor powers. A less cynical view, of course, is that the 'haves' must retain their arsenals to protect themselves against rogue states or other stakeholders (particularly terrorists) that may threaten them with WMD. Yet the vast size and sophistication of the WMD/CW arsenals of certain rich countries, plus their continued investment and research into various WMD (and CW that effectively function as WMD, such as fuel-air explosives), as well as their massive foreign arms sales programmes, mean that defensive measures against WMD could be taken with much less effort than they currently expend.

These behaviours then send mixed messages to would-be proliferators. Any signal that the NWS will continue to deploy WMD, and that friends of NWS such as Israel, India and Pakistan can get away with WMD proliferation, means that a potential proliferator is too easily tempted to develop WMD as quickly and secretly as possible to produce a *fait accompli* before it can be punished or opposed. This is why the cases of Iraq, North Korea and (potentially) Iran are so interesting: because they are the exception, not the rule, to this tendency of the major powers to disagree about whether to act. Each case further illustrates the practical dangers involved in policing the NPT regime when the major powers do decide to take action, in terms of punishing the wrong state (Iraq), waiting too long to punish a state (North Korea) or determining whether to punish a state that may already be too large, powerful or strategically important to succumb to such efforts (Iran). In addition, as WMD and other military capabilities serve multiple functions and interests for the stakeholders who develop, possess and desire them, any arms control regime that does not take a full range of these functions and interests into consideration is likely to run into problems. Yet these political difficulties should not blind us to the fact that some modest and demonstrable successes regarding arms control are still possible, primarily on a *regional* (nuclear weapons-free zones) or *bilateral* (US–Soviet/Russian cooperation), rather than global, basis. It is also worth noting that the use of chemical weapons during the Syrian civil war in 2013 was soundly condemned as 'unacceptable' by most of the international community. To the extent that these actions contribute to the security of their varied participants, overall international security may be enhanced, but only in a sub-optimal fashion. However, this is still much better than the alternative: 193 states armed to the teeth with every kind of fearsome weapon imaginable.

## Further reading

Gordon Adams (1992). *The Revolution in the Arms Trade: The Emergence of a Transnational Arms Industry*. Washington: Defense Budget Project.

Joseph Cirincione (2007). *Bomb Scare: The History and Future of Nuclear Weapons*. New York: Columbia University Press.

Jeanne Guillemin (2005). *Biological Weapons: From the Invention of State-Sponsored Programs to Contemporary Bioterrorism*. New York: Columbia University Press.

Robert Jervis (1990). *The Meaning of the Nuclear Revolution: Statecraft and the Prospect of Armageddon*. Ithaca: Cornell University Press.

William Langewiesche (2007). *The Atomic Bazaar: The Rise of the Nuclear Poor*. London: Allen Lane.

P. R. Lavoy, S. D. Sagan and J. J. Wirtz (eds.) (2000). *Planning the Unthinkable: How New Powers will use Nuclear, Chemical and Biological Weapons*. Ithaca: Cornell University Press.

Judith Miller, Stephen Engelberg and William Broad (2002). *Germs: Biological Weapons and America's Secret War*. New York: Touchstone.

William J. Perry (2015). *My Journey at the Nuclear Brink*. Stanford: Stanford Security Studies.

Scott D. Sagan (1993). *The Limits of Safety: Organizations, Accidents, and Nuclear Weapons*. Princeton: Princeton University Press.

Scott D. Sagan and Kenneth N. Waltz (2002). *The Spread of Nuclear Weapons: A Debate Renewed*. New York: W.W. Norton.

Kenneth N. Waltz (1981). *The Spread of Nuclear Weapons: More May Be Better*, Adelphi Paper No. 171. London: International Institute for Strategic Studies.

Lawrence S. Wittner (2009). *Confronting the Bomb: A Short History of the World Nuclear Disarmament Movement*. Stanford: Stanford University Press.

# Chapter 7

# Terrorism

Although terrorism has served as a political tactic for well over a century, its status as a major problem of international security is a more recent trend. In fact, no other contemporary problem so effectively demonstrates one of the core arguments of this volume: the role of politics in setting the international security agenda. The US has been the critical player in this regard, as it elevated its view of terrorism from a relatively minor threat to a major international concern following the attacks by al-Qaeda on American soil on 11 September 2001. This response was supported to various degrees by several American allies and led directly to US military attacks on Afghanistan and Iraq, plus a host of other, often controversial, domestic and foreign policies whose aftershocks persist. This increased attention by policy-makers has been accompanied by more activity on the part of security scholars and other experts, making the study of terrorism one of the major growth areas in the field since the end of the Cold War (Anderson, 2004). Before 9/11, the study of terrorism had been quite marginalized by many universities, book publishers and major academic journals (Jentleson, 2002; Cronin, 2002–3).

Unfortunately, however, much of this work is polemical or sensationalistic in nature, and often does not involve rigorous empirical research or sharp conceptual distinctions. Works that attempt to paint Islamic terrorism in particular as an uniquely violent or abhorrent type of political behaviour, as with studies of 'Islamikaze' attacks (Israeli, 2003) or the rise of 'Islamofascism' (Podhoretz, 2007), are especially suspect in this regard, even when such views are embedded in broader treatments of terrorism (Burleigh, 2008). In addition, even the more credible studies reveal a fairly high degree of discord involving some basic aspects of terrorism: how to define it, what causes it and whether to treat it as a criminal activity requiring a legal or judicial response, or as a form of asymmetric warfare – a 'weapon of the weak' – that requires or justifies far more aggressive measures (Silke, 2004; Carter 2016). However, and despite these analytical disputes, there is some degree of consensus that terrorism will remain a threat to international security for the foreseeable future for a number of reasons, which may be framed as root, or permissive/passive, causes. These might include the continued dominance of world politics by the developed states of the North in general, and of the US and its allies in particular;

the utility of global networks to organize attacks, circulate weapons and supply ideas/funds/recruits for terrorism; a growing backlash against globalization and its proponents/effects/instruments; the existence of weak and failed states; and a range of major demographic changes, such as migration, ethnic conflicts, border disputes, urbanization, limited natural resources and so on that can contribute to the politics of extremism and terrorist violence (Björgo, 2003).

That said, it is also important to recognize what may be the single most critical factor in considering terrorism as an *existential* security threat: how the political targets of terror – typically national governments – interpret, and respond to, a terrorist attack. The goal of terrorism is to provoke a response by the targets in the form of national policies based on the politics of fear. If national governments do not show fear and do not over-react to terrorist attacks, then terrorism will be undermined as a political tactic. Unfortunately, however, fear is all too often an emotional response rather than a measured choice and can very easily be manipulated by both terrorists and their targets, as well as by the media. This is why it is very important to subject terrorism to the same rigorous political analysis that we apply to the other modern security problems covered in this volume.

## Terrorism and international security

As always, we begin with some definitional issues, and right from the start it becomes clear that terrorism is a highly contested concept. There is no agreed universal definition of terrorism; in fact, many international treaties avoid defining it and instead adopt different terms or euphemisms, such as crime, low-intensity conflict, insurgency, asymmetric warfare or guerrilla/unconventional warfare. A new Comprehensive Convention on International Terrorism, proposed by the UN, is also deadlocked over the question of defining terrorism. The literature on the topic reveals well over 100 definitions of terrorism; a selection is summarized in Box 7.1.

As we can see, some definitions are fairly straightforward; the American view in particular seems relatively focused and concise compared to those of other states. The official and long-standing (from 1948) Israeli version simply focuses on 'violence', which can be perpetrated by any groups (including state actors) for any reason, while the British view is so broad as to include not just violent action but also other non-violent political behaviours if they cause a risk to 'health and safety' or 'damage property'. Indeed, in the UK a number of collective political actions might straddle the line, such as it is, between terrorism and intimidation: boycotts, strikes, protest marches, civil disobedience or politically motivated vandalism. The official UK definition (2006) also includes attacks against IOs and attacks against electronic systems, or cyberterrorism. Despite this

---

**Box 7.1   Over 100 definitions of terrorism: a summary**

1   *US view* Any premeditated politically motivated violence perpetrated against non-combatant targets by sub-national groups or clandestine agents.

2   *British view* Use or threat of an action (i.e. involving serious violence against a person, serious damage to property, endangering a person's life, creating a serious risk to the health or safety of the public, or one designed seriously to interfere with or seriously disrupt an electronic system) which is intended to: (1) influence the government or international governmental organizations, or to intimidate the public or a section of the public and (2) advance a political, religious or ideological cause.

3   *UN view* Criminal acts, including against civilians, committed with the intent to cause death or serious bodily injury, or taking of hostages, with the purpose to provoke a state of terror in the general public or in a group of persons or particular persons, intimidate a population or compel a government or an international organization to do or to abstain from doing any act.

4   *EU view* Terrorist offences may seriously damage a country or an international organization where committed with the aim of: seriously intimidating a population, or unduly compelling a government or international organization to perform or abstain from performing any act, or seriously destabilizing or destroying the fundamental political, constitutional, economic or social structures of a country or an international organization.

5   *Arab League view* Any act or threat of violence, whatever its motives or purposes, that occurs in the advancement of an individual or collective criminal agenda and seeks to sow panic among people, cause fear by harming them, or place their lives, liberty or security in danger, or seeks to cause damage to the environment or to public or private installations or property or to occupy or seize them, or seeks to jeopardize a national resource.

6   *Israeli view* A terrorist organization is a body of persons resorting in its activities to acts of violence calculated to cause death or injury to a person or to threats of such acts of violence.

---

range of opinion, however, there are at least four common features or debates regarding most definitions of terrorism.

The first involves its *methods or tactics*, in terms of whether violent acts or the mere threat of violence must be involved for an action to 'qualify' as terrorism. Most official definitions stress violent acts, and in fact six tactics comprise about 95 per cent of all terrorist incidents: bombings, assassinations, armed assaults, kidnappings, barricade/hostage situations and hijackings. The second aspect concerns the *nature of the terrorists* themselves, namely whether they involve states or non-state actors, or some combination (state-sanctioned or state-sponsored terrorism), and whether they might involve nationals of more than one state (international or transnational terrorism). Although states have used terror as a tactic, the modern treatment of terrorism tends to stress non-state actors as the main perpetrators. The third aspect involves the *nature of the targets*, or (again) the treatment of civilians/non-combatants versus military targets. Most definitions of terrorism stress the role of civilians as targets, yet the discussions in Chapter 4 and Chapter 5 remind us that the concept of a civilian is becoming increasingly problematic, as is the nature of a combatant. For example, are off-duty military personnel or armed PMC guards in a conflict zone considered civilians or military combatants? In other words, are they legitimate targets of military violence, or innocent victims of terrorist activity? In the US view of terrorism, for example, the phrase 'non-combatant targets' does in fact include unarmed and/or off-duty military personnel, even if serving in a conflict zone. Finally, there is some debate over the *motivation/objectives* of the terrorists. The specific or tactical motivation, of course, is to generate fear on the part of the target; broader or political motivations behind terrorism, however, can be far more complex. We shall return to this point throughout the rest of this chapter.

Overall then, most definitions of terrorism tend to incorporate these core elements: *organized* and *premeditated violence* against *people* in order to sow *fear or terror* for the purposes of gaining *political or criminal objectives*. A number of definitions also mention the targeting of innocent victims (i.e. civilians) in order to influence a broader audience or attract attention (i.e. a form of 'political theatre'). However, each of these factors can be interpreted to produce a specific definition of terrorism, which has often been the case over the years.

## Destructive scale

Relative to the number of deaths caused by other threats to international security, such as war or infectious disease, international terrorism actually ranks very low in terms of its destructive scale. The 9/11 attacks in the US, which resulted in nearly 3,000 fatalities, are the major exception to this fact. This event aside, one problem in the analysis of terrorism follows from the definitional disputes noted above: different sources count different types of political violence as terrorism, which then skews measures of the destructive scale of such violence. Including 'threats' as well as actual violence confuses the measurement even more. One widely cited source, the US State Department's annual list of terrorist attacks, has been prone to criticisms of political bias based on the variable ways it defines such attacks. Complicating this issue even further are the cases of

Afghanistan and Iraq since the US invasions of those states in 2001 and 2003 respectively, where analysts simply cannot agree on what types of political violence should be counted as terrorist attacks (made for the purpose of sowing fear) rather than as armed resistance to a foreign military occupation (as a type of insurgency or asymmetric warfare). If attacks in these states are counted as terrorism, which number in the hundreds each year, then the annual number of such attacks has increased markedly since 2001, especially in Iraq. If not, then the scale of terrorist destruction since 2001 falls accordingly.

With these caveats in mind, most terrorist attacks tend to result in deaths ranging from a few dozen to 100 or 200 fatalities, which is extremely low relative to other major threats to international security. Instead of its actual destructiveness, then, terrorism is more often framed in terms of its potential destructiveness – which is, ironically, precisely the response terrorist groups hope to provoke: a general fear that they could strike anyone, anywhere and anytime, with no warning or opportunity for countermeasures. The speed and extent to which this fear can manifest itself could be seen in a very dramatic fashion in the US after the 9/11 attacks, and it still informs policy-making to this day. When coupled with the fear that terrorists might use WMD, particularly nuclear weapons, the dread of death by terrorism becomes that much greater no matter how unlikely it really is. In fact, some analysts argue that nuclear terrorism is one of the most widely feared threats facing the international community today, and should demand an equally comprehensive response (Allison, 2006). The fact that foreign terrorists have struck a state as powerful as the US, on its own territory, also greatly amplifies perceptions that 'no one is safe' from this threat.

Overall, then, in terms of its objective destructiveness it is difficult to view terrorism as a major existential threat to the survival of major powers, although it may of course play a role in destabilizing weak states, as we saw in Chapter 5. Even if terrorists had access to a WMD, particularly a nuclear weapon, and a reliable way to deliver it, undetected, to a major population centre, the resulting damage would still pale in comparison to some of the other threats examined in this volume, such as a major power war, a deadly pandemic or the consequences of unrestrained global climate change. The threat of terrorism thus owes far more to the subjective emotions and politics of fear and uncertainty, particularly among citizens who believe themselves to be secure in the developed world, than to its objective destructiveness, whether real or potential. As such fears can be manipulated or inflated by terrorists and their targets (especially the media), a kind of 'echo chamber' effect can occur as the problem takes on a new life of its own as a security threat, which seems to be precisely what has happened in international security affairs since 9/11.

## Geographic and temporal scope

As suggested above, terrorism is primarily a domestic or regional phenomenon, and occurs most often in the less developed regions of the planet.
Statistical analyses also indicate that terrorist attacks within a state generally decline as economic development and foreign trade increase (Li and
Schaub, 2004). Most terrorist groups are in fact concerned with national,
and even sub-national, rather than global, political goals, and their
attacks are usually confined to the territories they hope to influence or
control, and in which they maintain a base of recruits and a supply chain
of resources to be used in their attacks. These factors lead terrorist groups
to favour operations in areas in which they feel relatively safe, which again
points to a fairly restricted geographic scope. The one major exception,
of course, is al-Qaeda ('the base') and its associations with other Islamic
extremists (such as the rise of Islamic State), which apparently operate as a
truly global network of terrorist cells (Anonymous, 2002; Byman, 2003).
However, it is not possible to determine precisely whether such groups are
being controlled by al-Qaeda, or are instead acting merely in sympathy
with its aims. There are in fact numerous terrorist groups, as well as so-
called 'lone wolf' attacks by individuals, associated with extremist Islam,
and the difficulty of disentangling the relationships between them can easily lead one to misconstrue or overstate the nature of al-Qaeda as a threat.

## Likelihood

Terrorism is now such an entrenched part of the discourse on international
security affairs that it seems as if we should expect a spectacular terrorist
attack, even one on the scale of 9/11, at almost any place and time. Some
media also contribute to this perception when they devote disproportionately more attention to the aftermath of terrorist attacks than to the death
and destruction associated with other problems discussed in this volume.
As noted above, this is precisely what some terrorists are trying to achieve,
and political and media elites seem only too willing to elevate terrorists and
their activities to a much higher political status than they probably deserve
relative to other contemporary threats to international security. In fact,
given this attention and the range of potential terrorist grievances against
powerful global actors, as well as the more general cultural and political
backlash against globalization, we might well ask why terrorist attacks do
not occur more often, rather than why they occur in the first place.

Some scholars have attempted to address this question in an indirect
fashion, by examining the possibility of terrorist waves or cycles, yet there
is no consensus on such an approach. Some argue that attacks peak on the
basis of two-year cycles (Enders and Sandler, 2004), while others adopt a
'generational' approach and identify cycles as long as 40 years (Rapoport,

2004), which involve more general transitions starting in the form of a backlash against *empires* (Austro–Hungarian, Russian and Ottoman) and then *colonial powers* (mainly European); to a more focused attack on the *US/West and its allies* (such as Israel) and the current *Islamic jihad* era of global 'sacred' terrorism (Rapoport, 2001a).

From a purely statistical perspective, however, these fears are either overstated or misplaced. As with the threat of war more generally, most terrorist attacks tend to occur in poor countries, even though the targets might be the symbols of rich countries, such as their embassies or businesses. The odds of someone located in a rich state becoming a victim of terrorism are extremely small, and pale in comparison to other real dangers, such as death or injury in an automobile accident. Some analysts even argue that the likelihood of a US citizen being victimized by terrorists is about as same as being struck by lightning – very long odds indeed (Mueller, 2005). Indeed, before 9/11, the US believed that terrorism was a moderate or manageable threat compared to problems such as nuclear proliferation and the epidemic of intrastate violence since the end of the Cold War. Throughout the 1990s, one of the most dangerous domestic terrorist organizations in the view of the US government was the Earth Liberation Front, a decentralized environmental movement known for property damage rather than for spectacular and deadly terror attacks.

What security specialists really need, of course, is more precise information regarding the nature of future terrorist attacks: when, where and made by whom. Except for rare groups, such as the Irish Republican Army (IRA), which often – but not always – warned the public a few hours before its attacks, most terrorist organizations tend to rely on shock and surprise in their operations. Predicting the likelihood of a specific attack (or forecasting) is thus extremely difficult in the absence of intelligence provided by individuals with direct knowledge of the group. This is precisely why the US and some of its allies, including the UK, were willing to engage in or support the kidnapping (or 'extraordinary rendition') and torture of suspected terrorists and their supporters as a way to gain this valuable intelligence (ICRC, 2007). I shall return to these policies in the sections below; here we need only note that the fact that they were used, and by states who normally proclaim their support for human rights and the rule of law, indicates the intense desperation and fear felt by these states in the aftermath of 9/11. Before these attacks, terrorism was treated by the US and its key allies as a fairly low-level threat: annoying but relatively manageable even though terrorist attacks had occurred against US interests on a fairly regular basis since the 1980s. During the 1990s, the CIA began issuing warnings that al-Qaeda might launch attacks on US soil, as did the US government's chief counter-terror official, Richard Clarke, in the months just before 9/11 (Clarke, 2004), yet these officials could not identify the precise target and date of such attacks. The threat was downplayed accordingly by the Bush administration until it was too late.

## Recovery

Finally, the small-scale nature of most terrorist attacks – so far – means that recovery efforts are quite manageable relative to other wider-scale threats discussed in this volume. Even in the exceptional case of the 9/11 attacks, the US economy and transportation system resumed functioning very soon after the event, and the stock market opened with no major problems a few days later thanks to the intensive public–private coordination between major stock exchange firms and the federal government. The attacks left a gaping hole where the World Trade Center used to stand, yet businesses in the surrounding area resumed their operations as soon as possible after the event, as did officials in the Pentagon (the US Department of Defence, or DoD) which had suffered an attack by one of the four aeroplanes on 9/11. Obviously this situation could change in the case of a *protracted* terrorist campaign against a single target, as in states such as Peru with attacks by the Sendero Luminoso ('Shining Path'), or with an attack involving WMD, particularly a nuclear weapon.

Still, our experience with most terrorist attacks suggests that ordinary citizens and firms in stable, developed states can not only return to business as usual after an attack, they can almost learn to live with terrorism as a normal threat in their everyday lives, provided that reasonable precautionary measures are taken, as with protecting oneself against any violent crime. This has been seen with protracted terrorist campaigns in the UK and Israel, which failed in both cases to either disrupt normal civilian activities or even to disrupt the political machinery charged with dealing with terrorism. This fact, as well as the points above regarding the overall destructive nature and likelihood of the average terrorist attack, also suggests that this problem probably receives a disproportionate amount of attention by citizens, politicians, the media and perhaps even some academics relative to other, far more likely and destructive, international security threats. To determine why this is so, we need to make a more focused political analysis of the phenomenon of international terrorism.

## Stakeholder factors

As terrorism is a specific behaviour of stakeholders who take it upon themselves to threaten (that is, 'terrorize') other stakeholders, particularly national governments, many of the disputes regarding the *nature of terrorism as a policy problem* are often rooted in disagreements about the *nature of terrorists as individuals*. Any credible analysis of terrorism therefore needs to be as clear as possible in terms of its assumptions about the goals and power resources of these individuals, especially in terms of the situational and dispositional causes of terrorism. Supposed situational causes include the nature of the international system (US or Western-dominated, or merely 'unjust'), while supposed dispositional causes include individuals who hold certain views about ideology, religion, ethnic identity/nationalism, and grievances against the prevailing order, as well as (to a much lesser extent) those who possibly have a psychological pathology. Distinguishing between, and then measuring, these multiple factors is precisely where various analyses of terrorism start to disagree, if not break down completely.

## Principal stakeholders

Most definitions of terrorism stress the highly organized nature of terrorist groups and their attacks; in other words, it is generally a *social* or *collective*, rather than a personal or individual, phenomenon (unlike, for example, serial murder or 'lone wolf' terror attacks) inspired by shared political goals (Rapoport, 2001b). This fact strongly encourages the creation of 'watch lists' of certain terrorist organizations as a first step in hunting them down, as we shall see later. However, terrorism apparently violates the sensibility of so many people that some researchers have closely examined the idea of a terrorist mindset or psychological personality that (supposedly) distinguishes such individuals from other normal, law-abiding, peaceful citizens (Crenshaw, 2000; Horgan, 2005). Some argue, for example, that terrorists have a martyr or vengeance complex, and that they organize their activities like a religious cult, even to the extent of requiring sacrifices, initiation rites or guilt-sharing behaviours, all of which keep the organization alive and help it recruit new members. Others have attempted to create a personality profile of the average terrorist, which might include traits such as: an oversimplification of issues; frustration about an inability to change society; a sense of self-righteousness; a utopian belief in the world; a feeling of social isolation; a need to assert his/her own existence (narcissism); and a cold-blooded willingness to kill (Davis, 2001).

This argument, however, can be problematic for the simple reason that there really is no such thing as an average or typical terrorist, or a 'terrorist mentality'. History and research clearly show that individual terrorists, like criminals more generally, have varied widely in terms of their socio-economic classes, education levels, cultural backgrounds, personality types, religious beliefs, ideological views and so on. However, it also seems that better educated individuals with a higher socio-economic status than others in their community might be more prone to all types of political involvement, including terrorism (Lee, 2011). Even so, and based on the list of all factors above, it would seem that almost any politically concerned individual could be capable of terrorism if circumstances allow, while other terrorist attributes – such as being 'cold-blooded' – are difficult if not impossible to measure. In fact, it could be argued that most adolescents share the first six personality characteristics noted in the previous paragraph, yet (fortunately) they do not engage in terrorism.

More recent psychological studies have attempted to shed light on a more focused type of political violence: the phenomenon of 'suicide terrorism' (Bloom, 2005; Gambetta, 2005; Oliver and Steinberg, 2005; Pape, 2005a; Pedahzur, 2005; Hafez, 2006). As always, we see major definitional and conceptual problems right from the start (Crenshaw, 2007), such as whether all attacks that result in the death of the attacker should be counted as suicide and as terrorism. For example, what about Japanese kamikaze attacks during WWII, or cases where the attackers did not realize they would die or were otherwise duped into their attacks? Many studies of suicide terrorism also focus on the Islamic variant when such attacks in fact have been perpetrated by a variety of groups, and not just religion-oriented ones, well beyond the Islamic world and the Middle East. The major example is the Liberation Tigers of Tamil Eelam, or LTTE, in Sri Lanka, which helped to pioneer the tactic. Even within this smaller class of suicide terrorists, as opposed to all terrorists, we can still find a wide range of motivating emotions, such as 'pride, anger, rage, frustration, humiliation, shame, hopelessness and despair' (Crenshaw, 2007). Overall, then, the perception that terrorism in general, and Islamic or suicide terrorism in particular, tends to involve religious fanatics or similar disturbed individuals, is highly mistaken, a conclusion also reached in a comprehensive report by the behavioural science unit of MI5, the UK's domestic security service (MI5 Behavioural Science Unit, 2008).

It is also worth keeping in mind the stakeholders responsible for responding to terrorism, and in doing so either elevating or marginalizing it as a threat. This involves primarily national government officials and, to a lesser extent, IOs that may have some counter-terror responsibilities, such as the UN, and the media. For example, studies of the media have shown that they devote disproportionately more attention to attacks in rich countries, which helps to amplify the threat perception relative to the situation in poor countries. As noted above, it is also not self-evident that all terrorist organizations pose an existential threat to either a specific national government or to the international community, so the stakeholders responsible for counter-terror policies must bear in mind the consequences of inappropriately inflating the threat posed by any single terrorist group, a task much easier said than done. However, the problem of threat inflation must be balanced against some evidence that increasing exposure to terrorist attacks (or the threat of such attacks) may increase public opinion in favour of 'get tough' policies often associated with conservative or right-wing parties (Getmansky and Zeitzoff, 2014), which can put pressure on public stakeholders responsible for counter-terrorism. Finally, we should note that terrorist organizations tend to have a fairly short life span; according to one study (Rapoport, 1992), 90 per cent of terrorist organizations are active for less than one year; of those that last for more than a year, more than half disappear within a decade. Although some more recent organizations, such as Islamic State, might demonstrate greater staying power, the odds that any single group will persist as a major global threat are still extremely low given the counter-terror resources now available to many states in the aftermath of 9/11 and the lower degree of state support for terrorism as compared to the Cold War era.

## Interests and preferences

Given the difficulties associated with analysing terrorists as flawed or even pathological individuals, it is possible to make more progress if we focus on a comparative analysis of terrorist *organizations*, and on their *political* goals. One critical debate regarding this issue is whether terrorism actually works as a political tactic, and here it is important to recognize that terrorist organizations, like states and other major stakeholders, have both external and internal interests. External interests are oriented towards the political targets of the terrorist attacks, such as changes in the policies of a specific national government, and can influence a group's decision to pursue smaller-scale terrorist attacks rather than more violent guerrilla warfare campaigns (Carter, 2016). Internal interests are oriented towards the needs of the organization itself, which in most cases simply means the desire to keep the 'movement' alive as a political force and, in doing so, outlast its political opponents. This latter objective is a key feature of terrorist campaigns and insurgencies, and many analysts fail to recognize that as long as the movement is alive and threatening, it is arguably 'winning' as a political force no matter how much the authorities may claim otherwise. Most studies of the effectiveness of terrorism therefore focus on its external objectives, and although some scholars continue to assert that terrorism 'does not work' (Abrahms, 2006; Fortna, 2015), others argue that terrorism can in fact result in significant political concessions by the target governments (Pape, 2005a; Kydd and Walter, 2006), which is precisely why it persists. The fact that the state of Israel was created after a series of terrorist attacks by various Jewish groups against the British in Palestine is just one critical example of how terrorist campaigns can achieve their political objectives.

More specifically, the preferences of most terrorist organizations tend to cluster around five priorities: regime change, territorial change, policy change, social control and maintenance of the status quo. Regime change (sometimes known as revolutionary terrorism) involves a replacement of a government with one favoured by the terrorist organization; territorial change involves the creation of new state boundaries, or even a new state, favouring the terrorist organization; policy change involves less dramatic political demands, such as the withdrawal of US forces from various places in the Middle East or the release of certain prisoners; social control involves enhancing the dominance of individuals by the terrorist organization; and status quo maintenance involves support for an existing regime, territorial arrangement or set of policies against any stakeholders who seek to change it (Kydd and Walter, 2006). Some groups may pursue several of these goals at once, which further complicates the question of whether any single terrorist group is effective or not: for example, it may be effective in facilitating policy change but not regime change.

This is why al-Qaeda is so difficult to evaluate as a political threat; some observers claim it seeks narrow, even 'reasonable', political goals, while others argue that it wants to provoke an apocalyptic, existential struggle between the West and the Islamic world, which justifies an equally dramatic response by the West. Specific concerns of al-Qaeda and most Islamist terrorist groups about American 'offences' include: its military presence in the Middle East, which is blasphemous in their eyes; its bias towards Israel at the expense of the Palestinians; its support for a range of corrupt and often authoritarian regimes in the Muslim world; its destruction of Afghanistan and Iraq; its subordination of the Muslim world to the interests of the US and its allies; its attempts to maintain cheap and steady flows of oil from Muslim states and its willingness to tolerate or inflict deaths in the Muslim world, as in Chechnya, Kashmir, Indonesia, Nigeria, Uzbekistan, the Philippines, the Xinjiang province in China and elsewhere (Anonymous, 2002; Benjamin and Simon, 2002; Berger, 2002). As more than one observer has noted, this list 'is not completely baseless' (Byman, 2003), and the US might want to reconsider some or all of these policies in an effort to combat terrorism. However, such an agreement, whether tacit or explicit, would also require al-Qaeda to determine which of its own goals are non-negotiable, and then to modify, if not abandon, them. Such a move might also fatally weaken the movement itself, which might be unacceptable to its grass-roots supporters. In fact, such a deal would almost certainly create a range of more extreme splinter groups, as has happened with several other major terrorist groups. Islamic State is just one example of such an al-Qaeda splinter group, and has arguably achieved a higher status than al-Qaeda as a major threat in Syria and Iraq, as noted in Chapter 5.

As always, preferences also can change depending on the response of targets and other factors, such as political windows of opportunity that might allow a terrorist organization to increase its status. Examples of groups with these various types of goals are summarized in Table 7.1.

Thus, of the 42 groups designated as Foreign Terrorist Organizations (FTOs) by the US State Department in 2005, 31 sought regime change, 19 sought territorial change, four sought policy change and one sought to maintain the status quo (Kydd and Walter, 2006).

Table 7.1  *Major goals of terrorist organizations, with examples*

| | |
|---|---|
| Regime change | FLN (Algeria); Shining Path (Peru) |
| Territory change | LTTE (Sri Lanka); Irish Republican Army (Northern Ireland) |
| Policy change | al-Qaeda (global) |
| Social control | Ku Klux Klan (US); anti-abortion terrorists (US); Taliban militants |
| Status quo maintenance | United Self-Defense Forces (Colombia); Ulster Defence Forces (Northern Ireland) |

*Source*: Adapted from material in Kydd and Walter (2006).

Finally, we must note the interests and preferences of counter-terror stakeholders. As always, these can vary widely, even among the main political targets of terrorists: national governments. Some government interests are more narrowly constructed, such as stopping the attacks and protecting lives and property, while others might be much broader in scope, such as completely eliminating the terrorists and their sympathizers as a political force. To protect these interests, however, governments have increasingly debated the appropriate policy preferences, which can involve virtually all the power resources of the state: rhetorical, legal, economic, police and military. Moreover, the citizens they mean to protect often expect counter-terror officials to use all resources necessary to stop the attacks and bring the terrorists to justice, which can give officials an unprecedented amount of leeway when deciding how to respond. This tendency regarding the perceived nature of the terrorist threat brings us to the next element in our analysis: preferences about the use of force.

## The use of force

To be defined as such, terrorist organizations obviously see the use of force, mainly against civilians, as necessary to achieve their objectives, particularly when matched against the superior resources of states. As noted above, one problem in the analysis of terrorism is the tendency to confuse the tactical use of force with the strategic political interests or preferences of terrorists. As a tactic, force can be used by terrorists for a variety of purposes, for example to: sow fear, send a message ('political theatre' or the 'propaganda of the deed'), exact concessions, build morale, advertise for recruits and supporters, disrupt order, provoke repression, discredit authority, exact revenge or enforce obedience (Crenshaw, 1981). However, acts of terrorism may be more effectively analysed in terms of

their strategic political ends, which mainly involve influencing two primary audiences: their own supporters or sympathizers, and the stakeholders whose behaviour they hope to influence. Accomplishing these goals
simultaneously usually requires a strategy of attrition, where the terrorist organization attempts to survive while demonstrating its ability and
willingness to attack its target indefinitely, which, in principle, will raise
the cost of non-compliance on the part of the target government to unacceptable levels.

If terrorists are willing to use deadly force against both civilians and
state stakeholders to attain their objectives, the same cannot always be said
regarding their political opponents, who must decide whether these highly
visible tactics require an equally forceful response. In fact, the history of
counter-terrorism shows that the response to terrorism can take a variety
of forms and produce a variety of outcomes. As with the discussion about
civil war in Chapter 5, the main targets of terrorism – usually national
governments – have a choice: whether to negotiate with the terrorists or
to attack them with various degrees of force. This is a crucial decision, for
negotiation, even if it fails, typically legitimizes the political interests of
the terrorists, and even the terrorists themselves, in the view of the public
and other stakeholders, such as foreign observers. This process may then
make it difficult for the government to resort to force or to discredit the
political goals of the terrorists. The first rule of US counter-terror policy,
for example, is to make no concessions and strike no deals, and many
other advanced states that suffer from terrorist attacks also seem to share
this view. However, the reality is much more complicated, and states, even
the US, have been known to make deals with or otherwise comply with the
demands of terrorists, either implicitly or explicitly (Bapat, 2006). Equally
controversial is the recent resort by some states, such as the US and the UK,
to adopt certain policies as noted above, such as extraordinary rendition
and torture, to gain intelligence about future attacks.

## Public–private domains and levels of jurisdiction

One very interesting but often overlooked aspect of terrorism, and counter-
terrorism, is the simple fact that most targets of terrorist *attacks* (not the
targets of their political goals) are actually *private* in nature, mainly firms
such as foreign-owned businesses. This is because such targets are much
'softer' than the hardened facilities controlled by states, such as embassies
and military bases. Thus, the first responders here, as with other contemporary threats to international security like infectious disease, are
typically private stakeholders rather than public officials. In other words,
the first line of defence in terrorist attacks is the general public. And the
second line of defence might often be PMCs or security firms hired by the
state or private stakeholders, plus larger paramilitary units composed of

private citizens who take up arms to defend their local territories against the acts of terrorist organizations (Pelton, 2007). As with our discussion of rebel movements in Chapter 5, terrorism and counter-terrorism activities often occur in the increasingly complicated grey area between 'purely public' and 'purely private' domains, which is precisely why such movements can be so difficult to defeat with normal legal and police methods. This task becomes even more difficult if the terrorists themselves can recruit or draw support from the ranks of public officials, as happened with the Ku Klux Klan in the American South, or if, conversely, the terrorists explicitly target the judicial officials and witnesses who attempt to bring them to justice using legal means, as occurs with various narco-terrorist groups, as well as organized criminals, in Colombia and elsewhere.

These considerations regarding counter-terror campaigns further complicate the issue of determining an appropriate jurisdiction, whether domestically or internationally. At the domestic level, local officials might be either sympathetic to, or direct targets of, terrorist campaigns, which might require greater national or federal attention to the problem. Things become even more complicated at the international level when multiple states attempt to coordinate their activities. Assuming a formal legal approach is adopted, states are typically expected to comply with bilateral extradition treaties or even broader mutual legal assistance treaties (MLATs), which can be very difficult to negotiate and which might not always be in place, particularly between states with difficult diplomatic relationships, such as the US and Libya. This is precisely why some states, including the US, are so easily tempted to bypass formal legal measures altogether and kidnap and even torture their suspects, or allow them to be interrogated and tortured in third countries such as Egypt or Pakistan, rather than pursue a frustrating, time-consuming and possibly unsuccessful extradition request (Gourevitch and Morris, 2008; Sands, 2008). Other states have pursued equally questionable tactics, such as the UK's unsuccessful attempt in 2005 to allow its police to hold terror suspects for up to 90 days without charging them, as well as a similar attempt in 2007 to extend the limit to 42 days; this type of extensive grant of state power was rejected by Parliament in favour of maintaining the current limit of 28 days without charge, which is still the highest legal limit for detention without charge in the Western world, where most states have a limit of less than a week.

## International terrorism as a policy problem

Based on the considerations above, it should be clear by now that analysing terrorism as an international security problem is extremely complicated and contentious, even if the actual threat in terms of damage to lives or property is small relative to other major threats. It also should be clear that the main threat posed by terrorism, in fact, is precisely to the legitimacy and authority of states themselves, rather than to other referent objects such as lives and property. Thus, even though states may agree on the need to prevent the physical damage created by terrorism, they may strongly disagree about whether terrorism poses an existential threat to their national interests. This tendency in turn then undermines the potential for international counter-terrorism cooperation, as we shall see throughout this section.

## Agenda-setting

The problem of terrorism in general has been on the international security agenda since the early 1970s, yet attention to specific groups or targets can vary widely depending on the context. Obviously the most overt and direct aspect of agenda-setting involves the choice of targets made by the terrorist organizations themselves; some states clearly suffer more than others from terrorism and therefore will adopt a different view about it. The degree of official international attention to certain terrorist groups also varies in terms of whether they are viewed as domestic or transnational/international terrorist organizations. In other words, then, there is still some contention over whether terrorism is really an international or more regional/local threat.

During the Cold War, for example, the US and its allies were especially concerned with state-sponsored terrorism that could be traced back to the communist world in general or the Soviet Union and its allies in particular. For terrorist groups that were not directly linked to communist activities, such as the IRA in Northern Ireland, the US took a much more passive view, even as its own allies such as the UK were struggling to defeat such groups. This situation has changed to some degree in the years since 9/11, which encouraged the Bush administration to put counter-terrorism at the top of the US security agenda. Yet even though many global stakeholders – the US and its major allies, the UN and the EU for example – all include terrorism as one of their top security priorities, there is still a high degree of contention over the best way to counter that threat.

One way around this problem is simply to identify and focus on the specific foreign terrorist organizations (FTOs) as the main targets of global policy, and then encourage other major global stakeholders to bring the individuals associated with those organizations to justice. The US in particular does this through its annual official designation of FTOs. The most recent such list of 59 FTOs is given in Table 7.2; this is an increase of about 30 per cent relative to the list of 45 FTOs released in 2009:

These FTOs vary extremely widely in terms of how lethal they are; some groups, such as the Revolutionary Nuclei in Greece, have been responsible for just a few attacks or deaths. As a result, they do not receive an equal amount of attention by the major international stakeholders, yet the regular updating of a list such as this – as well as securing some international consensus regarding the inclusion of certain groups on it – is a necessary first step down the path of effective international counter-terrorism cooperation. As the majority of the groups on this list are Muslim-related, and as nearly all of the new groups identified since 9/11 are Muslim as well, this type of terrorism naturally receives the bulk of attention by most policy-makers and scholars. A second step along these same lines involves the identification of state sponsors of terrorism, another US priority that has resulted in some cooperation by other like-minded states even though some have questioned whether such state 'sponsorship' actually helps terrorist groups survive (Carter, 2012) or why it occurs at all (Salehyan, Gleditsch and Cunningham, 2011). Even so, this designation makes it easier for state targets of terrorism to impose sanctions on other states as a way of deterring their support for terrorist activities. Currently, only Iran, Sudan and Syria are designated as state sponsors of terrorism; Afghanistan and Pakistan were considered for the list before 9/11 but were not included, while Iraq was on the list before the 2003 US attack on that state and has been taken off it since then, as have Libya (2006), North Korea (2008) and Cuba (2015).

## Framing policy alternatives

Assuming there is some agreement on the main FTOs and state sponsors to be targeted, which is not always the case, the question then turns to the tension between unilateral and multilateral responses, as well as the related problem of what policy instruments should be deployed. If terrorism really is a global threat, as most major powers and IOs agree it is, then it must require multilateral efforts to combat it. And it most certainly would benefit from a combination of passive/defensive measures and active/offensive measures given the overall complexity of the phenomenon. Most states in fact have enacted a wide range of defensive measures since 9/11, such as hardening potential targets, improving passenger screening at transportation facilities, working to deny dangerous weapons or materials to terrorists, issuing travel warnings to certain states, training civilian first responders to deal with terror incidents and enhancing public–private cooperation. There is relatively little discord regarding these approaches at the international level of analysis and they will not be considered further here, although the issue of airline passenger data privacy has provoked some transatlantic tension (along with some aspects of cybersecurity; see Chapter 8). The situation becomes far more difficult regarding efforts to improve multilateral counter-terror cooperation, and/or to enact more offensive measures, given the diffuse and varied nature of the threat. Thus, although multilateral cooperation on terrorism-related issues has existed

Table 7.2   *US-designated foreign terrorist organizations, 2016*

**Designated Foreign Terrorist Organizations**

| Month/Year Designated | Name |
| --- | --- |
| 10/1997 | Abu Nidal Organization (ANO) |
| 10/1997 | Abu Sayyaf Group (ASG) |
| 10/1997 | Aum Shinrikyo (AUM) |
| 10/1997 | Basque Fatherland and Liberty (ETA) |
| 10/1997 | Gama'a al-Islamiyya (Islamic Group) (IG) |
| 10/1997 | HAMAS |
| 10/1997 | Harakat ul-Mujahidin (HUM) |
| 10/1997 | Hizballah |
| 10/1997 | Kahane Chai (Kach) |
| 10/1997 | Kurdistan Workers Party (PKK) (Kongra-Gel) |
| 10/1997 | Liberation Tigers of Tamil Eelam (LTTE) |
| 10/1997 | National Liberation Army (ELN) |
| 10/1997 | Palestine Liberation Front (PLF) |
| 10/1997 | Palestinian Islamic Jihad (PIJ) |
| 10/1997 | Popular Front for the Liberation of Palestine (PFLF) |
| 10/1997 | PFLP-General Command (PFLP-GC) |
| 10/1997 | Revolutionary Armed Forces of Colombia (FARC) |
| 10/1997 | Revolutionary People's Liberation Party/Front (DHKP/C) |
| 10/1997 | Shining Path (SL) |
| 10/1999 | al-Qa'ida (AQ) |
| 9/2000 | Islamic Movement of Uzbekistan (IMU) |
| 5/2001 | Real Irish Republican Army (RIRA) |
| 12/2001 | Jaish-e-Mohammed (JEM) |
| 12/2001 | Lashkar-e Tayyiba (LeT) |
| 3/2002 | Al-Aqsa Martyrs Brigade (AAMB) |
| 3/2002 | Asbat al-Ansar (AAA) |
| 3/2002 | al-Qaida in the Islamic Maghreb (AQIM) |
| 8/2002 | Communist Party of the Philippines/New People's Army (CPP/NPA) |

$\rightarrow$

| | |
|---|---|
| → | |
| 10/2002 | Jemaah Islamiya (JI) |
| 1/2003 | Lashkar i Jhangvi (LJ) |
| 3/2004 | Ansar al-Islam (AAI) |
| 7/2004 | Continuity Irish Republican Army (CIRA) |
| 12/2004 | Islamic State of Iraq and the Levant (formerly al-Qa'ida in Iraq) |
| 6/2005 | Islamic Jihad Union (IJU) |
| 3/2008 | Harakat ul-Jihad-i-Islami/Bangladesh (HUJI-B) |
| 3/2008 | al-Shabaab |
| 5/2009 | Revolutionary Struggle (RS) |
| 7/2009 | Kata'ib Hizballah (KH) |
| 1/2010 | al-Qa'ida in the Arabian Peninsula (AQAP) |
| 8/2010 | Harakat ul-Jihad-i-Islami (HUJI) |
| 9/2010 | Tehrik-e Taliban Pakistan (TTP) |
| 11/2010 | Jundallah |
| 5/2011 | Army of Islam (AOI) |
| 9/2011 | Indian Mujahedeen (IM) |
| 3/2012 | Jemaah Anshorut Tauhid (JAT) |
| 5/2012 | Abdallah Azzam Brigades (AAB) |
| 9/2012 | Haqqani Network (HQN) |
| 3/2013 | Ansar al-Dine (AAD) |
| 11/2013 | Boko Haram |
| 11/2013 | Ansaru |
| 12/2013 | al-Mulathamun Battalion |
| 1/2014 | Ansar al-Shari'a in Benghazi |
| 1/2014 | Ansar al-Shari'a in Darnah |
| 1/2014 | Ansar al-Shari'a in Tunisia |
| 4/2014 | ISIL Sinai Province (formally Ansar Bayt al-Maqdis) |
| 5/2014 | al-Nusrah Front |
| 8/2014 | Mujahidin Shura Council in the Environs of Jerusalem (MSC) |
| 9/2015 | Jaysh Rijal al-Tariq al Naqshabandi (JRTN) |
| 1/2016 | ISIL-Khorasan (ISIL-K) |

*Source*: US Department of State, Bureau of Counterterrorism.

since the 1960s, until 9/11 these measures usually played a subordinate role compared to the efforts made by certain states (particularly the major powers) to deal with terrorist organizations that threatened them directly.

While a more unilateral legal approach is still in place for most major states, since 9/11 the range of options has expanded considerably thanks primarily, but not exclusively, to US leadership. There is now much more multilateral cooperation against terrorism in general and against specific terrorist activities, as we shall see in more detail in the discussion of policy effectiveness, as well as the use of more aggressive policies to deal with terrorism. These policies involve the greater use of military force to combat terrorism, whether in the form of covert action or overt military attacks, including bombing terrorist training facilities, targeting individual terrorist suspects with aircraft or drone strikes (sometimes known as 'decapitation' when terrorist leaders are targeted; see Jordan, 2009), and full-scale invasion and occupation, as with Afghanistan and Iraq. These methods also extend to the use of various extra-legal if not illegal measures, such as extraordinary rendition, torture and the imprisonment – without charge or trial – of terrorist suspects. Israel has also used such measures in attempting to stop terrorism campaigns, and has even resorted to the indiscriminate bombing of civilian populations during the 2006 war in Lebanon (against Hezbollah) and the 2008–9 war in Gaza (against Hamas). The defeat in Sri Lanka of the LTTE in 2009 also involved a high civilian death toll, while 300,000 others were left homeless. Taken together, these measures clearly indicate that these states believe that terrorism deserves the highest possible status, almost similar to interstate war, as a threat to domestic and/or international security.

Some analysts have advocated more positive, though still proactive, measures. One option is to negotiate to discourage terrorists from attacking; this option is often highly contentious, especially in states that have suffered from major terrorist campaigns. Another, and somewhat more acceptable, suggestion is that governments try to avoid overreacting to terrorism (Mueller, 2005; Kydd and Walter, 2006), even to the extent of using government education programmes to explain why terrorism is not as threatening as the public might otherwise think it is. Some analysts would apply such an approach to terrorism's possible root causes; for example, by undertaking a general 'charm offensive' throughout the world in general and the Muslim world in particular, whereby the US would deliberately attempt to improve its image as a protector of human rights and friend to Islam. This effort could be enhanced through related policies regarding development and humanitarian aid policies. Some further advocate the use of financial aid to states where terrorist groups operate, which could function as a kind of 'Middle East Marshall Plan' similar to the US effort to rebuild European economies after WWII. While these suggestions are creative and potentially effective, they are difficult to evaluate since the US and its major allies, as targets of terrorism, have very strong political incentives to inflate the terror threat and use more visible means to deal with it rather than try these less aggressive, and supposedly less well-proven, measures. These measures are also far too easily exploited by opposition parties and leaders in democratic states, which is why they tend to be found in the pages of academic articles rather than in formal policy statements by government officials.

## Policy choice

We have seen that the nature of terrorism often encourages states, especially the major powers, to take matters into their own hands, typically through the adoption of unilateral measures. This tendency also follows from the fact that terrorists are highly selective when linking the targets of their attacks to their political objectives. In other words, the terrorist threat is quite discriminatory, so states vary widely in their vulnerability to attacks by various groups. And most states are not prone to attacks by *any* groups, a condition which may decrease their willingness to assume the risks of joining a major counter-terror campaign. These factors, as well as the diffuse nature of the entire war on terrorism, mean that there is no dominant multilateral forum or approach to the problem. Instead, it is dealt with on multiple fronts, with multiple tools and varying degrees of commitment, and thus effectiveness, by the major players.

In terms of unilateral policies, some states with adequate power resources will act almost with impunity to counteract terror attacks. Here the US has clearly played a major role in enhancing the status of terrorism as a major global threat, with much support by some of its key allies, such as Israel and the UK. Among the advanced liberal democracies, most have tended to adopt a more legal/judicial approach, which involves police forces, due process of law and criminal trials. Before 9/11, for example, America's official counter-terrorism policy involved four elements: make no concessions and strike no deals; bring terrorists to justice for their crimes (that is, the prosecution and extradition of foreign suspects); isolate and apply pressure on states that allow or sponsor terrorism to eliminate the safe havens where terrorists hide out; and bolster the counter-terrorist capabilities of states that cooperate with the US, which has led to the training of over 20,000 police and military officials in over 100 states.

This more legal approach also involves the payment of rewards for information on terrorists, and the use of civil suits against state sponsors of terrorism under the 1996 US Anti-Terrorism Law. To help stem the financing of terrorism, the US Treasury Department created a new Foreign Terrorist Asset Tracking Center, which is linked to other measures regarding money laundering (see Chapter 9). The threat of bioterrorism in light of the anthrax attacks in the US after 9/11 has encouraged a greater role for public health officials in counter-terror policies (see Chapter 12). Finally, the US government quickly passed a controversial series of measures to permit much greater counter-terror intelligence gathering within the US itself, in the form of the 2001 USA Patriot Act. Although most of the Act's provisions were supposed to expire in 2005, nearly all of them were reauthorized twice by Congress and the president until 2015; these mainly relate to authority to conduct surveillance on various types of communications and to stop terrorist-related money laundering. An even more serious expansion of federal counter-terror authority, the 2006 Military Commissions Act, would have allowed the detention and prosecution by military tribunals (rather than criminal courts) of 'unlawful enemy combatants' in the US or captured elsewhere. However, the Act was struck down as unconstitutional by the US Supreme Court in 2008. In 2015 the USA Patriot Act itself was replaced with the USA Freedom Act, which kept many of the same provisions on surveillance but blocked the US National Security Agency (NSA) from conducting mass data collection activities (see Chapter 8).

In the UK, a legal response to terrorism has run into some difficulty in recent years. In addition to the problems, noted above, with extending the detention without charge period to 90 or 42 days, the British government created a Special Immigration Appeal Commission (SIAC) to hear immigration cases involving a question of national security, namely terrorism. The SIAC system allowed for detention without trial, but was ruled illegal in 2004; the current system of 'control orders' was created in 2005 to replace it (a similar approach exists in Australia). Such control orders allow the use of secret evidence to place terror suspects under what amounts to house arrest for up to 24 hours a day, without a chance to defend themselves. However, use of such secret evidence, or surveillance, informers and other forms of intelligence that must not be compromised in the face of a public trial was also ruled illegal in June 2009, so the government has struggled to find a way to deal with such cases, which is why the 28-day detention scheme noted above remains in effect. In 2011, the British government replaced control orders with Terrorism Prevention and Investigation Measures, which essentially involves many of the same powers.

The UK has also shown a clear willingness to negotiate with terrorist groups, as with former Prime Minister Tony Blair's offers of concessions to the IRA and its political arm, Sinn Fein, in order to keep the 1998 Good Friday Agreement peace process on track (Powell, 2008). This was the first time a British prime minister had agreed to meet Sinn Fein's leadership since the 1920s, and the decision seems to have produced positive results. The UK also worked with Libya (a former state sponsor of terrorism) prior to its civil war; the UK negotiated a prisoner transfer agreement with that state and then released one of the Libyan bombers of Pan Am flight 103 from prison in Scotland. Although the UK and Scottish governments claimed the decision to release and return Abdelbaset al-Megrahi to Libya was made on compassionate grounds alone and not part of a larger deal, it was still highly controversial as the Pan Am bombing had killed

270 people (the majority of whom were Americans), and UK government officials later admitted a link to a series of new oil and investment deals between Libya and the UK. The UK was also heavily involved in the military intervention in Libya in 2011, which is still an ongoing crisis.

Measures that are not ruled illegal in their home states are also coordinated with America's major allies, especially in the EU (Rees, 2006). For example, all major IOs (including regional ones), as well as related diplomatic forums, such as the annual G8 summits of the major powers, have discussed terrorism as a problem and have issued resolutions and other policies regarding how to combat it. At the international level, multilateral efforts have involved the condemnation of various terrorist groups and acts in the form of UNSC resolutions, plus specific treaties devoted to certain types of terrorist activities. As noted above, although a general UN Global Strategy on Counter-Terrorism was approved in 2006, a stronger UN-sponsored Comprehensive Convention on International Terrorism has run into difficulties because of disputes about distinguishing (for example) terrorists from liberation movements. Instead, most multilateral counter-terror cooperation attempts to target violent or criminal behaviours rather than the terrorist groups themselves, or indeed, the very idea of terror as a political tactic (the 'War on Terror', see Box 7.4). Some of the more important such measures are summarized in Box 7.2.

---

## Box 7.2  Major international treaties pertaining to the subject of international terrorism

International Civil Aviation Organization (ICAO), Convention on Offences and Certain Other Acts Committed on Board Aircraft.

ICAO Convention for the Suppression of Unlawful Seizure of Aircraft.

ICAO Convention for the Suppression of Unlawful Acts Against the Safety of Civil Aviation.

UN Convention on the Prevention and Punishment of Crimes Against Internationally Protected Persons, Including Diplomats.

UN Convention Against the Taking of Hostages.

International Atomic Energy Agency, Convention on the Physical Protection of Nuclear Material.

ICAO Protocol for the Suppression of Unlawful Acts of Violence at Airports Serving International Civil Aviation.

International Maritime Organization (IMO), Convention for the Suppression of Unlawful Acts Against the Safety of Maritime Navigation.

IMO Protocol for the Suppression of Unlawful Acts Against the Safety of Fixed Platforms Located on the Continental Shelf.

ICAO Convention on the Marking of Plastic Explosives for the Purpose of Detection.

UN International Convention for the Suppression of Terrorist Bombings.

UN Convention on the Suppression of Financing of Terrorism.

As we can see, these efforts not only target terrorist acts, but also some of the materials/weapons and support infrastructure that make terrorism possible. This strategy is very similar in fact to the fight against transnational organized crime, as we shall see in Chapter 9.

We can also see various complementary efforts by regional IOs to manage the threat of terrorism, as summarized in Box 7.3.

Most recently, the US, NATO and the EU are cooperating against terrorism, as part of a broader agenda to confront organized crime, data protection issues, travel security and other transnational security problems. While all of these multilateral efforts are admirable, they generally represent a kind of 'middle ground' consensus position regarding how to organize international counter-terrorism cooperation. They also must be considered in light of more aggressive measures (the War on Terror) already noted, as well as the use of bargaining or concessions *vis-à-vis* terrorist organizations, which often takes place on more minor issues, although this usually is not admitted publicly (Sederberg, 1995). Taken together, these measures clearly reveal a fairly high degree of global opposition to certain terrorist acts, such as bombing and hijacking, but much less consensus regarding how to deal with the root causes or specific political goals of terrorists.

---

### Box 7.3   Regional counter-terror agreements

League of Arab States, Arab Convention on the Suppression of Terrorism.

Organization of the Islamic Conference, Convention on Combating International Terrorism.

Council of Europe, European Convention on the Suppression of Terrorism.

Council of Europe Convention on Laundering, Search, Seizure and Confiscation of the Proceeds from Crime and on the Financing of Terrorism.

Organization of American States, Convention to Prevent and Punish the Acts of Terrorism Taking the Form of Crimes against Persons and Related Extortion that are of International Significance.

African Union (formerly Organization of African Unity), Convention on the Prevention and Combating of Terrorism.

South Asian Association for Regional Cooperation, Regional Convention on Suppression of Terrorism.

Commonwealth of Independent States, Treaty on Cooperation among the States Members of the Commonwealth of Independent States in Combating Terrorism.

EU Area of Freedom, Security and Justice (AFSJ): Multiple and comprehensive measures to deal with terrorism, organized crime and similar transnational threats in the area of Justice and Home Affairs, including the creation of an EU-wide arrest warrant and a European Police Office (Europol) after 1992.

## The politics of policy effectiveness

With such a high degree of discord regarding the nature of international terrorism as a global security threat, it is not surprising that policy effectiveness is equally difficult to evaluate. Beyond the problems noted above, there is a fairly high degree of both voluntary and involuntary defection regarding various domestic and international counter-terror policies. Voluntary defection is most prominent in the form of disputes among states and other stakeholders regarding whether to give terrorism a high priority as an existential threat, even though they may agree on various conventions and treaties about specific terrorist or criminal acts, as noted above. Involuntary defection is always more difficult to evaluate, yet we should be aware that some states simply do not have the financial, administrative and other resources to implement various counter-terror treaties, even though they may agree with them in principle. Even where they have such resources, other policy goals, such as economic development or public health, might take priority over the fight against terrorism. This is not just a problem for poor and less developed states; in fact, one of the most striking aspects of counter-terror policy is the high degree of involuntary defection among developed states owing to not just a lack of resources or political attention, but also to organizational politics and fragmentation across a number of law enforcement, military and other agencies.

In the US, for example, counter-terrorism policy is supposed to be coordinated by the National Security Council, but most major US agencies, both domestic and foreign, have their own offices or desks devoted to this topic, and they do not always cooperate. Domestic counter-terrorism investigations are supposed to be handled by the FBI, while the State Department and the CIA handle foreign ones. Large US police departments, such as the New York Police Department, also have their own counter-terror capabilities. In addition, some agencies are devoted to 'security' affairs while others are devoted to 'disaster management' or 'emergency response' (Falkenrath, 2001). These divisions beg the question: which agency is responsible for investigating or responding if a *foreign* group (such as al-Qaeda) plans or executes a *domestic* terrorist attack in the US? This is why 9/11 served as a major 'wake-up call' and led directly to the creation of a Department of Homeland Security (DHS) and brought together many security-related agencies scattered across the US government (Flynn, 2004; Shenon, 2008). However, the DHS does not possess its own intelligence capacity, while the FBI and CIA still exist as separate agencies and possess their original mandates. Thus, if the main leader of the War on Terror cannot organize itself very effectively to deal with this threat, then it can hardly expect other states, especially less developed ones, to do much better.

## Box 7.4    9/11 and America's 'War on Terror'

*The never-ending War on Terror, thanks to a single massive attack against the US.*

The terrorist attacks against the US on 11 September 2001 represent a major turning point in international security, in terms of the nature of the destruction but also America's response. Prior to 9/11, terrorism was merely one among a range of threats facing the US, and was overshadowed by other concerns, such as civil wars and the rise of China. In addition, the US often adopted an inconsistent view of terrorist/insurgent groups, especially during the Cold War if they took the form of anti-communist movements. Finally, America's approach to domestic (or 'homeland') security was highly fragmented, which may have undermined the possibility of predicting 9/11 despite several al-Qaeda attacks against US targets in the 1990s, including one at the World Trade Center (WTC) (Zegart 2007).

→

The UK's response is somewhat better coordinated by its long-standing (since 1909) domestic security service, MI5, and its subordinate agency, the Joint Terrorism Analysis Centre. Even then these agencies must compete to some degree with MI6 (the Secret Intelligence Service), the Metropolitan

→
These views changed dramatically after the 9/11 attacks, which took the form of an extraordinary day-long global spectacle on live television, beginning at 8:46 a.m. when the first aircraft flew into Building 1 of the WTC. The drama did not end until 5:21 p.m., when Building 7 of the World Trade Center collapsed. The entire day was filled with terror in the air and on land as three aircraft hit their targets on the ground (including the Pentagon), the Twin Towers of the WTC collapsed and a fourth aircraft – United Airlines Flight 93 – was crashed in a field after its passengers confronted their hijackers. With nearly 3,000 dead victims, 9/11 remains the deadliest terrorist attack in history, and it provoked an equally forceful response by the US. This involved domestic and foreign components, starting with the creation of the DHS and the adoption of extensive surveillance/spying measures as noted in the main text (also see Chapter 8). Internationally, the US first invaded Afghanistan to pursue al-Qaeda's leader, Osama bin Laden ('Operation Enduring Freedom-Afghanistan') and then extended its campaign across the globe: to the Philippines, the Horn of Africa, into Asia and the Middle East and eventually to more than 80 countries. The US also requested help from its NATO allies under Article V for the first time, and they responded in various ways.

The CIA was given a central role in coordinating this campaign, and it quickly became apparent that highly controversial, if not completely illegal, measures, such as assassinations, kidnapping ('extraordinary rendition'), torture and detention without charge were being used. These acts undoubtedly inspired other Muslims to join the fight against the US, which is precisely the kind of outcome many terrorists hope to achieve. America also invaded Iraq in 2003 partly out of fear that terrorists might obtain WMD from that country; this act quickly destabilized the entire region and provided more recruits for al-Qaeda. Thus, while the US has not (so far) suffered another major attack similar to 9/11, many other al-Qaeda attacks have taken place around the world since then, while hundreds of thousands of civilians have been killed in Iraq and beyond. And although bin Laden himself was killed by US forces in 2011, al-Qaeda has splintered into, or inspired, many other extremist groups around the world, such as Boko Haram and Islamic State. These trends indicate that while America's War on Terror clearly represents a major change in security strategy by the world's leading military power, the need for that campaign, the effectiveness of that campaign, and its definition of 'victory' when (or if) it ends, will remain contested issues for years to come (Anderson, 2004; Mueller and Stewart, 2012).

Police of London (Scotland Yard), the City of London Police, the new National Crime Agency (which replaced the Serious Organised Crime Agency, or SOCA; see Chapter 9) and other bodies. Both the US and the UK have also been criticized for their creation of a jointly aligned *public* terror threat notification system. The US/UK terrorism threat levels (or US Homeland Security Advisory System) are:

GREEN　　Low (US/UK) – an attack is unlikely
BLUE　　　Guarded (US)/Moderate (UK) – an attack is possible, but not likely
YELLOW　Elevated (US)/Substantial (UK) – an attack is a strong possibility
ORANGE　High (US)/Severe (UK) – an attack is highly likely
RED　　　Severe (US)/Critical (UK) – an attack is expected imminently

Beyond the obvious difficulty of distinguishing clearly between these levels (such as the use of the term 'severe' at two different levels of threat in the US and UK, and the fact that an attack is always *possible*, so that the Green or low level is unnecessary), the data and criteria on which threat level decisions are made are not available to the public and therefore do not inspire any confidence. In fact, the two lowest levels have never been used in either the US or the UK since the system was created (2002 in the US and 2006 in the UK). The system thus seemed tailor-made for sowing fear (at best) or ridicule (at worst) among civilian populations, and could easily be used to distract attention from other political problems. In response, it was replaced in the US in 2011 with a simpler, but not necessarily more useful, National Terrorism Advisory System, which only issues threat warnings when it has specific, credible information. If so, the system uses only three categories of threat: 'elevated', 'intermediate', and 'imminent'. The UK, however, continues to rely on the earlier five-level warning system.

Taking a closer look at various measures of policy effectiveness, a total victory standard against terrorism as a general threat clearly would produce a disappointing result if we take a global perspective (the War on Terror). The simple fact that the US itself has been at an elevated threat level or higher since 2002 clearly indicates what little overall progress has been made in this area. As noted above, we have also seen a proliferation of Islamic-related terrorist groups well beyond al-Qaeda in the past decade, operating across a much wider geographic scope (such as Africa). However, a number of individual terrorist organizations have diminished as major threats as a result of a variety of factors, only some of which actually involve policy initiatives by the global community. In fact, there are at least seven basic reasons why a terrorist organization would cease to exist as such: the capture or death of its leader; failure of transition to the next generation; achievement of the group's aims; transition to a legitimate political process (typically involving negotiations); undermining of popular support; repression; and transition from terrorism to other forms of violence, whether of lesser intensity (crime) or greater intensity (insurgency or warfare) (Cronin, 2006). These factors are not mutually

Table 7.3   *The demise of terrorist organizations*

| Key factors | Examples |
|---|---|
| Capture/kill leader(s) | Shining Path, Kurdistan Worker's Party, Real IRA |
| Failed generational transition | Red Brigades, Weather Underground, Red Army Faction, Aryan Resistance Army |
| Achievement of the cause | Irgun/Stern Gang, African National Congress |
| Transition to a legitimate political process | Provisional IRA, PLO, Moro Islamic Liberation Front |
| Loss of popular support | Real IRA, Basque Homeland and Freedom (ETA), Shining Path |
| Repression | People's Will, Shining Path, Kurdistan Worker's Party, LTTE |
| Transition out of terrorism | |
|   to criminality | Abu Sayyaf, Revolutionary Armed Forces of Colombia |
|   to insurgency | Khmer Rouge, Guatemalan Labour Party, Armed Islamic Group (Algeria) |

*Source*: Adapted from Cronin (2006).

exclusive, of course, and experiencing more than one of them can quickly bring a group to an end, as happened with Shining Path in Peru. This example and others are summarized in Table 7.3.

These examples clearly indicate it is possible to reduce or eliminate the threat posed by specific groups. This aim is most likely to be achieved by adopting a multifaceted as well as multilateral counter-terror strategy targeted at the vulnerabilities of specific groups, which can vary quite widely. The decentralized terrorist network al-Qaeda, for example, did not disappear following the May 2011 killing of its main leader, Osama bin Laden, by US forces in Pakistan. However, a more hierarchical organization based on the charisma or personality of a single leader (such as Abimael Guzmán of Shining Path) may suffer greatly after his/her death or capture, and scholars are currently debating about the true effectiveness of a 'decapitation' strategy that targets top terrorist leaders (Jordan, 2009; Johnston, 2012; Price, 2012; Jordan, 2014; Long, 2014).

A historical trends standard of effectiveness is equally mixed if recent years are any guide. The evidence indicates that terrorist attacks have not declined in the post-Cold War era; they are in fact either holding steady or on the rise in some parts of the world. Similarly, while the former Director of the CIA, General Michael Hayden, might point to a decline in attacks by a specific group in a specific state, such as those of al-Qaeda in Iraq following the US military surge after 2007, this must be balanced against evidence of a corresponding rise in activity in Afghanistan, North Africa, India, Indonesia, Iraq, Nigeria, Pakistan, Somalia, Syria, Yemen and elsewhere. As always, baseline figures for calculating these changes are not easily agreed, and when they are, they must be analysed in light of trends elsewhere, whether positive or negative, that would provide a true net assessment of the impact of any given policy. Similarly, if one defines Islamic State as a terrorist group rather than as a nationalist/insurgent movement, then the number of terror attacks rises much higher, especially those involving small groups or individual 'supporters'. Attacks of this type have increased since 2013, and have occurred in countries ranging across the globe, including the US and several states in Europe (particularly Belgium, France and Turkey). A single attack such as this, the November 2015 attack in Paris by supporters of Islamic State, killed 130 people.

Moreover, and as with statistics on casualties of war, the suppression or manipulation of data regarding terrorism trends by government officials seriously calls into question the use of any random benchmarking approaches for the purposes of demonstrating the supposed effectiveness of counter-terror policies. The same holds true for counterfactual approaches, such as arguing that the *absence* of a terrorist attack in a given state is due to the policies of the government rather than to other factors, as the Bush administration claimed during its final months in office, and as the UK government has claimed when attempting to give its police authorities more power, as occurred after the discovery in 2006 of an alleged plot to bomb UK airports. The only clear evidence of such government proactive counter-terror influence involves the arrest and successful prosecution of individuals who were actively planning an attack, as with the UK's conviction in September 2009 of the group intending to blow up several aeroplanes using liquid explosives concealed in drinks bottles.

Finally, the comparative metrics standard can be equally problematic since there are no such common standards regarding counter-terror policy. One standard, for example, might involve whether any terror attacks have involved WMD; since this has not been the case, except for one or two isolated examples, we could say that counter-terrorism cooperation is working well. Similarly, the US could use its own metric for success and argue that its policies have been working as there have been no major terrorist attacks on its soil since 9/11, as some Bush administration officials, such as Vice President Dick Cheney, asserted on leaving office. Although this approach is certainly appealing to the domestic US audience, it ignores the major terror attacks in other places (London, Madrid, Bali, Mumbai, Paris, Istanbul and so on) that have taken place since the War on Terror was initiated. This focus on major attacks also downplays several 'lone wolf' type incidents in the US and elsewhere (or 'home-grown terrorism'; Brooks, 2011), such as the mass murders by armed attackers in San

Bernardino in 2015 (14 killed) and Orlando in 2016 (49 killed). In addition, using the absence of 'major' attacks on US soil as positive affirmation of the success of a *global* War on Terror is extremely selfish if not outright callous, especially in light of the many thousands killed in Africa and the Middle East, and hundreds more in Europe noted above, since the rise of Islamic State in particular. This kind of attitude does suggest, however, that 'all politics is local', even in international security affairs.

Finally, these 'positive' metrics can easily be countered with other metrics, such as the nature of various terrorist groups: their strength in numbers and resources, what kind of support base they have, and whether these figures are trending upwards or downwards. Where reliable data exist on these matters, which is not always the case, they can easily counterbalance any claims that terrorism has declined as a threat simply because terrorists have never launched a major chemical, biological, nuclear or radiation attack, or because the US has not suffered a large-scale terrorist attack in recent years. As noted earlier, the only clear way to use comparative metrics is to identify specific groups that have declined or disappeared as a result of counter-terror policies (or related factors), and hope that other groups will not rise to take their place, as seems to have happened with the emergence of the Continuity IRA as a faction of the Real IRA, which itself split off from the Provisional IRA – which split from the Official IRA in 1969.

## Summary

Two major trends are evident regarding the nature of international terrorism as a threat and as a policy target. As a threat, international terrorism clearly has received a large, even disproportionate, share of attention ever since the 9/11 attacks in the US, thanks primarily to America's influence. As a policy target, it is also clear that America's own War on Terror rhetoric has been widely criticized, if not completely discredited, in light of the more militaristic and illegal policies of the Bush administration (some of which, such as drone strikes, have been greatly expanded by the Obama administration). More thoughtful political leaders seem to realize how important it is to clearly analyse the threat rather than be tempted to overstate and attack it blindly for political gain, which is still an extremely difficult temptation to avoid for most politicians in competitive electoral systems. In using the 'global War on Terror' language, the US created an expectation that a decisive victory in this realm could virtually eliminate terrorism as a security threat. This outcome is impossible based on the current global distribution of political and economic power, especially if the international community in general, and the US and its key allies in particular, continue to combat terrorism with such an *ad hoc* approach that tends to deal with its symptoms rather than its root political origins and objectives. As we shall also see with America's war on drugs in Chapter 9, these terms can be very misleading as policy goals. It is similarly confusing to conduct a war on a political tactic used by other stakeholders besides terrorists, such as states, organized criminals, and even certain political vandals or protesters such as anti-vivisection and anti-abortion activists, who have been known to threaten or use violence.

Moreover, the aggressive use of military resources, as well as tactics such as torture, rendition and detention without legal representation or trial, only compounds the problem by creating a larger pool of terrorist recruits and sympathizers than otherwise might be the case. This fact has been known at least since the French war against Algeria in the 1950s, when torture was used in an attempt to break the Algerian National Liberation Front, yet was quickly forgotten in the aftermath of the Palestinian *intifada* and the 9/11 attacks. It is also very worrisome that US/UK counter-terror cooperation with such measures seems to ignore the already highly negative reputations of each state in parts of the Middle East, as with Britain's promise of a Jewish homeland (through the 1917 Balfour Declaration) on land that was 90 per cent Palestinian-controlled at the time, and with forceful Anglo-American support for their oil interests in the region after WWII (see Chapter 11). More recent Anglo-American tolerance regarding Israel's aggressive counter-terror tactics, which have been responsible for the deaths and injuries of hundreds of civilians, also suggests ignorance of the role of Jewish militants, such as Irgun and Lehi (or the Stern Gang), who conducted terror/sabotage attacks against British forces in Palestine and helped bring about the creation of Israel in the first place.

Such tactics can also undermine more legal or judicial methods (policing and jury trials), which is precisely what happened in a 2006 incident when the US disrupted a British counter-terror case (Operation Overt) in Pakistan by prematurely rounding up suspects before enough evidence could be gathered to convict the suspects of a terror plot (Suskind, 2008). All counter-terror efforts therefore must be based on the realization that the potential pool of terrorists is not finite, and that misguided policies to kill or capture one terrorist (or to attack large areas indiscriminately) might produce hundreds or thousands of new terrorists, insurgents and local sympathizers – or 'accidental guerrillas' (Kilcullen, 2008) – so that the net benefit of the policy is actually quite negative. In other words, it does more harm than good.

The answer, then, may lie in confronting terrorism from a position of legal and moral strength rather than with military excesses (including, for example, torture), and focusing on the political goals of both sides rather than (or in addition to) the specific nature of terrorist crimes. In addition, and given the nature of terrorism as a North–South and often intra-Muslim conflict, the US and its allies in particular must remain aware of the counterproductive effects – or what the CIA calls 'blowback' – of controversial policies. President Obama's speech to the Muslim world in Cairo of 4 June 2009 was specifically intended to limit the damage caused by earlier US counter-terror (and other) policies, and could have heralded a new 'charm offensive' by the US towards the Muslim world, yet this approach was undermined by Obama's maintenance of Guantanamo prison and his escalation of drone strikes in several states, which often result in civilian deaths. US and European inattention to the situation in Syria since 2011 also has created a major window of opportunity for extremist groups such as Islamic State to expand their reach. Some officials, such as Tony Blair's chief of staff Jonathan Powell, who was instrumental in negotiating the Good Friday agreement with the IRA, have gone even further and argued for direct negotiations between the West and al-Qaeda. As this option is still politically unacceptable in the US, and probably across Europe as well, it may be that America and other major powers will have to focus more attention on changing their own attitudes (and those of their like-minded allies, such as Israel) than on attempting to 'pacify' the Muslim world.

## Further reading

Graham Allison (2006). *Nuclear Terrorism*. London: Constable & Robinson.

T. Björgo (ed.) (2003). *Root Causes of Terrorism: Findings from an International Expert Meeting in Oslo 9–11 June 2003*. Oslo: Norwegian Institute of International Affairs.

Mia Bloom (2005). *Dying to Kill: The Allure of Suicide Terror*. New York: Columbia University Press.

Audrey Kurth Cronin (2011). *How Terrorism Ends: Understanding the Decline and Demise of Terrorist Campaigns*. Princeton: Princeton University Press.

Audrey Kurth Cronin and James M. Ludes (eds.) (2004). *Attacking Terrorism: Elements of a Grand Strategy*. Washington: Georgetown University Press.

Diego Gambetta (ed.) (2005). *Making Sense of Suicide Missions*. Oxford: Oxford University Press.

Adrian Gulke (1995). *The Age of Terrorism and the International Political System*. London: I.B. Tauris.

John Horgan (2005). *The Psychology of Terrorism*. London: Routledge.

John Mueller (2006). *Overblown: How Politicians and the Terrorism Industry Inflate National Security Threats, and Why We Believe Them*. New York: Free Press.

Robert A. Pape (2005). *Dying to Win: The Strategic Logic of Suicide Terrorism*. New York: Random House.

Ami Pedahzur (2005). *Suicide Terrorism*. Cambridge: Polity Press.

David C. Rapoport (ed.) (2001). *Inside Terrorist Organizations*. London: Frank Cass.

Andrew Silke (ed.) (2004). *Research on Terrorism: Trends, Achievements, and Failures*. London: Frank Cass.

## Chapter 8

# Cybersecurity and Cyberwar

The internet has been widely known by the public for less than a generation, after it was heavily commercialized during the 1990s (Greenstein, 2015), yet in that space of time it has become so ubiquitous in world affairs that it now deserves attention as a major 'standalone' issue in international security; in fact, a new *Journal of Cybersecurity* was launched in September 2015 to study this issue. It is also a useful topic to mark the transition from traditional security problems towards the new security or human security agenda, beginning in Chapter 9. As suggested earlier in this volume, two factors help define the orthodox view of traditional international security problems: a focus on violence/military affairs and a focus on direct threats to the state or its major components, such as the economy or public infrastructure, for primarily politico-military rather than economic/criminal reasons. Conversely, the new security agenda involves broader issues, which often do not involve violence and that may not involve direct attacks against the state system but that still undermine national or international stability. International crime, including various forms of cybercrime, represents one focus of the new agenda, as it generally involves the pursuit of economic gain or personal satisfaction rather than political control, and will be discussed in the next chapter.

Accordingly, the rest of this chapter will examine the concepts of cybersecurity and cyberwar. These terms focus on the internet and its related components, such as databases, as a critical referent object to be protected from deliberate attacks (i.e. cybersecurity) and as a means to deliver such attacks to computers and other linked targets, which is essentially a form of sabotage (i.e. cyberwar, including cyberterrorism). More detailed terms will be provided below; for the moment it should be clear that this topic is both extremely complex and very fast-moving, so that some of what follows may be 'overtaken by events' by the time this book is published. However, it is still worth examining the internet as a security issue with the same framework used throughout this volume, to help contextualize our understanding of the problems and solutions involved in protecting it. Moreover, and beyond the technically complex and fast-moving nature of cybersecurity/cyberwar, the issue of internet security governance may be one of the most difficult problems of all contemporary topics discussed in this book (Mueller, 2002; Paré, 2003; Thierer and Crews, 2003), so we need to be very clear about its core political aspects before moving to the analysis of security threats.

## Information, the internet and international security

The twin concepts of cybersecurity and cyberwar are rooted in two major technological revolutions of the twentieth century, both of which involve electronics. The first was a revolution in electronic mass communications thanks largely to the radio and television; the second was a revolution in electronic computing. Both of these trends helped create and advance the concept of *electronic warfare* among states with advanced technical capabilities, as in the form of disrupting radar or radio signals against an adversary (for example). This concept expanded to encompass attacks on Command, Control, Communications, Computers and Intelligence (or C4I) systems, as well as the related concept of *network-centric warfare* (Stiennon, 2015), after the twin revolutions of electronic communications and computers came together during the late 1960s, along with other technologies, as part of what became known as the '*revolution in military affairs*' (Sloan, 2002). At this time, the Advanced Research Projects Agency (ARPA), an office of the US DoD, funded a project to link computers in a network so that they could share information more easily through existing communications lines; the high price of computing at the time was a major incentive for this. The US government also wanted a way to ensure that such a system could survive in the event of a disruption of parts of the network, as might occur during a war. The result was the ARPAnet, which went 'live' in 1969 with just a few institutions (or 'nodes') involved, mostly universities. The core innovation was the use of 'packet switching' protocols to divide a message up, send the parts across the network using the fastest routes, and reassemble the parts in the correct order at the point of reception. Once the system proved its effectiveness, in 1983 the military part of ARPAnet was split off as a separate network (MILNET) so that civilian networks could develop without compromising US national security; this decision, along with another new technical protocol (TCP/IP), allowed multiple networks in various countries to communicate with each other in what is now known as the internet. Since then, the system expanded rapidly and globally thanks to the advent of smaller, and far more affordable, 'microcomputers' and then 'personal computers' (PCs) that found their way into many firms and households by the late 1980s.

The final stage in the evolution of the modern internet, or the 'digital revolution' (Isaacson, 2014), involved the invention of a way for users to interface with the system more easily, especially for those (such as home PC users) who were not computer scientists. This solution took three parts: 1) creating a common language used to store, link and transmit information quickly across the internet (known as 'Hypertext Transfer Protocol', or HTTP); 2) creating a common language to display (or publish) linked computer-stored information in an clear manner (known as 'Hypertext Markup Language', or HTML); and 3) creating software to access the entire global internet (or 'World Wide Web') easily (i.e. 'browsers' such as Mosaic, Internet Explorer, Netscape Navigator, Safari and Google Chrome) and organize the search results (i.e. 'search engines' such as Google and Yahoo). These innovations made it much easier for non-computer scientists to not only access information on the internet, but also to provide content themselves. Thus, the entire system is based on three main pillars: *hardware* (computers, computer servers, internet-linked devices and communications links, both hard-wired and wireless), *software* (publishing/browsing/databasing) and actual *content* (information/data published, stored and shared by users). Once these components were in place, and once computers were found in most firms and many households (at least in the industrialized world), the stage was set for the commercial expansion of the internet during the 1990s, resulting in the system we use today (Hafner and Lyon, 1998; Ifrah, 2001).

However, the 'cyberworld' or 'cyberspace' can be defined in terms well beyond the internet itself, so it is important to keep in mind the roots of this concept in the wider area of mass communications and related concepts (public relations, public diplomacy, information awareness, data/information privacy, surveillance, encryption and so on) (Parker, 2000; Diffie and Landau, 2007; Bamford, 2008; Laidler, 2008). The key point is that any term or policy involving 'cyber' must be thought of as multifaceted in nature, involving a highly complex set of technologies that are understood by only a small proportion of the billions of people who use it regularly. These points will become clearer as we work through the twin concepts of cybersecurity and cyberwar in the rest of this chapter, using our political analysis framework. Much of the analysis will focus on threats and actions involving the three core pillars, or internet infrastructure, noted above (hardware, software, content), although there are clear ramifications beyond this realm as well (for example, involving print/radio/television media, intelligence, surveillance and warfighting of various types) (Hansen and Nissenbaum, 2009). Throughout the discussion, our focus on *international* cybersecurity and cyberwar should also be kept in mind, although some attention to other levels of analysis will be necessary.

## Destructive scale

One of the great ironies about cybersecurity is the massive rise in vulnerabilities in a system funded by the US DoD that was specifically designed to keep computers working in the face of a disruption, such as a deliberate attack. These vulnerabilities are a consequence of many factors, which can be summarized in terms of the types of attacks or disruptions involved (covered in this section) and the nature of the stakeholders who rely upon the internet (covered in the next section). Moreover, these are not necessarily new issues; long before the terms 'cybersecurity' and 'cyberwarfare' became popular, governments, researchers and firms were colluding to develop ways to use computers and networks to conduct surveillance, build databases and recognize voices. This occurred among leading Western powers such as the US and the UK, as well as among their Cold War adversaries, such as East German security authorities and their allies in the Soviet KGB (now the Russian Federal Security Service, or FSB).

In terms of destructive scale, the internet clearly is a global phenomenon and computer systems have been under attack in one form or another even before the internet itself was invented. Perhaps the easiest and therefore most prevalent threat is when an attacker discovers a previously unknown vulnerability in hardware or software and attempts to exploit it before others detect and fix it (i.e. a *zero day* attack). Direct computer-based attacks using harmful software, known generally as *malware* (i.e. 'malicious software'), also take various forms, such as *viruses, worms* and *Trojan Horses*. Like a disease virus, computer viruses replicate themselves across a network in order to harm it in various ways; they are often small parts of software, or bits of code, that require attachment to a larger system to function and replicate. Computer worms are more complex 'independent' software programs that can burrow through a computer network by themselves in order to access specific information or execute a specific function; they can also replicate themselves like viruses. Malware that allow a hacker to take remote control of the system are known as *Trojan Horses*; this approach accounts for roughly two-thirds of malware attacks. The rise in home computing in the 1980s was accompanied by a steady rise in malware attacks as well, since home computers could be more vulnerable to such attacks than better-protected systems at large firms, and attackers themselves could use home computers to launch such attacks. Table 8.1 gives major examples of the evolution of malware.

Although early malware efforts were mostly theoretical and experimental, the evolution of viruses and worms clearly indicates that attacks on various targets have become more frequent and more sophisticated, so that this problem can be regarded as part of the typical risks associated with connecting to the internet. Therefore every internet user, whether in the form of a person, firm or government, must rely upon a considerable degree of self-help in order to avoid these risks. In addition, while some malware attacks are made public very quickly once a virus or worm is detected, other cyberattacks can be far more sophisticated and/or focused in nature so that they are not easily detected – if at all. One major example involves 'denial of service' (or *DoS*) attacks, which attempt to bombard internet servers with so many requests for action that they shut down. More sophisticated DoS attacks can be engineered through the use of thousands of computers around the world, often without the knowledge

**Table 8.1**   *Evolution of major internet-related computer threats*

| Date | Name | Description |
|------|------|-------------|
| 1948–49 | 'Cellular automata' | Mathematician John Von Neumann develops theoretical basis for self-replicating computing functions. |
| 1971 | Creeper vs Reaper | Bob Thomas creates first computer virus (Creeper); it fails to replicate but inspires the first antivirus software (Reaper). |
| 1978 | First worm experiments | John Shock and John Hepps create several versions of worm software at the Xerox Palo Alto Research Center, but they fail to work properly. |
| 1982 | Elk Cloner | Created by a high school student; first Apple operating system virus to replicate itself outside a computer lab. Circulates via a game on floppy disk and puts up a poem on the computer screen. |
| 1986 | cBrain | Basit Farooq Alvi and Amjad Farooq Avli in Pakistan create the first successful computer virus for IBM-PC operating systems; it inspires John McAfee (then employed by Lockheed) to develop the first commercial antivirus security software under his name (now owned by Intel). |
| 1988 | Morris worm | Robert Morris creates first successful computer worm at Cornell University; although meant to be experimental, it accidently infects 5,000 computers and blocks their access to the internet. |
| 1992 | WinVir | First successful virus to target MS Windows. |
| 1992 | Michelangelo | Overwrote first hundred sectors of computer hard drives using MS-DOS. |
| 1996 | VLAD | Australian hacker collective Boza targets MS Windows95. |
| 1998 | SQL injection | First public mention of a new code injection technique used to attack data-driven applications; this involves using Structured Query Language (SQL) code to exploit vulnerabilities in databases and websites by executing certain queries. $\rightarrow$ |

of their users (i.e. *botnets*); this is known as a 'distributed DoS' (or *DDoS*) attack, which can be extremely difficult to counteract. This type of threat also brings us into the realm of cyberwar, which is typically conducted by stealth (even if governments are involved), so that a target might not even know it is under attack. This problem will be examined in more detail later in the chapter. Finally, given the heavy reliance on internet-linked databases by governments and firms, the threat of deliberate data leaks by hackers, employees or other users is also a major concern; this can also involve placing harmful code on a server to steal, destroy or corrupt sensitive data (known as an *SQL Injection*).

$\rightarrow$

| | | |
|---|---|---|
| 1998 | Back Orifice | Hacker collective 'Cult of the Dead Cow' creates first Trojan Horse, which allows remote system control of Windows98. |
| 1999 | Melissa | Overloads email servers through MS Word and Outlook. |
| 2000 | I love you | Overwrote files with copies of itself using the Windows Address Book; created by computer students in the Philippines. |
| 2001 | Code Red worms I and II Nimda worm | Worms designed to attack Microsoft's web server (Code Red) and Windows operating system (Nimda). |
| 2001 | Win32.05-0-1 | First virus to target social networking websites. |
| 2003 | Blaster | 18-year-old student invents a DDoS-type attack that crashes systems when they update Windows online. |
| 2003 | Slammer | Unknown source; DDoS-type attack to slow down global internet traffic. |
| 2004 | Sasser | German computer student slows down global internet traffic. |
| 2007 | Zeus | Unknown source; software designed to steal financial information. |
| 2008 | Conficker | Unknown source; creates and replicates botnets. |
| 2010 | Stuxnet worm | See this chapter's case study. |
| 2011 | Duqu | Unknown source; similar effects to Stuxnet. |
| 2012 | Flame | Cyberespionage software attributed to the US and Israel, targeted at the Middle East. |
| 2012 | Shamoon | Virus, possibly from Iran, used to attack 30,000 computers in the network of Saudi Aramco, Saudi Arabia's national oil and gas firm. |
| 2014 | Regin | Unknown source; software used to target data collection. |
| 2014– 16 | BlackEnergy | Trojan Horse, thought to be of Russian origin, targeted against news firms and industrial systems in the US and Europe. |

*Source:* Bronk and Tikk-Ringas, 2013; Cavelty, 2016; updated and expanded by the author.

## Geographic and temporal scope

However, the steady rise of malware and other threats since the late 1980s is just one aspect of defining cybersecurity as a concept. Another key issue involves the huge geographic range of the system. The internet, indeed, has become a central, if not *the* central, component of the global communications infrastructure. As with the spread of viruses and worms, this geographic expansion has developed well beyond the early stages of the internet in the US, and now includes every populated continent on the planet. In addition, Google is working on 'Project Loon', which will use high-altitude balloons to connect remote parts of the globe to the internet. This wide geographic scope must be considered along with the speed with which information flows through the network; the very fact that the internet is a complex high-speed network, with billions of access points across the planet, means that a single virus or worm can spread from one computer to thousands or millions of others before the damage can be stopped. However, this speed is also a virtue of the system, as information about new malware, and (hopefully) a means to detect and prevent it, can spread equally quickly, as long as users keep themselves informed of such issues on a regular basis and update their systems accordingly. Given the rapid pace of technological change and wide geographical scope in this domain, there is fairly wide consensus today that cybersecurity will be a major problem area as long as the internet itself exists, although experts still debate about the precise nature of the threat, as well as the evolution of cyberwarfare in particular (Gartzke, 2013; Kello, 2013).

## Likelihood

As noted above, cyberattacks are such a regular occurrence that we need not spend too much time debating whether they will occur. In fact, the number of such attacks has reached almost ridiculous proportions; since 2005 there have been over 5,000 major data breaches, while in 2014 alone more than 317 million pieces of malware were created – nearly one million a day. At that rate, it would seem nearly impossible to cope with the vastness of the threat, but the good news is that the vast majority of these attacks are based on versions of malware that have been around for years. One study, the Verizon Data Breach Investigations Report, suggests that up to 90 per cent of these millions of attacks have involved malware from 2002 which is already known to the cybersecurity community. This also suggests that, like much criminal activity in general, attackers are looking for easy targets and windows of opportunity in conducting their attacks, so that regularly updating antivirus software and operating system software, as well as using secure internet connections and relying on trusted websites, should prevent some harm from those millions of attacks. Even so, 87 per cent of company executives still cited cybersecurity as a major concern in a 2015 PricewaterhouseCoopers survey, a figure that has risen over the past decade, while states vary widely in terms of their vulnerability to attacks, as Box 8.1 indicates.

In addition to profit-driven cybercrime attacks (see Chapter 9), computer virus and DoS attacks as described above have risen steadily since the mid-1990s. Hacking into computer systems is viewed as an especially menacing threat; since 2003, targets like Lockheed Martin, the US National Aeronautics and Space Administration (NASA), the US DoD, the US Congress, the UK Houses of Parliament and Sandia National Labs have suffered electronic intrusions and/or thefts of critical secret

---

**Box 8.1   States most vulnerable to hacking attacks**

1   Belgium
2   Tajikistan
3   Samoa
4   Australia
5   China
6   Hong Kong
7   Dominican Republic
8   Afghanistan
9   South Africa
10   Ethiopia

Ranking is from most to least vulnerable.

*Source:* Rapid Exposure Index, Rapid7 (June 2016).

---

information ('cyberespionage'). Authorities on this topic also claim that a Chinese spy network has hacked into 103 countries and is thought to have stolen plans for the Joint Strike Fighter aircraft from Lockheed Martin in 2009. They also cite an alleged Chinese attack on the US electrical grid, as well as the emergence of the Russian Business Network, an organization specializing in DoS attacks and other crimes. In 2016, Russian hackers were even thought to be behind the release of thousands of emails from the Democratic Party in the US, possibly to discredit its presidential candidate, Hillary Clinton. Even LDCs are not immune to such threats; some experts at IT-focused NGOs estimate that as many as 80 per cent of all computers in Africa are infected by some type of virus, compared with about 30 per cent in the UK.

Even so, the growing pace of attacks, and other technological changes, means that cybersecurity will require eternal vigilance on the part of everyone who uses the internet. One major trend along these lines involves the increasing migration of content onto the *Cloud* (i.e. data held on servers rather than or in addition to PCs/personal devices). This makes it easier for users as well as government authorities and/or hackers to access private information. A second trend involves the rise of the *Internet of Things* (IoT), which refers to the growing network of products connected to the internet. This began with mobile 'smart' phones and game consoles/televisions, but is steadily expanding: wearable gadgets, home appliances, thermostats, toys, vehicles and so on. Already security researchers have demonstrated that internet-connected cars can be controlled remotely against the driver's will; for example, a Jeep has been 'paralysed' remotely with a driver still inside, while various controls in the Nissan Leaf, the world's best-selling electric car, have been manipulated by remote control. Security researchers have also accessed information from web-enabled baby monitors, including video feeds of children in homes, and some experts say the IoT will provide even more opportunities for hacking and surveillance than the 'original' internet (Howard, 2015). Similarly, the rise in data analytics (or *Big Data*), which involves processing the vast information from internet users and IoT devices in order to (for the most part), provide new goods and services, means that new vulnerabilities will continue to emerge from these internet-enabled goods and services. However, security services are also able to use algorithms driven by such data in order to predict and locate such activity (known as *predictive analytics*), so there are costs and benefits here. Even so, the possibility of abuse always exists, as shown by the Edward Snowden revelations about covert communication surveillance and data mining by the US NSA, or America's 'surveillance state' (Greenwald, 2014). Finally, and in addition to the emerging issue of deliberate cyberwar (see the case study below), a more important concern involves the question of a major cyberattack, launched by terrorists or a government, on parts of the internet that would render much of it useless; a kind of 'Cyber 9/11' as some security researchers put it. Although there is little consensus on when, or even if, this would happen, most experts agree that everyone will 'know it when they see it' and the event will serve as a major wake-up call regarding how the international community uses, and protects, cyberspace.

## Recovery

Leaving aside the issue of a 'Cyber 9/11' attack, one positive aspect of cybersecurity is that the system is able to recover fairly quickly from major malware attacks. As noted above, this is one of the central virtues of a decentralized, high-speed network with multiple access points: threats can spread quickly, but so can countermeasures. However, the 'collateral' damage caused by such attacks, such as damage to reputation or the release of personal financial data, could take much longer to repair. Even so, for the moment cyberattacks have not resulted in a catastrophic or irreversible event that could be viewed as an existential threat to a state or large number of humans; instead, the debates are more about the potential for such an attack. Similarly, as we are just entering the era of cyberwarfare it is difficult to determine the actual extent of damage that could be caused by a 'full-scale' cyberwar between equally equipped adversaries (such as the US and China). It is also not yet clear whether, or how, major attacks in the digital realm (whether involving states or non-state actors) could escalate into a 'hot war' with conventional weapons, although the potential certainly exists. These threats notwithstanding, it seems the best defence against cyberattacks is to avoid being hacked in the first place, which requires constant attention on the part of internet users. This fact raises additional problems owing to the varied nature of those users, as we shall see in the next section.

## Stakeholder factors

Like the global economic system itself, the modern digital world, or cyberspace, involves a system with no single source of authority/control (although the US plays a critical role) and with a huge range of stakeholders as varied and vast as global society. In this sense cyberspace is a reflection of humanity itself, with both lawful and unlawful 'netizens'. Also like the economic system more generally (see Chapter 10), cyberspace involves a very high degree of public–private interaction. Therefore, one major problem regarding the pursuit of cybersecurity (as well as with broader human security issues covered later) is the fact that this issue potentially involves or touches upon virtually every person on the planet. However, the key word here is 'potentially', as cybersecurity stakeholders do not participate and benefit equally, nor do they enjoy the same degree of influence.

### Principal stakeholders

Hard as it may be to believe, in 1995 less than one per cent of the global population had an internet connection. Currently (2015) that figure is around 40 per cent, which means over three billion regular users and around one billion websites (see internetlivestats.com for current figures). Although this is a dramatic increase in just two decades, and although the UN in 2016 declared that internet access is a basic human right, the data also clearly indicate that the internet has not reached the status of a truly global public good accessible to everyone. In terms of internet users by region, Asia clearly dominates, just as it does in terms of population more generally (see Table 8.2).

As we might expect, there are more users in the developed world relative to their population sizes; in this sense Asia and Africa still have some catching up to do regarding broad access to the network (i.e. the *digital*

Table 8.2   *Distribution of internet users*

| Region | Percentage of internet users | Percentage of global population |
|---|---|---|
| Asia | 48.4% | 60% |
| Americas | 21.8% | 14% |
| Europe | 19% | 12% |
| Africa | 9.8% | 15% |
| Oceania | 0.9% | 0.5% |

*Source:* internetlivestats.com

*divide*). Overall, however, roughly half of the current global population has some stake in the internet and its security, simply by virtue of the fact that they use it.

Determining the politico-security nature of these three billion or more stakeholders is far more complex. One key problem is that, as with society more generally, there are so many and changing political cleavages because of the differing interests noted in the next section below. These cleavages can involve states versus states (i.e. cyberwar), technology firms versus the government, citizens versus governments, citizens versus firms, non-state actors versus state actors (as with cyberterrorism), public versus private stakeholders, and so on. Equally problematic from a politics/policy perspective are the use of anonymity when accessing the internet (Lucas, 2015) and the fact that users can play different roles depending on the context: providers and consumers of content; malicious hackers who disrupt the internet versus 'ethical' hackers who attempt to improve it by exposing vulnerabilities (or *hacktivism*); governments that simultaneously attempt to protect cyberspace while also abusing their surveillance powers, hoarding information about network vulnerabilities, or launching their own attacks against foreign adversaries, and so on (Mitnick, 2011; Angwin, 2014; Segal, 2016). In some cases these various actors coordinate their activities to increase their impact; one prominent example is the 'cyber-vigilante' group Anonymous, which engages in various types of politically motivated activism in cyberspace, against public and private targets, in a manner that can be viewed as security threats by authorities or others (Olson, 2012). Similarly, security authorities, researchers and technology firms have organized themselves into various associations at the national and international levels; their activities often involve attempts to influence the global cybersecurity policy agenda. Such associations include the Center for Internet Security, the Cloud Security Alliance, the Information Security Forum, the Information Security Research Association, the Information Systems Security Association, the Internet Security Alliance and others. These varied and complicated, even contradictory, roles mean that those who attempt to police cyberspace must often bend or break their own rules regarding security clearances and similar precautions when hiring computer experts (hackers and otherwise), which may create additional security problems.

## Interests and preferences

The issue of a common interest in securing the internet for everyone will be discussed below in the context of public–private domains. In terms of more specific interests, most private firms, citizens and civil society groups share an interest in making the internet as secure and reliable as possible so they can engage in various activities, whether profit-seeking or otherwise.

However, even with these actors we see some conflicts regarding control and use of the internet, most recently in terms of debates regarding 'net neutrality' and privacy/surveillance.

Among government stakeholders, for example, views differ widely across (and even within) states regarding whether the internet should respect free speech norms in the manner of print media. For example, within the US, which established many of the initial technical rules governing cyberspace, the Federal Communications Commission (FCC) since 2005 has attempted to respect 'net neutrality' by promoting competition among ISPs and equal access to internet services among consumers ('open internet'). This goal, however, has run up against some firms who have attempted to give priority to internet users willing to pay a higher price to move their data faster than 'ordinary' users. It is also possible to discern a transatlantic cleavage that often pits the more *laissez-faire* US views on privacy/free speech against the more regulated continental European/ EU social model, with the UK positioned somewhere in between these approaches. States also differ regarding whether access to the internet itself should be regulated more forcefully, whether in terms of banning certain types of users/content and/or offering differing levels of access and/ or privacy based on varying prices paid by users (which would violate the norm of *net neutrality*). More importantly, we also see major disputes regarding how governments themselves use (or abuse) cyberspace. For some states, the internet is not just a referent object to be protected, it is also a powerful tool to exert national power in terms of intelligence collection, surveillance, censorship and even covert action against foreign adversaries (i.e. cyberwar). This means, in turn, that government agencies in most advanced countries possess an inherent conflict of interest in their policies regarding cybersecurity and the internet.

This fact influences the interests and role of private actors in helping to secure the internet, particularly those involved in developing or managing its infrastructure and the main devices used to access it. Given the extensive commercialisation of the internet since the 1990s, private technology firms have become key stakeholders in developing the system and they share a common interest in making it secure and reliable. However, after the Snowden revelations regarding extensive US data collection by its NSA (with collusion by the UK's corresponding agency, the GCHQ), many technology firms became reluctant to cooperate with US authorities in various aspects of security (internet or otherwise), such as helping to defeat encryption or giving government law enforcement authorities access to private data about suspects. These firms feared, quite rightly, that cooperating with such authorities in the face of the Snowden revelations might undermine their reputations with their customers and harm their businesses, especially as he revealed that some firms had actively helped the US government with its spying activities.

This problem also raises the question of how authorities should deal with Snowden and similar cases, such as the thousands of secret US documents provided to WikiLeaks by Bradley (now Chelsea) Manning, another US government employee who became upset at the way the US was acting in Iraq. When such individuals work for private contractors (as Snowden did for Booz Allen Hamilton), the potential for loss of control or conflict of interest (i.e. public security versus private profit incentives) becomes that much greater. In addition, democratic governments often claim to support such 'whistle-blowing' about misconduct regarding private firms, but when this involves secret government activities the rules change. In fact, under the Obama administration the US has prosecuted six whistle-blowers, more than any US presidential administration in history. Not only does this policy make it more likely that government misconduct will remain a secret, it also discourages others from helping the government for fear of jeopardizing their own reputations or freedoms (the same also holds true regarding private help to the government in other areas of security, such as terrorism and crime). Competing views of such activities not only divide countries, they even divide political parties within countries, which makes the formulation of policies based on democratic consensus even more difficult. We shall return to this issue below in terms of measuring the costs and benefits of various types of policy actions in this realm.

## The use of force

One of the most interesting and provocative questions regarding cybersecurity/cyberwar involves the extent to which actions in this realm will involve or change the use of military force, whether in terms of deterrence, compellence or defence/retaliation (Clarke, 2010; Singer and Friedman, 2014). Although cyberwar capabilities now involve the use of software attacks against physical targets (see the case study below), and although some government authorities in certain states claim the right to use military force in such situations, we have not yet encountered a situation where cyberwar leads to a 'hot' war. However, the linkages between these domains clearly are increasing, in terms of concepts or doctrines (such as 'hybrid warfare') and actual conflict behaviours among adversaries. Hybrid warfare, for example, involves explicit linkages between conventional warfare (air, land and naval forces), unconventional warfare (special forces and/or or paramilitary forces) and cyberwarfare. Some believe this type of warfare has occurred regarding Russian actions against former Soviet republics, such as Estonia and Ukraine, while the Stuxnet attacks against Iran clearly demonstrate the ability of foreign agents to attack the military/defence infrastructures (among other targets) of other states simply by using computer code (see the case study below). Between cyberwar, hybrid warfare and the rapid development of other technologies, such as drones, machine learning and automated weapons, clearly we are entering uncharted territory regarding the future of warfare (Krishnan, 2009; Manjikian, 2010).

## Public–private domains and levels of jurisdiction

As noted above, one major consideration regarding the policing of cyberspace is whether it is a global public good, as defined in Chapter 2 (i.e. use of the internet is non-excludable and indivisible). Although there is a general belief among the many technicians who manage the internet that the system is a global public good simply because it provides 'benefits' to 'everyone in the world' (Netherlands Scientific Council for Government Policy, 2015), a closer look clearly indicates that the situation is far more complicated (Thierer and Crews, 2003). In other words, the internet may function more like a club good or like a private good depending on various factors, such as how easily one can access it (in terms of general connections or specific websites/features), whether one has to pay for that access and whether governments can prevent or interfere with that access, or can block certain forms of content because of (for example) political concerns about freedom of speech. The ability of governments to use the internet and related technologies (such as mobile communications) to monitor their own citizens and launch attacks against others also indicates that internet access is not a 'cost-free' public good for its users, even if they pay nothing (in terms of money) to access it. In other words, simply by using the internet, you are exposing yourself to a range of vulnerabilities (particularly a loss of privacy) that are not 'priced in' to the monetary cost of using it (Marlin-Bennett, 2004; Newman, 2008).

The need to view the internet as a club good or private good is even more obvious when one considers that much of the global infrastructure on which it is based is found within the country that invented it: the US. Moreover, this infrastructure is dominated by a quasi-public international body, the Internet Corporation for Assigned Names and Numbers (ICANN), which determines how website names (i.e. domains) are assigned to those seeking a presence on the internet. Although ICANN, a non-profit technical organization, has become a more transparent and publicly sensitive body since it was established, and has established branch offices around the world, it is still headquartered in the US (Los Angeles) and has a close relationship with the US Department of Commerce. This Department relinquished 'official' control of ICANN in October 2009, yet the US still exerts considerable authority over the organization and has successfully (so far) fought attempts to turn ICANN over to the UN or to replace it with a fully independent IO. These issues, in turn, clearly indicate that the public–private relationships regarding the internet in general and cybersecurity in particular are far more complicated, and inherently politicized, than may be preferred by the technicians who maintain the system and by many internet users. This problem also has implications for international efforts to secure the internet, as we shall see in the next section.

Even more difficult to analyse is the quasi-public role of certain MNCs involved in internet governance and security, such as computer/software firms, ISPs, banks, insurance firms, credit reporting agencies and certain infrastructural firms (such as utilities, transport, and communications) (among others). Barriers to entry for new internet-related services are very low relative to building physical storefronts/offices, and a growing number of firms rely on the internet to provide personal data, so that they can provide goods/services and/or sell that data to advertisers. As a common saying puts it, if you aren't paying for an internet-linked service, then 'you' (i.e. your personal data) are the 'product' being sold to others when you use that service. Therefore there is a clear conflict of interest regarding how these firms handle the issues of privacy and personal data on the internet, and often they have been 'shamed' into revealing or modifying their privacy policies in the face of a public backlash. In fact, one could argue that private firms are mainly to blame for internet vulnerabilities after the commercialization of cyberspace: first, for attempting to collect as much data as possible in order to monetize everything their customers/users do (rules also tend to focus on data use rather than collection); and second, for the broader 'ship it then fix it' mentality, so that security vulnerabilities are not addressed adequately before internet-related products and services are sold. The founder of Sun Microsystems, Scott McNealy, admitted as much in 1999 when he said, 'You have zero privacy anyway. Get over it'. In fact, few people understand exactly how much data they produce on a daily basis, and not just online; this includes data derived from location, shopping, browsing/searching, audio/voice, photograph/video and other actions/services, all which add up to 'signature data' to identify potential customers – or surveillance targets (Schneier, 2015). This problem will only increase with the rise of Big Data and the IoT as firms try to collect then monetize more personal data; in fact, a 2016 AT&T survey revealed that only ten per cent of the firms planning to deploy IoT devices felt confident in securing them. Ethical hackers and independent security researchers often attempt to expose these vulnerabilities (without causing harm) to improve the system, yet governments often seem more interested in promoting the development of the internet rather than in regulating or securing it, especially as technology firms are spending increasingly large amounts of money to lobby for government policies supportive of their business models.

Beyond these conflicts of interest, there is also no escaping the fact that much of the access to, and content on, the internet involves private stakeholders of various types, whose involvement is crucial in securing the entire system. In the UK, for example, the Critical National Infrastructure – or the linked computers that control communications, water, energy, emergency services and public safety – relies on voluntary compliance to secure itself and is controlled mainly by large firms, so their involvement is absolutely necessary in helping to secure these networks. In the US, the government has maintained very close security-related links with the major American technology firms involved in the internet, whether as part of its architecture or as content providers. Other firms have a direct interest in selling security products to protect information systems, which makes this industry (like the weapons industry) prone to problems of threat inflation and conflicts of interest. In fact, the global cybersecurity industry is expected to grow at around $9 billion a year for several years, which provides a major incentive to keep this issue high on the policy agenda. Similarly, government reliance on private firms to provide public services results in the widespread use of outsourcing/contractors in this realm (as with PMCs), which led to the Snowden revelations noted above and the larger backlash against America's varied covert cybersecurity/surveillance programmes, such as PRISM.

This problem of public–private conflict also involves the business practices of certain firms, such as those selling encryption, hacking or surveillance technology to authoritarian regimes or possible criminal/terrorist organizations. In addition, the vast majority of these firms are global in nature, which raises the question of legal jurisdiction over their activities. As with the proliferation of weapons sales in the developing world noted in Chapter 6, we now see a kind of cybersecurity 'arms race' as governments around the world attempt to acquire the latest security-related computer technology, and possibly use it to harm or repress their populations. Such firms engaged in 'offensive cybersecurity' include Finfisher Spying Software/Gamra International and Hacking Team, whose 'DaVinci Hacking Suite' has been sold to Azerbaijan, Egypt, Sudan, Saudi Arabia, Kazakhstan, Lebanon and Nigeria (among other states). At present these products and services are not broadly defined as 'weapons', even though they can be used to conduct cyberwar, so once again global regulations are lagging far behind technological capabilities in this realm, as we shall see in detail in the next section. Some of these firms have voluntarily suspended their sales to certain governments believed to be misusing their products, but reliance on such self-policing among private, profit-driven actors raises the same difficult questions of effectiveness, legitimacy and accountability already present among PMCs and vigilante/mercenary groups.

## Cyberspace as a policy problem

Leaving aside the issues of variable access, costs and usage noted above, the steadily expanding role of the internet in the daily lives of billions of people around the world has created a kind of cybercommunity (or

multiple cybercommunities) that reflects the 'real-world' global community itself. In this sense, defining and controlling cyberspace, for reasons of
security or otherwise, is like defining and controlling the course of humanity itself: an extremely difficult proposition. More importantly, the rapid
pace of technological change, especially in this realm, means that any common rules or principles used to achieve security can easily be overtaken by
new innovations. This is especially problematic in light of the often glacial
pace of national and international deliberations about new regulations.
In other words, national and international authorities are always several
steps behind the curve not just in responding to, but even understanding,
the possibilities of new technologies like the internet. For example, the UN
did not create its first Working Group on Internet Governance until 2004,
more than a decade after the system had been commercialized. Finally,
as noted above, inherent conflicts of interest among major stakeholders
– such as a desire to protect the internet for their own use, but also to
use it to deliver attacks against adversaries – make it even more difficult to devise common rules regarding cybersecurity and cyberwar. Under
these conditions, and with the continued prevalence of anonymity on the
internet, maintaining trust in cyberspace can be nearly impossible, which
undermines our ability to develop robust policies based on stable international cooperation. Therefore the temptations of voluntary and involuntary defection (i.e. not even being aware of the rules/norms in this realm)
among a very wide range of stakeholders are extensive here, perhaps more
so than with any other security problems discussed in this volume.

## Agenda-setting

Given these various problems regarding the pursuit of international cybersecurity, it might be more helpful to begin with a discussion of the areas of
broad consensus here. In terms of agenda-setting, for example, the early
agenda on the topic was set by hackers: their attacks against various targets through cyberspace, and the development of computer viruses/worms
more generally, forced internet architects and security specialists to devise
technical countermeasures, and to work together across borders to deliver
them. In this sense the internet was already becoming 'internationalized'
soon after the system began to grow in the 1970s, even before it had grown
well beyond the borders of the US itself. The growing commercialization
of the internet through the 1990s also created a large market for internet security software and related technologies, and paved the way for the
extensive public–private collusion in this realm that persists to this day.
This also involves countermeasures regarding the advent of cybercrime
during the same period; this issue will be discussed in the next chapter.

Taking a closer look at political agenda-setting, the role of the US
government (as well as leading US technology firms) has been critical

given its position as the developer of the internet. As noted above, it created ICANN in 1998 to help develop international standards for the development of the internet, which also involve cybersecurity (Franda, 2001). The US also insisted on retaining control of ICANN until very recently; at present the international community is still debating how to achieve the so-called 'NetMundial Initiative' of 2014, which would (in principle) turn over control of the internet to an international community of experts (still working via ICANN). Even as this process of releasing direct US control over ICANN unfolded during the first decade of the twenty-first century, America continued to set the agenda on cybersecurity issues; for example, President Bush appointed the first US 'cyber czar' in 2001 (Richard Clarke) to serve as Special Advisor to the President on Cybersecurity. This position was upgraded in 2008 to Director of a new US National Cybersecurity Center under Rod Beckstrom, located within the DHS. Under President Obama in 2009, a new White House Office of Cybersecurity was also created, under its own Director (currently Howard Schmidt). That same year, a US Cyberspace Policy Review explicitly identified this threat, and suggested that America's digital infrastructure be treated as a strategic national asset. Attacks against it can lead to considerable domestic disruption of important communications, transportation, financial and other networks, so the US and other states have framed this threat as a security matter in general (as 'critical infrastructure protection'), or more specifically (as 'cybersecurity').

One major factor in national and international agenda-setting in this realm was the possibility of what is now known as cyberwar; a key 'wake-up call' in this realm occurred in April 2007 in Estonia, where computer networks of banks, the media, government ministries and other stakeholders were targeted by servers under Russian authority (see case study in Box 8.2). In response to this perception of threat, the Obama administration upgraded the post of 'cyber czar' to coordinate government responses across various agencies such as the DHS, the NSA and the DoD, all of which now battle each other for control of the issue. In May 2010 the US DoD activated its own military command for cyberspace (the US Cyber Command) in order to develop defensive and offensive measures in cyberspace. In the UK, the British government also recently created a new cybersecurity centre, as did several other major powers. For example, China has a strategic goal of becoming a major cyberspace power, and has created a range of institutional and technical capabilities towards this aim; some experts, however, doubt that China will become a major cyberpower owing to its inherent technological limitations and vulnerabilities relative to its main competitors, particularly the US (Lindsay, 2014–15). Table 8.3 lists several of the new national agencies involved in this issue.

**Table 8.3   *Major national authorities involved in cybersecurity and cyberwar***

|  | Cybersecurity | Cyberwar |
|---|---|---|
| United States | National Cybersecurity Division (DHS) (2003) | US CyberCommand (CYBERCOM, DoD) (2010) |
| United Kingdom | National Cybersecurity Centre (2016) | GCHQ and Ministry of Defence (2015) |
| China | CyberSecurity Association of China (2016) | Strategic Support Force (2016) |
| France | French Network and Information Security Agency (2009) | General Officer for Cyber Defence in Ministry of Defence (2011) |
| Russia | System for Operative Investigative Activities (SORM)(Federal Security Service and Interior Affairs Ministry) (1998) | Signals Intelligence Division of Federal Security Service (FSB) (2003) |
| Germany | National Cyber Defence Centre (2016) | Cyber Defence Station in the German intelligence agency (BND) (2013) |

## Framing policy alternatives

Since the rise of internet from the 1990s, two major debates have emerged regarding the international security of cyberspace. The first involves the balance between unilateral versus multilateral approaches to cybersecurity; the second involves the balance between passive/defensive measures and active/offensive measures in this area (including cyberwar). Although these debates persist in some ways, the consensus among many national cybersecurity policy-makers is that unilateral and passive/defensive measures alone are not likely to work here.

Even so, as with many international security problems, states and other major stakeholders still prefer to take unilateral measures to deal with cybersecurity, as this approach maintains the illusion of direct control and (in principle) allows a greater degree of secrecy regarding one's own vulnerabilities and capabilities (including the conduct of cyberwar attacks). However, cybersecurity is inherently a network-focused activity, and the network in this case is inherently global, so adopting a unilateral approach to defending yourself against that network, while maintaining broad access to it in your country, is, essentially, futile. Moreover, all major stakeholders with extensive internet-related policy-making authority, whether governments, firms or civil society (i.e. ICANN), possess not just different attitudes – namely in the form of base motives and economic ideologies – but also different capabilities and vulnerabilities about the pursuit of cybersecurity. Of course, some states have attempted to shut down or limit access to some or all parts of the internet in the face of certain threats (such as public unrest facilitated by social media); this has occurred in China, Egypt, Iran, Turkey and elsewhere. Even democratic states like the US have considered the idea of devising their own national internet 'kill switches' to shut down access to the network in the face of a major threat. However, for most states with open economies this is very much a 'last resort' option, if one at all, and opinion polls clearly indicate that citizens feel that access to the internet without government censorship is important to them; a 2015 poll by the Pew Research Centre found that majorities in 32 out of 38 states surveyed felt this way.

In addition to the preference for unilateralism, which involves the creation of national cybersecurity/cyberwar authorities noted above, we also see a proliferation of passive/defensive technical solutions to this problem (Gartzke and Lindsay, 2015). As noted above, cybersecurity is a huge industry today, and (as one might expect) the US dominates the market in terms of the number of firms: according to one recent (2016) survey, over half (827) of all such firms are based in America (mostly in California). Thus, despite growing fears of Chinese/Russian cyber-capabilities or state-sponsored hacking attacks (Gompert and Libicki, 2014; Inkster, 2016), the US still leads in this area thanks to its many innovative indigenous technology firms, its role in internet development/governance, and various CIA/NSA/DoD programmes. Israel follows behind the US with 228 firms, while other major states have less than 100 each (the UK, Canada, India, Germany, France, Australia) (IT Harvest Research). Besides the US and Israel, Estonia also has emerged as a leader in the realm of cybersecurity even though it lacks a large number of IT firms; instead, the Estonian government has worked to build national capacities and also successfully worked with its NATO allies in this realm (see the next section below) (Crandall and Allan, 2015).

It is also worth noting, in terms of multilateral/defensive policy debates, that as IT products can threaten cybersecurity, whether directly or indirectly, some stakeholders have called for new rules that treat exports of such products as weapons. For example, the Wassenaar Arrangement was developed in 1996 as a successor to the Coordinating Committee for Multilateral Export Controls, which attempted to block certain types of exports to the Soviet bloc during the Cold War. Under Wassenaar, exports of dual-use technologies must be controlled according to common rules by its signatories (currently 41 participating states, most of which are OECD member states); it covers not just weapons but also computers, telecommunications and information security products. Dutch MEP Marietje Schaake (among others) has called for a country-specific list, with licensing rules and human rights assessments. However, export controls are a limited means, even if many other states agreed to them, as it takes just one state to defect from the regime to undermine the entire system. Moreover, these kinds of products (among other illicit ones) are widely available on the *Dark Web* (or the *Dark Net*), which refers to websites or forums, such as (presumably now-defunct) Silk Road, that can be accessed only through the use of special software or other capabilities, and are extremely difficult to police (Glenny, 2012; Bartlett, 2015). This brings us to the option of more multilateral and offensive options, which are covered in the next section as they receive much of the attention in terms of cybersecurity/cyberwar as international security issues.

## Policy choice

For all stakeholders, whether public or private, the single most prominent approach to problems of cybersecurity and cyberwar is, essentially, to 'fight fire with fire': that is, develop new technologies to detect, deter and prevent attacks on cyberspace (cybersecurity), as well as to deliver such attacks against foreign adversaries (cyberwar) (Stevens, 2012). As noted above, private firms play a central role in cybersecurity more generally; for example, some sources estimate that over $600 billion will be spent on such efforts between 2015 and 2020. This spending would be targeted at protecting PCs ($386 billion), protecting IoT devices ($172 billion) and protecting mobile devices like phones ($113 billion); it would be focused on multiple areas of vulnerability: network systems, devices (including mobiles), the movement of data ('data in motion'), databases ('data at rest') and network/data analysis tools to detect problems (*Business Insider Intelligence* 2016).

In addition to the role of this spending directed specifically at threats, we also should remember the indirect role of ethical hackers and other specialists (such as those working with ICANN) in helping to secure the internet and other computer technologies; for example, the use of the 'ctrl-alt-del' keys to restart Windows-based computers was a 'secret' fix that spread by word of mouth rather than as part of user manuals. Even government authorities have accepted the importance of private stakeholders in securing the internet; the US DoD is now conducting regular competitions among ethical hackers to see if they can penetrate various computer defences, while in early 2016 Estonia conducted the world's largest multilateral 'cyberwargame' (known as 'Locked Shields') in Tallinn, with 550 participants from 26 states. It was intended to train those involved in cyberdefences and hybrid warfare through the use of simulated, but extremely realistic, attacks on replicas of national computer systems. Even China has realized the potential of using private stakeholders/civil society in helping to secure its own cyberspace by creating in early 2016 its first public cybersecurity organization, the CyberSecurity Association of China, which will bring together academics, researchers, technology firms and other key stakeholders; it also intends to become more involved in international cooperation.

In terms of bilateral/multilateral efforts, passive/defensive measures have been well underway for years. For example, in the realm of more general information security/privacy, the US and the EU in 2000 managed to establish a set of general rules (known as *Safe Harbour*) to govern their use of personal data collected from the internet and related devices. This approach was based on the principle of *mutual recognition* so that firms on each side of the Atlantic essentially had to trust each other to comply with the rules; this principle was based on existing rules for other products, such as pharmaceuticals (Heisenberg, 2005; Newman, 2008). However, Safe Harbour was declared in violation of EU law in a court case brought by an EU citizen against Facebook in 2015, and US/EU authorities are working out a new solution that may or may not be a real improvement on Safe Harbour. The EU, along with other states, is also attempting to enforce a new cyberspace norm – the 'right to be forgotten' – by removing personal content from the internet, while some EU member states, such as Germany, also oppose the more general role of US firms such as Google and Microsoft in the new digital economy.

At the global level, the UN, along with related IOs like the International Telecommunications Union (ITU), has organized working groups (in 2005 and 2010) and related conferences on the topic, such as one in 2011 devoted to cybersecurity and development, to help bridge the 'cybersecurity digital divide' between rich and poor states. In August 2013 a group of UN experts finally agreed and released a long-awaited report, 'On the Developments in the Field of Information and Telecommunications in the Context of International Security'. This document provided a consensus view that acknowledged the full applicability of international law to cyberspace and pledged UN member states to work together to devise specific rules in this realm. The EU has been equally active regarding passive/defensive cybersecurity; beyond raising awareness and sharing best practices like the UN/ITU/ICANN, the European Commission (the EU's executive arm) released an EU Cybersecurity Strategy in 2013, followed by an EU Directive on Cybersecurity in December 2015 (the 'Network and Information Security Directive') – a formal regulatory measure binding on all EU member states. Similarly, although the EU's overall cybersecurity capabilities remain weak relative to those of other stakeholders, such as the US (Sliwinski, 2014), the EU has developed the strongest multilateral data privacy protections available to any internet users on the planet. This effort in turn has provoked no small degree of transatlantic discord (Newman, 2008), as the EU's regulations are stricter and more comprehensive than those in the US (and elsewhere).

Even more interesting is the role of active/offensive measures. For example, the US and the UK have jointly developed a new *strike-back* policy to target hackers, mostly from China, North Korea and Russia, who break into national defence or commercial computers. Some internet experts say

## Box 8.2  Stuxnet and cyberwar

*The Stuxnet worm marks a new era in the realm of stealth warfare.*

The advent of networked military operations and cyberspace more generally was, seemingly inevitably, soon followed by the advent of government-involved, politically motivated international attacks within that space: cyberwar (Clarke, 2010; Gompert and Libicki, 2015; Stiennon, 2015; Kaplan, 2016). Although experts have speculated about this possibility for years, and some remain sceptical about it (Rid, 2013), the first possible example seems to have occurred in April 2007, from servers located in Russia targeted against Estonia. This was followed by a series of international attacks during the 2008 South Ossetia war between Russia and Georgia; several other countries around this period also claimed to have launched and/or been the target of similar attacks: India, Israel, Kyrgyzstan, North/South Korea, Pakistan, Russia, the UK, the US and others. These incidents,

$\rightarrow$

strike-back policies, such as a defensive DoS attack, could disrupt other law-abiding computer users. Equally troubling is that governments tend to resist supplying information about cyberattacks on government computers, so it is unclear how pervasive this threat really is, or what source is involved: is it cyberwar, cyberterrorism, cyberespionage, cybercrime or cybervandalism? Even so, this effort to develop offensive capabilities occurs on a multilateral basis as well; in 2008 seven states (Estonia, Germany, Italy, Latvia, Lithuania, the Slovak Republic and Spain) established a Cooperative Cyber

→

although important at the time, pale in comparison to the Stuxnet worm attack in September 2010, which heralded the beginning of not just a new weapon but perhaps a new era in warfare: the use of computers to attack the physical components of another country's military/defence infrastructure (Lindsay, 2014).

Stuxnet, as the worm became known, targeted a type of software used to control large industrial systems, such as power plants. Although the worm was found in several states, including the US, it seemed most prevalent in just one country: Iran. A team of security experts in Germany examined the code of Stuxnet and determined that it was a very complex type of malware based on a combination of several zero-days vulnerabilities and the encryption keys (likely stolen) from at least two private firms that manufacture software drivers for various types of hardware; Stuxnet was also able to work on all current Windows-based operating systems. More importantly, Stuxnet was designed to attack one particular type of target: a controller made by Siemens used to run a specific number (984) of linked nuclear centrifuges, which were used to enrich uranium for use as fuel in nuclear reactors – or weapons.

This number of centrifuges corresponded exactly with a site in Iran (Natanz) and once Stuxnet was delivered (via laptops and memory sticks) the facility began to operate very erratically, so that its managers were not able to detect the problem for over a year. In fact, they weren't even aware it was a cyberattack until after Stuxnet was exposed on a blog by the German researchers. Not surprisingly, Israel and the US are thought to have collaborated on the attack (code name: 'Olympic Games'), which effectively stalled uranium enrichment at Natanz (Farwell and Rohozinski, 2011; Singer and Friedman, 2014; Zetter, 2014). Beyond its sophistication and effectiveness, Stuxnet also deserves credit as a new type of weapon that can attack very specific targets rather than simply be 'unleashed' on the internet to harm everyone; in this sense it may have been the first-ever 'cyberwar surgical strike' or 'cyber smart bomb'. It certainly won't be the last, however, as many other states are developing similar capabilities, some of which are linked to other new technologies, such as machine learning or artificial intelligence. This is occurring even as several major cyberwarfare players – China, Russia and the US for example – also claim to be working together to build confidence in terms of securing cyberspace, which represents yet another mixed message or conflict of interest regarding official government actions in this realm.

Defence Centre of Excellence, based in Estonia. This is formally part of NATO and today 16 NATO member states (including the UK/US) are closely involved with it. Although it tends to focus on defence capabilities and passive measures, the Centre's growing capabilities can be retasked for offensive cyberwarfare or 'cyber-deterrence' (Stevens, 2012); this is especially likely as some US authorities have stated that Russia is now the principal cyberthreat to the US, according to the 2015 World Threat Assessment released by the US Director of National Intelligence, James Clapper.

## The politics of policy effectiveness

Growing attention regarding cybersecurity and cyberwar means that these issues will remain on the international policy agenda for the foreseeable future. However, it is also worth mentioning that many of the problems regarding the security of the internet are not entirely new; they are merely part of a much longer evolution of electronic communications methods going back well over a century. The advent of the telegraph in the 1830s forced policy-makers to develop common rules and standards within and across countries to make the system work; this process has evolved with every subsequent innovation: the telephone, radio, television, satellite communications, mobile/cellular communications and now digital/computer communications involving the internet and other networks. Some of these long-standing rules, which still influence current debates, have specifically involved security, privacy and freedom-of-speech issues, such as those involving wiretapping and political broadcasting. A similar evolutionary process is also occurring in the realm of cyberwar, which is only part of a broader historical focus on the role of command, control, communication and intelligence (or 'C3I') in conducting military operations. Therefore although certain elements of these technologies, services and military functions are new from an innovation standpoint, our thinking about them from a political/policy standpoint has very deep roots.

Yet it is also clear that the rapid rise of the internet in particular – a process which is still underway – represents one of the most significant technological transformations in the history of the world. It is equally remarkable how so many individuals, firms and governments now depend on the system on a daily basis yet fail to understand how it actually works or how to secure themselves effectively when using it. The internet effectively combines the best and worst features of traditional two-way telephone communications and radio/television broadcasting: like telephone systems, anyone with an internet-connected device can communicate simultaneously (i.e. 'full duplex') with others who have such a device, and like radio/television broadcasting, users can also broadcast/publish anything they want (more or less) to a global audience: text, software, photographs, audio and video. However, because the system is inherently two-way (unlike television and radio broadcasting), and because the system allows users to access and/or place information, including various types of harmful content, on other users' devices/databases (unlike traditional telephones), every connection made to the internet raises a range of complex security problems. The facts that access to the internet is becoming cheaper (especially relative to traditional radio/television broadcasting) and that it is becoming a truly global network as access spreads to more countries and people, mean that these problems will only intensify in coming years.

Under these circumstances, it is probably not even worth speaking of a total victory standard where cybersecurity is concerned; there is no 'magic bullet' in terms of a policy or technology (other than stopping access to the internet itself) that would address the problems noted above in an effective fashion. Deterrence in this realm in the form of (for example) threatened criminal charges or legal/contractual penalties can be extremely difficult since it may be impossible to identify the perpetrators in the first place, or to target perpetrators of attacks launched outside one's own jurisdiction. In the meantime, new viruses, worms, data leaks and other forms of attack appear on a daily basis across the system, so the only possible defence involves constant monitoring and information-sharing among IT security specialists and related policy-makers, followed by countermeasures to identify and block such harmful forms of content. This also involves educating all users of the system, especially those linked to favoured targets of hackers/cyberwarriors (such as government facilities), about the basic principles of cybersecurity. However, in many institutions this involves little more than reminding users to avoid opening unfamiliar file attachments and to change passwords frequently (a policy actually criticized by some IT experts, as it can result in weak passwords). This tendency is also linked to the broader problem noted above about how so few internet users actually know how the system works so that they can protect themselves and their institutions. This problem explains, too, why some form of a total victory standard regarding cybersecurity is almost certainly unrealistic here; this finding also applies to most of the human security problems addressed later in this volume. The same holds true of cyberwar more specifically, as this type of conflict (as well as hybrid warfare itself) is directly linked to the functioning of the internet itself. Therefore to the extent that the internet is inherently insecure because of its basic characteristics, various forms of cyberwar will only proliferate.

In terms of a historical trends standard in the realm of cybersecurity, the evidence is somewhat more mixed. On the one hand, IT security specialists and related policy-makers are steadily improving their capacity to detect security threats and share countermeasures, such as antivirus patches. However, on the other hand the overall number of cyberattacks has increased steadily since the 1980s; likewise, the destructive scale and scope of these attacks have increased as well. Large-scale data leaks, whether by accident or intentional attack, seem to happen on a regular basis now. In just one spectacular case, Mexico's entire voter database was found to be available on the internet; this security lapse exposed the names, addresses and other personal details of 87 million Mexicans. More recently, 21.5 million records regarding the staff of the US Office of Personnel Management were stolen in June 2015, perhaps the most sensitive data breach so far given the detail of information taken, while the 'Panama Papers' leak in April 2016 involved the financial records of 11.5

million people using the small Central American country as a tax haven. This problem will only get worse as more data find their way onto global networks via mobile devices, the IoT, the Cloud and the increasing ambitions of government and firms to digitally measure as much human activity as possible (Big Data) in order to serve their interests. Finally, growing capabilities in the realm of cyberwar also mean that direct attacks against physical targets are likely to occur more frequently in the near future; this can already be seen in terms of the evolution of cyberwar attacks in just the past decade.

Finally, if a total victory standard of policy performance is impossible, and a historical trends standard provides mixed evidence, what about the situation across various countries? Here the evidence is also very mixed and always problematic considering the fast pace of technological innovation in this realm, involving the internet more generally and cyberwar capabilities more specifically. For example, the so-called digital divide noted above regarding internet access also applies to the realm of cybersecurity, as richer and more technically advanced states certainly possess more cybersecurity (and cyberwar) resources as compared to poor states. However, it is also true that richer states tend to attract more attacks relative to major targets in poor states. The key point is that despite considerable variance in cybersecurity capabilities and vulnerabilities, no state is, or ever will be, absolutely safe here, even if it attempts to use 'kill switches' or other draconian policies to cut itself off temporarily from global computer networks.

## Summary

When a detailed history of the emergence of cyberspace is written years or decades from now, several dates will be particularly important in that story: 1969 (ARPAnet project launched in the US); 1972 (first public demonstration of ARPAnet); 1983 (ARPAnet becomes 'civilianized' into the early internet); 1992 (internet is commercialized under US law); 1998 (creation of ICANN) and 2010 (the Stuxnet attack). From a social/political perspective, this history of the early years of our Digital Age is especially interesting for two reasons: first, for the intensive and complex international collusion between governments and civil society (firms, associations, individuals) in developing cyberspace; and second, for the way this new virtual realm required close attention not just to security problems but also to the possibility, then reality, of cyber/hybrid warfare. As a domain so dependent on the evolution and diffusion of sophisticated technology, it is also important to remember the warning of ARPAnet/internet architect Vint Cerf in 2013: there is no simple technological cure for the ever-increasing privacy/security problems related to the internet, especially with the advent of Big Data, the IoT, the Cloud, devices/services enabled with geo-location, facial/voice recognition, biometrics, street mapping, machine learning, mobile sensors, robotics and so on.

Based on these factors, and the lack of a competent global authority to address the many problems discussed in this chapter from a policy coordination perspective, we clearly are living through a kind of 'wild west' or 'frontier justice' type of situation here, in which there is no legitimate single source of political power to provide effective cybersecurity or to devise common rules for cyberwarfare. Even though the internet was created and nurtured by the US, which gave it a quasi-hegemonic role in cybersecurity governance for about two decades, today the internet and related technologies represent a kind of global public infrastructure subject to only limited common authority (mainly in the realms of technical standards and property rights), thanks to the ongoing role of ICANN and the relatively limited involvement of IOs like the UN and EU. Under these circumstances, the realm of cybersecurity/cyberwar comes very close to functioning as an anarchic, self-help system of the kind theorized by realists. As realists would also expect, this self-help situation doesn't just involve a general vulnerability against cyberthreats among all stakeholders at the international level; it also now involves a major cyberwar arms race among those same stakeholders: technology firms offering protection as well as methods to defeat cybersecurity to anyone wanting to possess those capabilities, and governments attempting to protect the internet while also using it to spy on their citizens and launch offensive attacks against other targets.

Thus, living with cyberattacks is now just a normal part of living with the internet; therefore the more each of us does online, the more vulnerable we become. Similarly, as more countries, devices and individuals become connected to cyberspace, the potential for both positive and negative outcomes increases as well. In other words, this is one major area of international security, like environment/resources, where security depends on the concerted efforts of all stakeholders, ranging from individuals to households to civil society groups to firms to governments to international organizations. Given these considerations and the discussion above, problems in this realm are almost certainly likely to get worse before they will get better (if they ever do), regarding both cybersecurity and cyberwar. This outcome is especially likely as large states (China, Russia and the US) and small (Estonia and Israel) are deliberately attempting to become major players in this realm; they almost certainly will be joined by many others. Even as this book is being written, the US and its allies are devising various cyberattacks against Islamic State, an organization which itself has made very effective use of the internet to expand its reach and gain recruits. The advent of hybrid war may be the biggest open question, as we have not yet seen exactly how this doctrine would work in a major interstate conflict. Yet the indications in terms of technological capabilities and doctrines/concepts are already in place, so that the future governance of cyberspace will have to address not just the narrow cybersecurity/cyberwar issues noted in this chapter, but also perhaps the broader future of warfare, if not humanity, itself.

## Further reading

Julia Angwin (2014). *Dragnet Nation: A Quest for Privacy, Security, and Freedom in a World of Relentless Surveillance*. New York: Times Books.

Richard A. Clarke (2010). *Cyber War: The Next Threat to National Security and What To Do About It*. New York: Ecco.

Whitfield Diffie and Susan Landau (2007). *Privacy on the Line: The Politics of Wiretapping and Encryption*. Cambridge: The MIT Press.

Marcus Franda (2001). *Governing the Internet: The Emergence of an International Regime*. Boulder: Lynne Rienner.

Philip N. Howard (2015). *Pax Technica: How the Internet of Things May Set Us Free or Lock Us Up*. New Haven: Yale University Press.

Fred Kaplan (2016). *Dark Territory: The Secret History of Cyber War*. New York: Simon & Schuster.

Edward Lucas (2015). *Cyberphobia: Identity, Trust, Security, and the Internet*. London: Bloomsbury.

Kevin Mitnick (2011). *Ghost in the Wires: My Adventures as the World's Most Wanted Hacker*. New York: Back Bay Books.

Milton L. Mueller (2003). *Ruling the Root: Internet Governance and the Taming of Cyberspace*. Cambridge: MIT Press.

Abraham L. Newman (2008). *Protectors of Privacy: Regulating Personal Data in the Global Economy*. Ithaca: Cornell University Press.

Daniel J. Paré (2003). *Internet Governance in Transition: Who is the Master of This Domain?* Lanham: Rowman & Littlefield.

Adam Segal (2016). *The Hacked World Order: How Nations Fight, Trade, Maneuver, and Manipulate in the Digital Age*. New York: Public Affairs.

Peter W. Singer and Allan Friedman (2014). *Cybersecurity and Cyberwar: What Everyone Needs to Know*. Oxford: Oxford University Press.

Richard Stiennon (2015). *There Will Be Cyberwar: How the Move to Network-Centric War-Fighting Has Set the Stage for Cyberwar*. Birmingham, MI: IT Harvest Press.

Adam Thierer and Clyde Wayne Crews, Jr. (eds.) (2003). *Who Rules the Net? Internet Governance and Jurisdiction*. Washington, DC: The Cato Institute.

Kim Zetter (2014). *Countdown to Zero Day: Stuxnet and the Launch of the World's First Digital Weapon*. New York: Crown.

**Part III**

# The New/Human Security Agenda

# Chapter 9

# Organized Crime

As we have seen, criminal activities often play a supporting role in many traditional international security problems, as in the form of criminally financed terrorist and rebel movements, computer hacking or illicit arms trafficking (Rubin and Guáqueta, 2007; Cockayne and Lupel, 2011; Asal, Milward and Schoon, 2015). These and similar problems, which also reflect the growing importance of non-state actors in international relations, are becoming so widespread and prominent that some crimes and criminal organizations are increasingly being treated as international security concerns. As the previous chapter noted, this trend also inspires a conceptual transition towards a range of non-traditional (or human security) issues covered here and in the rest of volume, which can involve well-organized non-state (or private) actors, often using non-military power resources and motivated by a wide range of goals, political and otherwise. Thus, although some security specialists might still argue that crime is much less important than the problems covered earlier in this volume, most would nonetheless agree that certain types of criminal activities – beyond terrorism and cybersecurity – can pose a threat to international security. As always, however, we must be very clear in terms of analysing why certain crimes or criminals are invested with the status of international security threats, while others are not. One obvious answer to this puzzle involves the growing role of international or transnational *organized* crime, and this trend indeed provides much of the raw material for this chapter. Yet even within this realm of criminal activity there is much disagreement among global stakeholders about which specific organized crimes deserve more attention as security threats, as we shall see below in the case study on drug trafficking.

Disputes about how to identify specific crimes or criminal organizations as major global threats are only one part of the problem, however. For organized crime today represents an extremely complex, multi-jurisdictional, international security issue requiring considerable and ongoing coordination between domestic law enforcement and foreign/security policy officials, which in turn requires sustained inter-agency international cooperation among actors who may not be so familiar with the norms of global diplomacy and the legal cultures of other states (Andreas and Nadelmann, 2006; Glenny, 2008). Yet the need for such coordination, whether or not a crime is viewed as an *international* security threat, is becoming abundantly clear among law enforcement officials, owing to several trends discussed in previous chapters. One involves simple demographics: a rise in urbanization creates more concentrated and more valuable markets for criminal activities, as does a growing underclass of younger people, mostly in LDCs, who either target, or sell to, richer people in the developed world. A second trend involves the channels through which these criminal transactions are conducted: the same elements of globalization used by transnational firms are being exploited by criminals, and it is becoming increasingly difficult to distinguish between legal and illegal globalization. However, while all of these factors help to increase the general *demand* for global cooperation to effectively manage the problem of organized crime, the actual *supply* of that cooperation is another matter entirely, as we shall see.

## Organized crime and international security

To answer the question of whether to treat crime as an international security problem, we first must recognize the sheer range of criminal activities that could be viewed as major threats. Here we have a seemingly endless list of candidates (beyond terrorism and cybersecurity covered earlier), including, but certainly not limited to: various types of illicit trafficking (narcotics, arms, hazardous waste, humans), prostitution, pornography, illegal technology transfers, gambling, protection/extortion rackets, contract murders, loan sharking, various types of fraud (including identity theft), corruption, piracy, counterfeiting (including the illegal copying and selling of copyrighted or trademarked goods), cybercrime, forced labour/slavery and so on (Sandholtz and Koetzle, 2000; Berdal and Serrano, 2002). As noted above and in previous chapters, many of these crimes do involve transnational organized criminals to various degrees, and often can be linked to weak or failed states, terrorist or rebel movements, war zones, post-conflict situations or corrupt regimes. This fact in turn raises the issue of how to label various crime-related organizations, such as warlords, Mafiosi, gangs, Caudillos, bandits, pirates, drug and arms traffickers and so on. In addition, once we have determined that a major criminal problem has emerged, how do we prioritize among various transnational organized crimes and groups in terms of treating them as specific threats to international security?

### Destructive scale

One way to handle this question involves simply focusing on the proceeds generated by various global criminal activities, as a kind of proxy for measuring their destructive scale. Some recent data, compiled by the

Table 9.1   *Annual global costs of major criminal activities*

| | |
|---|---|
| Money laundering | $800 billion to $2 trillion |
| Corruption | $2 to 3 trillion |
| Narcotics trafficking | $435 billion |
| Cybercrime | $445 billion |
| Toxic/hazardous waste dumping | $10 to 12 billion |
| Auto theft (US/Europe) | $4 billion |
| Human trafficking | $7 to 10 billion |
| Illicit arms smuggling | $1 billion |

*Source:* Various US, UN and OECD reports.

author, show (in Table 9.1) the estimated annual revenues from selected criminal activities.

As we can see, money laundering, corruption, narcotics trafficking and cybercrime clearly account for the greatest costs as compared to other types of major crimes. Taken as a whole, and assuming these figures are not grossly deflated or inflated, which is always a possibility considering that they are only estimates, these four crimes alone could amount to anywhere between five and ten per cent of global GDP ($77 trillion in 2014), or at least $3–4 trillion per year. Thus it should be no surprise that these crimes in particular have stimulated a great deal of attention, as major threats, by the international community. Counterfeiting of various kinds of goods, especially media, is also extremely lucrative, amounting to anywhere between $650 billion and over $1 trillion a year depending on the source consulted, yet this is not considered a major *security* threat as compared to money laundering, corruption, narcotics and cybercrime.

In addition, various major powers attempt to calculate the costs of crime in their own countries using a variety of measures. The US, for example, once estimated the total costs of drug abuse to American society to be $160 billion a year; the vast majority of these costs are related to lost workplace productivity rather than to health care or property theft (Perl, 2006), which indicates the perception of organized criminal activity, at least in America, as primarily an economic security threat rather than a social-political one. In the UK, however, the government has refused to conduct a cost–benefit analysis of its drugs policy; it simply claims that its current approach – prohibition – is more cost-effective than the alternatives, such as an attempt to decriminalize, if not legalize, certain drugs. Although this is still a somewhat unpopular option in the UK (among other states), one attempt to make a cost–benefit analysis with government data sources has argued that the regulated legalization of certain drugs would be more cost-effective than the current approach, and could save UK taxpayers up to £14 billion a year (Transform Drug Policy Foundation, 2009).

Similarly, the economic costs of pirate attacks off the coast of Somalia, where about 20 per cent of world trade is shipped through the Gulf of Aden, have been interpreted as a major threat by the UN and its more powerful members. In weaker states, such activities can also contribute to domestic instability, or, in extreme cases, the prospect of state failure or collapse. Trafficking in human beings for the purposes of prostitution, illegal or forced labour, illegal immigration and even the sale of babies or children to 'adoptive' parents is also becoming more widespread (Williams, 1999), which adds a human rights/human security dimension to the problem. In the UK, one of the most lucrative human trafficking networks in Europe was broken in mid-2009; a trio smuggled at least 230 Afghans into Europe and possibly as many as 1,800, earning between £200,000 and £300,000 from 2005 to 2008. The US State Department also estimates that between 600,000 and 800,000 people are trafficked each year for various purposes, a problem with obvious implications for population-related security problems covered in more detail in Chapter 13.

Also on the rise are crimes associated with the internet and computer networks, such as identity theft, extortion (i.e. using 'ransomware' viruses to take over a computer or threatening to disclose sensitive data if a payment is not made) and various types of financial fraud using email solicitations ('phishing' scams) or false websites that mimic the real websites of banks or other firms. This problem in fact has become one of the more prominent global priorities in the past few years, and not just because of the threats associated with cybersecurity/cyberwar discussed in the previous chapter. As noted there, the key focus of cybercriminals is profit-seeking rather than attacking the internet simply to cause harm; in this case annual cybercrime costs have been estimated at $400–500 billion a year. Much cybercrime, in fact, involves crimes that had already existed long before the internet (such as fraud and extortion); in this case some criminal activities have simply migrated from the physical world to the cyberworld. However, even the term 'cybercrime' can provoke disputes among some stakeholders, as it overlaps with cybersecurity/ cyberwar, may not always be 'organized' and may not always involve profit-seeking. For example, the acts of some cybercriminals (such as vandalism, bullying/stalking, thrill-seeking and protest/vigilantism) may represent a grey area between politically motivated cyberwar attacks and economically motivated cybercrime attacks. This definitional problem in turn makes it difficult for authorities in various jurisdictions to cooperate effectively, although they are becoming increasingly focused in their efforts.

## Geographic and temporal scope

A second consideration regarding the treatment of organized crime as a threat to international security involves its very wide geographic scope and its persistence as a social and political problem for nearly all states. No inhabited continent is immune from the problem of crime, and modern criminal networks of various types are found or based in the Americas, Europe, China, Israel, Japan, Nigeria, Russia and other states/regions. It is also a misnomer to rely largely on ethnic labels to identify these groups, as they often do not confine their membership or operations to single nationalities or territories. In addition, they just as often may collude with each other as compete with each other, even to the extent of creating market-sharing arrangements in territories where they operate. Indeed, transnational organized crime is one of the few truly global security problems analysed in this volume, and it involves many loose alliances or relationships among many other 'traditional' crime-related groups, such as small-time criminals, white-collar criminals, terrorist or rebel movements and corrupt governments (Williams, 1994).

For example, most of the illicit drugs entering the two largest markets, Europe and the US, are sourced from other states (mainly in South America and central Asia), and traffickers rely on the same global transport and communications networks used by legitimate multinational firms. In fact, virtually all of the heroin and cocaine consumed in the US is foreign-sourced, which makes counter-drug efforts against those substances an international problem, at least from the US point of view, while the UN asserts that cannabis is produced in around 176 states, which is nearly the number of all states in the system, to satisfy the demand of over 150 million users of the drug. Developing states can serve as major markets as well; for example, much of the haul from the UK's biggest jewel robbery – to the amount of £40 million – was expected to end up in East Asia, as China in particular is expected to displace the US and Japan as the world's largest diamond market. The highly pervasive nature of transnational organized crime, however, also makes it a very diffused, fragmented and unpredictable threat, whose hazards can vary widely not just across states but within states as well, so it becomes very difficult for these various actors to prioritize specific crimes as security threats, and to devote appropriate public resources to tackling them.

## Likelihood

As with many of the threats associated with cybersecurity discussed in the previous chapter, transnational organized crime is a fact of life in the modern world, but it is not a completely new phenomenon; the roots of some criminal groups like the Japanese Yakuza or the Chinese Triad

Societies extend back for centuries. The rise of globalization, especially in communications and transportation, has dramatically increased the scope and intensity of their operations over the past several decades (Mittelman, 2000). Other factors, such as the existence of weak states, the collapse of the Soviet empire, the transition to market economies in Central/ Eastern Europe and the creation of large free trade areas, such as the North American Free Trade Agreement (NAFTA) and the EU, also help to facilitate their operations (Caldwell et al., 1999). The disintegration of the Soviet Union alone, which involved the creation of 15 new, and often weak, states (including Russia), has flooded the market with thousands of weapons and other illicit goods and services, as well as facilitated the rise of criminal gangs based in, or linked to, former Soviet states. Many high-profile cybercriminal activities, in fact, have been traced directly back to Russia and other former Soviet republics. As all responsible states measure and track criminal activities as part of their normal police operations, there is little doubt about the prevalence of this problem. Crime is especially notorious in or near conflict zones (or post-conflict zones) or other areas of state weakness (Cornell, 2007; Rubin and Guáqueta, 2007); however, organized crime also exists in most, if not all, developed states. Currently Afghanistan in particular is a major problem (Felbab-Brown, 2006), both as a conflict zone and as the world's main source (along with Myanmar) of raw opium.

It is also important to consider likelihood in terms of the presumed link between criminal activity and its real/potential harm or threat. This often raises the question of so-called 'victimless' crimes, such as drug use/ abuse, a topic that produces a great deal of controversy. Drug use in particular might seem to lend itself to the application of scientific or medical evidence about the dangerousness or addictiveness of some drugs, yet such evidence can be manipulated or ignored by politicians and policy-makers. For example, the UK's Advisory Council on the Misuse of Drugs (ACMD) once attempted to reclassify cannabis as a less dangerous drug, but this view was rejected by the British government; a similar outcome occurred with an analysis of MDMA (the active ingredient in ecstasy). The British government even fired the head of the ACMD in October 2009 after it disagreed with his views on these issues; this move prompted the resignation of five other ACMD experts. In another example, in 1995 the World Health Organization (WHO) conducted the largest study on cocaine ever undertaken, involving a survey of 22 states. Its report, the WHO Cocaine Project, said the use of alcohol and tobacco were more dangerous health risks, and that cocaine risks are rare for light users. The report, however, was never published after the US threatened to withdraw its funding for WHO research projects; it was later disowned by WHO and does not officially exist on WHO's website (although it is available elsewhere on the internet). The report was also extremely critical of US policies discussed below, especially supply reduction, and suggested a consideration of decriminalization and other harm-reduction strategies, such as those found in Australia, Bolivia, Canada, Colombia and the Netherlands. It even said the use of coca leaves appears to have no negative health effects and can have positive therapeutic, sacred and social functions for indigenous Andean populations – views which directly contradicted US (and UK) views about cocaine, and were summarily suppressed.

## Recovery

Despite the prevalence of transnational organized crime as a growing threat, the good news is that the recovery from crime is much less difficult and costly than recovering from other threats to international security covered in this volume, such as interstate war. This assumes, however, that the problem has been brought under control to some degree, which of course is not always the case. Although many experts cite the examples of Bolivia, Colombia, Peru, Somalia and other states that seem to suffer from what appear to be chronic crime-related problems, it is important to recognize that other states with similar problems – such as America during the 1930s – have managed to turn things around, although this might take a very high degree of political will and sustained leadership (not to mention violence). These factors are often in short supply at the international level, especially relative to the management of more destructive security threats. Where such will is lacking, as in a weak or failing state, the situation can remain a crisis for years or even decades, especially where the criminal activity is linked to intrastate conflict or other internal problems, such as environmental or public health disasters. Afghanistan and Colombia, for example, are still in a state of crisis thanks to their status as the world's largest producers of heroin and cocaine respectively, much of which is destined for the European and US markets through global transhipment cartels (see the case study in Box 9.1).

## Stakeholder factors

One major problem regarding the conceptualization of organized crime as an international security problem involves the very wide range of stakeholders who can be associated with criminal activities. Equally, the extent to which these individual stakeholders might be viewed as security threats can also vary widely, which makes the problem of choosing which crimes and which criminals to target that much more difficult.

## Principal stakeholders

Keeping our focus on major criminal organizations, we noted earlier that such groups are found in all inhabited regions of the world. They are also known to develop various relationships and alliances with each other, with smaller-scale criminals, with terrorist/rebel movements and with corrupt governments. And like terrorist or rebel movements, criminal organizations can vary widely in terms of their organizational scope (narrow/regional to wide/global) and complexity (loose/informal networks to tight/formal organizational hierarchies). In addition, some groups might have long organizational traditions and histories that help them survive and prosper, while others appear virtually out of thin air, often owing to some type of window of opportunity that creates a demand for their activities.

The rise of criminal activity in conflict zones, such as the Balkans and Afghanistan, is one major example of the latter trend. In these areas, international efforts to control flows of arms and other goods through the use of economic sanctions and arms embargoes (see the section on policy below) often have the perverse effect of facilitating the activities of criminal gangs who can provide those very goods (Andreas, 2005). The same pattern has occurred with other efforts, such as America's failed experiment with alcohol prohibition from 1919 to 1933 (Okrent, 2010) and its current war on drug trafficking. The corruption of government officials and other elites (such as union leaders or bankers/investors) is another common factor behind the rise of major criminal groups, in both LDCs and in more developed states. For example, drug-financed corruption is an ongoing problem among the US Customs and Border Protection officers who patrol the 2,000-mile-long US border with Mexico. Since 2004, dozens of such officers have been arrested on suspicion of taking bribes or committing other offences, resulting in over 50 convictions, and Mexican crime syndicates are even suspected of attempting to plant their own informers in the agency.

It is also worth noting the role of other stakeholders who might facilitate, and benefit from, the various activities of criminal gangs. In addition to corrupt officials and non-state actors, these supporting stakeholders include those who might sell to, or otherwise supply, criminal gangs (such as farmers who grow illicit crops), various types of 'middlemen' who facilitate criminal transactions (such as corrupt banks or pawn shops) and, perhaps most important of all, the actual customers who purchase the goods or services proffered by criminal organizations. The markets for pirated or counterfeit goods, not to mention the illegal downloading of music and videos, may also be linked to larger criminal enterprises. In short then, all major criminal organizations are part of much broader networks of corrupt officials, suppliers, middlemen, customers and other stakeholders, and they depend on these variable networks of supply and demand to survive and prosper. Devising an effective strategy to stop these activities thus requires a comprehensive approach that targets entire networks and not just the specific criminal gangs at their core. Otherwise new criminal gangs will simply rise up and take the place of the defeated ones.

## Interests and preferences

All criminal organizations as defined above have a primary, if not exclusive, interest in profit-making and will choose certain types of criminal activities to increase those profits. However, and although the discussion above suggests that major criminal organizations seem to operate in an almost random fashion according to the dynamics of the supply and demand of various illicit goods and services, it is still possible to make distinctions among them regarding their more specific preferences. For example, even though most such gangs typically oppose traditional forms of authority, such as states and/or state-sponsored IOs, in their operations, they can vary in terms of their relationship to that authority and how they balance internal cohesion against external challenges, such as a need for resources (Hastings, 2012). Some groups adopt a 'predatory' approach, which involves preying upon or appropriating the resources of local authorities on an *ad hoc* basis. Others are more sophisticated and adopt a more 'parasitic' approach to the state, a longer-term and more sustainable method involving the regular extraction of payoffs (that is, extortion/protection rackets). Finally, a 'symbiotic' approach involves the coexistence, and even co-constitution, of criminals and state officials, through overlapping memberships, corruption and even joint ventures or market-sharing arrangements involving criminal enterprises (Cockayne and Lupel, 2009). Some examples of criminal organizations that use these approaches are, according to Cockayne and Lupel:

> *Predatory groups*: Revolutionary United Front (Sierra Leone), Taliban-linked groups (Afghanistan).
> *Parasitic groups*: Italian Mafiosi, Russia Maffiya.
> *Symbiotic groups*: Balkan groups, Charles Taylor's group (Liberia), Kosovo Liberation Army.

Thus, prosecuting some of these groups, particularly parasitic and especially symbiotic ones, often involves prosecuting public officials and their social/political supporters, which could weaken or otherwise undermine the state if more honest and effective officials cannot be appointed. This may involve a longer-term process of legal/judicial reform in the state involved, which of course requires a much greater commitment by the international community.

Finally, it is worth noting the contrasting views of major global stakeholders regarding the problem of crime. Although major powers and state-based IOs may share a general interest in stopping crime, these stakeholders vary widely in terms of how they prioritize it as a *security* threat. They also differ widely regarding their preferences about which crimes or organizations, if any, should be targeted, and with what means. In recent years, many states have identified cybercrime as a major security threat, partly because of its linkages with the issues discussed in the previous chapter. However, the US, for example, also still prioritizes counter-drug efforts as a security threat, and has a policy preference for stopping the flow of illicit drugs into the US itself and maintaining a global drug prohibition regime (Herschinger, 2015). Other stakeholders might place a higher priority on corruption (as in many LDCs) or illegal migration/human trafficking schemes (as in Europe). And although it is not generally appropriate to speak of individual customers or law-abiding citizens as major 'stakeholders', their preferences can be aggregated under the right circumstances, especially in well-functioning democratic states. If so, they may push for more attention to be paid to some crimes over others, or for some crimes (such as drug use and prostitution) to be decriminalized; cross-national surveys, for example, have shown that victims of crime (as with victims of terrorism) often become more politically active (Bateson, 2012), so any major increase in crime in a state could lead to stronger preferences about international counter-crime policies. These views, which also may result in the formation of specific pressure groups (such as the US-based National Organization for the Reform of Marijuana Laws, or NORML) can either support or contradict those of official stakeholders at the national and international levels. Scientific or technical bodies, such as the WHO or the OECD, can play similar roles in challenging official views of criminal threats/harm, as we have seen. Finally, in large or federal states, such as the US, individual localities can easily undermine or contradict national counter-crime policies, as with the legalization of prostitution in Nevada and various political movements to decriminalize marijuana (cannabis) in more than a dozen US states ranging from California to Maine.

## The use of force

The existence of differences over interests and preferences in turn raises some difficult questions about what degree of force should be used against various criminal enterprises, especially when major stakeholders cannot agree on the severity of a criminal threat. Legal and police powers are the dominant approaches, yet should these methods also involve the death penalty? The vast majority of developed countries – including all EU member states – have formally outlawed the death penalty as a normal criminal punishment; the US thus stands against many of its own allies in having executed hundreds of convicted criminals since its death penalty was reinstituted in 1976 after a four-year hiatus. According to Harm Reduction International, an NGO, 32 states also permit the death penalty for drug trafficking (although about half of these states don't actually enforce this penalty). The US federal government permits the death penalty for trafficking in large quantities of drugs, as do two US states (Florida and Missouri), although no one in the US has been executed under these laws. Equally controversially, should the international community consider a military response to crime, in addition to, or instead of, legal and police powers? Given the close relationships between certain types of criminal organizations, which may blur the distinction between criminal enterprises and terrorist/rebel movements, plus the parasitic/symbiotic strategies of certain groups, some global stakeholders are often tempted to offer military resources to combat such groups. The US has been a major proponent of this approach regarding certain types of criminal activities, particularly drug trafficking, yet it also has other adherents around the globe, particularly in states, such as Colombia, that face criminally supported insurgencies (see case study below). The threat of piracy off the coast of Somalia has led to a major military response by a number of states, as we shall see later in this chapter, and the issue of human trafficking has inspired a similar response, as we shall see in Chapter 13. The use of the military in such circumstances is, however, still very controversial for many global stakeholders, and can undermine any consensus on how to deal with organized crime as a security problem.

One specific concern, beyond the simple question of whether military methods are more effective than non-military ones in counter-crime operations, is whether such methods might also facilitate human rights abuses, corruption and other negative externalities, either at home or abroad. Weapons, military training, surveillance equipment/techniques and other military services provided to certain states can also be used against innocent civilians, either deliberately (for example, to put down a peaceful protest) or accidently (for example, various shootings of civilian aircraft by US-supplied military aircraft in South America). The market for weapons in particular can be affected by indirect policies as well; for example, the 2004 expiration of the US Federal Assault Weapons Ban increased the supply of those weapons in northern Mexico, and therefore increased gun violence in that region (Dube, Dube and García-Ponce, 2013). This 'collateral damage' of the militarization of counter-crime operations and loose gun control policies can easily lead to higher levels of violent crime than might otherwise exist in the states involved, as seems to have occurred with the US drug war in Central and South America (Bartilow and Eom, 2009). A second, and somewhat more parochial, concern involves a blurring of the important distinction in certain states between (primarily domestic-focused) civilian law enforcement and (primarily foreign-focused) military forces. In the US, for example, an 1878 federal law, the Posse Comitatus

Act, is supposed to prohibit local law enforcement agencies from using any branch of the military to do their jobs. This act was designed to help end the federal military occupation of the Southern states during the post-Civil War Reconstruction period and to prevent future abuses of military power on US territory. The statute embodied a long-standing principle in Anglo-American law that there should be a total separation of the military from civilian law enforcement. As we shall see below, this act has almost certainly been violated in the context of America's militarization of the war on drugs and even the war on terrorism.

## Public–private domains and levels of jurisdiction

This question of civilian versus military approaches, as well as the distinction between domestic and foreign law enforcement activities, also points to the difficult problem of determining the most effective or appropriate jurisdiction in which to conduct counter-crime operations. As suggested above, there is now a huge grey area between legal and illegal (or 'extra-legal') domains and between criminals and law-abiding citizens. This problem of course relates to the more general blurred distinction between state and non-state actors. In certain 'soft security' or 'human security' areas like organized crime, both the US and the UK for example have increasingly relied upon not just private security forces but also public–private partnerships and even quasi-autonomous NGOs (or 'quangos' in the UK); these tactics, as with the use of PMCs, raise serious questions about accountability, effectiveness and legitimacy. This problem can also be seen, for example, with the 'deputization' of ISPs, banks, shipping firms and other private actors to carry out state security functions (see below).

The completely opposite problem – an apparent lack of *any* sovereign authority – applies in other places. Like terrorist organizations, criminal organizations thrive where they can find safe havens free of effective police and judicial forces, especially in areas where multiple states connect with each other (such as Ciudad del Este in South America), or where major suppliers congregate to meet a nearby demand (such as Cuidad Juárez, the drug murder capital of Mexico), or in sub-national areas where national authorities lack effective control (such as the Transnistria region of Moldova, certain regions of Afghanistan and Pakistan and the Nagorno-Karabakh region of Azerbaijan) or in so-called 'sovereign-free' places (also known as 'micronations') which are nominally independent tiny states that lack formal recognition as such by the international community. These problems are often grouped together in the literature as 'black spots' or 'quasi-states' or 'parastates', and have been linked to various types of criminal and terrorist activities (Jackson, 1990; King, 2001; Stanislawski, 2008). Similar dynamics apply in new 'virtual' territories (such as cyberspace), where it can be difficult for government authorities to assert effective control; as noted in Chapter 8, the Dark Web in particular is thought to be used for the specific purpose of facilitating various forms of criminal activity (Bartlett, 2015).

Even within relatively well-managed states, particularly federal ones such as the US, Canada and Germany, it can be extremely difficult to determine which legal jurisdiction should take precedence when building a case against a specific criminal organization. As we have seen, such organizations are often not just transnational in nature; they are also 'trans-jurisdictional', meaning their various activities can take place in multiple and overlapping legal or administrative jurisdictions, both *across* and *within* states. Many criminal groups in fact take advantage of different criminal laws, or differing degrees of enforcement, to conduct their operations, as in the case of various smuggling operations that exploit the free trade relationships of certain states, such as Puerto Rico or Mexico with the US/NAFTA, and Central/Eastern European EU member states with those in Western Europe. Adopting a legal approach to bring these groups to justice, which is typically the case, thus requires an extremely high degree of inter-agency coordination involving surveillance procedures, chains of evidence, prosecution rights, extradition treaties or other types of MLATs, assuming they are already in place, and trial/sentencing norms, which are primarily implemented on an *ad hoc* basis to deal with specific groups but only once a credible case has been made.

Compounding the problem even further is the issue of public versus private stakeholders involved in organized criminal activities. One question is how to deal with various secondary players, such as middlemen and customers. For example, many illicit funds are laundered through legitimate banks and offshore financial centres, which operate legally in their home territories. We also should emphasize that many customers of these illegal activities are located in advanced developed states. Should these stakeholders be prosecuted to the fullest extent of the law, or instead be allowed to plea bargain to get a lighter sentence, often in exchange for information about more senior criminals? The use of plea bargaining actually varies widely across states; for example, a majority of criminal cases in the US are decided by plea bargaining, which avoids the high costs of a jury trial, while in other states, particularly civil law ones such as France and Italy, plea bargaining can be difficult and controversial.

An equally difficult question involves the use, by *private* stakeholders, of PMCs and other private security services to combat organized crime. Many MNCs, both large and small, hire their own security providers and investigative forces to deal with certain criminal activities, such as the counterfeiting of their goods or other forms of intellectual property theft, as well as the kidnapping of their officials, which invests such firms, and their private security services, with a degree of quasi-public authority. PMCs have also started to offer their services to shipping firms to counter the threat of piracy off the coast of Somalia. For the first nine months of 2008 alone, the International Maritime Bureau reported 63 cases of piracy and robbery at sea in this area, and pirates began taking hostages and asking for millions of dollars in ransoms in addition to seizing cargoes. For the next few years, the thousands of ships that transit this area each year were being forced to decide whether to enhance their security or take an alternative (and far more expensive) route around the Cape of Good Hope. These trends also give insurance firms a supporting role in framing some international criminal threats: if such firms will not insure, at a reasonable cost, private stakeholders in crime- or conflict-rich zones, then public authorities may have to step in to protect the interests of those stakeholders.

## International crime as a policy problem

Not only do states vary in the importance they attach to certain crimes, they even disagree about whether certain undesirable activities should be treated as crimes in the first place. Even when states or other global stakeholders do agree on the threatening nature of a particular crime or criminal organization, they often strongly disagree about how to manage that threat. These factors, all of which stem from the widely varying domestic social and legal cultures of individual states as well as the diffuse, idiosyncratic and unpredictable nature of modern organized crime, can make the politics of international policy-making in this realm extremely convoluted and even contradictory or hypocritical, similar to the problem of weapons proliferation discussed in Chapter 6.

### Agenda-setting

As is often the case in international security, the major players – particularly states – tend to set the global agenda regarding the treatment of crime as an international security threat. This trend of defining a crime at the domestic level, then exporting that view or norm to the international level, extends well back to the era of British hegemony in the nineteenth century, when the UK acted not only to define certain practices, such as slave trading and piracy, as crimes, but also attempted to police those crimes on a global basis (Nadelmann, 1990). As the UK was also involved in its own criminal enterprises at the time (namely the Chinese opium trade), and had greatly profited from the slave trade, we can already see the emergence of the hypocrisy in this realm that persists to this day. That said, and despite the proliferation in recent years of transnational crimes and criminal organizations, most international attention is devoted to a more narrow range of activities beyond those discussed in previous chapters:

drug trafficking, money laundering, piracy and cybercrime. As with the UK in the nineteenth century, this is partly a direct result of US leadership in the 1980s and beyond, which has had a dramatic influence on how the international community understands crime as a global security threat.

Specifically, in the realm of drug trafficking, the US Comprehensive Drug Abuse Prevention and Control Act of 1970 has inspired most subsequent US drug legislation as it designates all controlled substances and their legal uses and prohibitions. During the 1980s the Reagan administration instituted a 'war on drugs' which paved the way for a 1988 UN Convention Against Drugs ratified by a large majority of states in the international system (161 states). This focus on drugs was broadened to some degree in 1995 when US President Bill Clinton defined 'international organized crime' as a security threat on the occasion of the 50th anniversary of the UN (reproduced as Presidential Decision Document 42). Two years later, the UN itself echoed this view when it merged the UN Drug Control Programme and the UN Centre for International Crime Prevention into a single unit, the UN Office on Drugs and Crime (UNODC). The UNODC now operates in all regions of the world through an extensive network of field offices (Perl, 2006). It led directly to the UN Convention on Transnational Organized Crime, which attempts to improve law enforcement cooperation and harmonize legal codes to deal with this problem. The UNODC also has asserted that organized crime can undermine peacekeeping efforts and fuel civil wars through corruption and illicit trafficking in arms and commodities (UNODC, 2004) and the G8, too, has increasingly included transnational organized crime on its policy agenda (Scherrer, 2009).

The US also took the lead in placing another crime-related issue on the global agenda: the problem of money laundering, defined as the processing of criminal proceeds to hide their illegal origin. Such processing can occur through the legitimate international banking system as well as through informal transnational foreign exchange networks, such as the Hawala system and the Black Market Peso Exchange. This is an extremely important development, as many criminal enterprises, and those of similar illicit groups, such as terrorists, must attempt to spend their funds without revealing their sources, which typically requires money laundering – the Achilles' heel of organized crime. As a major financial stakeholder, the US has special vulnerabilities here, which led it to push for more global attention to money laundering. These include the facts that: US banks are global, numerous and vulnerable; the US dollar is still the primary international reserve currency, accounting for about 63 per cent of all global foreign exchange reserves in 2014 (the euro accounts for about 22 per cent); and, in a system dominated by flexible (or floating) market-determined exchange rates, money laundering cases could ignite global financial crises. Moreover, some states, even in the developed world, either did not consider money laundering to be a crime, or did not think it was serious enough to warrant major attention. Even the US did not criminalize money laundering until 1986. However, one major case in 1999 helped to focus global attention on this issue: about $7 billion was laundered through the Bank of New York on behalf of Russian criminals and corrupt government officials, which set a record as the largest money laundering case in history. Since then, global cooperation against money laundering has greatly intensified, especially in light of its importance to both counter-crime and counter-terror efforts (Sharman, 2008).

## Framing policy alternatives

As with other new security issues, policy alternatives can be framed in multiple ways as the main policy targets – crime and criminal organizations – operate across multiple levels of jurisdiction and involve complex public–private linkages. In addition, all developed states as well as most properly functioning LDCs have well-established criminal justice systems to deal with this problem, so these stakeholders must be 'internationalized' to help them think about the threat on a global basis. Finally, as crime often targets weak individual citizens within any society, it is important not to underestimate the role of individual/communal self-help. Even in situations involving well-organized crime, it is possible, though sometimes dangerous and difficult, to confront such groups with coordinated grass-roots action, such as the *addio pizzo* ('goodbye protection money') movement in Palermo, Sicily. This effort puts racketeering mobs on notice and provides more links to police to help reduce or eliminate the payment of protection money to crime gangs. In addition, the Italian business group Confindustria has decided to expel any business found to be paying *pizzo* money.

Taking a closer look at state-led multilateral efforts, we first should note that this type of cooperation largely requires the translating and exporting of various unilateral/domestic methods to the international/regional/multilateral level, as well as a high degree of transnational judicial cooperation, which is why the US has pushed for stronger extradition pacts and other types of MLATs as part of its 'nowhere to hide' approach to organized crime (and terrorism). The EU has adopted an even more ambitious attitude, as reflected in the emergence of its own AFSJ (Area of Freedom, Security and Justice) concept, plus the creation of Europol, as noted in Chapter 7 (Anderson and Den Boer, 1994; Occhipinti, 2003; Fijanut and Paoli, 2004). These measures also involve the ability of criminal justice authorities in EU member states, under certain conditions, to serve cross-border arrest warrants, and even engage in the 'hot pursuit' of criminal suspects across borders without asking for permission from the national authorities of the EU member state being entered. This type of cross-border law enforcement cooperation, which is intended to avoid the delays and other problems associated with extradition, is more developed in Europe than in any other region (although some EU member states, such as Denmark, Ireland and the UK, have been reluctant to participate).

The US and the EU also attempt to export their own legal norms in their main areas of influence: the western hemisphere for the US and the EU/European periphery in the case of the EU, as through the ENP, which attempts to facilitate counter-crime/counter-terrorism cooperation among the EU and its bordering regions to the East and South (Smith and Webber, 2007; Occhipinti, 2007). The EU has also incorporated counter-crime goals in several of its Common Security and Defence Policy (CSDP) foreign missions in the Balkans, Ukraine/Moldova and sub-Saharan Africa (among other locales). These goals include fighting organized crime and corruption while also attempting to strengthen local security/judicial capacities, including border controls, in some of these countries (Smith, forthcoming). These regional efforts are supplemented by global policing cooperation through the International Criminal Police Organization (Interpol), whose roots extend back to 1923 (Anderson, 1989; Barnett and Coleman, 2005). Interpol is supported by other more informal forums, some of which, such as the UN's International Organization for Migration (IOM), deal with very specific problems like human trafficking. It also should be noted that ASEAN, the OAS and other regional IOs do attempt to deal with organized crime and related threats, though these efforts are not nearly as well-developed as the EU's programme. However, the OAS has attempted to devise its own Multilateral (Drug) Evaluation Mechanism to help counteract the imposition of America's own unilateral certification procedures, which are often opposed by major drug-producing states.

Beyond these general frameworks, the range of strategies to combat specific crimes and criminal organizations can vary quite widely from the passive/defensive to the more aggressive/offensive methods. Passive/defensive approaches can involve enhancing the security of enterprises or stakeholders that might become targets of criminals, the regular investigation and prosecution of criminals and criminal organizations through normal law enforcement activities, various types of education campaigns (including the offer of rewards) to solicit information about criminal activities and so on. More aggressive approaches can range along a continuum from weaker to stronger measures. The weaker measures might include international 'sting' operations (including in cyberspace) to lure criminals into the open, destruction of the resource base of criminal organizations (such as drug crop eradication programmes), enforced interdiction of trafficked goods and 'naming and shaming' campaigns to punish uncooperative supporting players such as banks and national governments with economic sanctions and other penalties. More aggressive measures include the use of special forces, covert operatives and various forms of military assistance to monitor, investigate, apprehend and even suppress or kill suspected criminals and their resource bases. Naturally there is a great deal of contention regarding the use of these more aggressive measures, so they tend to be used on a more *ad hoc* basis by single states (or small coalitions of states) rather than by the international community at large. However, some regional organizations, such as the EU, have attempted to devise stronger and more comprehensive counter-crime measures in their geographic areas of responsibility than currently exist at the international level, which may be a sign of things to come regarding international cooperation in this area.

## Policy choice

Given the various definition and coordination problems already noted regarding the treatment of crime as an international security threat, specific global policy choices, when actually made, often reflect the will and resources of the major players. This generally involves a combination of hegemonic leadership and coalitions of the willing. What tends to occur, in fact, is the direct transfer of various counter-crime policies from the domestic level to the international system level by leading states, particularly the US and its allies in the developed world such as other OECD member states. This can take the form of bilateral agreements between relevant parties (such as the US and Colombia) or more comprehensive multilateral conventions and programmes to target specific criminal activities, such as the UN International Drug Control Programme, which assists 67 developing states. It also involves the creation of transnational law enforcement academies, often sponsored by the US or the EU in states such as Hungary and Thailand, to help them train new personnel for the fight against crime.

As with the discussion of terrorist organizations in Chapter 7, one broad strategy involves naming the specific targets for action, which usually begins with the states suspected of harbouring or otherwise facilitating the activities of criminal organizations. For example, the US defines a major illicit drug-producing country as one that annually harvests 1,000 hectares or more of illicit opium poppy or coca, or 5,000 hectares or more of illicit cannabis (unless the US president determines that such illicit cannabis production does not significantly affect the US, which is obviously a very self-centred way of defining this problem). Moreover, a major drug-transit country is defined by the US as one that acts as a significant direct source of illicit narcotic or psychotropic drugs or other controlled substances significantly affecting the US; or through which such drugs or substances are transported. Based on these criteria, which are not only mainly unilateral but also somewhat arbitrary, the US Department of State regularly releases lists of such countries in its *Annual International Nar-cotics Control Strategy Report*, which helps to focus global attention on certain problem states. The most recent such list (2015) names the major drug-producing and/or drug-transit countries as: Afghanistan; Bahamas; Belize; Bolivia; Burma; Colombia; Costa Rica; Dominican Republic; Ecuador; El Salvador; Guatemala; Haiti; Honduras; India; Jamaica; Laos; Mexico; Nicaragua; Pakistan; Panama; Peru; and Venezuela. In addition, the US has determined that nearly all of these states are cooperating with US counter-drug efforts and are therefore eligible for various types of US foreign aid, except for Bolivia, Burma (Myanmar), and Venezuela. Bolivia and Venezuela, however, won Vital National Interest Certifications from the US, meaning they can still receive US aid, despite their supposed non-cooperation, because *other* US national interests are at stake. Burma, however, has been denied such certification owing to its non-cooperation, as determined by the US, and is not eligible for American aid. The US has also started to name 'foreign narcotics kingpins', starting with a list provided by the Bush administration to Congress in 2003. It also includes terror/insurgent-related organizations, such as Colombia's FARC and United Self-Defense Forces. More recently, the Obama administration intensified America's long-term policy of deporting illegal immigrants, especially those with criminal records (usually for drug offences or driving under the influence of alcohol or drugs). Over 100,000 such individuals were deported in 2008; this figure rose to around 400,000 a year after 2010. US Immigration and Customs Enforcement (ICE), a part of the DHS, takes the lead on this policy (also see Chapter 13). The vast majority of these individuals are sent to Central/South America.

On the global multilateral level, the main international legal instrument is the 1988 UN Convention Against Illicit Traffic in Narcotic Drugs and Psychotropic Substances. This effort is very comprehensive and includes rules about illicit cultivation, production, distribution, sale, transport, financing, money laundering, asset seizure, extradition, mutual legal assistance, law enforcement and transit cooperation, precursor chemical control and demand reduction. At present there are 189 state parties bound by this Convention, which means nearly the entire UN membership. This effort has been supplemented by the 2000 UN Convention Against Transnational Organized Crime, which managed to define a 'transnational crime group' as one comprising three or more members who are organized for a set period of time before and after they act in a coordinated manner to commit a serious crime for the purpose of obtaining financial or other benefit. Drug trafficking is a major target of this instrument. As noted in Chapter 2, the 2003 Final Report of the UN Commission on Human Security also lists several counter-crime goals on its agenda; these include protecting people from the proliferation of arms, protecting people in violent conflict and supporting the security of people on the move.

The global counter-drug effort led by the US has inspired a similar 'naming and shaming', or 'scarlet letter', approach regarding states that facilitate money laundering through their banking secrecy laws and other financial practices, such as serving as offshore tax havens (Palan, 2003; Paris, 2003). As we saw in Chapter 7, the US Treasury Department has operated a Foreign Terrorist Asset Tracking Center since 9/11 in part to handle this problem, and has attempted to stop the use of informal money transfer schemes and the use of charitable funds for terrorism or criminal activities. The larger strategy against money laundering involves the OECD's Financial Action Task Force (FATF), created in 1989, plus several other IOs (mostly controlled by the rich developed states) devoted to global financial matters: the International Monetary Fund (IMF), the UN, the Bank for International Settlements (BIS), regional groupings (the EU and OAS), the World Bank and annual G7/G8 meetings. Given the highly transnational nature of modern global finance, this effort, which focuses on naming and punishing non-cooperative countries and territories, cannot succeed without a very high degree of international support. This can involve denying foreign aid and loans to non-cooperative states, or reducing their credit ratings, which could affect their ability to borrow in private capital markets. In 2000–1 the FATF succeeded in creating an official list of non-cooperative countries/territories, including: Bahamas; Cook Islands; Dominica; Egypt; Grenada; Guatemala; Hungary; Indonesia; Israel; Lebanon; Marshall Islands; Myanmar; Nauru; Nigeria; Niue; Philippines; Russia; St. Kitts and Nevis; St. Vincent and the Grenadines; and Ukraine. More recently, a coalition of multinational banks working with the IMF has also attempted to crack down on internet child pornography; this 'Light a Million Candles' campaign targets the credit card payments used to fund that criminal activity.

Two somewhat related approaches to organized crime championed by the US and other OECD states in recent years attempt to target the global trade in criminally obtained or conflict-related commodities (such as gemstones), and to improve domestic governance through clear global rules (that is, 'zero-tolerance' laws) against corruption. Related initiatives of an explicit public–private nature involve measures directed at the banking industry, such as 'know your customer' laws designed to: identify the real beneficiary of bank accounts, appoint compliance officers, monitor transnational relationships among banks, report suspicious activity/transactions, improve record-keeping, ban secret accounts and so on. The US also offers various Industry Partnership Programmes to improve counter-crime cooperation with certain firms: the Carrier/Container Initiative, the Business Alliance for Secure Commerce, the Americas Counter-Smuggling Initiative, the Land Border Carrier Initiative and the Business Anti-Smuggling Coalition.

To cope with cybercrime, the Budapest Convention on Cybercrime entered into force in July 2004; it was drafted in cooperation between the Council of Europe and other major states with an interest in this issue (such as the US, Canada and Japan). In addition to targeting breaches of cybersecurity as defined in Chapter 8 (such as illegal access and data interception), it also attempts to harmonize and coordinate national law enforcement activities regarding certain cybercrimes, such as child pornography, fraud/forgery and copyright infringement. However, although 48 states (mostly European) have acceded to the convention, a number of other major stakeholders, such as China and Russia, have refused to do so, which clearly adds to the sense of ongoing international conflict in this realm as discussed in Chapter 8. The EU's Europol agency also created a European Cybercrime Centre in 2013; it deals with many of the same issues among the EU's 28 member states. Through other initiatives, Europol also attempts to coordinate EU counter-crime activities regarding narcotics trafficking, human trafficking, money laundering, intellectual property theft and similar major crimes that pose a threat across the EU. Some of these crimes even involve 'Mobile Organized Crime Groups' (MOCGs), whose activities cross multiple jurisdictions and therefore require international cooperation on the part of law enforcement authorities.

The threat of piracy off the coast of Somalia and elsewhere has also inspired a fairly high degree of international cooperation to stop it, thanks in part to US leadership through its Operation Enduring Freedom, which included two naval task forces: TF-151, which operates in the Strait of Hormuz, and TF-150, which operates at the Horn of Africa. Following the dramatic increase in the number of raids in 2007 and 2008, the UNSC passed several resolutions between May and December 2008 in order to manage this problem. The primary measure was UNSC Resolution 1816, which authorized states to use 'all necessary means to repress acts of piracy and armed robbery' within the territorial waters of Somalia. Various states have sent naval units to the region to deter pirates as well as to signify their support to the ships flying their flag. Between October and December 2008, NATO sent units from its Standing Maritime Group to protect ships carrying humanitarian aid to Somalia (Operation Allied Provider); the EU also launched its first-ever naval operation in November 2008 (Operation Atalanta, or EU NAVFOR Somalia) to stop piracy in the same region. These NATO/EU efforts were later supported by patrol forces provided by non-NATO and non-EU states, including China, Egypt, India, Japan, Malaysia, Pakistan, Russia, Saudi Arabia and Turkey. This response clearly indicates that piracy near Somalia was viewed as a serious threat to international security by a range of powerful stakeholders, involving both major powers and leading IOs: the UN, the EU and NATO. China's decision to contribute to the fight was especially interesting, as it was the first time in five centuries that Chinese naval forces were sent

## Box 9.1    The 'War on Drugs' in South America

*Many stakeholders have an interest in the ongoing 'war on drugs'.*

The US has been a leading proponent of the view that narcotics trafficking is a threat to security, beginning with President Nixon's creation of the US Drug Enforcement Administration (DEA) in 1973 and continuing with President Reagan's 'war on drugs' in the 1980s. The US also strongly supported the UN Convention Against Drugs in 1988, which gained wide approval among UN member states. Yet these measures seemed to have little effect on drug trafficking in one of the most turbulent narcotics-producing regions of the world: South America. Cocaine was the primary drug export of several countries in this region – such as Colombia, Bolivia and Peru – and most

→

beyond China's territorial waters to defend that state's interests (Germond and Smith, 2009; Shemella, 2016).

It is also worth keeping in mind that the major powers often use more aggressive *unilateral* actions to deal with the threat of crime. The most prominent examples are America's 1989 invasion of Panama to capture General Manuel Noriega, the 1993 killing of Colombian drug lord Pablo Escobar with the support of US Special Forces (see the case study, Box 9.1), and numerous kidnappings of drug traffickers by the US and its allies (Nadelmann, 1994). These counter-drug renditions inspired the later efforts targeted against terrorist suspects that have attracted controversy,

→

of these exports ended up in the US, along with a rise in trafficking-related violent crimes such as murder, kidnapping and corruption.

Yet how violent must criminal activity become before it turns into a direct threat to national and regional stability? Colombia in particular faced this problem head-on, when 'drug lord' Pablo Escobar assumed control of the powerful Medellin cartel. In the process, he became one of the richest men in the world and used his wealth to bribe or kill a number of high-profile officials who stood in his way: judges, police officers, army officers and politicians. He also may have been behind the murder of Colombian presidential candidate Luis Carlos Galán in 1989, a man who had vowed to oppose the cartels if he had been elected. Even more worrisome to Colombian authorities were the complex links between drug traffickers such as Escobar and various Marxist-inspired rebel movements in the country, such as the Revolutionary Armed Forces of Colombia (FARC).

Under these circumstances, which might have turned Colombia into a failed state, the US offered various forms of assistance to help reverse the tide. This included military aid and the offer of technical assistance to help capture traffickers like Escobar and bring them to justice. In Escobar's case, this led to his killing by Colombian authorities in 1993, thanks to the help of US surveillance (Bowden, 2001). Even so, the violence did not end, and the US instituted an even larger aid programme, Plan Colombia, to help eradicate coca crops and interdict drug shipments. Although this aid has not dramatically reduced drug trafficking in the western hemisphere, it may have paved the way for peace talks between Colombian authorities and the FARC, resulting in a ceasefire in July 2015. Even so, Plan Colombia has been criticized for fuelling human right abuses throughout Colombia, among not just by Colombian authorities but also by US military and DEA officials. The high level of violence of this war on drugs has also inspired a number of countries to focus more on harm reduction rather than eradication/interdiction, a move that increasingly includes the possibility of decriminalizing certain drugs (such as cannabis). Even some US states have pursued this approach, along with many other countries, although it is unlikely to be applied to stronger narcotics like heroin and cocaine.

as discussed in Chapter 7. In addition, in 1989 the US DoD created Joint Task Force Six (JTF-6) based at Fort Bliss, Texas. JTF-6 provides federal military support for domestic low-intensity conflict operations 'to detect, deter, disrupt and dismantle' drug trafficking organizations. It was briefly suspended in 1997 after an 18-year-old US civilian was killed, and remains a focus of controversy in light of the Posse Comitatus legislation noted above. The US also operates a regional drug interdiction centre in Panama, thanks to its successful invasion of that state, and spent over one billion dollars on Colombia's counter-drug effort through its Plan Colombia and associated programmes in Peru, which include the provision of military assistance in the form of equipment, training and hundreds of US personnel (both military and civilian contractors; see the case study above). As noted above, Colombia is *the* major source of heroin and cocaine into the US and has been targeted accordingly. Plan Colombia was later embedded in a broader Andean Regional Initiative in an effort to devise a more comprehensive approach to drug trafficking in South America.

## The politics of policy effectiveness

More so than with the case of international terrorism, the fight against international crime involves a very high degree of domestic institutional fragmentation since crime is handled in all modern states by various jurisdictions ranging from the local to the regional to the national levels. This fact in turn means that involuntary defection from formally agreed international policies – assuming they have been agreed, which is not always the case – is very prominent throughout this policy domain. Even in rich states, coordination problems abound, especially regarding crimes that have an international and/or digital dimension. The simple truth, however, is that organized crime is much less important to most major governments than other threats, such as terrorism, and public money is spent accordingly: billions of dollars against terrorism, but 'only' millions against organized crime.

In the US, counter-drug cooperation in particular involves a range of competing authorities, thanks to the convoluted history of Prohibition regulation, which went from the Department of the Treasury (DoT) (1915–30), to the Federal Bureau of Narcotics (within the DoT; 1930–68), to the Department of Justice (DoJ) in 1968, then to the creation of the US Drug Enforcement Administration (DEA) in 1973 as part of the DoJ. Yet even the DEA, which has offices in over 50 countries and the support of its own 'drug intelligence centre' (in El Paso, Texas), does not have a policy monopoly at the federal level; instead it shares authority with DHS offices devoted to customs enforcement, the Department of State's Bureau for International Narcotics and Law Enforcement Affairs, the US Office of National Drug Control Policy (ONDCP) in the White House (whose head is the US 'drug czar'), the Counter-Drug Technology Assessment Center, the National Drug Intelligence Center and various foreign US offices run by the FBI, the CIA and other crime-related agencies. In addition, these federal agencies must compete with state and local law enforcement, a difficult enough problem within the US, let alone when working with foreign agencies who have their own share of coordination problems. The UK has had similar coordination problems; it merged several counter-crime agencies into the Serious Organised Crime Agency (SOCA) in 2006, but this body had weaker authority in some parts of the UK, particularly Northern

Ireland and Scotland. In 2013 SOCA was dissolved and replaced by the National Crime Agency (NCA); this body is now the UK's leading authority in the fight against organized crime. Thus, if the US and the UK, among other rich states, have such chronic problems regarding the coordination of their domestic counter-crime policies, the situation in other states, especially LDCs, must be even more difficult.

A second problem related to involuntary defection is the increasingly prominent role played by private firms and other stakeholders as they are literally 'drafted' into public service and asked to police their own customers, a role which not only increases their operating costs but also exposes them to costly liability lawsuits in case they make a mistake. A final general problem is that the international crime policy agenda is still largely dominated by the US and its major allies, as many other states simply lack the resources, political and economic, to launch expensive foreign investigations or operate transnational police academies, although they do of course cooperate with individual investigations or make other contributions (as in counter-piracy operations) on a case-by-case basis. This domination by the US/OECD/EU means in turn that crimes are prioritized according to the needs of these stakeholders, which explains the global focus on drug trafficking (rather than consumption), money laundering and cybercrime rather than many other transnational criminal problems, such as poaching endangered species and trafficking in small arms or women/children.

There is also evidence of more voluntary defection regarding international counter-crime cooperation, most prominently in the case of specific extradition efforts, and even among close allies. This is precisely what happened in the Enron case, when public pressure in the UK attempted to prevent the extradition to the US of three British bankers who worked with the troubled energy firm. Despite this campaign, the bankers were extradited, tried and convicted in the US for fraud in 2008, and each sentenced to 37 months in prison. Another grass-roots campaign emerged in the UK to prevent London hacker Gary McKinnon from being extradited to the US for hacking into the US DoD. McKinnon has Asperger syndrome (a mild form of autism), which was not taken into consideration during his judicial proceedings, according to the campaigners. A final example involves the extradition to the US of another British citizen, Jeffrey Tesler, accused of taking part in a $130 million bribery scandal in Nigeria. Tesler worked for a subsidiary of Halliburton, formerly run by former US Vice President Dick Cheney, which agreed to pay a $579 million fine to the US government. However, some of his crimes may have occurred in the UK, so it wanted the right to try him rather than allow him to be extradited to the US. Thus, if close allies like the US and the UK cannot always agree on how to manage their extradition regime, there is very little hope for other such relationships, unless one party has a major power advantage over the other. And many states, such as China, France, Germany and Russia (among others), are extremely reluctant to allow the extradition of their own citizens under almost any circumstances.

Taking a closer look at various standards that might be applied to the evaluation of policy effectiveness, the problem of international crime is quite similar to that of terrorism and cybersecurity. In terms of a total victory standard, the war on drugs/crime is probably even more impossible to 'win' than the war on terrorism. Crime thrives in the hard-to-police zones between states, between governments and civil societies and between private, economic and social activities, and it is difficult to subject those grey areas to a single global set of rules, and then enforce them, without a much higher degree of international legal and police cooperation than currently exists. As one indicator of victory, authorities can frequently point to the disruption of large criminal organizations on a fairly regular basis, as well as the arrest or killing of some major drug 'kingpin' as evidence that counter-drug efforts are working, as happened with Pablo Escobar in the 1990s and more recently with the arrest of a major 'opium baron' in Afghanistan, Haji Abdullah, in August 2009. However, criminal activity can quickly reconstitute itself if enough demand for it exists, and long-standing major criminal organizations like the Yakuza, the Mafia and other nationally based groups show no sign of stopping their operations as a result of police activity or other factors. Thus the situation here is even more difficult than that of international terrorism, where a number of terrorist groups have ceased to operate as such for a variety of reasons.

Other standards based on historical trends or comparative metrics, such as measuring criminal activity over time within or across states, can vary widely depending on the crime at issue. Efforts against money laundering/offshore tax havens, for example, have been quite successful, as major tax havens such as the Bahamas, Luxembourg and Switzerland have agreed to change their policies, albeit somewhat reluctantly in certain cases. Similarly, all of the FATF-listed 'non-cooperative' countries/territories noted above have worked with the OECD to combat money laundering, and all were removed from the list by 2006. Beyond money laundering, the dramatic multilateral military response to piracy near Somalia has resulted in the release of hostages and the arrests of dozens of pirates. Thanks to intensive EU and NATO patrols in this area, as well as self-defence measures taken by vessels, pirate attacks near Somalia declined rapidly within just five years. By the end of 2014, only two ships were attacked during the entire year, which is a huge decrease from the period 2009–11, when *monthly* pirate attacks numbered in the range of 30–40 incidents (Smith, forthcoming). However, it is still too early to tell whether this effort will have a long-term impact, especially if the patrol missions end.

The issue of effectiveness regarding cybercrime and counter-drug polices, however, is far more problematic, as there are no widely agreed benchmarks against which to measure progress, although elected officials in particular like to point to short-term positive improvements on their 'watch'. As counter-drug cooperation receives the most attention and resources, it is first worth noting that drug abuse (legal and illegal) is certainly a chronic public health issue; in the US alone, there are at least 15 million users of illegal drugs (about five per cent of the population). This, however, is an improvement on earlier figures; peak use for example was in 1979, when 25 million Americans (14 per cent of the population) used them. In the UK, about nine per cent of the population has reported using illegal drugs within the past year, a figure that has fallen slightly from the level of about 12 per cent reported a decade ago. While UK counter-drug officials claim this indicates success, the UK still has the highest level of drug abuse among all EU member states, yet another example of how historical trends and comparative metrics can be used to show different degrees of success for a certain policy. Similarly, cybercrime has risen dramatically since the 1990s, in terms of the number and scale of attacks; as noted in the previous chapter, this problem will almost certainly grow as the internet and the IoT expand to more countries and users.

Other historical measures can also indicate a general failure to stem global drug trafficking in particular; since the late 1990s, production of illicit drugs has risen dramatically, and street prices have fallen, indicating enhanced availability. Thus, a government official might report an *annual decrease* in coca cultivation in Colombia of 15 per cent as an indicator of policy success, but then be contradicted by evidence of a *long-term increase* in Colombian coca cultivation. This is precisely what happened in the US in 2003 during US State Department testimony to Congress (Perl, 2006). One also might point to reduced production in certain areas, such as Colombia and Peru, even while it has risen elsewhere, as in Afghanistan and Bolivia. This is the so-called 'balloon effect' in a supply-focused approach to crime: squeeze production in one place and it simply expands somewhere else, so that the net supply remains the same. Bolivia in fact is now becoming a destination for 'cocaine tourism' thanks to its lax enforcement and high levels of corruption, not to mention a president (Evo Morales, since 2006) who used to head Bolivia's coca grower's union. A number of countries have made similar moves recently to decriminalize possession of small amounts of certain illicit drugs (particularly cannabis) and in Afghanistan even the former US envoy to that state, Richard Holbrooke, admitted to the press in March 2009 that US attempts to eradicate opium poppy crops had been wasteful and ineffective.

Yet another measurement might involve counter-crime policy spending over a period of time, and even here we have problems. Despite its leading role in this area, the US actually spends much less on counter-drug/ counter-crime operations as compared to other defence-related activities (except for cybersecurity/cybercrime, where spending is growing), so America cannot expect other states, especially less developed ones, to devote their scarce resources to problems often defined as health or public safety issues in their own countries rather than as 'international security' threats. In addition, the fact that the US makes a *unilateral*, rather than multilateral, determination of the 'majors list' of drug-producing/transiting states in light of their past cooperation (as it does with 'state terrorism' sponsors) causes much friction with the target states and with the international community. Finally, the fact that the US is the single largest source of demand for drugs, among other illicit goods/services, while the EU is not too far behind it, seriously compounds the resentment, as critics say the US and other rich developed states should spend as much or more on demand-reduction programmes at home rather than on supply-interdiction programmes targeted at other states, especially poor ones. The Obama administration seems to have acknowledged this problem with a slight move in the direction towards harm reduction and prevention strategies; however, it has also persisted with a plan to increase US access to military bases in Colombia as part of the war on drugs. This plan prompted cries of protest by most South American leaders after they had hoped for more peaceful relations with the new US government, and is likely to simply accelerate a shift in coca production from Colombia to Bolivia rather than permanently reduce it.

## Summary

Unlike the fight against international terrorism, where it is possible to point to the demise of specific terror groups, in the realm of international crime the struggle is likely to continue indefinitely, for two simple reasons. First, the general trend towards globalization discussed in Chapter 2 will undoubtedly expand the market for illicit goods and services far beyond where it is today, especially as the BRIC powers and other major states grow their economies and link their markets to the rest of the world. The rise of free trade areas, such as NAFTA and the EU, compounds the problem as it becomes increasingly difficult to search all vessels, vehicles and individuals travelling in these huge regions. For example, up to 70–85 per cent of all shipments to the US come in large transport trucks that are exempt from inspection under NAFTA's rules, so increased customs/ border patrols simply cannot cope with the problem. Traffickers, however, demonstrate continuing creativity and ruthlessness in attempting to serve their markets, as with the recent use of handmade 'semi-submersible' vessels crafted in the jungles of South America to elude US drug interdiction forces. The US passed a Drug Trafficking Vessel Interdiction Assistance Act in October 2008 to deal with such craft, nicknamed *el ataúd* ('the coffin') by Colombians, yet the scale of the problem is simply too vast for American military and coastguard forces to defeat effectively.

This fact in turn leads to the second problem: the failure of the leading global powers – the US, the EU, the BRIC bloc and so on – to agree to a more comprehensive approach to transnational organized crime, involving not just the definition and prohibition of such activity, but also the international enforcement of it. Multilateral counter-crime conventions are often ineffective owing to differing interpretations by various states and a lack of strong enforcement mechanisms; the Budapest Convention on Cybercrime is a case in point, as only about one-quarter of the world's 195 sovereign states have acceded to it. The EU seems to have learned this lesson on a regional basis; its development of the single European market has been accompanied by a steady expansion of EU-level customs and police authority. The same cannot be said for virtually any other region in the world, including the US-led NAFTA zone. A stronger regional policing and/or coastguard force, similar to Europol in EU, might help in the western hemisphere, but such a solution is a long way off as the US is unlikely to put its own forces into such a multilateral framework while other states might be reluctant to allow foreign patrols near their waters/borders. And even the European approach has run into problems regarding certain types of trafficking, such as refugees and migrants, even though multilateral EU maritime security cooperation is expanding and may include an EU border force and coastguard (see Chapter 13). In addition, America's 'certification' processes are likely to remain a unilateral political decision of the US, based on its own interests, rather than become a more legitimate and acceptable multilateral tool to encourage widespread counter-crime cooperation. The same holds true of efforts by the US and other stakeholders to use the internet to launch their own counter-crime/cyberwar attacks. Moreover, we can see increasing resistance by some states to American pressure: in 2006, Bolivian President Evo Morales actually appointed a coca leaf grower to head his government's counter-drug programme and evicted the US DEA from his country (Perl, 2006); this was a deliberate, and very telling, signal to the US and his own people about his pledge to resist US efforts to curb coca production in his country. If many other states, especially LDCs, adopt a similar attitude, as seems to be happening already with other South American states, then international efforts to curb various types of transnational organized crime could become even more difficult than they already are.

## Further reading

Malcolm Anderson (1989). *Policing the World: Interpol and the Politics of International Police Co-operation.* Oxford: Clarendon Press.

Malcolm Anderson and Monica Den Boer (1994). *Policing Across National Boundaries.* London: Pinter Publishers.

Peter Andreas and Ethan Nadelmann (2006). *Policing the Globe: Criminalization and Crime Control in International Relations*. Oxford: Oxford University Press.

Jamie Bartlett (2015). *The Dark Net: Inside the Digital Underworld*. London: Windmill Books.

Mats Berdal and Monica Serrano (eds.) (2002). *Transnational Organized Crime and International Security: Business as Usual?* Boulder: Lynne Rienner.

Mark Bowden (2001). *Killing Pablo: The Hunt for the World's Greatest Outlaw*. London: Atlantic Books.

James Cockayne and Adam Lupel (eds.) (2011). *Peace Operations and Organized Crime: Enemies or Allies?* London: Routledge.

Cyrille Fijanut and Letizia Paoli (eds.) (2004). *Organized Crime in Europe: Concepts, Patterns, and Control Policies in the European Union and Beyond*. Dordrecht: Springer.

Misha Glenny (2008). *McMafia: A Journey Through the Global Criminal Underworld*. New York: Knopf.

Misha Glenny (2012). *DarkMarket: How Hackers Became the New Mafia*. New York: Vintage Books.

Barnett Rubin and Alexandra Guáqueta (2007). *Fighting Drugs and Building Peace: Towards Policy Coherence Between Counter-Narcotics and Peacebuilding*. New York: Friedrich-Ebert-Stiftung.

Amandine Scherrer (2009). *G8 Against Transnational Organized Crime*. London: Ashgate.

Paul Shemella (2016). *Global Responses to Maritime Violence: Cooperation and Collective Action*. Stanford: Stanford Security Studies.

Phil Williams (ed.) (1999). *Illegal Immigration and Commercial Sex: The New Slave Trade*. London: Frank Cass.

# Chapter 10

# Economic Security

Although the term 'economic security' is often invoked by scholars and policy-makers to advance a specific agenda, there is virtually no consensus on how to define it. Some more traditional security analysts would argue further that 'economic security' is not even relevant to a text such as this, as it relates only indirectly, if at all, to the core international security problems of war and related forms of organized violence. However, it is also true that many traditional security issues can be linked to economic factors, such as the role of economic investment and technology in fuelling a political rivalry in the form of an arms race (Levy, 1989). There is also an ongoing debate regarding whether increased economic interdependence helps promote peace, as economic or commercial liberalism argues (Snyder, 2015–16). As we saw in Chapter 5, the relationship between weak states and intrastate war, particularly in less developed regions, can also be greatly exacerbated by economic problems. Violent conflicts over identity/ethnicity also might have a strong economic element to them, especially when certain economic classes or sectors have links to foreign stakeholders, such as former colonial states. In addition, the basic measures of globalization as presented in Chapter 2 are primarily defined in terms of cross-border economic transactions, which can easily facilitate the movement of illicit (and therefore threatening) goods, services and individuals. Finally, the possibility of a catastrophic financial crisis cannot be discounted and could easily have major security implications. In fact, the world is still recovering from a state of economic shock, and the major powers have struggled to devise a coordinated solution to the malaise (see this chapter's case study).

Accordingly, this chapter will attempt to summarize the contemporary debate regarding the issue of international economic security and its specific component elements: that is, what economic factors, or referent objects, are supposed to be protected from what threats? As we shall see, both of these dimensions are still greatly contested among scholars and policy-makers (Mastanduno, 1998), which is why we see so little proactive coordination among the major players, even when they all agree that something should be done about a specific economic security problem. In addition, the major powers tend to dominate the overall policy-framing aspects of economic security, yet we still see a fairly high degree of discord among these states regarding the appropriate response to these problems.

271

This most often takes the form of a trilateral debate between American, European/EU and Asian views regarding economics and security (Sandholtz et al., 1992; Thurow, 1992), three regions which together account for the vast majority of global economic production. In a highly globalized world, solutions that do not involve the active support of the major powers within these regions, which themselves are becoming more integrated, are not likely to succeed. Even so, over the past decade the policy agenda pushed by these major stakeholders has been challenged by others, such as China and some LDCs. A final general point involves the role of the US as a global economic hegemon, which often takes the form of providing monetary stability and liquidity/credit, plus serving as a major market for the production of other states. As we shall see, this role is increasingly being called into question in light of America's own domestic economic problems.

## International economics and international security

As with many new security or human security issues, there is very little consensus on what international economic security actually means. One area of contention involves the appropriate level of analysis, whether international/regional, national/domestic, societal/individual or some combination of these. For example, a focus on the international level would involve the global institutions, firms and networks that help facilitate cross-border economic transactions. A focus on the domestic level would stress the national competitiveness and economic well-being of particular states, while a focus on the societal/individual level would stress the viability and livelihoods of specific firms, local communities and even households or individuals. A second area of contention involves the question of exactly what economic value or good is to be protected from what threat. Again, one can conceive of this value–threat relationship in a very general sense (to protect the international economic system) or a very specific sense (to protect the economic livelihoods of certain stakeholders). Finally, no matter what level of analysis is chosen, an 'economy' is fundamentally a system, or a constant flow of goods/services and the means to produce and pay for them, so we must also ask whether 'economic security' is concerned with maintaining the current system, or with changing it into another, supposedly more secure and better, one. In other words, this involves the debate between a status quo versus a revisionist policy orientation, another major area of contention for those who attempt to analyse or promote economic security.

As this volume is concerned with *international* economic security rather than with the economic competitiveness or foreign economic policies of certain states (Tyson, 1993) or the security of individual firms or households (Zalewski, 2005), the rest of this chapter will focus primarily on the international/regional level of analysis. In addition, it will stress international economic security as it is defined and pursued by major global actors, not by how some well-meaning scholars or political activists would hope to define it. This means, in turn, a stress on the maintenance and functioning of the existing liberal global economic order (Cable, 1995; Sperling and Kirchner, 1997; Wolf, 2008) rather than on the creation of a new economic order based on other principles, such as equity or justice, or economic activity, such as the rise of the 'gig economy' or the 'sharing economy' through the internet. For example, some advocates of a human security agenda argue the need to ensure a basic standard of living for all humans, which generally means reducing poverty and hunger in LDCs (King and Murray, 2001–2). Similarly, others have advocated forcefully to 'reform' capitalism (Reich, 2015) and/or argued that equality within a society generally produces more happiness and overall social stability (Pickett and Wilkinson, 2010). While these ideas certainly resonate as political goals for many individuals and some states, and have resulted in some concrete international policy initiatives, they currently do not enjoy the same urgent status as other international economic *security* problems, and are more appropriately considered as central topics in disciplines involving domestic political economy/economic development. Similarly, this chapter is not concerned with the *economics of security* (or defence economics), a topic which generally concerns the national production, procurement and allocation of military and other resources for security purposes (Liberman, 1996; Dombrowski, 2005).

## Destructive scale

As the modern international economy is becoming so globalized according to the major indicators discussed in Chapter 2, most analysts would agree that a major disruption could have a catastrophic effect on the economic well-being of millions if not billions of individuals. Social and political unrest, if not outright conflict, becomes highly likely among those who suffer the most from such an economic crisis, and/or those who fear the seemingly unstoppable pace of economic globalization, as occurred during the 1999 'Battle in Seattle' World Trade Organization (WTO) protests and similar events since then. The experiences of the global economic depression of the 1930s, of the global monetary and energy crises of the 1970s and of assorted monetary crises in various states during the 1980s and 1990s also serve as major reference points in discussions regarding a breakdown or disruption of the international economy. Even the advanced industrialized states are not immune, as various EU member states discovered during the European monetary crisis of 1992–3 and the 2008 global economic crisis. The global monetary system in particular is a major vulnerability of the international economy since it is no longer backed by gold or the US dollar (Kahler, 2004), as we shall see. However, this begs the question of what exactly constitutes a 'disruption' or threat to the system. One major problem is that the capitalist economic order on which the global system is based is inherently subject to cyclical swings, or booms and busts. This means in turn that it may be difficult to distinguish between a normal recessionary cycle (defined as two consecutive quarters of economic contraction) and a more severe shock to the system. In addition, these problems do not affect states equally despite the increasing levels of globalization found across most industrialized economies. States that do not suffer as much from such problems are therefore easily tempted to refrain from participating in a coordinated response, or may even attempt to profit from the economic misfortunes of other states – as any good capitalist would.

There is slightly more global consensus regarding the question of deliberate shocks to the system, as opposed to accidental panics or cyclical recessions/depressions. Two major forms of such deliberate shocks, tariff or trade wars (i.e. raising tariffs or other trade barriers to foreign competitors; Conybeare, 1987) and competitive monetary devaluations (i.e. reducing the value of a currency to make one's exports more competitive), have been greatly reduced in scope since the dark days of the 1930s thanks to the rise of various global economic norms. Today such deliberate shocks are more likely to take the form of an attack on an infrastructural component of the system, such as an internet hacking that disrupts financial or other economic services (see Chapter 8) or large-scale financial fraud of the type that led to the 2008 global financial crisis (see the case study below). Threats to cut off energy supplies in exchange for political or other concessions might also qualify as a deliberate attack on the part of an economic system (see Chapter 11). However, even in these cases there is still some question as to whether such actions, even though they might disrupt the normal operation of the global market economy, actually constitute major threats to the international economic order, or are instead merely 'business as usual' among self-interested economic competitors. This lack of consensual knowledge about the nature of economic threats, plus the overall differences in vulnerability to economic shocks experienced by various states, generally means that the destructive nature of an economic crisis is not fully appreciated or realized by the international community until it is far too late to prevent it.

## Geographic and temporal scope

As suggested above, the geographic scope of threats to economic security can vary widely, from the local to the international level. The same holds true regarding temporal scope as well, from very short-term market panics or financial crises that last a few weeks to a long-term depression that lasts for years. Even if we focus our attention primarily on the international or regional level of analysis, states and other economic actors can still vary in terms of their vulnerability to various kinds of economic disasters or threats, as theorists of interdependence argue (Keohane and Nye, 1977). As we might expect, the poorer LDCs are the most vulnerable to economic crises, yet their economic problems can often be contained by the actions of more developed states. Even among the advanced industrialized democracies, whose business cycles and approaches to public financing might be assumed to be converging under the pressures of globalization (the so-called *convergence hypothesis*), we actually find considerable variation in terms of their framing of, and response to, global or regional economic shocks (Drezner, 2001), which then affects their propensity to cooperate with other states in such matters. This result should not be surprising given the lack of a single international economic regulator to manage the international economy, although some IOs are attempting to play such a role.

## Likelihood

One of the most critical problems regarding how to conceptualize international economic security involves the question of the likelihood that a major shock will occur. There is some consensus among economists that post-WWII business cycles – consisting of one period of expansion and one period of contraction – generally last for about three to five years on average, yet these are typically considered as part of the 'normal' functioning of capitalist economies and are not necessarily interpreted as critical international threats. In addition, these cycles – as well as the underlying levels of economic growth on which they are based – do not occur in a uniform pattern across national economies, even ones that trade extensively with each other, so a coordinated global response to such normal cycles or differential growth patterns can be very difficult. Monetary or credit crises, as well as deliberate attacks on the economic infrastructure by various types of actors, can be far more severe but are also much less regular or predictable.

The same holds true for major global depressions, as occurred during the 1870s and 1930s, and more minor global depressions, as occurred during the 1890s and 1970s. However, warning signs could be seen just prior to all of these events if one cared to look for them (Kindleberger, 2001; Wolf, 2008). Well before the recent 2008 economic crisis, for example, numerous authoritative sources – including central bank officials and government economists – warned of a potential problem in the form of loose credit and a major asset price 'bubble', namely in the form of rising house prices, seen in some advanced economies, especially the UK and the

US. Yet as with earlier crises, these voices were simply drowned out by others, inside and outside of government, who chose to believe that the good times would last indefinitely – an attitude referred to as 'irrational exuberance' by Alan Greenspan, the former chairman of the US Federal Reserve (America's central bank). Thus, although we have huge amounts of economic data at our fingertips today, the interpretation of that data is still far too easily politicized and skewed by powerful actors with competing interests, as we shall see later.

## Recovery

There are, however, two small rays of hope regarding the disputes noted above. The first is that recovery is possible in the face of most economic-related catastrophes, even the most severe ones. To be sure, such a recovery might take years, yet economic crises simply are not interpreted as severe threats relative to the physical destruction to life and property that occurs during a major power war or a global infectious disease pandemic. This is why some more traditional security scholars still believe that such economic problems, although they are important, are not really international *security* concerns. In addition, the recovery from such problems may not even require a policy response; more powerful or competitive economic actors will simply move in to pick up the pieces and rebuild the economy on a (hopefully) stronger foundation. Thus, as in medicine, the first rule in responding to an economic catastrophe may be the most simple: 'First, do no harm.'

Indeed, this rule – to avoid making matters worse – was explicitly violated during the 1930s economic depression, when most industrialized states, starting with the US, adopted 'beggar-thy-neighbour', or mercantilist, economic policies, such as tariff barriers and competitive monetary devaluations, in order to shift the costs of painful economic adjustments onto other states. However, if all states adopt such measures, which is exactly what happened at the time, economic activity can grind to a halt and make the depression last far longer than it might have otherwise. Thus, the contraction period of the Great Depression lasted about 43 months (1929–33), while an average recession lasts only about 11 months. Fortunately, this critical lesson seems to have been learned by the major economic powers, although there are always isolated examples of trade or monetary conflict in specific sectors, even among close trading partners such as Japan, the US and the EU. A second ray of hope is that most such economic problems, except for the most severe global economic depressions (which are in fact quite rare), can also be contained by the international community once it has determined the nature and extent of the problem. Once it has been contained, the process of recovery can begin, with or without the formal assistance of the international community.

## Stakeholder factors

As with many human security issues, one major problem regarding economic security is the fact that this topic potentially involves or touches upon virtually every person on the planet. All people are therefore potential economic stakeholders to the extent that they consume, produce, work or otherwise participate in economic activity. However, these stakeholders do not participate and benefit equally, nor do they enjoy the same degree of influence regarding major economic decisions. Even if individuals face personal hardship and might favour increased social welfare spending as a solution, this tendency seems to be short-lived according to one study of the 2008 global financial crisis (Margalit, 2013). This wide and shifting variance in vulnerability and attitudes among individuals requires us to pay closer attention to the more powerful stakeholders, or the major market players, in this realm. Indeed, it is often precisely because the many (and weaker) stakeholders do not feel as in control as the fewer (and more powerful) major players that economic crises can turn into political conflicts, whether domestic or international.

### Principal stakeholders

The primary stakeholders responsible for the management of the international economic order are states, international financial institutions (IFIs) and large private firms, particularly MNCs devoted to banking, investments/securities and insurance. Among states, the main players have grouped themselves in various forms over the past few decades for the specific purpose of dealing with global economic issues, such as financial crises. The major groupings include the G7, the G8, and, since 1999, the G20, which combines the G8 plus 11 other major economic powers, including several in the developing world, as well as an EU representative. The G20 states account for about 85 per cent of the world's wealth and could exert decisive influence if they act in concert. Most of the world's LDCs have been organized since 1964 into the G77; although this group has grown to 130 member states, it rarely enjoys the same political clout as the G7/G8. The more recent G20 may however address that political gap, given its membership as shown in Table 10.1.

These various groupings, it should be noted, are not based exclusively on economic indicators; if so, the Netherlands and Spain would be included, rather than Argentina and South Africa, if the G20 list were based strictly on GDP. Instead, these are also political groupings as decided largely by the original G7 states, which is why the G20 includes Saudi Arabia, Indonesia, Argentina and South Africa rather than several other states that would deserve to be included in the G20 if membership

Table 10.1   *The Group of 20 (G20), ranked by nominal 2014
GDP in US dollars at official exchange rates*

|  | GDP | Population | GDP per capita |
|---|---|---|---|
| European Union | $18.5 trillion | 506 million | $36,645 |
| United States | $17.3 trillion | 319 million | $54,370 |
| China | $10.3 trillion | 1.37 billion | $7,572 |
| Japan | $4.6 trillion | 127 million | $36,222 |
| Germany | $3.9 trillion | 81 million | $47,774 |
| United Kingdom | $3 trillion | 65 million | $45,729 |
| France | $2.8 trillion | 64 million | $44,332 |
| Brazil | $2.3 trillion | 203 million | $11,573 |
| Italy | $2.2 trillion | 60 million | $35,335 |
| India | $2.1 trillion | 1.26 billion | $1,608 |
| Russian Federation | $1.9 trillion | 146 million | $12,718 |
| Canada | $1.8 trillion | 36 million | $50,304 |
| Australia | $1.4 trillion | 24 million | $61,066 |
| South Korea | $1.4 trillion | 50 million | $27,970 |
| Mexico | $1.3 trillion | 120 million | $10,784 |
| Indonesia | $889 billion | 252 million | $3,524 |
| Turkey | $798 billion | 77 million | $10,381 |
| Saudi Arabia | $746 billion | 31 million | $24,252 |
| Argentina | $543 billion | 43 million | $12,735 |
| South Africa | $350 billion | 54 million | $6,483 |

*Source:* IMF website (2015).

were based on economic indicators alone, although the Netherlands and
Spain were allowed to attend the G20 London summit in 2009.

In addition, using GDP rankings as measures of economic power can
be highly misleading; at a minimum, they should be qualified with other
economic statistics, particularly regarding public or sovereign debt (i.e.
the amount owed by the government), government budget balances and
current account (or trade) balances. These indicators would reveal some
major problems among the supposedly more powerful states, as suggested
in Table 10.2.

As we can see, some of the most economically powerful states in the
system also have some of the most severe economic problems; US federal
public debt for example is 104.2 per cent of GDP, while that for Japan
has ballooned to over 200 per cent of GDP in recent years. Conversely,
China's public debt is 31.7 per cent of GDP while the figure for Russia

Table 10.2   *Public finance indicators of various G20 states*

|  | All public debt (as a percentage of GDP) | Government financial balance (as a percentage of GDP) | Current account balance (as a percentage of GDP) |
|---|---|---|---|
| 1 US (Federal) | 104.2 | – 5.8 | – 2.2 |
| 2 Japan | 229.2 | – 8.4 | 0.5 |
| 3 Germany | 79.9 | – 0.2 | 7.2 |
| 4 UK | 88.7 | – 5.3 | – 5.1 |
| 5 France | 89.9 | – 3.8 | – 1.0 |
| 6 Italy | 132.5 | – 2.7 | 1.9 |
| 7 Brazil | 54.9 | – 3.4 | – 4.3 |
| 8 China | 31.7 | – 1.2 | 2.1 |
| 9 Russian Federation | 12.2 | 0 | 3.1 |

*Sources:* Public debt (CIA World Factbook 2013); government financial balance (OECD Factbook 2014); current account balance (World Bank website 2014).

is only 12.2 per cent; both China and Russia also enjoy current account surpluses thanks to China's exports of manufactured goods and Russia's energy exports. It is also interesting that the top two global external debtors (that is, total public and private foreign financial obligations), as measured by absolute amounts owed, are the US ($19.2 trillion) and the UK ($9.6 trillion). These states are also supposed to be the financial engines of the global economy, and it is no surprise, then, that in the view of many observers these two states should be held responsible for the global economic crisis of 2008.

These states also are part of a large network of IFIs and related international economic regimes, many of which attempt, unilaterally and collectively, to 'manage' the global economy. Among major IFIs, the IMF, the World Bank (official name: the International Bank for Reconstruction and Development), the OECD, the BIS and various UN bodies (such as the UN Conference on Trade and Development) all help to set the rules of global economic relations. They are supported by the WTO and other trade-related IOs, such as the World Intellectual Property Organization. States have also organized themselves into regional IOs, of which the EU is the most powerful thanks to its size and composition, as it includes most of the richest and economically developed states in Europe, with a total GDP greater than that of the US. Finally, major private banking firms and institutional investors (such as large pension funds) also perform a quasi-public role by keeping up flows of money and credit, which act as the financial lubricants for the global economy. Large credit reporting agencies can play a similar role, by raising or lowering the cost of credit for various stakeholders, including states themselves, through the use of credit ratings; some agencies, for example, lowered the UK's rating after its vote to leave the EU in mid-2016. As seen in Table 10.3, many of the major banks in particular are headquartered in the G7 or G20 (or other EU) states, which gives those states an additional source of influence – and vulnerability – with regard to the global economy. Most importantly, the US and China currently dominate the list of largest banks ranked by annual revenue, which clearly reflects their leading status as financial powers as well as their close symbiotic relationship as major trading partners.

To summarize, when we speak of the 'market' or the 'global markets' as a proxy for the international economy, we are referring primarily to these large stakeholders, whose power is derived from their ownership or other control of most of the productive resources found on the planet. When these stakeholders act collectively, in the form of major swings in the markets for capital, commodities and foreign exchange, then no single actor – including the US – has enough economic power to counteract the effects for very long. In this respect all stakeholders in the global economy

### Table 10.3    *World's largest commercial banks, ranked by revenues, 2015*

| Bank (headquarters) | Revenues (US$) |
| --- | --- |
| 1 Industrial & Commercial Bank of China (China) | $166.8 billion |
| 2 China Construction Bank (China) | $130.5 billion |
| 3 Agricultural Bank of China (China) | $129.2 billion |
| 4 BNP Paribas (France) | $124.5 billion |
| 5 Bank of China (China) | $120.3 billion |
| 6 JPMorgan Chase (US) | $97.8 billion |
| 7 Bank of America (US) | $97 billion |
| 8 Citigroup (US) | $93.9 billion |
| 9 Wells Fargo (US) | $90.4 billion |
| 10 HSBC (UK) | $81.1 billion |

*Source:* Forbes World's Largest Banks list (2015).

are vulnerable to the mood of the markets, though to varying degrees, which is precisely how capitalism is supposed to function – in principle.

## Interests and preferences

Most stakeholders who possess significant economic power are very much in favour of the status quo orientation to the global economic order. Their basic interest is to preserve and expand the benefits they derive from the existing world capitalist system rather than replace it with something else, although some new players (like the BRIC bloc) are increasingly demanding more influence in the system. The US still claims some degree of primacy among the major players, based on its economic status and role since 1945. This involved the creation of the modern global economic order (or the *Bretton Woods* system; see Conway, 2015) based on commercial liberalism, and its major support institutions noted above, such as the General Agreement on Tariffs and Trade (the predecessor to the WTO), the IMF, the World Bank and the OECD. However, although the US played a more hegemonic role in the immediate post-war years and could force its preferences onto other states within its economic bloc, this condition no longer holds and America's role as economic hegemon is under stress in a number of ways. Even during the Cold War, the US faced serious difficulties in persuading its alliance partners – particularly the Europeans – to join its economic war against the communist bloc (Mastanduno, 1988). With the end of the Cold War, the EU and China in particular are presenting major challenges to America's ability to lead international economic relations, and their preferences will increasingly need to be taken into consideration.

More specifically, even if most major stakeholders prefer to work within the existing international capitalist order, and even if they all value the stable functioning of that order, it is still possible to discern several major cleavages among these players. The most obvious one is a North–South cleavage that pits the developed world against the developing world, although some states, such as the BRIC bloc and the so-called 'Asian tigers' (Hong Kong, South Korea, Singapore and Taiwan), may straddle the North–South divide. A number of LDCs in the South often attempt to resist the post-war 'Washington consensus' regarding the supposed benefits of free trade, balanced budgets and capital mobility, at least as long as such LDCs are attempting to catch up with the North. This is precisely how Japan and the Asian tigers managed to become industrialized economies within the space of a generation: by adopting more nationalist or mercantilist economic policies and thus flouting the Washington consensus, at least temporarily. This was permitted, however, because the need to maintain cohesion of the capitalist bloc during the early part of the Cold War was more important than forcing Japan and other newly industrializing states to become more liberal. This view began to deteriorate, however, once these states became more competitive *vis-à-vis* the US and Europe in the 1970s and beyond.

It is also possible to discern a transatlantic cleavage that often pits the more *laissez-faire* US views against the more generous continental European/EU social model, with the UK positioned somewhere in between these approaches. Finally, one can often point to a 'US versus the rest of the world' cleavage, and to some extent a 'West versus the rest' cleavage, where 'the West' generally refers to the OECD economies. Thus, when a specific global economic crisis occurs, it is by no means self-evident that the major stakeholders will share the same views and preferences when interpreting that crisis (who is at fault?) and when attempting to manage it (who is going to pay to solve it?). As there apparently is no desire among these players to radically change the system, this latter question often involves how much regulation can be tolerated in the global market economy. In general, the US and the UK tend to favour less global regulation of economic matters, while the continental European states favour stricter global rules. Other states fall somewhere in between these extremes depending on the specific crisis at hand, as we shall see in more detail below.

However, it also should be noted that all major players, including the US, do agree on the importance of protecting the global economy against major threats, and define that goal as part of their national security strategies. For example, immediately after the Cold War the first Clinton presidential administration expanded the US National Security Council to include the Treasury Secretary (equivalent to the UK position of Chancellor of the Exchequer or of Finance Minister in other states) and the new Assistant to the President for Economic Policy. Later, the US added the goal of enhancing America's economic prosperity as a core objective of its US National Security Strategy, a concern echoed in the EU's own European Security Strategy of 2003. The fact that terrorists specifically chose the World Trade Center as one of their targets in 1993 and again on 9/11 also indicates the importance of economic affairs, whether as a symbolic or a physical target, in the current global political order. Thus, and leaving terrorist attacks aside, the question of how to protect the global economic order often turns on the issue of using more proactive regulation and oversight (including various forms of taxation/redistribution) versus more passive or reactive market-focused solutions to head off or respond to economic crises.

## The use of force

Economic security issues, like most other non-traditional or human security issues discussed in this volume, are not particularly amenable to the use of force in attempting to manage them. This is the primary reason that some more orthodox security analysts do not consider economic security to be within the realm of international security studies. However, to the extent that the pursuit of economic security requires a certain degree of regulation and enforcement, there is certainly some scope for the use of police and other non-military forces (such as customs/immigration/tax authorities or fraud investigators) to serve those purposes. These forces, however, are intended to combat specific crimes rather than more general economic crises of the type discussed in this chapter. They are also generally associated with the domestic laws of the jurisdictions where they are based (see below), which can make international cooperation among such forces extremely difficult. One major exception, as noted in Chapter 9, is the EU, where we find a considerable degree of international cooperation – which may involve 'supranational' governance – among such authorities across most EU member states and, to a lesser extent, with the authorities bordering the periphery of the EU. Even in the case of the EU, however, investigations and punishments (if any) are still largely based on the domestic laws of a given EU member state, although the AFSJ measures discussed in Chapter 9 should help avoid this inconsistency as national authorities make greater use of them.

## Public–private domains and levels of jurisdiction

As with the discussion of crime in the previous chapter, this question is highly relevant in any consideration of how to police or otherwise manage the global economy. All human beings are stakeholders in the global economy to some degree, and their aggregate economic activities can easily balloon into a crisis under certain conditions. Given this degree of fragmentation in an economically globalized world, any international rules to govern economic behaviour must be rigorously enforced by the states against their own citizens and firms since such mechanisms are often lacking at the global level. When such global rules cannot be agreed – which is often the case – the system becomes prone to excessive risk-taking (at a minimum) and outright fraud or other criminal activity (at a maximum) on the part of various stakeholders. Such problems can become especially acute when one also considers the role of deception, manipulation and false advertising in modern economic affairs (Akerlof and Shiller, 2015).

As with the issue of cybersecurity/cybercrime, it can be even more difficult to analyse the quasi-public economic security role of certain MNCs, such as banks, insurance firms, credit reporting agencies and certain infrastructural firms (such as utilities, transport and communications). The US and the UK led a trend in the 1970s and 1980s towards the deregulation and privatization of many of these firms precisely when the globalized economy was beginning to require *more* state control – though not necessarily state ownership – of those firms. This situation has put many industrialized states, even those that did not go so far down the privatiza-tion/deregulation path (such as many continental European states), in a major bind: they want to allow their own economic stakeholders as much freedom as possible to compete against their foreign counterparts, but when all states share this attitude, and keep regulatory or other governing costs to a minimum (i.e. a regulatory 'race to the bottom'), the system can suffer dramatically from the excessive risks taken by these stakeholders, even if such risk-taking is completely lawful in the jurisdiction where it occurs. This is precisely what happened with the 2008 economic crisis, as we shall see in the case study below.

## International economic security as a policy problem

Most advanced industrialized states now generally realize that various forms of economic protectionism are not effective long-term solutions to global economic crises, as the situation only becomes worse if multiple states adopt such measures. This was one of the supreme lessons of the Great Depression of the 1930s, and inspired the creation of the GATT regime, which became the current WTO in the 1990s. A similar realiza-tion inspired the creation of the IMF to help provide emergency loans to states with balance of payments problems in their current accounts (i.e. those who owed more to the global economy than they earned from it through exports); the IMF's role as a 'lender of last resort' in such cases hopefully would help avoid the prospect of competitive trade wars and currency devaluations, another unfortunate legacy of the 1930s. Although the GATT/WTO and IMF regimes, supported by US leadership, have helped to bring about the modern globalized economic order we now live in, they are far less effective in managing other economic crises or shocks discussed in this chapter, which is why we need to analyse the global response to such problems on a case-by-case basis. Moreover, these regimes are intended primarily for short-term and smaller-scale problems (such as resolving tariff disputes or providing short-term lending for bal-ance of payments difficulties), not preventing or managing a widescale economic meltdown, whether local, regional or global.

### Agenda-setting

After a long period of global economic recovery during the generation after WWII, which saw the rise of the Asian tigers, the economic inte-gration of Europe and the decolonization of dozens of LDCs throughout the world, the international economy has suffered an almost continu-ous series of financial crises and related problems since the 1970s. Thus, the security agenda here almost sets itself, in the form of very general (a major economic recession or depression) to more specific (monetary and financial crises) types of economic security problems facing the international community. The global economy has in fact experienced all of these threats in the post-war era, and they have become even more prevalent since the end of the Cold War, a somewhat ironic result of the apparent triumph of market capitalism over communism. In addition, the source of these crises may be found in both the developed and developing worlds, so it is not possible to blame such problems on weak states or bad governance in LDCs. To put it quite bluntly, globalized capitalism based on pure economic liberalism is not the solution; it is in fact part of the problem.

Monetary crises are a particular concern since the US ended its policy in 1971 of backing US dollars with gold at a fixed price (a global monetary regime based on US dollars exchangeable for gold at a fixed exchange rate), which had been a cornerstone of the international economic order since WWII under the Bretton Woods system. In the modern world of (mostly) floating exchange rates, whereby global markets set foreign exchange rates based on the supply and demand of various currencies, the vast majority of states, including the US and the eurozone members, are not bound by any mechanism – such as their national gold supplies – to 'keep them honest' in how they conduct their monetary policies. In other words, public confidence in the currencies of all major states in the system is now based largely on a huge psychological illusion about the credibility of government monetary and fiscal policies. Even worse, after the 1970s the US and the UK also helped to institute a system of global financial capital mobility, which meant easing restrictions on the international flows of financial capital (i.e. involving foreign currencies, stocks/bonds and other short-term or liquid capital). This resulted in the growth of capital movements so vast and fast that *daily* foreign currency exchange trading alone by the end of 2007 amounted to about *$3.2 trillion*, a 71 per cent increase on the 2004 figure. This amount, which now exceeds $5 trillion a day, greatly exceeds the foreign exchange and gold reserves of any single state in the system, including the current economic hegemon, the US (see below).

The result of this combination of financial market power and limited reserves is that states with *domestic* monetary problems owing to loose monetary policies or excessive government spending (or both) now also face severe *international* pressures in the form of either speculative attacks by investors and/or capital flight by those seeking to retreat from a stricken economy; moreover, these problems cannot always be financed with domestic foreign exchange or gold reserves, even by very rich states. Equally worrisome is the so-called 'contagion effect' experienced among many LDCs in particular as a crisis in one poor country causes a crisis in another one, even if the economic fundamentals are positive in the second country, which is what happened during the 1997 South Asia/Thailand monetary crisis. Since there is no such thing as a global currency or a global central bank, or enough gold to back up all the currency in circulation to restore public confidence, the system is now especially prone to monetary crises in addition to the normal cyclical swings of market economies. To this volatile mix we must add the agenda-setting effects of outright criminal or terrorist activity, whether in the form of fraud or deliberate attacks on certain elements of the economic infrastructure.

However, even with this jumble of contemporary economic security problems, which might seem self-evident to a detached observer, states and other major stakeholders often still profoundly disagree on whether an economic problem constitutes a security threat or a major crisis, and therefore on whether a coordinated international response is necessary. As always, the major powers often take the lead here, sometimes with support from other stakeholders noted above. Even so, LDCs and other supposedly less powerful stakeholders can play an agenda-setting role here, in at least two ways. First, they have attempted to act in a collective fashion through the UN or other IFIs, a pattern which began in the 1970s in the form of UN discussions on a new international economic order that would be more fair and equitable to the LDCs. This has continued with global efforts to reduce or even write off the debt of many such states, particularly the 41 so-called Heavily Indebted Poor Countries (HIPCs), and thus hopefully prevent a future monetary crisis. The Jubilee 2000/Jubilee Debt Campaign and the 2005 G8 (Live 8) summit in Gleneagles, along with the Make Poverty History movement, pledged such debt relief as major policy goals. Second, highly indebted states can threaten to default on their debts or other economic obligations in order to improve their financial positions, as some Central and South American economies, such as Mexico and Brazil, attempted during the 1980s. These are more extreme measures but are certainly not unheard of when LDCs or other less powerful stakeholders feel they are not getting a fair hearing from the major powers and IFIs. A wide range of development and human rights NGOs also support reducing the debt burden on these countries, which adds to the political pressures on the (mostly rich) creditor countries. However, putting an economic security problem on the global agenda, and doing something constructive about it, are two quite separate things, as we shall see below.

## Framing policy alternatives

As noted above, the major economic players possess not just different attitudes – namely in the form of ideologies – and interests but also very different vulnerabilities about how to interpret and respond to these regularly occurring problems in the global economy. One way to think about vulnerability is the question of proximity: for example, the US helped Mexico during its financial crisis in 1994, but was less willing to aid certain Asian states, because of Mexico's proximity to the US. Both President Clinton and his Republican opponents in Congress worked together on this issue because they feared the consequences of Mexican instability, such as increased illegal immigration to the US. Another way to think about vulnerability is the question of autonomy: can any state, no matter how powerful, effectively manage the various problems discussed above in a unilateral fashion? Increasingly, the answer is: not a chance. One simple measure on this point involves the amount of foreign exchange reserves that could be used to finance one's way unilaterally out of a crisis. For example, as noted above China not only enjoys a fairly manageable level of public debt and a positive current account balance, it is also sitting on the world's largest supply of foreign exchange reserves, valued at over $3 trillion (including gold reserves), as seen in Table 10.4. Japan is also very strong on this indicator, with total reserves valued at over $1 trillion, while the 19 eurozone member states collectively possessed around $335 billion in foreign exchange reserves in early 2016.

By contrast, the US, representing the largest economy of any single state in the world, possesses foreign exchange reserves in the amount of only around $130 billion and is ranked at number 19 of all economies (including the EU and Hong Kong) on this indicator. The UK is ranked even lower, at number 21, with reserves of $108 billion. The figures for the US and the UK have improved since the 2008 financial crisis, but so have those for other major economies, so that the two countries most responsible for increased capital mobility since the 1970s still lag well behind their competitors on this measure of economic strength (among others).

This means, in turn, that many supposedly poorer states, such as all of the BRIC economies, are much better placed than the US and the UK to finance themselves out of a major economic crisis such as a monetary collapse. For example, Russia spent a staggering $100 billion or more during the 2008 crisis to prop up the value of its rouble, a policy that would be extremely difficult for most OECD states. Lacking these reserves, the US and the UK, among other advanced industrialized economies, must rely instead on more public borrowing or – even worse – increasing the money supply itself by lowering interest rates or creating more money (known by the euphemism of 'quantitative easing'). Once interest rates have been cut to nearly zero – which is where they stood in many advanced economies during the 2008 crisis – it is impossible to reduce them further to stimulate spending, and the only alternative is some form of quantitative easing. Since any increase in the money supply can result in inflationary pressures on the value of money itself, the

**Table 10.4  *Highest foreign exchange reserves (including gold), 2015***

|  |  |
|---|---|
| 1  China | $3.22 trillion |
| 2  Japan | $1.26 trillion |
| 3  Saudi Arabia | $660 billion |
| 4  Switzerland | $546 billion |
| 5  Taiwan | $426 billion |
| 6  Russia | $378 billion |
| 7  India | $371 billion |
| 8  South Korea | $369 billion |
| 9  Brazil | $359 billion |
| 10  Singapore | $262 billion |

*Source:* CIA World Factbook (2015). Reserves for China on this table do not include Hong Kong, which would add $341 billion to China's total reserves.

net effect of such a policy, if not managed carefully by simultaneously reducing public spending elsewhere, will be negligible if not actually counterproductive.

Ultimately, then, with most global economic problems the options of either (i) doing nothing (that is, letting the market 'work its magic' by allowing weak firms or states to fail) or (ii) acting in a unilateral fashion, are increasingly difficult to pursue if the major players also hope to satisfy their constituents – voters and investors – while maintaining the overall trend towards greater global economic liberalism: free trade and capital mobility. In short, more globalization ultimately means far more multilateral coordination (at a minimum) and far more international economic regulation (at a maximum) if the major powers really hope to avoid similar crises in the future. And although many of these stakeholders seem to prefer short-term crisis intervention rather than long-term regulatory solutions, the ongoing effects of the 2008 crisis seem to be pushing them in the direction of the latter approach, though there are still major divisions regarding the scope and degree of such a response.

## Policy choice

These dynamics can be appreciated more clearly by examining some of the most recent decisions regarding the security and stability of the global economy. As noted earlier, monetary crises occur on a fairly regular basis now, yet the response by the international community can vary widely depending on the state(s) involved in the crisis, and its proximity to other major stakeholders such as the US or certain European states. The US is far more willing to intervene unilaterally (that is, to offer a financial bailout in the form of aid and/or loans) in crises involving a state in the western hemisphere, and may therefore take a more passive role (letting a state suffer the effects of a monetary crisis) for crises located much further away. This is mainly because the US fears the social and political fallout related to such problems in its own backyard. Thus, states such as Indonesia, South Korea and Thailand, which faced a series of crises in 1997 and did not enjoy the same type of US-led bailout as Mexico, were forced to suffer disinvestment (or capital flight), deflation and the painful drop in living standards that follow from such economic problems. Table 10.5 lists a number of major financial crises since the end of the Bretton Woods monetary regime in the 1970s; as we can see, there is no typical response or solution.

The situation is especially complicated in the face of a truly *global* economic crisis, which is exactly what the world experienced in 2008 (see case study, Box 10.1). The crisis was so severe that a major summit of the G20 members was held in London in April 2009 to coordinate a global response. However, despite the scope of the problem, which was evident to all of the participants, there were still some major differences of opinion regarding an appropriate policy mix. Most G20 states advocated some

**Table 10.5** *Major financial crises after Bretton Woods*

| Crisis | Response |
|---|---|
| Central/South America (1980s) | US 'Brady Plan' (debt rescheduling) |
| US Savings & Loan collapse (1980s) | Bank failures; deposit protection by US government |
| European monetary crisis (1992) | Devaluation; deflation of weak EU economies |
| Mexico (1994) | US loan; Mexico repaid it |
| Japan (1997) | Devaluation; deflation |
| Rest of Asia (1997) | IMF loans (and then IMF riots) |
| 42 HIPCs (1990s) | 'Jubilee 2000' debt relief/forgiveness |
| Global financial crisis (2008) | See case study below |
| Eurozone (2009 onwards) | Hundreds of billions of euros as 'bailout' funds for struggling debt-laden eurozone economies (particularly Greece); austerity measures to curb government spending |

## Box 10.1   The 2008 global financial crisis

*Many stakeholders caused the 2008 financial crisis, but the losses were not shared equally.*

In the first decade of the twenty-first century the global economy suffered its worst downturn since the Great Depression of the 1930s. Although financial problems in poor countries often receive much attention, the global crises of the 1930s and 2008 can be traced in large part to the actions of the US, involving both private actors and policy-makers, and these decisions had a knock-on effect that spread the contagion around the world. The 2008 crisis was precipitated by America's 1999 decision to revise its own Glass–Steagall (or Banking) Act of 1933, which had maintained a clear division in the US between retail/commercial banking (involving home mortgage lending) and investment banking (involving securities) to prevent the kind of risk-taking that had led to the Great Depression. This change allowed US banks to engage in both activities, as well as grow through mergers and acquisitions, to increase the rewards – and risks – of new 'full service' financial firms. As a result, the US quickly became the world's largest source of high-risk financial products such as hedge funds, with nearly

→

degree of extra government spending to help boost the global economy out of its malaise. Yet several other participants – particularly Italy, Germany, Russia and France (plus the leadership of the EU, which is a member of the G20) – opposed this idea and threatened to upset the summit. They also tended to blame the US, and to a lesser extent, the UK, for

→

5,000 funds totalling \$1.098 trillion by 2008. The UK followed America with about \$177.6 billion in such funds at the time; other foreign banks joined the hedge fund rush as well.

The central cause of the crisis, however, involved a new financial product – collateralized debt obligations (CDOs) – which 'packaged' thousands of US mortgage loans into investment products, some of which ended up in the hedge funds (that is, mortgages were 'securitized'). Thanks to low interest rates after the 9/11 terrorist attacks, the US housing market grew dramatically between 2001 and 2008, until the supply of housing exceeded the demand and the real estate market began to stall. Yet investment banks continued to sell CDOs, which increasingly consisted of loans held by higher-risk borrowers (or 'sub-prime' loans). By 2006, over 20 per cent of the US mortgage market consisted of sub-prime loans. Even worse, the inherent risks in the CDOs were not fully understood by many investors (Nelson and Katzenstein, 2014), and in some cases the loans packaged into the CDOs involved fraudulent activity on the part of lenders, home appraisers and credit ratings agencies in order to keep the loan money flowing. When interest rates began to rise just before the crisis, some of these borrowers began to default on their loans, which threatened the investors holding billions of dollars' worth of CDOs (Lewis, 2010; Blinder, 2013).

Since these firms are globalized, the US crisis quickly became an international one as investors around the world lost money as 'housing bubbles' burst in various countries, which effectively froze up the global credit markets by late 2008 as banks attempted to limit their losses. US sub-prime lenders began to collapse in 2007, followed by the collapse of major US investment firms like Lehman Brothers in September 2008. Moreover, the US was facing a presidential election, with new candidates from both major parties, while President Bush faced opposition from his own Republican party in Congress when he requested action to prevent a financial meltdown before the end of his term. By this time the contagion had spread to UK banks like Northern Rock and the Royal Bank of Scotland, as well as to other countries across Europe that held large investment positions in CDOs. As a result, these banks and other large creditors were faced with writing off over \$4 trillion in bad loans and other 'toxic' assets before they would begin lending to each other, and then to the larger public, even after large firms in the US and Europe received billions of dollars' worth of government help (Sorkin, 2010). The crisis resulted in economic upheaval across the world that lasted for years, and the main solutions are not likely to prevent such an event from happening again (see main text).

precipitating the crisis through lax financial regulations, excessive risk-taking and excessive consumer debt.

Despite these disputes regarding the origins and solutions to the 2008 crisis, the G20 summit did result in some explicit governance measures. According to British Prime Minister Gordon Brown, the London summit effectively saw the end of the 'Washington consensus' noted above, which had been a long time coming. The summit's major result was the creation of a new global regulator, the Financial Stability Board (FSB), in April 2009 as an enlarged version of the Financial Stability Forum created in 1999 to promote financial cooperation and stability through information exchange. The FSB includes all G20 states, Hong Kong, the Netherlands, Spain, Switzerland and the EU's own executive arm, the European Commission. It is based at the BIS headquarters in Basel, Switzerland, to monitor risks in the global economy and conduct early warning exercises and other reviews to spot potential problems. It will cooperate closely with the IMF and other major IFIs and report its findings to the G20 finance ministers, the IMF and central bank governors. Its mandate will include overseeing all 'systematically important' financial institutions, instruments and markets, including (for the first time) the most important hedge funds, which will have to register and report their strategies, debt and risk levels. In addition, the FSB may also impose constraints on borrowing and the use of credit derivatives, which are investment products whose value is based on an underlying asset, such as pooled home loans. The creation of the FSB, however, was contingent on a larger, and somewhat controversial, plan of economic stimulus in the amount of over $1 trillion, which was supposed to ease up the credit markets and accelerate a global recovery. However, much of these funds went to protect the interests of troubled banks and other firms 'too big to fail', so that the benefit to the overall global economy (particularly ordinary citizens) was quite marginal. As a result of these controversial policies – bailouts for certain risk-taking firms but austerity for certain debt-strapped states – the effects of the 2008 crisis, like those of the 1929 stock market crash, have lingered for years. In fact, the years 2007–17 will almost certainly be viewed as a 'lost decade' for the global economy by future historians, especially after the UK's vote in June 2016 to leave the EU.

## The politics of policy effectiveness

Past experience with post-war financial crises in individual states shows that it is possible for governments to dig themselves out of a hole, even without the assistance of richer states. However, this approach – which effectively relies on global market forces of supply and demand to bring fiscal and monetary discipline to a state – can take years to see any positive results. Some states, such as Japan, Mexico and Thailand, have languished for more than a decade as they attempted to restore their economies in the absence of coordinated assistance from other players. When the international community does aid a particular state, as with the debt relief provided to certain LDCs in the 1980s–90s and the US loan to Mexico in 1994, financial credibility can be restored fairly quickly as such aid increases the confidence of wary investors and lenders. Mexico even managed to pay off its loan early during its recovery in the late 1990s, and remains one of only two Latin American member states of the OECD (the other one is Chile). More recently, the pledges made by the richer OECD states during the Jubilee 2000 and Live 8 campaigns to cancel the debts of many HIPCs were largely implemented in good faith; in principle, this should allow the governments of such states to spend more on their own citizens than on debt service.

The G20 response to the 2008 financial crisis, including the eurozone crisis after 2009, has had mixed results so far (Helleiner and Pagliari, 2011). Although it is true that the 2008 global downturn could have been worse, and that the eurozone could have forced the exit of its weakest member states (an outcome which is still possible), the response was still not as coherent as it could have been owing to transatlantic and intra-eurozone conflicts of interest, which have not abated. The new FSB, as well as tighter regional regulations as agreed by the EU, is somewhat akin to closing the barn door after the horses have bolted, as such measures cannot mitigate the current malaise but may help alleviate future crises if it functions as it was designed to. This effective functioning cannot be assumed, however; soon after the crisis the UK and Sweden (among others) were resisting stronger efforts in the EU and elsewhere to regulate financial services (especially hedge funds), as both states still lie outside the eurozone, although EU member states did establish a European Banking Authority (EBA) in 2011 to monitor the health of European banks, including through the use of regular 'stress tests'. More worrisome is that leading eurozone creditors (namely Germany) nearly forced Greece out of the eurozone during a major standoff in 2015 before a deal was reached: more bailout money for Greece in exchange for more austerity in that country, an outcome many Greeks opposed. This situation is far from resolved at the time of writing, and we may yet see a eurozone member state exit the system for one reason or another, which would have repercussions across the EU and beyond.

An equally serious problem on a more global scale is the use of deficit spending, in the amount of over $1 trillion, as a stimulus to get the global economy moving again, which is exactly how the London G20 summit elected to solve the current global financial crisis. As noted above, the primary weakness of the global economy is the sovereign ability of all states to print their own money without backing the entire supply of their currencies with a store of physical wealth, such as gold supplies or foreign exchange. If this approach – printing new money to stop a liquidity crisis caused by excessive debt and loose credit – is also used to bring about economic recovery, then a cycle of inflation is the guaranteed result, and governments will eventually have to increase interest rates and/or cut public spending to control that inflation, which will then choke the prospects for a recovery. Although interest rates among most OECD member states remain fairly low since 2008, public spending cuts (i.e. austerity) have hit hard in many states and the supply of credit (such as mortgages) is much tighter, which is why the 2008 crisis still lingers. As noted, however, not all advanced industrialized states agree with this 'solution', and even some LDCs such as China still maintain a separation between their various banking industries to avoid such problems and are likely to continue doing so in light of the current crisis.

Thus, in terms of a total victory standard, it seems possible for the international community to cope with the occasional national economic crisis if it can be contained to some degree. In these cases, such as Mexico and Japan, the economic pain is primarily localized. Similarly, it is also possible for the international community to spend or otherwise coordinate its way out of a more global crisis, which was attempted after the London G20 summit. Yet the repetitive nature of business cycles and of monetary meltdowns means that economic instability is an unfortunate fact of modern capitalism. This fact will continue to hold as long as the merits of free trade, capital mobility and weakly regulated markets are prioritized by certain stakeholders over the merits of a more robust, and possibly more equitable, global economic management system. Although the FSB may help deal with some of the symptoms of global economic and financial instability, it will do nothing to address the underlying cause of this problem: the lack of a single authoritative economic regulator to govern not just private transactions but public ones as well. Of course, the most severe solution to keep governments honest would involve a new global monetary system based on fixed exchange rates (at a minimum) or an actual 'world currency' that replaces national currencies (at a maximum). At the moment neither option is feasible at the global level since governments prefer to maintain their monetary autonomy (that is, to spend their way out of a crisis), although the creation of the eurozone suggests a possible regional solution to this problem. Even here there are problems, however, as eurozone member states have pushed for monetary integration (a single currency) in the absence of tighter integration regarding fiscal policy among themselves (taxing and spending). Many economists predicted this would be a problem at some point, just as many economists warned decades ago that raising tariffs after the 1929 stock market collapse was a mistake, and they were right in both cases.

In terms of a historical trends standard for economic security, the evidence is also mixed. On the positive side, it is certainly true that the global economy has expanded greatly since WWII, from a global GDP of around $5 trillion (in inflation-adjusted dollars) to over $70 trillion today. Tariffs have steadily declined to an average global tariff of about five per cent among developed states, and global trade has expanded accordingly, which has raised the living standards of hundreds of millions of people. On the negative side, however, many economists argue that many individuals today are actually worse off than a generation ago, even before the current crisis materialized. Inequality has increased between the rich and poor both within and between states, while large portions of humanity are still condemned to poverty and live on less than $1 a day. Equally troubling is the seemingly chronic nature of economic crises during the postwar period, whether within states or throughout the entire system. While some free market economists argue that this is the price we must pay for a capitalist system organized around nation-states, others – and not just Marxists – argue that capitalism itself is fundamentally flawed and must be replaced with a more equitable and regulated system, which may see less economic growth but greater levels of stability and opportunity. In the meantime, policy-makers must attempt to manage each crisis as it occurs and hope that the most critical such crisis – a total collapse of the US dollar – will never occur, even if American dominance over the global economy still seems to be declining in the long term (Layne, 2012). If a collapse of the dollar's value does occur, the world may look to China to help organize a bailout of the American economy as its holds the world's largest supply of foreign exchange reserves, and is a major lender to the US. The financial rescue of a capitalist superpower by a rising communist one would be quite an extraordinary event to witness, and is not outside the realm of possibility (Rickards, 2011).

A comparative metrics standard is perhaps the most interesting of all, as states and other stakeholders can devise a wide range of ways to demonstrate their stability or prosperity *vis-à-vis* other economic stakeholders, even during a recession or crisis. For example, competitiveness is often defined as steadily increasing economic growth, a rising standard of living and continued exposure to international trade flows (that is, no protectionist tariff or monetary policies). Yet states and other stakeholders can be extremely creative in framing national income statistics to suit their purposes. The US claims it is doing better than the UK or Germany, while the UK can claim it is doing better than Iceland, while Iceland can claim it is doing better than Russia, and so on. There is, it seems, a natural tendency for states and other stakeholders to compare themselves to each other especially in the area of economic performance; this practice is defined by realists as a relative gains problem but by politicians as business as usual.

The problem of comparative standards also applies to the national policies used to deal with economic crises. Recessions and economic crises do not have the same impact across states, and states vary quite widely in terms of their ability to cope with such problems. Both factors often work to prevent the coordination of an effective multilateral response to a given crisis, whether local or global. And when such coordination is attempted, a more interesting question is raised: how do we regulate or otherwise control the risky but legal behaviours of individual firms and consumers, risks that are then aggregated into financial products, sold worldwide, and can then easily precipitate a global financial crisis? We forget that the roots of the 2008 crisis extend back nearly a decade in the form of specific practices on the part of major MNCs – and not just banks – that were completely overlooked by US regulators and other public watchdogs at the time. The US energy firm Enron, for example, which collapsed spectacularly in December 2001, was named in that very year as the most innovative company in America for the sixth year in a row by *Fortune* magazine. Its CEO and president (Kenneth Lay and Jeffrey Skilling respectively) had even attended the inauguration of President George W. Bush 11 months before their firm filed for bankruptcy and laid off over 20,000 employees. Enron's collapse was followed by that of its accounting firm, Arthur Andersen, one of the 'big five' accounting firms in the US, which was supposed to have kept Enron honest about its business practices and clearly failed to do so. About 85,000 jobs were lost as a result.

Thus, the 2008 crisis was not just another cyclical downturn; it was specifically instigated by reckless, and sometimes fraudulent, practices by US firms and consumers that spread to financial MNCs, especially in the UK, and then to the entire global economy. These practices centred on the so-called 'NINJA borrowers' – people with No Incomes, No Jobs and No Assets – who could still borrow more than enough to buy or regularly refinance their homes and other purchases, thanks to the active collusion of financial firms. Once these borrowers began to default on their loans in the face of rising interest rates and collapsing house prices in 2007–8, their losses spread to the banking system and then to other global investors, resulting in the situation we have faced for nearly a decade. Beyond this problem, the fact that the US and the UK – which are supposedly two 'market friendly' states – were so willing to rescue certain firms with financial aid clearly violates their free market ideologies, which assert that if capitalism's process of 'creative destruction' is to work properly (Schumpeter, 1942), then weak or otherwise struggling firms must be allowed to suffer the consequences of their decisions. Instead, we saw massive government spending to save these reckless stakeholders, as with America's Troubled Asset Relief Program, which provided such support in the amount of nearly $250 billion to such firms in 2008–9, while many other less important industries (not to mention ordinary homeowners) had to suffer the harsh verdict of the market.

Yet by bailing out these firms, we then create a huge *moral hazard*, or the possibility that protecting stakeholders from a risk will make it more likely that they engage in risky behaviour sometime in the future, which starts another crisis. Such policies send a clear signal to certain firms or industries – particularly financial services but also large manufacturers, such as auto firms – that they are supposedly 'too big or important to fail' and therefore can rely on government support at some point (Sorkin, 2010). Even worse, this practice once again sends mixed messages to developing states, which have been lectured for years by the IMF and World Bank and major banks – the vanguard of the 'Washington consensus' – about the merits of fiscal and monetary discipline, deregulation and domestic markets free of excessive state invention. Thus, if major financial powerhouses like the UK and the US can be allowed to run record deficits, bail out their banks and print as much money as they need, why should we expect other states – LDCs in particular – to act differently?

Instead of these kinds of policies, then, the managers of the global economy should consider at least three alternative options: clearer and tighter global regulations to monitor the risky behaviours of major stakeholders; early warning systems to determine when state intervention is necessary to rein in those behaviours; and 'firebreaks' of some type between various aspects of the global economy, especially in the money/credit realm, to prevent a localized crisis in a particular state or industry from becoming a regional or global one. Although the new FSB touches upon some of these issues, it remains to be seen whether its member states will not just allow it to make economic policy recommendations, but will follow them as well. The same might also be said of the EU's own EBA, although it will have much greater legal authority (in the EU) as compared to the FSB. At present it is still far too easy for governments to reject or otherwise discredit the advice or information provided by major financial IOs, as the British government did in April 2009 by rejecting the IMF's figures regarding UK economic growth rates in favour of its more inflated – and optimistic – projections. A similar process occurred during the June 2016 British EU referendum, when a majority of voters rejected economic forecasts (which predicted problems if the UK left the EU) in favour of far more optimistic assessments by the media and others.

## Summary

There are two primary points to be taken from the discussion above. First, the global economy is prone to a range of chronic management problems that are becoming increasingly difficult to solve in an *ad hoc*, market-driven fashion. Overall, the system is oriented towards economic growth/efficiency (including risk-taking) even at the cost of equity and stability. When times are good, no one wants to raise the spectre of a downturn or collapse, which is precisely what can happen if various stakeholders ignore the fundamental truth of capitalist markets: what goes up must come down once supply exceeds demand. Second, the primary economic

hegemon – the US – no longer has the power either to protect itself unilaterally or to impose its more lenient regulatory wishes on other states
where these problems are concerned. Instead, we see the rise of other
major economic powers such as the BRIC bloc and the EU, as reflected
in the role of the G20 (rather than the G7 or G8) as the main forum for
responding to the current economic crisis. The US could not even hope
to control the participation or agenda of the 2009 London summit as it
may have done just a decade ago. Its massive debt, current account deficit and budget deficit, plus the rise of alternative currencies (such as the
euro) and other players with massive foreign exchange reserves and huge
banks (such as China) put the US at a major disadvantage compared to
its post-war hegemony. Moreover, not only has the US declined in relative terms against its major competitors while becoming more exposed to
global trade and capital flows, its hands-off approach to economic management and corporate governance has been discredited in the wake of
accounting scandals, reckless lending practices, fraud, banking crises and
the 2008 financial crisis. Finally, the management of globalization is inherently a multilateral responsibility, a point the US and other major powers
often seem to forget in light of their varied exposure and responses to
certain economic problems. In short, then, the US and its major partners
are largely powerless to control globalization on an *ad hoc* basis, which
is precisely the default response of these stakeholders in the face of each
economic or financial crisis.

These problems are precisely why the backlash against US-led globalization trends has become so potent in recent years. It is bad enough
that globalization always results in short-term winners and losers, even
though the long-term effects might be positive from an economic growth
standard. Now we must also contend with reckless and even fraudulent
behaviour on the part of the major, often US-based, foundation institutions of the global economy – banks and other MNCs – who led us into
a global financial meltdown under a very weak global regulatory regime.
A final irony here is that a truly liberal global economy would permit not
just the free movement of goods and services, but all factors of production (human, financial and physical capital) so they could move to areas
where there is a shortage of such factors. In principle, this should include
labour mobility as well, yet the major powers in particular are extremely
reluctant to allow people to move more freely across their borders. This
reluctance regarding free movement of labour also led many British voters
to choose to leave the EU in 2016. Thus, financial capital can still move
freely, but human capital is far more restricted. This situation will create
new economic stresses as globalization progresses, and will create pressures for migration reform in a range of rich states. However, this question of liberalizing the global movement of labour – which is difficult on a
global basis but may emerge on a regional basis (for example, in the EU)

– is closely linked to environmental/resource issues, public health issues and population issues. These problems – all of which relate to the broader human security agenda – are examined in the next three chapters.

## Further reading

Alan S. Blinder (2013). *After the Music Stopped: The Financial Crisis, the Response, and the Work Ahead*. London: Penguin Books.

Kimberly Ann Elliott, Gary Clyde Hufbauer and Jeffrey J. Schott (2008). *Economic Sanctions Reconsidered*. Washington: Peterson Institute for International Economics.

G. John Ikenberry, David A. Lake and Michael Mastanduno (eds.) (1988). *The State and American Foreign Economic Policy*. Ithaca: Cornell University Press.

Charles P. Kindleberger (2001). *Manias, Panics, and Crashes: A History of Financial Crises*. New York: John Wiley & Sons.

Michael Lewis (2010). *The Big Short: Inside the Doomsday Machine*. London: Allen Lane.

Michael Mastanduno (1993). *Economic Containment*. Ithaca: Cornell University Press.

Wayne Sandholtz, Michael Borrus, John Zysman and Steven Vogel (eds.) (1992). *The Highest Stakes: The Economic Foundations of the Next Security System*. Oxford: Oxford University Press.

James Rickards (2011). *Currency Wars: The Making of the Next Global Crisis*. New York: Portfolio Books.

Andrew Ross Sorkin (2010). *Too Big to Fail: Inside the Battle to Save Wall Street*. London: Penguin.

James Sperling and Emil Kirchner (1997). *Recasting the European Order: Security Architectures and Economic Co-operation*. Manchester: Manchester University Press.

Martin Wolf (2008). *Fixing Global Finance: How to Curb Financial Crises in the 21st Century*. New Haven: Yale University Press.

# Chapter 11

# Environmental and Resource Security

The relationship between security affairs, the protection of the environment and the conservation of certain resources is becoming one of the more complicated topics in world politics. If international security is fundamentally concerned with the protection of particular referent objects – whether physical or symbolic/institutional – valued by large numbers of human beings, then it would seem self-evident that environmental problems would loom large in such a context. And if a physical resource such as territory can be treated as an object to be protected or contested by various political actors, then the same should be true of other components of the earth's physical environment essential to human life, such as food and water. Yet the orthodox view of international security seems extremely reluctant to include consideration of the protection of the environment and critical resources, except in isolated circumstances to be discussed later in this chapter. Conversely, scholars who defend the new security/human security agenda are far more likely to treat environmental and natural resource problems as security issues in and of themselves, and have pursued this position in their work.

This chapter examines the case for what might be called 'international environmental security' from both perspectives: the orthodox/traditional view and the new security/human security view. The fact that this division even exists indicates that the initial framing of an environmental problem as a security concern can be a highly contentious process, and that consensual knowledge about such framing is often lacking even in the face of scientific evidence. However, there are at least two major examples – ozone depletion and global warming – where the international community has managed to find some consensus regarding an environmental security issue, and these cases provide some useful empirical material to help structure the analysis in this chapter. In a sense, they can be treated as true international public goods as defined in Chapter 3, as protection against ozone depletion and global warming provides indivisible and non-excludable benefits for the entire planet. In fact, of all topics discussed in this volume, global warming may represent the most critical current threat to international security, in terms of its destructive scale, scope, likelihood and irreversibility. The related question of natural resources also offers

300

two major examples – fossil fuels and water – where the lack of reliable supplies could be treated as security problems.

In all of these cases, the inherent transborder nature of such problems strongly encourages multilateral solutions, which in turn makes them possible topics in international security studies. Even then, the search for a clear solution often pits various coalitions against each other for one fundamental reason suggested in previous chapters: the different vulnerabilities and costs felt by various actors who claim to have a stake in the matter. Moreover, and as with other 'soft security' or human security threats, globalization greatly intensifies such problems, not just in the form of liberal markets but also in the form of newly industrializing states, demographics (growing middle-class families who travel and consume more), finite supplies of certain natural resources and greater urbanization. Thus, if trends regarding globalization and economic development continue over the next few decades, then the international community will have little choice but to manage environmental and resource problems far more effectively, or else risk permanently damaging the single most important physical object for sustaining all life: the earth itself.

## The environment, natural resources and international security

Although the term 'environment' has a variety of meanings, the term as used here refers to a biological system that sustains life (i.e. the 'natural environment'). The term 'system' in turn implies a network of feedback loops and equilibrium states, which can be disrupted if not destroyed by a range of factors, both human and non-human. Although such a system may include physical or natural resources, such resources are viewed more appropriately as a separate analytical category, as some resources (such as mineral deposits) do not relate to biological systems. Other resources, such as water and agricultural products, play a dual role as natural resources in their own right and as critical parts of a larger environmental system, which makes them especially important as a potential referent object of security studies. Thus, rather than examine very narrow questions regarding the environment and security, such as the adverse impact of weapons testing on the environment or the problem of toxic waste dumping, this chapter will focus on protecting larger-scale natural environmental systems and natural resources whose disruption, depletion or damage/destruction would have a critically adverse effect on life (Young, 1989; Hurrell and Kingsbury, 1992; Haas, Keohane and Levy, 1993; Zurn, 1998; Barnett, 2001; Dalby, 2002).

While this focus seems fairly straightforward, the relationship between the environment and security is actually quite contested among *security* scholars, and – as with other new security or human security topics – there is limited consensus on how to conceptualize this topic or interpret technical data regarding it. One final general point is that discussions of environmental problems can easily expand to encompass natural disasters, such as earthquakes, floods, hurricanes etc.. While these problems can be extremely large and destructive in scale – such as the 2004 Asian tsunami, which killed more than 225,000 people – in the environmental politics literature they are more often considered as random accidents or acts or nature rather than as manageable problems, so the discussion below will exclude such incidents. It should be kept in mind, however, that a state's failure to anticipate or effectively respond to such disasters can have an extremely negative impact on the credibility and reputation of its government, as with the Turkish earthquake of 1999 (Jacoby and Özerdem, 2008), Hurricane Katrina in the US in 2005 and the Burmese cyclone of 2008; such a situation may also result in a higher propensity of violent intrastate conflict (Nel and Righarts, 2008). Thus, this chapter will stress anthropogenic sources of environmental or resource depletion problems, or those resulting from human activities, such as consumption or wastemaking (Bernauer, 1995). This focus in turn implies that environmentally friendly changes in human behaviour should have a correspondingly positive effect on the problems discussed in this chapter.

## Destructive scale

The debate about international environmental security has been greatly complicated by discussions about the direct and indirect consequences of specific problems, which relate to the question of destructive scale. Direct consequences refer to environmental damage or resource depletion problems that undermine the quality of life – or even life itself – in various human communities. Indirect consequences refer to other problems that stem from, or can be exacerbated by, underlying environmental problems, such as conflicts over scarce water resources. This is precisely where more traditional and less traditional security scholars differ: whether to treat environmental issues as a security problem only if they can be linked to more conventional security concerns, mainly involving violence (the more traditional view), or whether they should be considered as security concerns *in and of themselves* as they might undermine the quality of, or prospects for, human life itself (the less traditional or human security view).

The most obvious example of the former, more traditional, type of thinking involves studies that attempt to demonstrate a link between environmental or resource problems and violent conflict, or the question of *resource wars* (i.e. 'water wars' or 'oil wars'). This question of environment-related conflict has generated a fairly lively debate, as some scholars argue that such wars do exist (Homer-Dixon, 1994 and 1999; Kahl, 1998; Väyrynen, 1998; Le Billon 2001a, 2001b and 2004; Klare 2002; Ross 2004); in fact, one recent study claims that between one-quarter and one-half of interstate wars since 1973 have involved oil-related causal mechanisms (Colgan, 2013). Including intrastate wars in the analysis might strengthen this argument even more. Others, however (Levy, 1995; Deudney and Matthew, 1999; Barnett, 2000; Diamond, 2004; McNeill, 2005; Meierding, 2016), remind us that any analysis of such a link must be embedded in a broader understanding of the multidimensional nature of modern conflicts and the problems of economic growth in LDCs, especially in terms of whether the resource dispute is a cause or merely a symptom of a conflict. This argument even applies in situations of severe water shortages (Theisen et al., 2011–12). In other words, most such conflicts, as in the Middle East and Africa, involve many other factors besides limited natural resources or severe weather events, and solving the resource problem alone might do little to mitigate the conflict. In addition, there are many other examples of disputes over resources that do not become resource wars, in both the developed and developing world.

A much broader approach to environmental *security*, as opposed to environmental *conflicts* (Detraz and Betsill, 2009), would examine the destructive potential of various environmental problems as threats to human welfare rather than limit the analysis by attempting to link such problems to interstate or intrastate wars. This is precisely why the four main issues – ozone depletion, global warming, fossil fuels and water – discussed in this chapter have been chosen: because of their inherent importance to global human welfare well beyond any specific link – actual or potential – to a traditional military conflict. For example, the science behind ozone depletion is quite straightforward: every one per cent reduction in the atmospheric ozone layer that covers the earth allows two per cent more ultraviolet-B (UV-B) rays to hit earth. High UV-B rays are known to be harmful to many species, as they increase cancers and depress immune systems (see this chapter's case study). The question of global warming is similarly straightforward: as carbon dioxide ($CO_2$) and other waste gases are released into the earth's atmosphere owing to the actions of humans and animals, more heat is retained on the earth's surface – the so-called *greenhouse effect*. Fossil fuel burning, for example, releases more than six billion tons of carbon into the atmosphere every year, while deforestation adds another one to two billion tons of carbon a year. If global temperatures rise as a result of these and other greenhouse gases (GHGs), the consequences could adversely impact all life on the planet, in the form of water shortages, rising sea levels, coastal erosion, reduced agricultural productivity, the loss of numerous plant and animal species, adverse weather conditions, desertification and other threats (Nordhaus, 2013). One study explicitly claims that climate change is already killing

Table 11.1   *World energy sources*

|  | 2009 | 2013 |
| --- | --- | --- |
| Petroleum (oil) | 36.8% | 31.1% |
| Coal | 26.6% | 28.9% |
| Natural gas | 22.9% | 21.4% |
| Hydroelectric | 6.3% | 2.4% |
| Nuclear | 6.0% | 4.8% |
| Biofuels and waste | 0.5% | 10.2% |
| Other (solar, wind, geothermal) | 0.9% | 1.2% |

*Source:* International Energy Agency, *Key World Energy Statistics* (2015).

300,000 people a year, while economic losses caused by this problem are calculated at more than $125 billion a year (Global Humanitarian Forum, 2008).

The two main natural resources discussed in this chapter involve slightly different calculations about the potential destruction or damage involved if they are disrupted or depleted. Although use of biofuels has risen while reliance on fossil fuels (oil, coal and natural gas) has declined slightly in recent years, products based on fossil fuels still supply the vast majority – about 81 per cent – of the world's energy, as indicated in Table 11.1.

Fossil fuels are also a finite resource critical to the development and functioning of modern economies, while water can be replenished through the normal functioning of the earth's crust and atmosphere, as well as the use of water treatment facilities and similar technologies. The problem of energy security is therefore typically framed as the prospect of a major *disruption* of fossil fuels around the globe (including the question of radical price instability), although states vary widely in terms of how they interpret 'disruptions' (Duffield, 2012), while water security can be analysed on a more region- or country-specific basis in terms of *distribution*, as states vary widely in their exposure to this problem even though global water supplies are generally adequate (Selby, 2005; Sedlak, 2014).

## Geographic and temporal scope

Although the geographic scope of international environmental problems can be framed in terms as narrow as the pollution of a single lake, we are concerned here with the other end of the scale: problems whose scale and persistence could negatively impact the well-being of millions if not billions of people. Clearly the two main environmental issues discussed here, ozone depletion and global warming, qualify in this respect, as they could result in widespread illness and death if they are not managed adequately.

Their temporal scope and geographic scale are equally problematic, as a failure to address them in time could require years if not decades of adaptation by humans, animals and plants around the world (if they survive, that is). However, it must also be noted that vulnerability to the problem of global warming does vary somewhat across states; small island states for example face a major threat from rising sea levels, while people living along the equatorial belt – roughly half of the world's population – are likely to suffer from severe food shortages (Battisti and Naylor, 2009). Even across a region as large and poor as Africa, vulnerability to climate change varies widely depending on local socio-political factors; the DRC, Guinea, Sierra Leone, Somalia and South Sudan are thought to be most at risk (Moran, 2011; Busby et al., 2013).

The situation with resource depletion is even more inequitable. The case of fossil fuels would suggest a common international interest, as such fuels are a finite resource traded as a commodity on a global market. In fact, oil is not just important for economic growth; it is also the single most valuable component of international trade, accounting for about ten per cent of such trade. This means in turn that wide price swings, not to mention the ultimate depletion of the resource at some point, can affect all fossil fuel consumers, even if those consumers are located many thousands of miles away from the source of the price surge. However, such consumers, whether in the form of entire states or individuals, are in fact not equally vulnerable to such problems, as their energy sources can vary quite widely. Some states, such as France, have invested heavily in nuclear power to reduce their dependency on fossil fuels, while individual consumers may adopt a similar approach to conservation, by purchasing fuel efficient or electric cars for example. Thus, the interpretation of 'energy security' as an international priority can vary according to the preferences of these actors, as we shall see.

The same proposition is even more relevant with water resources, which can be replenished, are not traded as a global commodity, and therefore are not subject to a single global price. Although there is more than enough water to serve the current global population, its distribution is extremely uneven owing to a combination of factors. Some areas, whether states or local communities, are clearly very 'water-stressed' and must pay close attention to their water supplies. In fact, up to half of the world's population may be water-stressed by 2015, mostly in Africa, the Middle East, South Asia and China. The UN Development Programme (UNDP) has similarly argued, in its annual Human Development Reports, that up to two million children a year – mostly in LDCs – die because of a lack of clean water and sanitation; this amounts to a staggering 5,000 dead children *per day*. Water shortage problems also exist in parts of certain large states with arid or desert climates, such as central Australia and the western US. Other states, however, can take a much more sanguine

## Table 11.2   *Daily water usage per capita*

| | |
|---|---|
| US | 600 litres |
| Australia | 500 litres |
| Italy/Japan/Mexico | 350–400 litres |
| Germany | 200 litres |
| UK | 150 litres |
| China | 80 litres |
| India | 135 |
| LDCs | less than 50 litres |

*Source:* UN FAO.

view about their water supplies and do not even think in terms of water security, although they certainly pay more attention during the occasional drought. In fact, figures from the UN FAO (2006 data) clearly reveal that states vary widely in terms of their average per capita daily water use, as shown in Table 11.2.

This variance in vulnerability to either energy or water security can greatly impact the prospects for international cooperation in such matters, as we shall see.

## Likelihood

One major consensual knowledge problem shared by environmental degradation and resource depletion involves their incremental nature, in that these problems are often imperceptible to the average citizen/consumer, so it can be very difficult to convince people that they are in fact occurring. This is especially critical when comparing such problems to other more orthodox security threats, such as a war or terrorist bombing. A second problem here involves the link between these problems and human or animal behaviour: if such behaviour changes over time, then calculations about environmental degradation or resource depletion must change as well. Thus, even if we have some consensus that a problem such as ozone depletion or fossil fuel depletion is happening, or will happen eventually, we must still base that finding in part on projections about future behaviour, and such projections or forecasts can be quite contentious.

On the positive side, however, and thanks primarily to modern technologies for monitoring the earth's geography and atmosphere, there is a very high degree of consensus on the likely consequences of ozone depletion, as the case study below discusses, and a growing consensus regarding the nature of global warming over the past decade. Although a fairly high degree of misinformation about climate change is still being spread by a range of actors (see below), for most policy-makers the scientific consensus about this issue is incontrovertible. However, compared to ozone depletion, which has been very credibly confirmed by satellite technology, it is difficult to point to any single piece of evidence regarding the root causes of global warming in terms of anthropogenic factors. In addition, accurate temperature records only go back for the past 100 years or so. Still, it does seem clear that average global temperatures have been rising over the past century, by about one to two degrees Celsius, and that the eight warmest years on record have all occurred since 1990. Based on trends over the past several decades, one major report by the UN Intergovernmental Panel on Climate Change (IPCC) predicted a gradual rise in global temperatures ranging from 1.4°C (2.5°F) to 5.8°C (10.4°F) between 1990 and 2100 if drastic action is not taken to control GHGs. It further concludes that most of this warming is attributable to human activities rather than other factors (Vrolijk, 2001). A more recent UN assessment by the World Bank's Global Facility for Disaster Reduction and Recovery (2016) claimed that 1.3 billion people and $158 trillion in economic assets will be at risk from climate-related disasters by 2050; these effects will be most severe in urban areas, particularly those close to the coastline.

Predicting the likely depletion or shortage of fossil fuels and water supplies poses additional problems. Although all fossil fuel analysts expect global supplies to run out at some point, and we know that world energy consumption is growing at about 2.3 per cent a year, there is no consensus whatsoever on when these supply/demand trends will collide. In addition to the problem of measuring actual supplies by adding known reserves to (projected) future discoveries, we must add the problem of measuring and then forecasting global demand. As most major actors – states and large firms – are attempting to diversify their energy sources to reduce dependency on fossil fuels, others, such as China and India, are expected to increase their demand considerably and will offset the reduced dependency on fossil fuels enjoyed by other actors. Therefore the net calculation – or the likely depletion of known fossil fuel reserves based on factors of supply and demand projected decades into the future – is extremely contentious. Proven crude oil reserves at the end of 2008 were 1,258 billion barrels (not including about 150 billion barrels in Canadian tar sands), while current annual consumption is about 30 billion barrels. Based on these figures, oil will run out in about 34 years from 2016 (around 2050) if production and consumption do not radically change. However, advocates of *peak oil theory* – which argues that the maximum rate of oil production has been reached already – suspect we will run out even sooner as the global population nears nine billion (see Chapter 13). Finally, we must factor in a related problem: the likelihood of major price hikes owing either to accidental factors (such as war) or to deliberate attempts by certain market players to control supplies, as through cartels (see below). Oil and gas in particular are volatile commodities, and very susceptible to swings in production and delivery that directly affect prices and profits. Psychology also plays a role here, as fears of energy shortages can cause major price spikes, even when there is no economic justification for them.

The case of water is even more difficult, as there is no single market price nor major market players, and vulnerabilities can vary widely across the international community, even within single states. The fact that water can be replenished and purified adds to the difficulty of predicting future water shortages, whether on a local or global basis. However, for areas where geographic factors already indicate a potential problem with water supplies, such as desert regions and areas undergoing desertification, it is reasonable to assume that water security will be an ongoing problem for the people (if any) living in or near such areas. Freshwater stress is typically defined as a situation in which the water withdrawal rate exceeds the renewable water supply by ten per cent or more; for most states, irrigation makes up most of this use (around 70 per cent). As we might expect, states in the Middle East with largely desert climates (Bahrain, Israel, Kuwait, Lebanon, Oman, Palestine, Qatar, United Arab Emirates and Saudi Arabia) are among the most water-stressed on the planet; in fact, some analysts have claimed that water stress among farmers and herders contributed to the social unrest behind Syria's civil war in 2011.

## Recovery

As with other aspects regarding the consensual knowledge of these problems, the prospects for recovery vary widely as well. Thanks to the efforts of the international community regarding ozone depletion (see the case study below), we know that such effects can be halted if not reversed when sufficiently effective action is taken in time. The fact that the ozone layer can apparently be repaired by human behaviours is indeed a very positive finding; however, the case of global warming is more contentious and difficult. It is in fact unclear whether enough action can be taken in time to slow, stop or reverse global warming to limit the damage caused by a two to four degree Celsius rise in the earth's temperature over the next century. The most recent forecasts predict that such warming will not be under control in the next few decades, so that any recovery (assuming it is even scientifically possible) will be that much more difficult to achieve by the concerted efforts of the international community.

For fossil fuels, the story is much simpler: depletion will occur at some point in the current century, so stakeholders will have a few decades to alter their behaviours in terms of conserving current supplies for as long as possible while also diversifying into other energy sources, such as nuclear power, solar power, wind power and others in various combinations.

Finally, water clearly is essential for life and cannot be substituted (unlike fossil fuels), so the international community should be very concerned about the long-term sustainable conservation of such a resource. However, the fact that water stress varies so widely means that this problem at present probably does not get the attention it deserves, even though we all recognize how difficult – if not impossible – life would be without assured access to a reliable source of clean water. Unfortunately this is still a fact of life for many human communities, and can easily spill over to other international security problems, such as public health and migration (see Chapters 12 and 13).

## Stakeholder factors

It should be clear by now that new security or human security issues are characterized in part by the presence of multiple stakeholders located at various levels of analysis, and this is especially true of the issues covered in this chapter. Indeed, every human being on the planet has a general interest or stake in protecting the ozone layer, preventing global warming and conserving life-critical resources such as energy and food/water supplies. In addition, the behaviours of every human being can contribute to these problems, whether in a positive or negative sense. However, we still need to take politics into consideration, and the fact is that a much narrower set of stakeholders is directly involved in setting the global agenda and influencing public policy on these problems. That said, and compared to more traditional international security problems, there does seem to be more scope for non-state stakeholders, such as NGOs, scientists and interest groups, to play at least a limited role in environmental security affairs thanks to a general rise in environmental consciousness over the past few decades and more specific physical evidence regarding the nature of the problem, as noted above.

### Principal stakeholders

Although the stakeholders and politics behind various environmental/resource problems can vary somewhat, it is still possible to briefly summarize the major coalitions involved in environmental and natural resource problems. As with many human security problems, one major cleavage pits the advanced industrialized states against LDCs or newly industrializing states, most of which belong to the G77. On ozone depletion, for example, when the problem was first identified the bulk of CFC production was concentrated in the advanced industrialized states, particularly the US, so the involvement of these states was absolutely critical to any discussions about a possible solution. On global warming, the US in particular has been reluctant to play a stronger leadership role (see below) so other stakeholders, such as the EU and Japan (Matsumura, 2000), have attempted to forge a global coalition to deal with it. Regarding fossil fuels, the problem to a large degree involves two major coalitions: the major energy consumers on the one hand and the major energy suppliers (namely oil and gas producers) on the other. The major consuming states are the largest and most industrialized economies, while the major suppliers are located in both the developed and the developing worlds. The issue of oil is especially contentious, as the major suppliers are located in one of the most volatile regions in the world: the Middle East.

A second major cleavage often pits firms and even entire industries, such as the fossil fuel and automobile industries, against environmental- or natural resource-related NGOs. With global warming, for example, the core problem – $CO_2$ and methane emissions – is far more diffuse in nature than in the ozone case, so the range of key stakeholders is much wider. To the extent that such emissions – of carbon in particular – are largely a product of advanced economies and modern consumer lifestyles, the role of carbon-emitting firms is especially important. Environmental politics has become so contentious that major firms and NGOs increasingly attempt to lobby international negotiations on this topic and use other methods, such as campaign financing, to influence the states involved in these talks (DeSombre, 2000). More recently, a new method – 'Astroturfing' – has emerged, which involves the deliberate creation, by energy firms and automakers, of fake grass-roots political movements (hence the term 'Astroturf', which is a brand of fake grass) to lobby the US Congress against taking action on climate change. Despite this kind of activity, it should not be assumed that all polluting firms reflexively oppose all international environmental standards; in fact, in some industries certain MNCs – mainly in the OECD states – have been known to support higher standards wherever they operate – mainly in LDCs – to ensure they do not suffer a disadvantage relative to local firms. This view is reflected for example in the Responsible Care programme of the International Council of Chemical Associations, which attempts to create a level international playing field for all chemical firms (Garcia-Johnson, 2000).

The critical link between the use of fossil fuels and the role of carbon emissions in global warming also presents a major challenge to environmental groups, as some states are now concentrating on the development of nuclear energy as a solution to both problems. For some environmental NGOs, this is a wise choice given the potentially catastrophic nature of global warming, while for other environmental NGOs there is no such thing as 'clean' or 'green' or 'safe' nuclear energy, and they oppose this choice as a solution to either the fossil fuel shortage or the problem of global warming. Finally, the issue of water scarcity is very difficult to frame in terms of major stakeholder coalitions, as supplies vary so widely not just across but within states as well; this problem in turn is compounded by other factors (such as the weather). As a result, it is not possible to speak of (for example) ongoing international conflict between chronically water-stressed states against those with fairly abundant supplies. Instead, the politics of water security is far more dynamic and diffuse than for other environmental/resource problems. However, as most chronic water stress occurs in LDCs, many advanced states, such as France, play a key role in providing water-related technologies or management practices to LDCs, which creates a kind of symbiotic, but also asymmetric, relationship between such states.

## Interests and preferences

The various sensitivities and roles of these stakeholders can be seen more clearly by examining their views on each separate issue. Although it would seem the entire planet is vulnerable to the adverse effects of ozone depletion, one of the key stakeholders in this case – the US – was still reluctant, at first, to take stronger measures. This was mainly because one of the largest producers of CFCs was a major American MNC: DuPont. On global warming, the US adopted a similar attitude, while other major contributors to global warming, particularly some EU member states, were more willing to consider a concerted effort to deal with the problem, even if certain other contributors, such as China and India, were exempted from such measures. To defend these positions, most parties to the various climate change talks discussed below have organized themselves into several major factions, some of which have overlapping membership by certain states. These factions include: the G77; the Alliance of Small Island States (43 members); the LDCs (49 members); the EU (28 members, including the UK); the Umbrella Group (Australia, Canada, Iceland, Japan, New Zealand, Norway, the Russian Federation, Ukraine and the US); the Environmental Integrity Group (Mexico, the Republic of Korea and Switzerland); the Organization of the Petroleum Exporting Countries (OPEC) and assorted other less formal groupings. As these groupings suggest, the policy positions among various stakeholders cannot be easily reduced to simple North–South, transatlantic, or East–West cleavages. This is largely due to their varying vulnerabilities and the distribution of the costs of combating climate change: the Alliance of Small Island States is naturally concerned about rising sea levels, while other stakeholders might be more concerned with desertification or deforestation or severe weather events caused by global warming. Similarly, states with large oil revenues or that depend excessively on fossil fuels may be reluctant to adjust their economies to cope with a carbon-free world (Grundig, 2006).

The problem of a growing scarcity of fossil fuels is equally complex, and is related to some degree to the same factions involved in climate change negotiations. Here the US enjoyed considerable hegemony over oil production starting as early as 1859, when the first reliably functioning oil well was drilled in western Pennsylvania. In fact, a US oil firm – John D. Rockefeller's Standard Oil Company – was the first modern MNC, and Rockefeller became the world's first billionaire in 1916. This situation held until a series of major oil (and later natural gas) discoveries in Russia, Iran, Iraq, Mexico and Venezuela, followed by the real 'mother lode' in Saudi Arabia in the 1930s. At first, these states were not advanced enough to exploit their own reserves and sell on world markets; instead, they had to sell their drilling concessions to more advanced states. As a result, several major powers – mainly the US, the UK and (to a lesser extent) the Netherlands – managed to maintain control of these new suppliers through their original Seven Sisters oil firms: Anglo-Persian Oil (now BP); Gulf Oil (now part of Royal Dutch/Shell); Royal Dutch/Shell; Socony-Vacuum (now ExxonMobil); Standard Oil of California (now Chevron); Standard Oil of New Jersey (now ExxonMobil); and Texaco (now part of Chevron). However, the leading producers in the developing world eventually joined together to resist such dominance and formed their own oil suppliers cartel, known as OPEC. The members of OPEC are: Iran, Iraq, Kuwait, Saudi Arabia, Venezuela (all founding members, 1960), Qatar (1961), Indonesia and Libya (1962), United Arab Emirates (1967), Algeria (1969) and Nigeria (1971), while Gabon (1975–94) resigned its membership. Ecuador was an OPEC member state from 1972 to 1992, then rejoined the cartel in 2007.

Currently OPEC's 12 member states produce about 40 per cent of the world's oil supply and possess about 81 per cent of the world's proven oil reserves, which means that these states tend to dominate discussions about oil production, although several non-OPEC states, such as Mexico and the US, continue to produce their own oil. OPEC attempts to manipulate oil prices by controlling production (supply) through output quotas assigned to each of its member states. However, there are strong incentives to produce more than you are allowed (or *quota cheating*); yet if everyone cheats, then all oil producers are worse off in the end as prices fall (Doran 1980; Danielsen, 1982). Under these circumstances OPEC's real influence over oil markets may be overstated (Colgan, 2014), especially in light of recent trends, such as shale oil and gas production (see below). In natural gas, the US and Russia are the largest global producers, and their interests are critical in any discussions regarding that commodity. The Russian government in particular exercises its preferences through a controlling stake in the firm Gazprom, which is the largest Russian company and the largest extractor of natural gas in the world; it also supplies Europe with natural gas. However, European vulnerability to Russian supplies varies widely; central and Eastern European states in particular are at risk of Russian disruptions.

Finally, we should note the importance of major consumers of fossil fuels (particularly oil), and here again the US has a major interest given its status as the world's largest consumer of oil at around 20 million barrels a day (mbd) out of a total global consumption of around 93 mbd, or about 22 per cent of all consumption (2011 figures). The EU is second in line behind America and accounts for just under 20 per cent of all global consumption; this figure has also declined gradually over the past decade, which is somewhat encouraging considering that the EU has a slightly higher GDP, and much larger population, than the US. The same holds true of natural gas consumption: in 2011 the US consumed 690 billion cubic metres, while the EU consumed 460 billion. As both the US and the EU must import some of their oil (and natural gas), they have a strong interest in maintaining steady supplies at stable prices. All other states fall well below these levels of consumption as a proportion of global consumption; even China consumes less than 10mbd (or just over ten per cent of the world total) despite possessing around one-fifth of the world's population. Obviously this situation will change gradually as China's economy expands, and there is already heavy Chinese investment in oil contracts in major foreign energy markets in the Middle East and Africa, as well as other mineral resources (Burgess and Bellstein, 2013), which may point to future conflict with other major consumers such as the US and the EU as supplies grow scarce. In addition, China has asserted territorial claims on its periphery, which has involved the use of military force (see below).

As noted above, stakeholder interests and preferences regarding water are the most diffuse of all, and the only real international cleavage is that between chronically water-stressed areas, such as northern Africa and the Middle East, and states in regions that do not suffer from such problems, such as the advanced industrialized economies whose water resources are far cleaner and more reliable. It also should be remembered that water supplies are contingent not just on geography and weather, but also on technology, as more advanced states can be more efficient in using water (for example, with modern irrigation methods) and can be more effective in recovering and treating water for reuse relative to the situation in many LDCs, which can exacerbate the politics of water scarcity between rich and poor states (as well as within states). As most of the chronic water-stressed states lack major influence at the international level, and as their water problems tend not to spill over to the developed world, these states must struggle to work together to keep the problem of water security high on the international agenda.

## The use of force

Although it might seem there is not much scope for the use of force regarding environmental and resource issues, other than policing certain criminal activities that might harm the environment, such as toxic waste dumping, the case of energy security in particular demonstrates the extent to which some states are willing to use force and other coercive methods to maintain steady supplies of fossil fuels. As noted above, the US and the UK in particular acted to maintain the Seven Sisters system through the use of boycotts, foreign aid, arms sales and armed intervention; in the most egregious episode they even colluded to overthrow the prime minister of Iran in 1953 after he threatened to nationalize the Anglo-Iranian Oil Co. This policy sowed the seeds of the Iranian revolution in 1979, which led to the installation of an Islamist anti-American regime in that state (Yergin, 1991). The impact of this antagonism is still felt to this day over a range of security issues, such as the current Iraq war, terrorism and nuclear proliferation.

More recently, the US-led war against Iraq in 1991 was motivated to a large degree by fears that Saddam Hussein's regime would control Kuwaiti oil supplies, and possibly threaten those of more pro-Western oil producing states, particularly Saudi Arabia. The same concern was undoubtedly a factor behind the 2003 US-led war against Iraq, although this war was also bound up in a larger argument (false, as it turned out) regarding Iraq's possession of WMD and its supposed links to terrorist activity (see Chapter 4). Recent Russian policies also suggest a continued potential for armed conflict in this area as it attempts to assert its near-hegemony over natural gas supplies *vis-à-vis* its major consumers, particularly Ukraine but also wider Europe, which is heavily dependent on Russian natural gas. Finally, the efforts of some oil firms to maintain their drilling concessions in certain LDCs have involved allegations of environmental damage and even human rights abuses on the part of local governments who control such rights. For example, the torture and execution in 1995 of Nigeria environmental activist Ken Saro-Wiwa along with eight other leaders (the 'Ogoni Nine') has been attributed to desires by the Nigerian government to maintain a good relationship with Royal Dutch/Shell Oil, which had been the target of environmental protests and lawsuits by people in regions where the firm operates. Families of these activists sued Shell Oil in a New York court, and Shell agreed to settle the case just prior to the trial for $15.5 million. More recently, tensions have risen in Asia in the past decade as Beijing has asserted various claims over oil-rich and gas-rich areas around the South China Sea, which pits China against other stakeholders in the region: Brunei, Cambodia, Indonesia, Malaysia, the Philippines, Singapore, Taiwan and Vietnam. Military aircraft and naval vessels from some of these countries, as well as from outside stakeholders like India and the US, have become involved in various incidents, although major violence has not occurred (yet). Thus it is by no means assured that environmental and resource problems are inherently soft security or human security issues where the use of force is either unthinkable or unlikely.

## Public–private domains and levels of jurisdiction

Security issues arising from environmental or resource problems are to a large extent a direct consequence of the aggregate activities of all humans on the planet, which gives rise to the phrase 'think globally, act locally'. However, as with risky or reckless economic behaviours (or sexual/health practices; see Chapter 12), the question here is how to police these behaviours on a global scale according to common standards, assuming they can be agreed. In other words, individual private practices can have damaging, and even catastrophic, public consequences.

For ozone depletion, the main solution involved stopping the production of CFCs by certain firms, which considerably narrowed the range of policy targets (see the case study below). For global warming, energy consumption and water consumption, the main targets encompass all individuals who release GHGs into the atmosphere and use fossil fuels or water – which essentially means all human beings. Thus, the required level of jurisdiction over these matters extends all the way down to local communities and even households – which again raises the question of how to police individual behaviours, such as excessive carbon emissions or wasteful energy and water use, that might undermine national or international security even though such behaviours may be quite legal in their local jurisdictions. The well-known 'polluter pays principle' is one approach to this problem, and involves the use of taxes and/or fines levied on those who pollute the environment. The same approach is now being extended with the use of carbon taxes or carbon offsetting, although it is highly questionable whether these methods will actually slow or stop global warming, as well as arrest fossil fuel depletion, rather than merely raise more revenues for national governments. Water supplying/metering is equally problematic, as this service (as with energy supplies and ISPs) can involve close government collusion with private water suppliers/treatment facilities, where profits are as important as maintaining safe supplies. In other words, we again see the inherent problem of conflicting public/private interests whenever private stakeholders are asked or allowed to take on a public role as a utility provider. In some countries, consumers have even strongly resisted the use of market mechanisms to control water supplies, especially where water is used intensively for agriculture (Simmons, 2016).

## The environment and resource depletion as policy problems

As we have seen, although it would seem that the international community has a common interest in the environmental and resource problems discussed in this chapter, the individual members of that community, particularly states, may have varying degrees of vulnerability to such problems, and therefore often pursue different preferences regarding their resolution. Thus, even though a truly global problem like ozone depletion or climate change apparently would require international cooperation to solve it, it does not automatically follow that such cooperation will be achieved thanks to the varying sensitivities, interests and preferences noted above, plus other pathologies associated with multilateral cooperation in complex issue areas, such as the free-riding problem noted in Chapter 3.

## Agenda-setting

The first step as always is the question of agenda-setting, and here the story varies depending on the specific problem at hand. While overall international environmental awareness has increased dramatically over the past two or three decades, particularly following the 1972 UN Conference on the Human Environment (Carroll, 1988; Caldwell, 1990), attention to individual environmental or resource issues can rise or fall considerably. For ozone depletion, agenda-setting required the involvement of a large transnational ecological network, or epistemic community, of policy experts (see this chapter's case study). For global warming, the key global agenda-setting phase began with the IPCC in 1988, which studied the scientific, economic and social aspects of global warming. At the time, a number of European states called for an early commitment to stabilize $CO_2$ emissions by 2000, but this effort was strongly opposed by the UK, the US and several other states. A follow-up meeting, at the 1992 Rio 'Earth Summit,' saw slightly more agreement on weak provisions to slow global warming in the form of the UN Framework Convention on Climate Change (UN FCCC), yet again there were no firm targets or commitments, unlike in the ozone case. At least by this point, however, the international community was paying far more attention to the topic than just a few years before, and agreed to stage a major conference to be held in Japan in 1997 (Litfin, 2000).

The question of fossil fuels depletion has been on the global agenda for decades, though mainly in terms of maintaining stable supplies rather than proactively confronting the looming problem of a complete depletion of these supplies. The most significant factor of the post-war period in this area involved two dramatic price hikes, in 1973 and 1979, engineered by OPEC, which vividly focused global attention on OPEC's potential as a political stakeholder. Similarly, a series of price hikes in the aftermath of the 2003 Iraq war, when oil hovered near $100 a barrel rather than around the post-war average of about $25 a barrel in constant dollars, plus greater attention to the problem of global warming – which is partly a product of fossil fuel burning – have stimulated a more explicit debate about a world without fossil fuels; this debate also takes place in the shadow of discussions about arresting global climate change. Even so, a dramatic recent decline in oil prices, to less than $60 a barrel after 2013, owing to oversupply, seems to have reduced some of the political pressures regarding how to cope with a post-carbon world, at least temporarily. Water depletion has received the least amount of attention relative to these other issues, although several security studies produced independently by major stakeholders, such as the UN, the EU and the US, have pointed to the potential for more water stress-related conflicts and other problems, such as public health. Yet the fact that most water-stressed regions exist in the less developed world means that global agenda-setting in this area will almost always be subordinated to other security concerns of the major powers, which are of course quite extensive.

## Framing policy alternatives

As all of the problems discussed in this chapter generally stem from the negative externalities of human behaviours, all policy alternatives in turn attempt to set global and/or regional standards to protect the environment and conserve scarce natural resources. Yet the scope and clarity of these multilateral environmental agreements (MEAs), if they can be agreed, can vary widely depending on the politics of each specific problem. For example, they may apply to varying levels of analysis, from states to firms to individual households/consumers, and they may specify very general or very specific behavioural targets, or none at all ('cheap talk').

The framing of the ozone depletion problem was relatively straightforward compared to the other problems discussed in this chapter: the international community would have to reduce or cease, as far as possible, the use and production of CFCs and other industrial gases that negatively impact the ozone layer. This understanding was clearly reflected in the 1987 Montreal Protocol, as discussed in the case study below. For global warming, the range of alternatives is far more complex owing to the wide variety of factors thought to be responsible for the problem, particularly the types and sources of various GHGs emitted worldwide. Potential solutions range from doing virtually nothing to allowing states to set their own targets to devising explicit global targets and mechanisms to achieve them. Another difficult question involves how the burden of adjustment should be distributed among the parties to any agreement. This debate was compounded by the persistence of various doubts regarding the scope and origins of the problem, particularly on the part of states and firms that had an interest in fossil fuels. During multilateral talks among 150 states in Bonn and Kyoto, it was generally agreed that the burden of adjustment would be placed upon the developed and developing industrialized states, whose utilities, major industries and general standard of living involve high $CO_2$ and methane emissions on a per capita basis. This approach, however, would put the industrializing LDCs at a major disadvantage relative to their more advanced, and richer, competitors. This concern was not confined to LDCs; several industrialized states such as the US and the UK also opposed such a treaty generally on economic grounds. And although President Clinton expressed his support for a treaty during the 1990s, the US Senate, which must ratify the treaty in the US, passed a resolution urging the government not to sign such an instrument. More recent efforts have been somewhat more successful, as we shall see at the end of this chapter.

Regarding fossil fuel depletion, after years of competition over energy supplies the shock of the oil price hikes in the 1970s led to several options considered by the major powers in particular rather than the international community at large. These included, as always, a range of unilateral energy policy changes, such as diversification of supplies and energy conservation, as well as new standards for fuel efficiency. In the US, these efforts were supplanted with the creation of a Strategic Petroleum Reserve, or oil stockpile, in the amount of around 600 million barrels (on average). This amount is too small to serve as a long-term unilateral solution to America's dependency on imported fossil fuels, as it amounts to only about one month's supply based on average US consumption levels since the 1980s. Instead, it is intended primarily as a way to release oil onto global markets in hopes of counteracting short-term price hikes, whether deliberate or market-generated. Given the limits of a strictly unilateral response to a global fossil fuel economy, the US also took the lead in arranging a series of negotiations on the problem in the 1970s, which led to some concrete results (see below).

In the case of water stress, there has been very little sustained debate about the nature of the problem at the global level compared to other problems discussed in this chapter, other than in the reports noted above. As a result, there is no consensus whatsoever on the range of possible alternatives to deal with water-stressed states or regions, other than on a more localized basis. One major question involves the extent to which such communities, which are often poor, should be made to pay for water and water-related technologies, including water treatment facilities, which are often supplied by more developed states. This issue is especially critical given the role of water-related diseases, such as dysentery and diarrhoea, in killing large numbers of people in the developing world, which could be viewed as a security problem in its own right (see Chapter 12). Still, the UNDP has urged all governments to set a minimum target of 20 litres per day of clean water per person, even if it must be provided for free. While admirable, this is still an extremely low target considering the amount consumed by rich states (see Table 11.2), and would require a major redistribution of water resources, especially in sub-Saharan Africa and the Middle East – currently the most chronically water-stressed regions of the world.

## Policy choice

Given the fairly straightforward nature of the ozone depletion problem relative to other anthropogenic threats to the environment, the international community wasted little time in attempting to deal with it (see the case study, Box 11.1). As a result of concerted global action since the 1980s, starting with the Montreal Protocol, the ozone layer has recovered enough to avoid the threats posed by excessive UV-B rays. For global warming, the situation has been more complex. The initial key instrument was the 1997 Kyoto Protocol to the UN FCCC, or simply the Kyoto Protocol, which entered into force in February 2005. Currently 192 parties (191 states plus the EU) have acceded to the Kyoto Protocol, which established legally binding commitments to reduce emissions of six types of GHGs. Under its terms, which involved some of the most complex negotiations in the history of diplomacy, industrialized states agreed to reduce, by 2012, their collective GHG emissions by 5.2 per cent as compared to the baseline year of 1990, but this target is distributed unevenly across these states: some were required to make no reductions, while others were actually permitted to *increase* their emissions. The initial (2008–12) emissions targets under the UN FCCC, which are measured against 1990 levels for the vast majority of these states, are summarized in Table 11.3.

To reach these targets, the Kyoto Protocol permits the use of several mechanisms, such as emissions trading, the Clean Development Mechanism and Joint Implementation. These rules generally allow the industrialized states (listed in Annex B to Kyoto) to meet their targets by either reducing their own emissions and/or by purchasing or trading credits from other states (particularly non-Annex B states, most of which are LDCs and do not currently face GHG emission restrictions).

**Table 11.3   *UN FCCC targets, various states***

| | |
|---|---|
| Australia | 10% increase |
| Iceland | 10% increase |
| EU | 8% reduction |
| US | 7% reduction |
| Japan | 6% reduction |
| Russia | 0% |
| LDCs (includes China and India) | No targets |

In principle, this approach means that states such as the US can earn credits that can be applied to its own GHG targets by purchasing credits from Annex B states (such as Australia) whose emissions fall below their targets, or from non-Annex B states that develop their own GHG emission reduction projects such as the protection of forests and other 'carbon sinks' that help remove GHGs from the atmosphere. The overall idea is that this combination of targets and credits will create financial incentives for all parties to reduce GHG emissions and develop new emission reduction projects around the globe. Finally, Kyoto was meant to be only the first major step towards the control of GHGs, and is supposed to be enhanced with additional measures. However, in the end the US and several other Annex B states did not ratify the Kyoto Protocol, although the US remains a party to the UN FCCC, and the entire Kyoto process effectively stalled since a major follow-up conference at the Hague in 2001 failed to produce a new 'grand bargain' regarding a more comprehensive, long-term approach to climate change (Grubb and Yamin, 2001). The next phase in the effort – the Copenhagen talks of December 2009 – failed to produce more ambitious targets owing to disputes between several major players (particularly China and the US) as well as a stalemate over how much aid the rich states should be required to provide to LDCs to help them reduce their emissions. The most recent UN FCCC instrument is the Paris Agreement of December 2015, which basically allowed participating states to name their own emissions targets, known as 'Intended Nationally Determined Contributions' (INDCs), in hopes of collectively limiting global warming to below two degrees Celsius relative to the pre-industrial temperature. However, although 176 states and the EU signed this agreement (including China, India, Russia and the US), it has not yet entered into effect as the ratification process is still ongoing, and the Paris Agreement itself will be reviewed again in 2023.

On a regional basis, and in addition to pledging to reduce its emissions by at least 40 per cent by 2030 under the Paris Agreement, the EU attempted to address the climate problem by creating a new rule (EU Directive 2009/28/EC), which set mandatory targets for renewable energy among EU member states so that the EU's overall renewable energy use is 20 per cent of all energy use. Although the EU is currently well on track to reach this target (the figure for the EU as a whole was at 16 per cent in 2014), some EU states still have much further to go than others if this target is to be reached in time. Even so, it is very encouraging that the figures for renewable energy use as a percentage of total energy production have risen steadily for every single EU member state over the past decade; Table 11.4 gives the amounts for various EU member states (Eurostat website, 2015).

**Table 11.4**   *Renewable energy usage, various EU member states*

|            | 2005  | 2014  |
|------------|-------|-------|
| Sweden     | 40.8% | 52.6% |
| Latvia     | 34.9% | 38.7% |
| Finland    | 28.5% | 38.7% |
| France     | 10.3% | 14.3% |
| Germany    | 5.8%  | 13.8% |
| Italy      | 5.2%  | 17.1% |
| UK         | 1.3%  | 7.0%  |
| Luxembourg | 0.9%  | 4.5%  |

These figures clearly indicate that multilateral targets for energy can be agreed and reached among highly energy-intensive modern economies. Conversely, America's share of renewable energy was 11 per cent in 2015, putting it ahead of the UK but well behind most other EU member states. Although this figure for the US has increased in recent years (up from seven per cent in 2007), it was fairly stagnant since the early 1980s, a massive missed opportunity to lead by example and confront both global warming and fossil fuel depletion, as fossil fuels have supplied about 85 per cent of US energy needs for over 30 years.

As for fossil fuel depletion itself, the first major multilateral effort involved the creation of the International Energy Agency (IEA) in 1976 to monitor global energy supplies and facilitate joint action as a kind of 'energy consumer's consortium'. Its obvious inspiration could be traced to a desire among the major oil importing states to counterbalance the earlier creation of OPEC as an oil producer's cartel, and its current membership consists of: Australia; Austria; Belgium; Canada; Denmark; Finland; France; Germany; Greece; Hungary; Ireland; Italy; Japan; Luxembourg; Netherlands; New Zealand; Norway; Portugal; Spain; Sweden; Switzerland; Turkey; the UK; and the US. The main purpose of the IEA, which is closely linked to the OECD in Paris, is to facilitate a coordinated response to major energy price hikes or shortages, whether engineered by OPEC or otherwise. However, like OPEC, the IEA possesses no real regulatory powers of its own and relies largely on the goodwill of its member states. Its main function is to monitor energy usage and resources, pool emergency supplies of energy sources and provide oil to its member states in times of dire need; in other words, it frames 'energy security' as maintenance of the status quo rather than as an inevitable and concerted shift to a world free of fossil fuels.

## Box 11.1    Protecting the ozone layer

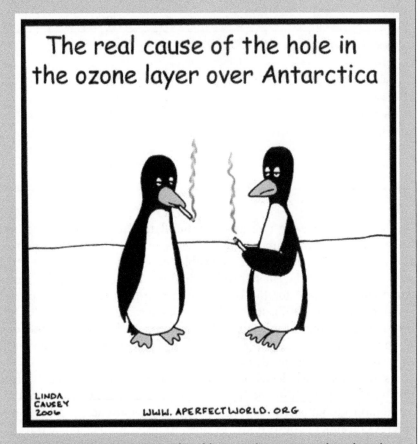

*Diagnosing severe environmental problems can be an extremely technical process.*

As noted earlier in this volume, very few international security problems actually represent a major threat to the entire global community. Instead, there are widely varying zones of stability and instability depending on the time period and problem under consideration. One exception to this involves certain global environmental issues, such as the threat posed by the emission of substances that deplete the ozone layer. How the international community realized, then acted upon, the nature of this particular threat reveals some important lessons about the use of scientific and technical expertise to address security problems.

In this case, the problem of ozone depletion is largely based on the scientific finding that the release into the atmosphere of CFCs gradually depletes

→

→

the ozone layer protecting the earth's surface from harmful UV-B rays. Hailed as safe and useful 'perfect chemicals' when discovered in 1931, CFCs are a type of industrial waste gas that can also be used as a refrigerant and propellant (as in aerosol sprays); ozone depletion due to extensive use of CFCs by consumers and firms is therefore an anthropogenic environmental problem. This finding, or the famous 'Rowland–Molina hypothesis' regarding ozone formation and decomposition, was so important that the three primary researchers behind it shared the 1995 Nobel Prize in chemistry, a clear endorsement of the problem by the scientific community after some years of controversy.

Even so, it took a high degree of activism by a range of authoritative stakeholders to convince government officials that urgent action was necessary to repair damage to the ozone layer. These stakeholders, who formed an epistemic community of scientific experts on the issue, included officials of the UN Environmental Programme, the US Environmental Protection Agency, the US State Department's Bureau of Oceans and International Environmental and Scientific Affairs, the World Meteorological Organization and other scientists from around the globe (Benedick, 1991; Haas, 1992b). In addition, their efforts were aided by the advent of new technological means of measuring the state of the ozone layer, such as satellite imagery. Growing consensus about the problem inspired the first UN international conference on the ozone layer in 1977.

However, it was not until nearly a decade later that the first major effort to reverse the damage was undertaken. This was the 1985 Vienna Convention for the protection of the ozone layer, which involved 20 states plus the European Community (later incorporated into the EU). This limited effort was followed by a more comprehensive multilateral instrument: the 1987 Montreal Protocol on Substances that Deplete the Ozone Layer, which included 27 states plus the European Community. The centrepiece of the Montreal Protocol, often called the 'most successful treaty in the history of the UN', was a firm agreement to freeze CFC levels at 1986 levels by 1990; followed by a 20 per cent reduction by 1993 and then 30 per cent more by 1998. The Montreal Protocol was followed by the 1989 Helsinki Declaration, where 86 states agreed further to gradually phase out the production and use of most ozone-depleting gases by the year 2000. Seven subsequent revisions throughout the 1990s helped to keep the agreement on track; the process also provided for a multilateral fund of over $2 billion to help LDCs phase out their use of CFCs. Thus, in this case we see some concrete measures and goals, despite some opposition among LDCs (including China and India) to the costs involved, and despite some lingering uncertainty among policy-makers, the public and even some scientists about whether there really was a problem. Even so, the level of international cooperation here was very high relative to another major anthropogenic environmental problem: global warming.

Finally, as we might expect given the discussion above, the question of water shortages has resulted in very little sustained international cooperation. The problem simply involves too much variance in vulnerability, mainly between the rich and the poor states of the globe, to permit any type of global water usage regime. Even worse, in some states endowed with fairly generous water supplies, water is not widely metered or monitored at the household level as a (potentially) scarce resource, so that individual levels of consumption can be extremely high compared to chronically water-stressed states. In the UK, for example, only about 40 per cent of water users in England and Wales are metered while the other 60 per cent of users in those countries have no way of determining their water consumption levels. This is one of the lowest levels of water metering among developed states, and a missed opportunity for the UK to lead by example regarding the conservation of water, as water utility studies have shown an average ten per cent decline in water usage after meters are installed. Conversely, about two-thirds of other OECD member states monitor the water usage of over 90 per cent of their single-family households. This wide degree of variance regarding measuring water usage across states, and even within regions of large states, means that water stress is likely to remain a 'think locally, act locally' problem for some time to come unless a major global catastrophe, such as a prolonged and severe drought in one or more rich states, focuses more attention on the problem.

## The politics of policy effectiveness

The effectiveness of multilateral responses to the types of problems discussed in this chapter is directly correlated with the willingness and ability of participating stakeholders to fulfil their obligations under specific international agreements, assuming, as always, that the agreements have targeted an appropriate solution (or solutions) to the problem, which may not be the case. In other words, stakeholders may meet their agreed goals, but those goals in turn may or may not actually impact the environment as intended. As the various stakeholders with an interest in these agreements often include not just states but also individual firms and even consumers, there is a high degree of both voluntary and involuntary defection from such agreements – again, assuming they have been negotiated and ratified in good faith in the first place.

In some cases, the stakeholders may deliberately refuse to join or ratify or implement certain agreements; in others, the stakeholders may wish to live up to their commitments but defect involuntarily because of administrative limitations, higher than anticipated costs of compliance, or simply because other political priorities demand more attention. In both cases, most environment and resource-protection agreements lack robust sanctioning mechanisms or other means of enforcement, other than 'naming and shaming', so the incentive to free-ride on the good behaviour of other stakeholders can be very tempting, and even politically rewarding, to governments who refuse to impose the costs of adjustment on their own citizens and firms. As always, these cooperative dynamics can vary widely depending on the specific environmental or resource problem under consideration. However, for the purposes of policy evaluation, it makes sense to focus primarily on whether the policy is in fact positively impacting the environmental or resource problem as defined by the international community (Bernauer, 1995); if so, we can presume that enough stakeholders have changed their behaviours to bring about this outcome even if other stakeholders have defected or refused to participate.

Taking a look at a total victory approach with our four cases covered in this chapter, only one environmental problem can be considered a possible success under this standard: global cooperation regarding the ozone layer. Although the 1987 Montreal Protocol allowed exceptions for the Soviet Union and many LDCs, these provisions did not prevent many other stakeholders – mainly the more advanced industrialized states – from implementing the agreement in good faith. Amazingly, all 193 UN member states, plus the EU, have ratified the Montreal Protocol, making it (and its successor pacts) the first and so far only universally agreed treaty in the history of the UN. Based on the high degree of compliance with this and subsequent measures, the expert assessment is that the ozone layer will return to its pre-1980 levels by around 2050 (World Meteorological Organization, 2007). A critical factor behind this very high degree of compliance is that alternatives to CFCs do exist, and the firms that rely heavily on CFCs can be retooled to adopt new types of refrigerants and propellants. As a result of this measure and similar efforts, ozone depletion has been slowed considerably relative to the situation in the 1980s, although all parties to these agreements will need to maintain their vigilance if the ozone layer is to be preserved indefinitely.

The historical trends standard is often applied to environmental problems, in the sense that some arbitrary past reference point is chosen as a baseline (such as freezing CFC emissions and phasing out the use/production of CFCs from a certain starting point), and future behaviour can be measured against it. The case of ozone protection has met this standard, which is why it may be approaching the level of success of a total victory standard. The case of global warming, however, is far more worrying, as most states have not even come close to fulfilling their obligations regarding GHG emissions under the Kyoto Protocol. Although most parties to Kyoto have created new national authorities to manage their commitments to the treaty, the market-creating aspects of the GHG emissions scheme have not developed as expected (Victor, 2001). Even states that strongly support such targets, such as many EU member states, have failed to comply with the standards expected of Kyoto because of the involuntary defection problems (or excuses) noted above. Moreover, according to the UN's own figures, the 5.2 per cent GHG reduction target against 1990 levels actually represents only a 29 per cent reduction in the GHG emissions that would have been expected by 2010 without the Treaty, so this instrument is in fact quite limited compared to the actual scope of the problem, even if all parties did meet their targets in 2012 (which did not happen). The figures used in the Kyoto Protocol also do not include international aviation and shipping, both of which contribute considerable amounts of GHGs into the atmosphere. Despite the hype surrounding it, the recent Paris Agreement does not do much better than Kyoto, as the emissions targets under Paris are determined on a national basis and there are no binding enforcement mechanisms. Even assuming it enters into effect, and even assuming that the leading polluters (particularly China and the US, which together account for 40 per cent of global emissions) live up to their obligations, many experts agree that the current INDCs are not ambitious enough to keep global warming below two degrees Celsius. In other words, the Agreement has already failed to force participants to take adequate measures to reach the main target, even before it has entered into effect.

The situation is even worse with the problems of fossil fuel and water depletion/distribution, where clear global targets for conservation and diversification have been difficult if not impossible to achieve and/or enforce. Although some individual states have adopted (for example) increasingly high fuel efficiency standards for cars and similar energy-saving measures, such as higher taxes on cars with less fuel efficiency, other states, particularly the auto-saturated US, continue to allow the production and sale of extremely fuel inefficient automobiles and similar products without seriously attempting to change the behaviour of individual consumers (although some individual US states, like California, have attempted to address this problem). The energy market has yet to settle on a clear, and much cheaper, alternative to fossil fuels (fuel cells, nuclear, solar, wind, electric cars and so on), so there is no strong market incentive to develop a new infrastructure to replace the current one based on fossil fuels. This aversion to fundamental change, which would have to be engineered by states in the absence of a broad market incentive, also affects the global warming problem, as greater fuel inefficiency, and continued reliance on fossil fuels in general, results in more GHGs.

Similarly, although the IEA during the 1980s seems to have prevented any major OPEC-orchestrated oil price shocks as experienced during the 1970s, oil prices have skyrocketed in recent years, especially following the wars in Afghanistan and Iraq. In addition, some individual energy-rich states (such as Russia) have deliberately used their supplies as a political tool, even to the extent of cutting off gas supplies to various parts of Europe. Equally remarkable is that some automobile manufacturers, particularly Volkswagen, were found recently to be falsifying the 'official' emission standards of their own products through the use of engine software. This indicates that behavioural standards for states and firms are not enough; they must be policed rigorously as well, which can vary widely depending on the state and/or the industry involved. The case of water depletion is perhaps the worst of all, as there are no stringent global standards or other mechanisms to encourage more water equity and conservation among states other than the UNDP's 20 litres per person per day target which the UNDP, of course, cannot enforce. In fact, some studies predict that nearly half of the world's population will face some degree of water stress by 2030; if so, the global political pressures behind this problem are likely to increase at some point. Until stronger international cooperation is agreed, many individual states, including most advanced states, have taken matters into their own hands by adopting household water metering and pricing, plus official water restrictions in certain temporarily water-stressed areas, to protect their aquifers. These unilateral and local measures are to be commended from the perspective of national or domestic water security, yet they should be leveraged much more by devising clearer global standards for states and other stakeholders, whether rich or poor, who continue to act as if fresh, clean water is a completely free and unlimited natural resource.

Finally, a comparative metrics approach can also be useful to judge the effectiveness of various policies covered in this chapter. This can take two general forms. First, one can simply compare states or other stakeholders against each other in terms of their performance regarding CFCs and GHG emissions, or energy/water conservation. This approach allows an analyst to identify the 'worst of the worst' or the 'best of the best' stakeholders in terms of various behavioural standards, which is often useful for naming and shaming. A second approach involves measuring behaviour against some current and/or future target rather than a historical benchmark. These targets can be very specific, as with the Kyoto Protocol goal of a 5.2 per cent reduction since 1990s levels of GHG emissions. Again, we see wide variance here under both standards – which can be easily combined into a single evaluation – across the four cases covered in this chapter. Only the case of ozone protection can be considered a success here, as most stakeholders have complied with their targets on CFC emissions. For global warming, Table 11.5 indicates which states were struggling to meet their Kyoto standards.

Of course, emissions from these states have been offset by states that have met or exceeded their targets, such as many central/East European states, Germany and the UK. Still, many of the all-important Annex B parties to the Kyoto Protocol ultimately failed to reach their emissions

Table 11.5    *Changes in GHG emissions, 1990–2004, selected Annex B*
*states*

|  | Kyoto target (2012 deadline) | Actual changes |
|---|---|---|
| Austria | 8% reduction | 15.7% increase |
| Canada | 6% reduction | 26.6% increase |
| Finland | 8% reduction | 14.5% increase |
| Greece | 8% reduction | 26.6% increase |
| Ireland | 8% reduction | 23.1% increase |
| Italy | 8% reduction | 12.1% increase |
| Japan | 6% reduction | 6.5% increase |
| Portugal | 8% reduction | 41% increase |
| Spain | 8% reduction | 49% increase |
| US | 7% reduction (not ratified by the Senate) | 15.8% increase |

*Source:* UN FCCC website.

reduction targets by 2012, and it seems fairly clear that the 2015 Paris Agreement is not ambitious enough, in its current form with its current INDC targets, to reach its own goals.

## Summary

As the discussion above demonstrates, a net assessment of international environmental security problems would vary quite widely. For ozone depletion, the assessment would focus primarily on the economic costs of adjustment, which were largely focused on the advanced industrialized states. These involved both adjustment costs derived from switching from CFCs to other types of refrigerants and propellants, and the opportunity costs of lost economic activity for a very narrow range of industries. As the threat posed by ozone depletion was so severe and clearly global in nature, and supported by sound scientific evidence, these costs have been well worth the benefits. For global warming, the assessment also primarily involves economic costs, yet these are diffused far more widely than in the case of ozone depletion, which is precisely why various stakeholders, whether states, firms or consumers, can be so tempted to free-ride on the adjustments made by others. Since the burden of policing GHG emissions is left to individual states, governments must become far more vigilant in their reduction of GHGs – which generally means imposing economic costs on firms and consumers – if they expect to meet their commitments. Such an effort need not become as draconian as it sounds; governments can use both carrots and sticks to encourage a reduction in carbon emissions within their states, as in the form of financial incentives or tax penalties (or both). At the moment, efforts such as voluntary carbon-offsetting payments made by airline passengers and similar measures are simply far too limited in scope to confront the problem, as the Stern Review on the Economics of Climate Change argues (Stern, 2009). Moreover, the exclusion from the Kyoto regime of the US and other major carbon emitters means that even if the more advanced economies eventually meet their targets, which is highly unlikely, the emissions of China, India and other growing states would easily offset those emissions cuts so that the net effect of the regime is negligible relative to the scope of the problem, even though all Annex B parties (that is, not including the US) taken together have collectively reduced their emissions by about 15 per cent between 1990 and 2004. Like the Kyoto Protocol, the recent Paris Agreement does reinforce the global understanding that climate change is a serious problem, but not in terms nearly as forceful as the Montreal Protocol on ozone. Thus, we are still largely in a 'wait and see' mode on climate change.

With fossil fuels and water depletion, the story is similarly very mixed in terms of an overall net assessment. Part of the assessment on fossil fuels involves implementation of the Kyoto Protocol and (potentially) the Paris Agreement, which as we have seen has been extremely uneven over the past decade and a half. Beyond these instruments, the benefits of more adjustment in the form of conservation and alternative energy sources would seem to justify the economic costs, yet many states in both the developed and developing worlds are simply not willing to make such an adjustment until the problem becomes far more acute. Most member states of the EU represent a major notable exception to this attitude. For the US in particular, the costs of foreign oil dependence over the past several decades seem to have been much greater than appreciated, so that a reduction in domestic demand through energy conservation or diversification could be far more beneficial than recent government policy, and the oil industry itself, suggests (Duffield, 2008). Some observers put their faith into advances in technology and new fossil fuel discoveries (including oil and gas recovered from shale), which may extend the time horizon a few more years or decades. This long-term nature of the problem coupled with the economic (and thus political) costs of adjustment make it highly unlikely that a new global agreement on the conservation of fossil fuels or the diversification of global energy supplies will be forthcoming.

For water depletion, a global net assessment is even more difficult as there are no binding global standards or agreements to analyse. Instead, performance here is measured in terms of individual states, and those with chronic water stress are often willing, though not always able, to adjust their water policies as necessary even while other states take a far more relaxed attitude. The idea of a more robust global policy, as in the form of comprehensive household water metering and/or the use of stockpiles or even transfers from water-rich areas to water-stressed areas, is well beyond the political will of most of the great powers in the system. As these states do not suffer to the same degree as severely water-stressed regions, as in Africa, there is little hope that the problem of water depletion will receive the sustained global attention it deserves considering the critical role of this resource in sustaining life on earth. In other words, water stress may remain a national, rather than international, security problem for some time to come.

In the final analysis, and like many aspects of international economic security, the global environmental and resource depletion problems discussed in this chapter are fundamentally linked to the 'normal' (i.e. not criminal or unusual) behaviours of billions of individual firms and consumers. The ultimate responsibility for policing these stakeholders rests with the individual states in the system, and their willingness and ability to assume that role varies extremely widely. Elected officials are often punished for imposing new costs on their constituents, even if there is general agreement that something should be done about the problems discussed in this chapter. The Montreal Protocol on ozone depletion is a very rare example of the type of global agreement required to hold states to specific obligations regarding environmental problems; such agreements can be very successful if states then follow through with their commitments. In this case, a unique combination – consensual knowledge over the problem itself, a high degree of *global* vulnerability and a firm solution that concentrates costs on several key stakeholders while providing assistance to LDCs – helped to move international cooperation forward. This combination, however, is conspicuously lacking in the other cases discussed in this chapter. Thus we may have to suffer a truly serious global or regional crisis involving climate change, fossil fuels or water shortages before the major powers, and thus the international community at large, adopt far more stringent measures to prevent an even worse future catastrophe.

## Further reading

Jon Barnett (2001). *The Meaning of Environmental Security: Ecological Politics and Policy in the New Security Arena*. London: Zed Books.

John E. Carroll (ed.) (1988). *International Environmental Diplomacy: The Management and Resolution of Transfrontier Environmental Problems*. Cambridge: Cambridge University Press.

Simon Dalby (2002). *Environmental Security*. Minneapolis: University of Minnesota Press.

Simon Dalby (2009). *Security and Environmental Change*. Cambridge: Polity.

Elizabeth R. DeSombre (2000). *Domestic Sources of International Environmental Policy: Industry, Environmentalists, and US Power*. Cambridge: The MIT Press.

Daniel H. Deudney and Richard A. Matthew (1999). *Contested Grounds: Security and Conflict in the New Environmental Politics*. Albany: SUNY Press.

Peter M. Haas, Robert O. Keohane and Marc A. Levy (eds.) (1993). *Institutions for the Earth: Sources of Effective International Environmental Protection*. Cambridge: MIT Press.

Thomas F. Homer-Dixon (1999). *Environment, Scarcity, and Violence*. Princeton: Princeton University Press.

Daniel Moran (ed.) (2011). *Climate Change and National Security: A Country-Level Analysis*. Washington, DC: Georgetown University Press.

William D. Nordhaus (2013). *The Climate Casino: Risk, Uncertainty, and Economics for a Warming World*. New Haven: Yale University Press.

Nicholas Stern (2009). *A Blueprint for a Safer Planet: How to Manage Climate Change and Create a New Era of Progress and Prosperity*. New York: The Bodley Head.

David G. Victor (2001). *The Collapse of the Kyoto Protocol and the Struggle to Slow Global Warming*. Princeton: Princeton University Press.

# Chapter 12

# Public Health

The analysis of problems related to public health in terms of their relationship to international security is very similar to the discussion of environmental issues in the previous chapter, and of population issues to be discussed in Chapter 13. Specifically, the more traditional or orthodox view of this topic would focus primarily on narrow or direct threats to international security, as in the form of a major infectious disease outbreak or a terrorist attack with biological weapons (i.e. 'biosecurity'; see Koblentz, 2010). A much broader view of this topic, framed in terms of the new security or human security agenda, would consider indirect health problems as well, such as high levels of infant mortality in LDCs or the role of public health issues in undermining government authority or stability. In this sense the human security agenda can become virtually indistinguishable from the international development agenda, which would stress health-related goals in LDCs such as access to clean water, adequate food, antenatal care and so on. Obviously these agendas are closely linked: vulnerability to a specific threat such as an infectious disease outbreak is strongly conditioned by vulnerability to broader problems involving sanitation, nutrition and adequate medical care. As always, however, our focus here is on the political framing and response (if any) to these problems as urgent international *security* threats rather than as long-term international development or human rights issues. From this perspective, it will become clear why certain public health problems are framed in such a manner while others are either ignored or marginalized by the international community despite their obvious negative impact on millions, if not billions, of human beings.

The question of framing public health problems as international security threats also raises important concerns regarding the more general relationship between LDCs, including rapidly developing states such as China and India, and the developed world. Public health and sanitation practices vary widely between these two worlds and this disparity can contribute to the spread of health-related security threats from LDCs to more developed states. This perception of diseases originating in, and spreading from, LDCs to the developed world can lead to attempts to contain the problem in LDCs, in the form of temporary travel restrictions or more comprehensive immigration policies. Conversely, efforts by the developed states to aid or otherwise improve public health or nutrition in LDCs can provoke a political backlash in poor countries, as these problems are often closely related to social and cultural norms involving childbirth, gender, sexual practices, burial rituals, food preparation and so on. Local populations, and even government officials, in LDCs might easily interpret public health aid policies promoted by rich states in terms of 'neo-colonial' or 'cultural imperialist' practices intended to control or even reduce the populations of LDCs; this problem will receive further attention in Chapter 13.

These views are not unreasonable considering the historical relationship between LDCs, particularly former colonies, and the developed world; moreover, an explicit rejection of such aid policies on the part of governments in LDCs can often improve their domestic political support, a very tempting option in the case of weak or failing states. In addition, public health issues can be viewed to some degree as anthropogenic threats: diseases and similar health problems may arise through natural biological processes, yet they can also be transmitted via the activities of human beings. Effective policies therefore must address both the underlying causes of such problems as well as the behaviours and perceptions of individual humans that may exacerbate the problem, such as poor hygiene or refusing to see a doctor or be vaccinated until it is too late. These factors, as with any other forms of intervention in the name of international security, must always be kept in mind when considering various policy options. If these policies are not handled carefully and sensitively, efforts by international security specialists could easily provoke more North–South conflict, and even a long-term backlash against Western medical treatments and social practices, and thus greatly undermine the prospects of handling any specific threat to international public health.

## Public health and international security

Multiple contextual factors are responsible for the gradual rise in international involvement in public health issues since WWII. These factors include: regular outbreaks of infectious disease on a national, regional and global scale; the development of new technologies and medicines to deal with such problems; growing awareness of the persistent gap in health, nutrition and sanitation standards between the developed and developing worlds; public concerns about the safety of foods and medicines traded among states and the threat of terrorist attacks involving chemical or biological weapons (Price-Smith, 2001a and 2001b; Kelle, 2007). The regular occurrence of intrastate wars over the past several decades is another contributing factor, as wars of any type tend to create public health problems in the forms of communicable diseases and the inadequate provision of nutrition and sanitation (Iqbal, 2006). Globalization and related demographic factors, such as urbanization, directly intensify all of these trends, in both negative and positive ways: globalization can make it much easier for an infectious disease to spread quickly, but can also make it much easier for public health authorities and other experts to share information and distribute potential remedies. However, these general factors alone cannot explain how the international community might interpret a specific public health problem as a threat to international security, so we need to take a closer look at the politics of threat perception in this domain.

## Destructive scale

There are various ways to frame health issues as international security threats. The simplest method involves measuring the direct human costs involved, in terms of the number of deaths attributed to a certain public health problem. From this perspective the problem of deadly infectious disease is especially salient (Peterson, 2002–3), as regional and global outbreaks, or epidemics and pandemics, of such diseases occur regularly across the globe. Table 12.1 summarizes some of the deadliest such outbreaks in modern history.

These figures clearly indicate that the potential destructiveness of a major outbreak is indeed serious enough to warrant attention by the international community, which is in fact exactly what we have seen in the past several decades of international public health policy. Two twentieth-century pandemics in particular – Spanish flu and HIV/AIDS – are often cited as major reference points in policy discussions regarding the security implications of infectious disease. Even the Asian and Hong Kong influenzas were each more than five times as deadly as normal seasonal flu; in the UK, for example, around 4,000–8,000 people die during a normal flu season, as compared to around 30,000 deaths during each of the 1957 and 1968 outbreaks. Smaller-scale outbreaks, such as Severe Acute

Table 12.1   *Major deadly pandemics*

| Pandemic | Estimated number of deaths |
|---|---|
| Black Death (1346–59) | 25 million |
| Bombay Plague (1898) | 6 million |
| 'Spanish' influenza (1918) | 40–50 million+ |
| Asian influenza (1957–8) | 2 million |
| Hong Kong influenza (1968–70) | 1 million |
| HIV/AIDS (1981–present) | 34 million |

Respiratory Syndrome (SARS) in 2003, which caused about 800 deaths worldwide until it was contained, as well as so-called 'avian flu' (more correctly known as influenza A virus subtype H5N1) and 'swine flu' (subtype H1N1) can also invite enough political attention to qualify as security threats if recent experience is any guide.

A second approach would take a much broader view, and examine the other human costs – beyond actual deaths – associated with public health problems such as infectious disease but also poor sanitation and nutrition, lack of adequate health care, lack of adequate education about nutrition and health practices and so on. These costs would include not just deaths but also injuries or chronic illnesses, loss of economic output, problems with human reproduction, the creation of orphans, a rise in poverty and crime rates and other problems associated with inadequate public health standards. For example, the spread of HIV/AIDS alone has produced more than 15 million orphans worldwide, which poses a major drain on social and government resources. This broader view of the inherent destructiveness of certain public health problems is linked very closely to the human security agenda; however, it will receive limited attention in the rest of this chapter as it is more closely associated with the politics and policies of international development, and humanitarian aid/human rights, rather than with international *security* affairs, although there are of course some overlapping concerns here, as we shall see.

Finally, a third approach would take the most orthodox and narrow view and measure public health security threats in terms of their specific impact on state strength/stability and/or levels of organized violence, in the manner of so-called 'resource wars' discussed in Chapter 11. In this view, the deaths attributed to a certain public health problem should be viewed as an international security threat only if they can be linked to more traditional security concerns, such as intrastate war or biological terrorism. In addition, a failure on the part of a government to deal adequately with certain public health problems or natural disasters could reduce its authority or stability, which might make it more susceptible to more traditional security problems. Some scholars have in fact attempted to demonstrate such a link, particularly involving the spread of HIV/AIDS in sub-Saharan Africa (Elbe, 2002; Price-Smith, 2004). In this case, HIV/AIDS has even been used as a kind of biological weapon when HIV-infected military personnel rape and thus deliberately infect enemy civilians as a way to destroy present and future generations of those poor individuals. This type of behaviour, for some scholars, helps to further justify the treatment of HIV/AIDS as a security problem as compared to other types of deadly infectious diseases. If no such link is evident, then we may be dealing with a standard domestic or international *public health problem* rather than a *public health-related international security problem*. There is of course no sharp line between these two categories, which are determined more by the views of various stakeholders discussed below rather than by the inherent destructive characteristics of the problem itself.

## Geographic and temporal scope

In terms of framing public health problems as international security concerns, the potential for such problems to spill over to other states, and/or to persist for fairly long periods of time, is nearly as important as the actual destructiveness associated with such problems. Here the truly global nature of a deadly infectious disease pandemic affecting a large number of states, as with the 1918 Spanish flu, is especially frightening to the average citizen as well as to the experts. Indeed, some have argued that there is an inherent, and even primal, human dread of death by poison or infection (Stern, 2002–3; Kittelsen, 2009), given humankind's long historical and cultural experience with infectious disease and related physical ailments. The image of an unstoppable deadly plague spreading throughout society or from one state to another, leaving thousands dead in its wake, is an especially powerful and frightening one for most people and therefore can be manipulated or exploited easily by the media, politicians, activists and others. Even the head of the WHO, Margaret Chan, has admitted that a major outbreak of a drug-resistant form of tuberculosis (TB) could be a huge challenge for the international community, and even take the world back to the pre-antibiotic era when there was simply no real possibility to treat such a deadly disease. In early 2008 the first-ever such case of extreme drug-resistant TB (or XDR-TB) was diagnosed in the UK, in a patient who had arrived from Somalia. Other isolated cases of XDR-TB, which kills 98 per cent of those infected within about two weeks, have already appeared throughout the world, including most OECD states.

A different threat calculation, however, is involved in public health problems that are confined to a single state or a single region within a state owing to health practices, prophylactic measures, geography/environment, cultural norms or other factors. Here is where the contrast between developed states and LDCs is most apparent, as many, if not all, LDCs suffer from chronic public health problems – such as malaria, TB, cholera, West Nile virus, syphilis, polio, dysentery, hepatitis and others – that are rarely, if ever, framed as international *security* concerns; for example, malaria alone kills around 450,000 people a year, mostly in Africa. Similarly, the Zika virus, which is spread primarily by mosquitoes and causes birth defects, has been confined to Africa for decades, but then made headlines when it spread to the Americas in 2015. This variance in vulnerability to certain diseases is why the policy of containment or quarantine is so tempting, but also so controversial for many LDCs and others sympathetic to the problems of the developing world: it may be effective in the short term to prevent an outbreak from spreading from LDCs to the developed world, but does little to assuage the longer-term health problems of people in LDCs. This fact is directly related to the more general debate between quarantine versus prophylactic measures versus treatment regarding international public health problems, as we shall see in the discussion of policy options below. Even in the case of HIV/AIDS, a pandemic which has killed tens of millions since its discovery in 1981, the fact that most infections and deaths are actually confined to a single region – sub-Saharan Africa – can help to undermine, for some, the sense of urgency required to frame it as an international *security* problem; currently 69 per cent of the 34 million HIV-positive people in the world (including 91 per cent of the world's HIV-infected children) live in sub-Saharan Africa.

## Likelihood

The question of containment (or geographic scope) above is related to, and certainly more straightforward than, the question of whether a public health problem will occur in the first place. Here we must find some degree of consensual knowledge regarding the nature of the problem itself, and the nature of the threatened population. For outbreaks of a known infectious disease, for example, it is usually possible to estimate the rate of spread (or rate of *morbidity* or *incidence*) and the rate of death (or *mortality*). For example, in January 2000 a US National Intelligence estimate projected that 25 per cent of Africa's population was likely to die of AIDS in light of figures available at that time (a 25 per cent mortality rate in the region). Most of these dead individuals are (or will be) adults, and up to three million people per year have died of AIDS-related illnesses in some years, a staggering figure compared to the number of deaths regularly caused by other security problems discussed in this volume, including intrastate war. It has also been estimated that the morbidity or incidence rate of HIV/AIDS in this region was around 5,000 new infections per day. These figures, which are collected by the WHO and the Joint UN Programme on HIV/AIDS (UNAIDS), can then be used to guide domestic and international policy to either prevent and/or treat the disease in question. Figure 12.1 shows how AIDS in particular grew steadily as a global threat, which had a corresponding effect on the public response to the disease.

The situation obviously becomes far more complicated when attempting to predict a future outbreak of any disease or similar public health problem, especially one whose features are unknown to us, such as a new flu strain, which can mutate as it infects a population. For example, for more than two decades, influenza experts have been predicting a major outbreak of a deadly new flu strain that could reach pandemic proportions; the recent outbreaks of avian flu (2006) and swine flu (2009) have also been mentioned in such terms by some experts. The WHO even took the rare step of declaring the swine flu outbreak to be a true pandemic, as

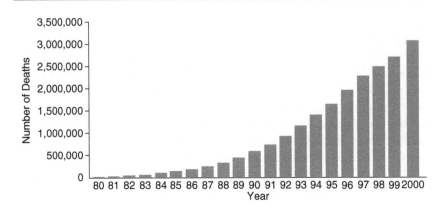

**Figure 12.1**    *Estimated AIDS-related deaths*

this flu strain was identified as a genetic descendant of the deadly 1918 Spanish influenza. Further, both avian and swine flu are thought by virologists to be related to industrial farming practices, especially in China, which greatly increases the occurrence of new viruses as they mutate among unhealthy animals heavily dosed with antibiotics. The worst combination would be a new virus as infectious as swine flu and as deadly as avian flu, which is a possibility but difficult to predict with any accuracy. Computer models are also possible, yet these can predict widely varying scenarios depending on the assumptions on which they are based. One model developed in the UK in 2006 predicted that over half of the UK population would become infected within three months of a flu pandemic; these figures and similar studies recommended that the UK increase its stockpiles of antiviral drugs to cope with such a crisis. This level of disaster certainly did not occur with the avian flu, and may not apply either to swine flu or any other flu pandemic unless it is especially contagious. Even so, the UK's chief medical officer still argued in mid-2009 that as many as 65,000 people in the UK could die from swine flu – in a worst case scenario, of course – after the virus had actually killed only 29 people at the time.

Even in the case of a better-understood disease such as HIV/AIDS, we can see disagreement about the likelihood of the threat. For example, some experts argue that sub-Saharan Africa is merely the 'tip of the iceberg' for this disease and will be followed by major outbreaks in Asia (particularly China and India) in the next few years; the former Soviet Union states are also mentioned as potential trouble spots (Piot, 2015). Similarly, both polio and smallpox have been the focus of major global eradication programmes using vaccines, yet both diseases stubbornly persist in certain parts of the world, such as India and Nigeria. More recently, in December

2013 an Ebola outbreak in West Africa caught local and international health authorities by surprise and killed over 11,000 people before it was contained (supposedly) after two years of turmoil in Guinea, Sierra Leone and Liberia. Thus, in all cases it must be kept in mind that health and disease figures can involve unreliable or unconfirmed data sources, and therefore can be contested or even wholly rejected by certain stakeholders, so they are unreliable *on their own* as indicators of the security implications of an international public health problem. Instead, they must be contextualized in light of various political considerations, as we shall see in the discussion of policy options. We should also note that the effective surveillance/containment of major public health problems such as HIV/ AIDS or flu is becoming one of the most sensitive but important questions regarding domestic and international security.

## Recovery

A final consideration regarding the consensual knowledge associated with international public health issues involves the potential to recover from such threats. Here the potential varies quite widely, which partly explains why the international community treats these problems in such a wide variety of ways. For deadly infectious diseases, a major pandemic that kills thousands if not millions of people could be as catastrophic as a major war: between 1346 and 1359 the Black Death plague killed about one-third of Europe's population – or 25 million people – and the recovery took decades, while HIV/AIDS has produced even greater casualties over the course of a single generation. However, and beyond human casualty statistics, the property damage from major pandemics is typically not as severe as that in a war; instead, the recovery can be undermined by the possibility that the disease has not been contained, or that it might soon flare up again, especially in a new, possibly more virulent, form, so that known infected regions remain cut off from the rest of the world for months or even years. This could delay or even prevent a recovery until the international community has regained confidence in the public health situation in that region (or state). Thus the recovery from a major public health problem can involve considerations well beyond those associated with war or natural disasters, as an open-ended aspect to such problems effectively stalls a full recovery until other major stakeholders – such as the WHO and the major powers – give the region/state a public health seal of approval and begin dealing with it again. This determination, however, involves major *political* considerations well beyond the inherent scientific or technical aspects of the problem at hand, and such a decision can even be used to embarrass or shame a government into cooperating with the international community, as happened with the controversial SARS outbreak in China in 2003 (see this chapter's case study).

## Stakeholder factors

Keeping a focus on the interpretation of public health problems as international security concerns, our treatment of stakeholders and preferences must be as varied as the nature of such problems themselves. Specifically, and as the discussion above suggests, vulnerabilities to such problems are not shared equally throughout the international community, unlike, for example, the case of ozone depletion. This variation in vulnerabilities or interests must then be coupled with the specific preferences and power resources of relevant political stakeholders to determine if and how the international community will define a public health problem as a security threat.

### Principal stakeholders

Problems related to public health obviously can be quite scientific/technical in nature, which creates a political opportunity for various experts to play a role in the international management of such problems. These experts might include physicians, epidemiologists, nutritionists, humanitarian aid workers with specialized knowledge (such as *Médecins Sans Frontières*), pharmacologists and other professionals whose technical training and experience may give them a unique degree of authority in interpreting and managing public health crises such as infectious disease (Vogel, 2013–14). To the extent that these individuals share their technical knowledge and assert common policy preferences regarding a certain health problem, they might be viewed as a kind of public health epistemic community, similar to those involving ozone depletion or climate change as discussed in Chapter 11. This community to some degree has been institutionalized in the form of the WHO and other UN bodies devoted to more general issues (such as the UN Food and Agriculture Organization, or FAO) or to more specific problems involving diseases (such as UNAIDS) or food safety (such as the FAO/WHO Codex Alimentarius Agreement). This UN network is linked to its regional equivalents in some areas, particularly the EU (such as the European Medicines Agency, or EMA, and the European Food Safety Authority, or EFSA). In addition, the trade-related aspects of food and medicines safety are dealt with by the WTO and its related agreements, such as the Agreement on Sanitary and Phytosanitary Measures (or SPS) and the World Organization for Animal Health (known by its original French acronym, OIE).

However, these international authorities, whose interests and preferences may vary (see the next section below), typically must cooperate with local and national authorities at the domestic level of analysis. If such cooperation is not forthcoming, the prospects for effectively managing a security-related public health issue may diminish considerably. Although domestic public health authorities may share the same views as their international counterparts – which is not always the case – local and national political leaders and other important domestic stakeholders, such as cultural or religious leaders, may attempt to play a role in such situations. This involvement can occur on the part of both aid-providing and aid-receiving states, and can either enhance or undermine the international response to a certain public health problem. The 2013 West African Ebola outbreak noted above involved such problems, as local and international authorities did not cooperate effectively and quickly enough to contain the problem. When we also factor in the varying vulnerabilities of different states to a wide range of potential public health problems, it should become clear that an optimal international response to even the most serious of health crises cannot always be taken for granted: it must be deliberately coordinated. To understand why this is so, we need to examine the interests and preferences of these stakeholders in more detail.

## Interests and preferences

In Chapter 11 we noted the major interest and preference cleavages between the developed world and the developing world regarding problems related to environmental protection and resource depletion. Specifically, much of the human suffering involving such problems occurs in LDCs, while the bulk of the political and financial capital available to solve them is located in the developed world. Even in the case of a truly global problem such as climate change, there are major differences in the abilities of states to adapt to such a threat. The same proposition generally holds here, with one critical caveat: the possibility of also containing public health-related damage in LDCs or other affected states. Such containment can occur through the use of outright travel or migration bans (or a *de facto* international quarantine) and/or the use of vaccines, antibiotics or other technologies more widely available in rich states as compared to poor ones. This fact, in turn, means that in cases where a public health problem can be confined, and/or is slow-moving enough to allow a more measured or conservative response on the part of most states (namely the major powers), then such a problem may be interpreted as a humanitarian aid issue rather than as an international security crisis.

This variation in general interests depending on who is suffering from a public health problem and whether it can spread to the rest of the world is compounded further by the policy preferences of the various stakeholders noted above. Even among international public health experts who generally share the same interest, as in the WHO or UNAIDS, we often find policy disputes regarding the question of 'securitizing' a public health problem (Elbe, 2006; Kelle, 2007; Hanrieder and Kreuder-Sonnen, 2014) or the most cost-effective way to manage it: whether through prevention or treatment, for example. This tension is especially prominent in the case of HIV/AIDS, yet it applies to a full range of public health issues. These experts in turn must often compete with other international authorities, such as WTO officials, who might be reluctant to impose trade or other restrictions because of their negative economic impact. Finally, once again we must consider the varying preferences of domestic stakeholders, whether health experts, political officials, advocacy groups for particular diseases or cultural/religious leaders, located in aid-providing and aid-receiving states (Fenio, 2011). As we shall see, there are unfortunately recurring cases of a conflict of policy preferences among these stakeholders, which can easily undermine the provision of assistance on the part of aid providers (usually rich states) and/or the acceptance of assistance on the part of aid-receiving states (usually LDCs). Further, even when the national public authorities on both sides may agree completely on the terms of a donor–recipient relationship, involuntary defection on either side can make implementation extremely difficult if local authorities, and even individual citizens, refuse to change their behaviours for a variety of reasons.

## The use of force

The extent to which force can and should be used in response to an international or domestic public health problem is one of the most underexplored and contentious topics under consideration in this volume. As we shall see, national authorities in well-developed states typically have little reluctance to impose and enforce a physical quarantine if a public health emergency is severe enough. This approach, however, might be difficult if not impossible in weak states; even if local and national authorities have the required resources and legitimacy to quarantine people, the problem may be too fast-moving for them to contain effectively. It has worked under certain circumstances, however, as with the 2003 SARS outbreak (see the case study) and the 2013 West African Ebola outbreak. It is also possible to impose restrictions on the movements of animals, as in the case of outbreaks related to influenza in birds or pigs (for example). An even more intriguing question involves the imposition of international quarantines imposed upon states or localities where a major public health crisis has occurred. States may be able to prevent ordinary travel on various types of transportation, but can and should they use military force to stop and investigate, for example, a ship suspected of carrying infected persons or cargo? In addition, what if the state or locality subject to an international quarantine refuses to abide by it, especially if it had little or no opportunity to play a role in deciding that quarantine? These are not just hypothetical questions; as we shall see below, several contemporary international public health emergencies have involved precisely these types of considerations, and they may deserve more attention in the literature on international security affairs than they currently receive.

## Public–private domains and levels of jurisdiction

The question of organizing and distributing public health assistance to states with such problems, as well as the question of organizing a more severe response in the form of enforced vaccinations or quarantines, are complicated further by this very simple question: who has the authority to make and enforce such decisions on the part of the international community? The answer to that question can vary widely depending on the nature of the problem and the actual states involved. Although international authorities such as the WHO have taken on more *de facto* authority in this area in recent years (see below), a great deal of the political implementation of WHO guidelines still takes place at the national level. Here there can be major problems, as public health authorities within states often share their responsibilities at various levels of jurisdiction; in the US, for example, such authorities exist at the local/city, county, state and federal levels – and they do not always agree or effectively coordinate their views for reasons discussed above. The US government response to the anthrax attacks in late 2001, for example, was plagued by inconsistent advice (such as the question of whether live anthrax spores could be distributed through the mail – they could!) and turf battles over policy, often between county/state officials and experts at the federal Centers for Disease Control (CDC). This problem was compounded by the fact that the targets of the attacks were located in multiple US states, and involved both public and private targets: the US Congress and the media.

This latter point raises an equally important concern: the relationship between public and private authorities regarding a health-related security crisis. Although most developed states have national health services to distribute advice, preventative care and treatment (such as vaccines and antibiotics) this is not always the case. In the US, for example, the health system is largely private and often involves profit-oriented firms, such as Health Maintenance Organizations (HMOs) and Preferred Provider Organizations (PPOs), whose prevention and treatment practices may differ from those suggested by local, state or federal authorities. Even more worrying is that many Americans are still not covered by adequate health insurance despite the advent of the US Affordable Care Act (i.e. 'Obamacare') in 2010, so they are likely to be at greater risk than the larger population. In the UK, the official response to avian and swine flu has varied across different regions (England, Northern Ireland, Scotland and Wales) even though each one is part of the public National Health Service (NHS). These disparities could easily produce a great deal of social and political tension in case of a major outbreak.

Moreover, the role of private pharmaceutical firms in developing vaccines, treatments and other public health-related goods and services must often be considered, as these firms are generally driven by a profit motive rather than by a selfless conception of international public health. Such firms may be unwilling to develop or provide certain products if they believe the sales profit will not offset their development costs (the so-called 'orphan drug' syndrome). As with the role of private firms in other security issues, there is also an inherent conflict of interest between the pursuit of profit thanks to private intellectual property rights and the need to secure resources, such as drugs and medical equipment, for the public good; this tension is especially prominent in the case of AIDS treatment regimes (Shadlen, 2007). These problems concerning how to coordinate the public/private balance of public health assistance are even more acute in LDCs, where we see a lack of both institutional arrangements and physical resources to address public health problems. Such a chronic and obvious disparity in access to health care in certain LDCs could easily cause those with more resources to either attempt to quarantine themselves or to flee the locality/state entirely – which obviously would violate any travel ban imposed by other states and create a new set of problems.

## International public health as a policy problem

These considerations should illustrate just how complicated and contentious it can be to devise an international response to a major public health crisis, whether involving a small number of states or the entire international system. On the positive side, however, we are much better positioned today than even just a decade or two ago to deal with such problems, and this change in awareness has occurred through the experience of several important public health emergencies since the early part of the twentieth century. We must also factor in the critical importance of major technological and scientific advances regarding the surveillance, diagnosis, prevention and treatment of such problems (including raising awareness), which make it more likely than ever before that an effective international response to a major health emergency can be organized, although it may take considerable time and effort depending on the case at hand.

### Agenda-setting

Although the international community is fully aware of the potential damage posed by major public health crises, this general awareness does not transform automatically or easily into a clear policy response for every single international health problem. Instead, agenda-setting for such problems can vary quite widely, and for reasons quite often unrelated to their scientific or medical characteristics.

For example, despite the well-known destructive potential of a global flu pandemic, and the devastating impact of various types of waterborne infectious diseases in the developing world, the first infectious disease to be considered a threat to international *security* was HIV/AIDS. This decision was taken by the UNSC in January 2000, only four years after UNAIDS became operational; three months later, President Clinton declared HIV/ AIDS to be a threat to US national security as well – a first for any disease. This action, which also included putting HIV/AIDS on the regular agenda of the US National Security Council, owed a great deal to the vociferous support of various domestic political activists, such as those supporting more assistance to Africa (where HIV/AIDS is very prevalent) as well as those who claimed to speak for the homosexual community in the 1980s and onwards, such as Queer Nation, the Gay Men's Health Crisis and the AIDS Coalition to Release Power (ACT-Up). These groups, among others, were especially motivated to advocate on behalf of HIV/AIDS sufferers following the extreme politicization of the disease in the US in the 1980s, where it had been marginalized as a threat by the conservative presidential administration of Ronald Reagan owing to its association with homosexuality and intravenous drug users (Shilts, 1987). This situation reversed somewhat during the 1990s under presidential administration of Bill Clinton, which began to issue official proclamations on World AIDS Day (1 December) starting in 1995 and increased federal funding for research into the disease. Today the problem of HIV/AIDS continues to receive a great deal of attention from the international community relative to many other diseases – but only until another infectious disease pandemic, such as flu or SARS or Ebola, temporarily displaces it.

This greater attention to new outbreaks has been facilitated by more effective means of health surveillance at the domestic and international levels. All states with moderately advanced health care systems now regularly collect domestic mortality and morbidity data to highlight patterns of disease, which could serve as an early warning system for a major outbreak. This more passive, 'low-tech' approach to surveillance is increasingly being supplemented in many states with more active and 'high-tech' approaches, such as the use of infrared thermal imaging devices at airports and other points of entry to detect the higher body temperatures of those possibly infected with a contagious disease. Some more developed states have developed even more sophisticated health surveillance systems, such as the BioWatch system of air quality monitors used in 31 American cities, to detect not just disease outbreaks but also chemical/biological terrorist attacks. The US DoD also developed its own system after 1999, known as ESSENCE (Electronic Surveillance System for the Early Notification of Community-Based Epidemics) to monitor such problems using its wide network of 400 military bases; since then, social media and related internet-enabled technologies are also being used for the surveillance of infectious disease. The crowdsourcing disease surveillance website www. crowdbreaks.com is just one example of this approach. Obviously some of these technologies and practices are almost completely lacking in the developing world, which again highlights the wide variance in vulnerability to an outbreak between the North and the South.

At the international level, the WHO in particular is responsible for monitoring and announcing the threat of epidemics and other public health emergencies, typically through its Global Alert and Response (GAR) system. A website affiliated with the Google internet search engine, www. Healthmap.org, is also used by the WHO, the CDC, the UK's Health Protection Agency and other authorities to monitor local reports of outbreaks of a range of infectious diseases. For flu pandemics in particular, in 2009 the WHO revised its alert system to distinguish between the phases of an outbreak (see Box 12.1).

---

### Box 12.1    Major pandemic phases

*Interpandemic period*

- *Phase 1*: No new influenza virus subtypes have been detected in humans. An influenza virus subtype that has caused human infection may be present in animals. If present in animals, the risk of human infection or disease is considered to be low.
- *Phase 2*: No new influenza virus subtypes have been detected in humans. However, a circulating animal influenza virus poses a substantial risk of human disease.

*Pandemic alert period*

- *Phase 3*: Human infection(s) with a new subtype, but no human-to-human spread, or at most rare instances of spread to a close contact.
- *Phase 4*: Small cluster(s) with limited human-to-human transmission but spread is highly localized, suggesting that the virus is not well adapted to humans.
- *Phase 5*: Larger cluster(s) but human-to-human spread is still localized, suggesting that the virus is becoming increasingly better adapted to humans, but may not yet be fully transmissible (substantial pandemic risk).

*Pandemic period*

- *Phase 6*: Pandemic. Increased and sustained transmission in the general populations.

*Postpandemic period*

- Return to interpandemic period.

*Source*: World Health Organization website.

This system may help to depoliticize the public debate regarding the nature of a new outbreak to some degree, although it does not, of course, lead automatically to a single set of policy options.

## Framing policy alternatives

Once a specific public health problem has been added to the international security agenda, the question then turns to the possible solutions available to deal with it. At this stage several considerations come into play. One involves the huge disparity in public health services between the developed and developing worlds, which often results in major North–South disputes regarding international public health problems. When LDCs in particular suffer from such a problem, as in the case of HIV/AIDS, the question of various types of aid transfers from the North to the South inevitably follows. This can involve not just the outright transfer of financial or technical aid to improve public health, sanitation and nutrition in LDCs, but also other policies that may be controversial, such as large-scale public education programmes to change individual behaviours or a relaxation of royalties on intellectual property rights for new drugs (or generic forms of existing ones) sold or produced in the developing world. Conversely, for problems that also affect the developed world, states with the means to engage in self-help may attempt to quarantine themselves from external threats and/or stockpile medical resources, such as vaccines and antibiotics, to protect their own populations. Obviously there are limited amounts of such resources at any given time, and the pressures of a crisis situation will inevitably lead to price hikes and shortages, which could disproportionately affect LDCs.

A second major consideration involves the debate over containment and prophylactic measures, including education programmes, versus treatment or curative measures (if available). The international community has limited resources to devote to an emerging public health crisis, so it must attempt to deploy those resources where they are – presumably – most cost-effective. This calculation, which obviously requires fairly reliable data about various alternative measures, may involve, for example, the shifting of resources from (possibly more expensive) treatment to (possibly less expensive) prophylaxis, such as vaccinations, which could be very controversial to certain populations. A drug treatment regime for HIV/AIDS, for example, may cost as much as $10,000 a year for one patient; the same funds could provide thousands of condoms to help prevent the spread of the disease. A treatment regime for XDR-TB is even more burdensome; it would take 12–18 months to administer and cost more than $150,000 per patient. For pandemics in particular, the WHO and other health authorities are typically more concerned with morbidity rates rather than mortality rates, which biases the global response in favour of containment rather than treatment. This view, however, may run counter to the views of the public and the media, who are more sensitized to mortality rates than morbidity rates. It may also require broader strategies to contain the outbreak, such as closing schools and transportation facilities; these can be controversial for large sectors of the public. Yet they are always worth considering; during the 1957 flu pandemic, for example, up to 50 per cent of schoolchildren across the UK caught the virus; in some schools the infection rate was as high as 90 per cent.

In addition, numerous factors can greatly complicate this calculation of cost-effectiveness, such as the interests of pharmaceutical firms, fears about medical treatments (such as vaccines) or the views of various activist groups, whether devoted to religious or cultural or other goals, who may support or oppose different types of assistance for certain problems, as in the case of certain Christian groups opposing the distribution of condoms to help prevent the spread of HIV/AIDS. Finally, it should be noted that even states with well-functioning public health systems, as in the developed world, can vary widely in terms of their approaches to the threat of epidemic disease. For example, in the US all children must be vaccinated against measles, mumps and rubella (MMR) to enrol in school; this legal requirement has resulted in a vaccination rate among US children of between 92 and 98 per cent. In the UK, vaccination is not legally required and the rate is around 78 per cent in England and Wales. This disparity resulted in 1,348 cases of measles in England and Wales in 2008, but only 135 cases during the first six months of 2008 in the US – even though the US has nearly five times the population. Although MMR infections are not nearly as deadly as other diseases discussed in this chapter, this difference in national approaches to MMR clearly indicates how the domestic political culture of a state can profoundly influence its vulnerability to public health problems, which can then influence its approach to international problems.

Even where common ground is found regarding the type of assistance or policy to be provided, local conditions at the point of delivery may undermine the effectiveness of such assistance. Local public health infrastructures must be involved to some degree, yet the priorities (and thus the spending, and thus the effectiveness) of these bodies can vary quite widely. Some drug regimens, for example, may require multiple doses of multiple drugs to work properly; these dosages must often also be calibrated to the needs of individual patients and closely monitored. If health care providers and/or patients are not able to follow such regimens for a variety of reasons, then such efforts may be completely ineffective and thus wasted. In some LDCs, private stakeholders in the form of charities, churches, aid groups and even drug firms may become involved in choosing and implementing various health policies to local populations; these groups are not equally effective or consistent. Local taboos and myths

Table 12.2   *Pandemic countermeasures*

| | |
|---|---|
| Personal measures | Health monitoring; hygiene; self-isolation during all illnesses |
| Private social/business measures | Crisis/continuity planning in large institutions (schools, universities, firms, government); alerts regarding voluntary closures and the private distribution of medical information/resources |
| Public health measures | Mandatory closures of institutions; cancelling public events/meetings; enforced 'social distancing' among large or vulnerable populations; infectious disease surveillance and quarantines/restrictions |
| General medical measures | Antibiotics, medical care for those infected |
| Specific medical measures | Antivirals and vaccines for particular diseases, if available |
| International public health measures | Surveillance/monitoring of outbreaks; sharing information on new diseases/strains; distributing/ developing antivirals and vaccines; recommending international quarantines and/or travel restrictions |

*Source:* Adapted by the author from information available at www.eurosurveillance.org (*Eurosurveillance* Vol. 12/No. 51, 20 Dec. 2007).

about sex, pregnancy, poverty, migration, gender, alcohol use and drug use can also easily undermine well-meaning global efforts to change the behaviours of threatened individuals. Even national government officials have been known to deliberately understate or even hide the nature of an emerging public health crisis, often for economic reasons (for example, to maintain tourism and foreign investment). Making decisions about these factors can therefore be extremely contentious, especially if they involve a fast-moving medical crisis and/or perceptions of a North–South conflict in the form of 'cultural imperialism'. Overall, an effective international response to a major pandemic requires coordination at multiple levels of analysis, from the individual to the international system, as summarized in Table 12.2.

## Policy choice

These dynamics can be better appreciated by taking a closer look at some recent major international public health issues. As noted above, the problem of HIV/AIDS still looms large as a major security threat according to the UN and several major powers, who attempt to coordinate their aid efforts to help bring this disease under control. The US has been the single largest aid provider in this area; official US assistance remained at about

$120 million a year since the end of the George H. W. Bush administration in 1992. On assuming office in 2001, his son George W. Bush initially requested $264 million for the fight against HIV/AIDS; in the face of criticism he then pledged $15 billion to be distributed over five years through a President's Emergency Plan for AIDS Relief. This aid and that of other stakeholders was further tied to various UN/WHO initiatives, such as the so-called 'ABC approach' public education programme, which involves teaching A (abstinence), B (being faithful to one's sexual partner) and C (using a condom) to people in infection-prone areas. Aid for treatment has been provided as well, largely in the form of the WHO's '3 by 5 plan', which committed the WHO to treating three million HIV-positive people in LDCs by 2005. Some private drug firms, such as Pfizer, also agreed to provide treatments for free or reduced prices to especially hard-hit populations. As we might expect, a major target of all these policies was sub-Saharan Africa, especially South Africa, which was reluctant to admit it had a major problem on its hands and declare a national emergency. South Africa has also seen the world's largest outbreak of XDR-TB, with over 300 cases by 2007; it was seriously considering the forceful detention and quarantine of XDR-TB patients, who are highly infectious, when the outbreak was brought under control.

In recent years, the problem of HIV/AIDS has often been overshadowed by more short-term, but potentially more serious and thus newsworthy, international public health crises. The SARS outbreak, which originated in China, is one notable example; SARS was first reported in February 2003 and resulted in about 8,000 infections and 800 deaths worldwide until it was contained by July 2003. SARS also prompted a major international coordination effort involving two major innovations: first, it involved the quick creation and input of an epistemic community of epidemiologists and other experts who attempted to understand the nature of SARS, which was a new disease at the time. This community put a great deal of pressure on Chinese authorities to cooperate with international public health specialists after they initially attempted to control the problem on their own. Second, the effort prompted the UN's first-ever announcement of global travel restrictions to prevent the disease from spreading further. Although the UN could not of course enforce such a recommendation, its 'seal of approval' for such a policy helped to convince its member states of the seriousness of the problem, and they became more likely to implement such a ban at the national level (see the case study below).

More recently, we have seen two smaller global outbreaks of avian flu and swine flu. Both viruses are believed to have originated in animals in Asia but mutated and spread to humans, sparking a threat of pandemic in each case. In fact, the Black Death and most major influenzas in the twentieth century have originated in Asia; even the Spanish flu of 1918 was misnamed and its origins are most certainly elsewhere (Barry, 2009), so Asia could become a major flashpoint in debates about international health security. The avian flu has killed about 250 people since the first outbreak in 1997, primarily in China, Indonesia, Laos, Romania, Russia, Turkey and Vietnam. The swine flu outbreak occurred in Mexico in April 2009 and was named by the WHO as a pandemic (Phase 6 on the scale in Box 12.1) on 11 June 2009; by that time it had spread to about 100,000 confirmed cases worldwide, with around 700 confirmed deaths in over two dozen states. Although only swine flu was named as an official pandemic by the WHO owing to its greater infectiousness as compared to avian flu, in both cases the international community attempted to implement a range of containment, treatment and prophylactic measures that varied quite widely from state to state. Given the fast-moving nature of swine flu, work on a vaccine was started well before the pandemic phase was reached. As such a vaccine would take months to develop, individual states had to adopt other measures to protect their own citizens.

These self-help measures varied quite widely, and included bans on imported animals and meat (especially pork) from Mexico and elsewhere, travel advisories, health advisories (including special flu hotlines and websites), airport surveillance, the suspension by some states of flights to and from Mexico and bans on airline passengers who are suspected of travelling with swine flu. China even provoked a diplomatic row with Mexico by quarantining dozens of visitors on flights from Mexico and holders of Mexican passports, even though they had not exhibited flu symptoms. By far the most prevalent measure involved the reliance upon national stockpiles of antiviral drugs, such as Tamiflu and Relenza. As Tamiflu is half the cost of Relenza, it is currently the antiviral of choice for most public health authorities. However, stockpile levels vary quite widely, even in the developed world, and this variance provides us with another critical indicator of how vulnerable different states are to outbreaks of avian or swine flu, beyond the actual morbidity/mortality rates of these diseases (Elbe, Roemer-Mahler and Long, 2014). Some examples of antiviral stockpiles as a percentage of population (quoted in *The Guardian*, 1 May 2009) are shown in Table 12.3.

These figures clearly indicate just how difficult it can be for certain states, such as Mexico, to cope with a major outbreak such as swine flu, which then greatly increases the likelihood that it will spread to other, hopefully more prepared, states. The WHO maintains its own stockpile of antivirals to treat about 3.5 million people; this amount clearly is far too small to decisively help people in more than a few poor states. Similarly, the pharmaceutical firm GlaxoSmithKline agreed to donate 50 million doses of swine flu vaccine to the WHO for distribution among LDCs; again, very admirable yet hardly enough to protect the nearly five billion people living in these areas. Determining which LDCs should benefit from these donations is likely to become a highly contentious process if swine

Table 12.3   *Antiviral stockpiles as a percentage of population*

| | |
|---|---|
| France | 52% |
| UK | 50% |
| Austria | 50% |
| Japan | 45% |
| New Zealand | 29% |
| US | 25% |
| Germany | 18% |
| Israel | 10% |
| Italy | 7% |
| Brazil | 5% |
| Mexico | 1% |

flu continues to spread. In addition to a lack of antivirals and other remedies, many LDCs do not even have basic contingency plans in place for such a health crisis; among over 50 states in Africa, for example, only one – South Africa – has filed a national contingency plan with the WHO.

## The politics of policy effectiveness

As we have yet to witness a significant international terrorist attack involving biological, chemical or nuclear weapons, our primary knowledge about the effectiveness of security-related international public health crises involves the question of deadly infectious diseases, especially those on an epidemic/pandemic scale. Before turning to such an evaluation, we first must consider the extent to which the international community has indeed followed through with the commitments noted above regarding various forms of international policy coordination to address major public health crises.

One critical point is the continuing prospect of voluntary defection on the part of many global stakeholders, whether aid providers or aid receivers. The US, for example, simply failed to follow through with its pledge to donate $15 billion over five years to the global HIV/AIDS campaign after the 9/11 terrorist attacks altered American security priorities in favour of the fight against terrorism. The US is not alone in shifting its spending priorities in the face of changing circumstances; all major aid donors, chiefly the OECD member states, have failed to live up to their global public health aid commitments in the past decade, and were struggling long before the 2008 global financial crisis strained budgets even further.

Equally problematic is the question of voluntary defection on the part of certain aid receivers. Several LDCs, such as Botswana, Indonesia, South Africa and Zimbabwe, which are known to be suffering from HIV/AIDS and similar health problems, have refused to accept certain forms of Western assistance for a variety of political and economic reasons: a fear of outsiders, an unwillingness to draw attention to certain negative aspects of their governance (such as nepotism and corruption), a fear of stigmatization, and the potential effects of outsiders on local cultures (such as the role of women) (Epstein, 2007).

Involuntary defection is equally important here, and again involves both major aid providers and receivers. In the US, although its National Security Council was charged with reassessing the government's HIV/AIDS programmes, and an Office of National AIDS Policy has existed since the mid-1990s, the US struggled to create a White House inter-agency group to consolidate the positions and policies of up to 16 agencies claiming some involvement in the issue. As there was no precedent in the US for linking a public health issue with the security establishment, turf battles and conflicts of interest frequently occurred. For example, the Department of Commerce was concerned about protecting US drug patents, so it inhibited the use of generic drugs and blocked temporary revocations of patent protection in areas suffering from major health crises. Similarly, the US Trade Representative created a 'watch list' of states facing trade sanctions if they did not uphold these property rights. The 1961 US Foreign Assistance Act also requires taxpayer-funded aid to come from American suppliers, even though other sources might be cheaper or more effective. The Act was, however, amended in 2004 to allow the president to provide aid to HIV/AIDS orphans in foreign countries. Similar problems have occurred in other major aid providers, whether in terms of general spending/direction and/or specific responses to disease outbreaks (see below). The '3 by 5' plan for HIV/AIDS treatment in LDCs, for example, suffered a funding shortfall of $5.5 billion soon after it was announced by the WHO. For aid recipients in LDCs, involuntary defection generally occurs through the lack of an effective public health infrastructure through which various forms of assistance can be channelled.

Despite these problems, there are some success stories in this area. One might even adopt a total victory approach to policy effectiveness in the sense that certain problems have been almost completely eliminated as public health threats, either on a global or local basis. For example, the WHO announced the global eradication of smallpox in December 1979, and today the only stocks of the virus are in two WHO reference laboratories: the CDC in the US and the State Research Centre of Virology and Biotechnology in Russia. Polio may be totally eradicated in the very near future; already the Americas, Europe and most states in the Western Pacific are polio-free. The global response to SARS noted above was very

## Box 12.2   The SARS outbreak

CHAPPATTE
Int'l Herald Tribune

*Gaining China's cooperation to stop SARS was a major challenge for the WHO.*

The 2002–3 outbreak of SARS in China, which spread rapidly around the world, provides unique lessons regarding the role of pandemic infectious disease as an international security issue. First, SARS clearly demonstrated that other new diseases besides AIDS were capable of becoming major global health threats. As such, SARS also exposed the limits of international authority to cope with the outbreak despite the supposed lessons learned in the two decades between the identification of AIDS and the SARS outbreak. Second, SARS is part of a recurring pattern of respiratory diseases with flu-like symptoms, which often can be traced to human–animal contact (as in 'wet markets' with live animals for sale), or a *zoonotic* origin (Quammen, 2013). Third, thanks to its flu-like nature, SARS is an airborne infectious

→

successful, and the disease was stopped (though not officially eradicated according to the WHO) in May 2006 after spreading to 37 states.

A historical or comparative trends approach provides other examples of improvement in dealing with major infectious diseases, whether over time and/or within specific states. For example, Botswana, Brazil, Senegal,

→

disease and spreads very easily even without close person-to-person contact, unlike AIDS or the 2013–16 Ebola outbreak in Africa, which was relatively contained, even though it has caused over 10,000 deaths so far. Fourth, SARS also revealed the critical role of health authorities and hospitals in actually spreading the virus, thanks to inadequate precautions and failed public health reporting practices, mainly in China.

The first evidence of SARS came in the form of a localized (endemic) outbreak in mainland China in November 2002, close to Hong Kong – a major transport hub. It spread to Hong Kong thanks to the travel plans of a physician, Dr Liu Jianlun, who had treated SARS cases on the mainland. Dr Liu infected over a dozen other victims during his stay on the 9th floor of the hotel Metropole in Hong Kong; this ability of a single victim to spread the illness to so many others, so quickly, became known as 'super-spreading'. Worse, some of these initial victims travelled by air to other countries, so that the virus spread to 37 countries in just a few weeks; SARS also has a longer incubation period compared to seasonal influenza, so that victims were not aware they were infected until they had already started spreading the disease. Finally, Chinese health authorities delayed reporting the new disease to the WHO, and then failed to take adequate measures to treat it as a crisis. China even hid some of its SARS patients from visiting WHO experts, so that the true extent of the crisis was not known until later.

Thanks to these factors, in the space of just a few months in 2003 over 8,000 infections were reported and around 800 deaths resulted from SARS (mostly in China/Hong Kong), which represents a mortality rate of about 10 per cent; the rate for seasonal influenza is about 0.1 per cent. This mortality rate is much lower than that for AIDS or Ebola of course, yet it could have been much worse, given the airborne nature of SARS and its incubation period, if the pandemic had not been stopped in time thanks to quarantine measures and mandatory health screening of international travellers. These measures were controversial as the WHO and other international authorities had never authorized such a travel ban; localized quarantines (as with the Amoy Gardens Apartments in Singapore) also required decisive effort by local authorities. This response also required the close involvement of private actors on the ground (churches, charities, volunteers, scientists, public health experts etc.). Thus, for major outbreaks of deadly infectious diseases with no known cure or vaccine, such as AIDS, SARS and Ebola, various measures such as accurate reporting, adequate precautions, passenger screening, travel bans and severe quarantines are not just the first, but also the only, line of defence.

Thailand, Uganda and Zambia saw significant declines in their HIV infection rates after adopting the ABC approach and accepting various forms of foreign assistance to deal with the problem. These examples, especially the case of Uganda, show that it is possible even for a very poor LDC to survey its HIV/AIDS sufferers, screen its blood supplies and direct foreign

assistance to where it is needed most, such as high-risk groups like pros-
titutes, soldiers and tourists. Uganda managed to cut its infection rate in
half, which is a major achievement by any reasonable standard.

These successful examples, however, must be balanced against other
historical or comparative trends, namely the continued persistence of a
North–South gap in levels of public health care. Although health standards have improved in many LDCs over the past few decades (a positive historical trend), they are still extremely low relative to the levels
achieved in the rich OECD member states (a negative comparative trend).
As we have seen above, whether this gap is viewed as a development/
humanitarian issue rather than an international security issue is due more
to the attitude of major political stakeholders than to the inherent destructive nature of such problems, which is why we see the persistence of this
gap – a policy failure – even in the face of successful efforts to deal with
other major outbreaks, such as SARS. The simple fact is that the chronic
and wide North–South gap in health care services is not viewed with the
same urgency as an occasional outbreak of a deadly infectious disease that
threatens the lives of people in the North as well as the South. Working to
narrow this gap while simultaneously managing major outbreaks and the
threat of terrorist attacks (not to mention other security problems) seems
beyond the political capacities of many global stakeholders, whether IOs
or states; this dynamic clearly was at work during the worst Ebola outbreak in history (West Africa in 2013), which killed hundreds and infected
thousands over a span of more than six months before the WHO took
serious action to combat it.

Beyond the general North–South gap, we should also note the limitations of specific responses to major outbreaks even in richer states, especially as revealed by the 2009 swine flu pandemic. One problem here
involved the varied levels of surveillance and high alert claimed by public
health authorities; in the UK, for example, where swine flu affected more
victims than the rest of Europe combined, NHS doctors complained to
the media that they had not been alerted at all to the threat of swine flu
even as the first British cases were being confirmed. Similarly, a pandemic
phone hotline to answer flu queries in the UK was supposed to be operational in October 2008; it was still not working in May 2009 when the
swine flu outbreak was occurring. A UK website designed to perform a
similar function immediately became overloaded when it went live in July
2009. If such failures can occur in the UK, which the WHO considers one
of the very best prepared states in the world given its large network of
NHS facilities and stockpile of antivirals, the situation must be even worse
in LDCs, where there is virtually no preparedness.

For example, Mexico had to send its swine flu samples to Canada for
genetic analysis, which delayed proper identification by nearly a week.
The CDC in the US, which attempts to monitor such problems on a global

basis, was also not aware of the outbreak until six days after Mexico had imposed emergency measures. A related problem concerns the mixed messages delivered by officials working for various institutions; the EU's health commissioner, for example, caused a political row by prematurely urging Europeans to avoid non-essential travel to the US and Mexico during the swine flu outbreak. In the UK, the same flu caused officials to publicly – and very confusingly – debate questions such as its risks to pregnant women and other vulnerable groups, whether to close schools, the alleged safety of a mass swine flu vaccine (which a majority of UK doctors and nurses do not want to take), the wisdom of allowing individuals to prescribe their own antivirals with an online diagnostic service and other critical issues.

This final point raises a more serious problem: the increasing reliance on antivirals as a prophylactic measure in the case of an influenza (or similar) pandemic. Such treatments must be given within two days of the appearance of flu symptoms to work most effectively, which is simply not always possible even when the drugs are available (especially in LDCs). In addition, the leading antiviral, Tamiflu, has been suspected of serious side effects, especially in children; during the 2004–5 flu season in Japan doctors were told not to prescribe it to patients aged 10–20 after 12 children died and 32 others exhibited abnormal behaviour after taking Tamiflu. Researchers in the UK also cautioned against prescribing antivirals to patients under 12 years old after the 2009 swine flu outbreak; however, these concerns did not prevent UK health care providers from giving Tamiflu to thousands of schoolchildren as a precautionary measure. The alternative, Relenza, is not licensed at all for use in children under the age of seven.

Even when such drugs can be used safely, over the long term their effectiveness is reduced; moreover, if a virus mutates to become resistant to these antivirals, then the only hope will be far more stringent quarantine measures until or unless a vaccine can be developed. Two older flu drugs, amantadine and rimantadine, are no longer used for precisely that reason, and at least one strain of flu in the US is now resistant to Tamiflu. In August 2009, government flu advisors in the UK specifically cautioned against the over-prescribing of Tamiflu as a measure to contain swine flu; this advice was then backed up by the WHO but rejected by the British government. Given these problems, it may be that the simplest measures – such as proper hygiene, hydration and staying home when you feel ill – are far more effective, cheaper and safer than the indiscriminate use of antivirals, especially when they are given to otherwise healthy individuals, particularly children. Yet this advice, which largely amounts to allowing the virus to run its course naturally, is politically unacceptable to some government officials if an apparent 'magic bullet' in the form of an antiviral pill is available.

## Summary

As with other non-traditional security threats like global warming and organized crime, the problem of international public health crises has become a major international security concern for most global stakeholders. No stakeholder can seriously dismiss the possibility of a deadly pandemic given the repeated experience of such incidents in human history; the possible use of chemical or biological weapons by terrorist groups lends additional urgency to this problem. As always, however, recognition of a common problem does not lead automatically to a common solution, and here we see the same problems associated with other non-traditional security threats: the lack of a consensus regarding an appropriate response to any specific public health crisis despite an increasingly high degree of attention on the part of an international epistemic community involving the WHO and other experts.

Moreover, this determination of an appropriate response can work both ways: in some cases very real threats are downplayed, while in others they are inflated thanks to computer models and alarmist headlines even though the real threat to the average citizen may be quite low. There is a very simple reason for this: politicians (rather than doctors) have a political (and often economic) interest in avoiding panic above all else, which can easily take precedence over the actual threat posed by a specific public health problem. Given the attention such outbreaks and attacks receive in the media, and the resulting levels of fear they inspire – no matter how irrational – political leaders can hardly ignore or dismiss the security implications of such problems. As with terrorism and other very unpredictable threats, the result is often worst case scenario planning and comforting panaceas, such as dispensing Tamiflu, rather than a measured attempt to explain the actual risks to the public as calmly, and truthfully, as possible.

Two other major political factors exacerbate this general problem. One is the existence of the North–South gap noted throughout this chapter, which produces political pathologies on both sides. Rich countries often hesitate to provide significant health assistance to LDCs, where most of the suffering occurs, because other priorities can easily take precedence (at best) or because they fear that such assistance may be ineffective or wasted in LDCs with corrupt governments and/or limited public health infrastructures (at worst). In fact, it is not uncommon today to speak of 'donor fatigue' among some major powers, especially in the face of economic crises, terrorism and many other security threats. Poor countries, on the other hand, may also resist such assistance for much the same reasons, resulting in a kind of vicious cycle between aid providers and aid recipients. They may also downplay the threat of a public health problem for fears of harming their economies, especially where foreign tourists and FDI are highly valued. This problem was in evidence during the 2003 SARS outbreak and the 2013 Ebola outbreak, among other examples.

The second factor is the persistent and widely varying levels of vulnerability to public health crises felt by states and other domestic stakeholders when an actual outbreak occurs. This variation quite easily translates into different national strategies – that is, self-help – as an outbreak works its way through individual states. As we have seen, this variance is due as much to the nature of the disease itself as it is to the different approaches to managing public health problems, including the public–private aspects of such problems, found throughout the international community. The result, unfortunately, is a very high degree of 'muddling through' and even policy incoherence as a major problem spreads throughout the system, as we have seen most recently with the swine flu virus and the Ebola outbreak. However, as long as humans (not to mention birds and other animals) attempt to move across borders, and thus unwittingly infect those in other states, such problems will not disappear. This question of controlling the free movement of individuals as a security measure leads us to our final topic: the question of international population trends.

## Further reading

John M. Barry (2009). *The Great Influenza: The Story of the Deadliest Pandemic in History*. London: Penguin.

Helen Epstein (2007). *The Invisible Cure: Africa, the West, and the Fight Against AIDS*. New York: Farrar, Strauss & Giroux.

Peter Piot (2015). *AIDS Between Science and Politics*. New York: Columbia University Press.

Andrew Price-Smith (2001). *The Health of Nations: Infectious Disease, Environmental Change, and Their Effects on National Security and Development*. Cambridge: MIT Press.

Andrew Price-Smith (2001). *Plagues and Politics: Infectious Disease and International Policy*. Basingstoke: Palgrave Macmillan.

Andrew Price-Smith (2004). *Downward Spiral: HIV/AIDS, State Capacity and Political Violence in Zimbabwe*. Washington: US Institute of Peace Press.

David Quammen (2013). *Spillover: Animal Infections and the Next Human Pandemic*. London: Vintage Books.

Randy Shilts (1987). *And the Band Played On: Politics, People, and the AIDS Epidemic*. New York: St. Martin's.

# Chapter 13

# International Population Trends

Our final problem area involves the international security aspects of human population trends based on changes in their size, composition, location or distribution/movements. As with many of the topics covered in this volume, the study of population, or demography, is an academic field in its own right, so our task here is to isolate various findings and arguments from this field and relate them to the question of international security. The most immediate problem in making such a linkage involves the inherently dual nature of certain demographic trends: populations can be framed as threats to security, or as referent objects to be protected. This can be seen most prominently with one major topic covered in this chapter: the question of mass population flows. Should these individuals be viewed as victims and welcomed by other states, or are they more appropriately viewed as threats? This is precisely where some aspects of the human security policy agenda begin to run into problems, as do national immigration policies in particular: because 'humans' can easily be interpreted as resources, victims or threats depending on the political context involved (Koslowski, 2002; Parker and Brassett, 2005). As we shall see throughout this chapter, the idea that the international community should provide greater human security for certain populations tends to ignore the hard political and economic calculations made by officials and others in the face of multiple security threats and limited resources.

## International population trends and international security

In international security, two population-related topics tend to dominate the literature and will be covered in this chapter: population growth/composition and mass population movements of the order of tens of thousands of people or more, whether cross-border (for instance, refugees and asylum seekers) or intrastate (such as internally displaced persons, or IDPs). Both issues, in turn, currently suffer from a lack of global consensual knowledge concerning both the nature of the threat and the nature of the referent object to be protected. This lack of consensual knowledge then complicates the search for common solutions, as we shall see in later sections.

360

## Destructive scale

The view that excessive population growth – or a 'population time bomb' – poses a general threat to international security has a long history that predates the existence of the field of study by some decades. This question in turn involves two types of forecasts: global population growth rates over the next generation or two (25–50 years) and the negative impact of such growth. In other words, what size population can the earth realistically sustain? We are on fairly firm ground regarding the former question; most experts currently predict a global population of about nine to ten billion people by 2050, or roughly a third more than the current (2016) population of about 7.4 billion. This is large, but not nearly as worrisome as the estimates – 12 to 15 billion people – made by some commentators in the 1990s, such as the former head of the World Bank, Robert McNamara (McNamara, 1992).

On the second question, however, there is much less consensus. One factor involves the *distribution* of this larger population between the developed and developing worlds: the vast majority of those nine or ten billion people in 2050 will live in LDCs, as is the case today with over five billion people living in LDCs. This large majority – perhaps up to seven or eight billion people – in 2050 will suffer from many of the problems already noted in this volume: civil conflicts, crime, economic instability, environmental and resource problems, infectious diseases and so on. A second factor involves the *composition* of these populations in terms of their age, income potential, residence (urban or rural) and other factors that help determine their sustainability. Thus it is not so much the size of the global population in 2050 but rather the increasingly uneven distribution and composition of it in coming decades that may negatively impact international (and national) security affairs in the form of concerns about social cohesion but also conflicts over increasingly scarce resources: land, homes, food, jobs, energy and so on (Rudolph, 2003). The negative environmental impacts must be considered as well, in terms of both resource depletion and global climate change. These stresses could lead to more conflict, but only if the amount of such resources does not also increase and/or if per capita consumption levels do not decline as a result of changing behaviours or new technologies.

The question of large-scale population movements is equally problematic in terms of finding consensual knowledge, mainly because of the dual nature of such movements as noted above. There is little doubt that a world free of migration controls would permit much greater population movements from LDCs to the developed world as a result of civil and interstate wars, secessionist campaigns, various types of discrimination and repression and economic stresses; however, at present such population movements can very easily be interpreted as damaging or destructive by the states targeted by migrants as potential homes (Weiner, 1993 and 1995; Adamson, 2006; Krcmaric, 2014). It is also clear that such movements seem to be increasing in recent years; for example, in 1969 there were less than ten million refugees in the world; since the end of the Cold War, refugees have numbered over 15 million in some years, according to the UN High Commissioner for Refugees (UNHCR).

In addition, there seems to be a general increase in the average number of refugees and IDPs produced by various conflicts as compared to a few decades ago (Weiner, 1992–3). However, one of the ironies of globalization is that most states are happy to facilitate the free movement of goods, services and capital but still balk at adopting more open immigration policies. Thus the framing of migration as an international (or national) security issue is subject to a range of complex political calculations made by individual states on the basis of their domestic circumstances rather than on the inherent nature of migrant populations as either threats or victims. The result of this mismatch between the empirical nature of the problem and the threat as framed by most political actors is, unfortunately but not unexpectedly, a set of contradictory and even hypocritical arguments made about migrants that typically result in equally contradictory and hypocritical policies, as we shall see.

## Geographic and temporal scope

This lack of consensual knowledge about the general demographic security threat is also apparent when examining more specific patterns of population growth and migration, which vary across the globe and can undermine any international sense of urgency about such threats. Regarding population, the general pattern noted above is complicated further by an actual *decline* in fertility rates in most OECD states, coupled with an *increase* in fertility rates in most LDCs. Population growth generally declines when the *total fertility rate* – or the average number of children a woman in a given population would bear if fertility rates remained unchanged during her lifetime – falls below the so-called *replacement rate*, which is an average of 2.1 children per woman.

As Table 13.1 indicates, most developed states are already either at or below this replacement rate, and will therefore experience not just a gradual decline but also a general ageing of their populations relative to the situation in LDCs, where the majority of people are under 24 years old. This trend is expected to put heavy stress on public services and natural resources; Africa alone is expected to increase its population by 116 per cent by 2050, according to the Population Reference Bureau, a US policy organization. This would amount to about two billion people; Uganda alone may have a population of over 130 million in 2050, even though its territory is much smaller than its near neighbours (Sudan and

**Table 13.1**   *Total fertility rates, world and selected regions*

|  | *1970–5* | *2015* | *2050 (projected)* |
|---|---|---|---|
| World | 4.47 | 2.5 | 2.25 |
| Africa | 6.72 | 4.7 | 3.1 |
| Asia | 5.04 | 2.2 | 2.0 |
| Europe | 2.16 | 1.6 | 1.7 |
| Latin America/Caribbean | 5.04 | 2.2 | 2.4 |
| North America | 2.01 | 1.9 | 2.0 |
| Oceania | 3.23 | 2.4 | 2.3 |

*Source: UN World Population Prospects (2015 Revision); UN World Fertility Patterns (2015).*

the DRC), while Nigeria may become the world's third most populous state, with a population of around 400 million by 2050. When these population stresses are added to the threat of global warming and the public health and economic problems already found in most LDCs, it is difficult to escape the conclusion that billions of individuals are likely to suffer more ills than they can be expected to cope with in the near future, and they may then adopt various forms of political action to solve their problems.

In rich states, however, the threat is framed differently: population trends may undermine the social contract or safety net (health and pension benefits) provided by most advanced capitalist states. As this system is generally financed by working citizens in their peak earning years, roughly ages 30 to 60, it requires a greater ratio of workers to retirees. In the 1940s, the ratio of workers to retirees in the developed world was about six to one. Today it is around three to one, and in the near future it could be as low as one to one. This trend is a direct result of the so-called 'baby boom' experienced by most developed states after WWII. The Baby Boomers, or those born between 1946 and 1964, in fact represent the largest single sustained growth of the population in the history of the US, when births increased from about 2.5 million a year to about 4 million a year and resulted in today's cohort of about 76 million American Baby Boomers; other OECD states experienced equally dramatic population growth rates. These individuals began to retire starting from 2011 as they reached 65 years of age; as they leave the workforce, greater economic and social stress will be placed on entire populations within states that experienced such a baby boom.

By around 2030 most 'Boomers' will have retired and will be in the 66–84 age range; most of their pension benefits, health care needs and other resources will be provided by the state, largely in the form of income transfers from workers to retirees, as a majority of people approaching retirement in all OECD states have not saved nearly enough to fund their lifestyles after they stop working. Some studies, in fact, have claimed that unfunded benefits for future retirees in the OECD states amount to about $35 trillion, or around half of the current global GDP. This situation will be especially problematic in the EU, where health and pension benefits (among others) are far more generous than in the US; some have argued further that this problem alone will prevent most great powers from over-taking America's global political role (Haas, 2007). In addition, many LDCs have seen their own populations expand over the past 50 years; China also experienced its own baby boom after the 1950s, when Mao Zedong encouraged his fellow citizens to have as many children as possible in order to help defeat capitalism. The result was an average fertility rate of about 5.8 children per woman, or hundreds of millions of extra children who gave China its current status as the most populous state on earth, with a population of nearly 1.4 billion, or nearly 20 per cent of the world total. Table 13.2 provides regional projections based on current (2015) UN forecasts; as we can see, Asia will dominate global population figures until 2050; after that, Africa's population is likely to equal that of Asia, while the figures for all other regions will be much smaller in comparison.

Another factor at issue is that the growing populations in LDCs tend to group into urban areas. For the first time in world history, more than half of

Table 13.2    *World population projections*

|  | 2015 | 2030 | 2050 | 2100 |
|---|---|---|---|---|
| World | 7.35 billion | 8.5 billion | 9.73 billion | 11.21 billion |
| Africa | 1.19 billion | 1.68 billion | 2.48 billion | 4.39 billion |
| Asia | 4.39 billion | 4.92 billion | 5.27 billion | 4.89 billion |
| Europe | 738 million | 734 million | 707 million | 646 million |
| Latin America/ Caribbean | 634 million | 721 million | 784 million | 721 million |
| North America | 358 million | 396 million | 433 million | 500 million |
| Oceania | 39 million | 47 million | 57 million | 71 million |

*Source:* UN World Population Prospects (2015 Revision).

all people living today now reside in towns and cities, and about 60 per cent of all people are expected to live in urban areas by 2030; this trend is known as the *urban millennium*. Many of these urban residents will live in so-called *megacities* of more than ten million people, such as Mexico City, Seoul, Mumbai and Cairo. There are now over 20 such megacities across the globe, the majority of which are located in Asia. In 1978, the United Nations Human Settlements Programme, or UN-Habitat, was specifically created to monitor and address the needs of these areas, and this agency provides forecasts about the populations of certain megacities. Table 13.3 shows the top ten projected megacities.

Based on these trends, we face the prospects of generational conflicts and urban–rural conflicts in addition to North–South ones in coming years (Urdal, 2006; also see the special issue of *Security Dialogue*, 40/4–5, 2009). In fact, increasing urbanization has now given rise to the phenomenon of *megaregions* or *endless cities* that cover hundreds of square kilometres of territory and house over 100 million people. The megaregion of Hong Kong–Shenhzen–Guangzoue in China, with about 120 million people, is the largest such example but others will follow. Moreover, the fact that nearly 80 per cent of city-dwellers in LDCs – or over one billion people worldwide – actually live in slums and shanty towns, with appalling sanitation conditions, adds a major public health element to this mix of concerns (Davis, 2006). Some scholars have also examined gender

### Table 13.3 *Top megacities, 2007 and 2025*

| | 2007 population (millions) | | 2025 projected population (millions) |
|---|---|---|---|
| 1 Tokyo | 35.7 | 1 Tokyo | 36.4 |
| 2 Mexico City | 19 | 2 Mumbai | 26.4 |
| 3 New York/Newark | 19 | 3 Delhi | 22.5 |
| 4 Sao Paulo | 19 | 4 Dhaka | 22 |
| 5 Mumbai | 18.8 | 5 Sao Paulo | 21.4 |
| 6 Delhi | 15.9 | 6 Mexico City | 21 |
| 7 Shanghai | 15 | 7 New York/Newark | 20.6 |
| 8 Kolkata | 14.8 | 8 Kolkata | 20.6 |
| 9 Buenos Aires | 20.8 | 9 Shanghai | 19.4 |
| 10 Dhaka | 13.5 | 10 Karachi | 19.1 |

*Source:* UN-Habitat website.

ratios in the context of these trends, and claim that a high imbalance of males to females in certain states, particularly China, may result in social problems – namely a lack of mates for men – that could turn into political ones (Hudson and Den Boer, 2002). Others have argued that traditions of gender inequality or discrimination can also predispose a state to internal conflict (Caprioli, 2005).

We see a similar degree of geographic variance in terms of mass population movements; although developed states tend to worry about movements from the South to the North, or from East to West after the Cold War, most such movements are in fact from one LDC to another. The vast majority of stateless persons, or those lacking a clear right of citizenship in any state, also come from less developed regions, as do those whose national identity is geographically dispersed across several states: Kurds, Palestinians and numerous African and Asian national groups. Moreover, some LDCs actually *encourage*, or at least do not actively discourage, illegal immigration for a variety of reasons, such as a need for low-cost labour or to change the composition of the electorate in ways that favour the government of the receiving state, as in the case of illegal Filipino emigration to Malaysia (Sadiq, 2005). The largest refugee flows also occur among LDCs, as in Africa, South Asia, South East Asia and the Middle East; South Asia alone has seen flows of up to 40 million people (Weiner, 1992–3).

Interstate and intrastate wars are largely responsible for these movements; environmental problems and resource shortages also contribute to their prevalence in LDCs, especially in Asia and Africa. Owing to these problems (particularly wars in the Middle East), refugee flows have increased by nearly 50 per cent in less than a decade, from 10.5 million in 2008 to over 14 million by the end of 2014, while over half of all refugees currently come from just three states: Somalia (1.11 million), Afghanistan (2.59 million) and Syria (3.88 million). The regional distribution of these refugees (and those in refugee-like situations) is as seen in Table 13.4.

Note that these UNHCR figures do not include the 5.1 million Palestinian refugees displaced after the 1948 Arab–Israeli War; another UN agency (the UN Relief and Works Agency for Palestine Refugees in the Near East) attempts to support these individuals.

As noted above, LDCs also tend to host the most refugees, which puts even greater stresses on the states least able to cope with large inflows of such individuals. Major refugee-hosting states by mid-2015 are listed in Table 13.5.

Regarding asylum seekers, the situation has become equally challenging in recent years; in 2014 at least 1.66 million such applications were lodged worldwide; the highest level ever recorded. Unlike with refugees, many of these claims are increasingly made in rich states; in 2014 Russia received

## Table 13.4 *Global distribution of refugees*

|  | 2008 | 2014 |
|---|---|---|
| Asia/Pacific | 3.6 million | 3.8 million |
| Middle East/North Africa | 2.3 million | 3.0 million |
| Sub-Saharan Africa | 2.1 million | 3.7 million |
| Europe | 1.6 million | 3.1 million |
| Americas | 803,500 | 770,000 |

*Source:* UNHCR website.

the most applications (274,700), followed by Germany (173,100) and the US (121,200). However, *taking* asylum applications and *approving* them are two separate things; some countries (such as Sweden and Denmark) tend to approve the majority of asylum claims they receive, while others (such as France, Germany, the UK and the US) typically approve fewer than half each year. Overall, then, given this distribution of refugee flows, asylum applications and the policies of hosting states for refugees/asylum seekers, it is quite clear that mass population movements are not shared equally around the globe, and the burden or benefits of hosting migrants/refugees therefore will be felt very differently across various states and regions.

## Table 13.5 *Major refugee-hosting states, 2015*

| | |
|---|---|
| Turkey | 1.59 million |
| Pakistan | 1.51 million |
| Lebanon | 1.15 million |
| Iran | 982,000 |
| Ethiopia | 659,500 |
| Jordan | 654,100 |
| Kenya | 552,300 |
| Uganda | 428,400 |
| Chad | 420,800 |
| Sudan | 356,200 |

*Source:* UNHCR website.

As with several other security threats examined in this volume, this critical difference often manifests itself as a general North–South conflict of interests. Developed states with long coastlines can be especially vulnerable to illegal migration inflows; Italy alone saw more than a 50 per cent increase in immigrants/refugees arriving by sea, from 20,000 in 2007 to 33,000 in 2008, mostly from Africa. This trend, which has intensified since the 2011 war in Syria, has put enormous stresses on Italian social, economic and political life, even to the extent of fostering the rise of vigilante groups permitted by the government. And throughout Europe in general, a great deal of attention, mostly negative, has been focused recently on the impact of Muslim immigrants, primarily from LDCs, who are feared by some to have a detrimental impact on not just the European economy but on European society and identity as well (Wæver et al., 1993; Caldwell, 2009). Such views were cited as a major reason for the UK's vote to leave the EU in 2016, as well as a more general rise of right-wing parties, particularly those with an anti-immigrant platform, during the 2009 elections for the European Parliament and various national European elections since then (McLaren, 2012). These rising parties include the Alliance for the Future of Austria, the Freedom Party (Austria), Flemish Interest (Belgium), National Union Attack (Bulgaria), the Party for Freedom (the Netherlands), the Slovak National Party (the Slovak Republic), the British National Party (UK), the National Front (France), Law and Justice (Poland), and Fidesz (Hungary).

## Likelihood

While it is fairly straightforward to measure population growth and migration patterns in various parts of the world, the question of linking those patterns to the propensity of specific security problems is more difficult. Regarding population growth in general, even if many experts predict a world of more than nine billion people by 2050, there is simply no consensus whatsoever on what type of world those people will inhabit. On this question we have nothing but pure speculation, informed and otherwise, about the risks – but also opportunities – of living in such a world. For every argument about the resource stresses and pollution likely to be created by nine billion people, there are counterarguments about the economic opportunities, new technologies and creative new solutions that could emerge from such global population growth. Some even argue that the world is moving towards a post-industrial or information-based economy whereby productivity is knowledge-intensive rather than labour-intensive. This also means that workers can learn new skills over a longer lifetime of employment and adapt as necessary in ways that might not be available in labour-intensive occupations. If so, then people should be able – and even willing – to work longer, and thus remain productive taxpayers as they age. This lack of consensus about the hazards of population growth, as well as the slow-moving and long-term nature of the supposed threats involved, contribute to the overall lack of urgency currently felt by the international community about this topic as compared to many other problems covered in this volume.

The same cannot be said, however, regarding the problems of migration and other cross-border population movements, which are far too easily used as scapegoats for a range of social problems that may be framed as national or international security threats. Beyond the general concern with preserving national identity or cohesiveness in a state facing migration pressures, especially from immigrants possessing a different ethnicity (Sniderman, Hagendoorn and Prior, 2004), we may also see a deliberate attempt to link migration to problems such as unemployment (at best) and crime/terrorism (at worst); the latter tendency has been especially apparent in the US and Europe since the War on Terror and the rise of Islamic State. Moreover, these problems are often linked: rising unemployment in the face of an economic recession is usually accompanied by rising crime rates, and it becomes very tempting for citizens and politicians to blame both trends on immigrants, whether legal or illegal. Such views can easily lead to extremist or fundamentalist political activism in all states, whether authoritarian or liberal. This tendency, finally, is not confined mainly to the question of emigration from very poor, southern LDCs; it has increasingly concerned East–West migration as well, mainly in Europe, since the end of the Cold War. Some authors explicitly, but wrongly, predicted a flood of economic migrants from the East to the West as communism collapsed in the late 1980s, which would put major stresses on the more advanced European states (Larrabee, 1993).

Also problematic, especially in or near LDCs, is the question of major refugee flows as a result of military conflict, natural disasters, economic/health crises or other problems (Neumayer, 2005; Prakash, 2012). Such flows are difficult enough to manage when confined to a single state; when they threaten to spill over to neighbouring states, many new stakeholders must then determine how to balance their treatment of such individuals as victims or threats. In some cases, such as Bosnia and Rwanda, populations have been driven out or killed deliberately by militias in actions that amount to ethnic cleansing or even genocide. In others, forced population movements are used as an instrument of foreign policy, as with Cuba's release of thousands of its 'undesirables', such as criminals and mental health patients, to the US in the Mariel boatlift of 1980. A failure to protect such refugees or IDPs has also been linked to a rise in the recruitment of child soldiers in some conflicts, as with the Lord's Resistance Army in Uganda, where minors made up almost 90 per cent of the soldiers (Achvarina and Reich, 2006). For LDCs in particular, which have scarce resources to begin with, the security imperative might quickly overshadow the humanitarian one on economic grounds alone.

## Recovery

It is somewhat inappropriate to use the term 'recovery', as opposed to 'adaptation' perhaps, with respect to dealing with the potential negative impact of a major change in global population, for 'recovery' implies some degree of return to a former state of affairs. Assuming global population levels are not controlled by radically altering birth or death rates in various parts of the world, the only real recovery here will depend on the amount and distribution of resources required to sustain the world's population. As there simply is no consensus on this question as noted above, there is similarly no consensus on how the international community would adapt to a global population expansion whereby up to eight billion out of nine or ten billion people reside in LDCs by the year 2050. There is more consensus, however, regarding the question of migration, as most economists agree that immigration provides a net long-term economic benefit to states that attract and assimilate migrants, although there are of course short-term costs (such as spending on education and health care). In other words, adaptation in this case is more a question of convincing most citizens in immigrant-receiving states about the net benefits of migration rather than a question of making major adjustments to cope with a large influx of migrants. Unfortunately, politicians are far less effective than economists in making the case for immigration in rich states, and opposition voices, as well as the media, are often readily available to blame problems on foreigners rather than on society at large or the government, which makes the question of adaptation much more difficult than it need be.

Finally, the question of recovering from or adapting to large cross-border refugee flows generally involves the issue of whether such individuals are to be returned home when conditions permit or allowed to stay as permanent residents in neighbouring states. Rich states are often much better placed (although not necessarily more willing) than LDCs to accept such refugees and thus assist the recovery from the crisis, yet for flows that occur among LDCs alone the question of recovery becomes far more complicated. In this case recovery is contingent on whether the receiving state views the refugees as victims or as threats, and whether the receiving state has the political and economic resources to accept the refugees on (potentially) a permanent basis, or to return them home (or to a willing third state) in as humane a fashion as possible. The same calculations also apply to the question of allowing illegal immigrants to become permanent residents in a host state. Economists often argue that the benefits of such an amnesty policy could outweigh the costs, mainly in the form of new tax revenues once the immigrants become documented workers. Several advanced industrialized states, including France, Greece, Italy, Spain, the UK and the US, have considered or adopted such policies to varying degrees in recent years, yet they remain controversial for reasons noted above.

## Stakeholder factors

International population trends pose special problems when framed in the context of security affairs, problems that are quite unlike those found in most other non-traditional security areas like crime, economic stability and environmental protection. These problems are primarily associated with the question of population growth and composition, as most societies and individuals generally agree that procreation – unlike crime or polluting or enjoying access to capital – is a basic human right. In this sense procreation also is somewhat similar to the question of public health: it involves a transformation of a normal human/biological activity into a security concern. Although all human beings therefore have a stake in any policies involving their procreative rights, they are not equally powerful in terms of exercising or defending those rights. Nor do procreative rights – such as they are – imply a right to free movement across any national borders to pursue better opportunities, except in certain circumstances. Instead, the constraints and vulnerabilities surrounding procreation and migration vary quite widely according to the populations at issue, which then greatly complicates any attempt to transform such factors or trends into international security problems.

### Principal stakeholders

Problems related to trends in population and migration can be fairly easily understood by interested laypersons, so it is difficult to speak of an authoritative epistemic community in this realm as compared to the topic of public health. Instead, we have a multiplicity of competing voices who claim to speak or act on behalf of certain populations, with varying degrees of authority. Some of these stakeholders are highly institutionalized at the international level, such as the WHO, the International Organization for Migration (IOM) and the UNHCR. Various human rights groups such as Amnesty International and CARE may also attempt to play a role in population/migration issues, although they may not always frame their involvement in terms of international security affairs. Very narrowly focused international groups may emerge in the context of related problems, such as those devoted to specific civil or international conflicts that generate population/migration problems. These include the Action Group for Peace and Justice in Rwanda and the Refugee Action Group, which focuses on Northern Ireland.

These international groups must often compete for attention with domestic interest groups in all major states, such as family planning groups, pro/anti-abortion groups, pro/anti-immigration groups (such as labour unions) and humanitarian aid groups that seek to assist or resist immigrants or refugees (Haus, 1995). Such groups can easily counteract each other's effects; in the US, for example, a private aid group (Paisanos al Rescate, or Countrymen to the Rescue) provides bottles of water to dehydrated immigrants attempting to cross the US–Mexican border, while on the Mexican side another American group, No More Deaths, provides assistance to those who have been deported back to Mexico. In the same region, however, a private border-watching group, the Minutemen Civil Defence Corps, keeps a lookout for illegal immigrants and informs the US Border Patrol when they are spotted. Illegal Mexican immigrants to the US can have their lives saved or their dreams trashed depending on which of these private American groups they happen to encounter in the desert.

With such a cacophony of competing voices and actions surrounding problems related to population trends, there is very rarely any clear consensus about how to respond to a certain population or migration/refugee problem, even when there may be security implications. This lack of consensus also allows state stakeholders – government bureaucrats and elected officials – to retain a central role as policy-makers over *international* population/migration issues, yet their attitudes to this topic are still strongly conditioned by the domestic political cultures of their own states. As with security issues related to public health, there is also a clear difference in vulnerability between the developed world and LDCs in the areas of population and migration/refugees. In fact, there are only limited circumstances under which the international community in general – meaning a coalition of both major powers and LDCs – will frame a demographic issue as an international security problem and respond accordingly.

## Interests and preferences

This divide can be seen more clearly by examining the specific interests and preferences of the major stakeholders noted above. Demography-oriented IOs and NGOs generally have a human rights or development-focused policy agenda that does not always translate into a clear set of international security concerns. The IOM in particular, for example, is devoted to humane and orderly migration; it was established in 1951 and now includes 162 member states plus nine states with observer status. It attempts to promote international cooperation in migratory affairs and provide humanitarian assistance for migrants, refugees and internally displaced people. The UNHCR was established in 1950 to help cope with the massive humanitarian consequences of WWII; the fact that it took five years of post-war stress for the international community to organize some degree of cooperation in this area speaks volumes about the difficulties involved here. Additionally, the UNHCR was expected to disband after its three-year mandate expired – another highly optimistic, and obviously very incorrect, assumption about the scale of the post-war refugee problem. The WHO also has an interest in health policies related to international demography, such as infant mortality, child health and ageing, as do other more general humanitarian NGOs. Overall, these groups generally resist the framing of their activities as international *security* missions, which in their view is a much too narrow way to address the humanitarian needs of certain populations and may even undermine their reputations as humanitarian organizations.

This framing is where the interests of major powers and LDCs tend to collide. Developed states tend to curb their population growth as they become industrialized: their citizens live longer, more infants survive and fewer children are needed to help support the family. As a result, families have fewer children and population growth levels gradually approach the replacement rate noted above. This simultaneous reduction of both birth and death rates in the developed world is known as the *demographic transition* (Chesnais, 2001) and is likely to occur in most LDCs as well, but only if they develop and modernize to the same degree as rich states, which will take years if not decades. Similarly, the major powers have adopted varying degrees of restrictions on their immigration policies to avoid the perceived social and economic costs of coping with large numbers of often poor incomers. Nor do major powers frequently suffer from the types of intrastate and interstate conflicts associated with large numbers of refugees and IDPs.

The opposite, of course, is true of most LDCs in the international system, which suffer from not just higher levels of population growth but also problems related to the movement of people, so once again we have a non-traditional security issue that must inevitably be seen in part as a clash of interests between North and South, or rich and poor states. Thus, international security in this realm can mean different things to different stakeholders: security for developed states may refer to the ability to isolate themselves from migrant/refugee related problems, while security for LDCs might involve a greater capacity to aid or even assimilate refugee populations and/or to cope with a loss of their own people as they migrate to other more stable or more developed states. When such migrants possess crucial skills, making them more attractive as immigrants to developed states, an LDC can suffer a type of economic loss known as *brain drain.* Overall, then, whether states will support or resist cooperation on any demography-related international security problem depends to a large degree on their own individual situations regarding population growth and the movements of people. As these situations – and thus vulnerability – vary so dramatically, it can take an extraordinarily high degree of leadership to create a critical mass of like-minded stakeholders powerful enough to act decisively in this realm.

## The use of force

The perception that procreation and freedom to pursue better opportunities or to avoid threats to one's life are normal human behaviours, if not formal human rights, seriously complicates the question of whether force should be used to either restrain or facilitate these activities. As always, the answer to this question depends on how the security threat, if any, is framed in these domains by powerful stakeholders, which typically means states. States are perfectly willing to use non-violent methods to cope with the pressures of population growth (or decline) and migration; as we shall see, these measures might involve tax incentives, immigration/citizenship criteria or quotas, foreign humanitarian aid and so on. Using force to deal with these problems, however, can be extremely controversial.

In the area of procreation, for example, while it would be somewhat absurd to use or threaten force to generate an increase in the birth rate (although the Nazis came close in their efforts to increase the German birth rate), force has been threatened in at least one state – China – to cope with the opposite problem: an excessively large population. China's highly controversial 'one-child policy', introduced in 1979, is a key example of the extent to which some states might act to address their population problems using highly controversial, if not draconian, measures. Although this policy is supposed to be phased out after 2015, and although it was typically enforced through economic measures such as fines and dismissals from jobs, rather than imprisonment, the heavy hand of the state was always present, and harsher punishments were not ruled out in the case of flagrant disobedience (Greenhalgh, 2008). Another large-population state, India, also uses financial incentives to encourage smaller families, preferably with two children at most.

The question of using force to deal with migration or refugees is as controversial and complicated as the forceful implementation of population policies. Most states normally use force to control their border crossings and to separate illegal visitors (or immigrants) from legal ones; such border/immigration authorities are faced with the difficult task of making such a determination in just a few seconds on the basis of a passport and a few questions. They can also use force to deport or imprison individuals who attempt to break the rules. Deportation can be deadly for immigrants whose asylum pleas are rejected by a host state; for example, in 2009 the UK resumed sending refused asylum seekers back to the DRC despite claims by lawyers and human rights campaigners that such individuals could be persecuted and tortured on their return. This policy could very negatively impact as many as 10,000 such asylum seekers in the UK.

Using force to cope with larger-scale situations, such as a mass flow of refugees fleeing a civil war, is even more complicated owing to the difficulties of balancing the humanitarian and security obligations of the state(s) involved. When such flows cross borders an international crisis may result, and states can very quickly and easily disagree about how to apply force to the problem (see this chapter's case study). This type of situation is difficult enough for states in the immediate neighbourhood; even more controversial is the option of organizing an international military intervention if such a mission is not supported by all the parties involved, which is typically the case. Finally, it should be noted that the use of force can also take the form of detention centres for undocumented immigrants waiting to be processed by the authorities, a practice which varies widely from state to state and is not subject to comprehensive international standards. For example, the UK government came under fire from children's advocacy groups in August 2009 when it was revealed that as many as 470 immigrant children were being detained for processing, nearly a third of whom were held longer than 28 days.

## Public–private domains and levels of jurisdiction

Individual decisions relating to procreation and various types of free movement are extremely private and personal. This is precisely why state involvement in such activities can be so controversial, even when they are framed as international security threats. In fact, the topic of demography raises a very important, yet unresolved, question about the political framing of security as a public versus private concern, and as a matter of personal jurisdiction versus national or international jurisdiction. Specifically, if one's personal security clearly depends upon, for example, having a larger family to work a plot of land, or moving to an area of greater economic opportunity or (especially) fleeing from a war/natural disaster, then such a choice is not just reasonable but even completely legitimate from a human rights perspective. Even illegal economic immigration can be viewed as a rational response to an unmet demand for labour in rich economies, as private firms and citizens in such states are willing to hire illegal immigrants despite possible penalties because legal citizens often are not willing to perform certain types of work at a certain wage and/or work at seasonal jobs, such as farming. However, when a great many individuals take such decisions, the collective result can easily generate a public interest, at best, and a security threat, whether national or international, at worst. Unfortunately, there are in fact no general guidelines to determine when the public security interest should trump the private/personal one, and such determinations are still generally made on an *ad hoc*, case-by-case basis by the major powers despite the best efforts of the international humanitarian aid community. This situation can change somewhat when a common perception of crisis exists (as with the outflow of Syrian refugees after 2011), yet even then it takes a great degree of deliberation and negotiation by the major stakeholders to coordinate a response, if any.

## Population trends as a policy problem

Given all the considerations above, it is no surprise that the international policy response to security-related population problems is still extremely contentious, confused and even counterproductive when a specific crisis emerges. As security threats related to population growth/composition/movements tend to inspire different types of policy responses, I shall consider them separately in each of the sections below.

### Agenda-setting

The question of excessive population growth has been on the global agenda at least since 1974, with the first meeting of the UN World Population Conference in Bucharest. This forum meets every ten years and the majority of the world's states participate in the discussions. The very first such conference saw arguments – mainly offered by the developed states – that excessive population growth in LDCs could become a major problem. The LDCs tended to resist this view, and argued that population control must not come at the expense of economic development. In their view, the best contraceptive in fact is economic development, as evidenced by the general demographic transition among developed states noted above. Once per capita income levels in LDCs begin to approach those of the OECD states, their citizens will have fewer children and the problem would almost take care of itself without resorting to drastic control measures. Moreover, it could be argued that, for rich states, the problem is not necessarily population growth but population growth among *poor* people, which is then framed in highly negative terms as a 'population explosion', 'people pollution' or a 'population plague' that must be brought under control. To a large degree, this general North–South divide has not changed very much over the past few decades, although it has been greatly intensified in recent years in terms of linking population growth in LDCs with specific patterns of crime and terrorism.

The question of mass population movements has been on the global agenda for the entire post-WWII period, although attention to specific problems in this realm varies quite widely. From a security perspective, the main concern involves forced or involuntary mass movements – refugees or IDPs – rather than the broader question of economic migration, which tends to be dealt with on a national/unilateral basis. The UN has gradually expanded its view of the nature of this problem; for example, the original (1951) UN Refugee Convention defined a refugee as a person who:

> is unable or unwilling to return to their country of origin owing to a well-founded fear of being persecuted for reasons of race, religion, nationality, membership of a particular social group, or political opinion.

This formulation was far too narrowly construed to encompass the actual nature of refugee movements in the post-war period, and today the UN's definition includes persons fleeing war or violence rather than only those who are specifically persecuted by their state of nationality. This expanded definition of 1967, which was a direct result of a continuing series of refugee movements, often brought on by civil war in LDCs, *in principle* brings a larger group of individuals under the protection of the international community (that is, the UNHCR) as compared to the original 1951 definition; *in practice*, however, the degree of protection they receive can vary widely depending on the political circumstances at the time. For example, humanitarian activists and some IOs, such as the EU (Montoya, 2008), have attempted to stress the need to protect 'women, children and other vulnerable groups' in part because this goal strongly resonates in discussions involving the broader R2P norm discussed in Chapter 5, even though most victims in conflict situations are men of all ages (Carpenter, 2005).

## Framing policy alternatives

As population pressure typically is framed in terms of excessive growth in LDCs rather than as a decline in developed states, the primary multilateral policy debate largely concerns the question of promoting population or birth control in the less developed parts of the world. The main target within LDCs is the so-called *absolute poor*, which refers to people suffering from problems such as chronic malnutrition, poor sanitation/health care, inadequate housing, illiteracy and/or disease at levels well below any reasonable definition of human dignity. These are the 'poorest of the poor', and not just in terms relative to the rich states. To deal with population pressures among these groups, the international community attempts to introduce or expand family planning programmes, which involve both educational aspects and aid/technology transfers in the form of contraception and care for infants. As we might expect, modern contraceptive measures are often rare in LDCs, especially the poorest ones, which tend to rely on pre-industrial methods: abstinence, abortion, infanticide/neglect and prolonged breastfeeding (which suppresses fertility). This attempt to modernize family planning in LDCs is also supposed to be embedded in a broader programme of aid to increase economic and social development in all LDCs, which should accelerate the onset of the demographic transition from higher to lower fertility rates as occurred among developed states over the past century.

It would be possible, of course, to replace or supplement a policy of more population control in LDCs with a policy of greater migration from LDCs to developed states. However, the question of using migration from LDCs to address population decline in more developed parts of the world creates another set of problems that may be framed as security threats depending on the situation at hand. Although it has become fashionable to refer to 'nationhood' as an 'imagined community' (Anderson, 1991) in the sense that national identity exists mainly in the minds of citizens – so that such identities can be learned, relearned and even layered on top of each other (for example, Catalan plus Spanish plus European identities) – this process is far more contentious and difficult when apparently 'too many' and 'too foreign' individuals attempt to integrate into a new community (McLaren, 2012). Even in a state as large, rich and culturally diverse as the US, the question of allowing more immigration has been one of the most sensitive political topics for well over 100 years. It is also worth remembering that the US and some European countries engaged in harsh forced sterilization programmes and restrictive immigration policies (as well as genocide in Nazi Germany) in the 20th century to socially engineer their populations according to the 'survival of the fittest' views of eugenicists (Hansen and King, 2001). For more culturally homogeneous and/or economically weaker states, immigration can be even more sensitive for both ordinary citizens and political officials, so that it is far easier to maintain the status quo – the use of varying degrees of restrictions on immigration – rather than attempt to liberalize migration to the same degree as has occurred with other economic factors of production since WWII. These restrictions can be easily targeted against certain states or ethnic groups/nationalities, so that discrimination among 'desirable' and 'undesirable' immigrants becomes national policy, whether explicitly or implicitly (Hainmueller and Hangartner, 2013).

The possibility of using migration to deal with population decline in the developed world can also be linked to the question of forced population flows. Specifically, periodic refugee crises often inspire calls to admit a certain number of refugees as permanent migrants to other LDCs or even to developed states. Although the UNHCR is nominally empowered to assist and protect such refugees and, to a lesser extent, IDPs, it cannot provide a permanent national home for these individuals if they cannot return to their state of origin. This would require other states to volunteer to accept such individuals, which can be an extremely difficult proposition owing to domestic politics in such states, especially in the developed world. Another option involves the payment of foreign aid to certain states to halt refugee flows; this option is typically reserved for states rich enough to afford such payments, and is targeted at states on or near their perimeter, such as US payments made to Haiti.

Even more controversial, finally, is the option of using various unilateral threats, typically made by population-receiving states against population-sending states. This could involve the usual tactics of disrupting aid/trade flows, but also could extend to the use of military force, which introduces an entirely new set of complications into the equation (Weiner, 1992–3). Some analysts have suggested no less than five possible military remedies for refugee crises: punishment of the assailants; the creation of safe zones in areas where refugee victims live; the creation of safe havens in areas to which refugees or IDPs have temporarily moved; an enforced truce between the parties (peacemaking/peacekeeping); or an offensive war to defeat the assailants and even topple the regime in power. These military options, which are typically framed in terms of compelling a reversal of a state's policy of forcing migration or harming refugees/IDPs rather than in terms of deterring such a policy in the first place (Dowty and Loescher, 1996; Posen, 1996), can generate all of the larger problems associated with interstate or intrastate wars, which very easily could make matters worse for both the rescuers and the rescued. However, the continued dilemma of forced refugee crises, particularly those involving genocide or ethnic cleansing, means this option – which could include bombing of the assailants – cannot be so easily discounted.

## Policy choice

Despite the controversial nature of population control in LDCs, such programmes have been agreed and implemented thanks to funding in the amount of several billion dollars, largely provided by developed states. Much of these funds are channelled through the UN Population Fund, a specialized agency of the UN established in 1969 as the UN Fund for Population Activities (UNFPA). The UNFPA provides assistance, when invited, to around 140 states organized into four major regions: Arab states/Europe, Asia/Pacific, Latin America/Caribbean and sub-Saharan Africa. This assistance is generally devoted to six specific population-related goals: universal access to services by 2015; universal primary education and closing the gender gap in education by 2015; reducing maternal mortality by 75 per cent by 2015; reducing infant mortality; increasing life expectancy; and reducing HIV infection rates. The vast majority of the world's states – over 170 at present – generally support these goals with voluntary contributions to the UNFPA; most of these goals form part of a broader human rights/development agenda – largely under the auspices of the UN's Millennium Development Goals for 2015 – rather than viewed in narrow security terms. However, the Millennium Development Goals do not specifically call for curbing population growth in LDCs, which is a major missed opportunity according to some population analysts; more importantly, although progress was made across some areas with some countries, the specific goals with the 2015 deadline were not achieved by then, so that the UN replaced the scheme with a similar list of 17 'Sustainable Development Goals' to be pursued between 2016 and 2030.

On a similar voluntary basis, many developed states have attempted to adjust their immigration and refugee/asylum policies in ways that could reduce the pressures on LDCs. Despite considerable domestic opposition, the US and Canada, for example, continue to maintain their extremely liberal policies of allowing automatic citizenship (and thus a right of immigration) for any persons born on their soil – even to illegal immigrant parents or temporary visitors. Regarding asylum, in July 2009 Obama changed America's policy in order to grant political asylum to foreign women who suffer severe physical or sexual abuse in their countries of origin, and who cannot escape such abuse because it is part of their home cultures. This decision reversed Bush's reversal of Clinton's policy on allowing domestic abuse as grounds for asylum, which clearly indicates how quickly and easily political changes can create reinterpretations of policy problems. For Obama, the deciding factor was the case of a Mexican petitioner whose husband had repeatedly raped her at gunpoint and tried to burn her alive when he found she was pregnant. Although US asylum policy is still fairly restrictive relative to other rich states, such as Sweden, it should provide more protection to such victims in the same manner as that already provided to women and girls fleeing forced genital mutilation, or female circumcision, in their home countries.

In 2000, Germany also revised its controversial, WWI-era citizenship policy to allow a right of citizenship by virtue of birth and residency in Germany, if the applicant is born to legal residents, rather than through blood kinship alone (that is, a mother or father with German citizenship). This policy helped to bring Germany's migration/citizenship policies more in line with its status as one of the more welcoming EU member states to refugees and asylum seekers (Geddes, 2008). As noted above, Germany also acted after the 2011 Syrian refugee crisis to accept more refugees and asylum seekers than the vast majority of other EU member states. In a related manner, most developed states have adopted selective immigration programmes to attract certain types of immigrants with special skills, such as scientists and engineers. The US H1B Visa programme and Germany's Green Card (now Blue Card) programme are two such examples, and tens of thousands of such immigrants have been admitted each year since these policies were established. Despite these efforts, states still vary quite widely in terms of their receptiveness to immigrants, as shown in Table 13.6.

Table 13.6  *Comparative immigration statistics, selected states*

| Rank/state | Population | Net migration rate |
|---|---|---|
| 1. Qatar | 2.2 million | 22.39 |
| 2. British Virgin Islands | 33,454 | 17.28 |
| 10. Turks and Caicos Islands | 50,280 | 9.94 |
| 13. Spain | 48.2 million | 8.31 |
| 22. Canada | 35.1 million | 5.66 |
| 23. Australia | 22.8 million | 5.65 |
| 25. Sweden | 9.8 million | 5.42 |
| 31. Ireland | 4.9 million | 4.09 |
| 34. US | 322 million | 3.86 |
| 40. UK | 64.1 million | 2.54 |
| 48. New Zealand | 4.4 million | 2.21 |
| 54. Russia | 142.4 million | 1.69 |
| 60. Germany | 80.9 million | 1.24 |
| 62. France | 66.6 million | 1.09 |
| 133. China | 1.37 billion | – 0.44 |
| 201. Lithuania | 2.9 million | – 6.27 |
| 220. Syria | 17.1 million | – 19.79 |

*Note:* 'Net migration rate' refers to the difference between the number of persons entering and leaving a state in a year, per thousand residents of that state. Rankings are based on the net migration rates.
*Source:* CIA World Factbook (2015 mid-year estimates).

Among all EU member states, for example, Spain has the highest net migration figures, while those for Lithuania are the lowest. The US and the UK are fairly similar on this measure, but they still fall behind many other OECD member states in terms of their receptiveness to migrants.

Developed states have also used targeted aid payments on a case-by-case basis to temporarily halt refugee flows, as with US aid to Haiti in the late 1980s, or with US/French aid to Thailand to encourage it to accept Vietnamese refugees. The UNHCR itself also channels aid to many LDCs, especially in Africa, to help them cope with refugees and IDPs, and thereby discourage refugees from attempting to move to the developed world (Weiner, 1992–3). The most generous approach to the refugee problem is for developed states to offer resettlement for 'worst case' persons fleeing repression or other threats to their lives; this often takes the form

## Table 13.7   *Official resettlement quotas*

| State | Quota (2001) | Year established |
|---|---|---|
| US | 80,000 | 1980 |
| Canada | 11,000 | 1978 |
| Australia | 10,000 | Unknown |
| Norway | 1,500 | Unknown |
| Sweden | 1,375 | 1950 |
| New Zealand | 750 | 1979 |
| Finland | 750 | 1979 |
| Denmark | 517 | 1989 |
| Netherlands | 500 | 1984 |
| UK | 500 | 2001 |

*Source:* UK Refugee Council.

of annual ceilings (or resettlement quotas) on the number of persons to be admitted. The largest such quotas are listed in Table 13.7.

These quotas are established by such states on the basis of their individual domestic political processes, and can be adjusted on a yearly basis depending upon domestic and international political factors, such as a war or famine. In this sense they are much closer to guidelines rather than formal targets, and states always reserve the right to control their immigrant numbers as they see fit. Since the 2011 Syrian crisis, for example, most rich states have temporarily increased their intakes; the EU in particular attempted to devise a formula for spreading Europe's share of refugees across its member states (see case study, Box 13.1).

Finally, the use of threats has been adopted by some states facing migratory pressures, as with India against Bangladesh or Bangladesh against Burma. In the former case, economic sanctions were threatened; in the latter case, the Bangladesh government threatened to arm Burmese Muslim refugees against the (majority Buddhist) Burmese state. A similar policy of arming refugees was made by Pakistan against Afghanistan after the 1978 communist coup in Afghanistan, which prompted the Soviet invasion of that state a year later. Unilateral military action has been attempted as well in certain cases, as with India against Pakistan, and with India against Sri Lanka. The US also used military force to create a safe zone for ethnic Kurds in Iraq during the 1991 Gulf War (Operation Provide Comfort); this policy was then repeated and greatly expanded after the 2003

US attack on Iraq. The UN similarly attempted to create safe havens for threatened populations in Bosnia during the 1990s and, on a lesser scale, in the DRC, Lebanon, Somalia and Sri Lanka. However, if the UN or any other IO creates such a safe haven but then fails to protect it, the potential for a massacre at the hands of the threatening force can arise, as in the killing of over 8,000 Bosnian Muslims at the 'safe haven' of Srebrenica, the largest mass murder in Europe since WWII. This tragedy clearly reminds us of the dangers involved when the international community makes a promise it cannot keep.

## The politics of policy effectiveness

As many of the remedies for population control in LDCs involve the provision of aid from developing states, the problem of voluntary defection always looms large and could negatively impact policy effectiveness. Refusing to disburse funds that had been publicly pledged does occur, and illustrates whether governments take seriously – or not – the threat of excessive population growth. One notable example was the refusal of the Bush administration to disburse about $34 million per year on international UNFPA population programmes between 2002 and 2008, even though the funds had been approved by Congress. Involuntary defection occurs far too frequently as well, particularly when states face other problems, such as the 2008 global economic crisis discussed in Chapter 10. Similarly, a comprehensive multilateral effort to deal with the potential ageing crisis in the developed world simply does not exist, so this problem will be dealt with on a unilateral basis for the foreseeable future. Finally, we continue to see wide variation in the implementation of international responses to specific migration or refugee problems; although a passive approach in the form of financial aid is often applied almost automatically in the more serious cases, a more active approach in the form of accepting refugees and/or intervening directly depends on the willingness of major powers to play such a role. As we have seen, this willingness depends on the nature of the problem as experienced by the major powers rather than on the experience of the refugees themselves or on the application of common multilateral norms in such situations.

Regarding various measures of effectiveness, it is very difficult to apply a total victory standard to demography-related international security problems given the multiple ways to frame such threats, and the wide variance in vulnerability to such threats as discussed earlier. However, some international goals, such as returning most if not all refugees or IDPs in a given conflict zone to their original homes, could be treated as a total victory standard, although this is very rarely achieved in the

**Box 13.1   Europe's refugee crisis**

*Major conflicts in poor states can lead quickly to refugee crises in other states.*

How might refugee flows become a matter of international security? The EU faced this question in a dramatic fashion after 2011 when another type of international security problem – intrastate war in Syria – spilled over to neighbouring states in the form of refugees fleeing the violence. By the end of 2014, Europe was facing its worst refugee crisis since WWII, with around four million extremely desperate people fleeing from Syria into other states nearby; around three-quarters of these individuals went to Turkey and Lebanon, but well over 100,000 headed to Europe, some via sea routes across the Mediterranean and Aegean Seas. These flows added to the growing numbers of migrants and refugees already coming to Europe from other parts of Africa, also mainly across the sea thanks in part to vessels commanded by human traffickers. Most tragically, large numbers of these

→

real world. More generally, the goals of universal access to services and universal primary education by 2015 could be treated in terms of a total victory standard, although such goals of course were not achieved by 2015 if 'universal' really means every person on the planet. Similarly, one

$\rightarrow$

people began to drown in the waters between Africa and Europe, sometimes within sight of EU member states, such as Greece and Italy. In just one notable incident in October 2013, 359 people drowned off the coast of the tiny Italian island of Lampedusa, which finally prompted the EU to take more action to deal with the crisis.

However, according to regular polls conducted by Eurostat, a majority of people in most EU states oppose non-European immigration; in fact, only a few EU member states, such as Sweden, demonstrate fairly strong support for such individuals (Geddes, 2008). Thus, thanks in part to security concerns (i.e. economic loss, cultural differences and fears of terrorism/crime) associated with migrants from African and Middle Eastern countries, some EU member state governments, supported by large numbers of their citizens, were reluctant to cooperate regarding efforts to rescue people on the seas in general and to distribute the Syrian refugee burden across Europe in particular. These fears were based partly on the fact that most EU member states participate in its free movement scheme (the Schengen Agreement), so it would be difficult to control movements of non-EU citizens once they entered, whether legally or illegally. The EU also had another rule in place, the Dublin Regulation, which required refugees to apply for help in the first EU member state in which they arrive. However, with several thousand people drowning each year since 2011 off the southern shores of the EU, in August 2015, Germany unilaterally suspended its compliance with the Dublin Regulation so that it could take more Syrian refugees even if they landed elsewhere first. Although this decision, news of which spread quickly via social media and other networks, was supported by human rights groups and even the European Commission, it increased the pressures on smaller EU states who still had to cope with thousands of refugees transiting their territories hoping to reach Germany or other like-minded EU states.

Thanks to continuing refugee pressures and divisions among its own member states, the EU still pursues a chaotic and incoherent approach to the crisis. It has launched a naval operation (EUNAVFOR Med) to deal with human trafficking on the seas, but failed to encourage all EU member states to share the intake of Syrian refugees based on a quota system devised by the European Commission. Worse, some EU member states have suspended their participation in Schengen and even have built walls to protect their borders against illegal migration of any type, while the UK voted to leave the EU partly because of fears about immigration. These acts show how quickly and easily the plight of foreign refugees can lead (supposedly) liberal states to violate their own humanitarian principles; this is especially ironic in the EU as it faces a widespread population decline and could probably use all the migrants and refugees it could take.

could argue for specific population growth or fertility targets; the zero population growth movement is one prominent example of this approach. Except for the example of China, however, it is difficult to believe that many other states would take such drastic measures to meet such targets, but this possibility cannot be ruled out given potential population stresses in the developing world. Even so, in China the one-child policy is being phased out as its costs may have outweighed its benefits, especially in the form of female abortion/infanticide and the resulting large numbers of young men (known as 'bare branches' in China) who will not be able to find a spouse; at present there are 117 men for every 100 Chinese women. China's government also has larger concerns about a lack of young workers to support an ageing population in the region thanks to the one-child policy. Similar problems are occurring in India, which uses cultural norms rather than official policies to devalue women relative to men; in that case, each year hundreds of thousands of female foetuses are aborted because of their gender even though this practice is illegal. Abandonment of female children and outright infanticide of females are also known to occur throughout India and other LDCs, a practice that could result in a socially unstable gender balance.

Given these problems, the application of standards based on historical trends or comparative metrics might be more appropriate. Regarding population growth, such measures are most often applied to LDCs where such problems seem most acute, and one can easily point to many positive general trends here, such as a reduction of infant and maternal mortality coupled with an increase in life expectancies throughout the developing world. It is also possible to isolate several success stories in terms of using international assistance to manage population-related problems, as in Bangladesh, Indonesia, Mexico and Thailand. One might also use counterfactual historical standards to prove the efficacy of certain policies; for example, European integration theorists could argue that the EU's enlargement to the East helped to reform former central/Eastern communist states into stable democratic ones, and thus prevent a major migration crisis between the two halves of Europe.

The question of managing mass flows of refugees and IDPs, however, is far more problematic. Based on the most recent (2015) comprehensive data from the UNHCR, the total number of refugees/IDPs (including Palestinians) worldwide has increased steadily since 2010, to nearly 60 million by 2015. Beyond the war in Syria, the civil conflict in Darfur, Sudan, has produced a major crisis of IDPs, yet the international community seems reluctant, as with Rwanda in the 1990s, to do much more than send financial aid (about $1 billion a year). An estimated 2.7 million IDPs are barely surviving in aid camps in Darfur, and there is still no end in sight even though some of these unfortunates have been homeless since the 2006 peace agreement in that state collapsed. The conclusion seems obvious: if turning refugees/IDPs into returnees is not possible for a variety of reasons, most of which are related to the ongoing intrastate conflicts discussed in Chapter 5, then they must be absorbed by other states, often as permanent residents (though not necessarily citizens).

Again, this problem is felt mainly within LDCs, and their tendency to circulate refugees among themselves provides a kind of safety valve to prevent much more emigration to richer states where there is very little political will to accept refugees/IDPs. However, this solution may create more problems than it solves in the long run, not only in the form of general population pressures in LDCs but also in the form of fears about social instability, transnational crime and even radicalization or terrorism on the part of such unwanted and despondent people, even though these outcomes actually are quite rare and/or inflated by certain states (Messina, 2014).

These chronic problems in turn also add to the overall 'security gap' between the developed and developing worlds, as noted in several previous chapters. As many of these problems can be effectively contained within LDCs, it can be difficult for the international community to respond in a more decisive manner in order to close this gap. Many observers advocate much more trade with, and aid to, LDCs to solve problems related to demography and other non-traditional security threats (Widgren, 1990); this option, however, is clearly a very long-term solution that may not show positive results – at least in security affairs – for quite some time. In fact, high growth rates in LDCs would have to be achieved independently of trade/aid for quite some time to have a positive impact on demographics; moreover, high rates of migration can still occur despite high growth rates, as with industrializing states in the nineteenth century (such as the UK) or more recent developing states in the twentieth century (the 'Asian tigers'). This means at least one or two generations of rising wages and standards of living are required in LDCs for the demographic transition to appear in terms of fertility rates and emigration levels, and it cannot be accelerated easily with trade or aid (Weiner, 1992–3), although temporary payments can entice governments of LDCs to halt forced emigration.

## Summary

Like intrastate wars, security problems generated by population growth and mass movements are a chronic feature of the post-Cold War era. In fact, the end of the Cold War itself is directly related to increased migratory movements in several parts of the world, while longer-term economic trends are responsible for the increasing disparities in population growth and ageing patterns between the developed and developing worlds. Yet the international community still finds it difficult to respond to such problems in a coherent and assertive multilateral fashion. In a sense, and of all problems covered in this volume, those related to demography seem to represent a kind of last bastion of state sovereignty, and most states seem very reluctant to abandon their unilateral approaches to population growth, social stability, migration and refugee flows in favour of a more concerted international effort. This general reluctance is compounded by the complexities involved in framing such concerns as international *security* threats; as there are multiple causes and multiple problems at work here, the international community can find it difficult if not impossible to settle on a single or dominant solution, even in the face of a crisis as severe as those in Darfur or Syria.

This situation is a direct result of the state-centric nature of the international system itself, as states – not private firms or IOs or NGOs – are ultimately responsible for managing their populations in terms of various factors or trends, including the questions of the terms of entry for foreigners or who enjoys a right of legal residency or citizenship, as well as control of borders (on border control in particular, see the special issue of *Security Dialogue*, 45/3, 2014). Yet this state authority can break down easily or otherwise fail in certain circumstances: populations can grow too large for their states, or can decline and put the state at risk from others. Mass movements of people can similarly, but far more dramatically, challenge state authority and stability, especially when they are forced by one state upon another. Such threats can be framed in terms of identity or economic loss, or more seriously as a matter of life and death. State-centrism also means that all people in the world, in principle, should be a citizen of at least one state and must turn to their own state for protection. Again, this practice can break down for a variety of reasons, which then generates IDPs, refugees, asylum seekers and stateless persons in numbers well beyond the managerial capacities of a single state, even a well-intentioned one. Questions of multi-ethnic states, dual or multiple citizenship, and intrastate wars, especially ethnic ones, can greatly complicate these determinations, as can the broader trend towards globalization.

As these problems are most acute in LDCs, more developed states can often afford to turn a blind eye to such problems until they arrive on their shores. However, rich states – most of which are liberal democracies – seem to want the best of both worlds: free movement of factors of production including, at least in principle, labour; they also attempt to promote the related idea of a right to citizenship and migration for all people, especially those living under authoritarian regimes. However, they are not so willing to accept many such migrants – except those with a high degree of education and/or special skills – for a variety of reasons discussed above. This contradictory, if not hypocritical, attitude is compounded by the variance in vulnerability to population pressures and mass population flows as experienced between the developed and developing worlds. Even so, various forms of containment and population control, especially among groups like the 'poorest of the poor', should be considered very carefully and sensitively considering the potential for such policies to be used as an informal or indirect type of ethnic cleansing and eugenics; we must always remember the early history of population control in developed states, including the US and in Europe, was linked closely to a desire to eliminate the 'feeble-minded' and other 'undesirables' from the gene pool (Black, 2003). Such programmes easily can run to tragic excesses even in liberal democratic states; in authoritarian regimes, such as China (and Nazi Germany before it), the problem could become even worse.

Despite these problems, the international community has managed to create some standards regarding the protection of these populations, and has organized limited cooperation to deal with them on a case-by-case basis. This *ad hoc* attention and intervention, however, is generally not replicated regarding the longer-term question of ageing populations in the developed world and younger (and larger) populations in LDCs. Yet if developed states cannot increase their own fertility rates to levels near or equal to the replacement rate, then the only solution might be a greater acceptance of migrants from LDCs, even if only on a temporary basis. This trend almost certainly will accelerate in coming decades, and may simultaneously reduce population pressures in the developing world even if it may increase social instability in the developed world if the OECD states do not take stronger measures to assimilate such populations, which should include educating their existing citizens about the positive benefits of immigration and refuting media reports about the 'imported problems' of immigrants. This could require far more political courage than is normally available in many rich states, however, where leaders are far too easily tempted to frame immigration as a crisis or threat rather than as an opportunity. If these leaders fail, the international security aspects of population growth and migration could easily become the defining issues of the twenty-first century if the demographic transition in LDCs lags too far behind their ability to cope with the needs of seven or eight billion people.

## Further reading

Alexander Betts and Gil Loescher (eds.) (2011). *Refugees in International Relations*. Oxford: Oxford University Press.

Edwin Black (2003). *War Against the Weak: Eugenics and America's Campaign to Create a Master Race*. New York: Basic Books.

Jean-Claude Chesnais (2001). *The Demographic Transition: Stages, Patterns, and Economic Implications*. Oxford: Oxford University Press.

Wayne A. Cornelius, Philip L. Martin and James F. Hollifield (eds.) (1994). *Controlling Immigration: A Global Perspective*. Stanford: Stanford University Press.

Andrew Geddes (2008). *Immigration and European Integration: Towards Fortress Europe*. Manchester: Manchester University Press.

Susan Greenhalgh (2008). *Just One Child: Science and Policy in Deng's China*. Berkeley, CA: University of California Press.

Jef Huysmans (2006). *The Politics of Insecurity: Fear, Migration, and Asylum in the EU*. London: Routledge.

Nana K. Poku and David Graham (eds.) (2000). *Redefining Security: Population Movements and National Security*. Santa Barbara: Praeger.

Ole Wæver, Barry Buzan, Morten Kelstrup and Pierre Lemaitre (1993). *Identity, Migration, and the New Security Agenda in Europe*. London: Pinter.

Weiner, Myron (ed.) (1993). *International Migration and Security*. Boulder: Westview.

Weiner, Myron (ed.) (1995). *The Global Migration Crisis: Challenges to States and Human Rights*. New York: HarperCollins.

# The Future of International Security Studies

When framed in terms of anthropogenic threats, as in this volume, the problem of international security basically amounts to saving humanity from itself. If so, then this seems to be a never-ending struggle, for every major security problem discussed in this volume – from war to drug trafficking to climate change to infectious disease and beyond – continues to receive attention from the world's media and political elites on a regular basis. Even in a single day, the news headlines may be dominated by several *simultaneous* international security problems, such as a terrorist attack, a global economic crisis, alarming new data about global warming and a flu pandemic. This range of coverage, on an average day, illustrates perfectly the single most important reason for framing international security studies as I have done in this volume: the problem of competing priorities. We live in a world of finite political and material resources, yet have an apparently endless list of global problems to manage. Under these circumstances, what topics will gain our attention as urgent international *security* concerns when the world's policy agenda is already so crowded? And how does the international community typically determine and manage these priorities? Without a sound and sophisticated understanding of these questions, we can neither effectively analyse current competing security issues nor confidently predict what types of issues are likely to become international security problems in the future.

This question of understanding, however, raises its own set of problems. Although the international security agenda now effectively includes all of the topics examined in Chapters 4–13 of this volume, our comprehension of these issues still varies quite widely as measured by their academic literatures. Thus, while we find hundreds of books and articles devoted to military-related topics in international security, this level of attention gradually tapers off as we move towards the analysis of non-traditional security threats such as economic crises, infectious disease and migration, which results in a much smaller common body of knowledge in these areas from an international security perspective. This situation is gradually changing, however, and it has been inspiring to discover more than enough compelling works on a number of non-traditional security threats to justify their inclusion in a volume such as this. Equally innovative has been the range of new concepts and theories developed to advance our understanding of both traditional and non-traditional security problems.

All of this attention and coverage, however, does not imply a higher degree of consensus regarding these topics, whether on the part of academics or policy-makers. Debates continue to rage among security specialists regarding the nature of various threats and the effectiveness of various policy options, as well as the utility of various explanatory frameworks drawn from realism, liberalism, constructivism and other theories. This discord can be seen not only in the context of individual topics but also in the importance of these topics relative to each other, whether as objects of academic analysis or as targets of international policy. When these disputes are coupled with our increasingly globalized modern communications networks, which put huge amounts of (often conflicting) data and opinions at our very fingertips, we face the clear danger of accumulating far too much information about security problems, and not enough cumulative knowledge or understanding about them. Again, this problem can be framed as a question of priorities, which in turn also involves *values*, as in the choice between various referent objects to be protected (such as national military forces versus a vulnerable refugee group), or in the choice between which types of policies to pursue (such as hard power versus soft power options). Finally, these debates can also be fuelled by more narrow considerations in the form of the types of evidence used to measure a specific security threat, or in the standards for effectiveness used to evaluate various security policies.

Given these trends, the study of contemporary international security may be in danger of becoming far more frustrating than stimulating. I believe it remains stimulating because questions relating to the protection of valued things continue to inspire innovative research across a range of disciplines, and because difficult problems of international security occur across the globe with regular, if not relentless, frequency. Framed most broadly, the study of international security represents no less than the study of the fate of humanity itself, which includes all of the resources, institutions and other factors that sustain human life or that make life worth living. However, the potentially unlimited breadth of security problems, the cacophony of varied opinions on the topic and the pace of global change also can make the study of international security very frustrating. Particularly since the end of the Cold War, a proliferation of theories, concepts and paradigms can make the topic difficult if not impossible to teach systematically in a coherent fashion across universities and countries. The interdisciplinary nature of contemporary international security studies also does not lend itself well to parsimonious explanations of cause-and-effect relationships, as competing disciplines often adopt different foundational assumptions, rely on different common bodies of knowledge and employ their own unique methodologies.

In short, then, international security is more relevant than ever before, yet the field is also in great danger of losing its analytical leverage as a discipline – assuming it ever had such leverage in the first place – as scholars increasingly contest the very definition and basic content of the field, and in turn unwittingly risk confusing rather than inspiring the next generation of educated graduates, informed citizens, official policy-makers and creative scholars who will need to contend with future security problems. A comparison of security-related textbooks easily confirms this assertion, as they vary widely in terms of their definitions of the field, foundational theories and concepts, organizational logics, historical breadth and topical subjects (Hough, 2004; Booth, 2005; Kolodziej, 2005; Sheehan, 2005; Morgan, 2006; Buzan, 2007; Hughes, 2009; Buzan and Hansen, 2011; Bourne, 2013; Browning, 2013; Dannreuther, 2013; Williams, 2013; Hough et al., 2015; Collins, 2016). Some of these texts focus more narrowly on traditional military-defence issues, while others are so broad and inclusive that they can be read as general introductions to international relations or world politics. It is encouraging, however, that two major new journals were launched in 2015: the *European Journal of International Security* and the *Journal of Global Security Studies* (although it is too early to tell whether they will make a major impact on the field). In the rest of this chapter, I revisit some of these issues, as first reflected by some important findings based on the academic work on the various topics covered in this volume. Following this discussion, I speculate on the near future of international security studies, based on several areas of opportunity for more research in the field. Finally, I revisit one specific real-world trend in international security affairs mentioned throughout this volume: the 'human security' agenda.

## The unsteady state of international security studies

This volume has focused on the framing and management of common security problems by the international community, defined in various ways depending on the topic at hand. My political analysis approach to this topic, which attempts to balance positivist and critical/normative epistemologies, inevitably involves the question of power and human agency: who has the power to determine how the international community should prioritize, and then deal with, a certain security problem? This approach, in turn, can easily be interpreted as realist in inspiration, and with good reason. Unlike other contending theories, realism seems far more coherent and consistent in terms of its core principles. And the empirical evolution of the state system itself certainly lends credence to the idea of a 'law of the jungle' approach to international security: actors who do not have enough power to protect themselves risk dominance or outright destruction at the hand of stronger players. National leaders who ignore this state of affairs, and its relationship to international security, might put their states at grave risk. Conversely, states that do survive may be able to play a role in setting international security policies, assuming they are powerful enough to assert their preferences. As we have seen throughout this volume, both traditional and non-traditional international security problems are defined in large part by the attitudes and policies of the major powers, which would seem to confirm a realist approach to international security.

However, we also see the tenacious persistence of more liberal approaches to certain international security problems, including those related to war. These approaches are inspired by ethical/normative liberalism, social liberalism, economic liberalism, legal/institutional liberalism and democratic liberalism. Thus, we see the use of arms control agreements, international criminal law and courts, MLATs, MEAs, formal IOs, democratization programmes, technical expertise and many other liberal-inspired attempts to manage international security affairs without first resorting to armed force. Moreover, these liberal approaches can interact with and strongly complement each other: the most peaceful of all worlds in the liberal view is one where enlightened and self-disciplined humans are embedded in well-functioning democratic states, which enjoy a high degree of social and economic interactions among each other, and are in turn embedded in a thick web of international laws and institutions to help manage their common problems through credible negotiated commitments. In this view, true international security is achieved through these interacting factors, which some have termed 'complex interdependence' or a 'community of democracies' or a 'zone of liberalism' (Keohane and Nye, 1977; Lipson, 2003), as opposed to the repetitive, and possibly dysfunctional, power-balancing dynamics stressed by realists.

Yet in the fairly short time span since the first edition of this book appeared (2010) we have seen a persistent recurrence, if not intensification, of major international security challenges that, again, seem to confirm the futility of relying too much on wishful thinking among enlightened stakeholders who fail to manage those challenges effectively, whether unilaterally or multilaterally. This verdict applies to major traditional threats such as interstate war, intrastate war and terrorism (i.e. Russia's annexation of Crimea, Syria's civil war and the rise of Islamic State) as well as to non-traditional threats such as economic security, pandemic disease and refugees/migration (the ongoing eurozone crisis, the 2013 Ebola outbreak and the Mediterranean refugee drownings). It also seems we will have to learn to live with rising cybercrime/cybersecurity threats (not to mention the advent of cyberwar) as well as with the various problems associated with a rise in global temperatures of two degrees Celsius or more. At the same time, major IOs involved in global/regional governance and security, such as the UN, the WHO, the IMF, the WTO, NATO and the EU, seem increasingly overburdened and under-resourced to cope with these challenges. Even in Europe, where the EU has worked for decades to manage complex interdependence, the system is under stress from social/economic malaise, from domestic and international terrorism, and from the UK's vote to leave the EU, which could destabilize European integration even more. Finally, it is also very uncertain, still, how the US and China will manage their increasingly contentious relationship in light of confrontations in the South China Sea, in cyberspace, in the global economy and even in outer space.

And herein lies the perennial paradox between realist and liberal approaches to international security: as individuals (rather than states in anarchy) are at the root of all liberal theories, liberal assumptions about the positive effects of norms, rules, institutions, commerce, democracy and similar factors are often highly contingent on what might be an unduly optimistic view of human behaviour. In other words, the various factors stressed by liberals – as well as some critical or normative theorists – strongly depend on the good faith and personal security, not to mention power resources, of the humans operating behind those factors. This good faith among like-minded, enlightened individuals might be taken for granted when actors feel secure and prosperous, yet under more insecure conditions liberal assumptions might be totally unwarranted. If so, then major powers and other stakeholders in the international community must consider alternative approaches – whether realist and otherwise – to manage the problems they identify as international security threats. Thus, while realism and liberalism can still be seen as ideal types of international political orders, with each one at the end of a hypothetical continuum of such orders, most recurring political interactions of interest to this volume have actually fallen somewhere between a pure realist and a pure liberal world depending on the issue and stakeholders in question.

These political interactions, framed as major international security problems, have become more numerous and complex as well since the end of the Cold War. This change largely involves the inclusion of non-traditional threats in international security affairs, often lumped together as the 'new security agenda.' Taken together, these issues represent one of the most important trends in contemporary international security studies. As these problems have always been with us, however, the critical question here is why, or whether, they are being treated as international *security* problems rather than as 'ordinary' global issues. Part of the answer here might involve the changing nature of these problems in recent years; for example, many such non-traditional problems can be linked, whether directly or indirectly, to broader globalization processes or to the more specific problem of weak or failed states – two major themes throughout this volume. Revolutions in transportation and communications in particular have helped to expand the potential for a local problem, such as a financial crisis, to be perceived as an international threat, especially if it undermines the national stability of a powerful state. Yet another part of the answer, however, involves the deliberate political framing of these sorts of problem by certain stakeholders, which is why such an analysis has been incorporated into this volume. This involves not just the 'securitization' of certain problems, such as economic stability, public health, environmental protection and migration, but also the internationalization of what used to be primarily domestic problems, such as organized crime.

This political framing, however, is not strictly limited to government stakeholders; nor does it always require political power in the form of material or hard power resources, as a realist might assume. This fact points to a second important trend in contemporary international security affairs: the expansion of political stakeholders and their associated types of power, whether acting as agenda-setters/advocates, threats, victims, witnesses or security providers. As the threat of major power war recedes relative to previous centuries, and as globalization expands, future security threats are more likely to be framed in terms of non-state stakeholders and factors. Naturally, these dynamics will vary widely depending on the topic at hand; however, even in the realm of a very traditional problem such as war, we have seen some important trends in the form of the expanded roles played by private actors such as PMCs, NGOs and even MNCs. The media and various internet communications, such as websites, social media and blogs, might also play a role in agenda-setting and in the evaluation of government claims, although such voices can adopt a variety of viewpoints and may cancel each other out. Still, non-state stakeholders of all types are especially prominent in the realm of non-traditional security problems, where banks, ISPs, public health officials, insurance firms, credit agencies and a host of other quasi-public actors might assert influence over the emergence of, and official response to, an international security threat. Increasingly, and in the name of security, banks and ISPs must report on their customers, health officials must report on their patients, university professors must report on their foreign students and so on – even if these actors do not wish to perform such functions.

These two trends – an expanded security agenda and an expanded range of major stakeholders – have directly inspired a third important development in the field: the apparent decline of grand paradigmatic debates about international relations and international security theories (for example, see the special issue on this topic in the *European Journal of International Relations*, September 2013). Especially in the analysis of many non-traditional security problems, it is possible to find theoretically informed works that make virtually no reference to realism or other general theories of international relations. Instead, we find an increasing number of more narrowly construed approaches, or middle-range theories, developed precisely to examine a single new international security problem rather than works that attempt to defend one grand theory over another. As noted in Chapter 2 of this volume, such grand theories are simply too general, and often too rigidly state-centric, to explain fully the core concerns of international security studies as defined in this volume. This point even applies to certain aspects of contemporary interstate and intrastate war, which can involve extremely complicated interactions between state and non-state stakeholders, between hard and soft power resources, and between various conceptions of effectiveness or victory that do not map easily onto the more traditional assumptions of grand theories such as realism. In response to such limitations, many scholars have become very adept at borrowing concepts, variables and even entire theories from many disciplines, such as economics, sociology, environmental studies and epidemiology, to fill in the gaps between the traditional grand theories of international relations or international security.

This theoretical expansion and eclecticism also point to a more specific conceptual trend in the study of international security: the apparent decline of strategic or defence studies relative to the rise of alternative approaches in the discipline (Betts, 1997). As discussed in Chapter 2, the rise of realism in general, and of strategic studies in particular, was a direct result of the emphasis on bipolar Cold War politics reflected in much of the scholarly literature on international security between the 1950s and the 1980s. Since then, the end of the Cold War and the rise in attention to non-traditional threats and non-state actors in international security makes it very difficult to reduce security relations to the type of game–theoretic or action–reaction relationships often assumed by classical strategists. Instead, we have not just an expanded and more diffuse range of threats and stakeholders to consider, but also far more complex and dynamic relations between those stakeholders and threats. For example, one stakeholder can act (or be treated) as a victim, threat and security provider within the context of a single security problem, even an inter-state war. This problem is difficult enough when dealing with obvious and direct anthropogenic threats, such as insurgents, terrorists or organized criminals; however, when one examines less obvious and indirect, but equally anthropogenic, threats, such as travellers infected with swine flu or a mass refugee exodus, the idea of a strategic international response to such a diffuse problem or threat becomes even more difficult.

That said, and although strategic/defence studies, not to mention realism more generally, seems like an easy target, especially in light of the non-traditional problems discussed in this volume, we still have no consensus on a leading alternative to these approaches. Increasingly it seems as if each individual international security problem requires its own unique theory to explain it. However, I have argued that it is possible to examine all of these problems through a common set of concepts and principles derived from political science, most of which centre on the collective definition of international security problems (or consensual knowledge about values and threats) and the processes of multilateral international cooperation (or principled collective political action) used to manage those problems. The importance of these two political processes can be seen in terms of examples taken from every chapter of this book, from intervening in certain intrastate wars to dealing with certain types of organized crime to attempts to stem the tide of certain infectious diseases. This approach also respects a range of major theories of international cooperation depending on the problem at hand, from more realist-based theories of hegemonic leadership to more liberal or constructivist theories involving institutions, regional cooperation, epistemic communities and so on (Milner, 1992).

## The future international security research agenda

In light of the considerations above, it is also possible to summarize several major areas of opportunity regarding the near-term international security research agenda. As scholars continue to investigate many past conflicts for insights into modern problems (for example, see the special issue of *International Security* on 'Reflections on WWI', Summer 2014), as well as develop new theories and methodologies, all of these efforts should involve giving far more systematic and rigorous attention to the full range of new or non-traditional security threats noted above. Although these topics can be gainfully analysed as individual threats, it is also worth examining their interrelationships in more detail than one often finds in the literature; for example, as with the links between intrastate war and organized crime, between public health and water resources, between economic stability and migration, between cybersecurity and terrorism and so on. As all international security problems require material resources to manage them effectively, understanding the political economy of security remains an important priority in the discipline (Mastanduno, 1998; Kapstein, 2002–3), especially in light of the role of various profit-seeking private stakeholders noted throughout this volume. For example, business interests beyond arms dealers and PMCs can be an important factor affecting the 'market' for security in conflict zones, even among Islamist stakeholders (Ahmad, 2014–15). This more comprehensive approach to analysing various interrelationships also could be framed as the 'securitization' of new public spaces, such as outer space and cyberspace, as well as the resurrection of erstwhile threats like maritime piracy or of former solutions such as the use of mercenaries or other private actors to provide security. Still another way to address these relationships involves the more general human security agenda, which will be examined in more detail later in this chapter.

A related area of opportunity involves more work on the political consequences of variation in vulnerability to certain international security problems, especially regarding non-traditional threats. As we have seen with multiple examples, it is difficult for any political stakeholder to make a case about a possible international security threat if states and other major stakeholders perceive wide dissimilarities in their exposure to that threat. This problem can be seen most prominently in the difference in vulnerabilities between the developed and developing worlds, yet also extends to differences within each of these main regions (such as American versus European vulnerabilities) and among major stakeholders within and across regions (such as state officials versus MNCs or NGOs). Even for apparently global threats such as economic crises and climate change, some stakeholders may believe they are immune for a variety of reasons; developed states in particular tend to believe they can spend or invent their way out of some security problems. The dramatic rise in drone strikes launched by the US and other states in recent years is just one prominent example of relying on technology when its effectiveness, not to mention harmful side effects and legality, are uncertain (McCrisken, 2013; Bergen and Rothenberg, 2014; Boyle, 2015; Gusterson, 2016). And if national differences about vulnerability matter, then more systematic comparative work is needed on how those differences might then transfer or migrate to the international system level. Such research on comparative vulnerabilities could be integrated with various types of forecasting models, such as related to state failure, economic crises, climate change and so on, to provide a more sophisticated analysis of how the international community is likely to respond to a certain threat.

The growing body of research on drones and cybersecurity/cyberwar in recent years also suggests another major path of enquiry: the role of knowledge in general and technology in particular in international relations (Skolnikoff, 1994; Tenner, 1997; Broderick, 2001; Chiles, 2001; Rappert, 2007; Simmons, 2011; Akaev and Pantin, 2014). Scholars have been concerned with weapons technology since the invention of this discipline a hundred years ago, yet the fast pace of technological change beyond the realm of armaments applies to a wide range of security problems, involving traditional and non-traditional threats. Social media is one prominent example, as it can be deployed by threatening stakeholders (such as Islamic State) to recruit followers and spread a consistent message (Klausen, 2015). Another example involves mobile phones, which can be used to organize political action, violent and otherwise; one study has argued that increased mobile phone coverage in Africa is associated with significantly higher levels of organized violent conflict (Pierskalla and Hollenbach 2013), while another asserts that such usage by insurgents also empowers counter-insurgent forces, who rely on signals intelligence to defeat them (Shapiro and Weidmann, 2015). However, new technologies are also used increasingly by vulnerable populations (such as refugees/migrants) to share information about transport and national policies, as well as by security authorities to monitor gang/criminal/terrorist/protest activity, control borders, conduct surveillance and, of course, spy on just about all of us (Morozov, 2011; Anderson, 2016; also see the special issue of *Security Dialogue*, 26/4, 2015). There is also scope for much more security-focused research on other emerging technologies that can protect or threaten (or both), such as robotics, Big Data, the Internet of Things, facial/voice recognition, geo-location, implants, biometrics, nanotechnology, biotechnology, space-based weaponry, automated weapons, machine learning, artificial intelligence, crowdsourcing and so on (Singer, 2009; Coker, 2015). Studies of critical military and technology gaps among major powers, as may be the case with the US–China rivalry (Brooks and Wohlforth, 2015–16), also are very much worth pursuing.

In addition to questions related to the perception of security problems based on non-traditional threats, new technology and other factors, we might also pay more attention to the management of those threats through the use of collective action, whether in the form of major power coalitions, IOs or some delegation to NGOs or epistemic communities. This volume has noted certain pathologies related to collective action, such as the free-rider problem and the difficulties in sanctioning defectors from agreements, yet there is more scope for work to be done on related topics, such as the harmful side effects (or negative externalities) noted above related to international security policies. Such research could take two forms: analysis of the more benign problems of collective action, such as the downside of certain policies, whether in the form of cost–benefit analysis or studies of unintended consequences ('blowback' or 'backlash' effects) (Johnson, 2002). Or it could involve research on far more malign or even illegal approaches to security, such as deliberate threat inflation or the overselling of security problems by political elites (especially in democracies); such elites can also attempt to downplay the costs associated with dealing with certain problems. These threat inflation/cost deflation dynamics have been especially acute in the War on Terror and the invasion of Iraq, but also involve other topics, such as the war on drug trafficking. Conversely, we might examine deliberate threat deflation/cost inflation on the part of some actors who are reluctant to confront a certain problem in the face of growing empirical evidence, such as economic crises or climate change or the ongoing civil war in Syria. Although LDCs have been known to deny such threats for various reasons, this problem is especially harmful when major powers or other stakeholders, such as large MNCs, attempt to downplay what seem to be obvious security threats or vulnerabilities because of their economic and/or political costs. Again, this is why a broader political, rather than narrow policy or strategic, approach to the topic is so necessary.

In light of these differences regarding vulnerability and threat/cost calculations, it is also worth taking a closer look at one of the major blind spots in the realm of international security studies: the role of area studies and comparative politics/history. We have seen this problem with regard to the failure to anticipate the end of Cold War and the potential for violence in Yugoslavia, yet it also extends to the ongoing instability in Iraq, Afghanistan, Syria, Ukraine and elsewhere, as well as to other looming problems (such as Pakistan and China) and the possibility of alternative, particularly non-Western, approaches to the topic (Acharya, 2014). Such work might also involve more attention to regional security architectures or even 'regional security governance' approaches (Lake and Morgan, 1997; Solingen, 1998; Diehl and Lepgold, 2003), as there is no realistic hope for a world government in the foreseeable future (Weiss, 2009). This area of research, which examines the emergence of security institutions and policies that are more authoritative and comprehensive – within a given region – than typified by traditional military alliances, is especially applicable to the case of the EU (Kirchner and Sperling, 2007), which has a far more sophisticated security architecture than any other region in the world. This arrangement generally involves NATO for traditional threats backed up by military force, and (increasingly) the EU for a full range of non-traditional threats such as organized crime, economic instability, migration, public health and similar problems, plus arrangements for the two institutions to work together (Cottey, 2007). Such research is also relevant in light of the debate over the relative decline of American hegemony (Kupchan, 1998) and in the rise, noted above, of non-traditional security threats that require the use of economic, legal, police and criminal justice approaches rather than, or in addition to, military force. These measures are precisely where the EU has a comparative advantage relative to other regional IOs in managing problems, security and otherwise, generated by complex interdependence and globalization. However, it also seems clear, based on its operational experience as a security actor since 2003, that the EU still has serious limits regarding its willingness and ability to project military force; this fact reinforces the point above about the practical division of labour between the EU and NATO (Smith, forthcoming).

As the potential for stronger regional approaches lags behind Europe in other parts of the world, it also might be worth taking a new look at an old solution: legal liberalism and the role of legal approaches to international security well beyond traditional arms control agreements and the LOAC (Goldstein et al., 2000). This work could involve not just the role of the ICC, which is still very uncertain, but also more specific national legal remedies such as criminal prosecution (by governments) and even lawsuits (by private citizens and firms) that have implications for international security affairs. In the UK, for example, military veterans who were harmed by nuclear testing in the 1950s can now sue the Ministry of Defence; more recently, military victims of alleged government negligence regarding their equipment have sued the government after a Nimrod aircraft crash in Afghanistan killed 14 soldiers. Lawyers in the UK also (unsuccessfully) attempted to force the British government to arrest Israel's defence minister, Ehud Barak, for war crimes in Gaza. In the US, criminal cases have been initiated by the government against Somali pirates, and civil cases have been pursued by Holocaust survivors and more recent victims of torture and state terrorism.

Legal issues also stem from government excesses, such as control orders and attempts to radically extend the detention without charge period in the UK, and abuses of power related to wiretapping, surveillance, torture and extraordinary rendition by the US government; in November 2009, for example, an Italian court convicted 23 Americans (including the former head of the CIA in Milan) in absentia for the crime of kidnapping, in the world's first trial involving extraordinary rendition. The militarization of what used to be criminal justice problems, such as drug and weapons trafficking, also raises legal problems. In a related manner, direct action and other forms of protest used by citizens and NGOs regarding security issues is likely to increase in the near future; this can even include vigilante or militia groups in various states who take it upon themselves to patrol borders and deter illegal immigrants or other perceived threats (Krause and Milliken, 2009; Schuberth, 2015). To some degree, these activities can be framed as a type of self-help by citizens and other less powerful actors in the face of globalized security threats that are not (in their view) managed responsibly by national governments.

This idea of personal self-help or direct action regarding security affairs raises an equally interesting area of opportunity for future research: understanding the role of new individual stakeholders, and the related idea of personal risk/responsibility, in international security affairs. Especially in the area of non-traditional security threats, individual citizens and firms really are the first line of defence; they must take specific measures to protect themselves when undertaking a range of ordinary tasks, as with using information technology, investing, consuming, conserving scarce resources and so on. If they fail to do so, or if governments fail to inform citizens about the consequences of their risk-taking, then international security in a globalized world can easily be undermined by the aggregate actions of millions of individuals and firms. Conversely, the rigorous self-help practices of individuals and firms can go a long way towards lowering the risks from these threats, whether in terms of preparedness beforehand or resilience afterwards (on resilience in particular, see the special of *Security Dialogue*, 46/1, 2015).

For example, the late Rick Rescorla, head of security for Morgan Stanley in the World Trade Center, has been immortalized for his critical role in quickly evacuating his co-workers during the 9/11 attacks and saving their lives before he perished in the building's collapse. This response was no accident, however: Rescorla – unlike the US federal government – had explicitly prepared for such an event in light of the 1993 bombing of that building, and he had conducted regular evacuation drills for his co-workers. The passengers of United Airlines flight 93 who fought back against their hijackers on 9/11 have almost certainly diminished the possible use of aeroplane hijacking as a terror tactic, while the disastrous US federal government response to Hurricane Katrina in 2005 also demonstrates the important role of individual preparedness in handling major disasters and threats. During the Cold War, this topic occasionally appeared in the security literature as 'civil defence' until scholars, and many citizens, realized there was no practical way to survive a thermonuclear war. However, this concept may need to be resurrected and re-examined in light of many of the international security problems – short of nuclear war – discussed in this volume.

This concern with individual risks and responsibility follows directly from a more general problem: the question of political leadership and political will in international security affairs. As we have seen throughout this volume, most if not all international security problems are defined as such by the major powers of the system: not just the P5 of the UNSC but also other groupings, such as the EU, NATO, the BRIC bloc and the G20. We therefore need a better understanding of the politics of coalition-building within and among these groups in matters of international security. Again, this can involve more traditional theories based on bargaining, or more unorthodox theories focused on the norms and values supposedly represented (and then defended) by these groups. A related and as yet unresolved debate concerns the general role and power of the US as an international security policy entrepreneur, whether on its own or relative to other competitors, such as China or the EU or the developing world. While we can see a general decline in US influence relative to its status during the early post-WWII era, there is, however, no firm consensus regarding a major alternative to American leadership, although several contenders do exist. If most modern security threats involve new/ non-traditional/human security issues, then the combination of unilateralism and the projection of military power – America's preferred approach – will be worse than useless; it will in fact be counterproductive as actors whose cooperation is necessary to solve the problem will simply refuse to participate in the face of what they see as American aggression. This is happening, or has happened, regarding a range of international security problems extending well back to the Vietnam era, and some more realist-oriented scholars have interpreted such obstructive behaviours as a form of 'soft balancing' against the US (Pape, 2005b; Paul 2005).

This focus on relations among the major powers, however, does not mean that international security is essentially what they say it is. Instead, it is more correct to focus on the political construction of a specific security

threat among a range of potential stakeholders; thus, under some circumstances it is possible for lesser powers, IOs and even NGOs to set the agenda
and to coordinate a multilateral response, which then may be joined by
the stronger powers or endorsed by the UNSC. Global campaigns regarding climate change, various types of inhumane weapons and the need for
debt relief in LDCs are prime examples. This tendency is a result of two
other underexamined phenomena in international security research: the
general impact of globalization on international security (in both positive
and negative terms) and the increasing disparity in threats facing the developed world versus the developing world (David, 1992–3). As we have seen
throughout this volume, LDCs overwhelmingly tend to suffer more from
both traditional and non-traditional security threats as compared to most
developed states such as the OECD members. Thanks in part to trends in
globalization, the developed world is certainly more aware of such problems, and may also become more vulnerable as countries continue to liberalize the movement of goods, services, labour, capital and ideas among
themselves. In fact, it may turn out that conflicts between the first and third
worlds will dominate the international security agenda in the medium-term
future. If this is so, then scholars and policy-makers must pay far more
attention to various trends in LDCs, not only in terms of defining security
threats but also in term of more fundamental values or ways of thinking.
More sophisticated and comparative studies of Asian or Islamic or African
views about international security would be especially welcome here (Callahan, 2008; Shani, 2008), assuming we also pay attention to whether and
how those views are then transformed into political power and action.

## From international security to human security – and back again?

This latter point about LDCs has inspired calls for more attention to
specific threatened populations as a way to frame international security
problems, and thus move the focus away from the state itself. As we have
seen throughout this volume, such views often appear in the literature
as societal security, gender security, food/water/energy/economic security,
and most recently human security. The human security agenda in particular still inspires considerable debate, and is partly related to the critical/
post-positivist academic agenda, in terms of bringing about the emancipation, or at least protection, of all human beings on the planet. Other scholars not associated with security studies have made a similar point about
how more equal societies tend to do better on a range of socio-economic
indicators, such as health, levels of violence and even overall happiness
as measured by public opinion polls (Wilkinson and Pickett, 2009; also
see Sennett, 2004 and Marmot, 2005). Once all humans have become

emancipated and more equal free agents, then peace, stability and (presumably) fairness and justice and other affirmative, universal values will naturally follow. This agenda is also linked to certain aspects of liberalism and Marxism given their concern with normative issues, such as inequality and justice, stemming from the anarchic international system in general or the pathologies of capitalism in particular. The idea that poor people (or states) remain marginalized because of the activities of rich people (or states) is also very seductive among certain populations, and provides a major impetus for political action among disadvantaged groups.

While a conceptual and empirical case can be made about the possible causal links between certain types of injustice, inequity or human suffering (such as famine or genocide) and a range of international security problems, a *political* analysis of the human security agenda would be far more critical (Paris, 2001; Chandler, 2008). As we have seen, some individual security threats discussed in this volume clearly are part of the larger human security agenda, and have been addressed by the international community with a range of policies. This point applies to traditional threats, such as intrastate war and terrorism, as well as certain non-traditional threats, such as environmental protection and public health. In other words, there does seem to be some political consensus among major stakeholders for managing certain aspects of the human security agenda. However, as defined by the UN, this agenda also includes goals such as ensuring a certain standard of living across the globe, encouraging free trade and fair markets among the poor, developing a more equitable system of patent rights, providing universal basic education and considering the need for a global human identity. More recently, some activists have called for even more goals to be added to the UN agenda, as with the Campaign for Global Road Safety. Yet these increasingly far-reaching goals, some of which clearly are inspired by social, normative and economic liberalism, as well as Marxism and even feminism, are simply not framed or addressed as international security concerns by most major stakeholders.

One reason for this, as we have seen, involves the question of global priorities: universal education and fair patent rights – not to mention more global equity – cannot compete at present with other international security agenda items such as intrastate war, terrorism, global warming, pandemic disease and so on. Another reason, as we have also seen, involves the question of varying vulnerabilities to these problems, which generally involves the North–South security gap discussed throughout this volume, but also can extend to differences between all kinds of states depending on the issue at hand. In fact, the idea of human security implies that all humans are part of the same political community, value system or public space, yet this simply is not the case; instead, we live in a world of multiple public spaces and value systems. It therefore can be not just naive but even counterproductive, from a public policy stance, to assume that seven billion humans will prioritize any of these values – including human life – in the same way across time and space. Religious differences alone clearly indicate that we cannot take any set of 'common values' for granted when attempting to explain or organize international security cooperation (Wald and Wilcox, 2006; Horowitz, 2009; Powell, 2015); the same also might be said regarding unique emotional responses to conflict situations (Eznack, 2013; Mercer, 2013) or distressing international events, such as the 9/11 attacks (Hall and Ross, 2015).

Finally, a third reason is far more parochial but still very important as a political consideration: the possibility of containment. If certain problems, no matter how serious they are to certain individuals or communities, are confined mainly to less developed areas of the planet or even to single states, as in the form of an endemic virus like Ebola for example, they simply will not receive adequate attention relative to other international security problems. When these three factors are combined, which is precisely the case with several aspects of the human security agenda, it becomes virtu-ally impossible to mobilize enough resources to deal adequately with such problems, although major stakeholders certainly might discuss the issue in various international bodies and thus produce mixed messages about what they plan to do about it. The fact that many supposedly liberal-minded EU member states, as well as other states like the US, are now erecting physi-cal barriers to limit their intake of vulnerable refugees, many of whom are women and children, clearly reflects this unfortunate tendency.

This tendency for many human security goals to stall at the agenda-setting phase also can be seen with general 'cheap talk' policies regard-ing the eradication of poverty around the globe, where most if not all advanced states – namely the OECD members – consistently fail to provide what they pledge during various UN funding campaigns and similar meas-ures. The G8 Live 8 summit in 2005, for example, provided debt relief to a number of HIPCs as noted in Chapter 10, yet failed to deliver on its promise to double aid to sub-Saharan Africa by 2010. It can also be seen during more specific human security-related crises; in 2008, for example, many LDCs were gripped by a major food crisis thanks to a combination of market and geographic factors. An emergency international food sum-mit took place Rome in June 2008 to deal with an estimated 963 million people, or 14 per cent of world's total, who were going hungry at the time. Yet the summit was easily overshadowed by the growing credit crisis, and the urgency quickly diminished as food prices fell along with everything else in the global economy, even though the problem is not really a global shortage of food but rather the unequal distribution of it (Stuart, 2009), as with the case of water resources. An even more absurd example of competing priorities and mixed messages can be seen with attempts to use military force to deliver humanitarian aid while simultaneously killing civilians in the same country, as in Kosovo (1999) and Afghanistan (after

2001) (Hills, 2003). These priorities collided in a tragically symbolic fashion in 2009 when a British military aircraft in Afghanistan killed a child by dropping a box of information leaflets on her, while others have argued that humanitarian aid, no matter how it is delivered, actually can prolong a civil war because it may influence calculations about the strength of various combatant groups (Nerang, 2015). To put it bluntly, the international community must be very careful about confusing the provision of international security – no matter how unfairly it may be defined – with the pursuit of development/humanitarian goals. This confusion of priorities is especially likely in multilateral military operations, although some actors – including the UN, NATO and the EU – are increasingly attempting to square this circle when conducting such operations.

Finally, as noted in Chapter 2, the human security policy agenda is currently being developed by the UN system, which means that state governments – the members of the UN – are charged with carrying out these policies. Unless the entire project is meant to be voluntary, national state authority will be necessary to transfer various resources from one policy agenda to another. Fundamental problems related to good governance at the national level, both in the developed and the developing worlds, should therefore take centre stage rather than any attempt to add even more goals to an already crowded international policy agenda in a world filled with weak, failed or otherwise ineffective governments. This fact means, in turn, that human security is *inherently contingent on the security of the state system itself*, which is precisely why the topic has been approached from such a perspective in this volume. In a far more peaceful and secure world than presently exists, it may be possible to elevate problems such as poverty and injustice to a much higher status than they currently enjoy. However, we do not live in such a world, so this wishful thinking must be tempered with rigorous and dispassionate analysis about what really motivates people to undertake collective political action. As important as questions of inequality and injustice have become in recent years, leading stakeholders still show very little propensity at present to reform the current international order into something more equitable and just. The ongoing failure to reform the membership of the UNSC, to strengthen the mandate of the ICC, or to create a stronger regulatory framework for the international economy are just three major examples of this tendency. Even worse, using the terms 'security' or 'crisis' too much robs them of their urgency as calls to action, as in the old story of the village boy who falsely cried 'wolf' too often, only to find that no one would help him when the wolf really did appear. Instead, perhaps we should simply revert back to the terminology of 'human rights' and 'human/international development' and promote those goals accordingly rather than repackage and devalue them in the form of potential security threats mainly of concern to the richer, and more powerful, developed world.

# Bibliography

Abrahms, Max (2006). 'Why Terrorism Does Not Work.' *International Security* 31: 42–78.

Acharya, Amitav (2014). 'Global International Relations (IR) and Regional Worlds.' *International Studies Quarterly* 58: 647–59.

Achvarina, Vera, and Simon F. Reich (2006). '"No Place to Hide": Refugees, Displaced Persons and the Recruitment of Child Soldiers.' *International Security* 31: 127–64.

Adams, Gordon (1992). *The Revolution in the Arms Trade: The Emergence of a Transnational Arms Industry*. Washington, DC: Defense Budget Project.

Adamson, Fiona B. (2006). 'Crossing Borders: International Migration and National Security.' *International Security* 31: 165–99.

Adler, Emanuel, and Beverly Crawford (1991). *Progress in Postwar International Relations*. New York: Columbia University Press.

Ahmad, Aisha (2014–15). 'The Security Bazaar: Business Interests and Islamist Power in Civil War Somalia.' *International Security* 39: 89–117.

Ahmed, Samina (1999). 'Pakistan's Nuclear Weapons Program: Turning Points and Nuclear Choices.' *International Security* 23: 178–204.

Akaev, Askar, and Vladimir Pantin (2014). 'Technological Innovations and Future Shifts in World Politics.' *International Studies Quarterly* 58: 867–72.

Akerlof, George A., and Robert Shiller (2015). *Phishing for Phools: The Economics of Manipulation and Deception*. Princeton: Princeton University Press.

Albright, D., and C. Hinderstein (2005). 'Unraveling the A. Q. Khan and Future Proliferation Networks.' *Washington Quarterly* 28: 111–28.

Allison, Graham T. (1971). *Essence of Decision: Explaining the Cuban Missile Crisis*. New York: HarperCollins.

Allison, Graham (2006). *Nuclear Terrorism*. London: Constable & Robinson.

Anderson, Benedict (1991). *Imagined Communities: Reflections on the Origins and Spread of Nationalism*. London: Verso.

Anderson, K. (2000). 'The Ottawa Convention: Banning Landmines, the Role of International Non-Governmental Organisations and the Idea of International Civil Society.' *European Journal of International Law* 11: 91–120.

Anderson, Lisa (2004). 'Shock and Awe: Interpretations of the Events of September 11.' *World Politics* 56: 303–25.

Anderson, Malcolm (1989). *Policing the World: Interpol and the Politics of International Police Co-operation*. Oxford: Clarendon Press.

Anderson, Malcolm, and Monica Den Boer (1994). *Policing Across National Boundaries*. London: Pinter Publishers.

Anderson, Ruben (2016). 'Hardwiring the Frontier? The Politics of Security Technology in Europe's "Fight Against Illegal Migration."' *Survival* 47: 22–9.

Anderson, Stephanie, and Thomas R. Seitz (2006). 'European Security and Defense Policy Demystified: Nation-Building and Identity in the European Union.' *Armed Forces & Society* 33: 24–42.

Andreas, Peter (2005). 'Criminalizing Consequences of Sanctions: Embargo Busting and Its Legacy.' *International Studies Quarterly* 49: 335–660.

Andreas, Peter, and Ethan Nadelmann (2006). *Policing the Globe: Criminalization and Crime Control in International Relations.* Oxford: Oxford University Press.

Andreski, Stanislav (1980). 'On the Peaceful Disposition of Military Dictatorships.' *Journal of Strategic Studies* 3: 3–10.

Angwin, Julia (2014). *Dragnet Nation: A Quest for Privacy, Security, and Freedom in a World of Relentless Surveillance.* New York: Times Books.

Annan, Kofi (1999). *Facing the Humanitarian Challenge: Towards a Culture of Prevention.* New York: UNDPI.

Anonymous (2002). *Through Our Enemies' Eyes: Osama Bin Laden, Radical Islam, and the Future of America.* Washington, DC: Brassey's.

Art, Robert J. (1996). 'Why Western Europe Needs the United States and NATO.' *Political Science Quarterly* 111: 1–39.

Asal, Victor, H. Brinton Milward and Eric W. Schoon (2015). 'When Terrorists Go Bad: Analyzing Terrorist Organizations' Involvement in Drug Smuggling.' *International Studies Quarterly* 59: 112–23.

Auerswald, David P. (2006). 'Senate Reservations to Security Treaties.' *Foreign Policy Analysis* 2: 83–100.

Avant, Deborah D. (2005). *The Market for Force: The Consequences of Privatizing Security.* Cambridge: Cambridge University Press.

Bailes, Alyson J. K. (2008). 'The EU and a 'Better World': What Role for the European Security and Defence Policy?' *International Affairs* 84: 115–30.

Baldwin, David A. (ed.) (1993). *Neorealism and Neoliberalism: The Contemporary Debate.* New York: Columbia University Press.

Baldwin, David A. (1995). 'Security Studies and the End of the Cold War.' *World Politics* 48: 117–41.

Baldwin, David A. (1997). 'The Concept of Security.' *Review of International Studies* 23: 5–26.

Baldwin, David A. (1999–2000). 'The Sanctions Debate and the Logic of Choice.' *International Security* 24: 80–107.

Bamford, James (2008). *The Shadow Factory: The Ultra-Secret NSA from 9/11 to the Eavesdropping on America.* New York: Doubleday.

Bapat, Navin A. (2006). 'State Bargaining With Transnational Terrorist Groups.' *International Studies Quarterly* 50: 213–29.

Barash, David P., and Charles P. Webel (2002). *Peace and Conflict Studies.* Thousand Oaks: Sage.

Barber, James David (1992). *Presidential Character: Predicting Performance in the White House.* New York: Prentice-Hall.

Barkin, J. Samuel, and Bruce Cronin (1994). 'The State and the Nation: Changing Norms and the Rules of Sovereignty in International Relations.' *International Organization* 48: 107–30.

Barnett, Jon (2000). 'Destabilising the Environment–Conflict Thesis.' *Review of International Studies* 26: 271–88.

Barnett, Jon (2001). *The Meaning of Environmental Security: Ecological Politics and Policy in the New Security Arena.* London: Zed Books.

Barnett, Michael, and Liv Coleman (2005). 'Designing Police: Interpol and the Study of Change in International Organizations.' *International Studies Quarterly* 49: 593–619.

Barnett, Michael, and Raymond Duvall (2005). 'Power in International Politics.' *International Organization* 59: 39–75.

Barnett, Michael, and Martha Finnemore (2004). *Rules for the World: International Organizations in World Politics*. Ithaca: Cornell University Press.

Barry, John M. (2009). *The Great Influenza: The Story of the Deadliest Pandemic in History*. London: Penguin Books.

Bartilow, Horace A., and Kihong Eom (2009). 'Busting Drugs While Paying with Crime: The Collateral Damage of US Drug Enforcement in Foreign Countries.' *Foreign Policy Analysis* 5: 93–116.

Bartlett, Jamie (2015). *The Dark Net: Inside the Digital Underworld*. London: Windmill Books.

Bateson, Regina (2012). 'Crime Victimization and Political Participation.' *American Political Science Review* 106: 570–87.

Battisti, David S., and Rosamond Naylor (2009). 'Historical Warnings of Future Food Insecurity with Unprecedented Seasonal Heat.' *Science* 323: 240–4.

Baum, Seth D. (2015). 'Winter-safe Deterrence: The Risk of Nuclear Winter and its Challenge to Deterrence.' *Contemporary Security Policy* 36: 123–48.

Beck, Nathaniel, Gary King, and Langche Zeng (2000). 'Improving Quantitative Studies of International Conflict: A Conjecture.' *American Political Science Review* 94: 21–35.

Beckley, Michael (2011–12). 'China's Century? Why America's Edge Will Endure.' *International Security* 36: 41–78.

Beer, Frances (1972). *The Political Economy of Alliances*. Beverly Hills: Sage.

Bellamy, Alex J., and Paul D. Williams (2005). 'Who's Keeping the Peace? Regionalization and Contemporary Peace Operations.' *International Security* 29: 157–95.

Bell, Sam R., and Jesse C. Johnson (2015). 'Shifting Power, Commitment Problems, and Preventative War.' *International Studies Quarterly* 59: 124–32.

Benedick, Richard E. (1991). *Ozone Diplomacy: New Directions in Safeguarding the Planet*. Cambridge: Harvard University Press.

Benjamin, Daniel, and Steven Simon (2002). *The Age of Sacred Terror*. New York: Random House.

Benjamin, Medea (2012). *Drone Warfare*. New York: OR Books.

Bennett, Andrew, Joseph Lepgold, and Danny Unger (1994). 'Burden-Sharing in the Persian Gulf War.' *International Organization* 48: 39–75.

Berdal, Mats, and Monica Serrano (eds.) (2002). *Transnational Organized Crime and International Security: Business as Usual?* Boulder: Lynne Rienner.

Bergen, Peter. L., and Daniel Rothenberg (eds.) (2014). *Drone Wars: Transforming Conflict, Law, and Policy*. Cambridge: Cambridge University Press.

Berger, Peter (2002). *Holy War, Inc.: Inside the Secret World of Osama Bin Laden*. New York: Simon & Schuster.

Bernauer, Thomas (1995). 'The Effect of International Environmental Institutions: How We Might Learn More.' *International Organization* 49: 351–77.

Betts, Alexander, and Gil Loescher (eds.) (2011). *Refugees in International Relations*. Oxford: Oxford University Press.

Betts, Richard K. (1997). 'Should Strategic Studies Survive?' *World Politics* 50: 7–33.

Biddle, Tami Davis (2002). *Rhetoric and Reality in Air Warfare: The Evolution of British and American Ideas about Strategic Bombing, 1914–1945*. Princeton: Princeton University Press.

Bigo, Didier (2013). 'International Political Sociology.' In Paul D. Williams (ed.), *Security Studies: An Introduction* (2nd ed.). London: Routledge.

Bitzinger, Richard A. (1992). 'Arms to Go: Chinese Arms Sales to the Third World.' *International Security* 17: 84–111.

Bitzinger, Richard A. (1994). 'The Globalization of the Arms Industry: The Next Proliferation Challenge.' *International Security*: 19: 170–98.

Björgo, T. (ed.) (2003). *Root Causes of Terrorism: Findings from an International Expert Meeting in Oslo 9–11 June 2003*. Oslo: Norwegian Institute of International Affairs.

Black, Edwin (2003). *War Against the Weak: Eugenics and America's Campaign to Create a Master Race*. New York: Basic Books.

Blainey, Geoffrey (1973). *The Causes of War*. New York: Free Press.

Blinder, Alan S. (2013). *After the Music Stopped: The Financial Crisis, the Response, and the Work Ahead*. London: Penguin Books.

Bloom, Mia (2005). *Dying to Kill: The Allure of Suicide Terror*. New York: Columbia University Press.

Bobbitt, Philip (2008). *Terror and Consent: The Wars for the Twenty-first Century*. London: Allen Lane.

Booth, Ken (ed.) (2005). *Critical Security Studies and World Politics*. Boulder: Lynne Rienner.

Bourne, Mike (2013). *Understanding Security*. Basingstoke: Palgrave.

Bowden, Mark (2001). *Killing Pablo: The Hunt for the World's Greatest Outlaw*. London: Atlantic Books.

Boyle, Michael J. (2014). *Violence After War: Explaining Instability in Post-Conflict States*. Baltimore: Johns Hopkins University Press.

Boyle, Michael J. (2015). 'The Legal and Ethical Implications of Drone Warfare.' *The International Journal of Human Rights* 19: 105–26.

Brands, Hal (2016). *Making the Unipolar Moment: U.S. Foreign Policy and the Rise of the Post-Cold War Order*. Ithaca: Cornell University Press.

Brandes, Stuart D. (1997). *Warhogs: A History of War Profits in America*. Louisville: University Press of Kentucky.

Braun, C., and C. F. Chyba (2004). 'Proliferation Rings: New Challenges to the Non-Proliferation Regime.' *International Security* 29: 5–49.

Breslauer, George W. (1987). 'Ideology and Learning in Soviet Third World Policy.' *World Politics* 39: 429–48.

Brito, Dagobert, and Michael Intriligator (1985). 'Conflict, War, and Redistribution.' *American Political Science Review* 79: 943–57.

Broderick, Damien (2001). *The Spike: How Our Lives are Being Transformed by Rapidly Advancing Technologies*. New York: Tom Doherty Associates.

Brodie, Bernard (1973). *War and Politics*. New York: Macmillan.

Bronk, Christopher, and Eneken Tikk-Ringas (2013). 'The Cyber Attack on Saudi Aramco.' *Survival* 55: 81–96.

Brooks, Risa A. (2011). 'Muslim "Homegrown" Terrorism in the United States: How Serious is the Threat?' *International Security* 36: 7–47.

Brooks, Stephen G., and William C. Wohlforth (2015–16). 'The Rise and Fall of the Great Powers in the 21st Century: China's Rise and the Fate of America's Global Position.' *International Security* 40: 7–53.

Brown, Archie (2009). *The Rise and Fall of Communism*. New York: The Bodley Head.

Brown, Michael E. (ed.) (2000). *Rational Choice and Security Studies: Stephen Walt and His Critics*. Cambridge: MIT Press.

Brown, Michael, Owen R. Coté Jr., Sean M. Lynn-Jones and Steven E. Miller (eds.) (2001). *Nationalism and Ethnic Conflict*. Cambridge: MIT Press.

Browning, Christopher (2013). *International Security: A Very Short Introduction*. Oxford: Oxford University Press.

Browning, Christopher, and Matt McDonald (2011). 'The Future of Critical Security Studies: Ethics and the Politics of Security.' *European Journal of International Relations* 19: 235–55.

Brownlee, J. (2007). 'Can America Nation-Build?' *World Politics* 59: 314–40.

Bueno de Mesquita, Bruce (1981). *The War Trap*. New Haven: Yale University Press.

Bueno de Mesquita, Bruce (1989). 'The Contribution of Expected Utility Theory to the Study of International Conflict.' In Robert I. Rotberg and Theodore K. Rabb (eds.), *The Origin and Prevention of Major Wars*. Cambridge: Cambridge University Press.

Bukharin, Oleg (1997). 'The Future of Russia's Plutonium Cities.' *International Security* 21: 126–58.

Bull, Hedley (2001). *The Anarchical Society: A Study of Order in World Politics*. New York: Columbia University Press.

Burgess, Stephen, and Janet Bellstein (2013). 'This Means War? China's Scramble for Minerals and Resource Nationalism in Southern Africa.' *Contemporary Security Policy* 34: 120–43.

Burleigh, Michael (2008). *Blood and Rage: A Cultural History of Terrorism*. New York: HarperCollins.

Burton, John W. (1987). *Resolving Deep-Rooted Conflict: A Handbook*. Lanham: University Press of America.

Busby, Joshua W., Todd G. Smith, Kaiba L. White and Shawn M. Strange (2013). 'Climate Change and Insecurity: Mapping Vulnerability in Africa.' *International Security* 38: 132–72.

Buzan, Barry (1993). 'From International System to International Society: Structural Realism and Regime Theory Meet the English School.' *International Organization* 47: 327–52.

Buzan, Barry (1997). 'Rethinking Security After the Cold War.' *Cooperation and Conflict* 32: 5–28.

Buzan, Barry (2007). *People, States, and Fear: An Agenda for International Security Studies in the Post-Cold War Era*. Colchester: ECPR Press.

Buzan, Barry, Ole Wæver and Jaap de Wilde (1998). *Security: A New Framework for Analysis*. Boulder: Lynne Rienner.

Buzan, Barry, and Lene Hansen (2011). *The Evolution of International Security Studies*. Cambridge: Cambridge University Press.

Byman, Daniel L. (2003). 'Al-Qaeda as an Adversary: Do We Understand Our Enemy?' *World Politics* 56: 139–63.

Byman, Daniel L. (2016). 'Understanding the Islamic State: A Review Essay.' *International Security* 40: 127–65.

Byman, Daniel A., and Matthew C. Waxman (2000). 'Kosovo and the Great Air Power Debate.' *International Security* 24: 5–38.

Cable, Vince (1995). 'What is International Economic Security?' *International Affairs* 71: 305–24.

Caldwell, Christopher (2009). *Reflections on the Revolution in Europe*. London: Allen Lane.

Caldwell, Gillian, Steve Galster, Jyothi Kanics and Nadia Steinzor (1999). 'Capitalizing on Transition Economies: The Role of the Russian Mafiya in Trafficking Women for Forced Prostitution.' In Phil Williams (ed.), *Illegal Immigration and Commercial Sex: The New Slave Trade*. London: Frank Cass.

Caldwell, Lynton Keith (1990). *International Environmental Policy: Emergence and Dimensions* (2nd ed.). Durham: Duke University Press.

Callahan, William A. (2008). 'Chinese Visions of World Order: Post-Hegemonic or a New Hegemony?' *International Studies Review* 10: 749–61.

Calleo, David P. (1987). *Beyond American Hegemony: The Future of the Western Alliance*. New York: Basic Books.

Cameron, M. (1999). 'Global Civil Society and the Ottawa Process: Lessons from the Movement to Ban Anti-Personnel Landmines.' *Canadian Foreign Policy* 7: 85–102.

Caprioli, Mary (2005). 'Primed for Violence: The Role of Gender Inequality in Predicting Internal Conflict.' *International Studies Quarterly* 49: 161–78.

Carpenter, R. Charli (2005). '"Women, Children and Other Vulnerable Groups": Gender, Strategic Frames and the Protection of Civilians as a Transnational Issue.' *International Studies Quarterly* 49: 295–334.

Carpenter, R. Charli (2011). 'Vetting the Advocacy Agenda: Network Centrality and the Paradox of Weapons Norms.' *International Organization* 65: 69–102.

Carr, Edward Hallett (1964). *The Twenty Years' Crisis, 1919–1939*. First published 1939. New York: Harper Perennial.

Carroll, John E. (ed.) (1988). *International Environmental Diplomacy: The Management and Resolution of Transfrontier Environmental Problems*. Cambridge: Cambridge University Press.

Carter, David B. (2012). 'A Blessing or a Curse? State Support for Terrorist Groups.' *International Organization* 66: 129–51.

Carter, David B. (2016). 'Provocation and the Strategy of Terrorist and Guerrilla Attacks.' *International Organization* 70: 133–73.

Cavelty, Myriam Dunn (2016). 'Cyber-Security.' In Alan Collins (ed.), *Contemporary Security Studies* (4th ed.). Oxford: Oxford University Press.

Cederman, Lars-Erik, Nils B. Weidmann and Kristian Skrede Gleditsch (2011). 'Horizontal Inequalities and Ethnonationalist Civil War: A Global Comparison.' *American Political Science Review* 105: 478–95.

Cederman, Lars-Erik, Andreas Wimmer and Brian Min (2010). 'Why Do Ethnic Groups Rebel? New Data and Analysis.' *World Politics* 62: 87–119.

Cha, Victor D. (2000). 'Globalization and the Study of International Security.' *Journal of Peace Research* 37: 391–403.

Chan, Steve (1984). 'Mirror, Mirror on the Wall: Are the Freer Countries More Pacific?' *Journal of Conflict Resolution* 28: 617–48.

Chandler, David (2008). 'Human Security: The Dog That Didn't Bark.' *Security Dialogue* 39: 427–38.

Chase-Dunn, Christopher (1981). 'Interstate System and Capitalist World-Economy.' *International Studies Quarterly* 25: 19–42.

Chatterjee, Deen, and Don Scheid (eds.) (2002). *Ethics and Foreign Intervention*. Cambridge: Cambridge University Press.

Checkel, Jeff (1993). 'Ideas, Institutions, and the Gorbachev Foreign Policy Revolution.' *World Politics* 45: 271–300.

Chesnais, Jean-Claude (2001). *The Demographic Transition: Stages, Patterns, and Economic Implications*. Oxford: Oxford University Press.

Chesterman, Simon (2001). *Just War or Just Peace? Humanitarian Intervention and International Law*. Oxford: Oxford University Press.

Chesterman, Simon, and Chia Lehnardt (eds.) (2007). *From Mercenaries to Market: The Rise and Regulation of Private Military Companies*. Oxford: Oxford University Press.

Chestnut, Sheena (2007). 'Illicit Activity and Proliferation: North Korean Smuggling Networks.' *International Security* 32: 80–111.

Chiles, James R. (2001). *Inviting Disaster: Lessons from the Edge of Technology*. New York: HarperCollins.

Chipman, John (1992). 'The Future of Strategic Studies Beyond Grand Strategy.' *Survival* 34: 109–31.

Christensen, Thomas J. (2001). 'Posing Problems Without Catching Up: China's Rise and Challenges for U.S. Security Policy.' *International Security* 25: 5–40.

Christensen, Thomas J. (2006). 'Fostering Stability or Creating a Monster? The Rise of China and U.S. Policy Towards Asia.' *International Security* 31: 81–126.

Christensen, Thomas J., and Jack Snyder (1990). 'Chain Gangs and Passed Bucks: Predicting Alliance Patterns in Multipolarity.' *International Organization* 44: 137–68.

Cirincione, Joseph (2007). *Bomb Scare: The History and Future of Nuclear Weapons*. New York: Columbia University Press.

Clarke, Richard A. (2004). *Against All Enemies: Inside America's War on Terror*. New York: Free Press.

Clarke, Richard A. (2010). *Cyber War: The Next Threat to National Security and What To Do About It*. New York: Ecco.

Clary, C. (2004). 'A. Q. Khan and the Limits of the Non-Proliferation Regime.' *Disarmament Forum* 4: 33–42.

Clausewitz, Carl Von (1968). *On War*. First published 1832. London: Penguin Books.

Cochran, Molly (2000). *Normative Theory in International Relations: A Pragmatic Approach*. Cambridge: Cambridge University Press.

Cockayne, James (2007). 'Make or Buy? Principal-Agent Theory and the Regulation of Private Military Companies.' In Simon Chesterman and Chia Lehnardt (eds.), *From Mercenaries to Market: The Rise and Regulation of Private Military Companies*. Oxford: Oxford University Press.

Cockayne, James, and Adam Lupel (2009). 'Introduction: Rethinking the Relationship Between Peace Operations and Organized Crime.' *International Peacekeeping* 16: 4–19.

Cockayne, James, and Adam Lupel (eds.) (2011). *Peace Operations and Organized Crime: Enemies or Allies?* London: Routledge.

Cohen, Dara Kay (2013). 'Female Combatants and the Perpetuation of Violence: Wartime Rape in the Sierra Leone Civil War.' *World Politics* 65: 383–415.

Coker, Christopher (2015). *Future War*. Cambridge: Polity Press.

Cole, Wade M. (2015). 'Mind the Gap: State Capacity and the Implementation of Human Rights Treaties.' *International Organization* 69: 405–41.

Colgan, Jeff D. (2013). 'Fueling the Fire: Pathways from Oil to War.' *International Security* 38: 147–80.

Colgan, Jeff D. (2014). 'The Emperor Has No Clothes: The Limits of OPEC in the Global Oil Market.' *International Organization* 68: 599–632.

Collier, Paul (2000). 'Rebellion as a Quasi-Criminal Activity.' *Journal of Conflict Resolution* 44: 839–53.

Collins, Alan (ed.) (2016). *Contemporary Security Studies* (4th ed.). Oxford: Oxford University Press.

Conybeare, John (1987). *Trade Wars: The Theory and Practice of Commercial Rivalry*. New York: Colombia University Press.

Conway, Ed (2015). *The Summit: Bretton Woods, 1944: J. M. Keynes and the Reshaping of the Global Economy*. New York: Pegasus Books.

Cornelius, Wayne A., Philip L. Martin and James F. Hollifield (eds.) (1994). *Controlling Immigration: A Global Perspective*. Stanford: Stanford University Press.

Cornell, Svante (2007). 'Narcotics and Armed Conflict: Interaction and Implications.' *Studies in Conflict and Terrorism* 30: 207–27.

Cottey, Andrew (2007). *Security in the New Europe*. Basingstoke: Palgrave.

Council of the EU (2003). *A Secure Europe in a Better World: European Security Strategy*. Brussels: Council of the European Union.

Cox, Robert W. (1981). 'Social Forces, States, and World Orders: Beyond International Relations Theory.' *Millennium* 10: 126–55.

Coyne, Christopher J. (2006). 'Reconstructing Weak and Failed States: Foreign Intervention and the Nirvana Fallacy.' *Foreign Policy Analysis* 2: 343–60.

Crandall, Matthew, and Collin Allan (2015). 'Small States and Big Ideas: Estonia's Battle for Cybersecurity Norms.' *Contemporary Security Policy* 36: 346–68.

Crenshaw, Martha (1981). 'The Causes of Terrorism.' *Comparative Politics* 13: 379–99.

Crenshaw, Martha (2000). 'The Psychology of Terrorism: An Agenda for the Twenty-first Century.' *Political Psychology* 21: 405–20.

Crenshaw, Martha (2007). 'Explaining Suicide Terrorism: A Review Essay.' *Security Studies* 16: 133–62.

Croft, Stuart (2012). 'Constructing Ontological Security: The Insecuritization of British Muslims.' *Contemporary Security Policy* 33: 219–35.

Cronin, Audrey Kurth (2002–3). 'Behind the Curve: Globalization and International Terrorism.' *International Security* 27: 30–58.

Cronin, Audrey Kurth (2006). 'How al-Qaida Ends: The Decline and Demise of Terrorist Groups.' *International Security* 31: 7–48.

Cronin, Audrey Kurth (2011). *How Terrorism Ends: Understanding the Decline and Demise of Terrorist Campaigns*. Princeton: Princeton University Press.

Cunningham, Kathleen Gallagher (2011). 'Divide and Conquer or Divide and Concede: How Do States Respond to Internally-Divided Separatists?' *American Political Science Review* 105: 275–97.

Daalder, Ivo H., and Michael E. O'Hanlon (2000). *Winning Ugly: NATO's War to Save Kosovo*. Washington, DC: Brookings Institution Press.

Dalby, Simon (2002). *Environmental Security*. Minneapolis: University of Minnesota Press.

Dalby, Simon (2009). *Security and Environmental Change*. Cambridge: Polity Press.

Danielsen, Albert L. (1982). *The Evolution of OPEC*. New York: Harcourt Brace Jovanovich.

Dannreuther, Roland (2013). *International Security: The Contemporary Agenda* (2nd ed.). Cambridge: Polity Press.

Dassel, Kurt (1998). 'Civilians, Soldiers, and Strife: Domestic Sources of International Aggression.' *International Security* 23: 107–40.

David, Steven R. (1991). 'Explaining Third World Alignment.' *World Politics* 43: 233–56.

David, Steven R. (1992–3). 'Why the Third World Still Matters.' *International Security* 17: 127–59.

David, Steven R. (1997). 'Internal War: Causes and Cures.' *World Politics* 49: 552–76.

Davis, Mike (2006). *Planet of Slums*. London: Verso Books.

Davis, Paul B. (2001). 'The Terrorist Mentality.' *Cerebrum: The Dana Forum on Brain Science* 3 (Summer).

Dawe, Hazel (2004). 'Euratom: The Toothless Treaty?' in Vassiliki N. Koutrakou (ed.), *Contemporary Issues and Debates in EU Policy: The European Union and International Relations*. Manchester: Manchester University Press.

Deporte, Anton W. (1986). *Europe Between the Superpowers: The Enduring Balance*. (2nd ed.). New Haven: Yale University Press.

Desch, Michael C. (1996). 'War and Strong States, Peace and Weak States?' *International Organization* 50: 237–68.

Desch, Michael C. (2008). *Power and Military Effectiveness: The Fallacy of Democratic Triumphalism*. Baltimore: Johns Hopkins University Press.

DeSombre, Elizabeth R. (2000). *Domestic Sources of International Environmental Policy: Industry, Environmentalists, and US Power*. Cambridge: The MIT Press.

Detraz, Nicole, and Michele M. Betsill (2009). 'Climate Change and Environmental Security: For Whom the Discourse Shifts.' *International Studies Perspectives* 10: 303–20.

Deudney, Daniel H., and Richard A. Matthew (1999). *Contested Grounds: Security and Conflict in the New Environmental Politics*. Albany: SUNY Press.

Deutsch, Karl W., Sidney A. Burrell, Robert A. Kann, Maurice Lee Jr., Martin Lichterman, Raymond E. Lindgren, Francis L. Lowenheim and Richard W. Van Wagenen (1957). *Political Community and the North Atlantic Area: International Organization in the Light of Historical Experience*. Princeton: Princeton University Press.

Deutsch, Karl W., and J. David Singer (1964). 'Multipolar Systems and International Stability.' *World Politics* 16: 390–406.

Diamond, Jared (2004). *Collapse: How Societies Choose to Fail or Succeed*. New York: Viking.

Diffie, Whitfield, and Susan Landau (2007). *Privacy on the Line: The Politics of Wiretapping and Encryption*. Cambridge: The MIT Press.

Diehl, Paul F. (1985). 'Contiguity and Military Escalation in Major Power Rivalries, 1816–1980.' *Journal of Politics* 47: 1203–11.

Diehl, Paul F., and Joseph Lepgold (eds.) (2003). *Regional Conflict Management*. New York: Rowman & Littlefield.

Dixon, William (1994). 'Democracy and the Peaceful Settlement of International Conflict.' *American Political Science Review* 88: 14–32.

Dobbs, Michael (2009). *One Minute to Midnight: Kennedy, Khrushchev, and Castro on the Brink of Nuclear War*. London: Arrow.

Dolan, Thomas M. (2013). 'Unthinkable and Tragic: The Psychology of Weapons Taboos in War.' *International Organization* 67: 37–63.

Dombrowski, Peter (ed.) (2005). *Guns and Butter: The Political Economy of International Security.* Boulder: Lynne Rienner.

Domke, William, Richard Eichenberg, and Catherine Kelleher (1987). 'Consensus Lost? Domestic Politics and the "Crisis" in NATO.' *World Politics* 39: 382–407.

Doran, Charles F. (1980). 'OPEC Structure and Cohesion: Exploring the Determinants of Cartel Policy.' *Journal of Politics* 42: 82–101.

Doran, Charles F., and Wes Parsons (1980). 'War and the Cycle of Relative Power.' *American Political Science Review* 74: 947–65.

Doswald-Beck, Louise (2007). 'Private Military Companies Under International Humanitarian Law.' In Simon Chesterman and Chia Lehnardt (eds.), *From Mercenaries to Market: The Rise and Regulation of Private Military Companies.* Oxford: Oxford University Press.

Downes, Alexander B., and Todd S. Sechser (2012). 'The Illusion of Democratic Credibility.' *International Organization* 66: 457–89.

Dowty, Alan, and Gil Loescher (1996). 'Refugee Flows as Grounds for International Action.' *International Security* 21: 43–71.

Doyle, Michael W. (1983). 'Kant, Liberal Legacies, and Foreign Affairs.' *Philosophy and Public Affairs* 12 (issues 3 and 4): 205–35; 323–53.

Doyle, Michael W. (1986). 'Liberalism and World Politics.' *American Political Science Review* 80: 1151–69.

Doyle, Michael W. (1997). *Ways of War and Peace: Realism, Liberalism, and Socialism.* New York: W.W. Norton.

Doyle, Michael W., and Nicholas Sambanis (2000). 'International Peacebuilding: A Theoretical and Quantitative Analysis.' *American Political Science Review* 94: 779–801.

Drezner, Daniel W. (2001). 'Globalization and Policy Convergence.' *International Studies Review* 3: 53–78.

Druckman, James N. (2004). 'Political Preference Formation: Competition, Deliberation, and the (Ir)Relevance of Framing Effects.' *American Political Science Review* 98: 671–86.

Dube, Arindrajit, Oeindrila Dube and Omar García-Ponce (2013). 'Cross-Border Spillover: US Gun Laws and Violence in Mexico.' *American Political Science Review* 107: 397–417.

Duelfer, Charles A., and Stephen Benedict Dyson (2011). 'Chronic Misperception and International Conflict: The U.S.-Iraq Experience.' *International Security* 36: 73–100.

Duffield, John S. (2008). *Over a Barrel: The Costs of U.S. Foreign Oil Dependence.* Stanford: Stanford University Press.

Duffield, John S. (2012). 'The Return of Energy Insecurity in the Developed Democracies.' *Contemporary Security Policy* 33: 1–26.

Duffield, Mark (1998). 'Post-Modern Conflict: Warlords, Post-Adjustment States, and Private Protection.' *Civil Wars* 1: 65–102.

Duncanson, Claire, and Rachel Woodward (2016). 'Regendering the Military: Theorising Women's Military Participation.' *Security Dialogue* 47: 3–21.

Dunn, D. J. (2005). *The First Fifty Years of Peace Research.* Aldershot: Ashgate.

Early, Bryan R. (2009). 'Sleeping With Your Friends' Enemies: An Explanation of Sanctions-Busting Trade.' *International Studies Quarterly* 53: 49–71.

Easton, David (1965). *A Framework for Political Analysis.* Englewood Cliffs, NJ: Prentice-Hall.

Edelstein, David M. (2008). *Occupational Hazards: Success and Failure in Military Occupation*. Ithaca: Cornell University Press.

Ekbladh, David (2011–12). 'Present at the Creation: Edward Meade Earle and the Depression-Era Origins of Security Studies.' *International Security* 36: 107–41.

Elbe, Stefan (2002). 'HIV/AIDS and the Changing Landscape of War in Africa.' *International Security* 27: 159–77.

Elbe, Stefan (2006). 'Should HIV/AIDS Be Securitized? The Ethical Dilemmas of Linking HIV/AIDS and Security.' *International Studies Quarterly* 50: 119–44.

Elbe, Stefan, Anne Roemer-Mahler and Christopher Long (2014). 'Securing Circulation Pharmaceutically: Antiviral Stockpiling and Pandemic Preparedness in the European Union.' *Security Dialogue* 45: 440–57.

Elliott, Kimberly Ann, Gary Clyde Hufbauer and Jeffrey J. Schott (2008). *Economic Sanctions Reconsidered*. Washington, DC: Peterson Institute for International Economics.

Elster, Jon (ed.) (1986). *Rational Choice*. Cambridge: Cambridge University Press.

Enders, Walter, and Todd Sandler (2004). 'Transnational Terrorism, 1968–2000: Thresholds, Persistence, and Forecasts.' *Southern Economic Journal* 71: 467–82.

Enloe, Cynthia (1990). *Bananas, Beaches, and Bases: Making Feminist Sense of International Politics*. Berkeley: University of California Press.

Epstein, Helen (2007). *The Invisible Cure: Africa, the West, and the Fight Against AIDS*. New York: Farrar, Strauss & Giroux.

Esty, Daniel C., Jack Goldstone, Ted Robert Gurr, Barbara Harff, Pamela T. Surko, Alan N. Unger and Robert Chen (1998). 'The State Failure Project: Early Warning Research for U.S. Foreign Policy Planning.' In John L. Davies and Ted Robert Gurr (eds.), *Preventative Measures: Building Risk Assessment and Crisis Early Warning Systems*. Lanham: Rowman & Littlefield.

Evans, Peter B., Dietrich Rueschemeyer and Theda Skocpol (eds.) (1985). *Bringing the State Back In*. Cambridge: Cambridge University Press.

Eznack, Lucile (2013). 'The Mood was Grave: Affective Dispositions and States' Anger-Related Behaviour.' *Contemporary Security Policy* 34: 552–80.

Falk, Richard (1997). 'State of Siege: Will Globalization Win Out.' *International Affairs* 40: 43–65.

Falkenrath, Richard A. (2001). 'Problems of Preparedness: U.S. Readiness for a Domestic Terrorist Attack.' *International Security* 25: 147–86.

Farber, Henry S., and Joanne Gowa (1995). 'Politics and Peace.' *International Security* 20: 123–46.

Farrar Jr., L. L. (1977). 'Cycles of War: Historical Speculation on Future International Violence.' *International Interactions* 1: 161–79.

Farwell, James P., and Rafal Rohozinski (2011). 'Stuxnet and the Future of Cyber War.' *Survival* 53: 23–40.

Fatton, Lionel P. (2016). 'The Impotence of Conventional Arms Control: Why Do International Regimes Fail When They Are Most Needed?' *Contemporary Security Policy* 37: 200–22.

Fazal, Tanisha M. (2004). 'State Death in the International System.' *International Organization* 58: 311–44.

Fearon, James D. (1994). 'Domestic Political Audiences and the Escalation of International Disputes.' *American Political Science Review* 88: 577–92.

Fearon, James D. (1995). 'Rationalist Explanations for War.' *International Organization* 49: 379–414.

Fearon, James D., and David D. Laitin (2004). 'Neotrusteeship and the Problem of Weak States.' *International Security* 28: 5–43.

Felbab-Brown, Vanda (2006). 'Kicking the Opium Habit? Afghanistan's Drug Economy and Politics Since the 1980s.' *Conflict, Security, and Development* 6: 127–49.

Fenio, Kenley Greer (2011). 'Tactics of Resistance and the Evolution of Identity from Subjects to Citizens: The AIDS Political Movement in Southern Africa.' *International Studies Quarterly* 55: 717–35.

Fijanut, Cyrille, and Letizia Paoli (eds.) (2004). *Organized Crime in Europe: Concepts, Patterns, and Control Policies in the European Union and Beyond.* Dordrecht: Springer.

Finnemore, Martha (2003). *The Purpose of Intervention: Changing Beliefs about the Use of Force.* Ithaca: Cornell University Press.

Finnemore, Martha (2009). 'Legitimacy, Hypocrisy, and the Social Structure of Unipolarity: Why Being a Unipole Isn't All It's Cracked Up to Be.' *World Politics* 61: 58–85.

Flockhart, Trine (2016). 'The Coming Multi-Order World.' *Contemporary Security Policy* 37: 3–30.

Flynn, Stephen (2004). *America the Vulnerable: How Our Government is Failing to Protect Us.* New York: HarperCollins.

Fordham, Benjamin O. (2008). 'Power or Plenty? Economic Interests, Security Concerns, and American Intervention.' *International Studies Quarterly* 52: 737–58.

Fortna, Virginia Page (2004). 'Does Peacekeeping Keep Peace? International Intervention and the Duration of Peace After Civil War.' *International Studies Quarterly* 48: 269–92.

Fortna, Virginia Page (2015). 'Do Terrorists Win? Rebels' Use of Terrorism and Civil War Outcomes.' *International Organization* 69: 519–56.

Fowler, James H., and Christopher T. Dawes (2013). 'In Defense of Genopolitics.' *American Political Science Review* 107: 362–74.

Franda, Marcus (2001). *Governing the Internet: The Emergence of an International Regime.* Boulder: Lynne Rienner.

Frederking, Brian (2003). 'Constructing Post-Cold War Collective Security.' *American Political Science Review* 97: 363–78.

Fromson, James, and Steven Simon (2015). 'ISIS: The Dubious Paradise of Apocalypse Now.' *Survival* 57: 7–56.

Fukuyama, Francis (1992). *The End of History and the Last Man.* New York: The Free Press.

Fukuyama, Francis (1998). 'Women and the Evolution of World Politics.' *Foreign Affairs*, September/October: 24–40.

Gaddis, John Lewis (1986). 'The Long Peace: Elements of Stability in the Postwar International System.' *International Security* 10: 98–142.

Gagnon, Jr., V. P. (1994–5). 'Ethnic Nationalism and International Conflict: The Case of Serbia.' *International Security* 19: 13–166.

Galtung, Johan (1996). *Peace by Peaceful Means: Peace, Conflict, Development, and Civilisation.* London: Sage.

Gambetta, Diego (ed.) (2005). *Making Sense of Suicide Missions*. Oxford: Oxford University Press.

Ganguly, Šumit (1999). 'India's Pathway to Pokhran II: The Prospects and Sources of New Delhi's Nuclear Weapons Program.' *International Security* 23: 148–77.

Garcia-Johnson, Ronie (2000). *Exporting Environmentalism: US Multinational Chemical Corporations in Brazil and Mexico*. Cambridge: The MIT Press.

Gardner, David (2009). *Last Chance: The Middle East in the Balance*. London: I.B. Tauris.

Garrett, Banning N., and Bonnie S. Glaser (1995–6). 'Chinese Perspectives on Arms Control.' *International Security* 20: 43–78.

Garthoff, Raymond J. (1985). *Détente and Confrontation: American-Soviet Relations from Nixon to Reagan*. Washington, DC: Brookings Institution Press.

Gartzke, Eric (2013). 'The Myth of Cyberwar: Bringing War in Cyberspace Back Down to Earth.' *International Security* 38: 41–73.

Gartzke, Eric, and Jon R. Lindsay (2015). 'Weaving Tangled Webs: Offense, Defense, and Deception in Cyberspace.' *Security Studies* 24: 316–48.

Gaubatz, Kurt Taylor (1991). 'Election Cycles and War.' *Journal of Conflict Resolution* 35: 212–44.

Gaubatz, Kurt Taylor (1999). *Elections and War: The Electoral Incentive in the Democratic Politics of War and Peace*. Stanford: Stanford University Press.

Gavin, Francis J. (2015). 'Strategies of Inhibition: U.S. Grand Strategy, the Nuclear Revolution, and Non-Proliferation.' *International Security* 40: 9–46.

Geddes, Andrew (2008). *Immigration and European Integration: Towards Fortress Europe*. Manchester: Manchester University Press.

Gent, Stephen E. (2008). 'Going In When It Counts: Military Interventions and the Outcome of Civil Conflicts.' *International Studies Quarterly* 52: 713–35.

Gentry, John A. (2006). 'Norms and Military Power: NATO's War Against Yugoslavia.' *Security Studies* 15: 187–224.

George, Alexander (1980). *Presidential Decisionmaking in Foreign Policy: The Effective Use of Information and Advice*. Boulder: Westview Press.

George, Alexander (1983). *Managing US-Soviet Rivalry: Problems of Crisis Prevention*. Boulder: Westview.

Gerges, Fawaz A. (2016). *ISIS: A History*. Princeton: Princeton University Press.

Germond, Basil, and Michael E. Smith (2009). 'Re-Thinking European Security Interests and the ESDP: Explaining the EU's First Anti-Piracy Naval Operation.' *Contemporary Security Policy* 30: 573–93.

Gerson, Michael S. (2010). 'No First Use: The Next Step for U.S. Nuclear Policy.' *International Security* 35: 7–47.

Getmansky, Anna, and Thomas Zeitzoff (2014). 'Terrorism and Voting: The Effect of Rocket Threat on Voting in Israeli Elections.' *American Political Science Review* 108: 588–604.

Gilpin, Robert (1981). *War and Change in World Politics*. New York: Cambridge University Press.

Gilpin, Robert (1989). 'The Theory of Hegemonic War.' In Robert I. Rotberg and Theodore K. Rabb (eds.), *The Origin and Prevention of Major Wars*. Cambridge: Cambridge University Press.

Ginsberg, Roy H., and Michael E. Smith (2007). 'Understanding the European Union as a Global Political Actor: Theory, Practice, and Impact.' In Kate McNamara and Sophie Meunier (eds.), *The State of the European Union, Vol. 8*. Oxford: Oxford University Press.

Glaser, Charles L. (1993). 'Why NATO is Still Best: Future Security Arrangements for Europe.' *International Security* 18: 5–50.

Glaser, Charles L. (2015). 'A U.S.-China Grand Bargain? The Hard Choice Between Military Competition and Accommodation.' *International Security* 39: 49–90.

Glaser, Charles L., and Chaim Kaufman (1998). 'What is the Offense-Defense Balance and Can We Measure It?' *International Security* 22: 44–82.

Glenny, Misha (2008). *McMafia: A Journey Through the Global Criminal Underworld*. New York: Knopf.

Glenny, Misha (2012). *DarkMarket: How Hackers Became the New Mafia*. New York: Vintage Books.

Global Humanitarian Forum (2008). *The Anatomy of a Silent Crisis*. Geneva: Global Humanitarian Forum.

Goldstein, Avery (1997–8). 'Great Expectations: Interpreting China's Arrival.' *International Security* 22: 36–73.

Goldstein, Avery (2013). 'First Things First: The Pressing Danger of Crisis Instability in U.S.-China Relations.' *International Security* 37: 49–89.

Goldstein, Joshua (2001). *War and Gender*. Cambridge: Cambridge University Press.

Goldstein, Judith, Miles Kahler, Robert O. Keohane and Anne-Marie Slaughter (2000). 'Introduction: Legalization and World Politics.' *International Organization* 54: 385–99.

Gompert, David C., and Martin Libicki (2014). 'Cyber Warfare and Sino-American Crisis Instability.' *Survival* 56: 7–22.

Gompert, David C., and Martin Libicki (2015). 'Waging Cyber War the American Way.' *Survival* 57: 7–28.

Gourevitch, Philip, and Errol Morris (2008). *Standard Operating Procedure: A War Story*. New York: Picador.

Gowa, Joanne (1995). 'Democratic States and International Disputes.' *International Organization* 49: 511–22.

Gowa, Joanne, and Nils Wessell (1982). *Ground Rules: Soviet and American Involvement in Regional Conflicts*. Philadelphia: Foreign Policy Research Institute.

Gray, Chris Hables (1997). *Post-Modern War: The New Politics of Conflict*. London: Routledge.

Gray, Colin (1992). 'New Directions for Strategic Studies: How Can Theory Help Practice?' *Security Studies* 1: 610–35.

Greenhalgh, Susan (2008). *Just One Child: Science and Policy in Deng's China*. Berkeley, CA: University of California Press.

Greenstein, Shane (2015). *How the Internet Became Commercial: Innovation, Privatization, and the Birth of a New Network*. Princeton: Princeton University Press.

Greenwald, Glenn (2014). *No Place to Hide: Edward Snowden, the NSA, and the U.S. Surveillance State*. New York: Metropolitan Books.

Greig, J. Michael, and Patrick M. Regan (2008). 'When Do They Say Yes? An Analysis of the Willingness to Offer and Accept Mediation in Civil Wars.' *International Studies Quarterly* 52: 759–81.

Grieco, Joseph M. (1990). *Cooperation Among Nations: Europe, America, and Non-Tariff Barriers to Trade*. Ithaca: Cornell University Press.

Grofman, Bernard (ed.) (2001). *Political Science as Puzzle Solving*. Ann Arbor: University of Michigan Press.

Grubb, Michael, and Farhana Yamin (2001). 'Climatic Collapse at the Hague: What Happened, Why, and Where Do We Go from Here?' *International Affairs* 77: 261–76.

Grundig, Frank (2006). 'Patterns of International Cooperation and the Explanatory Power of Relative Gains: An Analysis of Cooperation on Global Climate Change, Ozone Depletion, and International Trade.' *International Studies Quarterly* 50: 781–801.

Guéhenno, Jean-Marie (2015). *The Fog of Peace: A Memoir of International Peacekeeping in the 21st Century*. Washington, DC: Brookings Institution Press.

Guillemin, Jeanne (2005). *Biological Weapons: From the Invention of State-Sponsored Programs to Contemporary Bioterrorism*. New York: Columbia University Press.

Gulke, Adrian (1995). *The Age of Terrorism and the International Political System*. London: I.B. Tauris.

Gurr, Ted Robert (1994). 'Peoples Against States: Ethnopolitical Conflict and the Changing World System.' *International Studies Quarterly* 38: 347–77.

Gurr, Ted Robert, and B. Harff (2002). *Ethnic Conflict in World Politics*. Boulder: Westview.

Gusterson, Hugh (2016). *Drone: Remote Control Warfare*. Cambridge: MIT Press.

Haas, Mark L. (2007). 'A Geriatric Peace? The Future of U.S. Power in a World of Aging Populations.' *International Security* 32: 112–47.

Haas, Peter M. (1992a). 'Introduction: Epistemic Communities and International Policy Coordination.' *International Organization* 46: 1–35.

Haas, Peter M. (1992b). 'Banning Chlorofluorocarbons: Epistemic Community Efforts to Protect Stratospheric Ozone.' *International Organization* 46: 187–224.

Haas, Peter M., Robert O. Keohane, and Marc A. Levy (eds.) (1993). *Institutions for the Earth: Sources of Effective International Environmental Protection*. Cambridge: MIT Press.

Hadian, Nasser (2008). 'Iran's Nuclear Programme: Background and Clarification.' *Contemporary Security Policy* 29: 573–76.

Hafez, Mohammed M. (2006). *Manufacturing Human Bombs: The Making of Palestinian Suicide Bombers*. Washington, DC: United States Institute of Peace Press.

Hafner, Katie, and Matthew Lyon (1998). *Where Wizards Stay Up Late: The Origins of the Internet*. New York: Simon & Schuster.

Hagerty, Devin T. (1995–6). 'Nuclear Deterrence in South Asia: The 1990 Indo-Pakistani Crisis.' *International Security* 20: 79–114.

Hainmueller, Jens, and Dominik Hangartner (2013). 'Who Gets a Swiss Passport? A Natural Experiment in Swiss Immigration.' *American Political Science Review* 107: 159–87.

Hall, Todd H., and Andrew A. G. Ross (2015). 'Affective Politics After 9/11.' *International Organization* 69: 847–79.

Hameiri, Shahar, and Lee Jones (2013). 'The Politics and Governance of Non-Traditional Security.' *International Studies Quarterly* 57: 462–73.

Hanrieder, Tine, and Christian Kreuder-Sonnen (2014). 'WHO Decides on the Exception? Securitization and Emergency Governance in Global Health.' *Security Dialogue* 45: 331–48.

Hansen, Lene, and Helen Nissenbaum (2009). 'Digital Disaster, Cyber Security, and the Copenhagen School.' *International Studies Quarterly* 53: 1155–75.

Hansen, Randall, and Desmond King (2001). 'Eugenic Ideas, Political Variance, and Policy Variance: Immigration and Sterilization Policy in Britain and the U.S.' *World Politics* 53: 237–63.

Hastings, Justin V. (2012). 'Understanding Maritime Piracy Syndicate Operations.' *Security Studies* 21: 683–721.

Haufler, Virginia (2004). 'International Diplomacy and the Privatization of Conflict Prevention.' *International Studies Perspectives* 5: 158–63.

Haus, Leah (1995). 'Openings in the Wall: Transnational Migrants, Labor Unions, and U.S. Immigration Policy.' *International Organization* 49: 285–313.

Heisenberg, Dorothee (2005). *Negotiating Privacy: The European Union, the United States, and Personal Data Protection*. Boulder: Lynne Rienner.

Helleiner, Eric, and Stefano Pagliari (2011). 'The End of an Era in International Financial Regulation? A Postcrisis Research Agenda.' *International Organization* 65: 169–200.

Herbst, Jeffrey (1996–7). 'Responding to State Failure in Africa.' *International Security* 21: 120–44.

Herschinger, Eva (2015). 'The Drug *Dispositif*: Ambivalent Materiality and the Addiction of the Global Drug Prohibition Regime.' *Security Dialogue* 46: 183–201.

Herz, John H. (1950). 'Idealist Internationalism and the Security Dilemma.' *World Politics* 2: 157–80.

Hill, Christopher (2003). *The Changing Politics of Foreign Policy*. Basingstoke: Palgrave Macmillan.

Hills, Alice (2003). 'Dissolving Boundaries? The Development Marketplace and Military Security.' *Contemporary Security Policy* 24: 48–66.

Hoffman, Stanley (1977). 'An American Social Science: International Relations.' *Daedalus* 106: 41–60.

Holl, Jane (1993). 'When War Doesn't Work.' In Roy Licklider (ed.), *Stopping the Killing: How Civil Wars End*, New York: New York University Press.

Holsti, K. J. (1996). *The State, War, and the State of War*. Cambridge: Cambridge University Press.

Holsti, Ole, P. Terrence Hoppman and John D. Sullivan (1973). *Unity and Disintegration in International Alliances*. New York: Wiley.

Holt, Pat M. (1995). *Secret Intelligence and Public Policy: A Dilemma of Democracy*. Washington, DC: CQ Press.

Holzgrefe, J. L., and Robert O. Keohane (2003). *Humanitarian Intervention: Ethical, Legal and Political Dilemmas*. Cambridge: Cambridge University Press.

Homer-Dixon, Thomas F. (1994). 'Environmental Scarcities and Violent Conflict: Evidence from Cases.' *International Security* 19: 5–40.

Homer-Dixon, Thomas F. (1999). *Environment, Scarcity and Violence*. Princeton: Princeton University Press.

Hopf, Ted (1998). 'The Promise of Constructivism in International Relations Theory.' *International Security* 23: 171–200.

Horgan, John (2005). *The Psychology of Terrorism*. London: Routledge.

Horowitz, Donald L. (1985). *Ethnic Groups in Conflict*. Berkeley: University of California Press.

Horowitz, Michael C. (2009). 'Long Time Going: Religion and the Duration of Crusading.' *International Security* 34: 162–93.

Hough, Peter (2004). *Understanding Global Security.* London: Routledge.

Hough, Peter, Shahin Malik, Andrew Moran and Bruce Pilbeam (2015). *International Security Studies: Theory and Practice.* London: Routledge.

Housden, Martyn (2012). *The League of Nations and the Organisation of Peace.* Harlow: Longman.

Houweling, H., and J. Siccama (1988). 'Power Transitions as a Cause of War.' *Journal of Conflict Resolution* 31: 87–102.

Howard, Michael (1978). *War and the Liberal Conscience.* Cambridge: Cambridge University Press.

Howard, Michael (1983). *The Causes of Wars.* Cambridge: Harvard University Press.

Howard, Philip N. (2015). *Pax Technica: How the Internet of Things May Set Us Free or Lock Us Up.* New Haven: Yale University Press.

Howe, Herbert (1996–7). 'Lessons of Liberia: ECOMOG and Regional Peacekeeping.' *International Security* 21: 145–76.

Howorth, Jolyon (2003). 'ESDP and NATO: Wedlock or Deadlock.' *Cooperation & Conflict* 38: 235–54.

Howorth, Jolyon (2007). *Security and Defence Policy in the European Union.* Basingstoke: Palgrave.

Hudson, Valerie M., and Andrea Den Boer (2002). 'A Surplus of Men, a Deficit of Peace: Security and Sex Ratios in Asia's Largest States.' *International Security* 26: 5–38.

Hughes, Christopher, (ed.) (2009). *Security Studies: A Reader.* London: Routledge.

Hultman, Lisa, Jacob Kathman, and Megan Shannon (2014). 'Beyond Keeping Peace: United Nations Effectiveness in the Midst of Fighting.' *American Political Science Review* 108: 737–53.

Huntington, Samuel P. (1968). *Political Order in Changing Societies.* New Haven: Yale University Press.

Huntington, Samuel P. (1997). *The Clash of Civilizations and the Remaking of World Order.* New York: Simon & Schuster.

Hurrell, Andrew, and Benedict Kingsbury, (eds.). (1992). *The International Politics of the Environment.* Oxford: Clarendon Press.

Hussein, Seif (1987). 'Modeling War and Peace.' *American Political Science Review* 81: 221–30.

Huth, Paul K., Sarah E. Croco, and Benjamin J. Appel (2011). 'Does International Law Promote the Peaceful Settlement of International Disputes? Evidence from the Study of Territorial Conflicts Since 1945.' *American Political Science Review* 105: 415–36.

Huysmans, Jef (2006). *The Politics of Insecurity: Fear, Migration, and Asylum in the EU.* London: Routledge.

ICRC (2007). *ICRC Report on the Treatment of Fourteen 'High Value' Detainees in CIA Custody.* Geneva: ICRC.

Ifrah, Georges (2001). *The Universal History of Computing.* New York: John Wiley & Sons.

Ikenberry, G. John, David A. Lake, and Michael Mastanduno (1988). 'Introduction: Approaches to Explaining American Foreign Economic Policy.' In G. John Ikenberry, David A. Lake and Michael Mastanduno (eds.), *The State and American Foreign Economic Policy.* Ithaca: Cornell University Press.

Inbar, Efraim (2008). 'Iranians Like the Bomb: Some Tastes Are Dangerous.' *Contemporary Security Policy* 29: 565–68.

Inkster, Nigel (2016). *China's Cyber Power*. London: IISS/Routledge.

International Commission on Intervention and State Sovereignty (2002). *The Responsibility to Protect: The Report of the International Commission on Intervention and State Sovereignty*. Ottawa: International Development Research Centre.

Iqbal, Zaryab (2006). 'Health and Human Security: The Public Health Impact of Violent Conflict.' *International Studies Quarterly* 50: 631–49.

Isaacson, Walter (2014). *The Innovators: How a Group of Hackers, Geniuses, and Geeks Created the Digital Revolution*. New York: Simon & Schuster.

Isenberg, David (2007). 'A Government in Search of Cover: Private Military Companies in Iraq.' In Simon Chesterman and Chia Lehnardt (eds.), *From Mercenaries to Market: The Rise and Regulation of Private Military Companies*. Oxford: Oxford University Press.

Israeli, Raphael (2003). *Islamikaze: Manifestations of Islamic Martyrology*. London: Frank Cass.

Jackson, Robert H. (1990). *Quasi-States: Sovereignty, International Relations, and the Third World*. Cambridge: Cambridge University Press.

Jacoby, Tim, and Alpaslan Özerdem (2008). 'The Role of the State in the Turkish Earthquake of 1999.' *Journal of International Development* 20: 297–310.

Janis, Irving (1972). *Groupthink*. Boston: Houghton Mifflin.

Jentleson, Bruce W. (2002). 'The Need for Praxis: Bringing Policy Relevance Back In.' *International Security* 26: 169–83.

Jervis, Robert (1976). *Perception and Misperception in International Politics*. Princeton: Princeton University Press.

Jervis, Robert (1978). 'Cooperation Under the Security Dilemma.' *World Politics* 30: 167–214.

Jervis, Robert (1979). 'Deterrence Theory Revisited.' *World Politics* 31: 289–324.

Jervis, Robert (1990). *The Meaning of the Nuclear Revolution: Statecraft and the Prospect of Armageddon*. Ithaca: Cornell University Press.

Jervis, Robert (2009). 'Unipolarity: A Structural Perspective.' *World Politics* 61: 188–213.

Job, B. A. (ed.) (1992). *The Insecurity Dilemma: National Security of Third World States*. Boulder: Lynne Rienner.

Johnson, Chalmers (2002). *Blowback: The Costs and Consequences of the American Empire*. London: Time Warner.

Johnson, Loch K., and James J. Wirtz (2004). *Strategic Intelligence: Windows Into a Secret World*. Los Angeles: Roxbury Publishing.

Johnston, Alastair Iain (1995). 'Thinking About Strategic Culture.' *International Security* 19: 32–64.

Johnston, Alastair Iain (2013). 'How New and Assertive is China's New Assertiveness?' *International Security* 37: 7–48.

Johnston, Patrick B. (2012). 'Does Decapitation Work? Assessing the Effectiveness of Leadership Targeting in Counterinsurgency Campaigns.' *International Security* 36: 47–79.

Jones, Adam (1996). 'Does Gender Make the World Go Round? Feminist Critiques of International Relations.' *Review of International Studies* 22: 405–29.

Jones, Owen Bennett (2003). *Pakistan: Eye of the Storm*. New Haven: Yale University Press.

Jordan, Jenna (2009). 'When Heads Roll: Assessing the Effectiveness of Leadership Decapitation.' *Security Studies* 18: 719–55.

Jordan, Jenna (2014). 'Attacking the Leader, Missing the Mark.' *International Security* 38: 7–38.

Kahl, Colin H. (1998). 'Population Growth, Environmental Degradation, and State-Sponsored Violence: The Case of Kenya, 1991-93.' *International Security* 23: 80–119.

Kahler, Miles (1998). 'Rationality in International Relations.' *International Organization* 52: 919–41.

Kahler, Miles (2004). 'Economic Security in an Era of Globalisation: Definition and Provision.' *Pacific Review* 17: 485–502.

Kahn, Herman (1960). *On Thermonuclear War*. Princeton: Princeton University Press.

Kaldor, Mary (1999). *New and Old Wars: Organized Violence in a Global Era*. Stanford: Stanford University Press.

Kalyvas, Stathis N. (2001). ''New' and 'Old' Civil Wars: A Valid Distinction?' *World Politics* 54: 99–118.

Kaplan, Fred (2016). *Dark Territory: The Secret History of Cyber War*. New York: Simon & Schuster.

Kapstein, Ethan B. (2002–03). 'Two Dismal Sciences are Better than One – Economics and National Security: A Review Essay.' *International Security* 27: 158–87.

Kastner, Scott L. (2015–16). 'Is the Taiwan Strait Still a Flashpoint? Rethinking the Prospects for Armed Conflict Between China and Taiwan.' *International Security* 40: 54–92.

Katzenstein, Peter J., (ed.) (1996). *The Culture of National Security: Norms and Identity in World Politics*. New York: Columbia University Press.

Kaufmann, Chaim D. (1996). 'Possible and Impossible Solutions to Ethnic Civil Wars.' *International Security* 20: 136–75.

Kaufmann, Chaim D. (1998). 'When All Else Fails: Ethnic Population Transfers and Partitions in the Twentieth Century.' *International Security* 23: 120–56.

Kaufmann, Chaim D. (2004). 'Threat Inflation and the Failure of the Marketplace of Ideas: The Selling of the Iraq War.' *International Security* 29: 5–48.

Kay, Sean (2004). 'NATO, the Kosovo War, and Neoliberal Theory.' *Contemporary Security Policy* 25: 252–79.

Kaysen, Carl (1990). 'Is War Obsolete? A Review Essay.' *International Security* 14: 42–64.

Keck, Margaret E., and Kathryn Sikkink (1998). *Activists Beyond Borders: Advocacy Networks in International Politics*. Ithaca: Cornell University Press.

Kegley Jr., Charles W., and Gregory A. Raymond (2003). 'Preventive War and Permissive Normative Order.' *International Studies Perspectives* 4: 385–94.

Kelle, Alexander (2007). 'Securitization of International Public Health: Implications for Global Health Governance and the Biological Weapons Prohibition Regime.' *Global Governance* 13: 217–35.

Kello, Lucas (2013). 'The Meaning of the Cyber Revolution: Perils to Theory and Statecraft.' *International Security* 38: 7–40.

Kennedy, David M. (2004). *Over Here: The First World War and American Society*. Oxford: Oxford University Press (first published 1980).

Kennedy, Gavin (1979). *Burden-Sharing in NATO*. New York: Holmes & Meier.

Kennedy, Paul (ed.) (1991). *Grand Strategies in War and Peace*. New Haven: Yale University Press.

Keohane, Robert O. (1969). 'Lilliputians' Dilemmas: Small States in International Politics.' *International Organization* 23: 291–310.

Keohane, Robert O. (1984). *After Hegemony: Cooperation and Discord in the World Political Economy*. Princeton: Princeton University Press.

Keohane, Robert O. (ed.) (1986). *Neorealism and Its Critics*. New York: Columbia University Press.

Keohane, Robert O. (1998). 'Beyond Dichotomy: Conversations Between International Relations and Feminist Theory.' *International Studies Quarterly* 42: 193–97.

Keohane, Robert O., and Joseph S. Nye (1977). *Power and Interdependence*. Boston: Little, Brown.

Khong, Yuen Foong (2013–14). 'Primacy or World Order? The United States and China's Rise: A Review Essay.' *International Security* 38: 153–75.

Kilcullen, David (2008). *The Accidental Guerrilla: Fighting Small Wars in the Midst of a Big One*. Oxford: Oxford University Press.

Kim, Woosang (1989). 'Power, Alliance, and Major Wars.' *Journal of Conflict Resolution* 33: 255–73.

Kindleberger, Charles P. (2001). *Manias, Panics, and Crashes: A History of Financial Crises*. New York: John Wiley & Sons.

King, Charles (2001). 'The Benefits of Ethnic War: Understanding Eurasia's Unrecognized States.' *World Politics* 53: 524–52.

King, Gary, and Christopher J. L. Murray (2001–2). 'Rethinking Human Security.' *Political Science Quarterly* 116: 585–610.

King, Gary, and Langche Zeng (2001). 'Improving Forecasts of State Failure.' *World Politics* 53: 623–58.

Kirchner, Emil, and James Sperling (2007). *EU Security Governance*. Manchester: Manchester University Press.

Kittelsen, Sonja (2009). 'Conceptualizing Biorisk: Dread Risk and the Threat of Bioterrorism in Europe.' *Security Dialogue* 40: 51–71.

Klare, Michael T. (2002). *Resource Wars: The New Landscape of Global Conflict*. Basingstoke: Palgrave.

Klausen, Jytte (2015). 'Tweeting the *Jihad*: Social Media Networks of Foreign Fighters in Syria and Iraq.' *Studies in Conflict & Terrorism* 38: 1–22.

Koblentz, Gregory D. (2010). 'Biosecurity Reconsidered: Calibrating Biological Threats and Responses.' *International Security* 34: 96–132.

Kolodziej, Edward A. (2005). *Security and International Relations*. Cambridge: Cambridge University Press.

Koslowski, Rey (2002). 'Human Migration and the Conceptualization of Pre-Modern World Politics.' *International Studies Quarterly* 46: 375–99.

Koslowski, Rey, and Friedrich V. Kratochwil (1994). 'Understanding Change in International Politics: The Soviet Empire's Demise and the International System.' *International Organization* 48: 215–47.

Krain, Matthew (2005). 'International Intervention and the Severity of Genocides and Politicides.' *International Studies Quarterly* 49: 363–87.

Krasner, Stephen D. (1978). *Defending the National Interest: Raw Materials Investment and U.S. Foreign Policy*. Princeton: Princeton University Press.

Krasner, Stephen D. (ed.) (1983). *International Regimes*. Ithaca: Cornell University Press.

Krasner, Stephen D. (1995–6). 'Compromising Westphalia.' *International Security* 20: 115–51.

Krause, Keith, and Jennifer Milliken (2009). 'Introduction: The Challenge of Non-State Armed Groups.' *Contemporary Security Policy* 30: 202–20.

Krause, Keith, and Michael C. Williams (1997). *Critical Security Studies: Concepts and Cases*. Minneapolis: University of Minnesota Press.

Krcmaric, Daniel (2014). 'Refugee Flows, Ethnic Power Relations, and the Spread of Conflict.' *Security Studies* 23: 182–216.

Krebs, Ronald R., and Roy Licklider (2015–16). 'United They Fall: Why the International Community Should Not Promote Military Integration After Civil War.' *International Security* 40: 93–138.

Krauthammer, Charles (1990–1). 'The Unipolar Moment.' *Foreign Affairs* 70: 23–33.

Krishnan, Armin (2009). 'Automating War: The Need for Regulation.' *Contemporary Security Policy* 30: 172–93.

Kupchan, Charles A. (1988). 'NATO and the Persian Gulf: Examining Intra-Alliance Behavior.' *International Organization* 42: 317–46.

Kupchan, Charles A. (1998). 'After Pax Americana: Benign Power, Regional Integration, and the Sources of a Stable Multipolarity.' *International Security* 23: 40–79.

Kupchan, Charles A., and Clifford A. Kupchan (1995). 'The Promise of Collective Security.' *International Security* 20: 52–61.

Kuperman, Alan J. (2004). 'Is Partition Really the Only Hope? Reconciling Contradictory Findings About Ethnic Civil Wars.' *Security Studies* 13: 314–49.

Kuperman, Alan J. (2008). 'The Moral Hazard of Humanitarian Intervention: Lessons from the Balkans.' *International Studies Quarterly* 52: 49–80.

Kydd, Andrew H., and Barbara F. Walter (2006). 'The Strategies of Terrorism.' *International Security* 31: 49–79.

Lai, Brian, and Dan Reiter (2005). 'Rally 'Round the Union Jack? Public Opinion and the Use of Force in the United Kingdom.' *International Studies Quarterly* 49: 255–72.

Laidler, Keith (2008). *Surveillance Unlimited: How We've Become the Most Watched People on Earth*. Thriplow: Icon Books.

Lake, Daniel R. (2009). 'The Limits of Coercive Airpower: NATO's "Victory" in Kosovo Revisited.' *International Security* 34: 83–112.

Lake, David A. (1992). 'Powerful Pacifists: Democratic States and War.' *American Political Science Review* 86: 24–37.

Lake, David A. (2010–11). 'Two Cheers for Bargaining Theory: Assessing Rationalist Explanations of the Iraq War.' *International Security* 35: 7–52.

Lake, David A., and Patrick Morgan (eds.) (1997). *Regional Orders: Building Security in a New World*. University Park: Pennsylvania State University Press.

Lake, David A., and Donald Rothchild (1996). 'Containing Fear: The Origins and Management of Ethnic Conflict.' *International Security* 21: 41–75.

Lang Jr., Anthony F., (ed.) (2003). *Just Intervention*. Washington, DC: Georgetown University Press.

Lang Jr., Anthony F., Albert C. Pierce and Joel H. Rosenthal (eds.) (2004). *Ethics and the Future of Conflict: Lessons from the 1990s*. Upper Saddle River: Pearson Education.

Langewiesche, William (2007). *The Atomic Bazaar: The Rise of the Nuclear Poor*. London: Allen Lane.

Larrabee, F. Stephen (1993). 'Down and Out in Warsaw and Budapest: Eastern Europe and East-West Migration.' *International Security* 16: 5–33.

Lavoy, P. R., S. D. Sagan, and J. J. Wirtz, (eds.) (2000). *Planning the Unthinkable: How New Powers Will Use Nuclear, Chemical and Biological Weapons*. Ithaca: Cornell University Press.

Layne, Christopher (1993). 'The Unipolar Illusion: Why New Great Powers Will Rise.' *International Security* 17: 5–51.

Layne, Christopher (1994). 'Kant or Cant: The Myth of the Democratic Peace.' *International Security* 19: 5–49.

Layne, Christopher (2006). 'The Unipolar Illusion Revisited: The Coming End of the United States' Unipolar Moment.' *International Security* 31: 7–41.

Layne, Christopher (2012). 'This Time It's Real: The End of Unipolarity and the *Pax Americana.' International Studies Quarterly* 56: 203–13.

Leander, Anna (2007). 'Regulating the Role of Private Military Companies in Shaping Security and Politics.' In Simon Chesterman and Chia Lehnardt (eds.), *From Mercenaries to Market: The Rise and Regulation of Private Military Companies*. Oxford: Oxford University Press.

Le Billon, Philippe (2001a). 'The Political Ecology of War: Natural Resources and Armed Conflict.' *Political Geography* 20: 561–84.

Le Billon, Philippe (2001b). 'Angola's Political Economy of War: The Role of Oil and Diamonds, 1975–2000.' *African Affairs* No. 100: 55–80.

Le Billon, Philippe (2004). *Fuelling War: Natural Resources and Armed Conflict*. London: IISS Adelphi Paper No. 373.

Lebow, Richard Ned, and Janice Gross Stein (1995). *We All Lost the Cold War*. Princeton: Princeton University Press.

Lebow, Richard Ned, and Thomas Risse-Kappen (eds.) (1995). *International Relations Theory and the End of the Cold War*. New York: Columbia University Press.

Lee, Alexander (2011). 'Who Becomes a Terrorist? Poverty, Education, and the Origins of Political Violence.' *World Politics* 63: 203–45.

Legro, Jeffrey (1995). *Cooperation Under Fire: Anglo-German Restraint During World War II*. Ithaca: Cornell University Press.

Lehnardt, Chia (2007). 'Private Military Companies and State Responsibility.' In Simon Chesterman and Chia Lehnardt (eds.), *From Mercenaries to Market: The Rise and Regulation of Private Military Companies*. Oxford: Oxford University Press.

Leonard, Stephen (1990). *Critical Theory in Political Practice*. Princeton: Princeton University Press.

Lepgold, Joseph (1998). 'NATO's Post-Cold War Collective Action Problem.' *International Security* 23: 78–106.

Lévi-Strauss, Claude (1963). *Structural Anthropology*. Translated by Claire Jacobson and Brooke Grundfest Schoepf. New York: Basic Books.

Levy, Jack S. (1983). *War in the Modern Great Power System*. Lexington: University Press of Kentucky.

Levy, Jack S. (1984). 'The Offensive/Defensive Balance of Military Technology.' *International Studies Quarterly* 28: 219–38.

Levy, Jack S. (1985). 'Theories of General War.' *World Politics* 37: 344–74.

Levy, Jack S. (1989). 'Domestic Politics and War.' In Robert I. Rotberg and Theodore K. Rabb (eds.), *The Origin and Prevention of Major Wars*. Cambridge: Cambridge University Press.

Levy, Marc A. (1995). 'Is the Environment a National Security Issue?' *International Security* 20: 35–62.

Lewis, Michael (2010). *The Big Short: Inside the Doomsday Machine*. London: Allen Lane.

Li, Quan, and Drew Schaub (2004). 'Economic Globalization and Transnational Terrorism: A Pooled Time-Series Analysis.' *The Journal of Conflict Resolution* 48: 230–58.

Liberman, Peter (1996). 'Trading With the Enemy: Security and Relative Economic Gains.' *International Security* 21: 147–75.

Lichbach, Mark (1995). *The Rebels' Dilemma*. Ann Arbor: University of Michigan Press.

Licklider, Roy A. (ed.) (1993). *Stopping the Killing: How Civil Wars End*. New York: New York University Press.

Liff, Adam P., and G. John Ikenberry (2014). 'Racing Toward Tragedy? China's Rise, Military Competition in the Asia-Pacific, and the Security Dilemma.' *International Security* 39: 52–91.

Linden, Ronald H. (2000). 'Putting on Their Sunday Best: Romania, Hungary, and the Puzzle of Peace.' *International Studies Quarterly* 44: 121–45.

Lindsay, Jon R. (2014). 'Stuxnet and the Limits of Cyber Warfare.' *Security Studies* 22: 365–404.

Lindsay, Jon R. (2014–15). 'The Impact of China on Cybersecurity: Fiction and Friction.' *International Security* 39: 7–47.

Linklater, Andrew, and Hidemi Suganami (2006). *The English School of International Relations: A Contemporary Reassessment*. Cambridge: Cambridge University Press.

Lipson, Charles (2003). *Reliable Partners: How Democracies Have Made a Separate Peace*. Princeton: Princeton University Press.

Lischer, Sarah Kenyon (2003). 'Collateral Damage: Humanitarian Assistance as a Cause of Conflict.' *International Security* 28: 79–109.

Liska, George (1962). *Nations in Alliance: The Limits of Interdependence*. Baltimore: Johns Hopkins University Press.

Litfin, Karen T. (2000). 'Environment, Wealth, and Authority: Global Climate Change and Emerging Modes of Legitimation.' *International Studies Review* 2: 119–48.

Long, Austin (2014). 'Whack-a-Mole or Coup de Grace? Institutionalization and Leadership Targeting in Iraq and Afghanistan.' *Security Studies* 23: 471–512.

Long, D. (2002). 'The European Union and the Ottawa Process to Ban Landmines.' *Journal of European Public Policy* 9: 429–46.

Lowenthal, Mark M. (2003). *Intelligence: From Secrets to Policy*. Washington, DC: CQ Press.

Lucas, Edward (2015). *Cyberphobia: Identity, Trust, Security, and the Internet*. London: Bloomsbury.

Lundgren, Magnus (2016). 'Mediation in Syria: Initiatives, Obstacles, and Strategies, 2011–2016.' *Contemporary Security Policy* 37: 273–88.

Macdonald, Douglas J. (1995–6). 'Communist Bloc Expansion in the Early Cold War: Challenging Realism, Refuting Revisionism.' *International Security* 20: 152–88.

MacDonald, Paul (2003). 'Useful Fiction or Miracle Maker: The Competing Epistemological Foundations of Rational Choice Theory.' *American Political Science Review* 97: 551–65.

Maclean, Sandra J., David R. Black and Timothy M. Shaw, (eds.) (2006). *A Decade of Human Security: Global Governance and New Multilateralisms.* London: Routledge.

Manjikian, Mary McEvoy (2010). 'From Global Village to Virtual Battlespace: The Colonizing of the Internet and the Extension of Realpolitik.' *International Studies Quarterly* 54: 381–401.

Mansfield, Edward D., Diana C. Mutz and Laura R. Silver (2015). 'Men, Women, Trade, and Free Markets.' *International Studies Quarterly* 59: 303–15.

Mansfield, Edward D., and Jack Snyder (1995). 'Democratization and the Danger of War.' *International Security* 20: 5–38.

Margalit, Yotam (2013). 'Explaining Social Policy Preferences: Evidence from the Great Recession.' *American Political Science Review* 107: 80–103.

Marlin-Bennett, Renée (2004). *Knowledge Power: Intellectual Property, Information & Privacy.* Boulder: Lynne Rienner.

Marmot, Michael (2005). *Status Syndrome: How Your Social Standing Directly Affects Your Health.* London: Bloomsbury.

Martin, Pierre, and Mark R. Brawley (2001). *Alliance Politics, Kosovo, and NATO's War: Allied Force or Forced Allies?* New York: Palgrave.

Mason, T. David, and Patrick J. Fett (1996). 'How Civil Wars End: A Rational Choice Approach.' *Journal of Conflict Resolution* 40: 546–68.

Mastanduno, Michael (1988). 'Trade as a Strategic Weapon: American and Alliance Export Control Policy in the Early Postwar Period.' *International Organization* 42: 121–50.

Mastanduno, Michael (1993). *Economic Containment.* Ithaca: Cornell University Press.

Mastanduno, Michael (1997). 'Preserving the Unipolar Moment: Realist Theories and U.S. Grand Strategy After the Cold War.' *International Security* 21: 49–88.

Mastanduno, Michael (1998). 'Economics and Security in Statecraft and Scholarship.' *International Organization* 52: 825–54.

Matsumura, Hiroshi (2000). *Japan and the Kyoto Protocol: Conditions for Ratification.* London: Royal Institute of International Affairs.

McCrisken, Trevor (2013). 'Obama's Drone War.' *Survival* 55: 97–122.

McDermott, Rose (2015). 'Sex and Death: Gender Differences in Aggression and Motivations for Violence.' *International Organization* 69: 753–75.

McIntyre, Angela, and Taya Weiss (2007). 'Weak Governments in Search of Strength: Africa's Experience of Mercenaries and Private Military Companies.' In Simon Chesterman and Chia Lehnardt (eds.), *From Mercenaries to Market: The Rise and Regulation of Private Military Companies.* Oxford: Oxford University Press.

McLaren, Lauren M. (2012). 'The Cultural Divide in Europe: Migration, Multiculturalism, and Political Trust.' *World Politics* 64: 199–241.

McNamara, Robert S. (1992). 'The Population Explosion.' *The Futurist* (November–December).

McNeill, J.R. (2005). 'Diamond in the Rough: Is There a Genuine Environmental Threat to Security? A Review Essay.' *International Security* 30: 178–95.

Mearsheimer, John J. (1983). *Conventional Deterrence.* Ithaca: Cornell University Press.

Mearsheimer, John J. (1990). 'Back to the Future: Instability in Europe After the Cold War.' *International Security* 15: 5–56.

Mearsheimer, John J. (2001). *The Tragedy of Great Power Politics*. New York: W.W. Norton.

Meierding, Emily (2016). 'Dismantling the Oil Wars Myth.' *Security Studies* 25: 258–88.

Melander, Eric (2005). 'Gender Equality and Intrastate Armed Conflict.' *International Studies Quarterly* 49: 695–714.

Mercer, Jonathan (2013). 'Emotion and Strategy in the Korean War.' *International Organization* 67: 221–52.

Messina, Anthony M. (2014). 'Securitizing Immigration in the Age of Terror.' *World Politics* 66: 530–59.

Meyer, Stephen M. (1988). 'The Sources and Prospects of Gorbachev's New Political Thinking on Security.' *International Security* 13: 124–63.

MI5 Behavioral Science Unit (2008). *Understanding Radicalisation and Violent Extremism in the UK*. Behavioral Science Briefing Note BSU 02/2008. London: MI5.

Migdal, Joel S. (1988). *Strong Societies and Weak States: State-Society Relations and State Capabilities in the Third World*. Princeton: Princeton University Press.

Miller, Benjamin (2006). 'Balance of Power or the State-to-Nation Balance: Explaining Middle East War Propensity.' *Security Studies* 15: 658–705.

Miller, Judith, Stephen Engelberg and William Broad (2002). *Germs: Biological Weapons and America's Secret War*. New York: Touchstone.

Milner, Helen (1992). 'International Theories of Cooperation Among Nations: A Review Essay.' *World Politics* 44: 466–96.

Mitnick, Kevin (2011). *Ghost in the Wires: My Adventures as the World's Most Wanted Hacker*. New York: Back Bay Books.

Mittelman, James (2000). *The Globalization Syndrome*. Princeton: Princeton University Press.

Mittelman, James H. (2002). 'Globalization: An Ascendant Paradigm?' *International Studies Perspectives* 3: 1–14.

Mitton, John (2015). 'Selling Schelling Short: Reputations and American Coercive Diplomacy After Syria.' *Contemporary Security Policy* 36: 408–31.

Mitzen, Jennifer (2006). 'Ontological Security in World Politics: State Identity and the Security Dilemma.' *European Journal of International Relations* 12: 341–70.

Modelski, George (1963). 'The Study of Alliances: A Review.' *Journal of Conflict Resolution* 7: 769–76.

Modelski, George (1978). 'The Long Cycle of Global Politics and the Nation-State.' *Comparative Studies in Society and History* 20: 214–35.

Montoya, Celeste (2008). 'The European Union, Capacity Building, and Transnational Networks: Combating Violence Against Women Through the Daphne Program.' *International Organization* 62: 359–72.

Moore, Jonathan, (ed.) (1998). *Hard Choices: Moral Dilemmas in Humanitarian Intervention*. New York: Rowman & Littlefield.

Moran, Daniel (ed.) (2011). *Climate Change and National Security: A Country-Level Analysis*. Washington, DC: Georgetown University Press.

Morgan, Patrick M. (1985). 'Saving Face for the Sake of Deterrence.' In Robert Jervis, Richard Ned Lebow, and Janice Gross Stein (eds.), *Psychology and Deterrence*, Baltimore: Johns Hopkins University Press.

Morgan, Patrick M. (2003). *Deterrence Now*. Cambridge: Cambridge University Press.

Morgan, Patrick M. (2006). *International Security: Problems and Solutions*. Washington, DC: CQ Press.

Morgan, T. Clifton (1993). 'Democracy and War: Reflections on the Literature.' *International Interactions* 18: 197–203.

Morgenthau, Hans J. (1948). *Politics Among Nations: The Struggle for Power and Peace* (3rd ed.) (1963). New York: Alfred A. Knopf.

Morozov, Evgeny (2011). *The Net Delusion: The Dark Side of Internet Freedom*. New York: Public Affairs.

Morrow, James D. (1985). 'A Continuous-Outcome Expected Utility Theory of War.' *Journal of Conflict Resolution* 29: 473–502.

Morrow, James D. (1992). 'Signaling Difficulties with Linkage in Crisis Bargaining.' *International Studies Quarterly* 36: 153–72.

Moul, William (2003). 'Power Parity, Preponderance, and War Between Great Powers, 1816–1989.' *Journal of Conflict Resolution* 47: 468–89.

Mueller, John (1973). *War, Presidents, and Public Opinion*. New York: John Wiley.

Mueller, John (1988). 'The Essential Irrelevance of Nuclear Weapons: Stability in the Postwar World.' *International Security* 13: 55–78.

Mueller, John (1989). *Retreat from Doomsday: The Obsolescence of Major War*. New York: Basic Books.

Mueller, John (2000). 'The Banality of "Ethnic War".' *International Security* 25: 42–70.

Mueller, John (2005). 'Six Rather Unusual Propositions About Terrorism.' *Terrorism and Political Violence* 17: 487–505.

Mueller, John (2006). *Overblown: How Politicians and the Terrorism Industry Inflate National Security Threats, and Why We Believe Them*. New York: Free Press.

Mueller, John, and Mark G. Stewart (2012). 'The Terrorism Delusion: America's Overwrought Response to September 11.' *International Security* 37: 81–110.

Mueller, Milton L. (2002). *Ruling the Root: Internet Governance and the Taming of Cyberspace*. Cambridge: MIT Press.

Mullenbach, Mark J. (2005). 'Deciding to Keep Peace: An Analysis of International Influences on the Establishment of Third-Party Peacekeeping Missions,' *International Studies Quarterly* 49: 529–55.

Murphy, Craig N. (1996). 'Seeing Women, Recognizing Gender, Recasting International Relations.' *International Organization* 50: 513–38.

Nadelmann, Ethan A. (1990). 'Global Prohibition Regimes: The Evolution of Norms in International Society.' *International Organization* 44: 479–526.

Nadelmann, Ethan A. (1994). *Cops Across Borders: The Internationalization of U.S. Criminal Law Enforcement*. University Park: Penn State University Press.

Nel, Philip, and Marjolein Righarts (2008). 'Natural Disasters and the Risk of Violent Conflict.' *International Studies Quarterly* 52: 159–85.

Nelson, Stephen C., and Peter J. Katzenstein (2014). 'Uncertainty, Risk, and the Financial Crisis of 2008.' *International Organization* 68: 361–92.

Nerang, Neil (2015). 'Assisting Uncertainty: How Humanitarian Aid Can Inadvertently Prolong Civil War.' *International Studies Quarterly* 59: 184–95.

Netherlands Scientific Council for Government Policy (2015). The Public Core of the Internet. The Hague: Netherlands Scientific Council for Government Policy.

Neumayer, Eric (2005). 'Bogus Refugees? The Determinants of Asylum Migration to Western Europe.' *International Studies Quarterly* 49: 389–409.

Newman, Abraham L. (2008). *Protectors of Privacy: Regulating Personal Data in the Global Economy.* Ithaca: Cornell University Press.

Niou, E. M. S., P. C. Ordeshook and G. F. Rose (1989). *The Balance of Power: Stability in International Systems.* Cambridge: Cambridge University Press.

Nordhaus, William D. (2013). *The Climate Casino: Risk, Uncertainty, and Economics for a Warming World.* New Haven: Yale University Press.

Nordhaus, William D., John R. Oneal and Bruce Russett (2012). 'The Effects of the International Security Environment on National Military Expenditures: A Multicountry Study.' *International Organization* 66: 491–513.

Nye, Joseph (2005). *Soft Power: The Means to Success in World Politics.* New York: Public Affairs.

O'Brien, Kevin A. (2007). 'What Should and What Should Not Be Regulated?' In Simon Chesterman and Chia Lehnardt (eds.), *From Mercenaries to Market: The Rise and Regulation of Private Military Companies.* Oxford: Oxford University Press.

Occhipinti, John D. (2003). *The Politics of EU Police Cooperation: Toward a European FBI?* Boulder: Lynne Rienner.

Occhipinti, John D. (2007). 'Justice and Home Affairs: Immigration and Policing.' In Katja Weber, Michael E. Smith and Michael Baun (eds.), *Governing Europe's Neighbourhood: Partners or Periphery?* Manchester: University of Manchester Press.

Okrent, Daniel (2010). *Last Call: The Rise and Fall of Prohibition.* New York: Scribner.

Oliver, Anne Marie, and Paul F. Steinberg (2005). *The Road to Martyrs' Square: A Journey into the World of the Suicide Bomber.* Oxford: Oxford University Press.

Olson, Mancur (1974). *The Logic of Collective Action.* Cambridge: Harvard University Press.

Olson, Parmy (2012). *We Are Anonymous: Inside the Hacker World of LulzSec, Anonymous, and the Global Cyber Insurgency.* New York: Little, Brown.

Oneal, John R. (1990). 'The Theory of Collective Action and Burden-Sharing in NATO.' *International Organization* 44: 379–402.

Orbinski, James (2008). *An Imperfect Offering: Dispatches from the Medical Frontline.* London: Ebury.

Oren, Ido (1995). 'The Subjectivity of the Democratic Peace: Changing U.S. Perceptions of Imperial Germany.' *International Security* 20: 147–84.

Organski, A. F. K. (1968). *World Politics.* New York: Alfred A. Knopf.

Ostrom, Elinor (1990). *Governing the Commons: The Evolution of Institutions for Collective Action.* Cambridge: Cambridge University Press.

Ostrom Jr., Charles W., and Brian L. Job (1986). 'The President and the Political Use of Force.' *American Political Science Review* 53: 541–66.

Owen, John M. (1994). 'How Liberalism Produces Democratic Peace.' *International Security* 19: 87–125.

Oye, Kenneth A. (ed.) (1986). *Cooperation Under Anarchy.* Princeton: Princeton University Press.

Palan, Ronen (2003). *The Offshore World: Sovereign Markets, Virtual Places, and Nomad Millionaires.* Ithaca: Cornell University Press.

Pape, Robert A. (1996). *Bombing to Win: Air Power and Coercion in War*. Ithaca: Cornell University Press.

Pape, Robert A. (1997). 'Why Economic Sanctions Do Not Work.' *International Security* 22: 90–136.

Pape, Robert A. (1998). 'Why Economic Sanctions *Still* Do Not Work.' *International Security* 23: 66–77.

Pape, Robert A. (2005a). *Dying to Win: The Strategic Logic of Suicide Terrorism*. New York: Random House.

Pape, Robert A. (2005b). 'Soft Balancing Against the United States.' *International Security* 30: 7–45.

Pape, Robert A. (2012). 'When Duty Calls: A Pragmatic Standard of Humanitarian Intervention.' *International Security* 37: 41–80.

Paré, Daniel J. (2003). *Internet Governance in Transition: Who is the Master of This Domain?* Lanham: Rowman & Littlefield.

Parent, Joseph M., and Sebastian Rosato (2015). 'Balancing in Neorealism.' *International Security* 40: 51–86.

Paris, Roland (2001). 'Human Security: Paradigm Shift or Hot Air?' *International Security* 26: 87–102.

Paris, Roland (2003). 'The Globalization of Taxation? Electronic Commerce and the Transformation of the State.' *International Studies Quarterly* 47: 153–82.

Parker, Christopher S. (1999). 'New Weapons for Old Problems: Conventional Proliferation and Military Effectiveness in Developing States.' *International Security* 23: 119–47.

Parker, John (2000). *Total Surveillance: Investigating the Big Brother World of E-spies, Eavesdroppers, and CCTV*. London: Piatkus.

Parker, Owen, and James Brassett (2005). 'Contingent Borders, Ambiguous Ethics: Migrants in (International) Political Theory.' *International Studies Quarterly* 49: 233–53.

Park, Sunhee (2015). 'Power and Civil War Termination Bargaining.' *International Studies Quarterly* 59: 172–83.

Paul, T. V. (2005). 'Soft Balancing in the Age of U.S. Primacy.' *International Security* 30: 46–71.

Pedahzur, Ami (2005). *Suicide Terrorism*. Cambridge: Polity Press.

Pedersen, Susan (2015). *The Guardians: The League of Nations and the Crisis of Empire*. Oxford: Oxford University Press.

Pei, Minxin (2003). 'Lessons from the Past.' *Foreign Policy* 137: 52–5.

Pelton, Robert Young (2007). *Licensed to Kill: Hired Guns in the War on Terror*. New York: Three Rivers Press.

Percy, Sarah (2007). *Mercenaries: The History of a Norm in International Relations*. Oxford: Oxford University Press.

Perl, Raphael (2006). 'Drug Control: International Policy and Approaches.' *CRS Issue Brief for Congress IB88093*. Washington, DC: Congressional Research Service.

Perry, William J. (2015). *My Journey at the Nuclear Brink*. Stanford: Stanford Security Studies.

Peterson, Susan (2002–3). 'Epidemic Disease and National Security.' *Security Studies* 12: 43–81.

Phayal, Anup, Prabin B. Khadka and Clayton L. Thyne (2015). 'What Makes an Ex-Combatant Happy? A Micro-Analysis of Disarmament, Demobilization, and Reintegration in South Sudan.' *International Studies Quarterly* 59: 654–68.

Pickering, Jeffrey, and Emizet F. Kisangani (2005). 'Democracy and Diversionary Military Intervention: Reassessing Regime Type and the Diversionary Hypothesis.' *International Studies Quarterly* 49: 23–43.

Pickett, Kate, and Richard Wilkinson (2010). *The Spirit Level: Why Equality is Better for Everyone*. London: Penguin Books.

Pierskalla, Jan H., and Florian M. Hollenbach (2013). 'Technology and Collective Action: The Effect of Cell Phone Coverage on Political Violence in Africa.' *American Political Science Review* 107: 207–24.

Piot, Peter (2015). *AIDS Between Science and Politics*. New York: Columbia University Press.

Podhoretz, Norman (2007). *World War IV: The Long Struggle Against Islamofascism*. New York: Doubleday.

Poku, Nana K., and David Graham (eds.) (2000). *Redefining Security: Population Movements and National Security*. Santa Barbara: Praeger.

Posen, Barry (1984). *The Sources of Military Doctrine*. Ithaca: Cornell University Press.

Posen, Barry (1996). 'Military Responses to Refugee Disasters.' *International Security* 21: 72–111.

Posen, Barry R. (2000). 'The War for Kosovo: Serbia's Political-Military Strategy.' *International Security* 24: 39–84.

Powell, Emilia Justnya (2015). 'Islamic Law States and Peaceful Resolution of Interstate Disputes.' *International Organization* 69: 777–807.

Powell, Jonathan (2008). *Great Hatred, Little Room: Making Peace in Northern Ireland*. New York: The Bodley Head.

Powell, Robert (1991). 'Absolute and Relative Gains in International Relations Theory.' *American Political Science Review* 85: 1303–20.

Prakash, Adhikari (2012). 'The Plight of the Forgotten Ones: Civil War and Forced Migration.' *International Studies Quarterly* 56: 590–606.

Prentiss, Augustin M. (1937). *Chemicals in War*. New York: McGraw-Hill.

Press, Daryl G. (2004). 'The Credibility of Power: Assessing Threats During the "Appeasement" Crises of the 1930s.' *International Security* 29: 136–69.

Press, Daryl G., Scott D. Sagan and Benjamin A. Valentino (2013). 'Atomic Aversion: Experimental Evidence on Taboos, Traditions, and the Non-use of Nuclear Weapons.' *American Political Science Review* 107: 188–206.

Price, Bryan C. (2012). 'Targeting Top Terrorists: How Leadership Decapitation Contributes to Counterterrorism.' *International Security* 36: 9–46.

Price, Richard (1995). 'A Genealogy of the Chemical Weapons Taboo.' *International Organization* 49: 73–103.

Price, Richard (1998). 'Reversing the Gun Sights: Transnational Civil Society Targets Landmines.' *International Organization* 52: 613–44.

Price, Richard, and Mark W. Zacher (2004). *The United Nations and Global Security*. Basingstoke: Palgrave Macmillan.

Price-Smith, Andrew (2001a). *The Health of Nations: Infectious Disease, Environmental Change, and Their Effects on National Security and Development*. Cambridge: MIT Press.

Price-Smith, Andrew (2001b). *Plagues and Politics: Infectious Disease and International Policy*. Basingstoke: Palgrave Macmillan.

Price-Smith, Andrew (2004). *Downward Spiral: HIV/AIDS, State Capacity and Political Violence in Zimbabwe.* Washington, DC: US Institute of Peace Press.

Putnam, Robert D. (1988). 'Diplomacy and Domestic Politics: The Logic of Two-Level Games.' *International Organization* 42: 427–60.

Quammen, David (2013). *Spillover: Animal Infections and the Next Human Pandemic.* New York: Vintage Books.

Quester, George (1977). *Offense and Defense in the International System.* New York: Wiley.

Ramadan, Hisham, and Jeff Shantz (eds.) (2016). *Manufacturing Phobias: The Political Production of Fear in Theory and Practice.* Toronto: University of Toronto Press.

Randle, Robert (1973). *The Origins of Peace: A Study of Peacemaking and the Structure of Peace Settlements.* New York: Free Press.

Rapoport, David C. (1992). 'Terrorism.' In Mary Hawkesworth and Maurice Kogan (eds.), *Routledge Encyclopedia of Government and Politics*, Vol. 2. London: Routledge.

Rapoport, David C. (2001a). 'The Fourth Wave: September 11 in the History of Terrorism.' *Current History*, December: 419–24.

Rapoport, David C. (ed.) (2001b). *Inside Terrorist Organizations.* London: Frank Cass.

Rapoport, David C. (2004). 'The Four Waves of Modern Terrorism.' In Audrey Kurth Cronin and James M. Ludes (eds.), *Attacking Terrorism: Elements of a Grand Strategy.* Washington, DC: Georgetown University Press.

Rappert, Brian (ed.) (2007). *Technology and Security: Governing Threats in the New Millennium.* Basingstoke: Palgrave.

Rees, Wyn (2006). *Transatlantic Counter-Terrorism Cooperation.* London: Routledge.

Regan, Patrick (2002). 'Third-Party Interventions and the Duration of Intrastate Conflicts.' *Journal of Conflict Resolution* 46: 55–73.

Regan, Patrick, and Aysegul Aydin (2006). 'Diplomacy and Other Forms of Intervention in Civil War.' *Journal of Conflict Resolution* 50: 736–56.

Reich, Robert B. (2015). *Saving Capitalism: For the Many, Not the Few.* New York: Knopf.

Reiter, Dan (1995). 'Exploding the Powder Keg Myth: Preemptive Wars Almost Never Happen.' *International Security* 20: 5–34.

Richardson, Lewis F. (1960). *Statistics of Deadly Quarrels.* Chicago: Quadrangle Books.

Rickards, James (2011). *Currency Wars: The Making of the Next Global Crisis.* New York: Portfolio Books.

Ricks, Thomas E. (2006). *Fiasco: The American Military Adventure in Iraq.* London: Penguin Books.

Rid, Thomas (2013). *Cyber War Will Not Take Place.* Oxford: Oxford University Press.

Risse-Kappen, Thomas (1994). 'Ideas Do Not Float Freely: Transnational Coalitions, Domestic Structures, and the End of the Cold War.' *International Organization* 48: 185–214.

Roberts, Andrew (1999). 'NATO's "Humanitarian" War Over Kosovo.' *Survival* 41: 102–23.

Ron, James, Howard Ramos and Kathleen Rodgers (2005). 'Transnational Information Politics: NGO Human Rights Reporting, 1986–2000.' *International Studies Quarterly* 49: 557–87.

Rosato, Sebastian (2003). 'The Flawed Logic of Democratic Peace Theory.' *American Political Science Review* 97: 585–602.

Rosenau, James (1990). *Turbulence in World Politics*. Princeton: Princeton University Press.

Rosenau, James (1996). 'The Dynamics of Globalization: Toward an Operational Formulation.' *Security Dialogue* 27: 18–35.

Rosenau, James, and Mary Durfee Rosenau (2000). *Thinking Theory Thoroughly: Coherent Approaches to an Incoherent World*. Boulder: Westview Press.

Ross, Michael L. (2004). 'How Do Natural Resources Influence Civil War? Evidence from Thirteen Cases.' *International Organization* 58: 35–67.

Rothstein, Robert L. (1968). *Alliances and Small Powers*. New York: Columbia University Press.

Rubin, Barnett, and Alexandra Guáqueta (2007). *Fighting Drugs and Building Peace: Towards Policy Coherence Between Counter-Narcotics and Peacebuilding*. New York: Friedrich-Ebert-Stiftung.

Rudolph, Christopher (2003). 'Security and the Political Economy of International Migration.' *American Political Science Review* 97: 603–20.

Ruggie, John Gerard (1982). 'International Regimes, Transactions, and Change: Embedded Liberalism in the Postwar Economic Order.' In Stephen D. Krasner (ed.), *International Regimes*. Ithaca: Cornell University Press.

Rule, James B. (1988). *Theories of Civil Violence*. Berkeley: University of California Press.

Russett, Bruce M. (ed.) (1972). *Peace, War, and Numbers*. Beverly Hills: Sage.

Russett, Bruce (1990). *Controlling the Sword: The Democratic Governance of National Security*. Cambridge: Harvard University Press.

Russett, Bruce M. (1993). *Grasping the Democratic Peace: Principles for a Post-Cold War World*. Princeton: Princeton University Press.

Rutherford, K. (2000). 'The Evolving Arms Control Agenda: Implications of the Role of NGOs in Banning Antipersonnel Landmines.' *World Politics* 53: 74–114.

Sadiq, Kamal (2005). 'When States Prefer Non-Citizens Over Citizens: Conflict Over Illegal Immigration Into Malaysia.' *International Studies Quarterly* 49: 101–22.

Sagan, Scott D. (1989). 'The Origins of the Pacific War.' In Robert I. Rotberg and Theodore K. Rabb (eds.), *The Origin and Prevention of Major Wars*. Cambridge: Cambridge University Press.

Sagan, Scott D. (1993). *The Limits of Safety: Organizations, Accidents, and Nuclear Weapons*. Princeton: Princeton University Press.

Sagan, Scott D. (1996–7). 'Why Do States Build Nuclear Weapons? Three Models in Search of a Bomb.' *International Security* 21: 54–86.

Sagan, Scott D., and Kenneth N. Waltz (2003). *The Spread of Nuclear Weapons: A Debate Renewed*. New York: W.W. Norton.

Saideman, Stephen M. (2016). 'The Ambivalent Coalition: Doing the Least One Can Do Against Islamic State.' *Contemporary Security Policy* 37: 289–305.

Salehyan, Idean, Kristian Skrede Gleditsch, and David E. Cunningham (2011). 'Explaining External Support for Insurgent Groups.' *International Organization* 65: 709–44.

Sambanis, Nicholas (2000). 'Partition as a Solution to Ethnic War: An Empirical Critique of the Theoretical Literature.' *World Politics* 52: 437–83.

Sambanis, Nicholas (2004). 'What is a Civil War? Conceptual and Empirical Complexities of an Operational Definition.' *Journal of Conflict Resolution* 48: 814–58.

Sambanis, Nicholas, and Jonah Schulhofer-Wuhl (2009). 'What's in a Line? Is Partition a Solution to Civil War?' *International Security* 34: 82–118.

Sandholtz, Wayne, and William Koetzle (2000). 'Accounting for Corruption: Economic Structure, Democracy, and Trade.' *International Studies Quarterly* 44: 31–50.

Sandholtz, Wayne, Michael Borrus, John Zysman and Steven Vogel (eds.) (1992). *The Highest Stakes: The Economic Foundations of the Next Security System.* Oxford: Oxford University Press.

Sandler, Todd, and John F. Forbes (1980). 'Burden Sharing, Strategy, and the Design of NATO.' *Economic Inquiry* 18: 425–44.

Sands, Philippe (2008). *Torture Team: Deception, Cruelty, and the Compromise of Law.* London: Allen Lane.

Sands, Philippe (2016). *East West Street: On the Origins of 'Genocide' and 'Crimes Against Humanity'.* New York: Knopf.

Saunders, Frances Stonor (2001). *The Cultural Cold War: The CIA and the World of Arts and Letters.* New York: New Press.

Sauer, Tom (2003). 'Back to Arms Control: Limiting US National Missile Defence.' *Contemporary Security Policy* 24: 91–128.

Scahill, Jeremy (2008). *Blackwater: The Rise of the World's Most Powerful Mercenary Army.* London: Serpent's Tail.

Schelling, Thomas C. (1966). *Arms and Influence.* New Haven: Yale University Press.

Scherrer, Amandine (2009). *G8 Against Transnational Organized Crime.* London: Ashgate.

Schneier, Bruce (2015). *Data and Goliath: The Hidden Battles to Collect Your Data and Control Your World.* New York: W.W. Norton.

Schumpeter, Joseph A. (1942). *Capitalism, Socialism, and Democracy.* New York: Harper & Brothers.

Schuberth, Moritz (2015). 'The Challenge of Community-Based Armed Groups: Towards a Conceptualization of Militias, Gangs, and Vigilantes.' *Contemporary Security Policy* 36: 296–320.

Sederberg, Peter C. (1995). 'Conciliation as a Counter-Terrorist Strategy.' *Journal of Peace Research* 32: 295–312.

Sedlak, David (2014). *Water 4.0: The Past, Present, and Future of the World's Most Vital Resource.* New Haven: Yale University Press.

Segal, Adam (2016). *The Hacked World Order: How Nations Fight, Trade, Maneuver, and Manipulate in the Digital Age.* New York: Public Affairs.

Selby, Jan (2005). 'Oil and Water: The Contrasting Anatomies of Resource Conflicts.' *Government and Opposition* 40: 200–24.

Senese, Paul D. and John A. Vasquez (2003). 'A Unified Explanation of Territorial Conflict: Testing the Impact of Sampling Bias, 1919-1992.' *International Studies Quarterly* 47: 275–98.

Sennett, Richard (2004). *Respect: The Formation of Character in an Age of Inequality.* London: Penguin Books.

Shadlen, Kenneth C. (2007). 'The Political Economy of AIDS Treatment: Intellectual Property and the Transformation of Generic Supply.' *International Studies Quarterly* 51: 559–81.

Shambaugh, David (1996). 'Containment or Engagement of China? Calculating Beijing's Responses.' *International Security* 21: 180–209.

Shambaugh, David (1999). 'China's Military Views the World: Ambivalent Security.' *International Security* 24: 52–79.

Shani, Giorgio (2008). 'Toward a Post-Western IR: The *Umma, Khalsa Panth*, and Critical International Relations Theory.' *International Studies Review* 10: 722–34.

Shapiro, Jacob N., and Nils B. Weidmann (2015). 'Is the Phone Mightier Than the Sword? Cellphones and Insurgent Violence in Iraq.' *International Organization* 69: 247–74.

Sharman, J. C. (2008). 'Power and Discourse in Policy Diffusion: Anti-Money Laundering in Developing States.' *International Studies Quarterly* 52: 635–56.

Sheehan, Michael (2005). *International Security: An Analytical Survey*. Boulder: Lynne Rienner.

Shemella, Paul (ed.) (2016). *Global Responses to Maritime Violence: Cooperation and Collective Action*. Stanford: Stanford Security Studies.

Shenon, Philip (2008). *The Commission: The Uncensored History of the 9/11 Investigation*. Boston: Little, Brown.

Shilts, Randy (1987). *And the Band Played On: Politics, People, and the AIDS Epidemic*. New York: St. Martin's.

Silke, Andrew (ed.) (2004). *Research on Terrorism: Trends, Achievements, and Failures*. London: Frank Cass.

Simmons, Beth A. (2011). 'International Studies in the Global Information Age.' *International Studies Quarterly* 55: 589–99.

Simmons, Erica S. (2016). 'Market Reforms and Water Wars.' *World Politics* 68: 37–73.

Singer, J. David (ed.) (1980). *The Correlates of War II: Testing Some Realipolitik Models*. New York: Free Press.

Singer, J. David, and Melvin Small (1972). *The Wages of War, 1816-1965*. New York: Wiley.

Singer, Peter W. (2007). *Corporate Warriors: The Rise of the Privatized Military Industry*. Ithaca: Cornell University Press.

Singer, Peter W. (2009). *Wired for War: The Robotics Revolution and Conflict in the 21st Century*. London: Penguin Books.

Singer, Peter W., and Allan Friedman (2014). *Cybersecurity and Cyberwar: What Everyone Needs to Know*. Oxford: Oxford University Press.

Skolnick Jr., Joseph M. (1974). 'An Appraisal of Studies of the Linkages Between Domestic and International Conflict.' *Comparative Political Studies* 6: 485–509.

Skolnikoff, Eugene B. (1994). *The Elusive Transformation: Science, Technology, and the Evolution of International Politics*. Princeton: Princeton University Press.

Slim, Hugo (2008). *Killing Civilians: Method, Madness, and Morality in War*. New York: Columbia University Press.

Sliwinski, Krzysztof Feliks (2014). 'Moving Beyond the European Union's Weakness as a Cyber-Security Agent.' *Contemporary Security Policy* 35: 468–86.

Sloan, Elinor C. (2002). *The Revolution in Military Affairs*. Montreal: McGill-Queen's University Press.

Sloan, Stanley R. (1985). *NATO's Future*. Washington, DC: National Defense University Press.

Small, Melvin, and J. David Singer (1976). 'The War-Proneness of Democratic Regimes, 1816–1965.' *Jerusalem Journal of International Relations* 1: 50–69.

Smith, Michael E. (2003). *Europe's Foreign and Security Policy: The Institutionalization of Cooperation*. Cambridge: Cambridge University Press.

Smith, Michael E. (forthcoming). *Europe's Common Security and Defence Policy: Capacity–Building, Experiential Learning, and Institutional Change*. Cambridge: Cambridge University Press.

Smith, Michael E., and Mark Webber (2007). 'Political Dialogue and Security: The CFSP and ESDP.' In Katja Weber, Michael E. Smith and Michael Baun (eds.), *Governing Europe's Neighbourhood: Partners or Periphery?* Manchester: University of Manchester Press.

Smith, Thomas W. (2002). 'The New Law of War: Legitimizing Hi-Tech and Infrastructural Violence.' *International Studies Quarterly* 46: 355–74.

Snidal, Duncan (1991). 'Relative Gains and the Pattern of International Cooperation.' *American Political Science Review* 85: 701–26.

Sniderman, Paul M., Louk Hagendoorn and Markus Prior (2004). 'Predisposing Factors and Situational Triggers: Exclusionary Reactions to Immigrant Minorities.' *American Political Science Review* 98: 35–49.

Snow, Donald M. (1996). *Uncivil Wars: International Security and the New Internal Conflicts*. Boulder: Lynne Rienner.

Snyder, Glenn (1984). 'The Security Dilemma in Alliance Politics.' *World Politics* 36: 461–95.

Snyder, Glenn (1997). *Alliance Politics*. Ithaca: Cornell University Press.

Snyder, Glenn H., and Paul Diesing (1977). *Conflict Among Nations*. Princeton: Princeton University Press.

Snyder, Jack (1984). *The Ideology of the Offensive: Military Decision Making and the Disasters of 1914*. Ithaca: Cornell University Press.

Snyder, Jack (1990). 'Averting Anarchy in the New Europe.' *International Security* 14: 5–41.

Snyder, Jack (1991). *Myths of Empire: Domestic Politics and Strategic Ideology*. Ithaca: Cornell University Press.

Snyder, Jack (2001). *From Voting to Violence: Democratization and Nationalist Conflict*. New York: W.W. Norton.

Snyder, Jack (2015–16). 'Trade Expectations and Great Power Conflict: A Review Essay.' *International Security* 40: 179–96.

Snyder, Jack, and Karen Ballentine (1996). 'Nationalism and the Marketplace of Ideas.' *International Security* 21: 5–40.

Snyder, Robert S. (2005). 'Bridging the Realist/Constructivist Divide: The Case of the Counterrevolution in Soviet Foreign Policy at the End of the Cold War.' *Foreign Policy Analysis* 1: 55–71.

Soeters, Joseph, and Philippe Manigart (eds.) (2008). *Military Cooperation in Multinational Peace Operations*. London: Routledge.

Solingen, Etel (1994). 'The Political Economy of Nuclear Restraint.' *International Security* 19: 126–69.

Solingen, Etel (1998). *Regional Orders at Century's Dawn: Global and Domestic Influences on Grand Strategy*. Princeton: Princeton University Press.

Sorkin, Andrew Ross (2010). *Too Big to Fail: Inside the Battle to Save Wall Street*. London: Penguin Books.

Spearin, Christopher (2003). 'American Hegemony Incorporated: The Importance and Implications of Military Contractors in Iraq.' *Contemporary Security Policy* 24: 26–47.

Sperling, James, and Emil Kirchner (1997). *Recasting the European Order: Security Architectures and Economic Co-operation*. Manchester: Manchester University Press.

Spiro, David (1994). 'The Insignificance of the Liberal Peace.' *International Security* 19: 50–86.

Stanislawski, Bartosz H. (ed.) (2008). 'Para-States, Quasi-States, and Black Spots: Perhaps Not States, But Not "Ungoverned Territories," Either.' *International Studies Review* 10: 366–96.

Steans, Jill (1998). *Gender and International Relations*. Cambridge: Polity Press.

Stedman, Stephen John (1997). 'Spoiler Problems in Peace Processes.' *International Security* 22: 5–53.

Steele, Brent J. (2005). 'Ontological Security and the Power of Self-Identity: British Neutrality and the American Civil War.' *Review of International Studies* 31: 519–40.

Stein, Arthur A. (1976). 'Conflict and Cohesion.' *Journal of Conflict Resolution* 20: 143–72.

Stein, Arthur A. (1982). 'Coordination and Collaboration: Regimes in an Anarchic World.' *International Organization* 36: 299–324.

Stein, Janice Gross (1992). 'Deterrence and Compellence in the Gulf, 1990–91: A Failed or Impossible Task?' *International Security* 17: 147–79.

Stein, Janice Gross (1994). 'Political Learning by Doing: Gorbachev as Uncommitted Thinker and Motivated Learner.' *International Organization* 48: 155–83.

Stein, Rachel M. (2015). 'War and Revenge: Explaining Conflict Initiation by Democracies.' *American Political Science Review* 109: 556–73.

Stern, Jessica (2002–3). 'Dreaded Risks and the Control of Biological Weapons.' *International Security* 27: 89–123.

Stern, Nicholas (2009). *A Blueprint for a Safer Planet: How to Manage Climate Change and Create a New Era of Progress and Prosperity*. New York: The Bodley Head.

Stiennon, Richard (2015). *There Will Be Cyberwar: How the Move to Network-Centric War-Fighting Has Set the Stage for Cyberwar*. Birmingham, MI: IT Harvest Press.

Stevens, Tim (2012). 'A Cyberwar of Ideas? Deterrence and Norms in Cyberspace.' *Contemporary Security Policy* 33: 148–70.

Stigler, Andrew L. (2002–3). 'A Clear Victory for Air Power: NATO's Empty Threat to Invade Kosovo.' *International Security* 27: 124–57.

Stoll, Richard J. (1987). 'The Sound of the Guns: Is There a Congressional Rally Effect After U.S. Military Action?' *American Politics Quarterly* 15: 223–37.

Strange, Susan (1996). *Retreat of the State*. Cambridge: Cambridge University Press.

Stuart, Tristram (2009). *Waste: Uncovering the Global Food Scandal*. London: Penguin Books.

Suskind, Ron (2008). *The Way of the World: A Story of Truth and Hope in an Age of Extremism*. New York: Simon & Schuster.

Tadjbakhsh, Shahrbanou, and Anudura M. Chenoy (2007). *Human Security: Concepts and Implications*. London: Routledge.

Tannenwald, Nina (2005). 'Stigmatizing the Bomb: Origins of the Nuclear Taboo,' *International Security* 29: 5–49.

Tarar, Ahmer (2006). 'Diversionary Incentives and the Bargaining Approach to War.' *International Studies Quarterly* 50: 169–88.

Taylor, Brian D., and Roxana Botea (2008). 'Tilly-Tally: War-Making and State-Making in the Contemporary Third World.' *International Studies Review* 10: 27–56.

Tenner, Edward (1997). *Why Things Bite Back: Technology and the Revenge of Unintended Consequences*. New York: Vintage Books.

Theisen, Ole Magnus, Helge Holtermann, and Halvard Buhaug (2011–12). 'Climate Wars? Assessing the Claim that Drought Brings Conflict.' *International Security* 36: 79–106.

Thierer, Adam, and Clyde Wayne Crews, Jr. (eds.) (2003). *Who Rules the Net? Internet Governance and Jurisdiction*. Washington, DC: The Cato Institute.

Thompson, William R. (1983). 'Uneven Economic Growth, Systemic Challenges, and Global Wars.' *International Studies Quarterly* 27: 341–55.

Thomson, Janice (1990). 'State Practices, International Norms, and the Decline of Mercenarism.' *International Studies Quarterly* 34: 23–47.

Thurow, Lester C. (1992). *Head to Head: The Coming Economic Battle Between Japan, Europe, and America*. New York: Morrow.

Tickner, J. Ann (1992). *Gender in International Relations*. New York: Columbia University Press.

Tickner, J. Ann (1997). 'You Just Don't Understand: Troubled Engagements Between Feminists and IR Theorists.' *International Studies Quarterly* 41: 611–32.

Tilly, Charles (1978). *From Mobilization to Revolution*. New York: McGraw-Hill.

Toft, Monica Duffy (2007). 'Getting Religion? The Puzzling Case of Islam and Civil War.' *International Security* 31: 97–131.

Toft, Monica Duffy (2010). 'Ending Civil Wars: A Case for Rebel Victory?' *International Security* 34: 7–36.

Transform Drug Policy Foundation (2009). *A Comparison of the Cost-Effectiveness of the Prohibition and Regulation of Drugs*. Bristol: Transform Drug Policy Foundation.

Treisman, Daniel (2004). 'Rational Appeasement.' *International Organization* 58: 345–73.

Trumbore, Peter F. (2003). 'Victims or Aggressors? Ethno-Political Rebellion and Use of Force in Militarized Interstate Disputes.' *International Studies Quarterly* 47: 183–201.

Tyson, Laura D'Andrea (1993). *Who's Bashing Whom? Trade Conflict in High-Technology Industries*. Washington, DC: Institute for International Economics.

Ullman, Richard (1983). 'Redefining Security.' *International Security* 8: 129–53.

UN Commission on Human Security (2003). *Final Report of the UN Commission on Human Security*. New York: UN.

UN High Commissioner for Refugees (2009). *2008 Global Trends: Refugees, Asylum-Seekers, Returnees, Internally Displaced, and Stateless Persons*. New York: UNHCR.

UN Office on Drugs and Crime (2004). *A More Secure World: Our Shared Responsibility.* UN Doc A/59/565, 2 Dec. New York: UNODC.

Urdal, Henrik (2006). 'A Clash of Generations? Youth Bulges and Political Violence.' *International Studies Quarterly* 50: 607–29.

Valentino, Benjamin, Paul Huth and Sarah Croco (2006). 'Covenants Without the Sword: International Law and the Protection of Civilians in Times of War.' *World Politics* 58: 339–77.

Van Evera, Stephen (1984). 'The Cult of the Offensive and the Origins of the First World War.' *International Security* 9: 58–107.

Van Evera, Stephen (1986). 'Why Cooperation Failed in 1914.' In Kenneth A. Oye (ed.) *Cooperation Under Anarchy.* Princeton: Princeton University Press.

Van Evera, Stephen (1990–1). 'Primed for Peace: Europe After the Cold War.' *International Security* 15: 7–57.

Van Evera, Stephen (1994). 'Hypotheses on Nationalism and War.' *International Security* 18: 5–39.

Van Evera, Stephen (1998). 'Offense, Defense, and the Causes of War.' *International Security* 22: 5–43.

Van Evera, Stephen (1999). *Causes of War: Power and the Roots of Conflict.* Ithaca: Cornell University Press.

Van Meegdenburg, Hilde (2015). 'What the Research on PMSCs Discovered and Neglected: An Appraisal of the Literature.' *Contemporary Security Policy* 36: 321–45.

Vasquez, John (ed.) (2012). *What Do We Know About War?* Lanham: Rowman & Littlefield.

Väyrynen, Raimo (1983). 'Economic Cycles, Power Transitions, Political Management, and Wars Between Major Powers.' *International Studies Quarterly* 27: 389–418.

Väyrynen, Raimo (1998). 'Environmental Security and Conflicts: Concepts and Practices.' *International Studies* 35: 3–21.

Victor, David G. (2001). *The Collapse of the Kyoto Protocol and the Struggle to Slow Global Warming.* Princeton: Princeton University Press.

Vogel, Kathleen M. (2013–14). 'Expert Knowledge in Intelligence Assessment: Bird Flu and BioTerrorism.' *International Security* 38: 39–71.

Vrolijk, Christiaan (2001). 'Introduction and Overview.' *International Affairs* 77: 251–60.

Wæver, Ole (1998). 'The Sociology of a Not So International Discipline: American and European Developments in International Relations.' *International Organization* 52: 687–727.

Wæver, Ole, Barry Buzan, Morten Kelstrup and Pierre Lemaitre (1993). *Identity, Migration, and the New Security Agenda in Europe.* London: Pinter.

Wagner, R. Harrison (1993). 'The Causes of Peace.' In Roy Licklider (ed.), *Stopping the Killing: How Civil Wars End.* New York: New York University Press.

Wagner, R. Harrison (1994). 'Peace, War, and the Balance of Power.' *American Political Science Review* 88: 593–607.

Wald, Kenneth D., and Clyde Wilcox (2006). 'Getting Religion: Has Political Science Rediscovered the Faith Factor?' *American Political Science Review* 100: 523–9.

Wallerstein, Immanuel (1984). *The Politics of the World-Economy.* Cambridge: Cambridge University Press.

Walt, Stephen M. (1985). 'Alliance Formation and the Balance of World Power.' *International Security* 9: 3–43.

Walt, Stephen M. (1987). *The Origins of Alliances*. Ithaca: Cornell University Press.

Walt, Stephen M. (1988). 'Testing Theories of Alliance Formation: The Case of Southwest Asia.' *International Organization* 42: 275–316.

Walt, Stephen M. (1991). 'The Renaissance of Security Studies.' *International Studies Quarterly* 35: 211–39.

Walt, Stephen M. (1999). 'Rigor or Rigor Mortis? Rational Choice and Security Studies.' *International Security* 23: 5–48.

Walter, Barbara F. (1997). 'The Critical Barrier to Civil War Settlement.' *International Organization* 51: 335–64.

Waltz, Kenneth N. (1959). *Man, the State, and War: A Theoretical Analysis*. New York: Columbia University Press.

Waltz, Kenneth N. (1979). *Theory of International Politics*. New York: McGraw-Hill.

Waltz, Kenneth N. (1981). *The Spread of Nuclear Weapons: More May Be Better*, Adelphi Paper No. 171. London: International Institute for Strategic Studies.

Waltz, Kenneth N. (1989). 'The Origins of War in Neorealist Theory.' In Robert I. Rotberg and Theodore K. Rabb (eds.), *The Origin and Prevention of Major Wars*. Cambridge: Cambridge University Press.

Waltz, Kenneth N. (1990). 'Nuclear Myths and Political Realities.' *American Political Science Review* 84: 731–45.

Waltz, Kenneth N. (1993). 'The Emerging Structure of International Politics.' *International Security* 18: 44–79.

Weaver, Mary Anne (2003). *Pakistan: In the Shadow of Jihad and Afghanistan*. New York: Farrar, Straus & Giroux.

Weber, Katja, Michael E. Smith and Michael Baun (eds.) (2007). *Governing Europe's Neighborhood: Partners or Periphery?* Manchester: Manchester University Press.

Weber, Max (1918). 'Politics as a Vocation.' In H. H. Gerth and C. Wright Mills (eds.), *From Max Weber: Essays in Sociology* (1946 edition). New York: Oxford University Press.

Weede, Erich W. (1984). 'Democracy and War Involvement.' *Journal of Conflict Resolution* 28: 649–64.

Weeks, Jessica L. (2008). 'Autocratic Audience Costs: Regime Type and Signaling Resolve.' *International Organization* 62: 35–64.

Weiner, Myron (1992–3). 'Security, Stability and International Migration.' *International Security* 17: 91–126.

Weiner, Myron (ed.) (1993). *International Migration and Security*. Boulder: Westview.

Weiner, Myron (ed.) (1995). *The Global Migration Crisis: Challenges to States and Human Rights*. New York: HarperCollins.

Welsh, Jennifer M. (ed.) (2004). *Humanitarian Intervention and International Relations*. Oxford: Oxford University Press.

Wendt, Alexander (1992). 'Anarchy is What States Make of It: The Social Construction of Power Politics.' *International Organization* 46: 391–425.

Wendt, Alexander (1999). *Social Theory of International Politics*. Cambridge: Cambridge University Press.

Weiss, Thomas G. (2009). 'What Happened to the Idea of World Government?' *International Studies Quarterly* 53: 253–71.

Western, Jon (2002). 'Sources of Humanitarian Intervention: Beliefs, Information, and Advocacy in the U.S. Decisions on Somalia and Bosnia.' *International Security* 26: 112–42.

Widgren, Jonas (1990). 'International Migration and Regional Stability.' *International Affairs* 66: 749–66.

Wilkenfeld, Jonathan (ed.) (1973). *Conflict Behavior and Linkage Politics*. New York: Longman.

Wilkinson, Richard, and Kate Pickett (2009). *The Spirit Level: Why More Equal Societies Almost Always Do Better*. London: Allen Lane.

Williams, Michael (1998). 'Identity and the Politics of Security.' *European Journal of International Relations* 4: 204–25.

Williams, Paul D. (ed.) (2013). *Security Studies: An Introduction* (2nd ed.). London: Routledge.

Williams, Phil (1994). 'Transnational Organized Crime and International Security.' *Survival* 36: 96–113.

Williams, Phil (1999). *Illegal Immigration and Commercial Sex: The New Slave Trade*. London: Frank Cass.

Wittner, Lawrence S. (2009). *Confronting the Bomb: A Short History of the World Nuclear Disarmament Movement*. Stanford: Stanford University Press.

Wolf, Martin (2008). *Fixing Global Finance: How to Curb Financial Crises in the 21st Century*. New Haven: Yale University Press.

Wolfers, Arnold (1962). *Discord and Collaboration*. Baltimore: Johns Hopkins University Press.

Wood, B. Dan, and Arnold Vedlitz (2007). 'Issue Definition, Information Processing, and the Politics of Global Warming.' *American Journal of Political Science* 51: 552–68.

World Meteorological Organization (2007). *Scientific Assessment of Ozone Depletion: 2006*. Global Ozone Research and Monitoring Project – Report No. 50. Geneva, Switzerland.

Wright, Quincy (1965). *A Study of War*. Chicago: University of Chicago Press.

Wyn Jones, Richard (1999). *Security, Strategy, and Critical Theory*. Boulder: Lynne Rienner.

Yergin, Daniel (1991). *The Prize: The Epic Quest for Oil, Money, and Power*. New York: Simon & Schuster.

Young, Oran R. (1989). 'The Politics of International Regime Formation: Managing Natural Resources and the Environment.' *International Organization* 43: 349–75.

Yusuf, Moeed, and Jason A. Kirk (2016). 'Keeping an Eye on South Asian Skies: America's Pivotal Deterrence in Nuclearized India-Pakistan Crises.' *Contemporary Security Policy* 37: 246–72.

Zalewski, D. A. (2005). 'Economic Security and the Myth of the Efficiency/Equity Trade-Off.' *Journal of Economic Issues* 39: 383–90.

Zalewski, Marysia, and Jane Papart (eds.) (1998). *The 'Man' Question in International Relations*. Boulder: Westview Press.

Zartman, William I. (1993). 'The Unfinished Agenda: Negotiating Internal Conflicts.' In Roy Licklider (ed.), *Stopping the Killing: How Civil Wars End*. New York: New York University Press.

Zegart, Amy B. (2007). *Spying Blind: The CIA, the FBI, and the Origins of 9/11.* Princeton: Princeton University Press.

Zetter, Kim (2014). *Countdown to Zero Day: Stuxnet and the Launch of the World's First Digital Weapon.* New York: Crown.

Zimmerman, William (1969). *Soviet Perspectives on International Relations.* Princeton: Princeton University Press.

Zurn, Michael (1998). 'The Rise of International Environmental Politics: A Review of the Current Research.' *World Politics* 50: 617–49.

# Index

448